Teaching *and* Learning Languages

Teaching *and* Learning Languages

Selected reading from
Mosaic

edited by
Anthony Mollica

éditions **SOLEIL** *publishing inc.*

[09-09]

Cover Design: Frank Campion, Campion Marketing
Layout and Design: Anthony Mollica

ISBN   1-894935-34-9
       978-1-894935-34-0   Printed in Canada

éditions Soleil publishing inc.

In Canada   In USA
P. O. Box 847   P. O. Box 890
Welland, Ontario L3B 5Y5   Lewiston, NY 14092-0890
              Tel./Fax: [905] 788-2674
       Order Department: Fax 1-800-261-0833
       E-mail: soleil@soleilpublishing.com
              www.soleilpublishing.com

Library and Archives Canada Cataloguing in Publication

Teaching and learning languages : selected readings from Mosaic/ edited by Anthony Mollica. -- 3rd ed.

Includes bibliographical references.
ISBN 978-1-894935-34-0
1. Language and languages -- Study and teaching.
I. Mollica, Anthony, 1939 -
P51.T422 2008   418.0071   C2008-900478-7

Table of Contents

Preface to the 3rd Edition

The first issue of **Mosaic** appeared in the Fall of 1993. It was meant be an unpretentious publication devoted to the professional development of teachers of Heritage/International languages – languages taught in elementary schools, after school hours, or on Saturday mornings. It immediately became evident, however, that *all* language teachers were interested in a "reader-friendly" publication which combined both theory and practice.

We did a massive mailing – publishing some 25,000 copies of the first issue – reaching selected teachers, consultants, and supervisors in both Canada and the United States. Frankly, we were surprised at the enthusiasm which the issue generated.

We are fortunate to have had – and we hope that the trend will continue! – authors who successfully combine theory and practice and who write articles readily accessible to all readers.

The request to put a number of selected articles from **Mosaic** in book form came from two colleagues from the University of Toronto at Mississauga, Professors Charles Elkabas and Michael Lettieri, who were teaching a course on "Introduction to Second-Language Teaching." They felt that in the absence of a specific textbook, many articles would serve their purpose and form the basis for the course. As Editor, I was delighted to accede to their request and hence the first edition (1996) of 160 pages of *Teaching Languages. Selected Readings from* **Mosaic** was published.

The book was enthusiastically received and a handful of Canadian and American Faculties of Education adopted it as a textbook for their teacher education courses.

It soon became apparent that several other excellent articles which subsequently appeared in **Mosaic** should be included in any future edition of *Teaching Languages*. It also occurred to us that the readings provided in the first edition focused not only on teaching but also on learning. Hence, the new title, and an expanded edition (1998) – 480 pages – of *Teaching and Learning Languages. Selected Readings from* **Mosaic**.

The third, revised and expanded edition (2008, 624 pages) contains articles from the first nine volumes of the journal. Selecting the articles to be included has been a painful *embarras du choix*. We regret that several other excellent contributions had to be omitted because of space restrictions. Their absence from the current "Table of Contents" does not diminish their value and their contribution to language teaching and learning.

These fifty-one practical and theoretical chapters, written by distinguished North American second-language scholars, are invaluable professional readings for both beginning and seasoned teachers. Our purpose with this third edition is to make *Teaching and Learning Languages*, the *basic* textbook for language teaching and learning. Of great interest to researchers are not only the intersting and helpful articles but also the copious bibliographical references at the end of each chapter. These are invaluable to the readers who wish to expand their knowledge on the topic.

The selections in *Teaching and Learning Languages*

- *recognize the importance and benefits of language teaching and learning*

   (Mollica, "Language Learning: The Key to Understanding and Harmony"; Wodniecka and Cepeda, "Beyond the Classroom: Bilingualism, Cognitive Skills and Health"; Savignon, "A Letter to My Spanish Teacher"),

- *acknowledge the important role of the student, the teacher and the parent*

   (Mollica and Nuessel, "The Good Language Learner and the Good Language Teacher: A Review of the Literature and Classroom Applications"; Besnard, "Individual Differences in L2 Learning and the Good Language Teacher"; Ralph, "Motivating Parents to Support Second-Language Programs"),

- *identify students' anxiety and offer practical suggestions for studying*

   (Donley, "Language Anxiety and How to Manage It: What Educatiors Need to Know"; "Ten Ways to Cope with Foreign Language Anxiety"and Cankar, "Study Skill Suggestions for Students of Foreign Language Classes"),

- *discuss classroom environment*

   (Evans-Harvey, "Climate Setting in Second-Language Classrooms"; Heffernan, "Promoting the Development of Strategic Competence in the Language Classroom"),

- *provide practical teaching techniques which will assist teachers in their day-to-day teaching activity*

   (Chastain, "Planning for Instruction"; Mollica, "The Lesson Outline", "Classroom Expressions", "Questioning Strategies"; Richards, "Discipline in the Language Class"; Papalia, "Classroom Settings"; Bell, "The Challenge of Multilevel Classes"),

- *highlight the partnership between home and school*

   (Antonek, Tucker and Donato, "Interactive Homework: Creating Connections Between Home and School"),

- *identify the fundamentals of second-language teaching*
  (LeBlanc, "The Fundamentals of Second-Language Teaching"),
- *propose ways of improving our teaching*
  (Stern, "French Core Programs: How Can We Improve Them?"),
- *focus on mnemonic devices to teaching of a specific point of grammar*
  (Nuessel, "Mnemonic Acronyms: A Memory Aid for Teaching and Learning Spanish Grammar"; Janc, "Teaching French Using Mnemonic Devices"),
- *propose vocabulary expansion*
  (Mollica, Schutz and Tessar, "Focus on Descriptive Adjectives: Creative Activities for the Language Classroom"; Mollica, "Increasing the Students' Basic Vocabulary in French, Italian and Spanish through English Cognates"),
- *emphasize the fun element in language teaching*
  (Danesi and Mollica, "Games and Puzzles in the Second-Language Classroom: A Second Look"),
- *identify methods and approaches to language teaching*
  (Doggett, "Eight Approaches to Language Teaching"; Danesi and Mollica", Conceptual Fluency Theory and Second-Language Teaching"),
- *suggest caveats with print and non-print materials*
  (Hammerly, "What Visual Aids Can and Cannot Do in Second-Language Teaching"),
- *evaluate visuals in the classroom*
  (Hammerly, "A Picture is Worth 1000 Words and A Word is Worth 1000 Pictures"),
- *offer suggestions for creative activities*
  (Mollica, "A Picture is worth 1000 words… Creative Activities for the Language Classroom"),
- *discuss the importance of evaluation*
  (Ralph, "Teaching to the Test: Principles of Authentic Assessment for Second-Language Education"),
- *focus on three of the language skills:*
  speaking
  (Rivers, "Talking Off the Top of Their Heads"; Valette, "The Five-Step Performance-Based Model of Oral Proficiency"; Mollica, "French, Italian and Spanish Tongue Twisters in the Classroom"),

reading

(Krashen, "Immersion: Why Not Try Free Voluntary Reading?"; Valette, "Four Approaches to Authentic Reading"),

writing

(Nuessel and Cicogna, "Teaching Writing in Elementary and Intermediate Language Classes: Suggestions and Activities"; Besnard, Elkabas and Rosienski-Pellerin, "Students' Empowerment: E-mail Exchange and the Development of Writing Skills"; Colella and Urbancic, "'Dear Santa...': Santa Claus Helps with Communicative Competence"),

• *as well as on culture and body language*

(Runte, "The Problem of Passion and Culture"; Brooks, "Teaching Culture in the Foreign Language Classroom"; Wilcox, "Gestures and Language: Fair and Foul in Other Cultures"),

• *and conclude with background information on North American cultural festivities*

(Mollica, "Teaching Culture in a North American Context: An Introductory Note", "Thanksgiving"; Mollica, Séguin, Maiguashca and Valenzuela, "Halloween"; Lewin and Riesenbach, "Hannukka"; Onyschuk, "Ukrainian Easter"; Luo, "The Chinese New Year"; Mollica, Séguin and Valenzuela, "Valentine's Day"; Mollica and Sterling, "Mother's Day/Father's Day").

I should like to express my gratitude to the above colleagues for permission to reproduce the articles included in this anthology. Whatever success these readings will enjoy belongs to them.

It is with sadness that we announce that several colleagues passed away since permission was given to reprint some of the articles: Nelson Brooks, Philip Donley, Raffaella Maiguashca, Anthony Papalia, Wilga Rivers and H. H. Stern.

I would like to thank Maureen Smith, Faculty of Education, University of Western Ontario and René-Etienne Bellavance, Université d'Ottawa for their suggestions in the selection of some chapters and Virginia Plante and José Cortés for the preparation of this edition for press.

Anthony Mollica

1 Language Learning: The Key to Understanding and Harmony

Anthony Mollica

Teachers, parents and researchers can give a long list of advantage to be derived from studying a second language.

The incorrect translation of a word may have very well been responsible for the death of over 200,000 people. Towards the end of the Second World War, the United States had offered Japan an opportunity to surrender. The Japanese reply contained the word *mokusatsu* which means "withholding comment pending decision." Through mistranslation, the verb *mokusatsu* was rendered as "ignore." As a result, the allies believed that the ultimatum had been flatly rejected and President Truman ordered the use of the atomic bomb. I don't know whether the story is true or not, but it certainly is a good language anecdote...

Gaffes

Less tragic examples abound: *The Wall Street Journal* reported that General Motors was puzzled by the lack of enthusiasm the introduction of its Chevrolet Nova automobile aroused among Puerto Ricans. The reason was very simple. *Nova* means *star* in Spanish, but when spoken it sounds like *no va* which means "it doesn't go." GM quickly changed the name to Caribe and the car sold nicely.

Linguistic and cultural gaffes made by translators or by non-native speakers have often been a source of chagrin. One recalls the embarrassment President Carter faced when the interpreter stated that the President "lusted" for Polish women. A situation reported by the Canadian Press, involved Jean Drapeau, a former mayor of Montreal. At the end of a speech during a tour of China, the Mayor urged his audience "to beat up your brother when he is drunk." A glance at M. Drapeau's French text, however, showed that he had never advocated such violence! What he had said in French was "Il faut battre le fer pendant qu'il est chaud." The translator had obviously confused "fer" ("iron") for "frère" ("brother") and "chaud" for "ivre" ("drunk" in Québec).

Richard Lederer's "Lost in Translation" List

In his book, *Anguished English*, Richard Lederer (1987) identifies a number of incorrect translations which may very well lead to communicative… incompetence!

Teachers wishing to turn these mistranslations into a language activity can ask students to re-write them to convey the meaning intended.

In a Tokyo hotel:

> *It is forbidden to steal towels please. If you are not person to do such thing is please not to read this notis.*

In another Japanese hotel room:

> *Please to bathe inside the tub.*

In a Bucharest hotel lobby:

> The lift is being fixed for the next day. During that time, we regret that you will be unbearable.

In a Leipzig elevator:

> *Do not enter lift backwards, and only when lit up.*

Posted on a Belgrade hotel elevator:

> *To move the cabin, push button for wishing floor. If the cabin should enter more persons, each person should press a number of wishing floor. Driving is then going alphabetically by national order.*

In a Paris hotel elevator:

> *Please leave your values at the front desk.*

In a hotel in Athens:

> *Visitors are expected to complain at the office between the hours of 9 and 11 a.m. daily.*

In a Yugoslavian hotel:

> *The flattening of underwear with pleasure is a job of the chambermaid.*

In a Japanese hotel:

> *You are invited to take advantage of the chambermaid.*

In a lobby of a Moscow hotel across from a Russian Orthodox monastery:

> *You are welcome to visit the cemetery where famous Russian and Soviet composers, artists, and writers are buried daily except Thursday.*

In an Austrian hotel catering to skiers:

> *Not to perambulate the corridors in the hours of repose in boots of ascension.*

On a menu of a Swiss restaurant:

Our wines leave you nothing to hope for.

On the menu of a Polish hotel:

Salad a firm's own make: limpid reed beet soup with cheesy dumplings in form of a finger' roasted duck let loose' beef rashers beaten up in the country people's fashion.

In a Hong Kong supermarket:

For your convenience, we recommend courteous, efficient, self-service.

Outside a Hong Kong tailor shop:

Ladies may have a fit upstairs.

In Bangkok dry cleaner's:

Drop your trousers here for best results.

Outside a Paris dress shop:

Dresses for street walking.

In a Rhodes tailor shop:

Order your summers suits. Because is big rush, we will execute customers in strict rotation.

From the Soviet Weekly*:*

There will be a Moscow Exhibition of Arts by 15,000 Soviet Republic painters and sculptors. They were executed over the past two years.

In an East African newspaper:

A new swimming pool is rapidly taking shape since the contractors have thrown in the bulk of their workers.

In a Vienna hotel:

In case of fire, do your utmost to alarm the hotel porter.

A sign posted in Germany's Black Forest:

It is strictly forbidden on our black forest camping site that people of different sex, for instance, men and women, live together in one tent unless they are married with each other for that purpose.

In a Zurich hotel:

Because of the impropriety of entertaining guests of the opposite sex in the bedroom, it is suggested that the lobby be used for that purpose.

In an advertisement by a Hong Kong dentist:

Teeth will be extracted by the latest Methodists.

A translation sentence from a Russian chess book:

A lot of water has been passed under the bridge since this variation has been played.

In a Rome laundry:

Ladies, leave your clothes here and spend the afternoon having a good time.

In a Czechoslovakian tourist agency:

Take one of our horse-driven city tours – we guarantee no miscarriages.

Advertisement for donkey rides in Thailand:

Would you like to ride on your own ass?

In the window of a Swedish furrier:

Fur coats made for ladies from their own skin.

On the box of a clockwork toy made in Hong Kong:

Guaranteed to work throughout its useful life.

Detour sign in Kyushi, Japan:

Stop: Drive Sideways.

In a Swiss mountain inn:

Special today – no ice cream.

In a Bangkok temple:

It is forbidden to enter a woman even a foreigner if dressed as a man.

In a Tokyo bar:

Special cocktails for ladies with nuts.

In a Copenhagen airline ticket office:

We take your bags and send them in all directions.

On the door of a Moscow hotel room:

If this is the first visit to the USSR, you are welcome to it.

In a Norwegian cocktail lounge:

Ladies are requested not to have children in the bar.

At a Budapest zoo:

Please do not feed the animals. If you have any suitable food, give it to the guard on duty.

In the office of a Roman doctor:

Specialist in women and other diseases.

In an Acapulco hotel:

The Manager has personally passed all the water served here.

In a Tokyo shop:

Our nylons cost more than common, but you'll find they are best in the long run.

From a Japanese information booklet about using a hotel air conditioner:

Cooles and Heates: If you want just condition of warm in your room, please control yourself.

From a brochure of a car rental in Tokyo:

When passenger of foot heave in sight, tootle the horn. Trumpet horn melodiously at first, but if he still obstacles your passage then tootle him with vigour.

While examples of incorrect translations occur in English, there are several examples of misplaced modifiers and "perles" – "howlers" – which are no stranger to the French language. The following which first appeareed in *L'Eau vive* have been reprinted in *La presse à l'école* (Metford and Ottewell, 1996: 61).

Cet après-midi, il y aura des réunions au bout nord et au bout sud de l'église. Les bébés seront baptisés aux deux bouts.

Mardi à 4 h de l'après-midi, il y aura une rencontre sociale où on servira de la crème glacée. On prie toutes les femmes qui donnent du lait de venir tôt.

Mercredi, les dames de la société littéraire se rencontrent. Mme Johnson chantera « Mets-moi dans mon petit lit ». Le pasteur l'accompagnera.

Jeudi à 5 h, il y aura une réunion du club des petites mères. Toutes celles qui sont intéressées à devenir des petites mères sont priées de rencontrer le pasteur dans son bureau.

Les dames de la paroisse ont toutes rejeté leur linge et habillement. On peut les voir dans le soubassement de l'église vendredi après-midi.

Ceci étant dimanche de Pâques, nous allons demander à Mme Brown de s'avancer afin de déposer un œuf sur l'autel.

Le service se terminera avec « Petites gouttes d'eau ». L'un des hommes commencera lentement et ensuite toute la congrégation continuera.

Dimanche, une collection spéciale sera faite afin de payer pour le nouveau tapis. Tous ceux et celles qui désirent faire quelque chose sur le tapis sont priés de bien vouloir venir chercher un bout de papier.

Mesdames, n'oubliez pas la vente d'objets divers. C'est le bon temps de vous débarrasser de choses qui ne valent pas la peine d'être gardées. Amenez vos maris.

Je serai absent pendant quelques dimanches. Les prédicateurs seront collés sur le babillard de l'église et toutes les naissances, mariages et décés seront remis jusqu'après mon retour (le pasteur).

Cultural Meaning

Our ability to communicate effectively is dependent upon our skill in using language. But it is important to teach not only communication but also "cultural" meaning of words. *Language and culture are inseparable.* To teach one means to teach the other. Authors of second-language textbooks must not only identify the *denotation* of words, but also, where necessary, the *connotations* of those words and idioms. Where words seem to correspond lexically in their denotation, they may well diverge considerably in their connotation or the emotional association they arouse. While the English word *bread* and the French word *le pain* may correspond lexically in their denotation, they certainly do not correspond in their connotation. *Bread* is often found in a plasticized wrapping, is sliced and soft. The French *pain* brings markedly different association to mind!

As a publication of the College Entrance Examination Board (1986:22) stressed,

> Both at home and abroad, the linguistic skills that students need to communicate with speakers of other languages must be accompanied by knowledge about the culture. For example, students need to know not only words to use in greetings but also how to vary greetings according to the time of day, the social context, the age of the individual, and so forth, as well as what gestures to use, such as shaking hands or bowing.

It is a widely-accepted notion, then, that language skills must be taught integrally with cultural knowledge.

Heritage/International Languages in the Curriculum

Education in Canada falls under provincial jurisdiction. Each province or territory has its own ministry of education and is autonomous, although funds in some cases are channelled to the provinces from the federal government coffers. This is, in fact, the case for the expansion of both official languages, English and French as second languages.

Most, if not all, provinces recognize only two languages for study at the elementary level: English and French. All other languages generally fall under the category of Heritage Languages in English-speaking provinces and as *langues d'origine* in Quebec. Although only English and French are recognized as the official languages of instruction, Ontario has recognized the use of another language with a group of students in the classroom to acculturate them in either official language. The teaching of Heritage Languages is consistent with Canada's political ideology: the United States stresses the "melting pot," Canada favours the "multicultural mosaic."

Recent newspaper reports show that there is a political backlash not only for French but also to the cultural mosaic of which Canada is justifiably proud. Ethnic communities must not simply be passive observers of events but also take more than an active interest in issues which affect them. If ethnic groups are to keep their roots and not become entirely assimilated, a dispassionate, objective campaign on the preservation of one's ethnic identity must be fought at both the provincial and national levels.

The campaign to encourage and promote the learning of Heritage Languages must be fought objectively and not emotionally, educationally and not politically. My solution appears to be simplistic and I will readily agree that it is difficult to separate objectivity from emotions, or politics from education. Nevertheless, I feel that information about the advantages of learning a second or third language should be widely circulated in order to enlighten politicians and the general public on the values of Heritage Languages.

If Heritage Language programs are under attack, perhaps it is because the average person sees the introduction and the expansion of a Heritage Language as part of the maintenance of an ethnic group's identity and Canadian taxpayers, already overburden, do not feel that they should support the preservation of the language for the various ethnic groups. We must change this perception and emphasize the educational values of Heritage Languages. Certainly, the current term, Heritage Language, is not very appropriate in the current political situation and every effort should be made to change the term to International Languages, a term already used in other provinces. (*Editor's Note*: The Ontario Minister of Education, the Hon. David Cook, changed the term "Heritage languages" into "International Languages – Elementary"at a Heritage Language Conference held in Toronto in 1994).

The Value of Language Learning

Teachers and parents are quick to recite a whole litany of advantages and benefits to be derived from studying second or more languages:

✓   Second-language students perform better in English than non-second-language students.

✓   A second language helps students gain greater insight into their own culture.

✓   The self-concept of second-language students is significantly higher than that of non-second-language students.

✓   Studies have shown positive correlation between the study of a second language and the creative functioning of learners.

✓   A working knowledge of other languages is important for research.

✓   Reading skills are shown to be transferable from one language to another.

✓   Second-language learners have larger vocabulary.

✓   Today's students are career-oriented, and they must not overlook jobs that require second languages. The knowledge of a second or third language increases employment opportunities.

✓   The knowledge of the language of the region or country being visited, makes travelling more fun and more enjoyable.

Wilga Rivers (1968:8-9) identifies six classes of objectives for the study of another language (italics, mine):

✓   to develop the student's *intellectual powers* through foreign-language study;

✓   to increase the student's *personal culture* through the study of the great literature and philosophy to which it is the key;

✓   to increase the student's *understanding* of how the language *functions* and to bring him, through the study of a foreign language, to a great awareness of the functioning of his own language;

✓   to teach the student *to read* the foreign language with comprehension so that he may keep abreast of modern writing, research, and information;

✓   to bring the student to a *greater understanding* of people across national barriers by giving him a sympathetic insight into the life and ways of thinking of the people who speak the language he is learning;

✓   to provide the student with skills which will enable him *to communicate orally*, and to some degree in writing, with speakers of another language and with people of other nationalities who have also learned this language.

During a keynote address at the annual conference of the Ontario Modern Language Teachers' Association, Veronica Lacey (1993), a former Director of Education for North York and former Deputy Minister of Education for Ontario, stressed that,

> Learning a language is far more than an intellectual, cognitive challenge. It is a means to grow and mature through the experience of other cultures. It gives breadth and depth to our personalities. It allows us to approach problems differently because we have experienced different worlds; it allows us, as Proust says, to see with new eyes.

Endorsements for learning languages have come from thousands of writers or politicians. Napoleon is reported to have said, "The man who knows two languages is worth two people" and the German novelist-dramatist Goethe, "A man who is ignorant of foreign languages is ignorant of his own."

Tam Goossen (1994:5), a trustee with the Toronto Board of Education, is convinced that,

> an exposure to international languages in elementary school classrooms constitutes an important part of a forward looking up-to-date educational system.

Roseann Runte (1995:9), a former President of Victoria College, University of Toronto, and currently President at Carleton University, stresses that,

> Language is more than grammar. It is more than a way of structuring thought. It is a way of signifying our deepest feelings, our most sincere beliefs. Each time I learn a word which has no translation into another language, I feel that I have discovered a rare gift, a new idea, a fresh insight.

And, elsewhere, Runte (1996) concludes,

> If we want that part of our country which is humane and tolerant to continue on into the future, we need to educate the next generation to be tolerant, to be open. What better way to do this than through learning languages?

Edwin Ralph (1995), an associate professor of Education at the University of Saskatchewan, points out that,

> Recent global events have emphasized the critical importance of multinational communication. Growing trade and commercial relationships among European nations, among the Pacific rim countries, and among our own North American partners – plus the potential to forge further links between/among these larger international blocs – signal that people skilled in various languages will be required to help expedite these communicative relationships.

Even UNESCO's (United Nations Education, Science, and Culture Organization) report on *Our Creative Diversity* (1996), as quoted by Runte (1996), notes the importance of language learning. The "observable advantage of bilinguals" is that they are "more used to switching thought patterns and have more flexible minds." Their knowledge of language(s) makes them more familiar with "different, often contradictory concepts" and this, in turn, makes bilinguals or multilinguals more "tolerant than monolinguals, and more capable of understanding sides of an argument."

And the list of endorsements and advantages for language learning could continue.

But all these reasons can fall under four major objectives for studying a second language, as outlined by Jan Amos Komensky, known as "Comenius," a Czech writer and humanist (1592-1671),:

Political:
   to serve the nation's interests.

Cultural:
   to know the culture of other people for one's own personal enrichment.

Practical:
   to be able to communicate in the language of the foreign speaker.

Educational:
   to sharpen the mind and to shape the personality of the learner.

Heightened Abilities

The Canadian researchers, Elizabeth Peal and Wallace E. Lambert (1962), repeatedly pointed out that learning more than one language heightens the learners' ability to call into play a variety of learning configurations which will otherwise have been limited. "Figuring out" the sound system and grammatical rules in more than one language seems:

• to increase the learners' ability to organize perceptions of reality,

• to recognize concepts in several different forms, and

• to solve complex linguistic and cultural problems.

   Raymond Aron said,

   I have always felt that the ability to speak freely in two different languages provides us with a kind of personal freedom that no other means can provide. When I speak English or German, I don't think the same way as I think in French. This frees me from feeling like a prisoner of my own words (as reported in Mollica, 1984).

While the practical and educational values of learning two or more languages are readily recited what is not as well known is that, as psychological research has now documented beyond any doubt, learning another language brings about a whole series of psychological and affective benefits as a bi-product to the practical ones.

Myth

Before going into the kinds of research which pertain to this statement, it is perhaps useful, and probably necessary, to dispel a long-held myth about foreign language teaching, a myth which Marcel Danesi, a professor at the University of Toronto, in several studies has called the "neurological space myth." Essentially, this was a myth which was generated by research on bilingual children during the 1930s, 1940s and 1950s in the United States and which was connected to the socio-cultural variables rather than psychological ones. The subjects of study were always from lower class backgrounds which did not stress the learning of languages in the home. Nevertheless, this research generated the impression that the learning of another language, or the retention of the mother tongue as a second language, was detrimental to overall cognition because it was believed, or was hypothesized, that the brain had only so much space in it for language. To put another code into the brain, it was argued, would take away from the space the dominant language needed to be able to function and to operate normally in school environments.

This myth has now been debunked by whole series of neurological studies which show the exact opposite; that the insertion of another code into the brain, either in the primary ages during childhood or in the secondary ages during adolescence and adulthood, brings with it a re-organization of neurological linguistic operation so that, in fact, what another code does in the brain helps the brain to function more globally, more holistically and more completely than it otherwise would. Canadian researchers such as Wallace E. Lambert and G. Richard Tucker (1972), Jim Cummins and Merril Swain (1986) as well as many others have documented this phenomenon in several of their studies.

Social Convergence

In a 1984 study, B. McLaughlin observed that the research in Canada provides evidence that "bilingual education leads to a more liberal and enlightened perception of other ethnic groups."

Similarly, the research done by Jim Cummins and Merrill Swain (1986) of the Ontario Institute for Studies in Education (OISE), Toronot, finds that Heritage Language programs, for example, promote inter-ethnic cohesion by allowing ethnically diverse children an opportunity to adapt gradually to a new psycho-cultural way of living. By generating a favourable attitude to one's ethnic identity and background, these programs tend to produce what may be called a "social convergence" effect; that is, they promote cross-cultural understanding by inhibiting a natural tendency to reject cultural modes that might be perceived as being "different."

Other Worlds

In learning a second language, the students acquire new modes of thought, new ways of behaviour. They begin to understand those new modes and new ways. Understanding leads to acceptance. Acceptance leads to tolerance and diversification of one's world view. As I recently claimed in a slogan,

"Monolingualism can be cured!"

because it is, in a way, a type of cognitive disease. Monolingualism constrains. Monolingualism lessens our viewpoint and our *Weltanschauung*, the personal philosophy of the world. Learning other languages cannot help but diversify and broaden the point of view. Therefore, once we've come to see another person's point of view, we accept the other person. By accepting the other person, we accept that person's culture. Accepting another culture leads to increased tolerance and harmony and, ultimately, to peace in the world. This, after all, was the contention Alfred Korzybysky (1933), the founder of general semantics. The science and theory of general semantics was based on the view that knowing how other people talk is knowing how they think, how they behave, and this knowledge will lead to acceptance.

Language and Unity

This conclusion contradicts the waving placards of demonstrators against Canada's 1988 Official Languages Act: "One language unites, two languages divide." I am firmly convinced that only when the study of either official language or of Heritage/ International Languages is depoliticized and the learning of languages is accepted for its own intrinsic value, will we be able, in my opinion, to have linguistic peace and harmony in this country.*

References

College Entrance Examination Board. 1986. *Academic Preparation in For-*

eign Language. Teaching for Transition from High School to College. New York: College Entrance Examination Board.

Cummins, J. and M. Swain. 1986. *Bilingualism in Education.* London: Longman.

Danesi, Marcel. 1988. "The Utilization of the Mother Tongue in the Educational Experience of the Minority Language Child: A Synopsis of Research." *Multiculturalism*, 11: 6-10.

Goossen, Tam. 1994. "Should International Languages Be Part of the School Curriculum?" *Mosaic*, 1, 3: 19.

Korzybyski, A. 1933. *Science and Sanity: An Introduction to non-Aristotelian Systems and General Semantics.* Lancaster: Science Press.

Lambert, W.E. and G.R. Tucker, 1972. *Bilingual Education of Children: The St. Lambert Experiment.* Rowley MA: Newbury House.

Lacey, Veronica. 1993. "Modern Languages: Recognizing their Relevance." Keynote address at the Spring Conference on the Ontario Modern Language Teachers' Association. March. Mimeo.

Lederer, Richard. 1987. *Anguished English. An Anthology of Accidental Assaults Upon Our Language.* Charleston, NC: Wyric and Company.

McLaughlin, B. 1984. *Second-Language Acquisition and Childhood.* Hillsdale, NJ: Lawrence Earlbaum Associates.

Metford, Debirah and Suzann Ottewell. 1996. *La presse à l'école.* Welland, ON: éditions Soleil opublishing inc.

Mollica, Anthony. 1984. "Student Exchanges: Getting to Know One Another." *Dialogue, A Newsletter on the Teaching of English and French as Second Languages*, 3, 1 (November): 1-12. Toronto: Council of Ministers of Education, Canada.

Peel, Elizabeth and Wallace E. Lambert. 1962. "Relationship of Bilingualism to Intelligence." *Psychological Monographs*, 76 (whole issue).

Ralph, Edwin G. 1995. "Motivating Parents to Support Second Language Programs." *Mosaic*, 2, 4: 17.

Rivers, Wilga. 1968. *Teaching Foreign-Language Skills.* Chicago, IL: University of Chicago Press.

Runte, Roseann. 1995. "Learning Languages in the Context of Canada's Many Cultures." *Mosaic*, 2, 4: 8-11.

Runte, Roseann. 1996. "Surviving the Perils of Politics: The Language Classroom of the Next Century." *Mosaic*, 3, 2: 1, 3-7.

*Mollica *et al.* have published, through éditions Soleil publishing inc., (www.soleilpublishing.com) a series of 18"x24" posters identifying reasons for promoting/encouraging the study of languages.

CS-001 Why *you* should learn a second language
CS-002 No knowledge of a second language?
CS-003 Why learn a modern language?
CS-004 Important benefits of second-language learning
CS-005 Why learn French in Canada?
CS-006 Why learn a heritage language?
CS-007 Why learn French?
CS-008 Why learn German?
CS-009 Why learn Latin?
CS-010 Why learn Italian?
CS-011 Why learn Spanish?

Caption-only posters:
LP-001 Monolingualism *can* be cured!
LP-003 Italian. Don't leave *school* without it!
LP-004 Languages. A golden opportunity!
LP-005 Languages. The world at your fingertips!
LP-006 Learn a language. Share a culture. Change the world!

Editor's Note: This is a revised, expanded, and up-dated version of Anthony Mollica, "Language Learning: The Key to Understanding and Harmony," *Language and Society/Langue et société*, 26, Spring 1989. Published by the Office of the Commissioner of Official Languages. It is reprinted with permission of the Minister of Supply and Services, Canada, 1989.

The current article includes sections from Anthony Mollica, "*Traduttore, traditore!* Beware of Communicative Incompetence!" *Mosaic*, 3, 4(Summer 1996), pp. 23-24.

Reprinted from: Anthony Mollica, "Language Learning: The Key to Understanding and Harmony." *Mosaic*, 1, 1 (Fall 1993): 1, 3-5.

2 Beyond the Classroom: Bilingualism, Cognitive Skills and Health

Zofia Wodniecka and Nicholas J. Cepeda

The authors discuss the effects of bilingualism on cognitive skills, such as problem-solving, task switching, and ignoring irrelevant information, and health, including the onset of dementia during aging. They also examine the types of cognitive skills that are and are not likely to benefit from bilingualism.

Questions

There are many questions that teachers might want to ask about bilingualism:

- Is there a critical period of life during which language is most easily learned; consequently, at what age should children start learning a second (or third) language?
- When teaching a new language, should we intersperse communication across old and new languages, or immerse children in a new language to the exclusion of communication in the old language?
- Should we insist on keeping active the native languages of immigrant children?
- Finally, what are the effects of bilingual education beyond the classroom, including effects on basic cognitive skills and health?

These questions bear on the decisions educators make about when, whether, and how to implement bilingual education in both the classroom and the general curriculum.

Historically, the psychology literature has painted a splattered and complex picture and has been biased by researchers' agendas, making it difficult for psychologists to provide meaningful guidance to teachers. Part of the reason psychologists have failed to reach a consensus about major curriculum decisions, such as whether to use English immersion programs, stems from methodological flaws in the studies and reviews aimed at answering these questions. For example, Greene (1997) carefully examined Rossell and Baker's (1996; see also Baker and de Kanter, 1981) bilingual education literature review, which compared bilingual education to English immersion programs, during second-language acquisition, and found two major problems with the review.

- After carefully examining each of the 38 studies in the Rossell and Baker review, Greene concluded that only 11 of the original 38 studies were methodologically sound.
- Rossell and Baker used a non-rigorous review methodology – they counted the number of studies showing positive and negative effects.

Because more than half of studies in their review showed negative effects, Rossell and Baker concluded that English immersion is preferable to bilingual education. In contrast, using just the properly designed and controlled studies, and using more precise meta-analysis methodology, Greene showed overall positive benefits of bilingual education on reading and math ability. Recently, Krashen and McField (2005) reviewed six meta-analyses of English immersion programs and found that all six showed positive benefits for bilingual education during second-language acquisition.

In this paper, we discuss the effects of bilingualism on cognitive skills, such as problem-solving, task switching, and ignoring irrelevant information, and health, including the onset of dementia during aging. We focus on the history of bilingualism research, recent evidence about the cognitive and health consequences of bilingual-ism, possible reasons that bilingualism impacts intellectual functioning, and pedagogical implications of second-language acquisition and maintenance. Finally, we examine the types of cognitive skills that are and are not likely to benefit from bilingualism.

Research History

Psychologists became interested in bilingualism during the 1920s. The main goal at that time was to understand why bilingual children were performing more poorly at school than monolinguals (May, Hill, and Tiakiwai, 2004). Early research ended up confirming existing stereotypes that being bilingual meant being a lower-class citizen. In actuality, bilinguals often were immigrants or lived in economically depressed rural regions, where they did not receive a rigorous education. It comes no surprise that they performed worse than their monolingual peers, who came from families of higher socio-economic status.

Compounding these issues of bias, bilingualism itself was

rather poorly defined at that time; scientists treated language status as a dichotomous variable, and failed to acknowledge that language ability is graded and multi-dimensional. Tests of "mental capabilities" often were administered in the researchers' primary language, not the language with which participants felt most comfortable. One of the most spectacular examples of this rather loose attitude toward the methods of scientific inquiry is a study from the 1930s, in which children were classified as monolinguals or bilinguals based on the sound of their name (Pintner, 1932). The unfavorable view on mental abilities of bilinguals was still rather strong in the 1950s, when Darcy (1953), after reviewing earlier studies, came to conclusion that bilinguals always perform worse than monolinguals on verbal tasks, as well as on a majority of performance-based tasks. (A comprehensive review of the literature on this topic can be found in Peal and Lambert, 1962.)

A breakthrough came in the 1960s, when Peal and Lambert (1962) conducted a study in which they compared two carefully selected groups of children speaking French and English. When selecting participants, factors like socio-economic status and level of fluency in both languages were taken into careful consideration. In the context of earlier research, the results were surprising: Bilingual children outperformed monolinguals on the majority of tasks, measuring both verbal and non-verbal skills. Peal and Lambert explained this bilingual advantage by claiming that bilingual children are better at concept formation and cognitive flexibility. Further research supported Peal and Lambert's conclusions. For instance, Kessler and Quinn (1980; 1987) found a bilingual advantage on problem solving and creativity tasks.

Recent Evidence

Since the seminal study by Peal and Lambert (1962), bilinguals have been found to outperform monolinguals on variety of other tasks that tests that measure – most generally – effectiveness of attention, or the ability to focus on one thing and ignore another. In a series of experiments (reviewed in Bialystok, 2001), monolingual and bilingual children were asked to complete tasks that required flexibility in thinking, such as using the word "moon" to refer to daytime and focusing exclusively on grammatical aspects of sentences like "Apples grow on noses," ignoring the absurdity of the meaning. In both these tasks, bilingual children make considerably fewer mistakes than monolingual children.

Preschoolers and young children show great difficulty switching between tasks, such as from matching objects by shape to matching by color (Bialystok and Martin, 2004; Cepeda, Cepeda, and Kramer, 2000). Despite their repeated attempts to switch to a new task, and despite having knowledge of the new task, many preschoolers become stuck and unintentionally continue performing the first task, a problem called perseveration. Recent evidence shows that bilingualism moderates perseveration (Bialystok and Martin), helping to develop task control at an earlier age.

A bilingual advantage has been found on tasks that measure "theory of mind," a reasoning ability related to successful social interaction. In theory of mind tasks, children are shown objects that appear to be one thing (e.g., a rock), but actually are another thing (e.g., a sponge). After the actual nature of the object is revealed, children are asked whether their peer, upon first seeing the object, will think that the object is a rock (i.e., what it appears to be), or a sponge (i.e., what it actually is). Compared to age-matched monolingual peers, bilingual preschoolers are more likely to say "a rock," demonstrating that bilingual children develop theory of mind, or the ability to put themselves in somebody else's shoes, at an earlier age than monolinguals (Bialystok and Senman, 2004).

Older adults show some bilingualism benefits as well, demonstrating that the bilingual advantage extends well beyond childhood (at least in older adults who maintain use of multiple languages). For instance, young and old monolingual and bilingual adults were asked to pay attention to the color of a stimulus and ignore its location (Bialystok, Craik, Klein, and Viswanathan, 2004). Sometimes participants needed to press the same response key for each possible response (e.g., the same key for "red" and "left"), an easy task, and sometimes they had to press different keys for each task (e.g., one key for "red" and a different key for "left"), which created confusion. The results demonstrated that older bilinguals were almost as successful at ignoring the irrelevant aspect of a stimulus as young adults. In contrast, older monolinguals were slower and less accurate than their age peers.

Recent evidence suggests that bilinguals outperform monolinguals on memory tests. In one study, bilinguals were more successful at remembering episodic information, or the source from which they learned a fact, than their peers (Wodniecka, Craik, and Bialystok, 2007). Even more striking, older bilinguals show similar levels of recollection as younger monolinguals, suggesting that bilingualism may help offset age-related memory decline. In this study, the older bilingual group included individuals who acquired a second language in their 20s, which suggests that individuals can benefit from becoming bilingual and actively using both languages, even if they learn a second language later in life. At this point, it remains unclear whether regular practice using multiple languages is necessary to continue bilingualism benefits.

The cognitive benefits of bilingualism have been observed not only in children and older adults, but also in younger adults. Spanish-Catalan bilingual young adults were better at inhibiting irrelevant information and switching between tasks than their monolingual peers (Costa, Hernández, and Sebastián-Gallés, 2007).

Reasons

What is the source of the observed bilingual advantage on cognitive skills? One explanation suggests that when a bilingual prepares an utterance in one language, the other language is never "switched off" or waiting for its turn. This is supported by evidence from psycholinguistic experiments that both languages are always active to some degree. People who know and use more than one language can switch languages without intention or conscious recollection. Very often a bilingual becomes aware of this unexpected switch only after noticing the surprised faces of their listeners. The fact that such situations occur at all can be taken as evidence for the simultaneous activation of both languages. At least at the early stages of speech production, perhaps the bilingual mind activates translation equivalents in both languages. In this model, language production can be conceptualized as a race (Logan, 1988) or – using a more vivid metaphor – a battle, in which both languages are poised to seize power. This battle usually takes a fraction of a second, an era in mind-time.

Arguments in support of the "race" or "war" hypothesis have been provided by several psycholinguistic experiments. In one of them (Wodniecka, Bobb, Kroll, and Green, 2007), English-Spanish bilinguals named pictures in either English or Spanish. We asked participants to name pictures in one language, and then we repeated the pictures again, and asked participants to name them either in the same language as before, or in the other language. We also included a set of new pictures that were not named earlier. The time it took participants to name repeated pictures in the second language was longer, compared to when the first language was repeated. More importantly, the time to name repeated pictures in the second language was the same, and sometimes a bit longer, as the time to name completely new pictures. This result can be taken as evidence that there is competition between the two languages, and the conflict needs to be resolved by modulating relative activation of the languages. Because most of the time our mind makes the right decision (that is, the winner in the battle is the intended language), this suggests that there must be a mechanism that makes "the enemy withdraw its forces."

This proposed mechanism can explain the bilingual advantage observed in many studies discussed above: Bilinguals have massive practice using control mechanisms that help them negotiate the ever-present conflict between languages. Thus, they also are faster and more efficient at switching between tasks and modulating attentional control, compared to monolinguals. Bilinguals' superior performance on these tasks could be caused by increased ability to inhibit the undesired response (Anderson, 2005) and/ or increased activation of the desired response (Cepeda and Munakata, 2007). Green (1998) has argued that bilinguals recruit the same conflict-control mechanisms both when controlling competing languages and when performing other activities that require control (e.g., ignoring irrelevant distracting information). According to this argument, bilingual benefits observed in non-language-based cognitive tasks are side effects of bilinguals' frequent practice modulating speech production in each of their two languages.

Delaying Dementia

In case improved problem solving and reasoning skills are insufficient reason to learn and use a second language, throughout your life, bilingualism has been shown to have a sizable public health benefit – protection against the onset of dementia (Bialystok, Craik, Freedman, 2007). Knowing and using multiple languages, on an everyday basis, might delay some aspects of inevitable cognitive decline related to aging. The dementia-delay finding is perhaps the most spectacular bilingualism effect that has been demonstrated, to date.

Bialystok, Craik, and Freedman (2007) investigated the records of patients who were referred to a memory clinic with cognitive complaints. In the final analyses, they considered data from 184 patients; the group consisted of 132 patients who were diagnosed with Alzheimer's disease and 52 individuals with other forms of dementia. About half the patients were monolingual (the only language they knew was English), and the other half were bilingual, with a variety of different non-English first language backgrounds, most immigrants to Canada from Europe after World War II. The researchers looked at several variables, including: The age of first visit to the clinic, the age of onset of symptoms of dementia, and the rate of cognitive decline. The mean age at which symptoms of dementia occurred in the monolingual group was 71.4-years-old, and in the bilingual group – 75.5-years-old. The bilingual advantage – a 4-year delay in onset of dementia – was statistically significant, even when factors such as years of formal education, socio-economic status, gender, and immigration experience were taken into account (some of the monolinguals also were immigrants to Canada). According to Dr. Freedman, "There are no pharmacological interventions that are this dramatic."

It is important to bear in mind that this finding is preliminary, and more research is necessary before definite conclusions can be drawn. For instance, one limitation of the study stems from the methodology used; the study was correlational, and although it allows one to conclude that there is a relationship between linguistic experience and the age of onset of dementia, there might have been some unknown factors that contributed to the significant relationship. Another important issue that needs to be kept in mind is that the study did not show differential rates of decline between bilingual and monolingual groups. To the contrary, the rate of decline from diagnosis onset was the same for both patients groups. Thus, based on this study, we cannot infer that bilingualism is a remedy for dementia. Nevertheless, the results provide an important first step in establishing the exact influence of bilingualism on cognitive decline with aging. Notably, the beneficial impact of bilingualism on cognitive decline has only been established in individuals who make frequent use of both languages, and cannot yet be generalized to second language users who alternate between using each language on a less frequent basis.

How can bilingualism influence dementia? Bialystok et al. (2007) suggests that psychological factors (e.g., lifestyle, educational choices, and social engagement) may cause biological changes, such as increased generation of neurons or synapses, or reorganization of brain networks. For example, these biological mechanisms may increase working memory strength (Cepeda and Munakata, 2007), which undergoes developmental changes that are probably related to maturation of neural connections, thereby enabling the brain to better tolerate pathologies accumulated in the brain, such as dementia.

Caveats

Most things in life have a price attached. As it turns out, bilingualism may cause some problems, despite its benefits. A recent set of studies (Gollan, Montoya, Fennema-Notestine, Morris, 2005; Gollan, Montoya, Werner, 2002) showed that individuals who speak more than one language might have greater difficulty recalling words in each of their languages; they achieved lower scores than monolinguals in a task that required enlisting words from a given category. In addition, bilinguals have been found to experience the so-called "tip-of-the-tongue" phenomenon [where an individual remembers some aspects of a word (e.g., number of syllables or letters), but has difficulty retrieving the full word] more often than monolinguals (Gollan and Acenas, 2004). There are no known real-life implications from this deficit, but potentially it could mean that, on average, bilinguals speak less fluently than monolinguals.

Recently, prominent findings of a bilingual advantage (Bialystok et al., 2004) have been called into question (Morton and Harper, in press), based in part on making comparisons between immigrant and non-immigrant populations. Morton and Harper attempted to replicate one previous bilingual-advantage finding, while also carefully matching many background factors and comparing Canadian sub-populations that were not recent immigrants. Their replication failed to find a language-based performance difference in one cognitive control task, suggesting that further research using similarly matched groups is warranted. Most importantly, the Morton and Harper study suggests that even if the advantages of bilingualism are slightly smaller than previously thought, bilingualism does not appear to hurt cognitive skills.

Pedagogical Implications

As we have argued throughout this article, learning and regularly using a second language can improve not only cultural knowledge, but also cognitive abilities like problem solving, reasoning, attention, and cognitive control. In addition, bilingualism may have effects on long-term health, including possibly delaying the onset of memory decline during aging caused by dementia. We speculate that becoming proficient in a second language might either help children already diagnosed with ADHD develop improved ability to control their actions or reduce the chances of developing ADHD. Similar speculation has been made before, by researchers who examined the prevalence of ADHD in bilingual children and found that increased proficiency in a second language was associated with reduced ADHD symptom severity (Toppelberg, Medrano, Morgens, and Nieto-Castañon, 2002). It remains to be seen whether cognitive skill deficits that are associated with ADHD, such as difficulty switching between tasks (Cepeda et al., 2000; Kramer, Cepeda, and Cepeda, 2001), also are reduced by bilingualism.

While biased researchers and poor experimental design have plagued bilingualism research in the past, well-controlled studies suggest that, at worst, bilingual education is unlikely to produce significant cognitive deficits, and sometimes bilingualism leads to important cognitive benefits. On balance, the scales seem tipped far toward recommendations that schools implement bilingual education, for all students, at an early age, and that schools maintain bilingual education throughout the grade levels. To put it simply: Bilingualism probably improves cognitive skills and may delay the onset of dementia and reduce ADHD severity.

References

Anderson, M. C. 2005. "The role of inhibitory control in forgetting unwanted memories: A consideration of three methods." In N. Ohta, C. M. MacLeod, and B. Uttl, eds., *Dynamic cognitive processes* (pp. 159-190). New York: Springer.

Baker, K. A., and A.A. de Kanter. 1981. *Effectiveness of bilingual education: A review of the literature*. Washington, DC: U.S. Department of Education.

Bialystok, E. 2001. *Bilingualism in development: Language, literacy, and cognition*. New York: Cambridge University Press.

Bialystok, E., F. I. M. Craik, and M. Freedman. 2007. "Bilingualism as a protection against the onset of symptoms of dementia." *Neuropsychologia, 45*, 459-464.

Bialystok, E., F. I. M. Craik, R. Klein, and M. Viswanathan. 2004. "Bilingualism, aging, and cognitive control: Evidence from the Simon task." *Psychology and Aging, 19*, 290-303.

Bialystok, E., and M. M. Martin. 2004. "Attention and inhibition in bilingual children: Evidence from the dimensional change card sort task." *Developmental Science, 7*, 325-339.

Bialystok, E., and L. Senman. 2004. "Executive processes in appearance-reality tasks: The role of inhibition of attention and symbolic representation." *Child Development, 75*, 562-579.

Cepeda, N. J., M. L. Cepeda, and A. F. Kramer. 2000. "Task switching and attention deficit hyperactivity disorder." *Journal of Abnormal Child Psychology, 28*, 213-226.

Cepeda, N. J., and Y. Munakata. 2007. "Why do children perseverate when they seem to know better: Graded working memory, or directed inhibition?" *Psychonomic Bulletin and Review*, 14, 1058-1065.

Costa, A., M. Hernández, and N. Sebastián-Gallés. 2007. "Bilingualism aids conflict resolution: Evidence from the ANT task." *Cognition*. doi:10.1016/j.cognition.2006.12.013.

Darcy, N. T. 1953. "A review of the literature of the effects of bilingualism upon the measurement of intelligence." *Journal of Geriatric Psychology, 82*, 21-57.

Gollan, T. H., and L.-A. R. Acenas. 2004. "What is a TOT? Cognate and translation effects on tip-of-the-tongue states in Spanish-English and Tagalog-English bilinguals." *Journal of Experimental Psychology: Learning, Memory, and Cognition, 30*, 246-269.

Gollan, T. H., R. I. Montoya, C. Fennema-Notestine, and S. K. Morris. 2005. "Bilingualism affects picture naming but not picture classification." *Memory and Cognition, 33*, 1220-1234.

Gollan, T. H., R. I. Montoya, and G. A. Werner. 2002. "Semantic and letter fluency in Spanish-English bilinguals." *Neuropsychology, 16*, 562-576.

Green, D.W. 1998. "Mental control of the bilingual lexico-semantic system." *Bilingualism: Language and Cognition*, 1, *67-81.*

Greene, J. P. 1997. "A meta-analysis of the Rossell and Baker review of bilingual education research." *Bilingual Research Journal, 21,* 103-122.

Kessler, C., and M. E. Quinn. 1980. "Positive effects of bilingualism on science problem-solving abilities." In J. Alatis, ed., *Georgetown University round table on language and linguistics* (pp. 295-308). Washington, DC: Georgetown University Press.

Kessler, C., and M. E. Quinn. 1987. "ESL and science learning." In J. Crandall, ed., *ESL through content-area instruction.* Englewood Cliffs, NJ: Prentice Hall.

Kramer, A. F., N. J. Cepeda, and M. L. Cepeda. 2001. "Methylphenidate effects on task-switching performance in attention-deficit/hyperactivity disorder." *Journal of the American Academy of Child and Adolescent Psychiatry, 40,* 1277-1284.

Krashen, S., and G. McField. 2005. "What works? Reviewing the latest evidence on bilingual education." *Language Learner, 1,* 7-10 and 34.

Logan, G. D. 1988. "Toward an instance theory of automatization." *Psychological Review, 95,* 492-527.

May, S., R. Hill, and S. Tiakiwai. 2004. *Bilingual/immersion education: Indicators of good practice.* Wellington, New Zealand: New Zealand Ministry of Education.

Morton, J. B., and S. N. Harper. (in press). "What did Simon say? Revisiting the bilingual advantage." *Developmental Science.*

Peal, E., and W. E. Lambert. 1962. "The relation of bilingualism to intelligence." *Psychological Monographs, 76,* 1-23.

Pintner, R. 1932. *Intelligence testing: Methods and results.* 2nd ed. New York: Henry Holt.

Rossell, C. H., and K. Baker. 1996. "The educational effectiveness of bilingual education." *Research in the Teaching of English, 30,* 7-74.

Toppelberg, C. O., L. Medrano, L. P. Morgens, and A. Nieto-Castañon. 2002. "Bilingual children referred for psychiatric services: Associations of language disorders, language skills, and psychpathology." *Journal of the American Academy of Child and Adolescent Psychiatry, 41,* 712-722.

Wodniecka, Z., S. C. Bobb, J. F. Kroll, and D. W. Green. 2007. *Selection process in bilingual word production: Evidence for inhibition.* Manuscript in preparation.

Wodniecka, Z., F. I. M. Craik, and E. Bialystok. (in press). "Recollection and familiarity in monolinguals and bilinguals." *Brain and Cognition.* [Abstract].

Reprinted from: Zofia Wodniecka and Nicholas J. Cepeda, "Beyond the Classroom: Bilingualism, Cognitive Skills, and Health." *Mosaic,* 9, 3 (Fall 2007): 3-8.

3 Motivating Parents to Support Second-Language Programs

Edwin G. Ralph

Based on an assumption that second-language teachers provide the key motivating force facilitating this parental support, this paper presents several successful strategies – grounded both in second-language teachers' actual experiences and in related action-research – which have been shown to enhance parental support for school second-language programs.

The nineties are witnessing a growing societal demand for increased involvement by parents and the community in the improvement of education. Recent social, political, economic, and ecological events, worldwide – which often receive instantaneous exposure because of the advancement of global communication systems – have combined to exert pressure upon the educational establishment to become more effective, accountable, open, and collaborative with respect to the public they serve (Simpson, 1994).

Gone are the days when educators could "sidestep" demands from parents or could deflect societal pressure by arguing: "We are the trained professionals in education, parents are not. Just let us alone to do our jobs: we will teach your children what they need to know." Today's educators, on the other hand, are becoming increasingly pro-active in their deliberate solicitation of family involvement in education and are, as well, welcoming wider community participation by business, industry, and other agencies (Brandt, 1994).

Background and Rationale

The rationale supporting increased family and community involvement in schooling generally – ancsd in second-language education specifically – rests upon three key assumptions. Although these foundational premises are not necessarily new nor profound, they have recently regained prominence –

particularly in the light of the tenuous balance currently existing between the desire for international cooperation among nations, on the one hand, and the dangers of global competition, on the other.

The first assumption is rooted in the fundamental purpose of schooling in society. Schools were initially established by Western nations to be service agencies accountable to the families and citizens who financed them. The latter paid taxes to be used for the purpose of providing education for their children. Logically, then, those who pay for such educational services should have the right to be involved in examining the results of the enterprise, and in requiring improvements if necessary.

Traditionally, this involvement was secured in North America by several means:

- the election of representative school boards who set educational policy for groups of schools in a district;
- the establishment of school-division wide citizen advisory groups to provide school trustees with "grassroots input" about education from the community;
- the establishment of parent-teacher associations at each school; and
- other *ad hoc* committees set up from time to time, to provide information or to present concerns on educational matters to governing bodies at various levels.

In this paper, "second-language education" has a much wider scope than English-as-a-second-language (ESL), and French-as-a-second-language programs (FSL). Although the term includes ESL and FSL programs of all types, it also encompasses the so-called "modern languages" and the Heritage/International languages, as well as the First Nations languages.

With respect to second-language education in Canada over the past few years, the groups just described have pressured school districts in many regions to make policy-changes in favour of providing a variety of language-learning programs (See, for example, Ralph, 1979). In fact, it would be fair to say that – as a group – the parents of children in Canadian second-language programs, particularly those whose children are enroled in the various immersion options across the Nation, would tend to rate higher in "being motivated" about these school programs, than would comparable groups of parents whose children are not in these second-language programs. This is so because of the unique phenomenon in Canada that is unlike the experience in most parts of the world where people learn two or more languages, as a routine. In Canada, parents who choose immersion programs for their children must face several issues, some of which are:

- Will they and their children be stigmatized for "breaking neighbourhood ties" by sending pupils to centralized immersion schools?
- Will they be labelled as "elitist" because of this decision (and because of often receiving "free" bus transportation to and from the immersion schools that are often a distance away)?
- Will their children's scholastic achievement suffer, in their first language? in their second language? in the other subjects?
- How will parents ever know if they have made the right decision?

In short, because these parents, as a group, have risked "daring to be different", they will naturally tend to form a close-knit, supportive group, who become highly motivated in seeing their children succeed and thus will support the school program.

A second assumption underlying the principle of encouraging parental and community support for second-language programs is rooted in the fundamental biological/psychological basis of parenting. Parents care for their children, and they are ultimately the most important influence in their children's lives. While it is true that the make-up of the traditional family has recently shifted (Pawlas, 1994), it is equally true that the vast majority of parents, from all types of family units, are interested in being involved in assisting in their children's school experiences, but are often not sure of how to go about it (Elam, Rose, and Gallup, 1993; Epstein, 1993).

For example, Canter (1991) reports that in a recent poll, only 25% of parents reported receiving systematic requests/instructions from teachers with respect to assisting in students' learning activities at school or at home. In order to help remedy this situation, he consequently suggests – on the basis of his research in this area – that educators must capitalize on this ready parental desire to help, and that schools should initiate specific efforts to "turn parents into partners". The key to gaining and maintaining this support is effective teacher communication that expresses to parents a genuine interest in having *every* student succeed, and that treats the parent the way the teacher – if a parent – would want to be treated by her/his child's own teacher (Canter, 1991).

One of the clearest examples of organized parental involvement in second-language education has been the growth of Canadian Parents for French (CPF) over the past 20 years (Sloan,

1989; MacIsaac, 1990; Morissette, 1992). CPF, now numbering more than 18,000 members throughout Canada's 10 provinces and two territories, has been recognized as "the most successful educational lobby in history" (Hood, 1989)). This parental organization has been a major factor in exerting pressure:

(a) to increase access to improved FSL instruction (both core and immersion programs) for children in all regions of Canada;
(b) to promote para-educational activities for these students (e.g., FSL exchanges, trips, weekends, camps, media/materials, and interactive experiences); and
(c) to call for improved governmental second-language services for minorities in Canada.

A key result of CPF's efforts is that the current generation of Canadian school children ranks as the most bilingual in Canada's entire history (MacIsaac, 1990); and what is equally as notable, is that 90% of a recent survey of CPF members indicated that they would provide their children with the same FSL experiences, again, if they had the opportunity (Morissette, 1992). This association has not only demonstrated a consistently organized and powerful voice in presenting parental and community concerns to educational policy-makers, but they have been influential in helping establish and/or modify second-language policies/practices for individual schools and school districts.

In the United States, a comparable organization called "Advocates for Language Learning" (ALL), is a similarly powerful parental group that supports second-language school programs (Antonek, Tucker, and Donato, 1995). Erlich (1987), the founder of ALL, indicates – as does CPF – that immersion programs provide ideal means for children to learn a second language within regular school programs.

Another more recent example illustrating the increased importance of parental and community involvement in education on a broader front was the 1994 announcement by United States Secretary of Education, Richard Riley, of the formation of a nation-wide partnership among the U.S. Department of Education, the 45-member National Coalition for Parent Involvement in Education, and several prominent parent, religious, business, civic and community-based organizations (U.S. Department, 1994). This coalition is directly linked to one of the 8 National Education Goals recently enacted by the U.S. government as part of the *Goals 2000: Educate America* Act, which is to promote partnerships that will increase parental involvement and participation in the activities of the school.

These examples illustrate the underlying fundamental assumption with regard to parental support that is backed by 30 years of research:

> Greater family involvement in children's learning is a critical link to achieving a high-quality education and a safe, disciplined learning environment for every student" (U.S. Department, 1994, p. 1).

A third foundational premise underlying the need for family and community support of students' learning is that the classroom teacher is the key source in initiating and upholding the school-home relationship. Although government legislation, school-board policy, and school-site expectations are all needed to promote school-community bonding, it is essentially the responsibility of the teacher – and mostly through her daily interactions and relationships with students during the routines of school-life – to nurture and sustain this relationship. Parents promptly learn from their children – often even before the "September Open-House" is held – what the teacher is like (whether or not such an "assessment" is accurate). According to their children's descriptions, reactions, and opinions of the teacher's work, conduct, and attitude at school, the family's perceptions and views of the teacher and the program are soon formed, and the teacher's reputation becomes firmly established. Whether positive or not, this perception becomes relatively difficult to change. In fact, one director of education from a school district in Western Canada (on the basis of his 25 years' experience in education) recently advised a group of teacher-interns embarking on a job-search for their first teaching position that:

> If parents think you are effective as a teacher, then they will readily forgive you if you make a blunder – even a serious one! However, if they don't like you – on the basis of what their kids, and others, say about you – you will have an uphill struggle... You have to show that you really – not superficially care for their children... (Johnson, 1994).

Effective Ways to Involve Parents/Communities

Using the above rationale as a conceptual framework, I draw upon three sources from which to derive some specific practices that have proven successful in encouraging families and community to support second-language education. The three sources are:

1. responses both from practising and from retired educators (many in second-language education) (Ralph, 1994b);
2. recent findings reported in the related educational literature (Danesi, 1993; Mollica, 1993); and
3. my own 30 years' experience in education (as second-language

teacher, second-language program coordinator, school principal, career counsellor, president/director of a publishing firm marketing second-language instructional materials, college/ university professor, and supervisor of teacher-interns).

In many countries, government legislation and policy at both federal and provincial (or state) levels – together with local school district and individual school-site policies, regulations, and procedures – have all been combined to establish overall guidelines for second-language education. However, in recent years, the traditional top-down, hierarchical governance and administration of education has been displaced by: trends toward increased collaboration among stakeholders; more empowerment of school-based personnel to participate in decision-making and policy-formation that affects them; and transformational leadership, whereby administrative and supervisory tasks are shared among *all* professionals.

In the light of these reforms, and based on the assumptions undergirding quality parental cooperation, what specific practices have been shown to promote the involvement of the family and the community in second-language programs? Several practices are presented below. It should be noted, again, that even though some of these initiatives may be externally legislated, or bureaucratically mandated by various educational officials, it is the second-language teachers, themselves, who are key determinants in the degree of lasting success of these efforts.

Orientating Parents to Second-Language Programs

Several effective projects and programs that effectively link parents and the community to second-language programs have been reported. One initiative that invariably motivates parents and the school community – particularly in the case of immersion schools (or immersion programs within regular schools) is an "Orientation Evening" or "Open House" typically held early in the school year. At such sessions, school-based personnel describe the second-language program, answer parents' questions and allay their concerns about the program. Presentations on such topics as "Why Learn a second language?", or "What A Quarter-Century of Research Findings Tell Us About second-language Program Options" prove very valuable in clarifying misconceptions and/ or re-assuring parents that they have made sound decisions in enroling their children in particular programs.

With respect to the "Why learn a second language?" topic, I have found in my experience as a teacher of second-language and a coordinator of second-language programs in a Western

Canadian school district, that I was able to help defuse certain criticisms and fears of parents, students, and the community by first of all clearly articulating opponents' doubts about a specific second-language program, and then by deliberately refuting these misconceptions, one by one, using the well-established research results for second language programs. Furthermore, at these meetings, I was able to describe and clarify the strengths and comparative limitations of the various second-language program-options (i.e., early, intermediate, and late immersion; extended programs; and core and conversational courses) (Ralph, 1981).

Several current writers have synthesized the rationale supporting the study of a second language (Danesi, 1993; Mollica, 1993; Ralph, 1982, 1994a). A particularly valuable resource for this topic is Mollica's (1990) "The Clipboard Series" of eleven poster-size visuals presenting valid, practical reasons for learning a second language (e.g., Spanish, Italian, or Heritage Languages. See p. 14.).

A technique I found to be particularly effective in this vein was to present these concrete benefits of being bi- or multi-lingual to students and parents. Stating the following advantages proved to be a powerful means either to reduce negative attitudes or to bolster parent/student commitment towards various second-language programs:

(a) in general, people who know more than one language have a certain mental enrichment or cognitive stimulation about their personalities, not observable in comparable groups of monolinguals;

(b) bilingual/multilingual individuals' scores on psychological tests (both verbal and non-verbal) are as a rule higher for divergent thinking skills and diversified reasoning processes, than are similar scores for monolinguals;

(c) people who know more than one language typically get to know their mother tongue better than do comparable groups of monolinguals;

(d) bi- or multi-linguals, compared to their unilingual peers, tend to have a more socially relaxed and at ease reaction to meeting others from different cultures;

(e) they are generally less provincial, stereotypic, prejudiced, and biased in their views of other cultures or individuals, than are similar groups of monolinguals; and

(f) compared to unilingual peers, bilinguals as a group, enjoy more pragmatic benefits, such as being more disposed to travel to other countries overseas, and having access to wider job and career opportunities, because of their second-language abilities (Ralph, 1982, 1994a).

Furthermore, providing parents with attractive, concise print materials outlining the second-language program, its expectations, and its activities (and a time-schedule for these activities) – in the form of brochures, newsletters, and bulletins is typically well-received (Canter, 1991).

Capitalize on "Current Practicalities"

Recent global events have emphasized the critical importance of multinational communication. Growing trade and commercial relationships among European nations, among Pacific rim countries, and among our own North American partners – plus the potential to forge further links between/among these larger international blocs – signal that people skilled in various languages will be required to help expedite these communicative relationships. For example, because of expanding free-trade among Canada, Mexico, and the US on our continent, Spanish will no doubt become increasingly important, here.

With respect to the pragmatic benefits of knowing an second language, educators currently involved in Ukrainian language programs could especially use to their advantage in promoting the second-language program the recent events that have developed in Canada/Ukraine relations. For example, the 1994 visit to Canada by Ukraine's President Leonid Kuchma (Roberts, 1994) could be used by teachers to enhance the status of the study of Ukrainian in Canada. Not only did the two nations form an accord to increase their trade partnership, but Canada has agreed to share commercial and business information and to provide consultants in areas of Ukraine's economic growth, investments, and scientific/technological/ environmental concerns. During this visit, Canadian Prime Minister Chrétien noted that Ukrainian settlers helped to develop Western Canada a century ago, and now it is Canada's turn to reciprocate by assisting Ukraine to develop its newly acquired democracy and free-market system. He stated:

> We are the best country to benefit from Ukraine, because we can offer a lot of Canadian experts who speak Ukrainian... We are the best country to take advantage of the economic growth that will eventually come in Ukraine ("Canada Giving," 1994).

Kuchma later visited Western Canada, home of thousands of citizens of Ukrainian descent. He attended the G7 meeting in Winnipeg, and later met with Saskatchewan's Premier Roy Romanow, himself of Ukrainian ancestry. The two discussed establishing business and government ties to help Ukraine in the areas of energy, agriculture, and health care.

One interesting incident that second-language teachers could use a motivator for senior students and/or parents occurred near the end of this Kuchma-Romanow visit. The President invited the Premier to visit Ukraine, but jokingly advised that he would need to improve his Ukrainian first (Smart, 1994). Teachers could use this actual event to alert students that if native speakers of a language (even key politicians) need to work at ameliorating their linguistic skills, then second-language learners should not feel discouraged if their performance seems slow at times! These recent events graphically represent realistic possibilities for students of Ukrainian to pursue in order to prepare themselves to take advantage of future career opportunities. They will be able to use their bilingualism to assist the two nations in the fields of government, business, industry, labour, and education relations.

Such a pragmatic goal has also been recently highlighted by another Saskatchewan initiative involving the Ukrainian language (McMahen, 1994). In order to help Ukraine improve its schools and teaching since its 1991 independence, a joint initiative has been undertaken by representatives the Saskatchewan Teachers of Ukrainian (the only provincial association for teachers of this language in Canada), the Saskatchewan Department of Education, and the University of Saskatchewan. This project has established a growing number of educational exchanges (of teachers, professors, students, and administrators) between the two countries. During the past three years there has been a 1991 joint education conference in Ukraine, a 1992 student exchange, a sharing of resource materials, Saskatchewan educators' visits to Ukraine in 1993, Ukrainian officials' visits to Saskatchewan schools, and a second joint educational conference in Ukraine in 1994. All of these activities – and potential future developments – have combined to bolster the image of Ukrainian second-language education in Western Canada.

Building Bridges for Students' Second-Language Growth

Although a school's annual "Open House", "Back-to-School Night", or "Meet/Greet Treat" in September are basic means in attracting parents, additional ways have been recently reported to enhance these activities. Research by Epstein (1993) and Canter (1991), for instance, suggests that the school – through its individual teachers – must not only introduce but continue clear and interesting communication links with each family. Some of these initiatives are:

(a) "introductory letters" to parents in August to present briefly the teacher and the second-language program, and to invite them to the first September meeting;

(b) a short form sent to parents on which they are asked to de-
      scribe "What the teacher should know about my child" (e.g.
      his/her likes/dislikes, academic strengths/limitations, per-
      tinent background/experiences);
(c) occasional "positive" notes/memos/telephone calls home
      throughout the year to support, or acknowledge a child's par-
      ticular performance/ improvement/contribution in second
      language;
(d) specific teacher requests for parental assistance in: helping a
      child with a particular second-language homework project;
      being a classroom guest to share with students a unique ex-
      pertise/skill/trip concerning second-language; or filling out
      a brief check-list indicating the tasks/events/projects regard-
      ing second-language, in which the parents would be willing
      to assist during the school term; and
(e) invitations to assist children, individually or in groups – at
      home or at specific times at school – in practising their sec-
      ond-language skills (conversing, reading/listening to read-
      ing, and writing).

An excellent example of how interactive homework strategies are currently being used to promote home-school collaboration is the work reported by Antonek, Tucker, and Donato, 1994;
1995) related to a K-5 Japanese Foreign Language in the Elementary School (FLES) program in Pittsburgh. The researchers found
that the majority of parents completed and appreciated an assigned amount of interactive homework with children. It was also
found that even though the parents had not studied the target
language, themselves, prior to this project, they welcomed the
teachers' initiatives as helping:

> [...] them to understand, to participate in, and to support their
> children's learning experiences [...] They provided a valuable tool
> for enriching the partnership between home and school that has
> seemingly been ignored (Antonek, Tucker, and Donato, 1995, p. 9).

Although it is generally believed that this last initiative (i.e.,
parents helping children learn at home) is a common occurrence,
recent research suggests just the opposite! Devlin-Scherer and
Devlin-Scherer (1994) discovered in a study examining the 5779
tasks assigned over a 4-year period by 10 school boards in Ver-
mont, less than 2% of those tasks dealt with parent involvement
– and not one of these tasks dealt with assisting student learning
at home. Both Canter (1991) and Riley (U.S. Department, 1994)
believe that schools in the 90s must help remedy this problem by
implementing such projects as:

(a) recommending families to undertake a family learning project (e.g., to go on a "Walk 'n Talk", listing [using second language] 10 things that they saw/heard/smelled/felt);

(b) providing parents with brief but specific guidelines/tips for guiding children in their completion of [second-language] homework assignments (and having the parents, the student, and the teacher to sign a follow-up document as the student finishes it); and

(c) reinforce children's successful [second-language] achievements (and parents' assistance towards these) with short, genuine, and positive communications – by note, telephone, or in person.

With respect to Ukrainian-as-a-second-language programs, second-language teachers of Ukrainian, themselves, have found that having parents/grandparents, or other interested community-members who know the language, to take on tutor roles – either as occasional guests, or on a semi-regular basis at school has proved to be a powerful "win/win/win" motivator for all participants. That is,

(a) the visitors feel like worthwhile contributors to the second-language program;

(b) the students are permitted to practice their language skills with "authentic" speakers; and

(c) the teachers sense "a warm glow of satisfaction" from facilitating these successful experiences.

Involving Parents in Cultural Projects

As well as participating in linguistic activities with students, parents have been effectively involved with cultural activities and promotions in the second-language program. (In fact, this article contains several suggestions actually made by the conference attendees during a brainstorming session which I conducted as part of my presentation at the STU 1994 Conference in Saskatoon). Teachers of Ukrainian report high volunteer-rates by families of students for such projects as assisting teachers and their classes in:

(a) preparing traditional Ukrainian meals;

(b) helping or conducting cultural musical and/or dance programs;

(c) teaching/guiding special art projects; and

(d) providing assistance for Christmas Eve and Easter ceremonies (e.g., see Onyschuck, 1994).

A recent example that generated substantial parent and community interest in Ukrainian culture, in a non-Ukrainian school district where no Ukrainian second-language programs existed, occurred with one of my teacher-interns. The intern, who is of Ukrainian descent, and who is a skilled performer in a Ukrainian dance-troupe, was invited to have the sixth grade class, with whom he was working during his internship, to learn and perform a traditional Ukrainian dance-routine at the school's annual pre-Christmas, "Community Cultural Program". Not only did the teacher-intern and his students practice, prepare, and present an outstanding performance, but the reaction from the rest of the student body, the school-staff, the dancers' parents, and the "fullhouse" audience from the surrounding community was highly supportive.

This case reinforces the underlying theme of this present article: the teacher is the key agent to solicit parental involvement. In this case, the entire school community was positively disposed toward the Ukrainian culture by a single teacher, who through his own enthusiasm, motivated the students – and consequently their parents and the community at large.

Such teacher motivation is clearly essential – but insufficient – to achieve success in garnering continued community support for second-language programs. Indeed, to rouse parental motivation, initially, is one thing, but to sustain it over time it requires what effective teachers have always practised: persistence. creativity, and respect! My experience in establishing and maintaining parental and community support for second-language education has been consistent with what other educators and researchers have repeatedly confirmed (Brodkin, 1992; Canter, 1991, Epstein, 1993), and that is: teachers should deal with all second-language students as they would want their children to be treated if they were in that particular program.

References

Antonek, J., R. Donato, G. R. Tucker. 1994. "Japanese in elementary school: Description of an innovative Pittsburgh program." *Mosaic*, 2, 2: 5-9.

Antonek, J., G. Tucker, and R. Donato. 1995. "Interactive homework: Creating connections between home and school." *Mosaic*, 2, 3: 1-10. See Chapter 21, in this volume.

Brandt, R., ed. 1994. "The new alternative schools." *Educational Leadership*, 52, (September): 1.

Brodkin, A. 1992. "Parents and schools: Working together." *Instructor*, 101, 5: 6-7.

"Canada giving $50 million in help to Ukraine." 1994. *The Star Phoenix*, (October 25), p. C4.

Canter, L. and Associates. 1991. *Parents on your side*. Santa Monica, CA: Lee Canter and Associates.

Danesi, M. 1993. "Literacy and Bilingual Education Programs in Elementary School: Assessing the Research." *Mosaic*, 1, 1: 6-12.

Devlin-Scherer, R. and W. Devlin-Scherer. 1994. "Do school boards encourage parent involvement?" *Education*, 114, 4: 535-541.

Ehrlich, M. 1987. "Parents: The child's most important teachers." In J.M. Darcey, ed., *Commitment and collaboration*. Middlebury, VT: Northeast Conference on the Teaching of Foreign Languages.

Elam, S., L. Rose and A. Gallup. 1993. "The 25th annual Phi Delta Kappa/ Gallup poll of the public's attitudes toward the public schools." *Phi Delta Kappa*, 75 (2).

Epstein, J. 1993. "Make parents your partners." *Instructor.* 102 (8), 52-53.

Hood, Sarah. 1989. "The need for excellence in French language teaching." *Language and Society/Langue et société*, 27, pp. 19-20.

Johnson, R. 1994. "*Information for interns seeking teaching positions: views from a director of education.*" Presentation to teacher-interns at Internship Seminar #3, (October 26). McLurg High School, Wilkie, Saskatchewan.

MacIsaac, J. 1990. "The Commissioner speaks to Canadian Parents for French: Good news for the 90s." *Language and Society/Langue et société*, 33, p. 14.

McMahen, L. 1994. "Saskatchewan-Ukraine educational exchanges booming." *Saskatchewan Bulletin*, 61 3: 6. (Available from the Saskatchewan Teachers' Federation, Saskatoon.)

Mollica, Anthony, et al. 1990. "The Clipboard series", Posters. Welland, Ontario: *éditions Soleil publishing inc*.

Mollica, Anthony. 1993. "Language Learning: The Key to Understanding and Harmony." *Mosaic*, 1, 1: 1, 3-5. Chapter 1 in this volume.

Morissette, B. 1992. "Canadian Parents for French: 15 years later." *Language and Society/Langue et société*, 41, pp. 17-18.

Onyschuck, T. 1994. "Teaching culture in a North American context: Ukrainian Easter." *Mosaic*, 1, 3: 21-22. Chapter 49 in this volume.

Pawlas, G. 1994. "Homeless students at the school door." *Educational Leadership*, 51, 8: 79-82.

Ralph, E. 1979. *French-programming policy issues in a school jurisdiction: A case study*. Unpublished doctoral dissertation, University of Manitoba, Winnipeg.

Ralph, E. 1981. "*Immersion: Questions and answers.*" Presentation at Parents' Orientation Meeting, Assiniboine South School Division, Winnipeg, Manitoba. Mimeo.

Ralph, E. 1982. "The unmotivated second-language learner: Can students' negative attitudes be changed?" *The Canadian Modern Language Review/La revue canadienne des langues vivantes*, 38, 3: 493-502.

Ralph, E. 1994a. "Middle and secondary L2 teachers: Meeting classroom challenges via effective teaching research." *Foreign Language Annals*, 27, 1: 89-103.

Ralph E. 1994b. "On assembling the pieces: What do retired educators tell us?" *Action in Teacher Education*, 16, 2: 62-72.

Roberts, D. 1994. "Ukraine gets life line from G7." *The Globe and Mail*, (October 28), pp. B1, B4.

Simpson, J. 1994. "The future of society is knowledge, and schools are at the centre." *The Globe and Mail*, (November 4), p. A20.

Sloan, Tom. 1989. "Canadian Parents for French: Two Provinces," *Language and Society/Langue et société*, 26 (spring): 34-36.

Smart, S. 1994. "Premier, Ukrainian president discuss economic links." *The Star Phoenix*, (October 27), p. A8.

U.S. Department of Education. 1994. "Riley urges families to get involved in children's learning." *Goals 2000 Community Update*, 17, 1: 4.

Editor's Note: Portions of this paper formed the basis of an address to the Saskatchewan Teachers of Ukrainian annual convention in Saskatoon, November 3, 1994.

Reprinted from: Edwin G. Ralph, "Motivating Parents to Support Second-Language Programs." *Mosaic,* 2, 4 (Summer 1995): 1, 3-7.

4 The Fundamentals of Second-Language Teaching

J. Clarence LeBlanc

As second-language teachers do we agree on the fundamentals of our profession? Clarifying this question would help many beginning as well as seasoned teachers – not to mention curriculum developers and textbook authors. The article offers a number of elements for readers' consideration.

In sports, when a team is not winning, the coach often tells the players to get back to the fundamentals. Unlike many sports truisms, this one makes sense. Unless the fundamentals of an activity are mastered, respectable performance is impossible. One can hardly imagine a hockey player who skates poorly, or a ball player who can't throw, having much success no matter what other skills he might possess. What would we think of a coach who would make such athletes practice fancy manoeuvres that are beyond their level of development? Is there a lesson here for second-language teachers? What are the fundamentals of our activity? How well do we ensure their development before we take the students beyond them? Why do so many students, particularly in Core French (as opposed to Immersion or intensive programs)[1] seem to know so little after many years of second language study? They have been exposed to many aspects of the language but have retained little. Had they even learned one important function and notion per day, they would now have a considerable repertoire, enough for at least basic communication.

Before exploring the fundamentals of second-language teaching, mention must be made of another list that is even more vital to successful second-language teaching, the *working conditions* necessary for effective teaching and learning to take place (LeBlanc, 1990). It would include:

- a reasonable class size,
- administrative support for the program at the school, district and province/state levels,
- appropriate curriculum materials,

- competent teachers who believe in what they do,
- parental and societal valuing of language learning.

Without these conditions, discussion of in-class considerations is almost pointless. Without support, even good teachers can only struggle for so long before becoming exhausted and gradually losing focus. Decision-makers who fail to provide the conditions necessary for success in a school program should be fired for incompetence or better still, arrested for stealing (education) from children.

When existing conditions make successful teaching next to impossible, steps must be taken to improve the situation. Teachers, who are often isolated as individual employees of a bureaucratic system, have considerable power if they act in concert through their provincial/state language associations. Complaining in the staff-room may relieve stress but it does not improve conditions in the classroom. Professional associations can, and should, play a large role in educating decision-makers about the conditions necessary for an effective program. They could, for example, create a commission of experts to list reasonable conditions for effective second-language teaching, publish it widely, monitor how closely the schools or system meet them, and perhaps publish a yearly report card. At a more aggressive level they might research and publish the average class sizes in second-language classes attended by civil servants and business executives and compare the results with average second-language classes. For their own good and that of their students, teachers must be active members of their professional associations.

Assuming, then, that the system will provide at least reasonable conditions and support to the front-line staff who teach the students, I suggest that the following are fundamentals of second-language teaching.

Motivating Students

William Glasser (1990), the noted education theorist, makes the interesting observation that "being an effective teacher may be the most difficult job of all in our society" (p. 14). His rationale is that while many tasks are difficult, they involve no inherent resistance; patients want the doctor to cure them, clients want lawyers to defend them. The wood does not resist the carpenter, and the piano does not resist the musician. But...

> teachers are people managers, and most everyone will agree that students as workers seem to be the most resistant of all to being managed (Glasser, 16).

Yet, he also believes that students have an inner sense of what is quality work and that they can be encouraged to produce at that level. Managing thirty or so students (each a complex individual with a myriad of needs), and motivating them as learners, are basic teacher functions. Teachers require great skill, empathy, knowledge, organization, time, and supporting school and societal climates. Experience helps as well. While it is presumptuous to write about motivating students in one paragraph, my experiences in the classroom led me to the following beliefs:

- Students won't care until they know the teacher cares... about the subject and about them.
- On the first day of class teachers must sell their subject as useful to the students; otherwise why should they bother learning it? It is a challenging but essential task for which there are , fortunately, many supporting materials. Lacey (in Mollica, 1993) stressed that

  a language is far more than an intellectual cognitive challenge. It is a means to grow and mature through the experience of other cultures. It gives breadth and depth to our personalities. (p. 4).

Mollica (1993:5) identifies a number of reasons for the value of second-language learning and concludes that

only when the study of languages is depoliticized and the learning of languages is accepted for its own intrinsic qualities, will we be able to have linguistic peace and harmony...

Danesi (1993), in an article on the role of more than one language in literacy acquisition, points out that

The bilingual learner has access, therefore, to more than one way of processing information, and this cannot help but diversify and enhance the child's overall cognitive capacities.

Ralph (1995) stressed the "financial" advantages to language learning:

Recent global events have emphasized the critical importance of multinational communication. Growing trade and commercial relationships among European nations, among Pacific rim countries, and among our own North American partners – plus the potential to forge further links between/among these larger international blocs – signal that people skilled in various languages will be required to help expedite these communicative relationships.

Runte (1995) aptly points out that

Language is much more than grammar. It is more than a way of structuring thought. It is a way of signifying our deepest feelings, our most sincere beliefs. Each time I learn a word which has no translation into another language, I feel that I have discovered a rare gift, a new idea, a fresh insight... (p. 9).

Learning languages promotes interdisciplinarity and the ability to think in a creative fashion. It promotes creativity and discovery. Languages teach us new ways of seeing things, new perspectives (p. 10).

Today our students face many problems: change and instability, violence and lack of meaning, fragmentation and loss of identity. Communication, creativity and unity are the solutions to these problems, and they are all found in and promoted by the learning of languages (p. 11).

She asks

If we want to be part of a country which is humane and tolerant to continue on into the future, we need to educate the next generation to be tolerant and open. What better way to do this than through learning languages? (Runte, 1996a: 7).

Even UNESCO in a report favours the preservation of Languages (see Runte, 1996b:18).

The "observable advantage of bilingual over monolinguals" is that they are "more used to switching thought patterns and have more flexible minds." Their knowledge of language(s) makes them more familiar with "different often contradictory concepts" and this, in turn, makes bilinguals or multilinguals more "tolerant than monolinguals, and more capable of understanding an argument."

And even Canadian Parents for French (1995), a national association devoted to the promotion of French as a second language has produced a video, *Proud of Two Languages,* in which young people laud the acquisitions of a second or even third language (reviewed by Runte, 1996c:23).

Teachers must remind the students regularly that they are working for themselves, their own futures. Why should they get up in the morning and go work for teachers?

If the Coleman Study correctly concluded that the most important determinant of academic success is a willingness to defer gratification, i.e., to work now in order to have something later, students must learn how to do this. The finding of "deferred gratification" as a major determinant of success was a bit of a surprise. The expectation had been that school facilities, programs, etc. would largely explain the difference between "successful" students and less successful ones. Deferred gratification ought to be taught at home, but when it isn't, teachers must fill the gap, as usual. Students should learn to set short-term, intermediate and ultimate goals, and experience sequential success in meeting them.

Teachers must foster a climate where the focus is on the students, individually and collectively, not on the teacher or textbook (Evans-Harvey, 1993). I recommend "reverse onus" teaching, whereby students are made aware that they are the *raison d'être* of the system and that teachers help them acquire skills and knowledge. Off-task students are seen as disrupters of their own and other students' learning, not of the teacher. It creates a different dynamic vis-à-vis collaborative goal setting and behavioural expectations.

The classroom atmosphere must be so focussed on learning that risk taking and errors are almost stress free. Teachers should emphasize to students that not knowing something and making mistakes are central to learning. If students knew everything, they would not need the teachers who would then be unemployed. Students should also understand that most errors are smart, not dumb, because they involve logical inferences. For example, students who say

"Je suis 13 ans vieux"

in French are not saying something stupid; they are applying a correct syntactical structure from English. Much can be learned from such "mistakes" when students are taught that they are "smart mistakes."

Learning should be done in a context of "fun and games" as often as possible. Students are still children; they can learn without always knowing they are doing so. What involves more genuine communication than playing a game in the target language? Moreover, we know that second-language learning often involve attitudes and prejudices. When children have fun, they often forget that they "hate" the second-language (Danesi and Mollica, 1994).

Teaching in the Target Language

Many practices in education are matters of opinion, but the results of others have been demonstrated beyond discussion. One of these is the inefficacy of teaching a second language in the mother language. For decades in Canada, French as a second language was taught by the grammar-translation method with all real communication being in English. Most of its former students are living proof of its failure. "I can read it," they say, "I understand some, but I can't speak it." Dissatisfaction with that state of affairs, in an officially bilingual country, led to the creation of "immersion" classes, the communicative approach, the multidimensional curriculum, and [Canada's] National Core French Study (NCFS). The latter development is explained in some detail later. The NCFS's key conclusion was that second-language teaching should aim first and foremost at imparting communicative skills for real-life purposes.

With the proper introduction and attitude, students can be motivated to use the target language from the start. In fact, its use stimulates interest and motivation. Students want to communicate, and if the second language must be the medium of communication in that class, so be it. It has been said that "immersion" programs are not immersion at all since even the most intensive of them only involve a small fraction of the students' daily life. Nevertheless, immersion works because its key article of faith is target language use. Essentially, regular second-language classes should also be "immersion" during the class period. Of course these students would benefit from a more significant exposure to the language than one short period per day. A five-month intensive introduction has been proposed by some as a desirable common experience for all Canadian children, after which they could opt for immersion or regular French. Perhaps it will happen some day, but whatever the format, second language teachers who wish to be successful must quickly and systematically make the target language the norm in their classroom.

In a lead article published in *Dialogue*, Stern (1983a: 4) stresses that the teaching of Core French (i.e. "regular") requires a diversified approach. He points out that

> In the last few years a new view of language acquisition has resulted partly from research on second langauge learning and partly from the immersion experience. It underlines the fact that a language cannot be learned by formal practice alone. Much of it is learnt best in the process of doing something else.

Calvé (1985:278) echoes similar sentiments when he states that

> Ce n'est qu'en communiquant qu'on peut apprendre à communiquer.

Mollica (1985:490) wonders whether we are

> [...] truly fulfilling our task to teach students to communicate. Are we providing the classroom environment which encourages communication. How much English is *really* spoken in the French classroom? While in immersion classes we insist on French being the language for communication and are careful not to deviate from this norm, in the Core French class we appear to have adopted the slogan of the Commissioner of Official Languages: "English or French. It's your choice."

He suggests that teachers audiotape their lesson and listen to the recording to determine:

- How much time we spent trying to get the class's attention
- How much time we spent speaking English
- How much time we spent speaking French

- How much time was left for our students to speak French. (Mollica, 1985:490).

The Language Management System

Second-language teachers are regularly urged to teach in the target language, but when faced with a class that doesn't understand even the most rudimentary elements of the language they often dismiss the advice as unrealistic. Yet, little progress can be made in a language that isn't used for (real) classroom communication. So, *how* does one teach in a language not understood by the students? Many theorists promote an aural phase when the students hear the second language, its sound and cadence, for a period of time. They begin by processing and understanding, and then reach a readiness stage, a desire to speak. Whether one subscribes to that approach or not, when it is time for students to speak perhaps my Language Management System may be useful (LeBlanc, 1994). Used systematically, this mechanism allows a teacher to use the target language in class from the outset. Its key assumption is that the FIRST need anyone has when faced with a second language is acquiring the tools to cope with the linguistic situation itself. If they don't understand those strange French sounds, for example, the phrase "Je ne comprends pas." effectively sends the ball back to the other side of the court. While that could be accomplished with the traditional physical gestures, other language management tools such as "Comment dit-on ... en français?" and "Que veut dire le mot...?" are most effectively conveyed verbally. (See chapter 15, "Classroom Expressions" by Mollica in this volume.)

One of the most effective devices to develop teacher respect for the fundamentals, and empathy for the students' predicament, is a training session in which teachers become students of a language that they don't know at all, Mandarin or Russian, for example. They quickly experience what it is to have a person make unfamiliar sounds at you, then act as if you are stupid for not understanding right away and not assimilating strange structures after only one or two repetitions. Very early on, the students should be taught the verbal tools to slow the teacher down, to make him or her use basic vocabulary and to re-use words or functions a reasonable number of times in meaningful contexts. That is how the first language is learned, and how other languages are learned as well. The Language Management System is intended as a mechanism that students use to survive the initial phase of second language learning, then to acquire more language.

The Concept of Interlanguage

While the concept of interlanguage, the rudimentary form of language that concentrates exclusively on the message, is very simple, most theorists feel it has an important place in language development. It involves saying, for example, "Me hungry, where restaurant please," in any language. Language teachers all spoke that way as babies, and nearly all would use interlanguage spontaneously in a foreign environment, yet many make little room for it in the classroom. They forget that beginning students are at the baby stage in second language learning and that the classroom is a foreign environment for students. The active encouragement or tolerance of interlanguage in the classroom has been a matter of considerable debate, but in my view it has a place among second-language teaching's fundamentals. Some will point to the fossilized errors so endemic to immersion students, but that is more related to how long interlanguage should be tolerated rather than whether it is a normal first stage leading to more correct expression. As Chastain (1971: 316) points out,

> To learn a language, the students must reach a point at which they concentrate on *what* they are saying instead of *how* they are saying it, but often can not reach this point because the teacher places grammatical and phonological interruptions and stumbling blocks in their way. Language teachers tend to have an unwarranted obsession with perfection in their classroom. *They should remember that the initial goal is not native speech but the ability to communicate with the native* (italics mine).

And Grittner (1985:14) concurs that

> Teachers should apply the old adage "Practice makes perfect," in contrast to the tendency in the foreign language profession to say: "You've got to be perfect before you can practice." This means accepting errors as part of the learning process rather than making believe that they will not occur. Mistakes should be used to diagnose errors and prescribe remedial practice.

Le Vocabulaire Fondamental

The basic building block of linguistic communication is the word. When one reads, hears, writes, or speaks a language, it is done by means of words used individually or organized in some fashion. Whether they are used on the strict basis of communication, as in the interlanguage discussed above, or according to sophisticated rules sanctioned by the Académie Française, for example, each utterance is made up of... words. Therefore, language learning is fundamentally about vocabulary learning. Indeed, when one visits a second-language class one sees the vocabulary that the teacher sets as priority for that particular group. One might, for example, visit a grade three second-language class and see large posters of fruits with each part, from the outer skin to the innermost pit, listed and the vocabulary being drilled. If these students ever become fruit buyers for a produce company, they are ready; they know all the vocabulary. But, are those the words they most need to learn at that point in their language development? I doubt it. And unless next year's teacher asks them about fruits, they will appear to know little of the language.

As Robert Galisson pointed out (cited in Nemni, 1985),

> Jusqu'à preuve du contraire, les mots restent bien utiles pour communiquer.

The point is that vocabulary is central to second-language study and must be selected very judiciously. There are said to be more than half a million words in the French language, for example, and it is estimated that a university graduate knows perhaps 50,000 to 60,000 words, and a high school student perhaps 15,000. We also know that to be mastered, words must be reused often. (see Pellerin, 1996). How do we know which words should be prioritized? A most interesting research project was conducted by the Centre de Recherche et d'Étude pour la Diffusion du Français (CRÉDIF) and published in 1959 as *Le Français Fondamental*. Thousands of everyday conversations were recorded and word frequency lists were compiled. Naturally certain words appeared more often than others. The most basic words were organized a bit and it was deemed that with 1222 lexical words and 253 grammatical words (*Le Français Fondamental*), a person could function quite effectively in everyday life. The point for teachers is that the most basic words should be prioritized and re-utilized until they are assimilated by the students. Teachers should also teach the basic skill of circumlocution by which, if students don't know the exact word they want to say, instead of shutting down the communication they find a way to explain their meaning using the words they know.

Teachers can consult *Le Français Fondamental* or similar lists of basic words, but they can also create their own list by asking themselves if a word is an often used general one or a less used specific one. Another criterion for essential words are those needed to operate in the classroom. The vocabulary for classroom routines should be taught first and if, for example, the teachers want to play a game, the vocabulary and language functions needed to play should be taught beforehand. As soon as students have sufficient literacy skills to do so, the class-room vocabulary should be written in a special scribbler and reviewed regularly. It becomes their personal "dictionnaire fondamental."

Functions and Grammar

If vocabulary is important as the language's building blocks, and is organized in elemental fashion in interlanguage, we want to advance quickly to language forms that are like those that native speakers use. The question is, as usual... "How?" Most teachers itch to teach grammar for at least two reasons; they wince at the students' fractured structures and they personally relate to grammar because of their studies (which they chose because they liked to study language). But formal grammar is not what most beginning students need. Teachers should review the alternative view of language as evolved in *The Threshold Level* by a Council of Europe research group in 1975. It separates language in two basic components, the "functions", and "notions", as J. A. Van Ek (1976:6) explained:

> What people do *by means* of language can be described as verbally perform certain functions. By means of language people assert, question, command, expostulate, persuade, apologize, etc. etc. In performing such functions people express, refer to or – to use a more general term-handle certain notions.

Second-language teachers must initially think in terms of functions and notions (another word for "vocabulary") rather than in grammatical terms. If students want, for example, to perform the language function of asking permission to do something, let's provide the function rather than the grammar. Students should learn such functions as: "Est-ce que je peux aller...?" and the notion "aux toilettes" without learning to conjugate completely the irregular verbs involved. Teachers and students should think in terms of developing and expanding their repertoire of functions and notions. For the time and place of grammar, teachers might start by reviewing the theories of Stephen Krashen (1995) and Krashen and Terrell (1983) and the debates they stimulated, the Language Syllabus of the National Core French Study, and innumerable articles on the issue.

The National Core French Study

The National Core French Study[2] was created by the Canadian Association of Second-Language Teachers (CASLT) and supported by government, to meet the challenge of making regular (Core) French effective. The proposal for such a study was first outlined in a keynote address given by the late H.H. Stern (1983) on "French Programs in Canada: How Can We Improve Them?",at the annual CASLT convention held in Winnipeg, Canada. (See Chapter 8 in this volume). The project was originally chaired by Stern himself and, after his death, by Raymond LeBlanc. A strong cadre of second-language experts were enlisted and participated in various capacities. A central research group, supported by six task groups and schools committees, fleshed out Stern's multidimensional model for restructuring second-language teaching.

A five-year, seven-volume, national study cannot be fairly summarized in one paragraph. There exists an excellent synthesis written by Raymond LeBlanc (1990), and a comprehensive summary published as a special issue by *The Canadian Modern Language Review/La Revue canadienne des langues vivantes* (1990) that can easily be accessed. In the proverbial nutshell, the National Core French Study proposed that second language teaching integrate four aspects of language, each described in a separate syllabus:

- language
- communicative-experiential
- culture, and
- general language.

Two other work groups addressed the important questions of testing and teacher education. These are all part of the total package, six fundamentals, if you will. While each report contains a chapter on classroom approaches, the project was more geared to providing a blueprint for second-language teaching in Canadian schools. We are much gratified that ministries and publishers have accepted the basic concepts and are integrating them in their latest materials. In spite of the name, it is generally accepted that the principles of the multidimensional approach are equally valid for immersion teaching. Teachers who consult the study will find themselves better equipped to understand and deliver the latest programs.

Opportunity for oral testing

"Ok, students, take your pencils and paper and we'll see how well you speak the second language you have been studying." That doesn't seem reasonable but it is often what we do. How we test is very important because it is the ultimate motivator for many students. "Does it count?" they ask. However, to test orally there must be conditions in place that allow it. Asking teachers to give up most of their noon hours and preparation time to interview students individually is simply unreasonable. There are many things teachers can do in class to test orally, including monitoring a few students each day, having student presentations, mastery teaching, having students tape certain answers, etc. If your school is fortunate enough to have a language lab, it can make oral testing a breeze, especially at the middle and secondary levels. As well, aural comprehension tests can be administered to the entire class, and they should be part of any quality curriculum material. For oral testing beyond that, teachers will need assistants or release time.

A comprehensive package of field-tested testing instruments for the intermediate level is now available through the Canadian Association of Second Language (see address in Note 2.) It should provide a theoretical base and accessible materials for ensuring that testing is closely related to communicative teaching.

Conclusion

Second-language teaching in the public school context is a very demanding occupation. Reviewing and applying the fundamentals is no panacea, but it offers perspective and helps define the conditions for success. Once these are in place, second-language teaching can be a most stimulating task. Unlike other subjects, where teachers must follow a curriculum closely, communicative-experiential teaching allows teachers to discuss events and issues, play games, undertake projects, watch TV, listen to music, etc. Granted, most of these activities are conducted in a *vocabulaire fondamental*, but a great deal of variety is still possible. Second-language teachers who master the fundamentals of their profession can derive much satisfaction from effectively introducing students to a new language and culture.

Notes

1. In Canada, French is the main second language taught in schools due to the bilingual nature of the country. The regular second-language course, typically one class period per day up to 12 years in all other provinces and territories (except in Ontario up to 13 years), is called Core French. This involves a minimum of 40-minute daily classes. More intensive programs, involving up to 100 per cent of the school day in the initial years and lesser percentages at the middle and high school levels are called "Immersion" where the language of instruction for subjects is in French.

2. The materials related to the National Core French Assessment Project may be purchased from : The Canadian Association of Second Language Teachers (CASLT), 176 Gloucester St., Suite 310, Ottawa, Ontario, Canada K2P 0A6 E-mail: caslt@istar.ca

References

Calvé, Pierre. 1985. "Les programmes de base: des principes à la réalité." *The Canadian Modern Language Review/La Revue canadienne des langues vivantes*, 42, 2: 271-287.

The Canadian Modern Language Review/La Revue canadienne des langues vivantes. 1990. Vol. 47, 1. The entire issue is dedicated to the National Core French Study. Guest editors: Pierre Calvé, Anthony Mollica and H.H. Stern.

Canadian Parents for French. 1995. *Proud of Two Languages*. Ottawa, Ontario: Canadian parents for French. Video. 14 min., 52 sec. Reviewed by Runte (1996c).

Chastain, Kenneth. 1971. *The Development of Foreign Language Skills*. Philadelphia, PA: The Center for Curriculum Development, Inc.

Council of Europe. 1975. *The Threshold Level in a European Unit/Credit System for Modern Language Learning*.

Danesi, Marcel. 1993. "Literacy and Bilingual Education Programs in Elementary School: Assessing the Research." *Mosaic*, 1, 1: 6-12.

Danesi, Marcel and Anthony Mollica. 1994. "Games and Puzzles in Second Language Teaching: A Second Look." *Mosaic*, 2, 2: 13-22. See Chapter 31, in this volume.

Evans-Harvey. 1993. "Climate Setting in the Second-Language Classroom." *Mosaic*, 1,2:1,3-5.

Glasser, William. 1990. *The Quality School: Managing Students Without Coercion*. New York: Harper Perennial Press.

Grittner, Frank. 1985. "What Language Teachers Should Do to Improve Instruction." *Indiana Foreign language Teachers Association News*, (Fall): 14-15. The article was published originally in *Information* (1984), Wisconsin, 11, 3: 19.

Krashen, Stephen D. 1985. *The Input Hypothesis*. London: Longman.

Krashen, Stephen D. and Tracy Terrell. 1983. *The Natural Approach: Language Acquisition in the Classroom*. Oxford: Pergamon.

Lacey, Veronica. 1993. "Modern Languages: Recognizing their Relevance." Keynote address at the Ontario Modern Language Teachers' Association. Mimeo. Quoted in Mollica (1993).

LeBlanc, Clarence. 1990. "Administrative Conditions for Effective FSL Programs." *The Canadian Modern Language Review/La Revue canadienne des langues vivantes*, 46, 4: 783-787.

LeBlanc, Clarence. 1994. The "Language Management System." In "A Touch of... Class!" *The Canadian Modern Language Reviews/La Revue canadienne des langues vivantes*, 52, 2: 331-335.

Mollica, Anthony. 1993. "Language Learning: The Key to Understanding and Harmony." *Mosaic*, 1, 1: 1, 3-5 (1993). See Chapter 1 in this volume.

Nemni, Monique. 1985. "Les maux des mots." *The Canadian Modern Language Review/La Revue canadienne des langues vivantes*. 41, 6: 1020-1040.

Pellerin, Suzanne. "L'enseignement du vocabulaire en FLS niveau universitaire (débutant)." In R. Furgiuele and N. Naiman, eds., *The Converging of Two Visions: the Learning and Teaching of French and English as Second Languages at the University Level*. Toronto: Canadian Scholars' Press, p. 55, 104-105, 161-162.

Ralph, Edwin G. 1995. "Motivating Parents to Support Second Language Programs." *Mosaic*, 2, 4: 1, 3-7. See Chapter 3, in this volume.

Runte, Roseann. 1995. "Learning Languages in the Context of Canada's Many Cultures." *Mosaic*, 2, 4: 8-11.

Runte, Roseann. 1996a. "Surviving the Perils of Politics: The Language Classroom of the Next Century." *Mosaic*, 3, 2: 1, 3-7.

Runte, Roseann. 1996b. "UNESCO Report favours Preservation of Languages." *Mosaic*, 3, 4: 18.

Runte, Roseann. 1996c. "A Review of Proud of Two Languages. Video produced by Canadian Parents for French. *Mosaic*, 4, 1: 23.

Stern, H. H. 1983a "And Cinderella may yet go to the Ball: A personal view of the past, present and future of core French." *Dialogue. A Newsletter on the Teaching of English and French as Second Languages.* 2, 1: 1-4. Toronto, Ontario: Council of Ministers of Education, Canada.

Stern, H. H. 1983b. "French Core Programs across Canada: How can we Improve Them?" *The Canadian Modern Language Review/La Revue canadienne des langues vivantes*, 39, 1: 34-47. See Chapter 8, in this volume.

Van Ek, J. A. 1976. *The Threshold Level for Modern Language Learning in Schools*. London: Longman.

Reprinted from: Clarence LeBlanc, "The Fundamentals of Second-Language Teaching". *Mosaic,* 5, 1 (Fall 1997): 1, 3-8.

5 Individual Differences in L2 Learning and the Good Language Teacher

Christine Besnard

In order to understand fully today's issues such as in-dividual differences in L2 learning, it is important to start by setting them within an historical framework.

Thirty ears ago, L2 teaching was definitely more traditional, teacher-centered and unidirectional. Indeed, in those days, teachers were the sole owners of knowledge that they would share with their audience, and they considered that it was the full responsibility of the students to find the best way to learn, no matter how interesting, well organized and clear their presentations were.

The outcome was quite disappointing as students would drop out of L2 classes, little learning would happen, and even if they would know the grammar rules taught, they were unable to communicate in the L2 properly.

The sixties are also the time when both Europe and North America started to rethink the way L2 were taught mainly for political reasons.

In the linguistic spheres of the seventies, Chomsky severely criticized the central principles of the audio-lingual method which was based on Structuralism and Behaviorism which he considered as being flawed. Then the American anthropologist Hymcs who believed in an ethnographic vision of communication started to criticize Chomsky's theory which, he found, was too removed from social reality, and to underline the importance of the acquisition of a socially based communicative competence.

In the education spheres of the eighties, researchers and practitioners started to become more interested in the learners and in the way they learn L2. The specialists in L2 learning and teaching started to distance themselves from a model where the teacher was a semi-god, and they rallied around Comenius' theory based on the central principle that:

Teaching is an art which consists of making sure that students are able to learn what their master already knows (Germain, 1993: 88).

The researchers turned themselves towards the learners in an attempt to understand better the way they learn in order to help them become more efficient, and maximize their learning.

In doing so, L2 teaching and research became more learner-centered as more attention was being paid to the individual factors and differences which could explain why certain learners learn L2 with ease and why others have great difficulty doing so. It is the time when a number of individual differences were identified, and what's interesting about them is that they all account for an easy L2 learning or for an arduous one. They also fall into two categories:

- the ones which escape the influence of the learners and the teachers as they are intrinsic (age, gender, personality, self-esteem, anxiety, intelligence, and abilities),
- and the ones which are extrinsic (motivation, attitude, learning styles) and which can be positively influenced and slightly modified by either the learners or the teachers.

We firmly believe that the present research on individual differences is all the more essential as it provides an eye-opener to teachers who need to be fully aware of the different kinds of circumstances that profoundly impact on their students' motivation and attitude towards L2 learning. Indeed, only the teachers who are aware of individual differences between students will be able to become non-judgmental towards the ones who succeed the least as they will be adequately equipped to better understand them, and answer their particular needs in order to give them a chance to be successful in their learning an L2.

1. Age

It is widely believed that children have a strong advantage over the adults as far as L2 learning is concerned. But in fact, this belief should be measured. Indeed, as Ritchie and Bhatia (1996:127) say,

> adults are more cognitively advanced than children thus have a wider set of problem-solving skills available to them than children do.

And these "tools" help them to be more efficient in the L2 learning. Adults know and understand the world better, they know their L1 and therefore have a more mature and thorough understanding of the workings of their language. They already know the grammar, the lexicon and the syntax of their L1. They are better able to apply abstract knowledge to their learning, they are more able to abstractly conceive, generalize and classify rules so that they are more efficient and they learn faster than children.

As Ellis (1985:354) puts it, the effect of age on L2 learning still needs to be fully understood because as he insists, it is important to make a distinction between the effects of age on

> the route towards the acquisition of an L2, [...] the speed of the acquisition of an L2 [...] and the ultimate attainment of the L2 learning.

And as Ellis summarizes it (1985: 354), even though "age doesn't affect the route of acquisition" it does have an impact on the speed of acquisition and on the final results.

Concerning the speed of acquisition of grammar and vocabulary, teenagers are faster than adults and children, and adults are faster than children. But in the long run, as Lightbown and Spada write (2006:48-49), even though at first, adults and teenagers are more efficient and learn faster in the early stages of the L2 learning, later then, they are caught up by children (who do better with their pronunciation, oral comprehension and oral communication) if those are immersed in the L2. Confirmed by Bialystok and Hakuta (1994:80),

> Older learners and adults make more rapid progress than younger learners, but, overtime, the older learners reach a plateau earlier and are overtaken by younger learners.

As for the final results, researchers like Ellis (1985:106) agree that they are greatly influenced by the age you start learning an L2, and the number of years you are exposed to the L2. Indeed, the number of years you have been exposed to the L2 deeply influences the communication fluency, and the age you have started learning the L2 influences your level of proficiency and especially your pronunciation and how native-like you sound (Ellis:106). Not surprisingly, all this has to do with Lenneberg's "critical period" or "optimal period" as we prefer to call it today, and that so many researchers are still researching on.

Still, as Lightbown and Spada (2006) stress it, it is widely accepted now that the children of immigrants who were born in the country usually communicate like natives while their parents even if they are fluent, keep their accent, and their choice of words and expressions remain different from those of the natives. This could be partly explained by the fact that, as Brown and Gonzo put it (1995:82), adults

> don't have the cultural identification with the host country necessary to become fluent [...].

This difference in proficiency is not only due to the age they started learning the L2 at but also to the conditions they have learnt the L2; indeed, the young learners end up spending much more time than the adults being exposed to and immersed in the L2. Bialystok and Hakuta argue (1994:52) that

> if children are better language learners than adults, the reason may have nothing to do with their brains. It may just be that children have more opportunity to learn and practice the second language than adults.

That is why researchers now agree that the age you arrive in a country is the most important factor that will determine the level of proficiency one will arrive at.

Another major difference between children and adults is that the young learners are not expected to be perfect right at the start whereas adults are expected to be good with the L2 from the moment they start using it. They therefore feel self-conscious and confused and uncomfortable, and they will not take as many risks as children when learning the L2.

Finally, another major difference in L2 learning between adults and children are the cognitive processes used by both groups. Indeed, as Dekeyser (2000:499) points out:

> While children rely on language-specific mechanisms of implicit learning, adults have largely lost the ability to learn a language without reflecting on its structure, and have to use alternative mechanisms, drawing especially on their problem-solving capacities, to learn a second language;

in other words, their learning style is more explicit as opposed to the children's which is more implicit.

But despite all these differences between children and adults, one must remember, as Scovel indicates (1988:66) that

> biological constraints on language learning do not impede ultimate achievement in any linguistic skill except native like phonological fluency.

And Bialystok and Hakuta (1994:86) to add:

> There is no evidence at all to assign greater word learning power to children. Syntax [...] remains accessible throughout life.

Whether or not children attain higher levels of proficiency as adults, we mustn't forget that ultimately,

> [...] the amazing human ability to learn grammar remains with us as long as we remain human (Bialystok and Hakuta (1994:75).

And little by little, researchers reached the conclusion that there was not a single critical period but that there were multiple critical periods also called "sensitive periods" for phonology, morphology, syntax and semantic.

2. Gender

A number of research show that females are more sociable than males, and that they enjoy group activities much more than males who tend to be more individualistic. They tend to communicate and interact with their classmates more readily and more actively than male students who prefer working independently and individually. The fact that L2 classes are attended by a vast majority of female students clearly reflects a gender difference between female and male L2 students.

But as far as success is concerned, both female and male students can succeed despite their different learning styles. They all need to be given language activities which suit best their way of learning whether social or more individualistic.

3. Personality

Among the L2 student population, the two personality traits that are the most striking are

- the extroverts and
- the introverts.

While the extroverts enjoy working in groups, expressing themselves, sharing their ideas and opinions with peers, meeting with natives, the introverts prefer working individually and independently without having to interact and cooperate with others.

One area where personality plays an important role is in relation with anxiety. Indeed, according to Gregersen and Horwitz (2002:566), perfectionists, especially when they talk, feel constantly judged by their teachers and their peers, and therefore feel very anxious.

> With respect to language learning, perfectionist students would not be satisfied with merely communicating in their target language – they would want to speak flawlessly, with no grammatical or pronunciation errors, and as easily as a native speaker (2002:563).

But Lightbown and Spada (2006) still stress the fact that even today, research is not able to show a direct link between personality and second-language acquisition.

And so, once more, the responsibility of the good language teacher is to make sure that all types of personalities present in the L2 classroom are given a chance not only to fully participate in all the L2 activities but also to succeed in all language activities whether oral or written, individualistic or in groups.

4. Self-esteem

Self-esteem has a profound influence on the quality of L2 learning. Indeed, the learners with a good self-esteem and who are used to be successful are more active, more engaged and more ready to take risks when they learn an L2.

On the other hand, the learners who fail repeatedly lack self-esteem and self-confidence, and therefore tend to be more passive; they display signs of self-helplessness as they have become discouraged by constantly failing in their attempts to learn the L2 to the point that they do not want to try anymore because they are convinced they will fail again.

Once more, the good language teacher has a big responsibility in trying to help students strengthen their self-esteem as we know it is crucial to a solid L2 acquisition. And the best way to do so is by making sure that all students, whether good or weak, have a chance, once in a while, to succeed in their attempts to learn an L2. Therefore, the good language teacher has to present students reasonable and attainable challenges which are neither too easy as they may bore them nor too difficult as they may discourage them.

And if the good language teachers are aware that one of the main strategies good language learners use in order to succeed is taking risks, they will ascertain that they give their students ample opportunities to take risks with the L2 without fearing to be penalized. And in doing so, they will also help their students to strengthen their self-esteem and self-confidence.

5. Anxiety

Research clearly shows that the L2 classroom is a place that tends to generate a lot of anxiety that directly impacts on students' motivation and success or failure.

Interesting research on anxiety by Horwitz, Horwitz and Cope (1986) started to clearly show that the 3 most common types of anxiety are oral anxiety, test or exam anxiety and class anxiety. Oral anxiety is generated by the fact that the learners want to express intelligent ideas as in L1, but are greatly frustrated by their being deprived of a normal mode of communication. Class anxiety is constantly felt by students as it pervades all class activities; indeed, they feel judged, all the time, by their teachers and their peers. And tests/exams generate a lot of anxiety; whereas for the good students, this type of anxiety can stimulate them to achieve their best, for the weak students, it usually will interfere with and weaken their performances.

But still nowadays, no research has been able to show if it is anxiety that lowers the abilities of the students or if it is because their abilities are low that their performance is weak. In fact, studies still do not agree on the impact of anxiety on the learning of L2.

An interesting study by Verma and Nijhavan showed that there is a link between IQ and anxiety: "Higher states of anxiety facilitate learning at upper levels of intelligence, whereas they are associated with poorer performance at lower IQ levels." (Scovel, 1978:136).

Some researchers like Scovel (1978:139) said that there are two kinds of anxiety: a facilitating one which helps the learner to learn, and a debilitating anxiety that makes learning difficult. A few years later, Ely (1986:7) stated that quite often, students who want good marks will tend to participate much more than their counterparts in the L2 class, and will not let anxiety interfere with their progress.

Among all language activities, the oral ones are the ones which generate the biggest amount of anxiety as the students feel embarrassed to make mistakes in front of their peers and their teacher. This will then impact on their willingness to take risks as they want to avoid embarrassing themselves in front of the class.

In fact, researchers are now convinced that the quality of the learning experience which is strongly influenced by the different feelings learners experience when they study an L2 is as important as the methodology and the language materials used by the teachers. And that is why researchers like Scovel (1978) have been encouraging L2 students to write personal journals that enable them to identify the personal factors that strongly influence L2 learning.

For example, through the writing of her own journal, Bailey was able to discover that competitiveness ("Competitiveness being the desire to excel in comparison to others." Bailey, 1995:199) between students in L2 classes play a significant role in the quality of the learning and the degree of the motivation felt by students. In fact, thanks to this kind of personal journals, researchers have realized that there is a "complex relationship between competitiveness and anxiety" (Bailey, 1995:199), and then between "anxiety and language learning".

According to Bailey (1995:200), it seems that language classroom anxiety can be lessened if the learner views himself/herself as more proficient than his/her classmates, but anxiety is aggravated when he/she sees himself/herself as less proficient as his/her classmates. Therefore, it clearly appears that there is "a cyclic relationship between anxiety and negative competitiveness" (Bailey, 1995:200).

Age seems to also have a deep impact on the level of anxiety that the learners feel. As Gardner and McIntyre state (1989:94-95):

> [...] the few studies that have been done on pre-adolescents seem to show that foreign language anxiety is more relevant to language learning among adults.

So it seems that the older the students, the more anxious they feel, as the greater the gap between what they want to say and what they can say is, the more frustrated and anxious they feel (Gardner and McIntyre, 1989:96). While in the language classrooms, young L2 learners are allowed not to speak if they do not feel ready for it, teachers expect older learners to talk, and this kind of pressure and expectations definitely raise their level of anxiety. It is also important to keep in mind that while children feel free to take risks and make mistakes, adolescents feel constantly judged by their classmates, and they therefore tend to feel self-conscious about their performance in L2.

Anxiety is clearly an area where the good language teachers must rally their best skills in order to ensure that they create an atmosphere of cooperation and respect in their classes. It is also an area where they must ensure that they correct and evaluate their students in the least disruptive and degrading way by correcting them constructively. It is paramount that they keep in mind that every student needs to have a chance to succeed in the eyes of his/her classmates.

6. Intelligence

Everybody wonders if one needs to be intelligent to learn an L2. But if you ask people how they define intelligence, they all come up with many different definitions as it is still a concept that is unclear and divisive.

Whereas today, the school system continues to favor through the kinds of programs it offers, two traditional types of intelligence (the verbal/linguistic and the logico/mathematical), during the last twenty years researchers such as Gardner and his team of Harvard researchers (1996) have shown that there are other types of intelligences that should be recognized and taken into consideration in our teaching practices.

And indeed, in our language classes, we have different kinds of learners with different kinds of intelligences (verbal/linguistic, logico/mathematical, interpersonal, intrapersonal, visual/spatial, body/kinesthetic, musical/rythmic, and natural); and so, if we want to give all of them a better chance to maximize their learning and succeed, we have to do a better job at answering their needs and interests, by presenting them with a wide variety of language tasks and activities better geared to their types of intelligence.

7. Abilities

As our societies are becoming more and more inclusive, it is all too normal to wonder whether it is possible and desirable to include in our L2 classes students with different abilities ranging from the gifted to what is commonly called the LD students with learning difficulties who quite often show signs of language and communication impairments.

If we take the case of the province of Ontario (Canada), it is quite interesting to observe that the only subject LD students are automatically allowed not to take is French as an L2! It is quite perplexing as more and more research shows that the learning of an L2 can have a number of positive results not only on their L2 but also on their L1 proficiency, and also on their cognitive, social, cultural and psychological development. Indeed, succeeding in the learning of an L2 can positively boost their self-image and their self-confidence. It also gives them a better chance to becoming not only citizens of the world if they want to travel, but also to having a better chance to find a job if they live in one of the many countries, like Canada, which have several official languages.

8. Motivation

Researchers consider now that motivation is the most important factor for success, and yet, it is the biggest challenge that teachers face in their language classrooms. Indeed, can they motivate the students even if they do not want to learn the L2, and are not motivated?

For Tardif (1997), motivation at school greatly depends on the students' perception of the importance and the usefulness of the language tasks teachers present them; indeed, students who do not understand why they are asked to learn certain grammar rules, vocabulary or functions of the L2 will not put the effort into it. Their motivation also depends on their perception of the demands and the difficulty of the tasks; indeed, if it is too easy, they will be bored, and if it is too hard, they will be discouraged as in order to be motivated, interested and involved, they need to be presented with challenges, but challenges which are reasonable. Finally, according to Tardif (1997), their motivation will also depend on their perception of the controllability of the task; in other words, they need to feel that they are in control, and that, ultimately, they will be able to do it.

As early as the seventies, a study by Gardner and Lambert (1972) demonstrated that there were 2 major kinds of motivation: the instrumental and the integrative. The instrumental one motivates you to learn an L2 in order to reach a practical goal such as obtaining a job, traveling, attending a conference, etc. Whereas the instrumental motivation is short term, the integrative one is long term as it is triggered by a positive attitude of the L2 learner towards the target language community and culture, and a desire on his/her part to know and understand that community better, and to be part of it. And if you want to become an active and full member of it, you will be motivated and you will work hard in order to get a good command and a good accent of its language. As Ritchie and Bhatia stress it (1996:272), the learner's motivation and ultimate success depend a lot on his/her attitude towards the community and culture he/she is immersed in. In fact, research have shown that when learners want to establish and keep a great distance between them and the rest of the community they live in for all kinds of reasons whether personal, political, economic or social, they will not acquire a good accent and a good command of the L2. Indeed, research shows (Ritchie and Bhatia, 1996:271-272), the accent serves as a "powerful symbol of ethnicity", and depending on his/her accent, the learner will be more or less accepted by his/her community. Furthermore, it is important to point out that the learners' motivation also depends on their empathy to the other members of the target language community as well as to its culture. Another factor that needs to be taken into consideration as it strongly impacts on the learners' motivation to learn an L2 is their self-esteem, the "flexibility of (their) ego-boundaries" (Ritchie and Bhatia, 272) as to whether or not they fear they will lose their own language, culture and identity if they show interest in another one; in other words, do they feel threatened by the L2 language and culture?

An interesting study by Gardner and McIntyre (1991) emphasized that students who were instrumentally and integratively motivated learned much more than the others. It also clearly demonstrated that the integrative motivation has a long-term influence on the learners whereas the instrumental motivation stops as soon as the learners have reached their goals.

Keeping these principles in mind when considering the school children, it becomes clear that the L2 teachers have a number of powerful tools (internet, e-mail, films, videos, trips, films, music, exchange, etc.) provided by the new technologies as well as the communicative approach, and the globalization of our world that can adequately equip them to succeed in motivating their L2 students better than ever.

9. Attitude

As mentioned previously, repeated failures without ever being given a chance to succeed can only have detrimental effects on the students' self-esteem .Indeed, those who never succeed are discouraged, and become more and more passive overtime. Since they keep failing, they give up on trying again as they are convinced that they will fail again; they will not take risks and they fall into a state of self-helplessness as cogniticians like Tardif (1997:97) and Wenden (1991:57) point out. And the only way they can change their attitude to the better is to have teachers who understand that they have to give them a chance to be successful.

The teachers' expectations also have a strong impact on their students' attitude as studies by Tardif (1997), Brien (1990) and Bogaards (1988) have demonstrated. But it is important to stress the fact that these expectations need to be neither too high as they may discourage the learners, nor too low as they may bore them, but just reasonable to trigger the right attitude towards learning.

It is also paramount to stress that the L2 learners' attitude is deeply influenced by the socio-political situation of a country. If we take the case of Canada, we've been able to clearly see a major shift of attitude towards the learning of the country's second official language, French, over the last 30 years. Whereas during the Trudeau era, we could observe a real interest and motivation towards the learning of French throughout the country, the three Quebec referenda as well as the change in the immigrant population have dramatically altered the general attitude towards the learning of FSL. In the West of the country for example, where the economic and social relations are more North-South than West-East, the learning of French by the school children is more and more often questioned by families. In Canada which is regularly faced with the issue of the uniqueness and the distinctiveness of Quebec as well as its special status, families may develop a negative attitude towards French which they will pass on to their children who, at school, will display disinterest towards the learning of this language. Therefore today, many FSL teachers complain about spending much time and energy struggling with their students' lack of motivation and negative attitude towards French instead of teaching them the language.

As very briefly mentioned above, to fully understand how powerfully demotivating a negative attitude towards an L2 and its culture can be, one should have present in mind the very interesting study done in the late seventies by Schumann (1976). He studied a Costa Rican immigrant of 33 years by the name of Alberto whose economic and social status was considerably lower than that of the community he lived in, who tried to learn ESL while working in the United-States, and who failed to do so. He was first tested to make sure that he was not cognitively impaired and that he had a normal IQ. But despite the ESL courses he took over a period of one year, he made very little gains and only used a pidgin of English. In fact, it was clear in his case that his pidginization of English was his way of refusing to become a full member of the target language community he lived in for fear of losing his own identity, his own culture and his own language; by using a pidgin of English, he clearly established a social and psychological distance between him and the target language group he rejected, and feared to be assimilated in.

Schumann's study clearly points to the powerfully positive or, in this case, negative effects of motivation and attitude of a learner on the great or poor quality of his/her learning. To put it differently, the study shows that the more distant an L2 learner is from the community he/she is learning the language of, the more incomplete his/her L2 learning will be.

And so, in countries where there are many different linguistic and cultural groups, L2 teachers have to be aware of the many societal and psychological factors that impact on their students' attitude towards the target language, and have to try to use new strategies to counteract their negative effects.

10. Learning styles

Since the last 30 years when L2 teaching became more and more learner-centered, researchers have been particularly interested in the ways L2 students learn, so that they have managed to identify a number of different learning styles among the student population. Nunan (1989:52), for example, classified L2 learners into 4 categories : the concrete learners who love action, games, group work, and contacts with the natives, as opposed to the analytic learners who like to study grammar, to read, and to study on their own. He also opposed the communicative learners who like to use the L2 with their classmates and their teachers as well as with the natives, and who enjoy hearing it on TV, radio and CD, to those who like being in a structured L2 classroom, following their teachers' instructions, and who do their homework; in other words, the teachers' pets!

A few years later, Felder and Henriques (1995) offered a slightly more complex categorization of the students which we think is great as they identified 5 pairs of learning styles: the actives and the reflectives, the sensing and the intuitives, the visuals and the auditives/verbals, the serialists and the globals, the inductives and the deductives. To this taxonomy, Cyr (1996) and others added the extroverts and the introverts as well as the field dependents and the field independents, the reflectives and the impulsives. There are also a number of minutely detailed taxonomies with tens of different learning styles that were identified, but we favor the above taxonomies as they are not too complex and have identified the most common learning styles that all L2 teachers encounter in their language classrooms.

And as Besnard (1995) argues, these taxonomies offer precious tools to the good language teachers as they help them remain aware that learners do not learn the same way, and that they have to present them with a wide variety of language tasks and activities that will give a chance to every learning style and every student to succeed in his/her learning.

11. The good language learner

Another individual difference is that some language learners are naturally good and some others are not so good at learning an L2.

In 1978, when a wide scale research was done on the good language learner by a team of researchers (Naiman, Frolich, Stern and Todesco) at OISE (Ontario Institute for Studies in Education, Toronto, Canada), it was clearly established that some language learners learn languages easily while others experience many more difficulties.

Indeed, the good language learners seem to naturally be using about 7 good language strategies that enable them to become efficient in their L2 learning. As the study shows, they are actively involved in their learning, and they take advantage of every opportunity, in and out of the classroom, to use the L2 as they understand that such practice will facilitate their learning; they behave like detectives who look for the mistakes in their own written and oral productions, and they do not hesitate to ask teachers and the natives of the L2 to correct them; in other words, they do not shy away from making mistakes as they use them as learning tools towards a solid command of the language; they also manage to develop on their own strategies to improve their accent, their vocabulary and their grammar skills.

Since the time this major study was conducted that made language teachers aware of the efficient strategies good language learners use, we have also come to realize that these strategies can be taught to less effective language learners in order to improve their learning skills.

Furthermore, it has been shown (Besnard, 1995) how the good language teachers, by developing appropriate language tasks and activities, can firstly expose their students to these strategies, and secondly, can make them use these new learning tools in order to improve and maximize their learning. Indeed, the good language teachers should develop language exercises that make the poor language learners use the strategies described above in the hope that progressively and through proper practice, they will use them more naturally and readily so that they will become better language learners.

In the perspective of individual differences, the other essential insight the Naiman's study provided the L2 teachers with is that successful language learning is not achieved in a single way. Indeed, it was demonstrated that among the good language learners observed, some liked studying grammar while others hated it, some would memorize lists of vocabulary and grammar rules while others would hate doing that and would learn the L2 in a more intuitive and holistic way, some would seek the natives' company to practice the L2 while others would rather study with books. And consequently, the teaching community became aware that there is not a unique path to learning an L2, and that they have to accommodate the variety of needs of the students who take these different paths.

But despite these differences among the good language learners, the ingredients that all of them share were that they were all highly motivated, they were all actively involved in the L2 learning, and they all shared a positive attitude towards the L2, its culture and its people. And these are also qualities that good language teachers have to make all of their students, whether good or poor, become fully aware of in order to properly equip them in their learning.

12. Conclusion

Besides being fully aware of the individual differences that make each student unique, and of the need for a greater variety of teaching strategies, there is one more step that the good language teachers need to take in order to be able to maximize their students' learning. Indeed, they have to realize that their teaching style is directly influenced by their learning style, and that unconsciously, they tend to teach the way they like to learn.

They therefore need to analyze their own learning style and teaching style, and let themselves be inspired by the newest developments in the field of individual differences in order to then succeed in opening themselves up to new ways of teaching languages.

References

Bailey, K.M. 1979. "An Introspective Analysis of an Individual's Language Learning Experience." In S. Krashen and R. Scarcella, eds. *Research in Second Language Acquisition: Selected Papers of the Los Angeles Second Language Research Forum.* Rowley: Newbury House.

Bailey, K.M. 1995. "Competitiveness and Anxiety in Adult Second Language Learning: Looking at and through the Diary Studies." In H. Douglas Brown and Susan T. Gonzo, eds. *Readings on Second Language Acquisition,* pp. 163-205. Englewood Cliffs: Prentice Hall.

Besnard, C. 1995. "Les contributions de la psychologie cognitive à l'enseignement stratégique des langues secondes au niveau universitaire." *La Revue Canadienne des Langues Vivantes,* 51(3) : 426-443.

Besnard, C. 1995. "L'apport des sciences de l'éducation, de la cognition et du développement à l'enrichissement du répertoire méthodologique des professeurs de L2." *La Revue Canadienne les Langues Vivantes,* 52(1) : 7-21.

Bialystok, Ellen and Kenji Hakuta. 1994. *In Other Words: the Science of Psychology of Second Language Acquisition.* New York: Basic Books.

Bogaards, P. 1988. *Aptitude et affectivité dans l'apprentissage des langues étrangères.* Paris : Hatier-Crédif.

Brien, R. 1990. *Science cognitive et formation.* Québec : Presses de l'Université du Québec.

Brown, H. Douglas and Susan T. Gonzo, eds. 1995. *Readings on Second Language Acquisition.* Englewood Cliffs: Prentice Hall.

Cyr, Paul. 1996. *Le Point sur... Les stratégies d'apprentissage d'une langue seconde.* Anjou (Québec) : Les Éditions CEC inc.

Dekeyser, Robert M. 2000. "The Robustness of Critical Period Effects in Second Language Acquisition." *Studies in Second Language Acquisition,* 22: 499-533.

Ellis, Rod. 1985. *Understanding Second Language Acquisition.* Oxford: Oxford University Press.

Ely, Christopher M. 1986. "An Analysis of Discomfort, Risktaking, Sociability, and Motivation in the L2 Classroom." *Language Learning. A Journal of Applied Linguistics,* 36(1):1-25.

Felder, R. M. and E. R., Henriques. 1995. "Learning and Teaching Styles in Foreign and Second Language Education." *Foreign Language Annals,* 28:22-31.

Gardner, R. C. and W. E. Lambert. 1972. *Attitudes and Motivation in Second Language Learning.* Rowley: Newbury House.

Gardner, Howard. 1996. *Les intelligences multiples.* Paris: Éditions Retz.

Gardner, R. C., Smythe, P. C., Clement, R., and L. Glicksman. 1976. "Second Language Learning: A Social-psychological Perspective." *The Canadian Modern Language Review,* 32:198-213.

Gardner, R. C. and P. D. MacIntyre. 1989. "Anxiety and Second Language Learning: Toward a Theoretical Clarification in Language Learning." *A Journal of Applied Linguistics,* 39.

Gardner, R. C. and P. D. MacIntyre. 1991. "An Instrumental Motivation in Language Study. Who Says it Isn't Effective?" *Studies in Second Language Acquisition,* 13: 57-72.

Germain, C.. 1993. *Évolution de l'enseignement des langues : 5000 ans d'histoire.* Paris : Clé International.

Gregersen, Tammy and Elaine K. Horwitz. 2002. "Language Learning and Perfectionism: Anxious and Non-Anxious Language Learners'Reactions to their own Oral Performance." *The Modern Language Journal,* 86(4):562-570.

Horwitz, E. K., Horwitz, M. B., and J. Cope. 1986. "Foreign Language Classroom Anxiety". *Modern Language Journal,* 41:85-117.

Leather, J. and A. James. 1996. "Second Language Speech." In W. C. Ritchie and T. K. Bhatia, eds., *Handbook of Second Language Acquisition,* pp. 269-316. New York: Academic Press.

Lightbown, Patsy M. and Nina Spada. 2006. *How Languages are Learned.* Oxford: Oxford University Press.

Naiman, N., Frolich, M., Stern, H. H. and A. Todesco. 1978. *The Good Language Learner.* Toronto: Ontario Institute for Studies in Education.

Nunan, D. 1989. *Understanding Language Classrooms – A Guide for Teacher-initiated Action.* Hemel Hempstead: Prentice Hall.

Ritchie, Wlliam C. and Tej K. Bhatia. eds. 1996. *Handbook of Second Language Acquisition.* New York: Academic Press.

Schumann, J. H. 1976. "Second Language Acquisition: the Pidginization Hypothesis." *Language Learning,* 26:391-408.

Scovel, Tom. 1978. "The Effect of Affect on Foreign Language Learning: A Review of the Anxiety Research." *Language Learning,* 28:129-142.

Scovel, Tom. 1988. *A Time to Speak: A Psycholinguistic Inquiry into the Critical Period for Human Speech.* New York: Newbury House.

Seliger, Herbert W. 1978. "Implications of a Multiple Critical Period Hypothesis for Second Language Learning." In W. Ritchie, ed., *Second Language Acquisition Researc – Issues and Implications.* New York: Academic Press. 11-32.

Tardif, Jacques. 1997. *Pour un enseignement stratégique : l'apport de la psychologie cognitive.* Montréal : Éditions Logiques.

Towell, Richard and Roger Hawkins. 1994. *Approaches to Second Language Acquisition.* Clevedon: Multilingual Matters Ltd.

Wenden, Anita. 1991. *Learner Strategies for Learner Autonomy.* New York: Prentice Hall.

Reprinted from Christine Besnard, "Individual Differences in L2 Learning, and the Good Language Teacher." *Mosaic,* 9, 2 (Summer 2007): 3-10.

6 The Good Language Learner and the Good Language Teacher: A Review of the Literature and Classroom Applications

Anthony Mollica and Frank Nuessel

What are the characteristics of the good language learner? Knowledge of these traits can help the good language teacher create a classroom environment that will facilitate second-language learning.

The Good Language Learner

Nearly twenty-five years ago, in an important article, Stern (1975: 316) summarized the following ten learning strategies associated with the good language learner:

1. A personal learning style or positive learning strategies;
2. An active approach;
3. A tolerant and outgoing approach to the target language and empathy with its speakers;
4. Technical know-how about how to tackle a language;
5. Strategies of experimentation and planning, with the object of developing the new language into an ordered system and of revising the system progressively;
6. Constantly searching for meaning;
7. Willingness to practise;
8. Willingness to use the language in real communication;
9. Self-monitoring and critical sensitivity to language use; and
10. Developing the target language more and more as a separate reference system, and learning to think in it.

In the same year as Stern's (1975) article, Rubin (1975: 45-48) published an article on the same topic entitled "What the 'good language learner' can teach us." In that essay, Rubin enumerated the following seven strategies employed by the good language learner:

1. The good language learner is a willing and accurate guesser.
2. The good language learner has a strong drive to communicate, or to learn from communication. He [sic] is willing to do many things to get his message across.
3. The good language learner is often not inhibited. He is willing to appear foolish if reasonable communication results. He is willing to make mistakes in order to learn and to communicate. He is willing to live with a certain amount of vagueness.
4. In addition to focussing on communication, the good language learner is prepared to attend to form. The good language learner is constantly looking for patterns in the language.
5. The good language learner practises.
6. The good language learner monitors his own speech and that of others. That is, he is constantly attending to how well his speech is being received and whether his performance meets the standards he has learned.
7. The good language learner attends to meaning. He knows that in order to understand the message, it is not sufficient to pay attention to the grammar of the language or to the surface form of speech.

Subsequent Research on the Good Language Learner

Various follow-up studies on the good language learner have appeared since the publication of the initial essays by Rubin (1975) and Stern (1975). In their comprehensive review of this topic, Naiman, Fröhlich, Stern, and Todesco (1978: 25; cited in Stern 1983: 406), state that good language learners

> take advantage of potentially useful learning situations, and if necessary create them. They develop learning techniques and strategies appropriate to their individual needs.

These same researchers further observe that good language learners

> demonstrate that, contrary to popular belief, language success is not so much attributable to an 'innate' gift,' as to a conscious effort and constant involvement.

Reiss (1985: 512) pointed out that Rubin's (1975) and Stern's (1975)

> strategies are eminently plausible, but unfortunately empirical data supporting them is not available.

Reiss (1985: 513) also points out that if the term "strategy" is defined as a "conscious approach used by an individual to facilitate learning" then Rubin's strategy no. 3 [see item # 3 in the previous section] 'the good language learner is often not inhibited' is not a strategy but a personality variable.

Based on her own research on the good language learner, Reiss (1985: 518) concluded that

> the good language learner may or may not be inhibited. He [sic] is fairly comfortable with ambiguity. He uses a variety of strategies, including monitoring, inferencing, and practising. He pays attention to form and meaning. He likes to communicate and enjoys learning a foreign language. Above all, the good language learner is an *active* participant in the conscious-learning process. The word "active"' is of great significance because the successful language learner is constantly processing information whether called upon or not. Even when silent, he is active mentally and thus becomes a *silent speaker*. This may well explain why the successful language learner need not necessarily be an extrovert. He may not volunteer or take chances on errors "aloud" but this does not stop him from practising silently. This silent speaking is the cornerstone upon which many other strategies are built. Once a student is "speaking silently" he is ipso facto practising, inferencing, looking for meaning, etc.

As a means of ascertaining the specific attributes that second-language instructors deem pertinent to successful second-language learning, Lalonde, Lee, and Gardner (1987: 16) summarize a study by Naiman, Fröhlich and Stern (1975) by observing that

> teachers most often characterize the good language learner as being meticulous (perfectionistic), mature or responsible, and self-confident, as exhibiting classroom behaviours of attentiveness, active participation, and regularity in completing homework, and in demonstrating good memory, a good ear for sound, and general all-around ability.

These same researchers (Lalonde, Lee, and Gardner, 1987: 28) provided an exhaustive examination of the extant research on the relationship between personality traits and second-language achievement. The purpose of their research project was to determine if there was agreement by teachers on the personality traits and classroom behaviours of the successful language learner. The results indicate that teachers, in fact, agree on a cluster of personality characteristics and behaviours demonstrated by the good language learner. Nevertheless,

> no evidence of a relationship was found between these personality traits and classroom behaviours.

In their study, Lalonde, Lee, and Gardner (1987: 23) found that teachers identified three classroom behaviours as significant for the good language learner. In this regard, these researchers state that

> teachers perceived the good language learner to be an individual who actively vocalizes corrections, speaks out regardless of making mistakes, and focuses on getting an idea across in the second language.

They further state that (see also Politzer, 1983)

> the finding of only three behaviours being identified as important for good language learners could be due to the fact that teachers only relate to the communication aspects of second-language learning.

The Learner's Role

In her summary of strategies exhibited by the good language learner, Cook (1991: 80) suggests the following:

1. Find a learning style that suits you.
2. Involve yourself in the language learning process.
3. Develop an awareness of language both as system and communication.
4. Pay consistent attention to expanding your language.
5. Develop the L2 as a separate system.
6. Take into account the demands that L2 learning imposes.

Classroom Applications of Research on the Good Language Learner

The extant research on the good language learner by Lalonde, Lee, and Gardner (1987) reveals two important points:

- There are certain personality variables that play a role in good language learning.
- Good language learners display specific learning behaviours.

It is the latter aspect that has a direct classroom application, since strategies employed by this group are explicit learnable behaviours that may be acquired by any student enrolled in a language class. This language-learning or language-acquisition conduct involves both the instructor and the learner. The second-language teacher can teach students how to change inappropriate and ineffective learning. Such behaviour modification may help to improve the learner's strategies. Likewise, the learner must make a conscious effort to adapt the second-language learning demeanour that will be most helpful in acquiring another language.

The Instructor's Role in Developing Good Language Learners

In her article on the unsuccessful language learner, Reiss (1983:

265) concludes that instructors can help "less successful students increase their level of competency." In this essay, Reiss referred to Rubin's (1975) study on the good language learner and also addressed two other factors involved in the problems of the unsuccessful language learner, namely, personality and cognitive style variables.

In particular, Reiss states that teachers can:

1. inform students honestly of the task of learning a language, the work involved, and the rewards to be gained;
2. create the kind of classroom climate in which students feel comfortable and involved;
3. aid students in developing certain cognitive styles helpful in language learning by assigning tasks such as those suggested by Omaggio and Birckbichler (1978);
4. help students develop the art of inferencing by making them aware of clues for intelligent guessing;
5. personalize language instruction whenever feasible in order to motivate students to express themselves readily;
6. ask students to monitor each other's speech and thus take an active part, not only in learning, but also in teaching;
7. seek out opportunities for students to use the language outside the classroom;
8. present all material in a meaningful manner and, in turn, expect students to attend to both structure and meaning from the outset;
9. ask successful language learners to serve as informants regarding strategies, techniques, and study skills; and
10. encourage slow students to experiment freely until they find their own particular learning style.

As a concluding note, we highly recommend the following books on strategies employed by the good language learner:

1. O'Malley, J. M. , and A. U. Chamot. 1990. *Learning Strategies in Second Language Acquisition*. Cambridge: Cambridge University Press.
2. Pimsleur, Paul. 1980. *How to Learn a Foreign Language*. Boston, MA: Heinle and Heinle.
3. Stevick, Earl W. 1989. *Success with Foreign Languages: Seven Who Achieved it and What Worked for Them*. New York: Prentice Hall.
4. Wenden, Anita and Joan Rubin. 1987. *Learner Strategies in Language Learning*. New York: Prentice-Hall.

The Good Language Teacher

The good language teacher has a pivotal role in the second-language learning/acquisition task. The good language teacher at every educational level (elementary, secondary, and post-secondary) engages in behaviour and activities designed to provide an environment conducive to the acquisition and appreciation of a second language and its culture.

The good language teacher fulfills numerous important roles both in and out of the classroom that facilitate optimal second-language learning opportunities. The following summary specifies many of those varied and distinct roles:

Out-of-Class Roles
- Researcher
- Planner
- Manager
- Advocate
- Organizer
- Evaluator
- Communicator

In-Class Roles
- Teacher
- Motivator
- Evaluator
- Facilitator
- Innovator
- Communicator
- Disciplinarian

The roles enumerated above indicate that the good language teacher must dedicate a considerable amount of time outside the classroom to engage in activities that will maintain and enhance his/her professional status in terms of competency, fluency and proficiency. There is, of course, some overlap in the roles both in and out of class, namely, those of evaluator and communicator.

This provides teachers-in-training, neophyte teachers, experienced teachers, and people charged with evaluating the performance of second-language teachers with an overview of the professional development and behaviour exhibited by the good language teacher.

The following sections outline the ways in which the good language teacher maintains and enriches his/her professional status. The good language teacher must dedicate a significant part of his or professional life to the various roles specified above, because this person literally lives the profession of language teacher inside and outside the classroom.

1. Professional training and preparation

a. Personal library
b. Professional organizations
c. Professional journals
d. Professional meetings
e. Pedagogical textbooks
f. Library usage
g. Professional travel
h. Methodology
i. Oral proficiency training
j. Instructional trends and developments
k. Instructional techniques and strategies
l. The lesson plan and outline
m. Activities for student use during the brief classroom absence of the good language teacher.

2. The four skills and cultural comprehension

a. Listening comprehension
b. Speaking proficiency and performance
c. Writing techniques and strategies
d. Reading
e. Stages of presentation of materials for the four skills and cultural comprehension
f. Cultural comprehension
g. Vocabulary acquisition
h. Homework.

3. Instructional materials

a. Visual materials
b. Pedagogical graphics
c. Visual aids
d. Audio materials
e. Language teaching and learning technology.

4. Assessment and evaluation

a. Assessment of students
b. Self-assessment
c. Peer review
d. Professional testing.

5. Classroom environment

a. Reduction of second-language anxiety
b. Maintenance of classroom discipline
c. Improvement of student study skills
d. Activity-appropriate classroom seating
e. Sponsorship of language organizations.

Professional Training and Preparation

Obvious as it may seem, the good language teacher is enrolled in,
or has graduated from an accredited post-secondary institution.
At the elementary and secondary level, this means that the good
language teacher enrolls in appropriate accredited second-
language pro-grams and obtains the professional provincial or
state credentials and certification required to engage in licensed
instruction in the geographical area in which he or she seeks
employment. In addition to these requirements, the good language
teacher also willingly engages in related voluntary activities. This
section outlines some of the out-of-class professional development
carried out by the good language teacher.

a. Personal Library

The good language teacher builds a personal library of
professional resources. The following constitute a core of basic
resources that ought to appear in every good language teacher's
home library:

1. Bilingual dictionary
2. Dictionary in the target language
3. Grammar of the target language
4. Current textbooks used in the field
5. History of the target language
6. Popular literature (magazines, newspapers, comic books)
7. Collection of proverbs in the target language.

b. Professional Organizations

The good language teacher joins professional language
organizations and associations to keep abreast of current trends
and issues in second-language education. Moreover, the good
language teacher belongs to local and provincial or state language
organizations.

c. Professional Journals

The good language teacher subscribes to professional journals in
order to remain current in the field. As Heffernan (1987:6) aptly
wrote:

> the language teacher [graduate] who never reads a professional
> journal and participates only minimally, if at all, in professional
> meetings, will stagnate. There is an onus on the profession in all
> areas to upgrade and keep abreast of current developments in his
> field.

d. Professional Meetings

The good language teacher attends professional meetings on a regular basis to learn about innovations, and significant trends and issues in the profession. National. state or provincial language association sponsor annual professional meetings, with workshops and numerous sessions devoted to the scholarly study of literature, culture, pedagogy and methodology.

e. Pedagogical Textbooks

The good language teacher maintains, in his/her personal library, current textbooks in the target language designed for classroom usage. This part of the personal library allows the good language teacher to refer to other alternative presentations of materials for use in the classroom. In addition, such a collection of books allows the good language teacher to make informed decisions about the selection of a new textbook (see Nuessel, 1991-1992 for an objective approach for the evaluation of pedagogical textbooks).

f. Library Usage

The good language teacher possesses a library card for the local public library and local or regional college or university libraries. The good language teacher becomes familiar with and utilizes local public and academic libraries to carry out research on specific projects. By visiting the local college and university libraries, the good language teacher can determine which professional organizations best serve his/her needs.

g. Professional Travel

The good language teacher visits, vacations or lives in the countries in which the target language is spoken. Information about such trips of varying duration is available in the advertising sections of professional journals or through the local college or university.

The good language teacher utilizes foreign travel as a means of gathering authentic materials for use in the classroom (Nuessel and Cicogna, 1997, Omaggio Hadley, 1993: 82-3, 174-8, 383-94).

Rogers and Medley (1988: 468) define the notion of authentic materials as:

> language samples, either oral or written, that reflect a naturalness of form and appropriateness of cultural and situational context that would be found in the language as used by native speakers.

The following is a representative "shopping list" of such pedagogical resources:

1. Postage stamps at local philatelic shops
2. Samples of low denomination paper and metal currency at local numismatist shops

3. Recorded and published versions of popular songs and music (including folk music)
4. Advertisements from local shops and international companies, e.g., McDonalds®, etc.
5. Video cassettes of films in the target language and films originally in English with target-language dubbing
6. Video cassettes of television programs and commercials
7. Political announcements distributed in the streets
8. Newspapers and magazines (puzzle booklets, cartoons)
9. Popular icons of the target culture (*Astérix, Mafalda, Pinocchio*)
10. Books with collections proverbial language, humour, cartoons, tongue twisters
11. Greeting cards
12. Business cards.

h. Methodology
The good language teacher knows the current teaching methodologies and selects one approach or devises an eclectic strategy that draws the best techniques from each approach.

Larsen-Freeman (1986) describes eight of the most prevalent teaching methods in current use. In a recent article, Doggett (1994) summarizes Larsen-Freeman's list in schematic format. (See Chapter 22, in this volume):

1. The Grammar-Translation Method
2. The Direct Method
3. The Audio-Lingual Method
4. The Silent Way
5. Suggestopedia
6. Community Language Learning
7. The Total Physical Response
8. The Communicative Approach.

Given the widespread acceptance of the proficiency movement and the subsequent incorporation of its strategies into pedagogical textbooks, it is likely that many instructors will elect to include elements of the communicative approach in their methodology (Omaggio Hadley, 1993). Nevertheless, the good language teacher must review current methods and new strategies critically and incorporate the best elements of each methodology into his/her curriculum (Bancroft, 1996).

i. Oral Proficiency Training
The good language teacher will also be familiar with the ACTFL *Proficiency Guidelines* (see Omaggio Hadley 1993: Appendix A, pp. 501-11). Moreover, the good language teacher will seek formal training in the Oral Proficiency Interview (OPI) through ACTFL

(American Council on the Teaching of Foreign Languages 1001 N. Fairfax St., Suite 200 Alexandria, VA 22314). The good language teacher will also recognize that the OPI is neither a theory nor a method, but rather a procedure for measuring what a second-language learner can do functionally.

j. Instructional Trends and Developments

The good language teacher keeps up to date with the major trends and issues in the field of second-language education. One of the most important recent developments is the standards movement. In fact, the important publication *Standards for Foreign Language Learning: Preparing for the 21st Century* (Standards 1996: 35-63; available from ACTFL) enumerates five goals which summarize the most significant developments in the profession, and now commonly referred to as the "Five C's":

1. *Communicate*: in languages other than English.
2. *Cultures*: Gain knowledge and understanding of other cultures.
3. *Connections*: Connect with other disciplines and acquire new information.
4. *Comparisons*: Develop insight into the nature of language and culture.
5. *Communities*: Participate in multilingual communities at home and around the world.

k. Instructional Techniques and Strategies

The good language teacher keeps well informed with innovations and new ideas and developments in instructional materials for use in the classroom. This means that the good language teacher reads the current literature in the field, consults with colleagues about their successful strategies, and attends conferences and workshops to learn about meaningful innovations.

l. The Lesson Plan and the Lesson Outline

The good language teacher carefully plans for and organizes materials for classroom instruction. Chastain (1994: 16; 1988, see Chapter 13, in this volume) notes that lesson preparation involves three aspects:

1. Pre-planning analysis,
2. Textbook adaptation, and
3. Lesson planning.

With regard to the specific aspects of lesson planning, Mollica (1994a: 14, see Chapter 14, in this volume) proposes that a lesson outline include the following components:

1. Theme or topic
2. Aims and objectives
3. Warm-up period
4. Materials needed by
   a. Teacher
   b. Students
5. Presentation
6. Application
7. Summary
8. Assignment
9. Evaluation
10. Teacher's references
11. Motivation.

m. Provision for Temporary Classroom Absence of the Good Language Teacher

The good language teacher also prepares several packets of lessons for substitute teachers in the event of an absence due to illness or emergency, or for attendance at a professional conference. These packages should be easy to locate by the substitute teacher. Moreover, such materials should be self-contained and designed to be completed or viewed by students within one class period. These packets may include the following items:

1. A selection of guided essays (Nuessel and Cicogna, 1993 and 1994b).
2. A packet of problem-solving activities (Cicogna, Danesi and Mollica, 1992; Mollica and Danesi, 1994).
3. Video tapes with material that relates to the cultural content of the curriculum.

The Four Skills and Cultural Comprehension

The good language teacher devotes an appropriate amount of time to the four skills, including the so-called active skills (speaking and writing) and the receptive skills (listening and reading). Following are some recommendations concerning the presentation of these skills together with activities.

a. Stages of Presentation of Materials for the Four Skills and Cultural Listening Comprehension

The good language teacher recognizes that planning activities for the introduction and practice of the four skills (see section on lesson planning above) is very important. The following format will help the good language teacher to present these activities to help insure success:

1. Pre-activity Stage

a. Provide information appropriate to the actual activity, e.g., vocabulary, grammatical structures, cultural data (geography, history, and so forth).
b. Ask questions to assist students in anticipating the activity stage.
c. Ask students to summarize what they have learned.
d. Model the activities.

2. Activity Stage

a. Introduce the activities.
b. Practice the activities individually and in pair or group formats.

3. Post-Activity Stage

a. Apply the knowledge gained in the activity stage to novel situations.
b. Assess the activities to determine if students have learned the salient points, or to determine if they have developed the appropriate skills to demonstrate their knowledge of the topic.

b. Listening Comprehension

The good language teacher develops materials and adapts textbook materials that enhance listening comprehension (Davis and Rinvolucri, 1988; Karsenti, 1996; Krashen, 1995b; Rost, 1990; Rubin, 1994; see also questioning techniques and strategies Mollica, 1994b, Chapter 16, in this volume; Richards, 1995). To this end, the good language teacher will develop and utilize authentic materials that focus on different categories of listening experiences (Rost, 1990 11; see chart below).

Categories of Listening Experiences	
Type of listening:	*General purpose:*
Transactional listening	learning new information
Interactional listening	recognizing personal component of message
Critical listening	evaluating reasoning and evidence
Recreational listening	appreciating random or integrated aspects of event

c. Speaking Proficiency and Performance

The good language teacher introduces classroom activities that facilitate oral communication. Valette (1994) provides a five-step model to accomplish this goal:

1. *Guided observations*: Listening to the spoken word.
2. *Guided analysis*: Learning how the language works.
3. *Guided practice*: Building the skills.
4. *Simulated performance*: Participating in guided conversations and role play (see Di Pietro 1987 for his excellent Strategic Interaction Method).
5. *Performance*: Speaking in real-life situations.

Implicit in this recommendation is the presumption that the target language will be the exclusive medium of communication during the class time. Moreover, the good language teacher provides students with opportunities to use the target language outside the classroom through language clubs, language houses, language tables, and travel to areas where the target language is used.

d. Reading

The good language teacher incorporates diverse reading activities into the second-language curriculum. Grellet (1981: 4-5; cf. Munby 1978 as Grellet's source) notes that the following components are involved in developing an effective reading a text:

1. Recognizing the script of a language.
2. Deducing the meaning and use of unfamiliar vocabulary.
3. Understanding information that is stated explicitly.
4. Understanding implications not explicitly stated.
5. Understanding relationships within sentences.
6. Understanding relationships between parts of a text through cohesive devices both grammatical and lexical.
7. Identifying the main idea from the supporting detail.
8. Distinguishing the main idea from the supporting detail.
9. Extracting main points in order to summarize.
10. Understanding the communicative value and function of the texts.

A variety of activities may be utilized to facilitate the reading of novel texts in a class as discussed by Constantino (1995), Krashen (1989, 1995a, b), Mollica (1971), Swaffar, Arens, and Byrnes (1991), and Valette (1997).

e. Writing Techniques and Strategies

The good language teacher provides his/her students with opportunities to write. Writing tasks in the second-language course too often receive inadequate attention. The good language teacher recognizes that a writing assignment may be divided into achievable sub-components, and thus provides students with opportunities to engage in writing assignments that are feasible. In this regard, Hedge (1988: 21) points out that the act of writing consists of seven stages:

1. Initial motivation
2. Assembly of ideas
3. Planning and outlining
4. Note-taking
5. Preparation of a first draft
6. Revision and replanning of the initial draft
7. Formal presentation of the final product.

Several articles and books provide useful information and strategies for developing writing activities (Besnard, Elkabas and Rosienski-Pellerin, 1996, see Chapter 38, in this volume; Hedge, 1988; Laviosa, 1994; Mollica, 1995; Nuessel and Cicogna, 1993; Raimes, 1983).

f. Vocabulary Acquisition

The good language teacher employs a variety of strategies and techniques to enhance and enrich students' vocabulary.

Krashen (1989, 1995a, see Chapter 35, in this volume, 1995b) argues that voluntary free reading of authentic texts in the second language significantly enhances vocabulary acquisition and improves spelling in the target language.

The development of problem-solving activities such as crossword puzzles, word search materials, scrambled letters, word creation, tic-tac-toe, provide students with an interesting and amusing way of learning vocabulary (Mollica, 1981; Nuessel, 1992; Danesi and Mollica, 1994).

Carter (1987) and Carter and McCarthy (1988) specify seven procedures for enhancing vocabulary acquisition:

1. Utilize techniques that evoke visual images and associations.
2. Focus on phonological patterns as a strategy for lexical retention.
3. Develop a notion of core versus peripheral vocabulary.
4. Encourage lexical amplification in more advanced classes through semantic grids.
5. Teach fixed and idiomatic expressions.
6. Encourage students to guess by using contextual clues for ascertaining the meaning of new vocabulary in oral or written formats.
7. Teach words in discourse to develop an appreciation of syntactic, semantic and pragmatic functions of lexical items.

In two excellent articles focussing on vocabulary, Maiguashca proposes a variety of activities for figurative language (1984) and offers an overview of the various developments that have taken place during the last twenty years in the area of vocabulary research within the field of second-language education (1993).

g. Cultural Comprehension

The good language teacher includes meaningful and authentic cultural content in the curriculum. With regard to this dimension of classroom instruction, Stern (1992) has enumerated ten goals for cultural learning in order of difficulty:

1. Knowledge of the cultural connotations of words and phases
2. Knowledge of how to behave in common situations
3. The development of interest and understanding of the second culture
4. Understanding of crosscultural differences
5. Understanding of intercultural institutions and differences
6. Research-projects
7. Development of an integrated view of the second culture
8. Ability to evaluate statements about the second culture
9. Development of an empathy toward a second culture and its people
10. Academic research on the second culture.

One very helpful strategy for developing and maintaining an interest in the target culture is to conduct a class survey to determine which cultural facets to study. Dechert and Kastner's study on culture (1989: 180-2) reveals that the following topics belong to the following general domains that are of greatest interest to students:

1. Everyday life
2. Tourist attractions and travel tips
3. History
4. Landscape and climate
5. Social and political structure
6. Culture
7. Technology
8. School system
9. Church and religion
10. Social structure and classes in society
11. Production
12. Demography

h. Homework

The good language teacher gives meaningful and creative

homework assignments that reflect and reinforce classroom activities just discussed above. The assignment of such homework requires careful planning and effort so that such work is not just rote and tedious drudgery. In this regard, Antonek, Tucker, and Donato (1995: 1) discuss the innovative use of interactive homework that

> communicates to parents, *facilitates* classroom learning, and *mediates* the home/school relationship.

In today's world of institutional accountability, interactive homework in this type of school-home-parent communicative interaction and bridge-building strengthens important educational ties between the home and public institutions (Ralph 1995).

Instructional Materials

The good language teacher acquires over time a bank of appropriate instructional materials for use in the second-language classroom. This process is an ongoing and essentially lifelong task. The inventory should include published visual materials (posters, maps, etc.), teacher-created visuals, audio materials (recordings), and multi-media materials (computer software, CD-ROM, videos).

a. Visual materials

At a strictly theoretical level, Mollica and Danesi (1995; see also Danesi ,1988) have demonstrated that the bimodal model of second-language instruction benefits the acquisition of a second-language by stimulating both hemispheres of the brain (Danesi 1987, Nuessel and Cicogna, 1992: 291). In Danesi's (1987: 384-9) applications of this model to actual pedagogical situations, there are four key components for the classroom:

1. *Contextualization*: the appropriate environmental placement of an exercise to make it meaningful.
2. *Visualization*: the use of visuals (pictures, slides, overhead projections, film, interactive CALL [computer-assisted language learning] (Nuessel,1989; Smith, 1987, 1989) and interactive TELL [technology-enhanced language learning; see below] (Bush and Terry, 1997).
3. *Diversification*: the use of a wide range of learning activities.
4. *Personalization*: the direct inclusion of students in language learning activities.

b. Pedagogical Graphics

The good language teacher employs pedagogical graphics consistently when introducing grammatical structures with "in-house" materials developed. In this regard, Danesi (1983: 73-4) points out the importance of "pedagogical graphics" which he defines as:

> any symbol, figure, schema or chart (dots, lines, arrows, circles, braces, etc.) that can be used to enhance the presentation of a grammatical point; i.e., it is a visual device that can be utilized in conjunction with, or superimposed upon, target language data in order to highlight some structural feature, relationship or process.

There are three functions of pedagogical graphics:
1. They are time savers.
2. They are highly intelligible.
3. They enhance the learning of structure (Danesi 1983: 74-5).

c. Visual Aids

The good language teacher employs visual aids in the classroom setting in an appropriate manner. Hammerly (1995:12, 1994) defines visual aids as:

> drawings, photos, graphics or models of a nonverbal nature used to facilitate (second-language) teaching/learning.

With regard to pictures, Wright (1989:2) notes that these graphics add to:
1. interest and motivation
2. a sense of context of the language
3. a specific reference point or stimulus.

Selected examples of visuals include the following:
1. Gestures (Kirch 1979, Nuessel 1985, Wilcox 1994)
2. Postage stamps (Nuessel 1996)
3. Pictures (Wright 1989)
4. Problem-solving activities and puzzles (Mollica and Danesi 1994)
5. Videos (Donley 1996b, Stempleski and Tomalin 1990).
6. Graphic materials in general (Mollica 1979a, Hammerly 1994, 1995, Mollica and Danesi 1994, 1995, Stevick 1986, Wright 1989).

d. Audio Materials

The good language teacher uses appropriate examples of authentic audio materials to introduce a variety of listening experiences in the classroom. This strategy includes the following possibilities:
1. Music and songs (Anton, 1990; Karsenti, 1996; Nuessel and Cicogna, 1991).

2. Dictation activities (Davis and Rinvolucri, 1988).

e. Language Teaching and Learning Technology

The good language teacher uses technology-enhanced instructional materials as appropriate (see Tremblay 1996 for a discussion of the use of the Internet). Bush (1997: vii) points out in the "foreword" to *Technology-Enhanced Language Learning* a decade ago Smith (1987, 1989) used the acronym CALL (= Computer-Aided Language Learning) to refer to the use of technology in second-language instruction. Today, however, that acronym has been replaced by the newer and more apt designation TELL (= Technology-Enhanced Language Learn-ing). As Bush (1997: vii) further states:

> the change in emphasis from computer to *technology* places direct importance on the media of communication made possible by the computer, which itself often remains unseen, rather than on the computer itself. For example, it is possible to observe present technological evolution and conclude from different perspectives that on the one hand the computer is becoming a television, or on the other that the television is becoming a computer. Furthermore, the computer makes possible the Internet, that intriguing network of networks that enables communications of all sorts that have only recently become imaginable.

TELL requires continuing teacher education and the wise investment of resources in appropriate equipment that will be useful for a reasonable length of time before it becomes obsolete. In the ever-changing technological environment, multimedia instruction involves the following significant issues (Pusack and Otto, 1997: 6):

1. The combination of media types.
2. The dimension of control.
3. Aspects of help and guidance for interactivity.

Assessment and Evaluation

The good language teacher engages in periodic (formative) review and final (summative) review of his/her students to ensure that they have acquired the basic skills and knowledge associated with the study of a second language. The extent to which students succeed, i.e., demonstrate linguistic proficiency and cultural competency, is one measure of the good language teacher's effectiveness and competency.

At the same time, the good language teacher monitors his/her own performance to determine the effectiveness of specific activities and projects in the classroom. Finally, the good language teacher undergoes periodic professional review (most likely once a year) by his/her peers who will make additional, objective judgments about teaching performance and effectiveness, or through standardized tests of proficiency.

a. Assessment of Students

The good language teacher regularly assesses students in a fair and reasonable fashion to determine the effectiveness of classroom instruction in the four skills (listening, speaking, reading, writing) and cultural comprehension. This facet of instruction involves the use of a variety of assessment instruments to determine the retention of classroom content at various intervals in the course (formative evaluation) and at the end of the course (summative evaluation).

Specific suggestions for such assessment may be found in Boyd (1978), Nuessel (1991),Ralph 1994).

b. Self-Assessment

The good language teacher evaluates his/her own progress in the instructional task. Perhaps the most effective approach to this process is the use of the Glossodynamic Model first discussed by Roback (1955). As applied to second-language teaching, the Glossodynamic Model involves the following stages (Titone and Danesi, 1985: 167):

1. Familiarize (yourself).
2. Adapt.
3. Try out.
4. Adjust.
5. Evaluate.

c. Peer Review

The good language teacher also participates in assessment of his/her teaching effectiveness through peer review of classroom performance and materials (syllabus, handouts, and related materials). Moreover, the good language teacher also has his/her instruction rated by students with an official teaching rating instrument. These forms of evaluation allow the good language teacher to retain the positive elements of instruction, change the less than effective pedagogical strategies, and eliminate ineffective teaching practices.

d. Professional Testing

The good language teacher undergoes professional testing to assess his/her linguistic proficiency. Lewin, Flewelling, and Gagné

(1996) discuss a number of existing tests for second-language teachers.

Classroom Environment

The good language teacher seeks to provide a classroom environment that maximizes teaching effectiveness by reducing those problems that most often contribute to ineffective language learning (Evans-Harvey 1993): anxiety (Donley 1996a, Horwitz and Young 1991, Maceri 1995), poor study habits (Cankar 1996), discipline problems (Richards 1994), and activity-appropriate seating arrangements (Papalia 1994).

a. Reduction of Second-Language Anxiety

The good language teacher helps students to reduce their anxiety over learning a second language. One helpful strategy includes the distribution of Donley's (1996a, see Chapters 10 and 11, in this volume) list of ten ways to cope with foreign language anxiety (see also Horwitz and Young 1991; Maceri ,1995).

b. Maintenance of Classroom Discipline

The good language teacher maintains an orderly classroom. In this regard, Richards (1994; see Chapter 20, in this volume) advises the following plan of action:

1. Prevent possible problems.
2. Head off problems.
3. Discuss the consequences of serious misbehaviour.
4. Seek help for a crisis situation.

c. Improvement of Student Study Skills

Another way in which the good language teacher enhances effective second-language learning is to discuss with students effective study skills (see Cankar 1996, see Chapter 9, in this volume).

d. Activity-Appropriate Classroom Seating

The good language teacher is attentive to seating arrangement in the classroom. Different types of second-language activities require different seating arrangements (Papalia, 1994; see Chapter 17, in this volume.). The choice of classroom seating arrangements is directly related to the type of activity that occurs in the classroom (choral work, individual work, paired activities, group activities).

e. Sponsorship of Language Organizations

The good language teacher sponsors language organizations out-

The Good Language Teacher: Activity Performance Checklist		
✔	Activity:	Who: What: Where: When: Why:
	1. Professional Training and Preparation:	
	a. Personal library	
	b. Professional organizations	
	c. Professional journals	
	d. Professional meetings	
	e. Pedagogical textbooks	
	f. Library usage	
	g. Professional travel	
	h. Methodology	
	i. Oral proficiency training	
	j. Instructional trends and developments	
	k. Instructional techniques and strategies	
	l. The lesson plan and outline	
	m. Provision for Temporary classroom absence	
	2. The Four Skills and Cultural Comprehension:	
	a. Stages of presentation of materials	
	b. Listening comprehension	
	c. Writing techniques and strategies	
	d. Speaking proficiency and performance	
	e. Reading	
	f. Vocabulary acquisition	
	g. Cultural comprehension	
	h. Homework	
	3. Instructional Materials:	
	a. Visual materials	
	b. Pedagogical graphics	
	c. Peer review	
	d. Professional testing	
	4. Classroom Environments:	
	a. Reduction of second-language anxiety	
	b. Improvement of student study skills	
	c. Maintenance of classroom discipline	
	d. Activity-appropriate classroom seating	
	e. Sponsorship of language organizations	

side of the classroom. Language organizations, especially those affiliated with national organizations, are one effective way of maintaining and expanding interest in a second language outside the classroom. Such organizations may engage in a number of activities designed to promote the use of the language outside of the classroom:

1. Development of exhibits in public locations (libraries, commercial enterprises) to inform people of the numerous benefits associated with learning another language.
2. Sponsorship of language tables at meal time where the target language is the sole medium of communication.
3. Invitation of speakers who will provide lectures or talks in the target language.
4. Promotion of a language house at post-secondary institutions where the target language is the sole medium of communication, e.g., a section of a college or university dormitory.
5. Plans for work/study trips to a geographical area where the target language is spoken (Hershberg and Van Fleet, 1987).
6. Scheduling and planning for a teacher-guided educational trip to a location where the target language is spoken.
7. Memberships in honour societies affiliated with national organizations.
8. Awards for academic achievement by students from the national headquarters.

Conclusion

A review of the literature on the good language learner reveals certain conduct and personality traits associated with that type of learner. The good language teacher may utilize information about the behavioural characteristics of the good language learner to point out to the less successful language learner specific strategies for achieving second-language success.

This article enumerated those aspects of the good language teacher's teaching behaviour, administration, communication, and professional activities that contribute to a profile of a good language teacher. In particular, we examined the domains of professional training and preparation, the development of the four skills and cultural comprehension in the classroom, the creation of appropriate instructional materials, the assessment of student and teacher performance, and the building of a positive classroom environment where effective teaching and successful learning may take place.

A more specific purpose of our attention to the good language teacher is to inform teachers-in-training and neophyte teachers of their professional expectations. Finally, supervisors and administrators who evaluate a second-language teachers are provided with an objective and professionally-oriented set of guidelines to carry out such assessments.

References

Allen, V. F. 1983. *Techniques in Teaching Vocabulary*. Oxford: Oxford University Press.

Anton, Ronald J. 1990. "Combining Singing and Psychology." *Hispania*, 73: 1166-1170.

Antonek, Janis L., G. Richard Tucker, and Richard Donato. "Interactive Homework: Creating Connections between Home and School." *Mosaic*, 2, 3: 1-10. See Chapter 21, in this volume.

Bancroft, W. Jane. 1996. "SALT for Language Acquisition." *Mosaic*, 3, 3: 16-20.

Besnard, Christine, Charles Elkabas, and Sylvie Rosienski-Pellerin. 1996. "Students' Empowerment: E-mail Exchange and the Development of Writing Skills." *Mosaic*, 3, 2: 8-12. See Chapter 38, in this volume.

Boyd, J. Alvin. "Evaluating the Active Communication Skills: Writing." *The Canadian Modern Language Review/La Revue canadienne des langues vivantes*, 34, 4:735-745. Trans. into French with the title of "L'évaluation des habiletés de communication: écrire," in Pierre Calvé et Anthony Mollica, réds, *Le français langues seconde: des principes à la pratique*. Welland, Ont.: The Canadian Modern Language Review, 1987, pp.385-397.

Bush, Michael D. 1997. "Foreword." In Michael D. Bush and Robert M. Terry eds.,. *Technology-Enhanced Language Learning*. Lincolnwood, IL: National Textbook Company, pp. vii-ix.

Bush, Michael D. and Robert M. Terry, eds. 1997. *Technology-Enhanced Language Learning*. Lincolnwood, IL: National Textbook Company.

Cankar, Paul. 1996. "Study Skill Suggestions for Students of Foreign Language Classes." *The Forum of Phi Sigma Iota*, 18, 1: 11-12. See Chapter 8, in this volume. See Chapter 9 in this volume.

Carter, Ronald. 1987. Vocabulary: *Applied Linguistic Perspectives*. London: Allen and Unwin.

Carter, Ronald and Michael McCarthy. 1988. "Developments in the Teaching of Vocabulary: 1945 to the Present Day." In Ronald Carter and Michael McCarthy, eds., *Vocabulary and Language Teaching*. London: Longman, pp. 39-59.

Chastain, Kenneth. 1988. *Developing Second-Language Skills: Theory and Practice*. 3rd ed. San Diego, CA: Harcourt Brace Jovanovich.

Chastain, Kenneth. 1994. "Planning for Instruction." *Mosaic*, 2, 1: 16-17. See Chapter 13, in this volume.

Cicogna, Caterina, Marcel Danesi, and Anthony Mollica, eds. 1992. *Problem Solving in Second-Language Teaching*. Welland, ON: éditions Soleil publishing, Inc.

Constantino, Rebecca. 1995. "The Effects of Pleasure Reading." *Mosaic*, 3, 1: 15-17.

Cook, Vivian. 1991. *Second Language Learning and Language Teaching*. London: Edward Arnold.

Danesi, Marcel. 1983. "Pedagogical Graphics in Second-Language Teaching." *The Canadian Modern Language Review/La revue canadienne des langues vivantes*, 40,1: 73-81.

Danesi, Marcel. 1987. "Practical Applications of Current Brain Research to the Teaching of Italian." *Italica*, 64: 77-92.

Danesi, Marcel. 1988. "Neurological Bimodality and Theories of Language Teaching." *Studies in Second Language Acquisition*, 10: 13-31.

Danesi, Marcel and Anthony Mollica. 1994. "Games and Puzzles in Second-Language Teaching: A Second Look." *Mosaic*, 2, 2: 13-22. See Chapter 31, in this volume.

Davis, Paul and Mario Rinvolucri. 1988. *Dictation: New Methods, New Possibilities*. Cambridge: Cambridge University Press.

Dechert, Christiane, and Peter Kastner. 1989. "Undergraduate Student Interests and the Cultural Content of Textbooks for German." *The Modern Language Journal*, 73, 2: 173-191.

Di Pietro, Robert J. 1987. *Strategic Interaction: Learning Language through Scenarios*. Cambridge: Cambridge University Press.

Doggett, Gina. 1994. "Eight Approaches to Language Teaching." *Mosaic*, 1, 3: 8-13. See Chapter 22, in this volume.

Donley, Philip M. 1996a. "Ten Ways to Cope with Foreign Language Anxiety." *The Forum of Phi Sigma Iota*, 18, 1, 13. See Chapter 11, in this volume.

Donley, Philip M. 1996b. "Using Video to Promote Critical Thinking." *The Forum of Phi Sigma Iota*, 18, 2, 10.

Evans-Harvey, Cher. 1993. "Climate Setting in Second-Language Classroom." *Mosaic*, 1, 2, 1: 2-5. See Chapter 12, in this volume.

Evans-Harvey, Cher. 1994. "Planning for Effective Teaching: The Unit Plan." *Mosaic*, 2, 2: 10-12.

Garrett, Nina. 1991. "Technology in the Service of Language Learning: Trends and Issues." *The Modern Language Journal*, 75, 1: 74-101.

Giroux Collins, Rosemarie. 1994. "Group Work: From Process to Product." *Mosaic*, 2, 1: 6-9.

Grellet, Françoise. 1981. *Developing Reading Skills: A Practical Guide to Reading Comprehension Exercises*. Cambridge: Cambridge University Press.

Hammerly, Hector. 1994. "A Picture is Worth 1000 Words and a Word is Worth 1000 Pictures." *Mosaic*, 1, 4: 13-17. See Chapter 26, in this volume.

Hammerly, Hector. 1995. "What Visual Aids Can and Cannot Do in Second Language Teaching." *Mosaic*, 2, 3: 11-18. See Chapter 24, in this volume.

Hedge, Tricia. 1988. *Writing*. Oxford: Oxford University Press.

Heffernan, Peter J. 1987. "Core French Teacher's Continuing Professional Development: Balancing the Ideal and the Real." *Dialogue*, 5, 1:1,5-8.

Hershberg, David, and James A. Van Fleet. 1987. "Work Exchange Programs: Achieving More for Less." *The Modern Language Journal*, 71, 2: 174-179.

Horwitz, E. K. and D. J. Young. 1991. *Language Anxiety: From Theory and Research to Classroom Applications*. Englewood Cliffs, NJ: Prentice Hall.

Karsenti, Thierry P. 1996. "Bringing Songs in the Second-Language Classroom." *Mosaic*, 3, 4: 10-15.

Kirch, Max S. 1979. "Non-Verbal Communication across Cultures." *The Modern Language Journal*, 63, 416-23.

Krashen, Stephen. 1989. "We Acquire Vocabulary and Spelling by Reading: Additional Evidence for the Input Hypothesis." *The Modern Language Journal*, 73, 4: 440-464.

Krashen, Stephen. 1995a. "Immersion: Why Not Try Free Voluntary Reading?" *Mosaic*, 3, 1: 1, 3-4. See Chapter 35, in this volume.

Krashen, Stephen. 1995b. "The Reading/Listening Library." *Mosaic*, 2, 4: 20.

Lalonde, R. N., P. A. Lee, and R. C. Gardner. 1987. "The Common View of the Good Language Learner: An Investigation of Teachers' Beliefs." *The Canadian Modern Language Review/La revue canadienne des langues vivantes*, 44, 1: 16-34.

Larsen-Freeman, Diane. 1986. *Techniques and Principles in Language Teaching*. Oxford: Oxford University Press.

Laviosa, Flavia. 1994. "The Writing Process of Italian as a Second Language: Theory and Practice." *Italica*, 71, 4: 484-504.

Lewin, Louise, Janet Flewelling, and Antoinette Gagné. 1996. "Meeting the Challenge: The Creation of a Communicative Test for Evaluating the Proficiency of Second-Language Teachers." *Mosaic*, 4, 1: 9-14.

Maceri, Domenico. 1995. "Reducing Stress in the Foreign Language Classroom: Teaching Descriptive Adjectives through Humour." *Mosaic*, 2, 4: 21-2.

Maiguashca, Raffaella Uslenghi. 1984. "Semantic Fields: Towards a Methodology for Teaching Vocabulary in the Second-Language Classroom." *The Canadian Modern Language Review/La revue canadienne des langues vivantes*, 40, 2: 274- 97.

Maiguashca, Raffaella Uslenghi. 1993. "Teaching and Learning Vocabulary in a Second Language: Past, Present and Future Directions." *The Canadian Modern Language Review/La revue canadienne des langues vivantes*, 50, 1: 83-100.

Mollica, Anthony, 1971. "The Reading Program and Oral Practice," *Italica*, 48, 4: 522-544. Reprinted in Antony Mollica, ed., *A Handbook for Teachers of Italian*. Toronto: Livingstone, 1976, pp. 75-96.

Mollica, Anthony. 1978. "The Film Advertisement: A Source for Language Activities." *The Canadian Modern Language Review/La Revue canadienne des langues vivantes*, 34, 2: 221-243.

Mollica, Anthony. 1979a. "Print and Non-Print Materials: Adapting for Classroom Use." In June K. Phillips, ed., *Building on Experience – Building for Success*. Skokie, IL: National Textbook Co., pp. 157-198.

Mollica, Anthony. 1979b. "*A Tiger in Your Tank*: Advertisements in the Language Classroom." *The Canadian Modern Language Review/La Revue canadienne des langues vivantes*, 35, 4: 691-743.

Mollica, Anthony. 1981. "Visual Puzzles in the Language Classroom." *The Canadian Modern Language Review/La Revue canadienne des langues vivantes*, 37, 3: 582-622. Trans. into French with the title of "Casse-tête visuels dans la salle de classe," in Pierre Calvé et Anthony Mollica, réds, *Le français langues seconde: des principes à la pratique*. Welland, Ont.: The Canadian Modern Language Review, 1987, pp. 267-300.

Mollica, Anthony. 1992a. *A Picture is Worth... 1000 Words! Book 1*. Welland, ON: éditions Soleil publishing inc. With Teacher's Guides in English, French, German, Italian, Portuguese and Spanish. See Chapter 25, in this volume.

Mollica, Anthony. 1992b. *A Picture is Worth... 1000 Words! Book 2*. Welland, ON: éditions Soleil publishing inc. With Teacher's Guides in English, French, German, Italian, Portuguese and Spanish. See Chapter 25, in this volume.

Mollica, Anthony. 1994a. "Planning for Successful Teaching: The Lesson Outline." *Mosaic*, 1, 3: 13-15. See Chapter 14, in this volume.

Mollica, Anthony. 1994b. "Planning for Successful Teaching: Questioning Strategies." *Mosaic*, 1, 4: 18-20. See Chapter 16, in this volume.

Mollica, Anthony. 1995. "Creative Writing: Poetry in the Language Classroom." *Mosaic*, 3, 1: 18-20.

Mollica, Anthony, ed. 1997. Teaching Languages: *Selected Readings from Mosaic*. Welland, Ontario, Canada: éditions Soleil publishing, inc.

Mollica, Anthony, and Marcel Danesi. 1995. "The Foray into the Neurosciences: Have We Learned Anything Useful? *Mosaic*, 2, 4: 12-20.

Munby, John. 1978. *Communicative Syllabus Design*. Cambridge: Cambridge University Press.

Naiman, N., M. Fröhlich, and H. H. Stern. 1975. *The Good Language Learner*. Toronto: Institute for Studies in Education.

Naiman, N., M. Fröhlich, H. H. Stern, and A. Todesco. 1978. *The Good Language Learner*. Research in Education Series No. 7. Toronto: The Ontario Institute for Studies in Education

Nuessel, Frank. 1985."Teaching Kinesics through Literature." *The Canadian Modern Language Review/La revue canadienne des langues vivantes*, 41, 1014-19.

Nuessel, Frank. 1989."The Role of CALL in Second-Language Education." *Language Teaching Strategies*, 4: 3-12.

Nuessel, Frank. 1991."Foreign Language Testing Today: Issues in Language Program Direction." In Richard V. Teschner, ed., *Assessing Foreign Language Proficiency of Undergraduates*. Boston: Heinle and Heinle, 1-20.

Nuessel, Frank. 1991-1992."Criteria for the Objective Evaluation of Pedagogical Textbooks." *Language Teaching Strategies*, 5-6: 41-51.

Nuessel, Frank. 1996. "Postage Stamps: A Pedagogical Tool in the Second Language" Classroom." *Mosaic*, 3, 2: 12-17.

Nuessel, Frank and Caterina Cicogna. 1991. "The Integration of Songs and Music into the Italian Curriculum." *Italica*, 68, 473-86.

Nuessel, Frank, and Caterina Cicogna. 1992. "Pedagogical Applications of the Bimodal Model of Learning through Visual and Auditory Stimuli."In Jeanette

Beer, Charles Ganelin, and Anthony Julian Tamburri, eds., *Romance Languages Annual 1991*, Vol. III. West Lafayette, IN: Purdue Research Foundation, pp. 289-92.

Nuessel, Frank and Caterina Cicogna. 1993. "Teaching Writing in Elementary and Intermediate Language Classes." *Mosaic*, 1, 2: 9-11. See Chapter 37, in this volume.

Nuessel, Frank and Caterina Cicogna. 1994a. "Strategies for Teaching Vocabulary in the Elementary and Intermediate Italian Classroom." *Italica*, 71, 4: 521-547.

Nuessel, Frank and Caterina Cicogna. 1994b. "Writing in the Elementary and Intermediate Italian Class: Theory, Practice, and Assessment." In Jeanette Beer, Charles Ganelin, and Ben Lawton, eds., *Romance Languages Annual 1993*. West Lafayette, IN: Purdue Research Foundation, pp. 265-71.

Nuessel, Frank and Caterina Cicogna. 1997. "The Integration of Authentic Cultural Materials into the Elementary Italian Curriculum." *Romance Languages Annual* 8:254-264 .

Omaggio Hadley, Alice. 1993. *Teaching Language in Context*. 2nd ed. Boston: Heinle and Heinle.

Omaggio, A. and D. Birckbichler. 1978. "Diagnosing and Responding to Individual Learner Needs." *The Modern Language Journal*, 62, 336- 345.

O'Malley, J. M. and A. U. Chamot. 1990. *Learning Strategies in Second Language Acquisition*. Cambridge: Cambridge University Press.

Papalia, Anthony. 1994. "Planning for Effective Teaching: Papalia's Classroom Settings."*Mosaic*, 1, 3: 16. See Chapter 17, in this volume.

Pattison, Pat. 1987. *Developing Communication Skills: A Practical Handbook for Language Teachers, with Examples in English, French and German*. Cambridge: Cambridge University Press.

Politzer, Robert L. 1983."An Exploratory Study of Self-Reported Language Learning Behaviours and Their Relationship to Achievement." *Studies in Second Language Acquisition*, 6, 1: 54-68.

Pusack, James P. and Sue K. Otto. 1997. "Taking Control of Multimedia." In Michael D. Bush and Robert M. Terry, eds., *Technology-Enhanced Language Learning*. Lincolnwood, IL: National Textbook Company, pp. 1-46.

Raimes, Ann. 1983. *Techniques in Teaching Writing*. Oxford: Oxford University Press.

Ralph, Edwin. 1994. "Teaching to the Test: Principles of Authentic Assessment for Second-Language Education." *Mosaic*, 1, 4: 9-13.

Ralph, Edwin. 1995. "Motivating Parents to Support Second-Language Programs." *Mosaic*, 2, 4: 1-7. See Chapter 3, in this volume.

Reiss, Mary-Ann. 1981. "Helping the Unsuccessful Language Learner." *The Modern Language Journal*, 65, 2, 121-128.

Reiss, Mary-Ann. 1985. "The Good Language Learner: Another Look." *The Canadian Modern Language Review/La revue canadienne des langues vivantes*, 41, 3: 511-523.

Richards, J. 1976. "The Role of Vocabulary in Teaching." *TESOL Quarterly*, 10, 77-89.

Richards, Merle. 1994. "Discipline in the Language Class." *Mosaic*, 2, 1: 14-15. See Chapter 20, in this volume.

Richards, Merle. 1995. "Planning for Successful Teaching: Questioning in the Language Classroom." *Mosaic*, 2, 3: 21-22.

Roback, A. A. 1955. "Glossodynamics and the Present Status of Psycholinguistics." In A. A. Roback, ed., *Present-Day Psychology.* . New York: Philosophical Library, pp. 897-912.

Rogers, Carmen, and Frank W. Medley, Jr. 1988. "Language with a Purpose: Using Authentic Materials in the Foreign Language Classroom." *Foreign Language Annals*, 21, 5: 467-88.

Rost, Michael. 1990. *Listening in Language Learning*. London: Longman.

Rubin, Joan. 1975. "What the 'Good Language Learner' Can Teach Us." *TESOL Quarterly*, 9, 41-50.

Rubin, Joan. 1994. "A Review of Second Language Listening Research." *The Modern Language Journal*, 78, 2: 199-221.

Seelye, H. Ned. 1984. *Teaching Culture: Strategies for Intercultural Communication*. Lincolnwood, IL: NTC Publishing.

Smith, Wm. Flint, ed. 1987. *Modern Media in Foreign Language Education: Theory and Implementation*. Lincolnwood, IL: National Textbook Company.

Smith, Wm. Flint, ed. 1989. *Modern Technology in Foreign Language Education: Applications and Projects*. Lincolnwood, IL: National Textbook Company.

Standards for Foreign Language Learning: Preparing for the 21st Century. 1996. Yonkers, NY: ACTFL.

Stempleski, Susan, and Barry Tomalin. 1990. *Video in Action*. Englewood Cliffs, NJ: Prentice-Hall.

Stern, H. H. 1975. "What Can We Learn from the Good Language Learner?" *The Canadian Modern Language Review/La revue canadienne des langues vivantes*, 31, 4: 304-318.

Stern, H. H. 1983. *Fundamental Concepts of Language Teaching*. Oxford: Oxford University Press.

Stern, H. H. 1992. *Issues and Options in Language Teaching*. Oxford: Oxford University Press.

Stevick, Earl W. 1986. *Images and Options in the Language Classroom*. Cambridge: Cambridge University Press.

Stevick, Earl W. 1989. *Success with Foreign Languages: Seven Who Achieved and What Worked for Them*. New York: Prentice Hall.

Swaffar, Janet K., Katherine M. Arens, and Heidi Byrnes. 1991. *Reading for Meaning: An Integrated Approach to Language Learning*. Englewood Cliffs, NJ: Prentice-Hall.

Titone, Renzo, and Marcel Danesi. 1985. *Applied Psycholinguistics: An Introduction to the Psychology of Language Learning and Teaching*. Toronto: University of Toronto Press.

Tremblay, Roger. 1996. "Professional Development Via the Internet: A Proposal." *Mosaic*, 4, 1: 3-8.

Valette, Rebecca. 1994. "The Five-Step Performance-Based Model of Oral Proficiency." *Mosaic*, 2, 2: 1-4. See Chapter 34, in this volume.

Weinrib, Alice. 1997. "A Sampling of Information Sources in Second-Language
Pedagogy." *Mosaic*, 4, 3:20-21.

Wenden, Anita, and Joan Rubin. 1987. *Learner Strategies in Language Learning*. New York: Prentice-Hall.

Wilcox, Joanne. 1994. "Gestures and Language: Fair and Foul in Other Cultures." *Mosaic*, 2, 1: 10-13. See Chapter 40, in this volume.

Wright, Andrew. 1989. *Pictures for Language Learning*. Cambridge: Cambridge
University Press.

Reprinted from: Anthony Mollica and Frank Nuessel;, "The Good Language
Learner and the Good Language Teacher: A Review of the Literature and
Classroom Applications." *Mosaic,* 4, 3 (Spring 1997): 1, 3-16.

7 Promoting the Development of Strategic Competence in the Language Classroom

Peter J. Heffernan

Research into what strategies work best in second language learning has much to offer the classroom practitioner.

Overview of Learning Strategies Research

There exists a message embedded in dubious advertising appearing periodically in mainstream media beckoning the unaware to purchase language learning products with which they are guaranteed to learn a second language almost overnight, with limited or no effort and seemingly unconsciously. On the other hand, most teachers and learners of second languages are well aware that acquiring a new language takes considerable time, effort and focus, usually involving significant immersion in the target linguistic and cultural milieu combined with formal language/culture study at home and abroad.

Learners of other languages, like other learners, also vary tremendously in their predilections, predispositions and natural proclivities and abilities. Einstein-like, some students appear almost to have been born with scientific insight. Others produce works of visual art and interpret music apparently spontaneously and in the way of virtuosos. Language learning gurus, masters of dozens of languages, the current Pope John Paul II being one living example, have also been recorded in the annals of human history. Of course, talent counts for something in all such examples. Behind the façade of talent, though, there also exist strategies or approaches to learning which work much better than others and which account, most often much more than talent, for the seemingly easy success in learning of such individuals.

Twenty years ago, the Modern Language Centre of the Ontario Institute for the Study of Education (OISE) in Toronto undertook research on the good second language learner (Naiman et al., 1978). Like others in that period, such as Rubin (1975) and Stern

(1975), this team of researchers attempted to find the response to these nearly mystical and elusive questions: "what makes the good language learner tick?" or "what can the good language learner teach us?." We mused: if only all our students could be like the good language learner!

There is no need to downplay the significance and contribution of this research activity. As Vandergrift (1995:88) aptly suggests: "It is here that the study of language learning strategies finds its roots."

Indeed, among its most important findings, one reads that one-size-fits-all does not work as language teaching methodology. Among outstanding adult language learners, for example, it was found that development of learning techniques and strategies appropriate to their individual needs was common to all. The idea of individualization was also supported for public school classrooms where students' preferred activities and likes and dislikes were made explicit. Regarding good language learners, Rubin's work suggests they are:

- risk-takers who are willing to try informed guesses and make and learn from mistakes,
- driven communicators,
- metalinguists willing to attend to form,
- faithful practitioners who search out means to try and use the target language,
- self-regulating monitors of their new speech, contrasting it routinely with their native standard, and
- social animals with their antennae out and attuned to social context variables.

For his part, Stern identified ten learning strategies, as follows:
- *planning strategy*: a personal learning style or positive learning strategy,
- *active strategy*: an active approach to the learning task,
- *emphatic strategy*: a tolerant and outgoing approach to the target language and its speakers,
- *formal strategy*: technical savoir-faire of how to tackle a language,
- *experimental strategy*: a methodical but flexible approach, developing the new language into an ordered system and constantly revising it,
- *semantic strategy*: constant searching for meaning,
- *practise strategy*: eagerness to practise and learn by trial and error,
- *communication strategy*: willingness to use the language in real communication,

- *monitoring strategy*: self-monitoring and critical sensitivity to language use, and
- *internalization strategy*: developing second language more and more as a separate reference system and learning to think in it.

Cohen and Hosenfield (1981) have also strongly recommended the use of introspection and retrospection as important techniques in language learning. Moore's (1977), Rivers' (1979) and, more recently, Heffernan's (1992) writings are representative published examples of such introspections/retrospections.

The early work on identification of good language learning strategies, referred to above, spawned a plethora (Hosenfeld, 1976; Pimsleur, 1980; Reiss, 1985; Wenden and Rubin, 1987; Prokop, 1989; Stevick, 1989; Galloway and Labarca, 1990; O'Malley and Chamot, 1990; Oxford, 1990; Lawson and Hogben, 1996; Gu and Johnson, 1996; Robinson, 1997) of related research activity on:

- personality and cognitive styles (e.g., Prokop *et al.*, 1982),
- learner characteristics (Lalonde, Lee and Gardner, 1987),
- so called 'general language education' (Hébert, 1990; Heffernan, 1990; LeBlanc, 1990),
- multiple intelligences (Gardner, 1993),
- brain hemispheric learning research (Sousa, 1995; 1998),
- and so forth in the 1980's and 1990's and has had a major and widespread impact on current curricula for second language teaching (e.g., Alberta Education, 1991). Vandergrift (1995) provides a quite thorough synthesis of this research and theoretical focus to the mid-1990's.

Towards An Understanding of Strategic Competence

What is being focussed on essentially is the development of a specific competence in language learning, which is most appropriately called strategic competence. This concept is far from being new. Canale and Swain (1980) described such a competence, above and beyond Chomskyan (1966) linguistic and Hymesian (1972) communicative or sociolinguistic and sociocultural competence, as being the knowledge of communicative strategies, that is strategies that second language learners intend to make use of in order to get meaning across in spite of their imperfect command of the language:

- paraphrasing,
- avoidance of difficulties,
- circumlocution,
- simplifications,
- survival skills or

- coping techniques
- and so on.

Vandergrift (1995:88) further refines our understanding of the meaning of strategic competence by the distinction he makes between learning and communicative strategies. As he suggests:

> Language learning strategies are deliberate, cognitive steps used by learners to enhance comprehension, learning and retention of the target language; they can be accessed for conscious verbal report... Language learning strategies focus on techniques used to learn a language."

Communicative strategies, in contrast, focus on techniques used to communicate in the target language. In reference to the above, the former help the learner to assimilate language knowledge and skills, the latter help to negotiate meaning between speakers. In keeping with this evolving conceptual development, it is proposed here that strategic competence is manifest by second language learners' ability to exhibit, overtly and explicitly, what and how they implicitly learn to learn so as to function efficiently, effectively and creatively in a second language. Admittedly, as Wenden and Rubin (1987) point out, while some learner strategies employed may be non-observable, it is anticipated that they may be identified by learners via conscious probing, reflection, recall, introspection and retrospection, inter alia (for more such techniques, see Rubin, 1981).

Classroom Implications of Learning Strategies Research

The burgeoning research activity outlined above which has led to a current focus on the development of strategic competence has correspondingly given rise to a veritable industry of workshops, articles and monographs on coping strategies in the language classroom: helping our students learn how to learn, multiple intelligences and the second language learner, matching second language learners and their dominant learning styles, and so forth. All of this is, in fact, quite desirable, worthwhile professional activity and focus. However, for beleaguered neophyte and experienced language teaching practitioners, short on time and thirsty for practicable, theoretically sound ideas, what is essential to be retained?

The answer, it seems, is not provided easily. Learning strategy researchers and theorists, with their findings, perhaps not unsurprisingly, muddy the waters. Nothing in life is simple. Politzer and McGroarty (1985:118), for example, found that

> good behaviours may be differentially appropriate for the various types of skills related to the purpose of second language study.

Different variables can affect the choice of language learning strategies:

- achievement,
- level of language learning,
- years of language study,
- nature and difficulty of the task,
- motivation, goal of language study,
- method of teaching,
- ethnic or cultural background of the learner, and
- gender.

Prokop *et al.* (1982) had earlier arrived at similar conclusions and warn against any dogmatic statements about language learners without taking into account all the background variables. Indeed, subsequent researchers (particularly Oxford, Nyikos and Ehrman, 1988; Ehrman and Oxford, 1989; 1990; Oxford and Nyikos, 1989) suggest teachers consider use of a personality test, such as the Myer-Briggs-type indicator or MBTI, the results which can serve as a signpost to describe personality traits and assign the preferred type of training for that personality type. A couple of adaptations of such learning style tests, originally developed for an Ontario ministerial publication (1996), are included in the appendices appearing at the end of this chapter.

Learning strategies research is very extensive. Oxford's exhaustive classification scheme, for example, consists of 60 language learning strategies incorporating every strategy cited in the voluminous language learning strategies literature. Additionally, the cautionary remarks noted above must be taken into account. Accordingly, the ideas which follow regarding how to promote the development of strategic competence in the language classroom are intended as tentative and exploratory only, though research-informed and reasonably grounded in evolving theory on the subject.

Classroom practitioners need to be aware that:

- Like linguistic and communicative competence, strategic competence can be developed through teaching and learning.
- Language learning strategies can become automatic through explicit instruction and convert to implicit linguistic knowledge [or procedural knowledge], thereby facilitating language competence (Vandergrift, 1995: 98).
- Less successful differ from more successful language learners in their more limited range of language learning strategies use and in their deployment of language learning strategies not always most appropriate to the task. Hence, what successful language learners intuit to a greater degree needs

to be taught explicitly to weaker language learners.
- Notwithstanding weaker language learners' more limited repertoire of language learning strategies, like successful language learners, they do use, albeit not always most appropriately, different language learning strategies and are capable of describing the strategies they use. Their strategic competence can be enhanced through explicit instruction.
- Language learning strategies can be categorized in three groups, all of which warrant explicit classroom instructional focus – cognitive, socio-affective and metacognitive language learning strategies (Oxford, 1985; 1990; O'Malley and Chamot, 1990; Vandergrift, 1995). Some specific, representative examples of each category are repeating/imitating, matching, memorizing, making associations and applying knowledge from one's maternal language (cognitive); developing a positive attitude in using the language, taking risks, cooperating with peers or the teacher, asking questions for assistance or verification/clarification (socio-affective); and using selective attention, organizing one's learning, monitoring one's learning and evaluating one's own progress (metacognitive). These are described in more detail in Alberta Education (1991: 30-34) and Vandergrift (1995: 95).

Cognitive language learning strategies can be made operative, for example, in the following ways/contexts in the classroom:
- developing sound pronunciation skills/habits.
- imitation, mimicry.
- building vocabulary – using the dictionary to determine the meaning of a word, activation of newly learned words, matching vocabulary words with pictures, using informed guessing to devise meaning of words similar in the mother tongue and target language.
- developing grammatical awareness/precision in use – making complete sentences from two column lists, matching sentences that have the same meaning but are said or written differently, such as, "I have lots of books/I have many books."
- developing aural comprehension (listening) skills – contextual guessing, clumping together of known material so as to attend to the unknown, recognizing semantic patterns, using one's ability and experience to anticipate contextual elements, inferencing.
- developing oral production (speaking) skills – rehearsing an oral text produced by the students themselves or by others, using circumlocution or asking for help with a word or phrase

(just as one would in one's mother tongue).
- developing reading comprehension skills – using contextual classes to assist in the comprehension of a text, skimming or scanning written texts for information (e.g., headlines, sub titles, keywords, italics), using one's knowledge about text genre to determine the type of text.
- developing written expression skills – note-taking for future reference, transferring style features for forms of writing from the mother tongue that are appropriate to the target language.

Socio-affective language learning strategies might be made operative in ways such as the following:
- developing sound pronunciation skills/habits – openness by way of exposure to regional and other dialect varieties, understanding and accepting that approximative pronunciation patterns may not be understood and may be corrected or need to be repeated.
- building vocabulary – recognizing and accepting semantic differences and similarities across languages (e.g., cognates, 'faux amis').
- developing grammatical awareness/precision in use – openness to feedback, willingly entering activities with peers and the teacher which are designed to reinforce/develop automatisms in grammar patterns, seeking clarification/ verification regarding the grammaticality of a sentence.
- developing aural comprehension (listening) skills – tolerance of ambiguity, openness to cultural clues and patterns that might differ from those in the mother tongue, actively searching out opportunities to hear the target language spoken (e.g., radio and TV broadcasts, second-language clubs).
- developing oral production (speaking) skills – active participation in cooperative learning activities, participation in impromptu skits/debates, acceptance in self and others of pause, hesitations, backtracking and such as normal practices in oral discourse, actively searching out situations in which to use the target language.
- developing reading comprehension skills – tolerance of ambiguity, openness to cultural clues and patterns that might differ from those in the mother tongue, self-selecting outside class reading opportunities in the target language.
- developing written expression skills – openness to feedback, peer review, self-evaluation (using grids, for example).

Metacognitive language learning strategies might be promoted in the following ways:

- developing sound pronunciation skills/habits.
- contrasting one's own approximative patterns of pronunciation with those of a native speaker role model, self-correcting.
- building vocabulary – paying attention to word formation, skillful use of dictionaries, vocabulary building using semantic maps.
- developing grammatical awareness/precision in use – conscious awareness of one's own errors.
- developing aural comprehension (listening) skills – going from getting the main idea (gist) to understanding specific details, hypothesizing, attending to key information in a text.
- developing oral production (speaking) skills – brainstorming, group problem-solving.
- developing reading comprehension skills – going from getting the main idea (gist) to understanding specific skills, attending to key information in a text/ using selective attention.
- developing written expression skills – discerning differing written styles/patterns in diverse written genres, note-taking.

Conclusion

Teachers ignore at their peril focusing on development of strategic competence among learners in their second language classroom. Considerable research demonstrates that language learning strategies vary in their usefulness and applicability dependent on such variables as: achievement, motivation, level of language learning, years of language study, method of teaching, nature and difficulty of the task, ethnic or cultural background of the learner and gender, among possible others yet to be identified. All the same, it is clear that all language learners, successful and less successful, use a variety of language learning strategies and are capable of describing them. Moreover, developing strategic competence enhances over time learner's linguistic and communicative competence. It is clearly the second language teacher's responsibility, given what is known at this time about cognitive, socio-affective and metacognitive strategies for language learning, to help students become cognizant of strategy use and subsequently apply this knowledge. Teachers can help both more and less successful students broaden their strategies repertoire (i.e., enhance their strategic competence) and, in particular, help weaker language learners learn to make choices of strategies use more appropriate to the task at hand.

It is likely that second language classrooms where teachers focus tentatively and carefully on the development of strategic competence, in addition to linguistic and communicative competence, will result also in less frustrated learners and more satisfied teachers. This seems a reasonable payback for some worthwhile, research-substantiated and theoretically-sound activity in the classroom.

Questionnaire on Learning Styles

Teachers should present this questionnaire in a way that is not threatening to students and does not make comparisons among them. It is recommended that the teacher read the questions aloud with the students and clarify them if necessary.

Learning Styles Questionnaire

Editor's Note: The information which appears in the "Appendix and the "Questionaire on Learning Styles" is taken from *French for Basic Communication 1987*: A resource document for grade 9 and 10 basic level Core French. Toronto. Ontario Ministry of Education 1987. The information in chart format was done by Anthony Mollica.

This is a questionnaire to help you find out how you learn best. There are no wrong answers.

Answer the following questions quickly. If you agree strongly, circle A. If you sometimes agree, circle B. If you disagree, circle C.

A = strongly agree   B = sometimes agree   C = disagree

1. Once I hear a song, I can recognize the tune the next time I hear it.   ☐A ☐B ☐C
2. I recognize a voice on the phone very quickly.   ☐A ☐B ☐C
3. I understand the person speaking if I watch him/her closely.   ☐A ☐B ☐C
4. I enjoy watching others dance.   ☐A ☐B ☐C
5. I pour and carry full cups easily and do not spill liquids.   ☐A ☐B ☐C
6. When I climb stairs, I look ahead rather than at my feet.   ☐A ☐B ☐C
7. I think a diagram or picture is better than an explanation.   ☐A ☐B ☐C

8. Noises from the outside interfere with my ability to concentrate. ☐A ☐B ☐C

9. If an article is illustrated with pictures, it helps hold my interest. ☐A ☐B ☐C

10. When riding a bicycle, I can look to the side without turning the handlebars in the direction I am looking. ☐A ☐B ☐C

11. I can walk in the complete dark and not bump into anything. ☐A ☐B ☐C

12. When I dial a telephone number, I notice if there is an unusual ring. ☐A ☐B ☐C

13. I am very aware of the fine tuning and colour on the TV. ☐A ☐B ☐C

14. I decide that my hair needs washing by the way it feels. ☐A ☐B ☐C

15. I can easily remember faces. ☐A ☐B ☐C

16. I do well on a test if it is about information we have talked about in class. ☐A ☐B ☐C

17. Good sound quality is important to me when I listen to the radio or stereo. ☐A ☐B ☐C

18. I enjoy going barefoot and walking in sand or grass, if it is safe. ☐A ☐B ☐C

19. I can remember a license-plate number long enough to write it down an hour later. ☐A ☐B ☐C

20. The texture of the material is important to me when I buy clothes. ☐A ☐B ☐C

21. I would rather receive a phone call from a friend than get a letter. ☐A ☐B ☐C

Scoring the Questionnaire

If most of your answers to statements 5, 6, 10, 11, 14, 18, and 20 are A, you tend to learn by doing.

If most of your answers to statements 1, 2, 8, 12, 16, 17, and 21 are A, you tend to learn by listening.

If most of your answers to statements 3, 4, 7, 9, 13, 15, and 19 are A, you tend to learn by seeing.

If most of your answers are B in one of these three groups, that is probably your backup system.

If most of your answers are C in one of these groups, that is probably not the way you prefer to learn.

Appendix

Kinaesthetic Learning Style	Auditory Learning Style	Visual Learning Style
tries things out, touches, feels, and manipulates	talks about what to do	looks around and examines situations
expresses feelings physically, jumping for pushing, tugging pounding	expresses emotion by shouting for joy, blowing up verbally, or varying tone, pitch and volume	is less exuberant than the kinaesthetic/tactual joy, learner
shows emotion through facial expression, staring when angry and beaming when happy	enjoys listening but cannot wait to get a chance to talk	thinks in pictures and detail
asks questions during and after a presentation	likes to recite information	may be quiet
seems easily distracted easily distracted by movement	thinks in sounds and is by visual disorder or sounds	can easily be distracted
is a poor listener and loses interest in a long speech		may be impatient when asked to a question
stands very close to a person to whom he/she is listening or speaking	may mouth the words silently while reading	
	recalls lists of words better when they are presented orally	can recall lists of words better when they are presented visually
may start the day off looking neat and tidy but becomes dishevelled through physical activity		is neat in appearance
gestures while speaking		
may write neatly initially but loses that neatness as he/she runs out of space on the paper		has good handwriting
needs to write down words to determine if they "feel" right	uses a phonics approach in spelling	recognizes words by their configurations
	tends to remember names but forgets faces	has a vivid imagination
		likes to take notes

References

Alberta Education. 1991. _French as a Second Language Teacher Resource Manual._ Edmonton, Alberta: Alberta Education.

Canale, M. and Swain, M. 1980. "Theoretical bases of communicative approaches to second language teaching and testing." _Applied Linguistics_, 1, 1: 1-47.

Chomsky, N. 1966. "Linguistic Theory." In R.B. Mead Jr., ed., _Language Teaching: Broader Contexts. Northeast Conference on the Teaching of Foreign Languages: Reports of the Working Committees._ New York: MLA Materials Centre, 43-49.

Cohen, A. and C. Hosenfeld.1981. "Some uses of mentalistic data in second-language research." _Language Learning_, 31: 285-313.

Ehrman, M. and R. Oxford. 1989. "Effects of sex differences, career choice and psychological type on adult language learning strategies." _The Modern Language Journal_, 73, 1: 1-13.

Ehrman, M. and R. Oxford. 1990. "Adult language learning styles and strategies in an intensive training setting." _The Modern Language Journal_, 74, 3: 311-327.

Galloway, V. and A. Labarca. 1991. "From student to learner: Style, process and strategy." In D. Birckbichler, ed., _New Perspectives and New Directions in Foreign Language Education._ Lincolnwood, Illinois: National Textbook Co., 111-158.

Gardner, H. 1993. _Multiple Intelligences: The Theory in Practice._ New York: Harper Collins.

Gu, Y. and R. K. Johnson. 1996. "Vocabulary learning strategies and language learning outcomes." _Language Learning_, 46, 4: 643-679.

Hébert, Y., _et al._ 1990. _Syllabus formation langagière générale._ Ottawa, Ontario: Canadian Association of Second Language Teachers.

Heffernan, P.J. 1990. _National Core French Study: Summary Report/Étude nationale sur les programmes de français de base: Abrégé de l'Étude._ Ottawa, Ontario: Canadian Association of Second Language Teachers.

Heffernan, P.J. 1992. "Language learning remembered." _Alberta Modern Language Journal_, 29, 1: 16-19.

Hosenfeld, C. 1976. "Learning about learning: Discovering our students' strategies." _Foreign Language Annals_, 9: 117-129.

Hymes, D. 1972. "On communicative competence." In J.B. Pride and J. Holmes, eds., _Sociolinguistics: Selected readings._ Harmondsworth: Penguin Books, 269-293.

Lalonde, R.N., P.A. Lee, and R.C. Gardner. 1987. "The common view of the good language learner: An investigation of teachers' beliefs." _The Canadian Modern Language Review_, 44, 1: 16-34.

Lawson, M.J. and Hogben, D. 1996. "The vocabulary-learning strategies of foreign-language students." _Language Learning_, 46, 1: 101-135.

LeBlanc, R., _et al._ 1990. _National Core French Study – A Synthesis/Étude nationale sur les programmes de français de base – Rapport synthèse._ Ottawa, Ontario: Canadian Association of Second Language Teachers.

Moore, T. 1977. "An experimental language handicap (personal account)." *Bulletin of the British Psychological Society*, 30: 107-110.

Naiman, N., M. Frölich, H.H. Stern, and A. Todesco. 1978. *The Good Language Learner*. Toronto, Ontario: OISE.

O'Malley, J.M. and A.U. Chamot. 1990. *Learning Strategies in Second Language Acquisition*. Cambridge: Cambridge University Press.

Ontario Ministry of Education. 1996. *French for Communication*. Toronto, Ontario: Ministry of Education.

Oxford, R., M. Nyikos, and M. Ehrman. 1988. "Vive la différence? Reflections on sex differences in use of language learning strategies." *Foreign Language Annals*, 21, 4: 321-329.

Oxford, R. and M. Nyikos. 1989. "Variables affecting choice of language learning strategies by university students." *The Modern Language Journal*, 73, 3: 291-300.

Oxford, R. 1985. *A New Taxonomy of Language Learning Strategies*. Washington, DC: ERIC Clearinghouse on Languages and Linguistics.

Oxford, R. 1990. *Language Learning Strategies: What Every Teacher Should Know*. New York: Newbury House.

Pimsleur, P. 1980. *How to Learn a Foreign Language*. Boston, MA: Heinle and Heinle.

Politzer, R.L. and McGroarty, M. 1985. "An exploratory study of learning behaviours and their relationship to gains in linguistic and communicative competence." *TESOL Quarterly*, 19,1: 103-123.

Prokop, M., D. Fearon, D. and B. Rollet, 1982. *Second Language Learning Strategies in Formal Instructional Contexts*. Edmonton, Alberta: University of Alberta.

Prokop, M. 1989. *Learning Strategies for Second Language Users*. Queenston, Ontario: Edwin Mellen Press.

Reiss, M. 1985. "The good language learner: Another look." *The Canadian Modern Language Review*, 41: 511-523.

Rivers, W.M. 1979. "Learning a sixth language: An adult learner's daily diary." *The Canadian Modern Language Review*, 36: 67-82.

Robinson, P. 1997. "Individual differences and the fundamental similarity of implicit and explicit adult second language learning." *Language Learning*, 47, 1: 45-99.

Rubin, J. 1975. "What the good language learner can teach us." *TESOL Quarterly*, 9: 41-51.

Rubin, J. 1981. "Study of cognitive processes in second language learning." *Applied Linguistics*, 11, 2: 117-131.

Sousa, D. A. 1995. *How the Brain Learns*. Thousand Oaks, CA: Corwin Press.

Sousa, D.A. 1998. *Learning Manual for How the Brain Learns*. Thousand Oaks, CA: Corwin Press.

Stern, H.H. 1975. "What can we learn from the good language learner?" *The Canadian Modern Language Review*, 25: 9-21.

Stevick, E. 1989. *Success with Foreign Languages: Seven Who Achieved It and What Worked for Them*. New York: Prentice-Hall.

Vandergrift, L. 1995. "Language learning strategy research: Development of definitions and theory." *Journal of the CAAL/Revue de l'ACLA*, 17, 1: 87-104.

Wenden, A. and J. Rubin. 1987. *Learner Strategies in Language Learning*. Englewood Cliffs, N.J.: Prentice-Hall.

Reprinted from: Peter J. Heffernan, "Promoting the Development of Strategic Competence in the Language Classroom." *Mosaic*, 5, 4 (Summer 1998): 1, 3-8.

8 French Core Programs: How Can We Improve Them?

H.H. Stern

In this article the author proposes a multi-dimensional curriculum which formed the basis for the National Core French Study. The project was continued after the Author's untimely death.

Introduction

I am very happy to have been asked to address the Canadian Asssociation of Second Language Teachers (CASLT) at this meeting and at this time. The symbolism of your theme "Take a second language to heart in Manitoba, the heart of the continent" has not escaped me. Here we are indeed in the heart of Canada, a geographically central spot at which one is ideally placed to look west and east and north and to get a sense of perspective. In language teaching, no less than in other branches of education, our habits of thinking tend to be provincial rather than continental. Most of us have become so imbued with the idea of education as a provincial concern and not a national one or, heaven forbid, a "federal" one, that we quite forget that this educational separatism applies, above all, to educational administration and organization. Our thoughts, our ideas, and our ideals hardly stop at the provincial boundaries. Nor do the problems we face or even the rhythm of our concerns which is remarkably similar across the country from east to west. But unfortunately we lack sufficient mechanisms for cooperation, and the enormous distances which separate us prevent us from getting together often enough to share our ideas and to deal with our problems by joint action.

This is why I believe that an association like CASLT is so important. CASLT – we ought to remember – was founded in Manitoba twelve years ago at the initiative of Dr. Robert Roy, and we should pay tribute to his vision. As an organization, CASLT is probably more important than we may yet have realized. In these twelve years it has not yet played the role it rightly ought to play in matters of second language teaching and learning in Canada. CASLT should take a leaf out of the book of another association, Canadian Parents for French, whose activities range right across the continent. It has become a truly national force in promoting French as a second language. There is no reason why CASLT should not in due course become equally influential in its own way and for its own purposes.

The Council of Europe Modern Languages Project

At this point I am going to digress for a moment and say something about the Council of Europe Modern Languages Project, because I believe it presents an interesting parallel and has an important lesson for us. Europe, as we all know, also has its language problems. Over ten years ago, at the initiative of the Council of Europe, scholars from different European countries came together and during the subsequent years developed a new basis for language curricula for adults in Europe. Some of the linguists and teachers working on this project have become well known to us in Canada; to name only a few of them: John Trim, David Wilkins, Eddy Roulet, Daniel Coste, René Richterich and Jan van Ek. Out of their deliberations grew the *Threshold Level, Niveau-seuil, Kontaktschwelle,* and their equivalents in several other European languages.[1] The writings arising from the Council of Europe project constitute some of the finest and most significant studies on language questions produced anywhere during the last ten years.

In February this year, (1982) the Council of Europe organized a meeting at the Palais de l'Europe in Strasbourg which was of considerable importance for the future of this remarkable project. It was attended by delegations from 22 European countries. Canada was able to send a small delegation of six observers of whom I was one, at the invitation of the Department of the Secretary of State. The specific purpose of the February meeting was to take stock and review the project that concluded the first ten years, and now to advance to a new and even more ambitious project, wider in scope and more diversified than its predecessor, but again involving the voluntary cooperation of many people from the different member states of the European community. The most recent publication of the Council of Europe, Modern Languages 1971-1981, presents a fascinating review of the past of the project, of current trends of thought and developments, and above all, it gives a glimpse of future directions.[2] There is a lot one could say about this project. I am not, at this point, proposing to discuss it further or to elaborate on the new directions that the Council of Europe intends to embark on, interesting though this might be. Nor do I wish to imply by talking about the Council of Europe project at some length that this project or its findings could be transferred to Canada lock, stock and barrel. In the present context I have dwelt on this experience for a different reason. What struck me in Strasbourg as wholly admirable, and what I want to draw to your attention is, first of all, the fact itself of this cooperative international language venture; it is, secondly, the existence of an imaginative and committed group of language teachers and scholars sharing with one another the task of tackling jointly the language problems of a continent. It occurred to me that we have nothing of similar scope and dynamism across the provinces. And I wonder why we don't.

Interprovincial Cooperation

Yet, there are indications of a similar spirit here, as well; of a great willingness among us to cooperate on language questions. Take, among several instances, *The Canadian Modern Language Review* which has a national editorial board representing different provinces and which under the dynamic editorship of Tony Mollica has become the leading national, and indeed an internationl, language teaching review. It is now in the process of deliberately loosening its ties with the Ontario Modern Language Teachers' Association in order to emphasize its national character. Other examples of interprovincial cooperation are the much valued Monitor program administered by the Council of Ministers of Education; or SÉVEC, the recently created Society for Educational Visits and Exchanges in Canada (Société éducative de visites et d'échanges au Canada). The predecessors of SEVEC, *Visites Interprovinciales* and the Bilingual Exchange Secretariat, had for many years successfully organized student exchanges between Quebec and Ontario. The new society, which has been brought about by the merger of the two former organizations, is now extending these activities nationally and diversifying its program.[3] Other examples are the Canadian Association of Immersion Teachers (Association canadienne de professeurs d'immersion) which has attracted teachers from all across Canada, and the Canadian Association of Applied Linguistics (Association canadienne de linguistique appliquée). Finally, there are the two associations I already mentioned, Canadian Parents for French and this association, CASLT. All these organizations and activities are evidence that our thinking on language questions in Canada is not narrowly provincial. We are no doubt ready to make Canada-wide cooperative efforts in the interest of second language teaching.

A National Language Centre?

If we tried to make such a national effort now, what would most

clearly demand our energies? There are many projects one could
think of. It could be argued that at this stage the most important
thing to do is not to launch into this or that project, but to create a
mechanism of national interprovincial cooperation, a national
language centre or institute, of the kind first proposed many years
ago, in the Report on Bilingualism and Biculturalism. Such a centre has been asked for again and again, for example, by the Canadian Teachers' Federation, by Canadian Parents for French, and
most recently, and quite concretely, by the Office of the Commissioner of Official Languages.[4] However, these efforts have so far
not come to fruition, for various reasons, partly of course financial, but mainly, I fear, because of the reluctance on the part of
provincial ministries to allow an educational body to be created,
however benevolent, which transcends the provincial framework.
Some people might also be reluctant to support the creation of a
new national language centre, but for different reasons. They
would like to know beforehand what such a centre would be doing
that is not being done by existing language centres, such as the
International Centre for Research on Bilingualism at Laval,
language groups or centres at various other universities, e.g.,
McGill, Ottawa, Carleton, or the University of Western Ontario,
or the Ontario Institute for Studies in Education Modern Language Centre. For all these reasons it is perhaps more fitting than
to dream about a new national language centre to do some hard
thinking about the issues or problems that should receive attention nationwide.

The Plight of the French Core Curriculum

If I were asked to pick out one issue I would have little hesitation
in making my choice. It would be the second language curriculum, and more specifically, the French core curriculum. In my
view, curriculum is the key issue for a renewal and a strengthening of second language teaching in Canada at the present time.
To some extent this is already recognized by the provincial ministries and many school boards. Several of them have produced
for their own jurisdictions, or are in the process of doing so, new
language curricula, particularly for French as a second language.
I am familiar with a few interesting efforts in this direction, for
example, the FSL and ESL programmes d'étude of the Quebec
Ministry of Education and the Core Curriculum Guideline for
French of the Ontario Ministry of Education.[5] But where everybody works in the same direction, would we not gain a great deal
if we – like the Europeans did ten years ago – got together and
pooled our ideas through a Canadian modern language curriculum project? This would in no way interfere with the freedom of

the ministries to act as they wished, but it would give all the ministries, and not only the ministries, but also school boards, provincial language associations, leaders in the profession, and anyone else concerned with language program development access to a common pool of ideas and practices. This would not only save time and money, but it would also meet a genuine need and at the same time establish a cooperative principle from which all the provinces could benefit. Such a project should be much easier to establish in Canada than it must have been in Europe because our traditions and systems are so much more alike.

Let me turn to the substance of this proposal and ask why curriculum is so central. I am going to illustrate with French what I want to say, but I am sure it equally applies to other languages. All languages taught as subjects in school and university are at risk in the present juncture of events, and I suggest that all of us would be well advised to rethink our approach to the language curriculum.

What is meant by curriculum in this context comprises three things:
- *content* (what we teach),
- *objectives* (what we aim to achieve), and
- *teaching strategies* (how we approach teaching).

Underlying any view of the language curriculum is a philosophy or theory of language teaching, a view of language, a view of learning and a view of education, and this certainly applies to the curriculum concept I propose to sketch.

Why then should we focus on French, and more specifically, the French core curriculum (not immersion)? I believe that core French has been neglected because we have become mesmerized by immersion. The success of French immersion is undisputed; but it has been the undoing of the French core curriculum. "Immersion is the only way of learning another language" has, during the last ten years, become a Canadian credo of second language learning. Much as I like and support immersion as an exciting, and, indeed, essential alternative program in school systems, we do language teaching a disservice by overstating its success and, incidentally, also by overlooking its problems, but above all by deprecating, devaluing, and disregarding the potential of regular/core language programs. The majority of French language learners will have to learn French in a non-immersion core program. Most language teachers operate in regular programs. Language learning in other languages at school or university level is inevitably done in regular language courses. In other countries, for example throughout Europe, where immersion as a form of schooling does not exist, all language teaching is "regular," or "core" in our terms. We would therefore be seriously remiss if we overlooked the importance of all these conventional language courses. The plea to you of this address is that we should join together across provinces, hopefully through the medium of this association or with the help of some other agency, and over the next few years make determined attempts to make a thorough improvement in the curriculum of core programs so that the French core program becomes a true alternative to immersion and is no longer its "parent pauvre."

How can this be done? Rather than turning our back on the core program we should, to begin with, ask ourselves what are its major shortcomings. Can they be remedied? Or is the French core program (along with other regular language programs) a "lost cause"? Is perhaps language teaching in the conventional sense no longer a practical proposition? I firmly believe that the negative views, implied in the last two questions and sometimes voiced today even by language teachers themselves, are unjustified.

What then are the criticisms that we or others make of core programs and to which we have to respond? In a sweeping way and without qualifying them, they can be characterized as follows: French core programs and other conventional language courses can be criticized for taking too narrow a view of language and for operating with too limited a conception of the language learner and language learning process. They confine the role of language teacher too much to that of a drillmaster, and thus often fail to realize the educational potential of second language learning. Courses are accused of being repetitive and not well "articulated." The substantive content of programs has been described as unsubstantial, the narratives and dialogues in them as trivial and insipid. Students sometimes complain that they go over the same ground again and again and make no headway, and teachers feel frustrated and lose professional satisfaction.

At this point let us remember, in case these rather sweeping judgements are misinterpreted, that what I have characterized are expressions of self-criticisms among the professionals themselves as much as criticisms made by others. They are not accusations of "incompetence" directed against the teachers. What we attempt to do is to improve the quality of our work, and therefore, from time to time, we take a critical look at our own practices. The public would only have something to worry about if we were complacent and did not recognize shortcomings or were unwilling to do anything about them.

The shortcomings in language programs which I have

sketched can of course be explained. Broadly speaking, the way French is taught in Canada today has been very much the result of the audiolingual revolution of the sixties which aimed at making language training simple, direct and thoroughly practical, and many of us teach a language in the way we were at that time taught to do it. The techniques which were perfected during those years have considerable merit, and I am not engaging in the common pastime of "bashing" audiolingualism.[6] However, we must recognize that in the last twenty years there have been changes in views on language and language learning. There have been major advances which we cannot ignore. One such development has been the immersion experience which has important implications for regular language teaching. Another has been the Council of Europe Project with its challenging approach to new language curricula. A third has been research on second language learning. Here I am thinking of "interlanguage" studies, or Stephen Krashen's stimulating work on the distinction between language "acquisition" and "learning,"[7] and the growing insights on learners' own perceptions, initiatives, and individual ways of coping with a new language.[8] We must also bear in mind changes in the organization of language teaching which apply particularly to French in anglophone school systems and to English in francophone systems: a much bigger time allowance is given to the second language in school programs.[9] Core programs last much longer; they often begin in the primary or junior grades and often take five, eight, or even ten and twelve years. Moreover, more time per day or per week is allowed for. This means that a program cannot be confined to a limited drill routine for years on end. It places upon the curriculum developer the obligation to make sure that the French core program makes a significant contribution to the educational offerings of the school curriculum.

Framework for a New Language Curriculum

With these considerations in mind I would now like to present to you a curriculum framework which is intended to reflect these changes and which is also meant to respond to some of the current criticisms that language programs have provoked.[10] This is not the time and place to discuss the whole scheme in full detail. The accompanying diagram (Figure 1, on the following page) and a few explanations may, however, provide the necessary orientation.

As will be seen, it is a multidimensional curriculum that is proposed. This curriculum has four components, or, a fourfold focus:

An FL Curriculum Model

Content	Objectives				Main strategies
	Proficiency	Knowledge	Affect	Transfer	
Language Syllabus (L2)	(major)	(minor)	(minor)	(minor)	Analytical: Study & Practice
Culture Syllabus (C2)	(minor)	(major)	(minor)	(minor)	Analytical: Study (knowledge about C2)
Communicative Activity Syllabus (L2/C2)	(minor)	(minor)	(major)	(minor)	Communicative Activities (Experimential)
General Language Education Syllabus	(minor)	(minor)	(minor)	(major)	Comparative (Crosslingual/ Crosscultural)

Key   Suggested major elements ☐   Suggested minor emphasis ▨

Figure1

- language,
- culture,
- communicative activities, and
- general language education.

That is to say, the curriculum is not based on an undimensional conception of proficiency as purely linguistic knowledge. Its content is not just language, narrowly conceived. It consists in fact of four interacting content areas or "syllabuses." To each of these syllabuses we can ascribe certain basic teaching strategies, because the different content areas require different approaches which complement each other. Let me now briefly sketch these four content areas:

1. The *language syllabus* is familiar enough, at least in parts. It would have those vocabulary and grammatical components that language programs have always had and which no doubt are necessary for a thorough acquisition of the second language. In addition, however, it would incorporate new elements that derive from semantics, discourse analysis and sociolinguistics, in short, elements that the Council of Europe Threshold Level and other "notional-functional" syllabuses have already demonstrated. They would be taught with the techniques of study and practice familiar to most experienced language teachers, and therefore include "cognitive-" as well as "audiolingual-" type teaching strategies. This syllabus,

then, is the least controversial aspect of this proposal, except for the fact that the sociolinguistic and semantic components are relatively new and are still not well integrated with the teaching of the grammar and vocabulary of traditional programs.[11]

2. The second syllabus, *culture,* is in principle also widely recognized in most language curricula but is usually very subsidiary and is often completely ignored. It is this syllabus which would orient the French course openly and consciously towards one or several French communities. In the case of French as a second language in Manitoba, this would inevitably include the Franco-Manitoban community. In addition one would select other francophone communities in Canada, particularly Quebec, as the primary centre of francophone culture in North America, while also taking into consideration France and French-speaking territories across the world. The main teaching strategies for this syllabus are likely to be information sharing and discovery procedures. Culture should of course not only be learnt about; it should also be experienced at a more personal level. However, in this scheme, the "experiential" aspect is taken care of under the next heading. The cultural component is much harder to implement than is often realized because of a lack of solid information and accessible documentation. There is a shortage of appropriate materials to meet the requirements of this syllabus. It is a deficiency area which needs development. One would hope that French departments in Canadian universities will increasingly help in making good this deficiency.

3. The third syllabus, *communicative activities,* is most commonly overlooked and is perhaps the most novel contribution of our own time. It demands a change of approach. It is designed to ensure that all learners are exposed to the experience of natural, unedited and unrehearsed language use. The key concepts for this syllabus are contact, communication and authentic experience. This syllabus guarantees that the learner does not only learn about the language as if it were a separate object, but that he/she also "lives" the language in a personal and direct way. In this syllabus we apply to the core French program the lessons gained from the immersion experience, and from other recent so-called communicative approaches to language teaching. In the context of this syllabus, learners are encouraged to involve themselves as persons with the target language community in whatever way they can. Students should be given the opportunity to relate their own lives,

their activities, their predominant interests and concerns to the second language. The emphasis in this syllabus is on topics, on information – not on language as such. One of the most readily available ways of doing this is to offer a subject other than the language itself in French or to draw on the other subjects of the school curriculum; in this way the language is used as a means of communication for something else. This has been of course the "secret" of the immersion story. Another important aspect of this syllabus is to create opportunities for students to make direct personal contact with one of the target language communities: visiting, meeting target language speakers, taking up residence, taking part in student exchanges. Another approach to this syllabus is possible through reading books, magazines, and newspapers produced for French-speaking audiences, as well as through watching movies, or listening to the radio. In this context we may come to reconsider the role of literature in language teaching. In short, these are all different ways for students to move closer to the target language community. From this perspective, student travel and exchanges are not frills; they are an important part of this syllabus, because they involve students (as well as teachers) and, in the case of class exchanges or visits, whole schools in communicative activities.[12] The main teaching-learning strategy for this syllabus is one of communicative action rather than formal language study or rehearsal-type practice. Students become directly involved as participants in some worthwhile activities. While many teachers have already encouraged such activities and have gained experience in them, these enterprises are not usually fully incorporated in the French program. As a syllabus, communicative activities need pioneering development.

4.   With the fourth and final component of the curriculum, which we have called the *general language education syllabus,* we change our perspective again. We stand back from learning French and from learning about French-speaking communities. Instead, in this syllabus we attempt to think about language and languages in general, about language learning, about cultures and societies, using the experience of learning French as a jumping-off ground for generalizing and for relating learning French to what we know about English and other languages.

This syllabus would deal with general linguistic and cultural phenomena, make learners alert to the process of language learning ("learning how to learn"), and might even include discussions of a philosophical nature about the relations between language and thought, language and society, or language and reality. Other topics might be child language, language families, language varieties, questions of language and ethnic prejudice, or political and economic issues in language learning. The main teaching strategy for this syllabus is likely to be a highly cognitive one that involves students in making "crosslingual" and "crosscultural" observations and comparisons and that will encourage them to think about their own language learning. Here again we are treading on new ground – at least in the context of French for anglophones at school level.[13]

These four syllabuses jointly make up the framework for a second language curriculum. The important difference between this curriculum framework and more familiar ones lies in the fact that the language syllabus is not given automatic priority. The other three syllabuses are not treated as less important aspects. They are considered as of equal worth, offering different but complementary approaches to the second language.

To summarize:

in *syllabus 1* we study the language itself, acquire the skills of listening, speaking, reading, and writing; in syllabus 2 we are concerned with the communities that speak the language and get to know something of their lives,

but in *both syllabus 1 and 2* we quite legitimately look at language and life as if they were objects which we examine, and become familiar with;

with *syllabus 3*, communicative activities, we change our perspective and become personally involved, as human beings, in language use, and experience the target language and the target communities as directly as possible.

In *syllabus 4* we stand back from it all and relate French (or whatever other language we learn) to what we know and learn about language, language learning, and people in general.

These four syllabuses are mutually supporting, each contributing to the other three, and to the general school curriculum. They should not be thought of as completely separate from each other: "On Mondays, we have language, on Tuesdays, culture, and on Wednesdays, etc..." They are more in the nature of different ways of tackling a language from various angles. The success of these syllabuses would be greatest if they were completely integrated. This type of curriculum fits in well with the idea of "language across the curriculum" as well as with recent attempts to integrate French with other general school subjects.[14] Through this fourfold approach, I believe, we can give the second language curriculum greater strength, more balance, and greater educational impact, and thus, we would meet one of the main criticisms of current language curricula: triviality of content, lack of substance, lack of impact, and in addition, inadequate language proficiency.

The objectives (see Figure 1) to be reached with the help of this curriculum can be expressed in terms of four broad categories, which are loosely derived from Bloom's well-known taxonomies of educational objectives and their adaptations to language teaching by Valette:[15]

1. Proficiency in the language as well as cultural proficiency: the proficiency objective.

2. Knowledge about the language, culture and society: the cognitive objective. Learning a language should be an intellectually stimulating experience and should offer worthwhile new knowledge to the students.

3. Attitudes and values in relation to the language, the country or region and its people and culture: the affective objective. The students should feel good about the language and the countries or regions concerned. It is in this respect that the theme of this conference, "Take a language to heart", is particulary relevant.

4. The ability to transfer and generalize the experiences with French to other languages, other countries, and to a more general and multiethnic education: the general education objective.

These objectives, I contend, can be pursued with much greater chance of success with this kind of multidimensional curriculum than if we persisted in a narrowly unidimensional linguistic program.

It should be understood that in this scheme the different strategies only briefly referred to are not just an eclectic potpourri, but they are relevant to the different content areas and the main objectives identified.

Applications

What I have outlined does not claim to be entirely novel. In nucleus one can find something of these features in many French programs and classes. These are aspects which are more or less developed in the repertoire of many language teachers; but most curriculum developers, textbook writers, and teachers regard only the language syllabus as their real concern, and they tend to treat the other content areas as peripheral. The object of the present scheme is to develop these peripheral activities more systematically, and by giving them more weight language teachers would be enabled to deliver a more interesting, more varied and an educationally more substantial program which, hopefully, will also be more effective.

Because this scheme is not in itself completely new and merely gives emphasis to features of language programs which are commonly neglected, it is something that any teacher interested can introduce into his or her own teaching almost immediately, tentatively and on a small scale at first, but as one gains confidence in going beyond the conventional restrictions of the usual language programs, more boldly and in a more deliberate way.

Let me deal at this point with one objection that some teachers are likely to raise: "Where should I take the time from for these other syllabuses? I can hardly cover my regular course work." Hammering away at language practice in isolation and non-stop (even if it is made attractive with fun and games) is not enough, nor does it lead to proficiency. In the long run it merely frustrates teachers and students. Moreover, educationally, it is far less justifiable than a multidimensional curriculum.

At the same time, I should point out that I look upon this proposal not as a foolproof recipe for instant success, but as a direction to be explored. On theoretical and educational grounds a strong case can be made for it. Nevertheless, in education we should introduce innovations through experimentation, research and development, and systematic evaluation. It is in this spirit that I offer you this suggestion for your consideration.

In this presentation I have thought primarily of French as a second language at the school level. But, in my view, this scheme is equally applicable to teaching French at the university as well as to the teaching of any other language at school or university. I am not saying that in all language programs and at all stages of a particular program the weight of emphasis should always be the same. Thus, the diagram illustrates only one possible interpretation of major and minor emphases. The priorities can shift from one syllabus to another, and the learner objectives, too, can vary according to the age, experience, proficiency level and other learner characteristics; they are likely to vary also in different learning settings.

What I have described is only a framework or outline. As is obvious from my account, the content areas, the different syllabuses, do not exist in their entirety in any ready-made form. They have not been sufficiently developed. Here and there we can find useful examples of the kind of items to incorporate in a syllabus. The Modern Language Centre of the Ontario Institute for Studies in Education in Toronto has, for several years, produced prototype "modules" in French and English which illustrate some points on these syllabuses.[16] Existing programs and new curricula, such as the Ontario Core French Guideline or the Quebec programmes d'études in French and English, are helpful for different aspects in curriculum development, and no doubt other provinces have useful experiences to contribute. But much remains to be done.

Here I want to anticipate a possible misunderstanding. I am not suggesting a single French curriculum for Canada, a megaproject, an "Alsands" of language teaching. What is envisaged is a pool or bank of ideas, items, and examples of techniques, practices, and materials at different levels of language instruction to which many people from across Canada would contribute and on which teachers, ministries, school boards, publishers, and even learners themselves could draw.

Towards Action

If the idea of this scheme appears to be promising, one could envisage an organization like taking it up to study it more closely. If, on further scrutiny, it holds up well, one could imagine that CASLT or some other organization would take the initiative and set up national committees, workshops, or "task forces." These committees could then be asked to make themselves responsible each for one of the content areas. Alternatively, committees might be constituted so as to take charge of all four syllabuses at a specific level of education: primary, junior, intermediate, senior, adult or university. At all these levels and in all four curriculum areas (as well as in other languages besides French) language education could only benefit from such inter-provincial cooperation.

These committees would of course not work in isolation. They could be expected to cooperate with one another. In addition they would enlist the help of the different provincial language associations, of the ministries of education, the Secretary of State, the Council of Ministers of Education, the Canadian publishers, of centres like the OISE Modern Language Centre, the Centre for International Research on Bilingualism at Laval, or the language centres at Ottawa and Carleton Universities, and, last but not least, one would of course count upon the help of the language departments in the universities. Similar ideas to the scheme developed here have recently been expressed also in USA; and cooperation with American language teachers, for example, the American Council on the Teaching of Foreign Languages (ACTFL), can also be envisaged.[17]

Conclusion

The scheme I have outlined needs more elaboration than I can offer on this occasion. But I hope I have said enough to convince you that this is meant to be a concrete proposal which now needs thorough discussion. Let us examine whether, from different perspectives, it makes sense in the present situation. Consider its implications for the classroom, for materials development, for the professional development of language teachers, and for research. if we come to the conclusion that this proposal has something going for it, let us do something about it.

This is what I mean when I said "Let us use our heads to win their hearts." My conviction is that with this approach to the curriculum we would not only win the hearts of our students. Our students would probably also learn a lot more French (or whatever other language we teach); and they would learn lots of other things besides. Their present second language program may or may not be in reasonably good shape, but my belief is that the multidimensional curriculum I have outlined is worth considering as a move in the direction towards a more valid and a more effective second language education. What I have proposed is of course a long-term development. Even if it is not a quick miracle cure, I am convinced that if we tried something along those lines, an important step would have been taken to lift French core programs out of the doldrums.*

Notes

1. J. van Ek, *The Threshold Level in a European Unit/Credit System for Modern Language Learning by Adults* (Strasbourg: Council of Europe, 1975); D. Coste et al., *Un niveau-seuil* (Strasbourg: Council of Europe, 1976); M. Baldegger, M. Muller, and G. Schneider, *Kontaktschwelle Deutsch as Fremdsprache* (Strasbourg: Council of Europe, 1980); and P.J. Slagter, *Un nivel umbral* (Strasgourg: Council of Europe, 1979). For recent discussions of the Council of Europe Project and additional references see, among others, articles by L.G. Alexander, W.M. Rivers and B.J. Melvin, and H.H. Stern in J.E. Alatis, H.B. Altman, and P.M. Alatis, eds., *The Second Language Classroom: Directions for the 1980's* (New York: Oxford University Press, 1981).

2. Also available in French under the title of *Langues vivantes 1971-1981*, both versions published by the Council of Europe, Strasbourg, 1981. The conclusions and recommendations of this important meeting, held in Strasbourg from Feb. 23 to 26, 1982, were published by the Council for Cultural Cooperation of the Council of Europe as a separate document, dated April 20, 1982 (reference number: CC-GP4 (82) 3).

3. SÉVEC, which is set up as an independent, charitable organization, has its head-quarters at 1580 Merivale Road, Suite 505, Ottawa, Ontario, K2G 4B5. Its first annual meeting and conference is due to be held in Winnipeg in October 1982.

4. See, for example, an article by E. Sarkar, "When it comes to a national clearing-house, Canadians are still house hunting," *CPF National Newsletter,* No. 11 (Sept. 1980), 1-2.

5. Quebec Ministry of Education, *Programme d'étude: Primaire – Français, langue seconde (1980); Programme d'étude: Primaire – Anglais, langue seconde (1980); Programme d'étude: Secondaire – Français, langue seconde* (1981), all issued by the Quebec Ministry of Education.

   Ontario Ministry of Education, *French, Core Programs 1980: Curriculum Guide-line for the Primary, Junior, Intermediate and Senior Divisions.* (Toronto: Ontario Ministry of Education, 1980). I have recently discussed the approach of both min-istries to the second language curriculum in Issues in Early Core French: A Selec-tive and Preliminary Review of the Literature: 1975-1981 (Toronto: Research Department of the Board of Education for the City of Toronto, 1982).

6. The need for reassessing the contribution of audiolingualism was recently pointed out by J.P.B. Allen in "The Audiolingual Method: Where did it come from and Where is it going?" mimeographed (1981).

7. See, for example, S.D. Krashen, *Second Language Acquisition and Second Lan-guage Learning* (Oxford: Pergamon Press, 1981).

8. For a recent review of studies on second language learning, see H.H. Stern and J. Cummins, "Language Teaching/Learning Research: A Canadian Perspective on Status and Directions," in J.K. Phillips, ed., *Action for the '80s: A Political, Pro-fessional, and Public Program for Foreign Language Education.* The ACTFL For-eign Language Education Series. (Skokie, Ill.: National Textbook Company, 1981), pp. 195-248.

9. The importance of increased time allowance has been strongly advocated by the Ontario Ministry of Education; see, for example, *The Report of the Ministerial Committee on the Teaching of French (Gillin Report)* (Toronto: Ontario Ministry of Education, 1974), and the same Ministry's policy statement in *Teaching and Learning French as a Second Language: A New Program for Ontario Students* (Toronto: Ontario Ministry of Education, 1977). Recent literature on the time is-sue is discussed in my report to the Toronto Board of Education, cited in note 5 above.

10. The conceptions underlying this curriculum scheme have been developed over a number of years going back to the early 1970s. They have found concrete expres-sion and application in the products of the French Modules Project of the OISE Modern Language Centre. In its present form this scheme is the result of pro-longed cooperation with Rebecca Ullmann, OISE Research Associate and Princi-pal Investigator of the French Modules Project. For earlier statements along simi-lar lines, see H.H. Stern, "Mammoths or Modules," *Times Educational Supple-ment,* October 8, 1976 (special inset on modern language teaching, p.44); H.H. Stern, R. Ullmann et al., *Module Making: A Study in the Development and Evalu-ation of Learning Materials for French as a Second Language* (Toronto: Ontario Ministry of Education, 1980). For more recent statements, see H.H. Stern, "Direc-tions in Foreign Language Curriculum Development," in American Council on the Teaching of Foreign Languages, *Proceedings of the National Conference on Pro-fessional Priorities, November 1980* (Hastings-on- Hudson: ACTFL Materials Center), pp. 12-17; R. Ullmann, "A Broadened Curriculum Framework for Sec-ond Languages: Some Considerations," *English Language Teaching Journal,* 36, pp. 255-262. See also note No. 17.

11. This issue of language syllabus design is discussed, among others in articles by H.G. Widdowson and C.J. Brumfit as well as in the already mentioned article by L.G. Alexander in Alatis et al., op. cit.

12. For a study of student exchanges from this educational perspective see Hanna, G. et al., *Contact and Communication: An Evaluation of Bilingual Student Exchange Programs.* (Toronto: OISE Press 1980). See also H.H. Stern, "Language Learning on the Spot: Some Thoughts on the Language Aspect of Student Exchange Programs", *The Canadian Modern Language Review/La Revue canadienne des langues viuvantes,* 36, No. 4(May 1980), pp. 659-669.

13. This aspect of the language curriculum has also recently been emphasized by E. Hawkins, *Modern Languages in the Curriculum* (Cambridge: Cambridge University Press, 1981).

14. See E. Roulet, *Langue maternelle et langues secondes: vers une pédagogie integrée.* (Paris: Hatier, 1980).

15. See, for example, R.M. Valette "Evaluation of Learning in a Second Language" in B. Bloom, J.T. Hastings, and G. Madaus, eds., *Handbook on Formative and Summative Evaluation of Student Learning* (New York: McGraw- Hill, 1971) pp. 817-853.

16. See note No. 10 above or an illustration of an ESL module combining elements of aspects of the language syllabus with a communicative activity, i.e., focus on a school subject area, in this case geography, see J.P.B. Allen and J. Howard, "Subject-Related ESL: An Experiment in Communicative Language Teaching," *The Canadian Modern Language Review/La Revue canadienne des langues vivantes,* 37, No. 3 (March 1981), pp. 535-550.

17. ACTFL in a recent national priority statement on foreign language curriculum and materials endorsed the multi-dimensional curriculum conception and also proposed "a linguistic syllabus", "a cultural syllabus", "a communicative syllabus", and "a general language education syllabus". (See p. 28 of the *Proceedings*, cited in note No. 10 above).

*Adapted version of the keynote address entitled,"Let's use our heads to reach their hearts," delivered May 7, 1982, at the 12th Annual Conference of the Canadian Association of Second Language Teachers (CASLT), held in Winnipeg, Manitoba. It was published in *The Canadian Modern Language Review/La Revue canadienne des langues vivantes*, under the editorship of Anthony Mollica, with the title, "French Core Programs Across Canada: How can we Improve Them?" Vol. 39, 1 (October 1982): 34-47.

Reprinted from: "French Core Programs across Canada: How Can We Improve Them?" *Mosaic,*7, 1 (Fall 1999): 11-20. By permission of Rhoda Stern.

9 Study Skill Suggestions for Students of Foreign Language Classes

Paul Cankar

As a part-time instructor at Austin Community College I have had the opportunity to conduct Study Skills Workshops for students taking foreign language classes. In my workshops, I have focused mainly on three topics:

1. Tips on how to study effectively at home for the class;
2. How to benefit from in-class time; and
3. What many foreign language instructors expect from their students.

Here are some of the ideas and suggestions I have shared with students in the workshops.

Tips on how to study effectively at home for the class:

1. *Find an atmosphere which works best for you.*

   Study with friends or a study group vs. studying alone.

   Study at home vs. the library.

   Study with quiet vs. having music in the background or headphones.

   Always have good lighting.

   Have ready supplies and reference materials (books, dictionary, pens, paper, etc.)

2. *Know exactly what it is you should be concentrating on.*

3. *Periodically reward yourself.*

   Don't feel guilty about taking a short break to have a snack, make a telephone call, watch the news, look at a magazine or the newspaper or watch a television program.

   By rewarding yourself during study sessions, you'll study for a longer period   of time and you'll accomplish a lot more. Sometimes you need to get away from the material to clear your mind and/or relax. Or course, take breaks in moderation!

4. *New vocabulary words.*

   Learning new vocabulary is an important part of learning a foreign language. You might want to try a few of these ideas:

   Flash cards: Using index cards, write the word in the target language on one side and the English equivalent on the other.

Lists: Using the vocabulary lists in your textbook, or those supplied by your teacher, cover the target language column. Begin at the top of the list, working your way down. At each English word, write and say its equivalent in the target language. Each time you miss a word, go to the top of the list and repeat the procedure.

Categorize: If the vocabulary lists aren't already in categories (such as nouns, adjectives, verbs – or – places, foods, etc.), you may want to group your new words into categories to help you learn them.

Colour: On your flashcards, use one colour for all masculine nouns and another colour for all the feminine nouns.

Sentences: Create sentences with the new words you want to remember.

Label: Label objects in your house or apartment.

Repeat: Repeat the new vocabulary words aloud.

Write: Write the new vocabulary words over and over.

Record: Record on tape the new words and their definitions.

Use context: Let the context help you. Use the phrase or sentence to help figure out the meaning of a new word or expression.

5. *Work with new verbs:* Learning and working with new verbs is an important part of learning a foreign language. You might want to try the following ideas:

    Use colour: On your flash cards (or any other method you choose) use certain colours for certain verb infinitive endings. The use of colour can also be incorporated into conjugating the verbs by using specific colours for specific subject-related endings.

6. *Keep up with the material.* Don't let things go by without looking at the book or supplementary materials, such as the workbook.

7. *Remember that you cannot cram the night before for a foreign language exam!*

8. *Get used to spending some time every day with your foreign language textbook.* Try to devote extra time on the weekends to studying. Since language learning is a gradual, continual process, you need to approach the material with steady, consistent study habits.

9. *If you have cable TV, watch some shows in the target lan-*

guage. Don't worry about understanding everything that is said. Practise your listening skills concentrating on the rhythm and sounds of the language.

10. ***Rent foreign films from the video store.*** If possible, watch the films with other students.

11. Since language learning is a building process, ***review past materials*** while you're learning new materials.

12. ***Don't think that you have to be perfect.*** Set some short goals that are challenging but not unreasonable.

How to benefit from in-class time:

1. ***Never feel embarrassed or afraid to ask questions.*** If your teacher makes you feel uncomfortable, he or she has a problem – not you.

2. ***Come to class prepared.*** Read over the materials to be covered before coming to class.

3. ***Listen attentively and pay special attention to points which the teacher refers to as "important or significant."***

4. ***Sometimes, referring to your native language can be helpful, but at other times it isn't.***

   You'll often be faced with structures, vocabulary, sentence structure, etc., in the language that seem odd, even ridiculous. Keep an open mind and remember that you're dealing with a new language and its contents – not your native language.

5. ***Don't feel awkward, silly or embarrassed about trying to pronounce the new language as your teacher does or as you hear it on tape.***

6. ***When working in pairs or groups, speak in the target language, avoid going off task or reverting to English and chatting.***

   Take advantage of the time in class (with your classmates and teacher present) to work with the language.

7. ***Listen for mistakes of your classmates.***

   Paying attention to their mistakes may help you avoid making them yourself.

8. ***Paraphrase.***

   If you don't know the target language equivalent for a certain word, use other words to describe it or to get your point across. For example, if you couldn't remember the word for "party", you could say "a celebration with food and music."

This is called circumlocution.

What many foreign language instructors expect from their students.

1. *Since teachers have different expectations, pay attention to what is in the class syllabus.*

   There are a variety of things which instructors may deem important: attendance, participation, no late homework or compositions, no make-up quizzes or tests, etc. Focus on what it is that your instructor expects from you and give it back to your instructor.

2. *Attend all classes, and be on time.*

   All instructors would love to have every student attend every class session. If for any reason you cannot attend class, notify your instructor before the class period.

3. *Come to class as well-prepared as possible.*

   This doesn't necessarily mean that you have the new material down completely, but that you have made an attempt to learn the material before coming to class.

4. *Since language is communication, try to get used to participating actively in class.*

   This involves answering questions when called on, volunteering answers, and asking questions when you don't understand something.

5. *Do the workbook activities and the lab book activities.*

   This involves taking time to go to the library and listening to (or borrowing copies of) the audio or video cassettes.

6. *Cooperate and be flexible with your instructor, and be supportive of your fellow classmates.*

7. *Keep the lines of communication open between you and your instructor.*

   For example, if you're having problems keeping up due to your heavy work schedule or you were "less than perfect" in class because you were up all night writing a paper, let your instructor know. Don't let your instructor draw false conclusions about you.*

*The article was originally published in *The Forum of Phi Sigma Iota*, 8, 1 (Spring 1996), p. 11-12. It is reprinted in *Mosaic* with permission of the Editor, Pennie A. Nichols-Alem.

Reprinted from: Paul Cankar, "Study Skill Suggestions for Students of Foreign Language Classes." *Mosaic*, 4, 3 (Spring 1997): 18-19.

10 Language Anxiety and How to Manage It: What Educators Need to Know

Philip Donley

Anxiety is a formidable obstacle that many students face when trying to learn a new language. The author provide basic information about language anxiety and how to manage it.

Anxiety and its Effects on Learning and Performance

Lesse (1970) defines anxiety as a

phenomenon experienced as a foreboding dread or threat to the human organism whether the threat is generated by internal real or imagined dangers, the sources of which may be conscious or unconscious, or whether the threat is secondary to actual environmental threats(p. 13).

Researchers (e.g., Spielberger, 1975) further define the anxiety construct by distinguishing between trait anxiety and state anxiety. Simply put, trait anxiety refers to a person's inborn tendency to have anxious feelings or not; state anxiety is considered to be transitory, caused by exposure to stressful experiences.

A number of researchers have examined the effects of anxiety in academic situations. Learners have been found to be anxious about test-taking (Sarason, 1980) and when studying specific disciplines, such as math (Tobias, 1978) and science (Mallow, 1981). Tobias (1986) suggests that anxiety interferes with learning by impeding the intake and processing of information and the retrieval of learned information. Test anxiety researchers Alpert and Haber (1960), however, assert that anxiety may in fact enhance performance (facilitating anxiety) or interfere with it (debilitating anxiety). It seems probable that a moderate level of emotional arousal (which does not necessarily equate with anxiety) is helpful in academic situations, whereas extremely low or high levels of arousal are not conducive to learning or performance.

What is Language Anxiety?

Early studies (e.g., Chastain, 1975; Swain and Burnaby, 1977) conceive of language anxiety as a simple transfer of other types of anxiety, such as trait anxiety and test anxiety, to language learning. More recently, scholars have generally agreed that language anxiety is a special and distinct phenomenon caused by the unique stresses imposed on students in language classes. Researchers do not entirely agree, however, about the role that the various types of anxiety play in the language anxiety construct. In their landmark article, Horwitz, Horwitz and Cope (1986) argue that language anxiety is related, but not limited, to communication apprehension, test anxiety, and fear of negative evaluation by fellow students and the instructor. Aida (1994) agrees with Horwitz and colleagues that communication apprehension and fear of negative evaluation are important components of language anxiety, but suggests that test anxiety is an unrelated construct. MacIntyre (1999), however, concludes that language anxiety is not strongly related to other types of anxiety; language anxiety develops when students have a series of uncomfortable experiences during the language learning process (i.e., multiple instances of state anxiety) and begin "to associate anxiety arousal with the second language" (p. 31).

What causes language Anxiety?

In order to understand and manage language anxiety, it is helpful to know what causes it. Researchers have identified the following as possible causes of language anxiety.

Speaking and Being Called On

Many students feel anxious when speaking the target language or being called on in language class. Horwitz, Horwitz, and Cope (1986) assert that communication apprehension may cause anxiety in some students; they may feel uneasy speaking publicly in their own language, much less in a language in which they do not feel confident. Horwitz and colleagues note that some students fear that others will think less of them if they make mistakes while speaking, and they may feel frustrated about their inability to communicate their ideas and their personalities in the target language. Students may worry about their non-native accents (Price, 1991) and fear being "put on the spot" to answer questions in a foreign language (Young, 1990). In addition, anxieties about speaking the second language in class may be related to teachers' harsh error correction styles (Horwitz, Horwitz, and Cope, 1986; Young, 1990; Young, 1991; Price, 1991).

Listening

Learners may feel nervous if they do not understand what they hear in the second language (Vogely, 1998; Campbell, 1999). They may feel anxious when the language is spoken to them too quickly (Vogely, 1998) or at great length (Donley, 1997). Vogely notes that students may have a similar reaction if the language they hear contains unknown vocabulary or difficult sentence structure, or deals with an unfamiliar topic. Anxious listeners may approach the listening task in unrealistic ways, believing they have to decipher the input word for word (Vogely, 1998). Students who have listening comprehension difficulties may also feel isolated because they cannot understand what their classmates understand, and they may fear that they will miss the instructions they need to complete assigned tasks (Donley, 1997).

Test-taking

Horwitz, Horwitz, and Cope (1986) note that nervousness about tests is a part of many students' experience of learning a new language. Students may feel anxious

- if diligent study before a test doesn't produce the desired results,
- if they are not familiar with an examination's format, or
- if they are tested in a way that does not reflect how classroom time is utilized (Young, 1991).

Reading

Reading in the second language may be linked to language anxiety. Lee (1999) posits a spiraling process in which anxiety siphons cognitive resources away from the reading task, causing reduced comprehension, which in turn causes even higher levels of anxiety.

Lee notes that educators and students commonly approach academic reading tasks in ways that may be counterproductive. He points out that students are typically asked to read a passage individually or at home, then answer a list of comprehension questions. This may cause anxiety by limiting the students' familiarity with the text (they may know only enough to answer the comprehension questions), and students may feel isolated as they struggle through a reading without the help of their classmates or instructor. Students may feel frustrated if they try to read in a word-for-word, linear way, and they may engage in all-or-nothing thinking, castigating themselves when they do not understand every aspect of the text.

Writing

Some learners may feel anxious when required to write in the target language. Teachers may force students into a defensive position by treating writing assignments as a test of grammar knowledge rather than as a communicative venture in which students meld language and ideas (Leki, 1999). Leki also suggests that students may find writing to be a daunting task because they lack strategies and procedures for the process of writing.

Learning grammar

Grammar learning may also be related to language anxiety. VanPatten and Glass (1999) note that learners may feel overwhelmed by the amount of grammar they are expected to master. Students may feel uneasy, VanPatten and Glass believe, if their evaluation is heavily based on their ability to use grammar correctly, or if classroom activities focus on communication, but tests elicit only grammar knowledge. VanPatten and Glass also state that students may feel nervous if they expect grammar to be a substantial part of learning a language but are enrolled in a course that downplays its importance.

Learning style issues

Anxiety may result if students' learning styles are not congruent with their instructors' ways of teaching. Oxford (1999) mentions several teacher-student style clashes that may produce anxiety. For example, students may be anxious if they dislike ambiguity but their instructor prefers a loosely structured class atmosphere. It is also possible that introverted students will feel threatened by an extroverted teacher and that students who are not detail-oriented will feel pressured by a teacher who is a stickler for detail. In addition, students may feel anxious if they have strong sensory preferences (e.g., learning by seeing or doing, rather than by simply listening) that are not taken into account by their instructors.

Competitiveness

Competitiveness is a personality factor that may contribute to language anxiety. Competitive students may be overly concerned about the performance of others, comparing their own achievements in a very self-deprecating way with those of their classmates (Bailey, 1983; Young, 1991).

Unrealistic beliefs

Learners may feel anxious because they have unrealistic beliefs about the language learning process. For example, students may believe they should avoid speaking until they can speak perfectly and that they shouldn't guess the meaning of words they don't know (Horwitz, Horwitz, and Cope, 1986), or that they simply lack the aptitude that they need to learn a new language (Price, 1991).

Native language problems

Sparks and Ganschow (1991) believe that students who have difficulties with the systems of their native language will have similar problems when trying to learn a second language. They assert that

> low motivation, poor attitude, or high levels of anxiety are . . . a manifestation of deficiencies in the efficient control of one's native language (p. 10).

What does Anxiety do?

Language anxiety can have an impact on students in the psychological and physical realms, and it can affect their academic performance as well.

Horwitz, Horwitz, and Cope (1986) note that anxious language students may display a variety of physical and psychological symptoms, including impaired concentration, nervousness, increased perspiration, and palpitations. Students may also "freeze" when asked to speak in language class and inexplicably forget information when taking tests or during oral practice.

A number of researchers have investigated the relationship between anxiety and performance in language classes. Although some scholars (Dunkel, 1947; Chastain, 1975; Kleinmann, 1977) have suggested that anxiety may not always be harmful, it has been linked to diminished performance on oral interview examinations (Young, 1986; Phillips, 1992), oral examinations (Scott, 1986), and reading tasks (Oh, 1990).

Researchers have also linked anxiety to lower course grades (Horwitz, 1986; Aida, 1994; Saito and Samimy, 1996) and to performance decrements on a variety of measures of achievement (Gardner, Smythe, and Brunet, 1977; Sánchez-Herrero and Sánchez, 1992).

Moreover, students' attempts to avoid anxiety-provoking situations (e.g., skipping class, not completing assignments, avoiding opportunities to speak in class) may deprive them of opportunities to learn (Horwitz, Horwitz, and Cope, 1986). In fact, Horwitz and colleagues believe that some anxious students may avoid language classes altogether by choosing degree plans that don't require foreign language study.

Identifying Students Who Have Language Anxiety

Teachers and schools have an obvious stake in identifying students who suffer from language anxiety in order to provide them with appropriate assistance and support.

Educators should be aware of the verbal and non-verbal ways that students communicate their feelings. Sometimes students speak to their teachers privately about their anxieties; such conversations may be initiated by either party. Students may also leave messages about their feelings on work that they turn in to the teacher. Instructors should be attentive to outward signals of anxiety (e.g., blushing, trembling, stammering, "freezing") and should also watch for anxiety-related avoidance behaviors (e.g., skipping class, avoiding eye contact with the instructor, sitting on the back row).

Those who prefer more formal means of gauging their students' language anxieties may want to use scales developed specifically for this purpose. Probably the two best known scales for measuring situation-specific language anxiety are the Foreign Language Classroom Anxiety Scale (Horwitz, 1983b) and the French Class Anxiety Scale (Gardner, 1985). The Foreign Language Classroom Anxiety Scale (FLCAS) is a 33-item instrument that asks students to rate their degree of agreement with statements related to language anxiety. The validity and reliability of the FLCAS have been established (Horwitz, 1986). The French Class Anxiety Scale is a 5-item questionnaire in which students indicate their degree of agreement with statements about speaking French in the classroom (Gardner, 1985).

Managing Language Anxiety

Because of the many negative consequences of language anxiety, Horwitz and colleagues (1986) conclude that

> if we are to improve foreign language teaching at all levels of education, we must recognize, cope with, and eventually overcome, debilitating foreign language anxiety as a factor shaping students' experiences in foreign language learning (p. 132).

Here are some of the suggestions that researchers have made about managing language anxiety.

Skill-building

Several researchers believe that students' anxieties will decrease as their knowledge of the language and strategic sophistication increase.

Foss and Reitzel (1988) suggest that students may feel less anxious if they are allowed to speak the second language in a structured context. Specifically, Foss and Reitzel advocate oral interpretation based on rehearsed material, believing that students will build confidence as they master the linguistic and cultural nuances of the material. Similarly, Lucas (1984) recommends the teaching of dialogues, language patterns, and gambits, reasoning that students will be able to use them to manage communicative situations more effectively.

Skill-building is also addressed in Beauvois' (1999) suggestions about implementing real-time computer chat on local area networks. Students gain valuable practice in communication during target language computer chats; at the same time, anxiety is reduced because students have time to process incoming language and plan their responses. Also, as Beauvois notes, learners who participate in computer chats develop a reassuring sense of community.

For students who have native language coding deficits, skill-building may be particularly important. Since such students may have problems with phonology, Ganschow, Sparks and colleagues (1994) advocate

> multisensory structured language approaches focusing on direct teaching of the sounds and symbols of the foreign language (p. 52).

Workshops and outreach programs designed to increase students' strategic sophistication and improve their study skills may help alleviate language anxiety. An anxiety workshop given at the Defense Language Institute (Campbell and Ortiz, 1991), for instance, provided instruction about language learning strategies (e.g., circumlocution, paraphrasing, guessing the meaning of words from the context), and workshop participants were asked to discuss their own successful strategies for language learning. Educators may also want to investigate the various university outreach programs described by Cope Powell (1991). These programs, designed to teach time management, build language skills, and reinforce good study habits, include support groups, adjunct classes, and a written course supplement containing learning tips and information about language anxiety.

Self-regulation of anxiety

Several scholars have advocated teaching students to control their own reactions to anxiety-provoking events. McCoy (1979) and Foss and Reitzel (1988), for example, suggest that the principles of rational-emotive therapy be used to manage anxiety. Foss and Reitzel recommend that students identify the thoughts or beliefs that make them feel anxious, analyze the logic of these cognitions, and substitute thoughts that are more logical and productive. McCoy (1979) and Schlesiger (1995) note the benefits of systematic desensitization; students can be taught to imagine stressful events and then associate them with relaxing thoughts or images of handling the stressful event successfully. Teachers may also wish to encourage students to manage their own anxieties by distributing Donley's (1996) list of 10 ways to cope with anxiety (e.g., discussing their feelings, getting enough food and rest, being prepared for every class, and keeping the language class in proper perspective). Other suggestions for self-regulation of anxiety, including progressive relaxation, deep breathing, meditation, self encouragement, and being aware of how one's body registers physical and emotional discomfort, are detailed in Oxford (1990).

Raising students' awareness about language learning
Since students may have inaccurate, anxiety-provoking beliefs about language learning, Phillips (1991) advises teachers to help students form realistic expectations about language learning. This can be accomplished by informing students that second language acquisition is a gradual process in which errors are to be expected, that language acquisition follows predictable patterns, and that what they learn about the language may not be immediately transferable to spoken and written communication (VanPatten and Glass, 1999).

Educators may also wish, as Phillips (1999) suggests, to administer Horwitz' (1983a) Beliefs about Language Learning Inventory and use students' responses as a springboard for discussion. Phillips (1999) notes as well that students' responses to Horwitz' (1983b) FLCAS can be used to make students aware that they are not alone in their anxieties and to generate discussion about their feelings.

Changing classroom procedures
A number of recommendations have been made about changing classroom procedures in order to reduce students' anxieties about speaking, listening, reading, writing, test-taking, and learning grammar. Some advice has also been offered about minimizing anxiety caused by learning style conflicts between teachers and students.

Speaking
Making mistakes in front of others is some students' greatest fear. For this reason, teachers' treatment of oral errors is important. Phillips (1999) recommends that teachers remind students that errors are a natural part of language learning. Phillips also encourages teachers to employ gentle error correction techniques, noting that modeling correct forms may be more effective than overt error correction, which draws unpleasant attention directly to the student who produces an incorrect form.

Some students feel anxious when they are called on in language class. To reduce this type of anxiety, Daly (1991) suggests calling on students in a predictable order or allowing students to volunteer to answer questions.

Students may also feel less anxious when participating in enjoyable, non-threatening classroom activities. With this in mind, Young (1990) recommends classroom discussion of engaging themes; she also suggests employing group activities because they don't single individual students out. Phillips (1999) advocates and gives examples of several kinds of affectively oriented oral activities:

- recognition activities that require students to understand but not produce targeted forms,
- cued response activities that give students possible answers while still permitting original responses,
- task-focused (not form-focused) information gap activities in which each person has part of the information necessary to complete the task,
- interviews and surveys that ask students about things they are familiar with, and
- role play activities which inject an element of humor into the class.

Listening

Vogely (1999) lists several ways to reduce listening comprehension anxiety. She recommends that teachers make students aware of regional pronunciation variations so that they will understand individual speakers better. Vogely also advocates making listening input more comprehensible by offering advance organizers and activating students' prior knowledge. Since listening tasks that require students to listen for more than one thing may provoke anxiety, Vogely suggests using concise and structured tasks in which students listen for very specific information (see examples in Vogely, 1999). Vogely also notes that students may find listening comprehension less stressful if they are aware of specific listening strategies (e.g., guessing through context, listening for specific information, listening for the main idea, recognizing cognates) and if teachers make use of visuals (e.g., photos, videos, posters, expressive body language) during listening tasks.

Reading

Several ways that teachers can minimize students' anxieties about reading are proposed in Lee (1999). Lee counsels against relying solely on comprehension questions to gauge students' understanding of a text; he suggests that teachers use a variety of activities that allow students to interact with the text. Lee recommends that students not be isolated during reading tasks: they should be allowed to work cooperatively with other students and with the teacher. Students should, Lee believes, be reminded that comprehension is never absolute and that reading is not a linear, word-for-word activity. Lee also notes that students may benefit from employing strategies like skimming, scanning, recognizing cognates, identifying the structural features of a text, and examining illustrations and photographs for clues about meaning.

Writing
Leki (1999) discusses a number of ways to address anxiety about writing in language class. So that students will have clear expectations, Leki advises teachers to let students know to what extent their grades are based on correctness of form rather than on content. Leki suggests that students will feel more comfortable if they learn more about how to write: students can become more skillful writers by participating in a full range of process writing activities, including brainstorming, freewriting, outlining, drafting, and peer editing. Leki also notes that students' confidence may grow if they are assigned sequenced writing projects in which each step of the project builds their knowledge of a particular topic and the language needed to write about the topic.

Test-taking
Educators can take several common-sense steps to help students manage their anxieties about tests. Teachers may, for example, wish to inform students about the format of each test and the number of points allotted to each section of the test; students are less likely to feel anxious if they know how they are going to be tested and what to study. To defuse anxieties about testing formats, teachers can distribute short sample tests. Moreover, teachers should ensure that examinations test what students are being taught and that they correspond to the types of activities students do in class. In other words, there should be no surprises: "test the way you have taught."

Learning grammar
The use of processing instruction involving structured input has been suggested by VanPatten and Glass (1999) as a way to deal with students' anxieties about heavy grammar loads as well as a lack of explicit focus on grammar. VanPatten and Glass believe the structured input should focus on a single form and function at a time, require the student to focus on both meaning and form, and progress from the sentence level to the paragraph level.

VanPatten and Glass recommend the use of both oral and written input

- in any combination across activities or within the same activity if it contains various steps/stages (p. 99),
- and they stress that the learner should process the input in a meaningful fashion. Also, VanPatten and Glass recommend that teachers ensure that students attend

to the grammatical feature rather than to some other part of the utterance when cues are in competition (p. 100).

Learning style conflicts

As Oxford (1999) notes, there is no "magic bullet" that will eliminate anxiety about learning style conflicts. Oxford simply recommends using a variety of activities that will appeal to students' sensory modalities (e.g., visual, auditory) and learning styles (e.g., analytic vs. global, intuitive-random vs. concrete-sequential).

Conclusion

There is little doubt that anxiety plays a role in many students' language learning experiences and that its role is multifaceted and complex. However, as teachers become familiar with the language anxiety literature, they will feel empowered to help anxious students understand and address their fears. As a result, language learning may become a more enjoyable process, and ultimately a more successful one.

Bibliography

Aida, Y. 1994. "Examination of Horwitz, Horwitz, and Cope's construct of foreign language anxiety: The case of students of Japanese." *Modern Language Journal,* 78: 155-168.

Alpert, R., and R. N. Haber. 1960. "Anxiety in academic achievement situations." *Journal of Abnormal and Social Psychology,* 61: 207-215.

Bailey, K. M. 1983. "Competitiveness and anxiety in adult second language learning: Looking at and through the diary studies." In H. W. Seliger and M. H. Long, eds., *Classroom oriented research in second language acquisition.* pp. 67-102. Rowley, MA: Newbury House.

Beauvois, M. 1999. "Computer-mediated communication: Reducing anxiety and building community." In D. J. Young, ed., *Affect in Foreign Language and Second Language Learning: A Practical Guide to Creating a Low-Anxiety Classroom Atmosphere.* pp. 144-165. Boston: McGraw Hill.

Campbell, C. M. 1999. "Language anxiety in men and women: Dealing with gender difference in the language classroom." In D. J. Young ed., *Affect in Foreign Language and Second Language Learning: A Practical Guide to Creating a Low-Anxiety Classroom Atmosphere.* pp. 191-215. Boston: McGraw Hill.

Campbell, C. M., and J. Ortiz. 1991. "Helping students overcome foreign language anxiety: A foreign language anxiety workshop." In E. K. Horwitz and
D. J. Young, eds., *Language anxiety: From theory and research to classroom implications.* pp. 153-168. Englewood Cliffs, NJ: Prentice Hall.

Chastain, K. 1975. "Affective and ability factors in second language learning."
Language Learning, 25: 153-161.

Cope Powell, J. A. 1991. "Foreign language classroom anxiety: Institutional
responses." In E. K. Horwitz and D. J. Young, eds., *Language anxiety: From
theory and research to classroom implications.* pp. 169-176. Englewood
Cliffs, NJ: Prentice Hall.

Daly, J. 1991. "Understanding communication apprehension: An introduction
for language educators." In E. K. Horwitz and D. J. Young, eds., *Language
anxiety: From theory and research to classroom implications.* pp. 3-13.
Englewood Cliffs, NJ: Prentice Hall.

Donley, P. M. 1996. "Ten ways to cope with foreign language anxiety." *The
Forum of Phi Sigma Iota,* 8, 13. Reprinted in *Mosaic* 4, 3:17, 1997 and in
Teaching and Learning Languages. pp. 115-116. Anthony Mollica, ed.,
Welland, ON: éditions Soleil publishing inc., 1998.

Donley, P. M. 1997. The foreign language anxieties and anxiety management
strategies of students taking Spanish at a community college. Doctoral dissertation: University of Texas at Austin.

Dunkel, H. B. 1947. "The effect of personality on language achievement." *Journal of Educational Psychology,* 38: 177-182.

Foss, K. A., and A. C. Reitzel. 1988. "A relational model for managing second
language anxiety." *TESOL Quarterly,* 22: 437-454.

Ganschow, L., R. L Sparks, R. Anderson, J. Javorsky, S. Skinner and J. Patton.
1994. "Differences in language performance among high-, average-, and
low-anxious college foreign language learners." *Modern Language Journal,* 78: 41-55.

Gardner, R. C. 1985. *Social psychology and second language learning: The
role of attitudes and motivation.* London: Edward Arnold.

Gardner, R. C., P. C. Smythe and G. R. Brunet. 1977. "Intensive second language study: Effects on attitudes, motivation, and French achievement."
Language Learning, 27, pp.243-261.

Horwitz, E. K. 1983a. Beliefs about language learning inventory. Unpublished
instrument. Austin: University of Texas.

Horwitz, E. K. 1983b. Foreign language classroom anxiety scale. Unpublished
instrument. Austin: University of Texas.

Horwitz, E. K. 1986. "Preliminary evidence for the reliability and validity of a
foreign language anxiety scale." *TESOL Quarterly,* 20, 559-562.

Horwitz, E. K., M. B. Horwitz and J. Cope. 1986. "Foreign language classroom
anxiety." *Modern Language Journal,* 70: 125-132.

Horwitz, E. K. and D. J. Young, eds. 1991. *Language anxiety: From theory and
research to classroom implications.* Englewood Cliffs, NJ: Prentice Hall.

Kleinmann, H. H. 1977. "Avoidance behavior in adult second language acquisition." *Language learning,* 27, 93-107.

Lee, J. F. 1999. "Clashes in L2 reading: Research versus practice and readers' misconceptions." In D. J. Young, ed., *Affect in Foreign Language and Second Language Learning: A Practical Guide to Creating a Low-Anxiety Classroom Atmosphere.* pp. 49-63 Boston: McGraw Hill.

Leki, I. 1999. "Techniques for reducing second language writing anxiety." In D. J. Young, ed., *Affect in Foreign Language and Second Language Learning: A Practical Guide to Creating a Low-Anxiety Classroom Atmosphere.* pp. 64-88. Boston: McGraw Hill.

Lesse, S. 1970. *Anxiety: Its components, development, and treatment.* New York: Grune and Stratton.

Lucas, J. 1984. "Communication in the ESL classroom: Getting our students to talk." *Foreign Language Annals,* 17: 593-598.

MacIntyre, P. D. 1999. "Language anxiety: A review of the research for language teachers." In D. J. Young, ed., *Affect in Foreign Language and Second Language Learning: A Practical Guide to Creating a Low-Anxiety Classroom Atmosphere.* pp. 24-45. Boston: McGraw Hill.

Mallow, J.V. 1981. *Science anxiety: The fear of science and how to overcome it.* New York: Thomond Press.

McCoy, I. R. 1979. "Means to overcome the anxieties of second language learners." *Foreign Language Annals,* 12: 185-189.

Oh, J. 1990. On the relationship between anxiety and reading in English as a foreign language among Korean university students in Korea. Doctoral dissertation: University of Texas at Austin.

Oxford. R. L. 1990. *Language learning strategies: What every teacher should know.* Boston: Heinle and Heinle.

Oxford, R. L. 1999. "Style wars" as a source of anxiety in language classrooms." D.J. Young, ed., *Affect in Foreign Language and Second Language Learning: A Practical Guide to Creating a Low-Anxiety Classroom Atmosphere.* pp. 216-237. Boston: McGraw Hill.

Phillips, E. M. 1991. "Anxiety and oral competence: Classroom dilemma." *French Review,* 65: 1-13.

Phillips, E. M. 1992. "The effects of language anxiety on students' oral test performance and attitudes." *Modern Language Journal,* 76: 4-26.

Phillips, E. M. 1999. "Decreasing language anxiety: Practical techniques for oral activities." D. J. Young, ed., *Affect in Foreign Language and Second Language Learning: A Practical Guide to Creating a Low-Anxiety Classroom Atmosphere.* pp. 124-143. Boston: McGraw Hill.

Price, M. L. 1991. "The subjective experience of foreign language anxiety: Interviews with highly anxious students." In E. K. Horwitz and D. J. Young, eds., *Language anxiety: From theory and research to classroom implications.* pp. 101-108. Englewood Cliffs, NJ: Prentice Hall.

Saito, Y. and K. K. Samimy 1996. "Foreign language anxiety and language performance: A study of learner anxiety in beginning, intermediate, and advanced-level college students of Japanese." *Foreign Language Annals,* 29: 239-251.

Sánchez-Herrero, S. A. and M. Sánchez. 1992. "The predictive validation of an instrument designed to measure student anxiety in learning a foreign language." *Educational and Psychological Measurement,* 52, 961-966.

Sarason, I. G. 1980. *Test anxiety: Theory, research and applications.* Hillsdale, NJ: Lawrence Erlbaum.

Schlesiger, H. 1995. The effectiveness of anxiety reduction techniques in the foreign language classroom. Doctoral dissertation: University of Texas at Austin.

Scott, M. L. 1986. "Student affective reactions to oral language tests." *Language Testing,* 3: 99-118.

Sparks, R. L., and L. Ganschow. 1991. "Foreign language learning differences: Affective or native language aptitude differences?" *Modern Language Journal,* 75: 3-16.

Spielberger, C. D. (1975). "Anxiety: State-trait process." C. D. Spielberger and I. G. Sarason, eds., Stress and Anxiety, vol. 5. pp. 115-143. Washington, DC: Hemisphere.

Swain, M., and B. Burnaby (1976). "Personality characteristics and second language learning in young children: A pilot study." Working Papers on Bilingualism, 11: 115-128.

Tobias, S. (1978). Overcoming math anxiety. New York: W.W. Norton and Co., Inc.

Tobias, S. (1986). "Anxiety and cognitive processing of instruction." R. Schwarzer, ed., *Self-related cognitions in anxiety and motivation.* pp. 35-54. Hillsdale, NJ: Lawrence Erlbaum.

VanPatten, B., and W. R. Glass. 1999. "Grammar learning as a source of language anxiety: A discussion." In D. J. Young, ed., *Affect in Foreign Language and Second Language Learning: A Practical Guide to Creating a Low-Anxiety Classroom Atmosphere.* pp. 89-105. Boston: McGraw Hill.

Vogely, A. 1998. "Listening comprehension anxiety: Students' reported sources and solutions." *Foreign Language Annals,* 31: 67-80.

Vogely, A. 1999. "Addressing listening comprehension anxiety." In D. J. Young, ed., *Affect in Foreign Language and Second Language Learning: A Practical Guide to Creating a Low-Anxiety Classroom Atmosphere.* pp. 106-123. Boston: McGraw Hill.

Young, D. J. 1986. "The relationship between anxiety and foreign language oral proficiency ratings." *Foreign Language Annals,* 19: 439-445.

Young, D. J. 1990. "An investigation of students' perspectives on anxiety and speaking." *Foreign Language Annals,* 23: 539-553.

Young, D. J. 1991. "Creating a low-anxiety classroom environment: What does the anxiety research suggest?" *Modern Language Journal,* 75: 426-439.

Young, D. J., ed. 1999. *Affect in Foreign Language and Second Language Learning: A Practical Guide to Creating a Low-Anxiety Classroom Atmosphere.* Boston: McGraw Hill.

Reprinted from: Philip Donley, "Language Anxiety and How to Manage It: What Educators Need to Know." *Mosaic,* 6, 3 (Spring 1999): 3-9.

11 Ten Ways to Cope with Foreign Language Anxiety

Philip Donley

Although most of our readers do not suffer FLA (Foreign Language Anxiety), as tutors and teachers, many of us know people who do. Pass these helpful hints on to FLA afflicted students!

- Do you frequently feel nervous or apprehensive in your foreign language class?
- Do you often freeze when your instructor calls on you?
- Do you inexplicably go blank when taking a test in the foreign language?
- Do you dread your foreign language class so much that you are tempted to skip class or drop the course?

If you answered "yes" to one or more of these questions, you may suffer from foreign language anxiety.

If foreign language anxiety is a serious problem for you, you may want to use a few strategies to help you manage your anxious feelings. Ten coping strategies are listed below. Some of the strategies may be more effective for you than others, and you may find that certain combinations of strategies are especially useful for you. The right strategies to use are, of course, the ones that feel right and work best for *you*.

Coping strategies

1. *Discuss your feelings with other students.*

   You may feel more comfortable in your language class if you find out that other students empathize with your feelings.

2. *Tell your instructor how you feel.*

   Your instructor may be able to give you a different perspective on your learning experience. Also, your instructor may be much more understanding than you expect; remember, your instructor has probably been a language student too.

3. *Do something fun and relaxing.*

   Go for a walk, go to a movie, listen to your favourite music, participate in a sport. The possibilities are endless. Sometimes all you need do to alleviate your anxiety is to take your mind off your class for a few minutes or hours.

4. *Eat healthful food and get enough rest and exercise.*

   If you haven't been taking care of your body, you may be especially susceptible to anxiety.

5. *Make sure you're prepared for class.*

   You will probably feel less nervous while taking a test or when your instructor calls on you if you feel well-prepared. You may want to prepare an organized study and practice schedule for yourself.

6. *Attend every class.*

   Learning a language is less stressful if you learn a little bit every day. If you skip class, you will miss important information and valuable practice. When you return to class and have to catch up with your classmates, you may feel anxious and overwhelmed.

7. *Keep your foreign language class in perspective.*

   If you're doing poorly in one facet of the class, take some time to think of other parts of the class in which you *are* doing well. Also, remember that your life consists of more than your foreign language class. Remind yourself of those areas of your life in which you do feel relaxed and confident.

8. *Seek out opportunities to practise the foreign language.*

   The more confidence you gain in using the language, the less apprehensive you will be about using it in class. You may want to build your skills by conversing with native speakers, practising with more advanced students, or writing a pen pal.

9. *Remember that errors are a part of language learning.*

   Errors are a natural part of language learning. Even educated native speakers make errors occasionally, so don't expect yourself to be perfect. Don't be afraid to take a few risks in order to learn.

10. *Develop your own standards and rewards for success.*

    While grades are important, what you learn is more important. Set reasonable learning goals for yourself, and reward yourself for small successes along the way.*

*The article was first published in *The Forum of Phi Sigma Iota*, 8 (Spring 1996), p. 13. It is reprinted in this issue of *Mosaic* with permission of the Editor, Pennie A. Nichols-Alem.

Reprinted from: Philip Donley, "Ten Ways to cope with Language Anxiety." *Mosaic*, 3 (Spring 1997): 17.

12 Climate Setting in Second-Language Classrooms

Cher Evans-Harvey

A positive classroom climate enhances language acquisition, but how do teachers create an atmosphere conducive to learning? This paper suggests ways of establishing a positive classroom climate.

Introduction

In recent years there has been a lot of discussion about effective schools. Three studies refer directly to the climate or culture within the school as having an impact on learning. Mark Holmes, Kenneth Leithwood and Donald Musella (1989) outlined the following characteristics of effective schools:

- strong leadership aimed at academic achievement,
- an academic climate of high expectations,
- regular monitoring of student achievement,
- a safe, orderly and pleasant environment.

J. Howard Johnston (1984) and his colleagues also found that:

> Effective schools emerge from a complex set of cultural and social factors that focus attention on academic performance, support academic growth in a manner consistent with the developmental stage of the youngster, and build an intellectual community that rewards and reinforces academic pursuits in its public rituals and in its private interactions. It is the creation of the culture […] that will enhance student learning and produce long-term school improvements. (p. vii)

Johnston and Ramos de Perez (1985) also identified positive (not remedial) school environments as one of fourteen characteristics of effective schools. Although more information is available on school climate, very little has been written on classroom climate and on how to establish a positive, relaxed and happy climate that is conducive to learning. Language teachers are very aware that a positive classroom climate enhances language acquisition. Authors such as H. D. Brown (1987), Adelaide Heyde (1979), Marjorie MacKinnon (1988) and Moos and Tricket (1987) make reference to positive classroom climate enhancing second-language acquisition.

The purpose of this paper is:
- to clarify the meaning of classroom climate,
- to relate four aspects of school climate to the climate in language classrooms, and
- to suggest ways of establishing a positive climate in the language classroom.

Definition

Lawrence Lezotte *et al.* (1979) define climate as the norms, beliefs and attitudes reflected in institutional patterns and behavioral practices that enhance or impede student achievement. Borich (1988), in his commonly used text in teacher education programs, defines classroom climate as

> the atmosphere or mood in which interactions   between teacher and students take place. Classroom climate, for example, will determine the manner and degree to which a teacher will exercise authority, show warmth and support and allow for independent judgement and choice. (p. 277)

Malcolm Knowles (1984), a leading theorist of adult education contends that

> There are seven elements or procedures which the teachers of adults have to consider. The first, and the prerequisite one, deals with establishing a climate that is conducive to learning. This means providing experiences in an atmosphere in the classroom, workshop or institute in which the learners feel respected and in which they feel secure, supported, non-threatened, collaborative rather than competitive, trusting of one another and trusting of the teacher, liked, cared about, cared for, comfortable, informal, relaxed. These conditions are more conducive to learning than their opposites: cold, aloof, rigid, one-way transmission, judgemental, competitive. Creating such a climate conducive to learning is a step not usually considered in traditional education. The students walk into the room and the transmission of content starts. No time is given to creating feelings of respect and trust. (p. 92)

Four Dimensions of Classroom Climate

J. Howard Johnston and Maria Ramos de Perez (1983), in their paper "Four climates of Effective Middle Level Schools" outlined four climates common to effective schools:
- the physical climate,
- the academic climate,
- the organization climate, and
- the social-emotional climate.

Discussion of the four climates with direct reference to language classrooms offers language teachers ideas for improving the climate in their classrooms.

Physical Climate

Although language teachers teach in a variety of settings that range from their own classrooms to makeshift facilities, they should work towards providing learning areas that are well-lit and bright. The area should be well-maintained, safe and clean. Furniture should be appropriate to the age of the children. The air temperature and ventilation should be considered. It should be visually appealing with pictures and posters of the target language as well as student work displayed in an attractive manner. Given good facilities and evidence that learning the language is valued, the classroom environment is enhanced.

Academic Climate

There are five features to consider in improving the academic climate.

1. *People talk about academics.*

   Language teachers should ask students questions about their academic performance and show their interest in student success. They should talk about strategies for learning languages and organizing materials. They should ask students to help them solve problems.

2. *Academic achievements are recognized and rewarded.*
   Language teachers should display student work in the classroom and in the halls. Achievement should be rewarded liberally. Smiles, encouraging words, stickers, happy-grams, certificates, medals, and graduation gifts for top students should be given for learning languages.

3. *Academics form the basis for leisure pursuits.*
   Language clubs provide students with the opportunity to socialize in the target language and explore the culture in cooperative projects. Inter-provincial and international exchanges and visits provide similar opportunities.

4. *Expectations are high but reasonable, and failure is tolerated.*

   Language teachers should be aware of the abilities and feelings of the students. They should ask students to demonstrate new skills without an audience, or practice with their peers in a small group setting.

5. *Teachers use time wisely.*
   Language teachers should provide for maximum engaged learning time by organizing activities that are intrinsically interesting, require active cognitive engagement and are at a level that will benefit the student.

Organizational Climate

Four characteristics of organizational climate within effective schools can be related directly to the language classroom.

In these schools there are few rules, but those that exist are clear reasonable and fair. In the classroom, rules such as respect yourself and others, cooperate, do your best and treat other people the way you would like to be treated indicate values that promote learning.

The Student Council plays a dual role of influencing school policy and securing opportunities for student participation in the events of the day. The language teacher should promote the activities and events organized for the language program, making sure that class representatives and the Student Council are aware of what is planned so they, in turn, can promote them in the school. Activities such as field trips, concerts by singers, musicians, actors or storytellers, special assemblies or invited guests will have a more positive impact if the students themselves are involved in the planning and promotion of these activities.

Another important feature of effective schools is the belief students hold that the school is responsive to their concerns and feelings. This is manifest in the language classroom. The teacher should talk to the students and be responsive to their concerns about learning the language, the type and difficulty of assignments and evaluation.

Finally, with respect to organizational climate in effective schools, Johnson and Ramos de Perez (1983) found that teachers make major decisions about curriculum, students, special events and finances. Language teachers should make decisions that promote the language program. Examples could be integrated units, decisions about which students would be placed in split grades, what special events could be planned for the year, how the language budget would be spent and whether fundraising activities would be appropriate.

Social-Emotional Climate

Johnston and Ramos de Perez (1983) found that the social-emotional climate has a profound effect on the life of the school, the academic quality of its programs and the effectiveness of the teachers and students. These characteristics will be discussed with direct application for a language classroom.

The classroom should be encouraging, welcoming, supporting and positive. Teachers should try to find the good in each student even though their strengths may not lie in language learning. Valuing student achievement in language learning as well as in other subject areas, in sports, dance, music or drama, helps students increase their self-esteem. Adelaide Heyde (1979), suggests that teachers really can have a positive and influential effect on both the linguistic performance and the emotional well-being of the student.

The classroom should be a secure place where students feel safe from physical, psychological and emotional harm. A classroom should have a high level of comfort where students feel free to take risks, make mistakes and learn with each other without fear of put-downs or being laughed at by their peers or criticized by the teacher.

Language teachers should anticipate student needs and fill them without fanfare. Attention should be given to grouping students, to adjusting curriculum for gifted and for disabled learners, to making each person feel like a valued and important member of the class. Attention to student needs is proactive as many disruptive situations can be prevented.

Classrooms should be trusting places. Students are trusted to make important decisions about their learning in terms of choices, behaviour and evaluation of their progress. Language teachers could build in choices of activities, assignments and presentations. They could include a self-evaluation component into the course as well as contracts for learning and comportment.

Finally, classrooms should be civil places. Teachers should emphasize excellence, reward achievement and offer students intellectual tasks that are appropriate for their development in a comfortable learning environment. The students would be relaxed, happy and friendly.

Johnston and Ramos de Perez (1983) conclude that climate affects the quality of schooling to a great degree and that the creation of a school culture is mostly dependent on the behaviour of the adults in the school. It follows, then, that the climate in the language classroom affects the quality of the language learning and that the creation of a positive climate is dependent on the behaviour of the language teacher.

What can language teachers do to create and promote positive climates in the classroom?

A key factor is to know the students well: their characteristics, interests, needs, aspirations, learning styles and expectations. Before the course starts, teachers should inform themselves of the characteristics of the students by reading *Observing Children* (Metropolitan Toronto Board of Education, 1980) or *Observing Adolescents* (Metropolitan Toronto Board of Education, 1984) or by checking ministry documents that have sections relating language learning to the developmental stage of the student.

- To discover student interests, teachers could distribute an interest questionnaire, or organize activities such as asking the students directly or having them create lists of interests.
- Learning about student needs deals with physical, intellectual and social needs. Teachers should find out if students have physical handicaps, learning disabilities or social disadvantages.
- Knowing the aspirations of the students provides the teacher with the means to motivate. Asking students, providing communicative activities dealing with aspirations, creating lists or drawing are strategies that help teachers discover what aspirations the students have.
- Knowing the way students learn is also of vital importance for the teacher to provide appropriate resources for the visual, auditory or kinaesthetic learners. Distributing a single learning styles questionnaire helps the students and the teacher become more aware of how they like to learn. The Canfield Learning Styles Inventory (1976) may be appropriate for older students.
- Finally, near the beginning of the course the teacher should ask each person, through private conversation or though written comments what they expect to learn from the course in order to adjust strategies and resources.

This is the background information a language teacher needs to know to maximize the learning. The next step is to implement activities that are positive and create trust such as:

1. Getting to know student names by memorization, name tags or seating plans.
2. Sharing personal information about yourself, your background, interests and aspirations. An easy way to do this is through activities such as *Getting To Know Me, A Personal Coat of Arms* or a *Class Book*.

   To organize *Getting To Know Me*, the teacher brings in a bag or box of personal items to share with the class such as a photograph of his or her family, a favourite novel, a stuffed animal representing the family pet, their favourite word (e.g. respect) or something humorous. The students are then invited to bring in items to share with others to introduce themselves. They can present individually in front of the class or within a small group.

   To organize *A Personal Coat of Arms*, the teacher presents his or her family, shares personal interests, aspirations and preferred ways of learning. This is presented on a large sheet of graph paper cut in the shape of a coat of arms. Drawings, photographs or pictures from magazines can be used. The students are invited to prepare their own copy to present themselves to their classmates. If displayed in the classroom, they are visually attractive and provide information for communicative activities that help the students learn about each other. For example, "Who enjoys downhill skiing?" "Who wants to become a professional hockey player?" "How does Susan enjoy learning?"

To organize a *Class Book*, the teacher introduces himself or herself by reading a few short paragraphs about his or her family, personal interests, dreams or goals etc. Students are then invited to interview a partner, write a short paragraph, peer edit, produce the final copy and introduce their partner to the other students. The teacher then takes a picture of each student, glues it on the bottom of the page, laminates all the pages and assembles them in book form. This is more appropriate for students who are able to write in the target language. If any of these three activities are used at the beginning of the course, the teacher gets to know the students quickly, the students learn about each other and the teacher in a relaxed and friendly way.

3. Simple activities such as "Autographs", "Name Bingo" or "Introduce the person next to you" are also effective.

4. Distributing and discussing the course outline in detail -the objectives, the content, the process and the evaluation procedures.

5. Organizing simple communicative activities that stress the positive such as: discussing with a partner the best thing that has happened today, or the funniest thing that happened last week.

6. Working on building the individuals' self-esteem by having them identify their strengths, things they're good at, and nice things people have said about them.

7. Developing their appreciation of others by thinking and saying nice things about each other and by having them learn to give compliments to others when good things happen in the classroom.

8. Building team spirit by having them choose a name for their class or group to develop commitment and have a *sense of ownership and belonging*.

Many of these activities take only a few minutes of class time

but help to establish a positive and effective climate in the classroom.

References

Borich, G. 1988. *Effective Teaching Methods*. Toronto: Merrill Publishing.

Brown, H. Douglas. 1987. *Principles of Language Learning and Teaching*. Englewood Cliffs, NJ: Prentice Hall Regents.

Canfield, A. and Canfield, S. 1976. *Canfield Learning Styles Inventory*. La Crescenta, CA: Humanics Media.

Heyde, A. 1979. *The relationship between self-esteem and the oral production of a second language*. Unpublished doctoral dissertation, University of Michigan.

Holmes, Mark, Kenneth Leithwood and Donald Musella, eds. 1989. *Educational Policy for Effective Schools*. Toronto: Ontario Institute for Studies in Education Press.

Johnston, J. Howard Glenn C. Markle and Maria Ramos de Perez. 1984. "Effective Schools." In J . H. Johnston and G.C. Markle, 1986, *What Research Says to the Middle Level Practitioner*. Columbus, Ohio: National Middle School Association. p. 9.

Johnston, J. Howard and Maria Ramos de Perez. 1985. "Four Climates of Effective Middle Schools". In *Schools in the Middle: A Report on Trends and Practices*. (January),p. 1. As quoted by Oppenheimer, 1990.

Johnston, J. Howard and Maria de Perez. 1983. "Four Climates of Effective Middle Level Schools." A Paper presented at the Middle School Invitational IV, Chicago. Mimeo.

Knowles, M. 1984. *The Adult Learner: A Neglected Species*. Houston, Texas: Gulf Publishing Co.

Lezotte, L., Douglas Hatheway, Stephen Miller, Joseph Pasalacqua and Wilber Brookover, 1979. *School Learning Climate and Student Achievement*. Centre for Urban Affairs, College of Urban Development and Institute for Research on Teaching. East Lansing, Michigan: Michigan State University.

MacKinnon, M. 1988. "Creating Environment for Learning." *University of New Brunswick Training Bulletin*, 1, 2. Fredericton: University of New Brunswick.

Metropolitan Toronto School Board. *Observing Children*. 1980. Toronto: Metropolitan Toronto School Board.

Metropolitan Toronto School Board. 1984. *Observing Adolescents*. Toronto: Metropolitan Toronto School Board.

Moos, R. H. and E. Trickett. 1987. *Classroom Environment Scale Manual*. Second Edition. Palo Alto: Consulting Psychologists Press, Inc.

Oppenheimer, Jo. 1990. *Getting It Right: Meeting the Needs of the Adolescent Learner*. Toronto: Federation of Women Teachers' Associations of Ontario.

Reprinted from: Cher Evans-Harvey, "Climate Setting In Second-Language Classrooms." *Mosaic*, 1, 2 (Winter 1993): 1, 3-5.

13 Planning for Instruction

Kenneth Chastain

Adapting textbooks and preparing lesson plans require innumerable decisions. How do teachers select the explanations, the exercises and the activities and put them in the order that will be the most effective? Upon what bases do teachers make these choices?

Introduction

Planning for instruction includes a large number of considerations such as student characteristics, teacher characteristics, course goals, etc. However, I will limit my focus in this discussion to three that have direct bearing on each lesson:

1. pre-planning analysis,
2. textbook adaptation, and
3. lesson planning,

and I will treat them in reverse order, proceeding from the most to the least familiar based on the amount of time allocated to each in methods classes, conferences, and journal articles.

Lesson Planning

All of us are aware of lesson plans. We know what they are and why they are important. Although an amazing number of formats exist, they consist basically of goals and sequenced activities to help students achieve those goals.* They are important because they help teachers bring structure and direction to the teaching-learning process. With a properly prepared plan, each part of the class becomes a beneficial activity fitting perfectly into the instructional mosaic preparing the students for each subsequent activity and enabling them to perform it successfully. That is, lesson planning helps teachers make the teaching-learning process efficient and effective.

Textbook Adaptation

Textbook adaptation is a less common topic in second-language learning but certainly one that deserves greater attention. Current materials contain explanations that are clearer and more concise, exercises that are more focused and easier to complete, and larger numbers of more interesting communication activities than previous textbooks. However, no set of materials is perfect for all teachers and all students in all situations. A basic text written for a large number of students is a general purpose tool that teachers must adapt to their own particular situation. Classroom teachers are the ones who are aware of their own preferences and who are familiar with their students' knowledge, interest, and capabilities, and they have the responsibility to make justifiable changes in the   text in order to use it most effectively with their students. They may, and often should, delete from the text, add to the text, or alter explanations, exercises, and activities in the text. As a general rule, they should not require the students to cover all the material in the given order.

Adapting textbooks and preparing lesson plans require innumerable decisions. Planning for instruction is not easy. Plans that are appropriate to the students and that are well organized require considerable forethought, time, and energy. How do teachers select the explanations, the exercises and the activities and put them in the order that will be the most effective? Upon what bases do teachers make these choices?

Pre-planning

If they ask themselves these two fundamental questions, teachers will realize that adapting texts and preparing lesson plans are not the first steps in planning for instruction. The basis for both involves two prerequisite analyses:

1.   learning analysis and
2.   teaching analysis.

Teachers can best prepare themselves to make rational choices regarding the text and the lesson plans if they first have a clear conception of the learning task facing the students. Therefore, the first step is to consider the answers to three student-related questions.

1. What do the students already know in their native language?

What students already know is the single most influential factor in how they learn most effectively and in what they are able to learn. Therefore, what they know about their native language can be an asset in learning the second if teachers base their instruction on students' linguistic knowledge rather than on their knowledge of traditional grammar. (Implied in this cognitive principle is that students by definition know their native language and how it functions in communicative contexts even thought they may not be able to analyze it using traditional grammatical terminology.) Teachers can offer their students clearer explanations of grammatical concepts if they base their presentations on students' native-language knowledge.

2. What have the students already learned in the second language?

Everything that they have learned up to the point at which the present material occurs may provide support for the material to be learned. A brief analysis of what the students have previously learned enables teachers to relate the new material to the old, thus reducing the learning load and increasing the likelihood of comprehension and retention.

3. What else, other than the related concepts that the students already know in their native language and in the second, do they need to know in order to understand the new material?

The important concept inherent in this question is that rarely do students need to learn all the material in each chapter or lesson as if it were completely new. Either from their first or second language they already have much knowledge that can be of assistance in completing successfully the learning tasks of the current chapter. One of the teacher's responsibilities is to relate new material to old knowledge, thus reducing the learning load to its absolute minimum.

Teaching Analysis

The first step in teaching analysis is to evaluate the authors' presentation of new material. Normally, each teacher has the insights to incorporate some helpful alterations, and he/she should always proceed on the assumption that he/she can improve the presentation in the text.

The answers to the following questions serve as a guide to appropriate deletions, helpful additions, and/or needed changes.

- What alterations are advisable in the authors' presentation of the new material?
- What is correct, comprehensible, and helpful? What is not?
- What changes might improve the presentation?
- What deletions are advisable?
- What additions would be helpful?

The second step is to assess the strengths and the weaknesses of the drills and exercises in the text. They may be either too difficult or too easy. They may be uninteresting or unrelated to the topic. They may have no useful pedagogical value, or they may be organized in an inappropriate sequence, i.e., they may be arranged in a random fashion rather than in a hierarchy of increasing difficulty leading from knowledge to communication.

The answers to these questions help teachers decide which

exercises to use, which to replace, and which to alter.

*   What changes are desirable in the authors' practice drills, exercises, and communication activities? Which will stimulate learners and help them improve their ability to communicate in the language? Which will not?
*   What improvements should be made?
*   Do the exercises and activities progress from easier to more difficult, from less to more communicative?
*   Is completion of all the exercises necessary?
*   Are there too many exercises? Too few?

The third step is to study the communication activities to determine their interest and their value for the students in the teacher's classes. Can the students do them? Will completing the activity successfully help the   students develop their communication skills?

As part of the teaching analysis, teachers evaluate all communication activities, prepared to make needed changes.

Many texts do not provide a sufficient number of communication activities. How many should be added?

Conclusion

Obviously, the answers to these questions serve as guides for adapting the text and for preparing the lesson plans. The resultant adapted course materials will be more attuned to the learning needs of the students if teachers first complete a learning and teaching analysis of the chapter content, while the resultant lesson plans will be better coordinated with the text and more specifically geared toward the students in the class.

My impression is that when teachers consider planning for instruction, they think of lesson plans, which is certainly appropriate. However, my experience has been that planning for instruction is more efficient and more effective if it emerges logically and naturally from a careful and complete analysis of the learning and teaching tasks and if it also includes adapting the erials to the teachers' beliefs and the students' needs.*

* Interested readers will find additional information on the preparation and organization of lesson plans in:

Chastain, Kenneth. 1988 *Developing Second-Language Skills: Theory and Practice* Third Edition. San Diego: Harcourt Brace Jovanovich, Chapter 12. and Mollica, Anthony. 1994 "The Lesson Outline," Chapter14 in this volume.

Reprinted from: Kenneth Chastain, "Planning for Instruction." *Mosaic*, 2, 1(Fall 1994): 16-17.

14   The Lesson Outline

Anthony Mollica

Effective teaching requires planning and organization. Lesson outlines play a very important role in the planning for successful teaching/learning.

The Oxford dictionary defines a lesson as

> a continuous portion of teaching given to a pupil or class at one time; one of the portions into which a course of instruction is divided.

At the elementary and secondary school level, the lesson is based on the school board's curriculum guidelines which, in turn, are based on the provincial or state curriculum in that field. While the following outline focuses on language teaching, there are elements which are also of interest for lectures and seminars.

Successful teaching requires planning and organization. Rare are the teachers who can walk into the classroom with little or no planning. While some experienced teachers may not require lengthy, detailed lesson plans, there is a need even for these teachers to keep materials and methods current and relevant to the needs and the expectations of the students. Teachers must be versatile enough to be able to change plans and outlines (and, in some cases, even activities,) for no two classes are the same, and special attention must be paid to the students' learning styles and interests. As Henson (1993:58) points out,

> Often a class will become very interested and enthusiastic about a particular part of the lesson. When this happens, you should be willing to deviate from your plan and let the class explore their interests. On the other hand, when the planned lesson seems boring to a particular class, change your approach drastically.

For young teachers, lesson outlines play a very important role. Classroom routines and discipline problems often tend to disrupt the learning environment and teachers should be well prepared if they do not wish to be affected by such distractions. Henson (1993) stresses the importance of lesson planning by pointing out that

> A teacher who attempts to teach without a lesson plan is like a pilot taking off for an unknown destination without a map. Like the map, the lesson plan provides direction toward the lesson objectives. If

the lesson begins to stray, the plan brings it back to course. This may be difficult without a plan. (p. 39).

Callahan and Clark (1988:103) identify many uses for the well-written lesson plan:

1. It gives one an agenda or an outline to follow as one teaches the lesson.
2. It gives substitute teachers a basis for presenting real lessons to the class they teach.
3. It is very useful when one is planning to teach the same lesson in the future.
4. It provides one with something to fall back on in case of a memory lapse, an interruption, a distraction such as a call from the office or a fire drill.
5. Above all, it provides beginners security for, with a carefully prepared plan, a beginning teacher can walk into the classroom with the confidence gained from having developed, in an organized form, a sensible framework for that day's instruction.

Borich (1992:140) cautions teachers that before a lesson plan can be prepared, they must decide on:

- instructional goals
- learning needs
- contents, and
- methods.

Lesson outlines vary with each individual teacher. Arguing which type of lesson plan is best would be a waste of time and space. Nothing is sacred about any of them. The lesson plan is simply a tool which is as effective as the person using it.

The following is a *proposed* outline. Different teachers may use other headings, but ultimately the end result should be the same: to impart and to acquire knowledge. Along with the outline itself, the teacher should also keep in mind questions and questioning techniques as well as classroom expressions which help the student to participate in the learning process.[1]

What are the divisions of a lesson plan? What should the teacher's lesson plan look like? It is very useful to identify at the beginning of each lesson outline:

1. *the date*
   (This will be useful to compare, the following year, whether the teacher is "ahead" or "behind" in the course of study.)
2. *the grade*
3. *the title of the textbook used*
4. *the number of students in the class*

(It is obvious that the same teaching methods cannot be used with a class of thirty and a small class of ten students, or a class of mixed ability).

The above information should be followed by the following suggested divisions:

1. Theme or Topic
2. Aims or Objectives
3. Warm-up period
4. Materials needed by
   a) teacher
   b) students
5. Presentation
6. Application
7. Summary
8. Assignment
9. Evaluation
10. Teacher's References
11. Motivation.

1. Theme or Topic

Unlike the aims or objectives, which are specific, the theme or topic is general. It is something that may take several lessons to complete. For example, a topic might be "The Present Tense." In order to deal completely with this topic, several lessons may be required. Teachers may need to familiarize the students with various conjugations of regular and irregular verbs, with positive, negative and interrogative forms, as well as combinations of the latter: positive-interrogative and negative-interrogative. In other words, the topic/theme is general and will involve many individual lessons.

2. Aims or Objectives

The aims or objectives, on the other hand, are more specific. This section will focus on what the teacher will teach within a timeframe on a given day to a specified class. For example, the aim might be: "To teach the present tense of the first conjugation verbs in the positive form." However, teachers often write this aim in terms of *behavioural objectives*. If this is the case, all statements of performance objectives must meet at least three criteria (Henson, 1993:66):

- Objectives must be stated in terms of expected student behaviour (not teacher behaviour).
- Objectives must specify the conditions under which the students are expected to perform.

- Objectives must specify the minimum acceptable level of performance.

Stating objectives in terms of expected student behaviour is important because all teaching is directed toward the students. The success of the lesson will depend on what happens to the student. In writing performance objectives, Henson suggests that teachers avoid using verbs that cannot be observed or measured, such as *learn, know and understand*. Instead the plan should contain specific, action-oriented verbs such as *identify, list, explain, name, describe,* and *compare*. (Henson, 1993:68).

What is to be learned should be made apparent to the students in the title of the lesson. It should be clear to the teachers also when they develop their aim for the lesson.

3. Warm-up period

Before beginning the day's lesson, teachers should involve the students in some "warm-up" activity. This warm-up period may consist of:

- *general questions*
  These questions may focus on current events, school activities, news broadcasts, etc. Please avoid asking of every class the day's date and/or inquiring about the weather, unless these questions are used communicatively! (Mollica, 1985.)
- *personal questions*
  These questions may be directed to individual students to show interest on the part of the teacher for an activity in which the student might have been involved:
  "Did you see the hockey game last night?"
  "Who won?"
  etc.?
- *review questions*
  These questions are directed at reviewing the lesson of the day before. They may serve as a basis for introduction to the item(s) about to be presented or may be necessary as a prerequisite to the new lesson.
- *a combination of the above.*

4. Materials

a. needed by the teacher

Teachers should list the material(s) needed in order to teach a particular lesson. What print, non-print materials, audio and visual equipment are required to teach the lesson effectively? Does the teacher require

- a textbook, notebook,

- illustrations, flashcards,
- coloured chalk,
- an overhead projector (make sure there is a spare bulb!),
- a slide projector,
- an extension cord,
- etc.?

b. needed by the students

What do the students need in order to perform well in class? Have they been told to bring the right textbook and workbook? Do they have extra sheets of paper? Do they have their notebooks? Do they have pencils, ball-point pens to write with? (Keep a few spare ones aside; students have frequent memory lapses...)

5. Presentation

This is the part of the lesson in which the "item" to be learned is presented. The presentation should proceed step-by-step from the simple to the complex. In providing examples in the target language, teachers should use vocabulary which is already known to the student. Every effort should be made to avoid distractions so that students will be able to focus on what is being taught and on what the teacher wants the students to learn. Language should be kept simple and examples meaningful. The language of the teacher should enable the student to follow the teacher and be able to comprehend the presentation of the lesson, and finally to absorb the material with a feeling of understanding and accomplishment. Students should never be left "up-in-the-air" over a lesson.

Teachers should make every effort to *involve* students in the presentation. Where possible, the lesson should be developed by both teachers and students. Teachers may wish to jot down a number of key questions to be asked during the presentation which will help to develop the item to be learned.

Four-by-six index cards are very helpful in providing the teacher with additional examples or vocabulary lists which are useful to keep the lesson moving at an engaging pace.

6. Application

Once the teacher has presented the item to be learned, it is important that students be given an opportunity to *apply* what has been taught/presented. This activity should be done while both the teacher and students are together. While the students are practising (this is often an exercise found in their textbook or workbook), teachers should circulate about the classroom and see that the application is taking place,. They may stop here and there, complimenting a student for his/her good work or assisting students who may have not completely grasped the notion of the item to be learned. Application is doing something about the item taught while the group and teacher are still together.

7. Summary
The summary should terminate the formal instruction and should immediately follow the presentation or follow the application. In the latter case, the summary will serve as a reinforcement of what has been presented. The teacher, by means of the summary, brings together and emphasizes the main points made during the lesson presentation. The summary is meant to crystallize the learning and to highlight the presentation.

8. Assignment
The assignment phase of the lesson may be considered as a continuation of the application. Assignments provide a meaningful extended application of the item just learned. The assignment is an aid to retention. It differs from application, as it may consist of preparation for the next lesson. It may be done at home or in class. Whenever possible, an assignment should be started in class and continued at home. This process will allow the student an opportunity to ask the teacher any questions about the assignment while both teacher and student are present in class. The time spent with a student can never be regained or recaptured. It is time well spent.

9. Evaluation
Teachers should be familiar with the principles and techniques of evaluation in order to discover whether what has been presented/taught has been learned or not. Formative evaluation through observation, check-lists, student self-evaluation, peer evaluation, and comments by the teacher on oral and written work provide concrete information on the day to day learning. For formal evaluation, teachers should perhaps adopt the well-known Holiday Inn slogan "No surprises!" In other words, the method of evaluation should reflect the method of teaching. Simply put, "Test the way you've taught!"

10. Teacher's references
Teachers should identify in their lesson plan other textbooks which have similar explanations or exercises as the lesson just presented. These sources are invaluable for providing additional exercises on the same topic and may show the teacher how the same lesson has been presented by another textbook writer.

11. Motivation

As Paolo E. Balboni (1994: 75) stated, "There is no [language] acquisition without motivation." Motivation plays a crucial role in the lesson presentation. In fact, motivation should play a role not only in the presentation, but also should be pervasive throughout the class period. Teachers cannot say to students, "This activity will motivate you for the next five minutes..." (The implication being that teachers will bore the students for the rest of the class...) Motivation means to stimulate something or someone. Motivation is one of the prime tasks of teaching. Motivation should be constant and should not stop at any given point. Motivation is important at the beginning of the lesson as a means of introducing the material, stimulating interest, arousing curiosity and developing the specific aim; but it is equally important for teachers to provide motivational activities which will arouse and retain the interest of the students.

Conclusion

Lesson outlines may vary from teacher to teacher but essentially many of the components will be the same even though the headings and the language may change. There is no question in my mind that the lesson plan is an excellent guide which will assist both beginning and seasoned teachers to effective and successful teaching.

References

Balboni, Paolo E. 1994. *Didattica dell'italiano a stranieri*. 3ª ed. Roma: Bonacci editore.

Borich, Gary D. 1992. *Effective Teaching Methods*. Second edition.New York: Macmillan.

Callahan, Joseph E. and Leonard H. Clark. 1988. *Teaching in the Middle and Secondary Schools. Planning for Competence*. Third edition. New York: Macmillan.

Henson, Kenneth T. 1993. *Methods and Strategies for the Teaching in Secondary and Middle Schools*. Second edition. New York: Longman.

Mollica, Anthony. 1985. "Communication in the Second-Language Classroom." In Anthony Papalia, ed., *A Communicative Syllabus. Teaching for Proficiency. A Practical Guide*. Schenectady, NY: New York State Association of Foreign Language Teachers.

Reprinted from: Anthony Mollica, "Planning for Successful Teaching: The Lesson Outline." *Mosaic*, 1, 3 (Spring 1994): 13-15.

15 Classroom Expressions

Anthony Mollica

Every effort should be made to conduct the language class using the target language extensively. The following list is by no means exhaustive but permits students to communicate effectively and carry out classroom routines.

In preparing this list of classroom expressions, we have opted to place into groups a number of expressions. Certainly, they do not necessarily fall always in that category. They are so categorized for easier access. The list is by no means exhaustive. It is, nevertheless, a good start.

Greetings
- Good morning.
- Good afternoon.
- Good-bye.
- Hello.
- Until tomorrow.

Formulas of Courtesy
- Please.
- Thank you.
- You're welcome.
- Excuse me.
- I beg your pardon.

Warm-up Period
- What is your name?
- My name is...
- Where is (name of student) to-day?
- Present. / Absent.
- He/She is ill.
- Come in!
- Close the door.
- Open the window.
- Turn off the lights.
- Turn the lights on.
- Erase the blackboard.

Inquiry questions
- What is this?
- How do we say (word) in (target language)?
- How do you spell (word)?
- Use the five "W"s:
  Who...?
  What...?
  Where...?
  When...?
  Why...?

Classroom Management
- Are you ready?
- Quiet! / Silence!
- Distribute these sheets.
- Collect the test.
- That's enough!
- Pay attention.
- No talking.
- Listen.
- Stop talking to (name of student).

- One at a time, please.
- Faster. / More quickly.
- Stand up.
- Sit down.
- Read quietly.
- Read aloud.
- Louder.
- Come up in front of the class.
- Go back to your seat.
- Line up here.

Praise

- Excellent!
- Very good!
- Bravo!
- Good!
- Well done!
- Correct!
- Perfect!
- Great!
- Terrific!
- Congratulations!

Audio-Visual Equipment

- Blackboard / Chalkboard
- Overhead projector
- Slide projector
- LCD projector
- Extension cord
- Cassette taperecorder
- Videocassette recorder
- Tape
- Plug in the overhead projector, please.

Presentation

- Repeat after me.
- All the boys.
- All the girls.
- All together.
- Everybody.
- For example…
- Close your notebooks.
- Close your books.
- Is this clear?

- Do you understand?
- Look at the blackboard.
- Look at the screen.
- Answer the question.
- Look at the bottom of page…
- Look at the top of page…
- Look at the middle of page…
- Once more.

Application

- Copy down the examples in your notebooks.
- Open your notebooks.
- Open your books.
- Open your books on page…
- Turn to page…
- Open your workbooks on page…
- Write. / Do not write.
- Continue…
- Repeat once more.
- It's (name of student's) turn.
- Go to the blackboard.
- Write the answer on the blackboard.
- Go back to your seat.
- Choose a partner.
- Play the role of…
- Look it up in the dictionary.
- For homework, do Exercise…

Students' favourites…

- May I sharpen my pencil?
- I don't have a pencil (pen).
- I forgot…
- I don't remember.
- I don't know.
- I don't understand.
- I left the book in my locker.
- I can't hear.
- May I get a drink of water?
- May I go to the bathroom?

Teachers may wish to illustrate some of these expressions and place the illustrations and the text on the bulletin board as a constant reminder and as an aid to learning . It follows that each illustration would be identified accordingly and the writing in the target language would reinforce the visual.

Editor's Note: The illustrations are taken from: Anthony Mollica, *À l'école.*Welland, ON: éditions Soleil publishing inc. 2006. Illustrations by George Shane.

Reprinted from: Anthony Mollica, "Planning for Successful Teaching: Classroom Expressions." *Mosaic*, 2, 1 (Fall 1994): 18.

16   Questioning Strategies

Anthony Mollica

Questioning is an art. Questions can stimulate conversation and discussion. Precise questions will normally elicit precise answers.

As a university student, I worked during the summer months as a Customs officer at the Fort Erie/Buffalo border. I was in the Customs yard one day when a car pulled up. It had a note on the windshield. It read: "Check under front seat." I took the paper and asked the driver:

"Where do you live?"

"Welland," he replied.

"How long have you been away?"

"A couple of hours."

I checked under the seat. There was nothing there. However, on the front seat there were two bottles of liquor, some bedsheets, some pillow covers.

"Do you have anything to declare?" I asked.

"Yes," he replied. "Two bottles of liquor, some bedsheets and some pillow covers."

"Why did you not declare these items to the officer on the line?" I inquired.

"Because he asked me if I had anything special. And this is not special."

I couldn't help smiling. The man was right. My colleague had asked an incorrect question. What the officer should have said was: "Do you have any thing to declare?" (or the equivalent in French, "Avez-vous quelque chose à déclarer?")

At which point the "smuggler" could have (would have?) identified the items. But the officer, obviously bored from asking the same question, tried to change it and thus obtained unacceptable results.

Questions such as: "Did you buy anything today?" are not appropriate. The traveller could easily reply negatively and then be discovered to have his car trunk filled with TV sets. His explanation to the Customs officer could be very simple. "You asked if

I *bought* anything. Well, I didn't *buy* these items. My uncle owns a TV store and he *gave* them to me free of charge."

I remember a similar scene from the movie *All the President's Men*. A senior *Washington Post* reporter asked the two investigative reporters, Woodward and Bernstein, why Hugh Sloan had not told the Grand Jury that Haldeman had been involved in the secret slush fund used to re-elect President Nixon. "He was never asked," was the reply.

Questions may be used to solve problems. I recall my practice-teaching days at the Faculty of Education at the University of Toronto. There was a young man in the Latin class by the name of Alvin who was determined to try the patience of even the most courteous student teacher! What seemed to be on the surface the most innocent of questions, turned out to be the most intricate and difficult queries with which he tried to stump enthusiastic future teachers. I was determined to put Alvin in his place, but to do so gently without declaring open warfare.

I had just finished teaching the ablative absolute. I had explained the function of the past participle which, together with the noun in the ablative case, provided a variety of possible translations:

> *Gallis victis, pacem fecit.*
> After defeating the Gauls, he made peace.
> The Gauls being defeated,…
> Having defeated the Gauls,…
> After he had defeated the Gauls,…
> Since he had defeated the Gauls,…
> etc…

Alvin, eager to stump me, asked:

"Can an adverb modify a past participle?"

The eyes of all my colleagues turned on me. I could have simply answered with a "yes/no". I decided instead to use Alvin's question as a springboard for problem solving.

"What is a participle, Alvin?"

Alvin was determined and eager to show off his newly acquired knowledge.

"A participle is part adjective and part verb."

I praised his answer.

"Very good, Alvin," I said. "Can an adverb modify an adjective?"

"Yes," replied Alvin, knowledgeably.

"Can an adverb modify a verb?"

"Of course," said Alvin, annoyed.

"Does that answer your question?" I asked.

Alvin didn't know what had hit him.

"Why... uh... Yes! Thank you, sir," he blurted out.

I had turned Alvin's question to my advantage and he had learned something.

Then there is the classic story of the teacher who, having spent some time trying to obtain class control, noticed that "Johnny" was still continuing to disrupt the class. Being short of patience and wanting to start the lesson, the teacher sarcastically asked:

"Would you like to take over the class, Johnny?"

At this point, Johnny stood up, went to the front of the class and solemnly announced:

"Class dismissed!"

Additional anecdotes and examples abound. The reader has only to watch any TV courtroom drama (*Perry Mason, Matlock, Street Legal, Family Law, Law and Order*) to see immediately the importance of asking questions which produce the response the lawyer requires. Precise questions will normally elicit precise answers. Teachers should frame their questions in such a manner as to ensure the answer they want, at least within the context of what they are teaching.

Why Ask Questions?

In the classroom, teachers should ask questions:

- to obtain information
- to spark and/or encourage discussion
- to stimulate and encourage participation
- to check facts and to reinforce recently learned material
- to probe more deeply after an answer is given
- to help recall specific information
- to arouse interest
- to gain a student's attention
- to diagnose specific learning difficulties
- to encourage reflection and self-evaluation
- to help determine individual differences
- to focus attention on an issue
- to determine what the students know
- to test learning
- to solve problems

- to teach via students' answers.

During the presentation of the lesson, the teacher may want to ask questions:

- to review content already learned
- for review or for drill
- to bring out or re-affirm the aim of the lesson
- to reinforce recently learned material.

What Types of Questions?

Teachers should ask questions which:

- are brief and clear
- are specific
- are consistent with students' abilities
- call upon the students' past experience
- help develop concepts and thoughts
- are relevant to the lesson
- are suitable for diagnostic purposes
- call for judgement.

Method

Teachers should ask questions:

- in a varied rather than a predictable order
- of several students rather than several questions directed to the same student
- in a courteous manner and expect the same courtesy in return
- in a familiar way rather than always formally
- as a teacher, not as a judge in a courtroom
- during class, but enter marks later
- in a sincere manner
- within the scope of students' acquired linguistic skills and using good target language
- according to the students' needs
- according to the ability of the group.

To Whom Should Questions be Asked?

Teachers should ask questions:

- of the slower as well as the rapid learner
- of the inattentive student

Suggestions and Techniques

Teachers should keep the following suggestions in mind:

- Ask the question. Pause a little. Only then identify the student who will answer the question.

- Allow a reasonable interval of time before the student answers.
- From time to time, ask questions which may require group response.
- Recognize volunteers.
- Praise a good response.
- Praise a good effort even if the answer needs a bit of polishing or correcting.
- Encourage students to ask as well as answer questions in the target language.

Key Words in Questions

Practically all questions, whether intended to recall factual information or stimulate discussion, consist of or include one of the following key words:

- Who...?
- What...?
- Where...?
- When...?
- Why...?
- How...?

Questions To Be Avoided

Teachers should avoid asking questions which:

- can be answered with a simple "yes" or "no"
- are vague
- are double-barrelled; i.e. two questions in one
- suggest the answer
- do not have a worthwhile purpose
- can be answered by guessing.

    Following are some examples of questions to be avoided:

1. Can you answer question No. 7?
    (*Yes, of course I can, but I don't feel like it...*).
    Better:
    Question Number 7. Johnny.
    (An elliptical question in the form of a command.)

2. Has anyone finished the exercise?
    (*No, of course no one has finished it!*).
    Better:
    Who has finished the exercise?

3. Who killed Julius Caesar and why?
    (*One question at a time. First I have to figure out who killed him, let alone try to imagine the reason...*).
    Better:

Who killed Julius Caesar?
(Teacher first obtains response and then proceeds with:) Why?

4. It was Brutus who stabbed Caesar, was it not?
    (I guess so, if you say so. You're the teacher; I'm not going to dis-agree with you...).
    Better:
    Who stabbed Caesar?

5. Who wants to erase the blackboard?
    (Thirty students rush to the front of the classroom...).
    Better:
    Please erase the blackboard, Mary.

Convergent vs. Divergent Questioning

Questions can be either narrow or broad. A narrow question is often referred to as a memory question, direct question, closed question or convergent question.

A *convergent* question limits the answer, for all the learner has to do is to recall certain facts either read or heard. This type of question generally requires a short answer and little reflection or thought on the part of the respondent. It is based on memory rather than on knowledge and understanding and may even encourage guessing.

The *divergent* question – a broad or open question – encourages an open response. It has no single correct or best answer, but can have wrong answers. Like the convergent question which involves memory, the divergent likewise entails memory, but also requires that the student explain, think about the topic and produce a logical, correct answer. Guessing, therefore, is held to a minimum. Divergent questions challenge the student's efforts and command greater attention and reflection for they stimulate further activity calling for judgment, analysis, organization, comparison, understanding and logical thinking. It follows that the teacher can expect more diverse responses from the divergent question than the convergent one.

Question Classification Scheme

Borich (1992) identifies the types of student behaviours associated with each level in the cognitive-domain taxonomy suggested by Bloom *et al.* (1956):

- Knowledge
- Comprehension
- Application
- Analysis
- Synthesis

Level of Behavioral Complexity	Expected Student Behavior	Instructional Processes	Key Words
Knowledge (remembering)	Student is able to remember or recall information and recognize facts, terminology and rules.	repetition memorization	define describe identify
Comprehension (understanding)	Student is able to change the form of a communication by translating and rephrasing what has been read or spoken.	explanation illustration	summarize paraphrase rephrase
Application (transferring)	Student is able to apply the information learned to a context different than the one in which it was learned.	practice transfer	apply use employ
Analysis (relating)	Student is able to break a problem down into its component parts and to draw relationships among the parts.	induction deduction	relate distinguish differentiate
Synthesis (creating)	Student is able to combine parts to form a unique or novel solution to a problem.	divergence generalization	formulate compose produce
Evaluation (judging)	Student is able to make decisions about the value or worth of methods, ideas, people, or products according to expressed criteria.	discrimination inference	appraise decide justify

Figure 1. A question classification scheme

Reprinted with the permission of Macmillan College Publishing Co. from *Effective Teaching Methods*, 2nd ed., by Gary D. Borich. Copyright © 1992 Macmillan College Publishing Company.

- Evaluation

and offers this excellent chart (Figure 1).

Conclusion

There is no doubt in any teacher's mind that the art of questioning is crucial and plays a major role in the process of teaching and learning. Postman (1979) went so far as to urge

> Let us... make the study of the art of question-asking one of the central disciplines in language education (p.140).

and to suggest that

> all our knowledge results from questions, which is another way of saying that question-asking is our most important intellectual tool (p. 140).

References

Bloom, Benjamin, M. Englehart, W. Hill, E. Furst, and D. Krathwohl. 1956. *Taxonomy of Educational Objectives. The Classification of Educational Goals. Cognitive and Affective Domains*. New York: David McKay Company, Inc.

Borich, Gary D. 1992. *Effective Teaching Methods*. Second Edition. New York: Macmillan Company.

Morgan, Norah and Juliana Saxton. 1993. *Teaching Questioning and Learning*. London and New York: Routledge.

Orlich, Donald C., Robert J. Harder, Richard C. Callahan, Constance H. Kravas, Donald P. Kauchak, R. A. Pendergrass and Andrew J. Keogh. 1985. *Teaching Strategies. A Guide to Better Instruction*. Lexington, MA and Toronto, Ontario: D.C. Heath and Company.

Postman, Neil. 1979. *Teaching as a Conservative Activity*. New York: Laurel Press, Dell. Delacorte.

Reprinted from: Anthony Mollica, "Planning for Successful Teaching: Questioning Strategies." *Mosaic,* 1, 4 (Summer 1994): 18-20.

17   Classroom Settings

Anthony Papalia

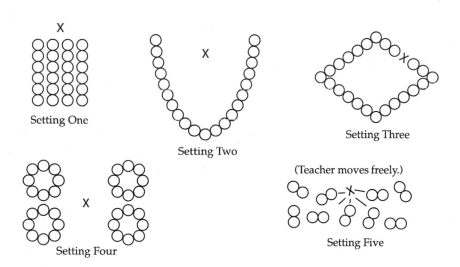

Setting One

Setting Two

Setting Three

Setting Four

(Teacher moves freely.)

Setting Five

In his book, *Learner-Centered Language Teaching. Methods and Materials.* (Rowley, MA: Newbury House, 1976), the late Anthony Papalia, identified a variety of learning styles (p. 15) and proposed various classroom settings (pp. 34-35).

Teachers realize, as Phillips (1976) points out, that

the neatly wrapped package for uniform distribution to a group of potential language learners has failed to live up to its advertising. There is no one right method for all learners at all stages. Alternatives in pace, content, goals and learning strategies require teachers and students to make choices – choices about how they learn and what they learn, all within the foreign language context.

Papalia firmly believed that it is necessary to understand and identify the learning styles that the student utilizes in order to enhance motivation and increase learning.

Is the student

- an *incremental learner* who likes to learn step by step?
- an *intuitive learner* who leaps to generalizations?
- a *sensory specialist* who learns better by seeing or hearing?

- an *emotionally involved learner* who depends heavily on interpersonal relationships?
- an *eclectic learner* who is able to adapt to any learning style?

In seeking answers to these questions, teachers acknowledge that each student is an individual who learns in a unique way and that options in learning should be provided for all students. By seeking these answers, they can better adjust their teaching materials and classroom pacing and grouping, and tailor instruction to the needs of each individual. Individualizing the mode of learning is as essential as individualizing the rate of learning.

Language teachers interested in individualizing instruction should design learning environments which provide varying degrees of structure, and should use different strategies and materials compatible with the individual differences of the learner.

Setting One:

To facilitate

1. the introduction of new material
2. the use of audio-visual aids
3. testing
4. activities where everyone is doing the same thing
5. independent work and
6. choral work.

Setting One

Setting Two:

To facilitate

1. teacher mobility
2. eye contact
3. pupil attention
4. communication
5. game playing and
6. teacher control.

Setting Two

Setting Three:

To facilitate

1. the introduction of new material
2. participation of the teacher as an equal
3. an informal atmosphere for oral presentations and
4. communication directed to all, not just to the teacher.

Setting Three

Setting Four:

To facilitate

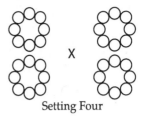

Setting Four

1. remedial activities
2. tutoring
3. use of tape recorders and media
4. reinforcement of learned material
5. use of self-instructional materials
6. peer teaching
7. skit planning
8. games
9. one-to-one teacher-pupil interaction
10. self-pacing
11. teacher awareness of individual learning problems and
12. grouping according to interests or needs.

Setting Five:

To enhance

(Teacher moves freely.)

Setting Five

1. peer interaction
2. peer teaching
3. "specific skill" grouping
4. variable pacing
5. tutorial work
6. games, simulations and role playing in a competitive or noncompetitive setting
7. group projects and
8. oral practice.

References

Papalia, Anthony. 1976. *Learner-Centered Language Teaching. Methods and Materials.* (Rowley, MA: Newbury House.

Phillips, June K. 1976. "Fun! Not for Fridays Only." Paper presented at the Northeast Ohio Teachers' Conference. Cleveland, October. Mimeo.

These pages are reprinted with kind the permission of Judith Papalia.

Reprinted from: Anthony Papalia, "Planning for Effective Teaching: Papalia's Classroom Settings." *Mosaic,* 1, 3 (Spring 1994): 165.

18 A Letter to My Spanish Teacher

Sandra J. Savignon

In this letter to her teacher, the Author shares her experiences in the classroom and her reasons for studying Spanish.

To my dear Spanish teacher,

You have been such a warm and enthusiastic teacher for me that I want to thank you for letting me join your class and to let you know how much you have helped me. I am especially eager to thank you because, as a language teacher myself, I have often wondered at the end of a term just how successful I had been in helping my students toward the competence they were seeking. Did I give them enough grammar? Was I too easygoing about errors? Should I have been more conscientious in sticking to the departmental syllabus? The opportunity you gave me to get on "the other side of the desk" has helped me to remember what it is like to be a language learner. The result is a renewed sense of direction as I resume my role as a language teacher.

I came into your second semester college class, Spanish 102, because I wanted to learn Spanish. A group of teachers of English as a second language had invited me to Barcelona to talk about ways of teaching for communicative competence. Inasmuch as I had been to Barcelona for the same purpose two years earlier, I thought it would be nice if I could show my hosts that in the meantime I had made some progress in Spanish. I wanted, at least, to be able to order my own *paella* and to ask my own directions. I further reasoned that with a better understanding of the basic structure of the Spanish language I would find it easier, once in Spain, to interact with native speakers and profit even more from my two-week stay.

I cannot begin to describe my anxiety as I walked into your class that first day. For one thing, I was plunging into a second semester course without having had the benefit of the first semester program. I chose your class, however, because I had heard from your supervisor what a very good teacher you were and because I planned to study hard and catch up on the grammar I had missed. As I was already a fluent speaker of French and had spent a little time in Spain, I thought I could keep up. Another reason for my anxiety was that I was not only older than the other students – most of them undergraduates fulfilling the language requirement – I was a professor of French as well. You and the others might well expect me to excel in an elementary Spanish class.

The class arrangement did not help to put me at ease. We sat around tables arranged in a semi-circle with our first names spelled out on big cards in front of us. The idea was a good one. This way we could all see each other and begin to get acquainted. But it was clear there was going to be no place to hide, no inconspicuous back row. I was going to have to speak Spanish!

What a relief it was when, as our first task, you had us introduce ourselves to our neighbor. I was sitting next to a friendly young woman who helped me to say my name, my age, and what I was doing in life. She was patient and very encouraging, virtues I know we try to stress in teaching of all kinds but which suddenly took on a special significance for me. I had a friend on whom I could count in the weeks ahead.

It was also nice the way you, the teacher, walked about the room as we were conversing, giving us help in Spanish whenever we asked. You did this often, dividing us into groups of two or three to work on specific assignments – writing answers to questions, writing a little story to describe a picture you had put on the overhead projector, finding out about how the others had spent the weekend. This was one of the best parts of the class. At these times we could count on each other and on you for help in completing the task. I know the classroom became somewhat noisy at times with eight or so groups at work, but the noise never distracted me. It was at these times, rather, that I felt I was learning the most Spanish. I could try things out I wanted to say, find out how to say them, and get the feeling that everyone was there to help me rather than to see how much Spanish I remembered.

When it came time to introduce my neighbor to the rest of the class on that first day, however, I was far from comfortable. I rehearsed what I was going to say over and over in my head, much as I do when speaking out in a public forum in English. When my turn came, I made my introduction more or less as I had practised it. When you corrected an error I had made, I repeated after you as best I could, but I was really too flustered to understand what I was doing. The experience was simply too intense to allow me to focus on the form you were trying to teach me. On the other hand, I gained many insights from your corrections of the other students. Once out of the limelight, it was easier for me to re-hearse forms and check them against the other's responses and your corrections.

What I liked best was when you spoke Spanish to us. You explained grammar, told us stories about a funny drawing, talked about class activities, shared your slides of beautiful places to visit in Spain. These were all marvelous opportunities for the listening experiences I craved, and you made the most of them. I became anxious again, though, when you pointed on the map to Andorra and asked me what it was called. I know you were being nice and giving me a chance to speak, but I did not know the answer. When I could just relax and listen while you talked, without fear of being called on, so much vocabulary and points of grammar seemed to start coming together. At these times I could feel myself learning Spanish. It was at once a powerful and exciting feeling.

Then came our first written test. It was a rather typical test as language tests go, requiring us to complete sentences, conjugate verbs and write answers to questions as they were read aloud. We did not do well as a class, and you were disappointed. You became uncharacteristically angry. I am not suggesting that your anger was unwarranted, but it definitely changed the ambience of the class. Seven out of seventeen of us had scored lower than 70 per cent, and you lectured us on how important it is not to get behind, on how miserable we would be in the two semesters ahead of us if we did not get down to work. I was very uncomfortable wondering how the seven in question must have felt. An added irritation was the student who had turned in a perfect paper! It turned out she had studied Spanish for three years in secondary school before entering a beginning Spanish course at the university. As we talked among ourselves later, in the corridor, I learned that there were several other students who had done the same, deliberately scoring low on the placement examination so as to give themselves an advantage in subsequent coursework. They said it was the only way to get through; there was no way to get all the grammar otherwise. While this practice helps to explain why so many of our incoming students do poorly on language placement examinations, it must also create considerable resentment from those who are trying to absorb all the vocabulary items and grammar rules for the first time.

The Unit 15 test we took a week later went fairly well. I felt good about understanding the oral comprehension questions although the others thought that part was hard. The grammar part was hardest. I thought of all the things I had done wrong after I had handed in my paper and felt as though I had really put my ego on the line. As it turned out, I got a grade of C (73 per cent) on the test. Our scores were all rather low, and you told us how weak we were, how much we needed to study. You were understandably frustrated because we continued to make so many errors. No doubt your syllabus said that we were to have "covered" a certain amount of material by then. The text book, after all, included all of basic Spanish grammar in a one year course. I was quite angry, however, about having lost so many points for wrong spellings and missing accents. Where I thought I had done well because I was beginning to understand, I had missed points because of what looked to me like minor errors. I was angry with you, angry at Spanish ... and feeling rejected by those I wanted to join. For me, the tests we took did much to destroy the productive, supportive atmosphere you had created in class.

Class discussions were always fun, but I had to concentrate hard on forms. One day you went around the table asking us questions so we would learn to change sentences from interrogative to declarative. The questions were no doubt interesting as you tried to ask things that related to us individually. I did not have time to listen to the questions asked of others, however, because I was busy counting the number of people ahead of me and rehearsing the forms silently to myself so as not to be caught off guard. When my turn came you asked me, "*¿Cómo se llama el presidente de Francia?*" I could not for the life of me fill in the name, so intent was I on verb endings! Now I know what my own students mean when they say they prefer not to talk about anything "heavy." They are so busy concentrating on forms they do not want their intelligence to be brought into question as well.

The birthday surprise was marvelous! Enrique had a birthday, and you brought in a little cake with a candle. We sang a song you had written on the board, and you told us about birthday celebrations in Mexico. It was a nice relief of tension after an hour of verb drills. We perhaps forget that even adults in a second-language classroom enjoy the frivolous. Songs, parties, and games which might seem unsophisticated to us in our native language are such a welcome way to relax in a second language. They also help to build the camaraderie we need in order to learn from each other.

I got bogged down in the subjunctive. We spent so much time learning the verb forms and examples of expressions requiring the subjunctive, yet there were so few things I sould say in Spanish on my own that I knew I did not have use for all those forms. I was sympathetic with your view that it would help if we got these "down pat," but that would have required a sheer feat of memory. It was one, frankly, to which I just could not push myself.

My own learning strategy was to prepare lots of vocabulary cards with Spanish verb infinitives. I then added some expressions I had heard that reminded me of endings, use of subjunctive and various prepositions and other vocabulary I liked. My best sources of expressions were:

1. the things you said in class,
2. a magazine you had given me of current events in Barcelona, and
3. a book of poetry by García Lorca.

The Lorca poems were so beautiful I had a friend record them so that I could listen and practice them at home. It might seem curious to you that someone interested in Spanish for travel would want to spend time reading poetry. It certainly is not in step with the language for special purposes movement so popular now in our profession. The language was, however, beautifully simple and authentic. I could read the poems at home, silently or aloud, and feel I was in touch with something, with someone really Spanish. Many of my private vocabulary words came from these poems. I think if we had studied them as a class it might have spoiled it for me.

Everyone told me I spoke with a French accent but that it sounded fine. This made me feel a part of the group. I could speak Spanish with my own accent and be accepted. I was happy you did not insist on the finer points of pronunciation. The pronunciation of /v/ as /b/ was still a major hurdle, and I was also busy attending to all kinds of lexical and syntactical matters.

The nicest thing you did for me was to introduce me to a Venezuelan woman who had recently arrived in the United States. She was looking for American contacts, and I needed someone with whom to practice my Spanish. Inasmuch as I was the hostess, it was up to me to take the initiative and arrange a meeting – *"a las cuatro y media, el diez y ocho de julio, aquí."* I used lots of gestures, repeated myself frequently but the *señora* was most gracious. I found I was able to listen to her Spanish as she spoke because we were working together to solve a problem. I did not have to be concerned with how to correct any errors in my Spanish. From this first and subsequent encounters I realized I was on my way. I could have some fun in Barcelona and show others I was eager to talk with them.

And talk I did. Once in Barcelona I even succeeded in phoning friends of yours to make a date to meet them. I spent hours in

Spanish, listening mostly, but smiling and speaking up enough to let my companions know I enjoyed their company and was following the conversation. You could never have anticipated all my needs. How could you have known I would need to have a new heel put on my boot and would have to let the shoe-maker know I wanted a rubber, not synthetic, heel? As it was, I enjoyed going into the shop and waiting my turn. This gave me a marvelous opportunity to eavesdrop. From the signs posted on the walls I was able eventually to figure out what I wanted and communicate it with some degree of self-assuredness. Victory!

I never earned above a B in our class exams, and my average was probably closer to a C. Errors in spelling and grammar kept my marks down. But you were my bridge to the Spanish-speaking world. In your classroom I was able to make friends with other learners and feel that together we were working and learning. You were my model. I trusted you and was grateful for your encouragement. You see, my dear Spanish teacher, test scores do not really matter to me. An A in Spanish is not what I want. I want Spanish speakers from Puerto Rico, Spain, Cuba, and Mexico to know that I respect them and their language and that I am going to meet them half way. Thank you for your help.

Reprinted from *The Canadian Modern Language Review,/La Revue canadienne des langues vivantes.* Vol. 37, No. 4 (May, 1981), pp. 747-750. By permission of Prof. Sandra J. Savignon.

Reprinted from: Sandra J. Savignon, "A Letter to My Spanish Teacher." *Mosaic,* 7, 1 (Fall 1999): 21-23.

19 The Challenge of Multilevel Classes

Jill Bell

Every language class is a multilevel class! How could it be otherwise when language learning is affected by so many personal variables? The author discusses how language teachers can find ways to accommodate and capitalize on this classroom diversity.

One of the most common challenges facing teachers in language classes, particularly in ESL and heritage programs, is the wide variety of language competence which students may have. Even classes which appear relatively homogeneous at the outset soon display varying rates of progress, as factors such as age, levels of prior education, exposure to the target language and so on, all have their effect.

Developing a curriculum which allows each student to make the best possible progress is extremely challenging in such conditions. As well as offering learning opportunities for all students, the teacher must be concerned with the social atmosphere in the classroom so that learners are at ease and comfortable in the group. Splitting students up into permanent groups of advanced, intermediate and basic level learners tends not to promote the kind of group identity which allows learners to feel comfortable. In addition, it prevents the teacher from capitalizing on the various strengths of the students and allowing them to work together and help each other. Ideally then, in each session, the teacher will plan to have the whole group work together for at least part of each lesson.

There are three basic ways in which this can be accomplished:
a) start-up activities suitable for everyone;
b) whole group activities where students perform the task at different levels; and
c) whole group activities which incorporate a variety of different tasks.

a. Start-up activities

By beginning each class with the whole group working together, the tone is set for the rest of the session. Ideally the start-up activity should have a strong visual component, so that even learners with minimal language skills can understand what is going on. It should involve significant oral discussion so that stronger learners get a chance to express their oral competence and beginners hear a variety of spoken language richer than they would encounter in their small group, but with the content knowledge which allows them to comprehend at least some of what is said. Some possible ideas include the following:

- filmstrip
- LEA (Language Experience Approach) story: Students recount a story or an experience. The teacher   writes it down on a chart. Once this is done, the students read it back.
- field trip
- demonstration of any subject of interest, maybe jewelry making or car maintenance
- showing of family snapshots, baby photos, etc.
- discussion of strip story, or large poster-type photograph
- photo story where photos carry the dialogue.

A slightly different but highly successful starter is the use of interview questionnaires where students are given a class list and a simple question such as "When is your birthday?" Students must circulate around the room, interviewing each other and recording the results. This activity helps students get to know each other's names and breaks down the barriers between students of different ages or levels. To increase the challenge for the advanced students, a second, more open-ended question can be assigned, to be attempted only when the first set of interviews are successfully completed.

b. Whole group activities where students perform the task at different levels

The level of difficulty of many language tasks is determined less by the complexity of the language being presented than by the complexity of the task which the student is required to perform. A beginner may not be able to totally comprehend the TV Guide for instance, but may still be able to find and circle a favourite program. Meanwhile, a more advanced student might be planning an evening's viewing for a history buff or analyzing the intended audience for different channels. With this principle in mind, many activities can be developed where everyone in the class listens to or looks at the same piece of language but is assigned a task to perform which varies according to interest or ability. Some examples follow:

- Have the students listen to a taped conversation or similar.

Develop three or four different sets of follow-up activities.
The easiest might be a cloze where students decide which of
two words they hear. Slightly more difficult would be simple
yes/no questions on factual items. More advanced students
might be asked to write a paraphrase.

- Have students read a fairly simple piece, probably a strip or
photo story, with different questions to answer. (The task
could be copying for literacy students). Advanced students
are asked to create the dialogue or continue the story.

- Distribute newspapers or magazine ads. Have students skim
or scan to identify different pieces of information. Easy tasks
might be to find out whether a certain item is listed for sale.
More challenging activities include identifying sources, bud-
geting, etc.

- Have in-class discussions, choosing topics such as generation
problems which all learners will understand, rather than topics such as politics which require reading   skill. Allow all
students to contribute at their own level.

- Play team games, such as spelling bees, with the teacher choosing words at the appropriate level of difficulty for each student. Another successful game is Who am I, if students take
turns to ask questions, and sample questions (such as "Male
or Female?") are provided for lower level students.

c. Whole group activities which incorporate different tasks

Major class projects give everyone an opportunity of working
towards the same goal and taking pleasure in the joint final product while incorporating a wide enough variety of tasks for everyone to be involved at their own level. One useful idea is to issue
regular editions of a class newspaper. This can be mounted on a
bulletin board, or printed up for distribution if the class is not
always held in the same classroom. The strongest students might
interview people and write articles. Others with good literacy skills
might work as editors helping reporters to improve their text.
Less advanced students might do horoscopes and weather reports,
provide captions for photos, or be responsible for lay-out.

Other whole class projects which will involve a wide variety
of tasks at different levels of difficulty include organizing, planning and advertising a field trip, making a slide tape show, making a photo story account of a class activity, or planning a bring-
a-guest morning.

The activities I have described so far are all designed to help
the class develop a sense of being part of a group, and to help
them recognize that everyone in the class can contribute. Keep-

ing the whole group working together all the time is not entirely practical, however, and most teachers with multilevel classes find it is fruitful to also have the students work in various patterns of smaller groups.

One general principle to bear in mind when planning small group activities is that the makeup of the small group should be adjusted, depending on whether the focus of the activity is on accuracy or fluency. Accuracy activities will include any work which has as its aim improving the form of what is said. It may focus on learning a new piece of grammar such as a verb tense or the formation of plurals. It may be a pronunciation exercise, or an activity which helps people recognize the most socioculturally appropriate form of an utterance. For activities like these, it makes sense to have students work in groups of more or less equal ability, so that every member of the group is learning a specific item which they do not currently have control of, and which is appropriate for their level of language development. It is also, however, very important that students have the chance to work on their fluency, that is on using language to express oneself, where the task is to get the message over, not to worry about the form by which that is achieved. Such activities are better performed in mixed level groups. The advanced speakers are challenged to find alternate ways of expressing themselves which can be understood by the beginners. The weaker students benefit from hearing a much richer range of language than they would be exposed to in a group composed entirely of beginners.

Equal Ability Groupings

Equal ability small groups will often be doing the same type of tasks as you would assign to a whole class, but this is the teacher's chance to do some accuracy work focusing on a specific language item or function. There are also certain tasks which can be assigned to a small group of five or so which cannot be done with a whole class.

- *problem solving*
  "Who gets thrown out of the life-boat?" type decision making. Suitable problems might include planning the best meal for a particular occasion based on a set of food ads, choosing the best apartment for a specified tenant from the want ads, deciding on the best course of action for an immigrant with aging parents in the native country, and so on.
- *process writing*
  have students read their stories to each other, and edit based on the feedback they receive.

- *group work based on sequencing*
  e.g. deciding on the best sequence for a series of photos which tell a story, cut up comic strip stories, narrative strip stories and so on.
- *planning activities*
  working with a map to plan a route, organizing an end of term party, planning refreshments, etc.

Cross Ability Groups

As with whole group activities described above, this is best for project type tasks where jobs can be assigned based on ability. For example, students might contribute their favourite recipes to make a recipe book, with one responsible for the index, another for sorting, another for the title page, one for proof reading recipes, etc.

Pair Group

Pair work is another useful tool for the teacher of a multilevel class. Asking students to complete even basic seat work in pairs encourages the use of language and makes rather dull exercises into interesting oral interactions. The pairs may be composed of students of roughly equal ability or widely different.

Cross Ability Pairs

Sometimes teachers are reluctant to ask advanced learners to work with beginners as they feel that the stronger students are wasting their time. However, there are quite a few ways in which both students can really benefit from this mix, as many activities put heavier demands on one partner in the pair. The task for the teacher is to ensure that the stronger student does not take over the activity, by making it necessary for the less advanced student to have input. You might try some of the following ideas:

- have one student transcribe the LEA story of the other student and help the writer read it back.
- have the stronger student complete a form on the other student, which will require an interview of the other student.
- assign puzzle type activities where one student has to give instructions to the other. The weaker student is given for instance a set of pictures cut from a catalogue. The stronger student is given a matrix that is a completed grid with the same pictures pasted in a particular order. The task is for the weaker student to duplicate the matrix without looking at the original. The stronger student must give oral instructions as to how to arrange pieces appropriately. (The weaker the

lower level student is, the more demanding this is for higher level student).
- the lower level student selects an object, or famous person. The more advanced student has to find out who or what has been chosen. The beginner student need answer only "Yes/ No" or "I don't understand."
- assign a role play such as phoning for information, where one role is dominant or more demanding.

Equal Ability Pairs

Almost any activity which one person can do turns into a more communicative activity if the students work in pairs. Some particularly useful ideas include:
- interviewing each other, perhaps recording responses on some kind of form
- read aloud dialogues, especially those where a choice of answers is provided so that learners must focus on the content of what is said as well as the pronunciation task
- role plays where both parts are equally challenging.

Also useful are information gap activities where both students are given the same text but with different omissions and must question each other to discover the missing information.

Individual Work

A significant problem with multilevel classes is to make the students more responsible for their own learning. Because the class varies so widely in ability it is often difficult for the teacher to be sure that all students are working at their optimum level, and some students will tend to coast along doing easier activities than are really appropriate.

Ideally, students need to be able to select materials which suit not merely their language skill level but also their interests, age, cultural needs, etc. Building up a self access centre in a multilevel classroom is a great help for teacher and student. Some teachers work almost exclusively with self access materials. Others prefer to use it as one component of an overall program. The self access centre should be a large box or cupboard from which students select their own activity. Ideally the materials should provide correct answers for any accuracy based activities so that students can check their own performance and do not have to wait until the teacher is free to discover how well they did.

A self access centre should include materials which address all the skill areas.

Reading Materials

The teacher selects and mounts a variety or reading matter from comic stripsto hydro bills to short stories. A few comprehension questions are provided on each with an answer key on the back. Students select whatever interests them, and check their own work.

Listening

The teacher will need to provide at least one cassette player plus a selection of tapes with accompanying print material. The tapes might include spontaneous native-speaker conversation, recorded simplified language dialogues, radio broadcasts of news, weather or chat shows, songs for use with cloze text, work lists for dictation practice, letter lists for dictation practice.

Writing

A simple way to build up a variety of writing activities is to pull apart your favourite workbooks and laminate the pages. Provide washable felt markers so that the learners can write in their answers and then the sheets can be wiped clean for use by another student. You can also laminate cheques, deposit slips, birthday cards, etc. Pictures, comic strips and photos are also useful to stimulate free writing, with suggestions for vocabulary provided on the back which students can refer to if they wish.

Speaking

Provide puzzles and games calling on speaking skills which students can do in pairs. Provide blank cassettes for students to record whatever they wish, either individual rehearsal or pair role-play or conversation.

Grammar/Vocabulary Development

Again, laminated pages from a favourite text are the easiest way to provide a wide variety of activities.

The Overall Curriculum

As the suggestions above show, there is no shortage of activities for a multilevel class. The problem is not really what to do, but to find a way of organizing these apparently unconnected activities into a well-planned syllabus. Ideally we would consult with each student and with them determine their goals and the time frame in which they hope to achieve them. However, in practice this can mean 25 students all doing different things which require teacher input. For larger classes, therefore, we have to compromise. Although students should still have input into the goal-setting process they will select goals from a curriculum designed by the teacher.

Such a curriculum is normally based on process, where the activities are arranged to ensure that the student is developing all the required skills. This is not just a matter of listening, speaking, reading and writing but also of improving syntax, building vocabulary, inferring meaning from context, watching for nonverbal communication while following a conversation, etc. It also suggests breaking the traditional four skill areas down into the various subskills and ensuring, for example, that reading instruction includes not only detailed comprehension, but quickly grasping the gist of a passage, index skills, familiarity with layout, scanning for specific information, etc. A curriculum which focuses onthese sorts of skills should be applicable to all students at all

levels.

Editor's Note: A more detailed discussion of ideas and activities for miltilevel classes can be found in Jill Bell's book *Teaching Multilevel Classes in ESL* (Toronto: Pippin Publishing, 1988) from which these ideas are drawn. This material is reproduced by permission of the publisher.

Reprinted from: Jill Bell, "The Challenge of Multilevel Classes." *Mosaic*, 2, 1 (Fall 1994): 1, 3-5.

20 Discipline in the Language Classroom

Merle Richards

Language teachers need clear routines and practical rules to maintain discipline. The article offers some tips for encouraging good conduct and a positive attitude to language learning.

Second-language teachers often seem to have more than their share of classroom discipline problems. Often, these difficulties appear to be associated with pupils' lack of ability or interest in language learning. However, modifying one's teaching style can improve both discipline and interest, and can even seem to increase the students' language abilities (Gruenewald and Pollak, 1990), thus solving several difficulties at once.

Classroom observation shows that not all language teachers encounter discipline problems. When parents exclaim, "Hey, my kid loves Tamil (Polish, Mohawk, French)!", chances are the language class is not spent in rote repetition, word lists, grammar rules, or uninviting content. More likely, the learners are using language to talk about their lives and interests, building knowledge and skills slowly, but with increasing competence. As their capacity increases, they are encouraged to use the language, however badly, to express their ideas and feelings. Gradually, with feedback and help from the teacher, their form improves and approaches more closely the model of the fluent speaker.

Discipline and Respect

"Discipline" in the language class is the same as in any other. It implies guidance, limits, firmness, and leadership, not harshness, humiliation, or autocratic control.

Good discipline is based on respect: the teacher earns respect by being prepared and knowledgeable, and modelling consideration for self and learners. Children develop respect through example and practice; with it they gain self-control and responsibility.

Since schools have the mandate to teach alternatives to violence, physical punishment is not an acceptable method of discipline. Hence, teachers need to have a system of sanctions, rewards, and penalties to be used as needed. Rewards and incentives are nearly always more effective than punishment, but punishment may be necessary if a serious or harmful behaviour has occurred which must not be repeated. Punishment must work immediately if it is to work at all.

Best of all is to help the student take responsibility for correcting the situation, rather than directing blame or applying punishment. A useful maxim is "When you hurt someone, you have to make them better; when you do damage, you make repairs." Demanding apologies often just teaches children that "you can do whatever you wish if you apologize later".

A Discipline Plan

A discipline plan involves an escalating system leading from unobtrusive signals to outright penalties. Punishments that will cause lasting resentment or defiance should be avoided, but "punishments that fit the crime" or imply a bit of humour can be highly effective.

Step One: Prevention

Misbehaviour is easier to prevent or "nip in the bud" than to change. Observation shows that pupils misbehave when they are bored, confused, uncomprehending, or idle. The teacher who maintains involvement in activities through interest avoids most pupil misconduct. *Prepare thoroughly for each class*!

The same class may behave quite differently with different teachers. Usually the difference lies in the teacher's style and preparation. Active learning methods leave little time for misbehaviour. Using Total Physical Response (TPR) and language experience daily focuses the pupils on the learning task, avoiding "goofing off". Moreover, these approaches ensure that the pupils are comprehending and using the language, so that they do not become frustrated by lack of understanding.

Some kids are rowdy, inattentive, or defiant; a few are difficult under any circumstances. But most pupils' behaviour is guided by the situation – if it is clear. Make your rules simple and explicit: don't expect kids to "just know" what you want. Develop routines to avoid problems, making the rules and limitations clear (Ornstein, 1990). Children will push to try those limits: be cheerfully firm in enforcing them. For example, if pupils wander around during worktime, bring in a few language games. Then state, "When your work is finished, put it in my basket, then you may get a book or a quiet game." Similarly, state, "When I am addressing the whole class, stay in your seat and pay attention. You can sharpen your pencil or get a drink later".

Step Two: Heading Off Problems

1. When small misdemeanours occur just once, you can ignore them. But if they are repeated, you must react: the third time may establish a habit.

    Reaction should be low-key: Say the pupil's name, move to stand nearby, use "the eye". These serve as notice that the misconduct has been noted.

2. For more serious infractions, issue a warning: "We do not like our opening prayer to be interrupted. The next time you are late, please wait at the door until we finish." "If you fight over points, the game will stop." Then, the next time the same behaviour occurs, carry out your promise. Do not give another warning.

    Caution: Don't make threats you won't carry out. Someone will call your bluff, and the kids will think you don't mean what you say.

3. Have some boring jobs to use as punishments. Picking up scraps, straightening the boots, sharpening the pencils, or even writing lines may work.

    For some kids, these may be agreeable tasks; this is okay if they break the pattern of misconduct. In this case, tell the child, "I see you are looking for something useful to do; here's a job for you until you're ready to work properly." Make clear that the academic work still needs to be done; this is not an escape.

4. Realize that many problems are due to attention-seeking (Dreikurs, 1982). Tell the pupil you know this, and give much attention when the child is behaving well. (You have to notice good behaviour too!) Don't be embarrassed to praise when praise is due.

5. Avoid sarcasm or humiliation. They are effective controls, but arouse hostilities that may make the pupil want to get even, thus creating new discipline problems. Worse, the student may simply "opt out", withdrawing from learning or participating, and you will have a hard time recreating a relationship that will involve the student in learning again.

6. Restructure your program. Change the schedule or routines so that pupils have time to finish their tasks and do not have to spend time waiting for your attention or assistance. Use

games to provide practice and objects and pictures to ensure that pupils always catch the meaning.

Step Three: Consequences Matter!

1. Serious problems need immediate measures. A "time-out" corner may help some kids to cool off. If you use the hallway, don't leave the pupil alone; try to keep her/him in sight. If you send a student to the office, be sure s/he is expected, or act as escort yourself.

2. Talking with kids about their behaviour helps if you don't nag or blame. "It makes me really mad when I see you marking our books. We all need to use them. How are you going to fix them up?"

3. Discuss consequences of misbehaviour and decide with the class how to deal with repeated problems: "If you can't work with others, you'll have to work alone".

4. Establish incentives and bonuses for good conduct. Privileges can be lost if abused. (But be sure that kids are able to earn the rewards that are promised.)

5. You can use tokens or play money for rewards and for fines for infractions. "You forgot your homework? That will be one dollar. I'll see the homework after school, please". This works well with older children, especially if they can use their "money" for privileges.

6. Discuss problems with the class, and have them suggest solutions they can live with. For example, one group decided they could avoid provoking the class bully and "help him to be good". Some children even said they would allow him one poke, but that if he got really bad, he should be excluded from the room. This tactic was agreed to and acted upon.

7. Don't use tests, homework, or schoolwork as penalties. Learning is not a punishment. But writing "lines" is effective with some pupils.

Step Four: Crisis Management

Chronic and serious misconduct usually implies that something is wrong in the child's life. Document all offenses and get help! Talk with the principal and the parents to decide on a consistent discipline plan for that child. If behaviour problems are serious enough to threaten others or prevent learning, the miscreant may have to be removed from the class. The parents should be called to pick up the child; until they arrive, an adult should remain with the child. Emotional disorders are beyond most teachers' field of expertise, and the other children have a right to feel – and be – safe at school.

Step four cases are rare; most discipline problems can be dealt with in common-sense ways. The teacher needs to realize that most children want to behave well, and will if they know how. By planning interesting lessons with purposeful learning tasks, the teacher solves most problems before they begin.

These strategies apply to any teaching situations, but especially to the language class, because language learning often seems to be superficial and uninvolving. Switching from drills to practice games, from textbook exercises to language experience, and from recitation to TPR helps to get learners "onside". Then when discipline problems do arise, they are less likely to escalate.

Finally, maintain your sense of humour. Often one can choose to be affronted or to laugh. Ornstein (1990) mentions that choosing humour to defuse a tense situation shows that the teacher is secure and in charge. The students relax and can then return to their real business, learning and using the second language.

References

Dreikurs, Rudolf. 1982. *Maintaining Sanity in the Classroom*. New York: Harper and Row.

Gruenewald, Lee J. and Sara A. Pollak. 1990. *Language Interaction in Curriculum and Instruction: What the Classroom Teacher Needs to Know*. 2nd ed. Austin, Texas: PRO-ED.

McNeil, John D. and Jon Wiles. 1990. *The Essentials of Teaching: Decisions, Plans, Methods*. New York: Macmillan.

Ornstein, Allan C. 1990. *Strategies for Effective Teaching*. New York: Harper and Row.

Reprinted from: Merle Richards, "Discipline in the Language Classroom." *Mosaic*, 2, 1 (Fall 1995): 14-15.

21 Interactive Homework: Creating Connections Between Home and School

Janis L. Antonek, G. Richard Tucker
and Richard Donato

How can the awareness of foreign language programs in elementary schools be increased among parents? Interactive homework – the involvement of parents and child – may be one solution.

Introduction

Developing, funding, and maintaining elementary foreign language programs are complex tasks which routinely confront educators seeking to broaden the curriculum in the area of world languages and cultures.[1] Once a program of study is established, however, it is important to ensure that support is maintained, interest and enthusiasm are kept alive, and information regarding the contents of the elementary foreign language program is regularly communicated to everyone involved.[2] McLoughlin Carter (1993) states that to ensure future support of foreign language in the elementary school (FLES), teachers must engage in public awareness activities, tasks often deemed by teachers as unrelated to instruction and classroom learning. McLoughlin Carter (1993, p. 389) urges that

> we must force our programs into the awareness of our primary constituents – the students and parents whom we serve.

Rosenbusch (1991) further argues that parental support is crucial for second language programs and suggests that parental involvement can mobilize parents into program advocates.

Evidence of the powerful role that parents play in second language advocacy can be seen in the American organization Advocates for Language Learning (ALL) and the Canadian organization Canadian Parents for French (CPF). ALL was founded in 1983 by Madeline Ehrlich, a Culver City, California parent of three immersion students, because she "began to envision an educational environment where every child would have the opportunity to learn a second language as part of the regular school program" (Erlich, 1987:98-99). CPF, founded in 1977 by parents in Ottawa, has played a significant role in the advancement of French immersion schooling across Canada (Sloan, 1989). Both continue to flourish.

Not all parents are equally convinced of the importance of foreign language education. McLoughlin Carter (1993) outlines four public awareness activities foreign language educators may consider when trying to convince communities that their programs are as important as other more time-honoured subjects. She suggests

- Parent-Teacher Association programs,
- articles in local newspapers,
- vocabulary newsletters, and
- displays of student work.

The purpose of this article is to explore one additional means of increasing parental awareness of FLES programs – the use of interactive homework assignments. We will present a rationale for the use of homework that involves the parent[3] and child, report on an interactive homework project in a Japanese FLES program (Donato, Antonek and Tucker, 1994; Tucker, Donato and Antonek, 1994, Antonek, Donato and Tucker, 1995), discuss parental reactions to these interactive assignments, and provide guidelines for constructing interactive homework assignments for the foreign language class.

Considering the "Home" in Homework

Although a routine practice in school, homework is often assigned with little thought regarding its function, role, or connection with classroom instruction. A brief review of the most commonly used methodology textbooks in foreign language instruction (Curtain and Pesola, 1994; Nunan, 1991; Oller, 1993; Omaggio Hadley, 1993; Richard-Amato, 1988; and Schrum and Glisan 1994) reveals that the issue of homework is never presented or discussed. Why this issue has not been treated more fully in the professional literature is not the purpose of this article. In our investigation of the role and function of homework we question the tacit assumption that homework is exclusively the activity of an individual or merely an opportunity for independent practice. We have been led to explore the role of homework as a powerful and valuable tool and now recommend that systematic guidance be provided to teachers concerning its multiple purposes.

We maintain that the role of homework may be viewed differently from solitary activity of the learner or independent practice opportunities. Assignments a child brings into the home create a vital link between the classroom and outside world and should also be understood for their potential to inform and raise awareness about language instruction in the classroom. We argue that homework implicitly communicates information to parents about two important aspects of the child and the school.

- If attentive to home assignments, parents learn directly about the contents of the curriculum. While observing children completing assignments, the parent can gain access to what the child is being taught, the mode of presentation, and the child's level of mastery with the particular skill or concept. Children who take homework assignments seriously and appear to enjoy and take pride in their work inspire confidence about the school and teacher in parents and demonstrate to them that their children are most likely equally enthusiastic about their classroom learning. Conversely, parents can experience negative feelings or scepticism toward course content and the effectiveness of instruction while observing their children completing assignments that are tedious, needlessly complicated, or for which the child is unprepared.
- Further, assignments communicate directly to parents how the child feels about a particular task. A child's differential enthusiasm, eagerness, or lack of interest across subject areas tells the parent how the child reacts affectively to school activities, in general, and to a specific subject area, in particular.

In short, apart from homework's primary goal as a tool to increase learning opportunities and develop responsible students, it also can have a hidden function – to link the classroom with the home and to communicate implicitly to the parent what children know and can do, their level of mastery and comfort with the information, and their feelings about the subject area.

We suggest, therefore, that homework functions on three interrelated levels:

1. Homework communicates to the parent what and how well the child is learning in the classroom, the child's affective reaction to this learning, and the contents and scope of the curriculum. For this reason, it is curious that no attention whatsoever has been paid to the potential roles of homework in even the most current language teaching methodology textbooks.
2. Second, Homework facilitates classroom learning if it is linked to what the child can realistically carry out in the absence of the teacher and other students, and if the child has been prepared to complete the assignment independent of the myriad

forms of assistance a classroom can provide. Homework can also be conceptualized as incorporating other forms of assistance found in the home and community and thus reinforce or extend the child's learning outside the boundaries of the classroom.

3.   Homework mediates the relationship of school and home. Homework is an implicit public awareness mechanism which at the same time informs parents of the curriculum and the child's progress and level of engagement. In considering its mediational role, we feel that teachers would be well advised to consider carefully the communicative value of homework and its impact on parents who monitor their children completing assignments in the home. We maintain that well conceived homework has the potential to increase awareness and support for a program through the implicit messages it sends concerning a child's schooling. This message can be either negative or positive and for this reason homework is an important element of schooling and a topic worthy of our attention.

The Concept of Interactive Homework

Homework can build a bridge between the classroom and the home and can serve as an instrument of awareness and ultimately advocacy and support for foreign language programs. If this is so, how can homework be re-conceptualized to benefit both child and parent? Rather than view homework as an independent activity to be completed by the child, assignments can be designed to involve the parent in ways that benefit the child and inform the parent directly about what the child is learning in the classroom. The concept of interactive homework has recently been reported by Epstein (1993) at The Center on Families, Communities, Schools, and Children's Learning at the Johns Hopkins University where interactive homework assignments in math, science, English language arts, and health have been written and piloted. Referred to as "Teachers Involve Parents in Schoolwork" (TIPS), the process includes talking with students about homework in the classroom, asking them to describe the type of homework they like best, and inviting them to tell how their parents help them with their schoolwork at home (Epstein, 1993, p. 73). Central to the TIPS process is the interactive homework assignment which invites parents to work with their child on something they are learning in the classroom. In the discussion that follows, we will extend the concept of interactive homework to the foreign language classroom and present our work on incorporating interactive homework in the context of a Japanese FLES program.

Additionally, we believe that interactive homework is well suited to foreign language learning where

- opportunities for functional practice and interaction (Ellis, 1988; Long, 1981; Swain, 1985),
- the need to reflect on language (Brooks and Donato, 1994; Donato, 1994; Swain, 1994), and
- the importance of assessing one's own linguistic achievements (Donato and McCormick, 1994)

are central to the language learning process.

Epstein (1993) states that recent studies indicate that the home directly influences students' skills and achievements but that parents need guidance from schools on how best to assist their children. This assistance is all the more necessary in the case of subject areas where parents do not possess the necessary background or have the requisite knowledge to help their children at home. Foreign language represents a case in point since many parents may have never studied the language or the culture being taught to their children. Foreign language is also set apart from other subjects in that parents may not be able to learn along with their children without sufficient guidance concerning pronunciation, rudimentary knowledge of structure, or cultural information. This need for knowledge of a foreign language is all the more necessary in cases where parents have never studied the language in question. Unlike other subjects where parents may be able to inform themselves on the topic of study, parents have few resources to rely on to help them understand the language their children are acquiring. A further problem is the cumulative nature of language learning. Learning a language requires remembering vocabulary, pronunciation, etc. Parents may find it difficult to retain information from one assignment to the next. If they do remember aspects of the language represented across interactive assignments, this knowledge is, at best, fragmentary. However, given the apparent difficulty of actively incorporating the parent into the foreign language learning activity of their children, we believe that creative planning and thoughtful implementation of interactive assignments can result in the spread of information about foreign language curriculum to parents, parental support for foreign language programs, and the promotion of positive attitudes in children and increased learning.

Interactive Homework and the Japanese FLES Program
After the first year of a three year pilot program (1992-1995) to introduce a Japanese FLES program in grades K-5 at the Falk Laboratory School of the University of Pittsburgh, our team of

researchers collected data on the language development of students and the attitudes of parents, teachers, and children concerning this innovative program. Analysis of questionnaires distributed to the parents of the children participating in the program revealed two important findings. First, parents were concerned that they were not well enough informed about what their children were learning and the type of instruction they were receiving. Second, it was apparent that parents had no basis for accurately assessing their children's progress in Japanese. This second finding was manifested when we queried parents regarding how they perceived their children's achievement in Japanese. Comments ranged from extreme satisfaction and enthusiasm for the child's ability to carry out a small but appropriate number of language functions for a 75 minute a week FLES program to scepticism regarding the limited range of topics a child could handle. Curiously, we found that often parents would react differentially toward exactly the same behaviours exhibited by the child. For example, one parent expressed satisfaction that her child could count, name colours, and engage in a few greeting protocols. Conversely, another parent citing almost the same language abilities questioned whether this skill was a sufficient return for the time invested in learning Japanese. We concluded that due to their lack of information about the curriculum, parents needed to be directly connected to the activities of the classroom. This conclusion prompted us to explore the use of homework that would involve the parent in observing and assisting the child's use of Japanese. The goal of these assignments was, therefore, to help the child review classwork in the home and to make parents aware of the contents of the Japanese curriculum and the skills their children were developing in the classroom.

Interactive homework assignments were developed by the Japanese teacher, Ms. Mari O'Connell. As previously mentioned, the first task was to address the problem of providing the necessary resources for parents to work with children on a topic about which the vast majority of them had no knowledge. It was decided that vocabulary and culture would be the focus of each interactive assignment and that parents would be supplied with a guide to help them in pronouncing words with their children. Tasks included sharing vocabulary with parents or teaching the parent a few words or expressions in Japanese. Brief cultural information in English, previously discussed in class, was also included. Simple line drawings were used to cue vocabulary practice or to illustrate cultural notes (see Appendix).

After some initial experimentation with format and length during the first semester, we decided upon a one-sided, 8 1/2 x

14″ interactive homework sheet presented every other week during the second semester. The interactive homework assignments were generally consistent in format in an effort to minimize time expended on learning how to do each new assignment.

Section 1 of each homework sheet began with a title introducing the topic of the homework such as personal information, courtesy expressions, school subjects, classroom objects and greetings. Following the title was a statement to the family indicating that the homework topic reflected class work and curricular objectives (e.g., "In class we are studying how to greet different people in Japanese. In this homework assignment I will show you

---

Name: _____ Class: _____ Date: _____

Japanese: Greetings

Dear Family,
In Japanese class we have learned how to greet people. This activity will let me show you how I do it. This assignment is due _____

Sincerely, _____
Student's signature

In Japanese I am able to say and respond greetings and courtesy expression properly.

O.high.yo!	"Good morning!"
Cone.knee.chi.wa!	"Hello, Good afternoon!"
Cone.ban.wa!	"Good evening!"
Sa.yo.(o).na.la!	"Good bye!"
Are.lee.ga.toe!	"Thank you!"
Dough.e.ta.she.ma.she.tay.	"You are welcome."
ao.men.na.sigh.	"I am sorry."
Ee.des.yo!	"It's OK!"

To your parent, how do you...
greet him or her in the morning? afternoon? evening?
greet him or her when you go apart?
thank him or her? or respond when he or she says "thank you"?
apologize? or respond when he or she says "I'm sorry"?

Teach your parent how to greet in Japanese!

With your parent, exchange greetings and courtesy expressions.

1. AM   2. early PM   3. Evening   4. Gift   5. Oops!   6. Bye!

The tradition of bowing in Japan is a common gesture used in introductions, greetings, partings, apologizing, and thanking.

Student's name _____ Class _____ Date _____
How well do you think your child performed this skill?
1. ____ Child seems to perform this skill well.
2. ____ Please check work. Child needs some help on this.
3. ____ Please note (other comments below):

_____
Parent's signature

how I can say hello and good-bye to different people in Japanese."), a notice of the due date, and a space for the child's signature.

Section 2 featured from one to four language functions thus alerting the parent to what the child should be able to say in Japanese. This section provided all of the phrases necessary for carrying out the language functions in the homework. In this way, parents were provided with a helpful reference tool to use while working with the child. The Japanese examples were written in a modified form of roomaji to assist the parent with pronunciation. We had hoped that this presentation would alleviate pronunciation difficulties. In many ways it proved useful but as one parent noted "Victor (her son) corrects my pronunciation. He speaks so beautifully...but I don't remember the pronunciation from one time to the next." We will return to the problem of pronunciation under guidelines for creating interactive homework.

Section 3, entitled "Let's warm up," asked the students to display their knowledge to their parent by carrying out 3-5 language functions (e.g., "Tell your parents how you would greet them in the morning, in the afternoon, and in the evening. Apologize to your parents.").

In Section 4, the students would teach their parents how to carry out the language functions in the homework. Section 5 provided an opportunity for the parents and children to interact by communicating in Japanese (e.g., "With your parents, exchange greetings and courtesy expressions."). Section 6 presented cultural information relevant to the interactive homework topic.

The last section contained a response form for the parent to sign and provide feedback on the child's performance. Parents were asked to detach this last section and return it to the teacher. The response form was kept simple to allow parents simply to check off whether the child performed the task well or still needed additional practice. A space for other comments completed the interactive homework sheet. Students were encouraged to keep the interactive homework sheets to use for future reference.

The interactive homework was short and printed on a single page, followed a regular format, linked to the curriculum, included language resources to help the parent work with the child, included a cultural component, contained simple, direct instructions, provided for practice and interaction, and allowed the parent to respond concerning their child's performance and progress.

Parental Reactions to Interactive FL Homework

Parental reactions to the interactive homework assignments were sought on two different occasions – at the middle and end of the academic year. Mid-year questionnaires revealed that the length of the assignments and the child's level of comfort in completing the homework was problematic. In response to this observation, future assignments were shortened and only material that all children could be expected to complete without the assistance of the teacher was included, i.e., material that was adequately covered in class and was relatively familiar. It was hoped that this familiarity with the material would allow the children to showcase their ability rather than their frustration, which is often the case when assignments are given prematurely or without regard for pre-requisite skills and knowledge needed to work independently or with a parent. To shorten the assignments, language function practice was decreased and there were more activities at the word-level (e.g. "Say the names of the 12 body parts to your parents."). Cultural information was omitted; however, soon after this decision had been made, several parents voiced concerns that the cultural information was one of the most interesting aspects of the interactive homework. For this reason, cultural information was reinstated.

Of the parents who responded to the items regarding the interactive homework on the end-of-year parent survey, 33% stated that both they and their children enjoyed completing the homework together. Forty-two percent of the parents noted, however, that the assignments were frustrating for them and their children. Twenty-five percent of the parents observed that the first round of assignments were too long but since they had been shortened they enjoyed working with their children on Japanese homework. We found these responses encouraging since over half the parents (58%) stated that they and their children enjoyed completing the revised assignments.

We were also interested in determining how consistently parents participated in interactive Japanese homework with their children. Thirty-eight percent of the parents reported having completed all the assignments and 20% estimated that they had completed almost half of the interactive homework. Forty-two percent reported that very few or none of the assignments were undertaken with their children most likely because of the frustrations expressed in the previous question. It is striking that the same percentage of parents who expressed satisfaction with the interactive homework also represents the percentage of parents who report actually "doing homework" with children. That is, these parents' judgments seem to be based on practice and behavioral commitment rather than on merely providing a socially and educationally appropriate answer.

When asked whether interactive homework should continue, a high percentage (76%) of the parents responded affirmatively. The remaining parents (24%) who responded negatively need some qualification however, since this number included several parents of kindergarten students to whom homework is never given in other subject areas. In some cases, parents of kindergarten children felt that homework was not appropriate at all for any subject at this level of schooling. As one parent stated "kindergarten children have too many other things to do after school. They should not be assigned homework." Therefore, the interactive nature of the assignment may not have produced the recommendation to discontinue the project but a belief that kindergarten is not a time for bringing formal academic work into the home.

Anecdotal comments of the parents taken from the end-of-year questionnaires also shed light on the use and function of interactive homework, the characteristics of effective assignments, and their potential to inform and raise awareness about the contents of the curriculum. One parent stated that he liked the interactive assignments because "I'd have an idea of what was going on in class." The majority of the narrative comments centered on the pronunciation issue. Several parents requested that tapes be sent home even at a nominal fee. Another parent observed that her "two children argued over pronunciation and who would teach it." She added "I am bad at languages and found it frustrating to be grilled about it by my children." For this parent, audio tapes keyed to the assignments would have certainly helped to relieve frustration at interactive homework time.

Other comments reflected the need for a consistent format and clear objectives and directions. "Interactive homework should continue if it is made clearer concerning its purpose – to explore? to meet set goals? to assess progress?" All these questions deserve our attention if building interactions between parent and child in the home is to become a reality. Length of assignment also surfaced as a concern –

"Homework should be very short and more frequent (weekly) and they should focus on just one thing a week."

Finally, for a few parents, receiving the assignments was problematic.

"I never received assignments due to my child's not making them available without me asking for them."

Clearly this problem can be solved if parents are informed in advance concerning dates of interactive homework distribution. All the above comments were extremely helpful in refining our homework project. We were also encouraged by the comments of some parents who enthusiastically added "I learned some Japanese too!"

Recommendations and Guidelines for Creating Interactive Homework Assignments

Based on our experience, we offer the following recommendations and guidelines for the construction of interactive homework assignments for the foreign language class. In this section, we will make recommendations concerning the use of interactive homework and will then conclude with a reference checklist to use in designing interactive homework assignments.

Information

The first step in initiating an interactive homework project is to inform all participants on the nature of the project. Epstein (1993) emphasizes the importance of sending a letter of introduction to the parents describing the frequency, goals, objectives, and procedures of the interactive homework assignments. In turn, parents should be encouraged to provide their observations, comments, or questions to the teacher (Epstein 1993, p. 74). Including a response form at the end of each assignments allows the teacher to monitor the degree of participation in the project and provides the parent with a direct way to communicate with the classroom teacher.

Homework Format

As previously discussed consistency is critical. Although covering different material, each assignment should follow a similar format. (e.g., title, note to parent signed by child, objectives, language material used in assignment, child-parent interaction activity, cultural information, response form for parent). This predictable pattern of homework activity will help the parent to focus on the content of the assignments rather than the procedures for its completion. The format should be "user-friendly" by avoiding technical language, complicated or wordy directions, illegible printing and a dense or "busy" layout. In deciding on a format, it is equally important to consider the length of the assignment. It is unrealistic to expect parent and child to spend long periods of time on homework for a single subject. We have found that short 10 minute assignments work best and are viewed by parents as feasible and realistic rather than oppressive and inconvenient. Epstein (1993) also suggests that interactive homework be kept to one-page and be reproduced on coloured paper for easy identification by the parent and child.[4]

Language Resources

Make every effort to assist the parent to assist the child. Foreign language represents a subject area different from others whose contents are taught through a language already known to the parent. Provide clear, easy to use pronunciation guides. This year we are sending parents audio tapes of Japanese stories and songs and parents are responding quite favourably to this tool. Additionally, parents can not be expected to learn the language along with their child. Although parents will develop some knowledge of the language through their interactions with their children, an interactive assignment sent home twice a month will simply not provide the necessary input for a parent to make significant language gains. Moreover, parents will not have the continual language exposure and practice necessary for second language acquisition. Therefore, ensure that each assignment is self-contained. Make no assumption that information used in an assignment during the first week of the month will be retained by the parent for use in an assignment during week three of the same month. Each assignment needs to provide the necessary resources to be completed independent of all others.

One way to ensure parent-child interaction at homework time and avoid the problem of the parent who, for whatever reason, believes he or she is incapable of helping in a foreign language is to include activities that can be conducted in the home language of the parent and child. Children can share cultural information with their parents or tell their parents their favourite part of a story they have heard in the foreign language class. This interaction can be conducted in the first language and can serve a useful purpose in introducing the study of the foreign language into the everyday discourse of the family.

Consider the Child

Like the parent who requires resources for assisting and interacting with the child, the child also needs to be prepared to enter into the interaction with the parent. Among its multiple purposes, one aim of the interactive homework is its public awareness role to inform, inspire confidence and build enthusiasm for the accomplishments of the child and the foreign language program. The teacher needs, therefore, to consider the level of preparedness of the child for a particular homework assignment. Assignments should be written with the children in mind to allow them to showcase their abilities and developing knowledge. Little positive impact will come from assignments that consistently yield child-parent frustration or leave parents with the impression that their children are confused and learning little from the instruction of the teacher. One innovative aspect of interactive home-work is that the children become the spokespersons for the FLES program and have the potential to teach the parents. Therefore, like teachers, they need to have the background knowledge and confidence to instruct. Considering the learners and what they can realistically do on their own without teacher support should motivate and drive the contents of the interactive homework as-signment.

In deciding at which grade level foreign language homework should begin, the FLES teacher should consider school policy re-garding homework. As found in our program, offering foreign language homework in kindergarten when it was not given in other subjects was a contentious issue.

Consider the Contents

What can be included in an interactive assignment? We are still experimenting with the contents of interactive homework but our experience has shown that work on vocabulary and simple lan-guage functions works well and directly informs the parent of what the child is learning in the classroom. Children may dem-onstrate to the parent a language function they have learned and teach the parents a few phrases to allow them to engage in a brief 2-4 line dialogue with them. Pictures on the homework sheet can be used to cue vocabulary. Parents can use these images to help children practice and remember new words and expressions. We have also discovered that cultural information is greatly appreci-ated by parents. Sample activities might include a discussion about a target culture's holidays, a retelling of a legend or folktale, a discussion around a piece of realia, or information concerning daily cultural practices such as schooling, shopping, meals, and family life. As previously discussed, cultural information can be discussed in the child's home language thus avoiding the prob-lem of the parent's lack of proficiency in the target language.

In the spirit of the TIPS project (Epstein, 1993), the contents of the assignments may also connect directly with the home. That is, rather than try to duplicate the classroom in the home, the home itself may be used as a learning environment. Activities that in-volve the child and parent in information-gathering or observa-tions of persons, objects, and events in the home are excellent ways to take advantage of the unique contribution the home can make in a child's learning. For example, following a lesson on transpor-tation, children may be asked to interview the parent to gather information on the modes of transportation found in their home or neighbourhood (car, bike, motorcycle, roller-skates, sled, truck, wagon, etc.). After a lesson on rooms of the house, a child may be asked to take a parent on a tour of his own home by identifying as many rooms as possible in the target language. This information can then be used in class for additional projects. Comparisons of a child's home with homes found in the target culture can also be carried out in collaboration with a parent. An illustration of the interior of a house in Japan or Mexico, for example, can be used as a point of departure for a discussion of housing differences. In this case, it will be equally interesting for parents to learn about the dwellings of others in a culture unlike their own. In all the examples above, the important point is that the children make use of their immediate environment by connecting some aspect of the home with school, thus strengthening learning and extending the curriculum beyond the walls of the classroom.

The ideal scenario would be for the FLES teacher to consider grade and language level when developing interactive homework assignments. However, in a program like ours, where the staffing option is the language-specialist model – one FLES teacher for all children K-5, multiple versions of interactive homework may not be logistically realistic. Among our parents and students, there were no complaints regarding all students receiving the same homework. Conversely, parental feedback indicated that siblings, enrolled in the same program, were able to participate on the homework together, an unanticipated interaction.

Consider the Parent

In the best case scenario, an interactive homework project will result in unanimous, enthusiastic participation on the part of the parents. But as educators we would be naive to assume that parental support for a child's study exists uniformly in all homes. It is not the intention of the authors to pass judgment on parents who, for whatever reason, do not participate in helping a child with home assignments or monitoring their completion. Professional obligations, travel, health, educational background of the parent, work schedules, etc. all bear on the parent's ability or willingness to complete assignments with a child. However, we think that two issues are raised by the case of a non-participating parent.

- First, children cannot be held responsible for completion of an interactive assignment in cases where the parent refuses or is unable to participate. Unlike independent homework assignments where the onus is entirely upon the child for their completion, the interactive homework requires the participation of two individuals. Teachers need to be sensitive therefore to the feelings of the child whose parents, for whatever reason, have not participated in the assignment. In discussing interactive homework in class, care needs to be taken not to call attention to or embarrass those children who have nothing to turn in to the teacher due to parental non-involvement. Where parents refuse to interact around homework, the child is truly powerless to fulfill course requirements or to promote positive educational exchanges in the home.

- Second, we believe that the knowledge the teacher has of parental involvement in interactive homework can contribute positively to her better understanding of the child, individual differences in the classroom, and possible reasons for the child's achievement or lack of it. Just as interactive homework has the potential to inform parents about school, it can serve equally as a source of critical information about the support a child receives for schooling in the home. Thus interactive homework creates a bi-directional exchange of information from teacher to parent and from parent to teacher. We believe, however, that information concerning interactive homework shared in newsletters, parent night meetings, and communications from the teacher to the parent can alleviate some of the problems of non-participation by showing parents the importance of home support and the value of the project.

Checklist for Constructing an Interactive Homework Assignment

The following checklist is intended as a reference when writing interactive homework assignments.

Procedural considerations

- ☐ 1. Has a letter been sent to parents explaining the goals and purposes of the interactive homework?
- ☐ 2. Are parents aware of the dates of distribution and return of inter active homework?
- ☐ 3. Are the objectives clearly stated on the interactive home work sheet?
- ☐ 4. Are directions clear and brief? Have they been piloted on a few individuals before distribution to parents?
- ☐ 5. Has a brief statement introducing the assignment been written from the point of view of the child and signed by her?
- ☐ 6. Is a parental response form included at the end of the assignment?

Formatting considerations

- ☐ 7. Is the physical layout of the homework clear and easy to follow?

☐   8. Is the interactive homework on a single page?
☐   9. Is format consistent across assignments?

Content considerations

☐   10. Have parents been given the necessary background in formation to help the child (pronunciation guides, glosses, etc.)?
☐   11. Is the homework self-contained?
☐   12. Has care been taken to include only that content with which the child is most familiar and capable of completing at home?
☐   13. Is the assignment representative of what the child can do?
☐   14. Can the homework be successfully completed in a short time?
☐   15. Do the activities promote interaction?
☐   16. Does the assignment include activities involving the home?
☐   17. Has cultural information been included?

Self-assessment

☐   18. Do you feel the assignment is a good reflection of your competence as a teacher?

Conclusion

This report focuses on the seldom-explored topic of creating and strengthening connections between home and school through the use of interactive homework assignments in the foreign language program. Three factors triggered our interest in this topic: the complete absence of any discussion of homework in contemporary methodology texts, a desire to provide parents of children in a Japanese FLES program with information about their children's program and with a basis for assessing their children's progress, and a belief that the establishment or strengthening of a home – school partnership would significantly enrich the child's educational experience.

We have adapted, piloted, and revised the TIPS model developed by Epstein (1993) for use in the foreign language classroom. During the 1993-1994 school year, we found that a majority of parents completed and appreciated the interactive homework, but that they had a number of suggestions to offer for improving the form and content of assignments. Based upon our experience last year, and parental, student, and teacher feedback, we have revised the form and content of the assignments for this year, developed some supplementary material for parents, and devised a set guidelines and a checklist for others who may wish to develop their own assignments.

We particularly wish to encourage others who develop similar materials to ensure that the assignments encourage the children to showcase their abilities, and that they establish, extend, and solidify linkages between the home and the school. Some will argue that this is difficult to do when the parent does not speak and has not studied the target language; we disagree. We believe that our data indicate that such parents welcome a teacher's initiatives which help them to understand, to participate in, and to support their children's learning experiences. The use of interactive homework assignments, then, provides a valuable tool for enriching the partnership between home and school that has seemingly been ignored.

Notes

1. The preparation of this report was supported in part by a grant from the US Department of Education to G. R. Tucker and R. Donato, and in part by the Department of Instruction and Learning at the University of Pittsburgh.

2. Thanks to Claire Donato, age 8, for the child's perspective on the non-participating parent.

3. We will use he word "parent" to include caretakers who play a significant role in the life of children assuming primary responsibility for their upbringing, and emotional, physical, and educational needs. The word "parent" is intended to encompass all individuals present in the home who have the daily responsibility of nurturing and caring for children.

4. For sample interactive homework assignments in mathematics, science, English language arts, and health, see *Instructor* (1993, 1994).

References

Antonek, J. L., R. Donato and G. R. Tucker. 1994. "Japanese in the elementary school: Description of an innovative Pittsburgh program." *Mosaic*, 2, 2: 5-9.

Brooks, F. B. and R. Donato. 1994. "Vygotskyan approaches to understanding foreign language learner discourse during communicative tasks." *Hispania*, 77, 2: 262-274.

Curtain, H. A. and C. A. Pesola. 1988. *Languages and children – making the match*. Reading, MA: Addison-Wesley.

Donato, R. 1994. "Collective scaffolding in second language learning." In J. P. Lantolf and G. Appel eds., *Vygotskian approaches to second language research*. Norwood, NJ: Ablex. pp. 33-56.

Donato, R. and D. McCormick. 1994. "A sociocultural perspective on language learning strategies: The role of mediation." *The Modern Language Journal*, 78, 4: 453-464.

Donato, R., J. L. Antonek and G. R. Tucker. 1994. "A multiple perspectives analysis of a Japanese FLES program." *Foreign Language Annals*, 27, 365-378.

Ellis, R. 1988. "The role of practice in classroom language learning," *Teanga*, 8: 1-25.

Epstein, Joyce. 1993. "School and family partnerships." *Instructor*, 74-76.

Ehrlich, Madeline. 1987. "Parents: The Child's Most Important Teachers," in John M. Darcey, ed., *Commitment and Collaboration*. Middlebury, VT: Northeast Conference on the Teaching of Foreign Languages.

Long, M. 1981. "Input, interaction and second language acquisition," in H. Winitz, ed., *Native language and foreign language acquisition*, pp. 259-278. Annals of the New York Academy of Sciences 379.

McLoughlin Carter, Eileen. 1993. "Safeguarding our programs through public awareness." *Hispania*, 76, 388-391.

Nunan, D. 1991. *Language teaching methodology*. New York, NY: Prentice-Hall.

Oller, Jr., J. W., ed. 1993. *Methods that work – ideas for literacy and language teachers*. Boston, MA: Heinle and Heinle.

Omaggio Hadley, A. 1993. *Teaching language in context*. Boston, MA: Heinle and Heinle.

Richard-Amato, P. A. 1988. *Making it happen*. New York, NY: Longman.

Rosenbusch, Marcia H. 1991. "Elementary school foreign language: the establishment and maintenance of strong programs." *Foreign Language Annals*, 24: 297-311.

Shrum, J. L. and E. W. Glisan. 1994. *Teacher's handbook – contextualized language instruction*. Boston, MA: Heinle and Heinle.

Sloan, Tom. 1989. "Canadian Parents for French: Two Provinces," *Language and Society/Langue et société*, 26, spring, 34-36.

Swain, M. 1985. "Communicative competence: Some roles of comprehensible input and comprehensible output in its development." In S. M. Gass and C. G. Madden eds., *Input in second language acquisition*, (pp. 235-253). Rowley, MA: Newbury House.

Swain, M. 1994. "Three functions of output in second language learning." Paper presented at the meeting of the Second Language Research Forum, Montreal, Canada.

Tucker, G. R., R. Donato and J. L. Antonek 1995. "Documenting an exemplary Japanese FLES program: In pursuit of Goals 2000," Unpublished manuscript, Carnegie Mellon University and University of Pittsburgh.

Reprinted from: Janis L. Antonek, G. Richard Tucker, and Richard Donato, "Interactive Homework: Creating Connections Between Home and School." *Mosaic,* 2, 3 (Spring 1995): 1-10.

22 Eight Approaches to Language Teaching

Gina Doggett

What is the "best" method for teaching languages? The article presents a summary of eight language teaching methods in practice today.

There there was once consensus on the "right" way to teach foreign languages, many teachers now share the belief that a single right way does not exist. It is certainly true that no comparative study has consistently demonstrated the superiority of one method over another for all teachers, all students and all settings.

Presented here is a summary of eight language teaching methods in practice today:

- the Grammar-Translation Method
- the Direct Method
- the Audio-Lingual Method
- the Silent Way
- Suggestopedia
- Community Language Learning
- the Total Physical Response Method, and
- the Communicative Approach.

Of course, what is described here is only an abstraction. How a method is manifest in the classroom will depend heavily on the individual teacher's interpretation of its principles.

Some teachers prefer to practice one of the methods to the exclusion of the others. Other teachers prefer to pick and choose in a principled way among the methodological options that exist, creating their own unique blend.

The summary provides a brief listing of the salient features of the eight methods. For more details, readers should consult *Techniques and Principles in Language Teaching* by Diane Larsen-Freeman, published in 1986 by Oxford University Press in New York, on which this summary was based. Also see references listed at the end of the article.

Grammar-Translation Method

The Grammar-Translation Method focuses on developing

students' appreciation of the target language's literature as well as teaching the language. Students are presented with target language reading passages and answer questions that follow. Other activities include translating literary passages from one language into the other, memorizing grammar rules, and memorizing native-language equivalents of target language vocabulary. Class work is highly structured, with the teacher controlling all activities.

Direct Method

The Direct Method allows students to perceive meaning directly through the target language because no translation is allowed. Visual aids and pantomime are used to clarify the meaning of vocabulary items and concepts. Students speak a great deal in the target language and communicate as if in real situations. Reading and writing are taught from the beginning, though speaking and listening skills are emphasized. Grammar is learned inductively.

Audio-Lingual Method

The Audio-Lingual Method is based on the behaviourist belief that language learning is the acquisition of a set of correct language habits. The learner repeats patterns until able to produce them spontaneously. Once a given pattern – for example, subject-verb-prepositional phrase – is learned, the speaker can substitute words to make novel sentences. The teacher directs and controls students' behaviour, provides a model, and reinforces correct responses.

The Silent Way

The theoretical basis of Gattegno's Silent Way is the idea that teaching must be subordinated to learning and thus students must develop their own inner criteria for correctness. All four skills – reading, writing, speaking, and listening – are taught from the beginning. Students' errors are expected as a normal part of learning; the teacher's silence helps foster self-reliance and student initiative. The teacher is active in setting up situations, while the students do most of the talking and interaction.

Suggestopedia

Lozanov's method seeks to help learners eliminate psychological barriers to learning. The learning environment is relaxed and subdued, with low lighting and soft music in the background. Students choose a name and character in the target language and culture, and imagine being that person. Dialogues are presented to the accompaniment of music. Students just relax and listen to them being read and later playfully practice the language during an "activation" phase.

Community Language Learning

In Curran's method, teachers consider students as "whole persons," with intellect, feelings, instincts, physical responses, and desire to learn. Teachers also recognize that learning can be threatening. By understanding and accepting students' fears, teachers help students feel secure and overcome their fears, and thus help them harness positive energy for learning. The syllabus used is learner-generated, in that students choose what they want to learn to say in the target language.

Total Physical Response Method

Asher's approach begins by placing primary importance on listening comprehension, emulating the early stages of mother tongue acquisition, and then moving to speaking, reading, and writing. Students demonstrate their comprehension by acting out commands issued by the teacher; teacher provides novel and often humorous variations of the commands. Activities are designed to be fun and to allow students to assume active learning roles. Activities eventually include games and skits.

The Communicative Approach

The Communicative Approach stresses the need to teach communicative competence as opposed to linguistic competence; thus, functions are emphasized over forms. Students usually work with authentic materials in small groups on communicative activities, during which they receive practice in negotiating meaning.

THE GRAMMAR-TRANSLATION METHOD

Goals

> To be able to read literature in target language; learn grammar rules and vocabulary; develop mental acuity.

Roles

> Teacher has authority; students follow instructions to learn what teacher knows.

Teaching/Learning Process

> Students learn by translating from one language to the other, often translating reading passages in the target language to the native language. Grammar is usually learned deductively on the basis of grammar rules and examples. Students memorize the rules, then apply them to other examples. They learn paradigms such as verb conjugations, and they learn the native language equivalents of vocabulary words.

Interaction: Student-Teacher and Student-Student

Most interaction is teacher-to-student; student-initiated interaction and student-student interaction is minimal.

Dealing with Feelings

n/a

View of Language, Culture

Literary language seen as superior to spoken language; culture equated with literature and fine arts.

Aspects of Language the Approach Emphasizes

Vocabulary, grammar emphasized; reading, writing are primary skills, pronunciation and other speaking/listening skills not emphasized.

Role of Students' Native Language

Native language provides key to meanings in target language; native language is used freely in class.

Means for Evaluation

Tests require translation from native to target and target to native language; applying grammar rules, answering questions about foreign culture.

Response to Students' Errors

Heavy emphasis placed on correct answers; teacher supplies correct answers when students cannot.

THE DIRECT METHOD

Goals

To communicate in target language; to think in target language.

Roles

Teacher directs class activities, but students and teacher are partners in the teaching/learning process.

Teaching/Learning Process

Students are taught to associate meaning and the target language directly. New target language words or phrases are introduced through the use of realia, pictures, or pantomime, never the native language. Students speak in the target language a great deal and communicate as if in real situations. Grammar rules are learned inductively – by generalizing from examples. Students practice new vocabulary using words in sentences.

Interaction: Student-Teacher and Student-Student

Both teacher and students initiate interaction, though student-initiated interaction, with teacher or among themselves, is usually teacher-directed.

Dealing with Feelings

n/a

View of Language, Culture

Language is primarily spoken, not written. Students study common, everyday speech in the target language. Aspects of foreign culture are studied such as history, geography, daily life.

Aspects of Language the Approach Emphasizes

Vocabulary emphasized over grammar; oral communication considered basic, with reading, writing based on oral practice; pronunciation emphasized from outset.

Role of Students' Native Language

Not used in the classroom.

Means for Evaluation

Students tested through actual use, such as in oral interviews and assigned written paragraphs.

Response to Students' Errors

Self-correction encouraged whenever possible.

THE AUDIO-LINGUAL METHOD

Goals

Use the target language communicatively, overlearn it, so as to be able to use it automatically by forming new habits in the target language and over coming native language habits.

Roles

Teacher directs, controls students' language behaviour, provides good model for imitation; students repeat, respond as quickly and accurately as possible.

Teaching/Learning Process

New vocabulary, structures presented through dialogues, which are learned through imitation, repetition. Drills are based on patterns in dialogue. Students' correct responses are positively reinforced; grammar is induced from models. Cultural information is contextualized in the dialogues or presented by the teacher. Reading, writing tasks are based on oral work.

Interaction: Student-Teacher and Student-Student

Students interact during chain drills or when taking roles in dialogues, all at teacher's direction. Most interaction is between teacher and student, initiated by teacher.

Dealing with Feelings

n/a

View of Language, Culture

Descriptive linguistics influence: every language seen as having its own unique system of phonological, morphological, and syntactic patterns. Method emphasizes everyday speech and uses a graded syllabus from simple to difficult linguistic structures. Culture comprises everyday language and behaviour.

Aspects of Language the Approach Emphasizes

Language structures emphasized; vocabulary contextualized in dialogues but is limited because syntactic patterns are foremost; natural priority of skills – listening, speaking, reading, writing, with emphasis on first two; pronunciation taught from beginning, often with language lab work and minimal pair drills.

Role of Students' Native Language

Students' native language habits are considered as interfering, thus native language is not used in classroom. Contrastive analysis is considered helpful for determining points of interference.

Means for Evaluation

Discrete-point tests in which students distinguish between words or provide an appropriate verb for a sentence, etc.

Response to Students' Errors

Teachers strive to prevent student errors by predicting trouble spots and tightly controlling what they teach students to say.

THE SILENT WAY

Goals

To use language for self-expression; to develop independence from the teacher, to develop inner criteria for correctness.

Roles

Teaching should be subordinated to learning. Teachers should give students only what they absolutely need to promote their learning. Learners are responsible for their own learning.

Teaching/Learning Process

Students begin with sounds, introduced through association of sounds in native language to a sound-colour chart. Teacher then sets up situations, often using Cuisenaire rods, to focus students' attention on structures. Students interact as the situation requires. Teachers see students' errors as clues to where the target language is unclear, and they adjust instruction accordingly. Students are urged to take responsibility for their learning. Additional learning is thought to take place during sleep.

Interaction: Student-Teacher and Student-Student

The teacher is silent much of the time, but very active setting up situations, listening to students, speaking only to give clues, not to model speech. Student-Student interaction is encouraged.

Dealing with Feelings

Teachers monitor students' feelings and actively try to prevent their feelings from interfering with their learning. Students express their feelings during feedback sessions after class.

View of Language, Culture

Language and culture are inseparable, and each language is seen to be unique despite similarities in structure with other languages.

Aspects of Language the Approach Emphasizes

All four skill areas worked on from beginning (reading, writing, speaking, listening); pronunciation especially, because sounds are basic and carry the melody of the language. Structural patterns are practised in meaningful interactions. Syllabus develops according to learning abilities and needs. Reading and writing exercises reinforce oral learning.

Role of Students' Native Language

Although translation is not used at all, the native language is considered a resource because of the overlap that is bound to exist between the two languages. The teacher should take into account what the students already know.

Means for Evaluation

Assessment is continual; but only to determine continually changing learning needs. Teachers observe students' ability to transfer what they have learned to new contexts. To encourage the development of inner criteria, neither praise nor criticism is offered. Students are expected to learn at different rates, and to make progress, not necessarily speak perfectly in the beginning.

Response to Students' Errors

Errors are inevitable, a natural, indispensable part of learning.

SUGGESTOPEDIA

Goals

To learn, at accelerated pace, a foreign language for everyday communication by tapping mental powers, overcoming psychological barriers.

Roles

Teacher has authority, commands trust and respect of students; teacher "desuggests" negative feelings and limits to learning; if teacher succeeds in assuming this role, students assume childlike role, spontaneous and uninhibited.

Teaching/Learning Process

Students learn in a relaxing environment. They choose a new identity (name, occupation) in the target language and culture. They use texts of dialogues accompanied by translations and notes in their native language. Each dialogue is presented during two musical concerts; once with the teacher matching his or her voice to the rhythm and pitch of the music while students follow along. The second time, the teacher reads normally and students relax and listen. At night and on waking, the students read it over. Then students gain facility with the new material through activities such as dramatizations, games, songs, and question-and-answer sessions.

Interaction: Student-Teacher and Student-Student

At first, teacher initiates all interaction and students respond only non-verbally or with a few words in target language that they have practised. Eventually, students initiate interaction. Students interact with each other throughout, as directed by teacher.

Dealing with Feelings

Great importance is placed on students' feelings, in making them feel confident and relaxed, in "desuggesting" their psychological barriers.

View of Language, Culture

Language is one plane; non-verbal parts of messages are another. Culture includes everyday life and fine arts.

Aspects of Language the Approach Emphasizes

Vocabulary emphasized, some explicit grammar. Students focus on communicative use rather than form; reading, writing also have place.

Role of Students' Native Language

Translation clarifies dialogues' meaning; teacher uses native language, more at first than later, when necessary.

Means for Evaluation

Students' normal in-class performance is evaluated. There are no tests, which would threaten relaxed environment.

Response to Students' Errors

Errors are not immediately corrected; teacher models correct form later during class.

COMMUNITY LANGUAGE LEARNING

Goals

To learn language communicatively, to take responsibility for learning, to approach the task non-defensively, never separating intellect from feelings.

Roles

Teacher acts as counsellor, supporting students with understanding of their struggle to master language in often threatening new learning situation. Student is at first a dependent client of the counsellor and becomes increasingly independent through five specified stages.

Teaching/Learning Process

Non-defensive learning requires six elements: security, aggression (students have opportunities to assert, involve themselves), attention, reflection (students think about both the language and their experience learning it), retention, and discrimination (sorting out differences among target language forms).

Interaction: Student-Teacher and Student-Student

Both students and teacher make decisions in the class. Sometimes the teacher directs action, other times the students interact independently. A spirit of cooperation is encouraged.

Dealing with Feelings

Teacher routinely probes for students' feelings about learning and shows understanding, helping them overcome negative feelings.

View of Language, Culture

Language is for communication, a medium of interpersonal sharing and belonging, and creative thinking. Culture is integrated with language.

Aspects of Language the Approach Emphasizes

At first, since students design syllabus, they determine aspects of language studied; later teacher may bring in published texts. Particular grammar, pronunciation points are treated, and particular vocabulary based on students' expressed needs. Understanding and speaking are emphasized, though reading and writing have a place.

Role of Students' Native Language

Use of native language enhances students' security. Students have conversations in their native language; target language translations of these become the text around which subsequent activities revolve. Also, instructions and sessions for expressing feelings are in native language. Target language is used progressively more. Where students do not share the same native language, the target language is used from the outset, though alternatives such as pantomime are also used.

Means for Evaluation

No specific means are recommended, but adherence to principles is urged. Teacher would help students prepare for any test required by school, integrative tests would be preferred over discrete-point tests; self-evaluation would be encouraged, promoting students' awareness of their own progress.

Response to Students' Errors

Non-threatening style is encouraged; modelling of correct forms.

TOTAL PHYSICAL RESPONSE METHOD

Goals

To provide an enjoyable learning experience, having a minimum of the stress that typically accompanies learning a foreign language.

Roles

At first the teacher gives commands and students follow them. Once students are "ready to speak", they take on directing roles.

Teaching/Learning Process

Lessons begin with commands by the teacher; students demonstrate their understanding by acting these out; teachers recombine their instructions in novel and often humorous ways; eventually students follow suit. Activities later include games and skits.

Interaction: Student-Teacher and Student-Student

Teacher interacts with individual students and with the group, starting with the teacher speaking and the students responding non-verbally. Later this is reversed; students issue commands to teacher as well as each other.

Dealing with Feelings

The method was developed principally to reduce the stress associated with language learning; students are not forced to speak before they are ready and learning is made as enjoyable as possible, stimulating feelings of success and low anxiety.

View of Language, Culture

Oral modality is primary; culture is the lifestyle of native speakers of the target language.

Aspects of Language the Approach Emphasizes

Grammatical structures and vocabulary are emphasized, imbedded in imperatives. Understanding precedes production; spoken language precedes the written word.

Role of Students' Native Language

Method is introduced in students' native language, but rarely used later in course. Meaning is made clear through actions.

Means for Evaluation

Teachers can evaluate students through simple observation of their actions. Formal evaluation is achieved by commanding a student to perform a series of actions.

Response to Students' Errors

Students are expected to make errors once they begin speaking. Teachers only correct major errors, and do this unobtrusively. "Fine-tuning" occurs later.

THE COMMUNICATIVE APPROACH

Goals

To become communicatively competent, able to use the language appropriate for a given social context; to manage the process of negotiating meaning with interlocutors.

Roles

Teacher facilitates students' learning by managing classroom activities, setting up communicative situations. Students are communicators, actively engaged in negotiating meaning.

Teaching/Learning Process

Activities are communicative – they represent an information gap that needs to be filled; speakers have a choice of what to say and how to say it; they receive feedback from the listener that will verify that a purpose has been achieved. Authentic materials are used. Students usually work in small groups.

Interaction: Student-Teacher and Student-Student

Teacher initiates interactions between students and participates sometimes. Students interact a great deal with each other in many configurations.

Dealing with Feelings

Emphasis is on developing motivation to learn through establishing meaningful, purposeful things to do with the target language. Individuality is encouraged, as well as cooperation with peers, which both contribute to sense of emotional security with the target language.

View of Language, Culture

Language is for communication. Linguistic competence must be coupled with an ability to convey intended meaning appropriately in different social contexts. Culture is the everyday lifestyle of native speakers of the target language. Nonverbal behaviour is important.

Aspects of Language the Approach Emphasizes

Functions are emphasized over forms, with simple forms learned for each function at first, then more complex forms. Students work at discourse level. They work on speaking, listening, reading, and writing from the beginning. Consistent focus on negotiated meaning.

Role of Students' Native Language

Students' native language usually plays no role.

Means for Evaluation

Informal evaluation takes place when teacher advises or communicates; formal evaluation is by means of an integrative test with a real communicative function.

Response to Students' Errors

Errors of form are considered natural; students with incomplete knowledge of form can still succeed as communicators.

For Further Reading

General

Bowen, D., H. Madsen, and A. Hilferty. 1986. *TESOL techniques and procedures*. Rowley, MA: Newbury House.

Larsen-Freeman, D. 1986. *Techniques and principles in language teaching*. New York: Oxford University Press.

Richards, J. and T. Rodgers. 1986. *Approaches and methods in language teaching*. Cambridge, MA: Cambridge University Press.

On the Grammar-Translation Method

Chastain, K. 1976. *Developing second-language skills* 2nd ed., Chapter 5. Chicago: Rand-McNally.

Kelly, L. G. 1969. *25 centuries of language teaching*. Rowley, MA: Newbury House.

On the Direct Method

Diller, K. C. 1978. *The language teaching controversy*. Rowley, MA: Newbury House.

On the Audio-Lingual Method

Chastain, K. 1976. *Developing second-language skills* 2nd ed., Chapter 5. Chicago: Rand McNally.

Rivers, W. 1968. *Teaching foreign-language skills*, Chapters 2-4. Chicago: University of Chicago Press.

On the Silent Way

Gattegno, C. 1972. *Teaching foreign languages in schools: The silent way* 2nd ed.. New York: Educational Solutions 95 University Place, New York, NY 10003.

Gattegno, C. 1976. *The common sense of teaching foreign languages*. New York: Educational Solutions.

Stevick, E. 1980. *Teaching languages: A way and ways*, Chapters 3-6. Rowley, MA: Newbury House.

On Suggestopedia

Lozanov, G. 1982. Suggestology and suggestopedia. In R.E. Blair Ed., *Innovative approaches to language teaching*. Rowley, MA: Newbury House.

Stevick, E. 1980. *Teaching languages: A way and ways*, Chapters 18-19. Rowley, MA: Newbury House.

On Community Language Learning

Curran, C.A. 1976. *Counselling-learning in second language*. East Dubuque, IL: Counselling-Learning Publications.

Rardin, J. 1976. A counselling-learning model for second language learning. *TESOL Newsletter* 10 2.

Stevick, E. 1980. *Teaching languages: A way and ways*. Chapters 7-17. Rowley, MA: Newbury House.

On the Total Physical Response Method

Asher, J. 1982. *Learning another language through actions. The complete teacher's guidebook* 2nd ed.. Los Gatos, CA: Sky Oaks Productions.

Blair, R.W., ed. 1982. *Innovative approaches to language teaching*. Rowley, MA: Newbury House.

Krashen, S., and T. Terrell. 1983. *The natural approach*. San Francisco, CA: Alemany Press.

On the Communicative Approach

Brumfit, C.J. and K. Johnson, eds. 1979. *The communicative approach to language teaching*. Oxford: Oxford University Press.

Johnson, K.and K. Morrow, eds. 1981. *Communication in the classroom*. Essex, UK: Longman.

Littlewood, W. 1981. *Communicative language teaching*. Cambridge, MA: Cambridge University Press.

Savignon, S. 1983. *Communicative competence: Theory and classroom practice*. Boston: Addison-Wesley.

Widdowson, H.G. 1978. *Teaching language as communication*. Oxford: Oxford University Press.

Wilkins, D.A. 1976. *Notional syllabuses*. Oxford: Oxford University Press.

Editor's Note: The above summary, compiled by Gina Doggett, is based on Diane Larsen-Freeman, *Techniques and Principles in Language Teaching*. New York: Oxford University Press, 1986. The report was prepared with funding from the Office of Educational Research and Improvement, U.S. Department of Education for ERIC Clearing House on Language and Linguistics.It is reproduced here with the permission of ERIC Clearing House on Language and Linguistics.

Reprinted from: Gina Doggett, "Eight Approaches to Language Teaching." *Mosaic*, 1, 3 (Spring 1994): 10-12.

23 Conceptual Fluency Theory and Second-Language Teaching

Marcel Danesi and Anthony Mollica

In order for the student to be able to converse "naturally", in a conceptual accurate manner, the authors propose the application of conceptual metaphor theory to second-language teaching.

Introduction

The second-language classroom today has never before been so sophisticated in terms of instructional methodology and the use of advanced technology. This is because the teaching of second languages has been informed throughout this century by theories and findings coming out of psychology and linguistics, aiming to validate or refute teaching practices. This interplay between the research domain and instructional practices has produced teachers who are among the most informed and pedagogically-knowledgeable teachers of all time. As we approach the end of the twentieth century, it is, in fact, difficult to think of the second-language classroom in high school, college, or university as anything but a highly-advanced learning environment.

So, why is there, despite the apparent sophistication, still so much discussion going on in scholarly journals, and among practitioners, about what to do to make student discourse more native-like? The recent literature has even rekindled an old debate:

* Should we continue to focus on developing in the learner a functional knowledge of the uses of the target language (*communicative competence*), as we have been doing over the last three decades? Or,
* Should we return to the traditional deployment of techniques that aim to foster control of linguistic structure (*linguistic competence*)?

This debate has been reignited, no doubt, because teachers continue to be frustrated by the inability of their students to speak in ways that go beyond the "textbook literalness" of classroom discourse. The nagging and persistent problem of second-language teaching can be articulated as follows:

> Despite considerable research in second-language learning in class-room environments in this century, and despite the many pedagogical applications that such work has made possible, teachers still complain about the fact that the student's autonomous discourse lacks the conceptual accuracy that characterizes native-speaker discourse.

The manifestations of second-language discourse bear witness to the fact that learners have had little or no opportunity to access directly the conceptual structures inherent in the target language and culture.

The purpose of this article is to present an overview of a paradigm that was put forward a few years ago labeled *conceptual fluency theory* (e.g. Danesi 1993a, 1993b, 1994, 1995, Russo 1997) that aimed to address this very problem. Several practical projects applying conceptual fluency theory have been undertaken recently, leading to the development of various textbooks and related materials (Danesi, Lettieri, and Bancheri 1996, Danesi 1998).

In our view, conceptual fluency theory has important implications for methodology, material development and syllabus design in second-language teaching.

The Primary Claim

The notion of conceptual fluency was derived in large part from the research initiated in 1977 by Howard Pollio and his associates which showed that metaphor is hardly a frill in discourse. The average speaker of English, for instance, invents approximately 3000 metaphors per week and employs over 7000 idiomatic forms (Pollio, Barlow, Fine, and Pollio 1977). This discovery led in the 1980s to the development of two significant trends:

1. *conceptual metaphor theory* (Lakoff and Johnson 1980, Lakoff 1987, Johnson 1987), and
2. a branch of linguistics that now comes under the rubric of *cognitive linguistics* (Langacker 1987, 1990. Taylor 1995).

But conceptual fluency theory was also born of classroom experience with student discourse. Over the last seven years, the authors of this article have undertaken several research projects designed to gear second-language teaching in all its components – methodology, materials development, testing, etc. – towards imparting conceptual fluency to the student, without underplaying the roles of both grammatical and communicative competence. The latter two, in fact, are to be considered constituent aspects of verbal fluency. Using these two notions, the *problem* of second-language teaching enunciated above can now be rephrased as follows:

> While student discourse often manifests a high degree of verbal fluency, it invariably seems to lack the conceptual fluency that characterizes the corresponding discourse of native speakers. To put it another way, students "speak" with the memorized formal and communicative structures of the second language, but they "think" in terms of their native conceptual systems: i.e. students typically use second-language words and communicative protocols as "carriers" of their own native language "concepts." When the native and second-language conceptual systems coincide in an area of discourse, then the student discourse is assessable as "natural"; when they do not, the student discourse manifests an asymmetry between language form and conceptual content. What student discourse often lacks, in other words, is conceptual fluency.

Conceptual Fluency Theory

The research in cognitive linguistics suggests rather strongly that to be conceptually fluent in a language is to know, in large part, how that language "reflects" or encodes concepts on the basis of metaphorical reasoning. This kind of knowledge, like grammatical and communicative (pragmatic) knowledge, is by and large unconscious in native speakers. If one were to speak about "time" in English, our mind would scan conceptual domains that typically reveal metaphorical reasoning. So, if one were to say something like

> *That job cost me an hour,*

the conceptual reasoning enlisted by the speaker can be seen to have the form *time is money*. Of course, the speaker could have enlisted other appropriate metaphorical ideas – e.g.

1. He's wasting my time.
2. That's not worth the time or the effort (= *time is a valuable commodity*).
3. Build in some time for her too. (= *ideas are buildings*); etc. –

or combine them in various ways. The grammatical forms and categories that are used in actual discourse are, according to this line of research (e.g. Lakoff and Johnson 1980), consistently linked cohesively to such metaphorical forms.

This kind of conceptual programming is exactly what seems to be lacking in student discourse (Danesi 1993a, 1993b, Russo 1997). This implies that students have had little or no opportunity to access the metaphorically-structured conceptual domains inherent in the second language. *Metaphorical competence* – to coin an analogous term to linguistic and communicative competence – is almost completely lacking from second-language learners.

The work on metaphor in anthropology and linguistics over the past three decades (e.g. Dundes 1972, Beck 1982, Lakoff and Johnson 1980, Kšvecses 1986, 1988, 1990, Lakoff 1987, Johnson 1987) has demonstrated the validity of metaphorical competence and thus can be used to sustain the notion of conceptual fluency in second-language acquisition. The implications of this line of research for second-language teaching are quite clear. The cognitive programming of discourse in metaphorical ways is a basic property of native-speaker competence. As a competence, it can be thought about pedagogically in ways that are parallel to the other competencies on which teaching methodology has traditionally focused (linguistic and communicative).

Particularly influential in getting metaphorical competence onto the agenda of the social and cognitive sciences was George Lakoff and Mark Johnson's 1980 book, *Metaphors We Live By*. The innovative claim of that book was that metaphor is the cornerstone of discourse.

First, Lakoff and Johnson assert what Aristotle claimed two millennia before, namely that there are two types of concepts – *concrete* and *abstract*. But the two scholars add a remarkable twist to this Aristotelian notion – namely that *abstract concepts* are built up systematically from *concrete* ones through metaphor. They refer to abstract concepts as *conceptual metaphors*. These are generalized metaphorical formulas that define specific abstractions. For example, the expression "John is a gorilla" is really a token of something more general, namely, *people are animals*. This is why we say that *John* or *Mary* or *whoever* is a gorilla, snake, pig, puppy, and so on. Each specific metaphor ("John is a gorilla," "Mary is a snake," etc.) is not an isolated example of poetic fancy. It is really an example of a more general metaphorical idea – *people are animals*. Such formulas are what Lakoff and Johnson call *conceptual metaphors*:

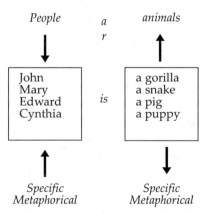

Each of the two parts of the *conceptual metaphor* is called a *domain: people* is called the *target domain* because it is the abstract topic itself (the "target" of the conceptual metaphor); and *animals* is called the *source domain* because it is the class of vehicle that delivers the metaphor (the "source" of the metaphorical concept). An *abstract concept* can now be defined simply as a "mapping" of one domain onto the other. This model suggests that abstract concepts are formed systematically through such mappings and that specific metaphors are traces to the target and source domains. So, when we hear people talking, for instance, of *ideas* in terms of *geometrical figures and relations*

1. Those ideas are circular.
2. I don't see the point of your idea.
3. Her ideas are central to the discussion.
4. Their ideas are diametrically opposite. etc. –

we can now easily identify the two domains as ideas (= target domain) and geometrical figures/relations (= source domain) and, therefore, the conceptual metaphor as: ideas are geometrical figures and relations.

Conceptual metaphors pervade common discourse. A few examples will suffice to make this evident.

Happiness is up/Sadness is down
1. Today she's feeling *up*.
2. Generally she feels *down*.
3. His comment *boosted* my spirits.
4. My mood *sank* after she told me what happened.
5. His joke gave me a *lift*.

Health and life are up/Sickness and death are down
1. Everyone in my family is at the *peak* of health.
2. Unfortunately, my cousin *fell* ill.
3. My job is an *uphill* struggle.
4. Lazarus *rose* from the dead.
5. They're *sinking* fast.

Light is knowledge/Dark is ignorance
1. The whole class was *illuminated* by that professor.
2. I was left in the *dark* about what happened.
3. Her explanation is very *clear*.
4. Quantum theory is *obscure*.
5. His example *shed light* on several matters.

Theories are buildings
1. Hers is a *well-constructed* theory.
2. His theory too is on solid *ground*.

3. But that theory needs more *support*.
4. Otherwise the theory will *collapse* under criticism.
5. Alexander put together the *framework* of a very interesting theory.

Ideas and theories are plants
1. My professor's ideas have come to *fruition*.
2. That's a *budding* theory.
3. Plato's ideas have contemporary *offshoots*.
4. That idea has become a *branch* of mathematics.

Ideas are commodities
1. My friend certainly knows how to *package* his ideas.
2. However, that idea just won't *sell*.
3. There's no *market* for that idea.
4. That's a *worthless* idea.

As Lakoff and Johnson emphasize, we do not detect the presence of metaphor in such common expressions because of repeated usage. We no longer interpret the word *see* in sentences such as

1. I don't *see* what you mean.
2. Do you *see* what I'm saying?

in metaphorical terms, because its use in such expressions has become so familiar to us. But the association between the biological act of seeing outside the body with the imaginary act of seeing within the mind was originally the source of the conceptual metaphor *seeing is understanding/believing/thinking*, which now permeates common discourse:

1. There is more to this than *meets the eye*.
2. I have a different *point of view*.
3. It all depends on how you *look* at it.
4. I take a dim view of the whole matter.
5. I never *see eye to eye* on things with you.
6. You have a different *worldview* than I do.
7. Your ideas have given me great insight into life.

The next important point made by Lakoff and Johnson is that there are three general kinds of psychological processes involved in conceptualization:

1. Mental orientation
2. Conceptualization process
3. An elaboration of the two above.

1. Mental orientation
The first psychological process involves mental orientation. This produces concepts that are derived from our physical experiences of up vs. down, back vs. front, near vs. far, etc. For example, the

experience of up vs. down underlies such conceptual metaphors as:

- *Happiness is up* = I'm feeling up.
- *Sadness is down* = She's feeling down today.
- *More is up* = My income rose (went up) last year.
- *Less is down* = Her salary went down when she changed jobs.

In later work, Lakoff and Johnson referred to orientational patterns such as *up vs. down, near vs. far, etc. as image schemas* (Lakoff 1987, Johnson 1987). These are defined as largely unconscious mental outlines of recurrent shapes, actions, dimensions, etc. that derive from perception and sensation. Image schemas are so deeply rooted that we are hardly ever aware of their control over conceptualization. But they can always be conjured up easily. If someone were to ask you to explain an idiom such as *spill the beans*, you would not likely have a conscious image schema involving beans and the action of spilling them. However, if that same person were to ask you the following questions

1. Where were the beans before they were spilled?
2. How big was the container?
3. Was the spilling on purpose or accidental? etc.

then you would no doubt start to visualize the appropriate schema; that is, you would see the beans as kept in a container; the container as being about the size of the human head; etc.

2. Conceptualization process
The second type of conceptualization process, according to Lakoff and Johnson, involves *ontological* thinking. This produces conceptual metaphors in which activities, emotions, ideas, etc. are associated with entities and substances:

1. *Time is a valuable commodity* = That is not worth my time.
2. *The mind is a container* = I'm full of memories.
3. *Anger is fluid in a container* = You make my blood boil.

3. An elaboration of the two above
The third type of process is an *elaboration* of the other two. This produces structural metaphors that distend orientational and ontological concepts. A structural metaphor is a conceptual metaphor built from existing conceptual metaphors of an orientational or ontological nature: for example, the structural metaphor *time is a resource* is built from *time is a resource = a quantity*:

- *Argument is war* = I demolished his argument.
- *Labor is a resource* = He was consumed by his job.
- *Time is a resource* = Time is money.

To get a firmer sense of how such abstract concepts shape

discourse, consider the argument is *war* metaphor. The target domain of *argument is* conceptualized in terms of *warlike activities* (the source domain), and thus in terms

- of battles that can be won or lost,
- of positions that can be attacked or guarded,
- of ground that can be gained or lost,
- of lines of attack that can be abandoned or defended,
- and so on.

These warlike images are so embedded in our mind that we do not normally realize that they guide our perception of arguments. But they are nonetheless there, surfacing regularly in such common expressions as the following:

1. Your claims are *indefensible*.
2. You *attacked* all my *weak points*.
3. Your criticisms were *right on target*.
4. I *demolished* his argument.
5. I've never *won* an argument.
6. She *shot down* all my points.
7. If you use that *strategy*, I'll *wipe you out*.

The last relevant point made by Lakoff and Johnson in their truly fascinating book is that culture is built on metaphor, since conceptual metaphors coalesce into a system of meaning that holds together the entire network of associated meanings in the culture. This is accomplished by a kind of "higher-order" metaphorizing – that is, as target domains are associated with many kinds of source domains (orientational, ontological, structural), the concepts they underlie become increasingly more complex, leading to what Lakoff and Johnson call *cultural* or *cognitive models*. To see what this means, consider the target domain of *ideas* again.

The following three conceptual metaphors, among many others, deliver the meaning of this concept in three separate ways:

Ideas are food

1. Those ideas left a *sour taste* in my mouth.
2. It's hard to *digest* all those ideas at once.
3. Even though he is a *voracious reader, he can't chew all those ideas*.
4. That teacher is always *spoonfeeding* her students.
5. That idea has *deep roots*.

Ideas are persons

1. Darwin is the *father* of modern biology.
2. Those medieval ideas continue to *live on* even today.
3. Cognitive linguistics is still in its *infancy*.

4. Maybe we should *resurrect* that ancient idea.
5. She *breathed* new life into that idea.

Ideas are fashion

1. That idea went out of *style* several years ago.
2. Those scientists are the *avant garde* of their field.
3. Those revolutionary ideas are no longer in *vogue*.
4. Semiotics has become truly *chic*.
5. That idea is old *hat*.

Recall from examples of everyday discourse cited above that there are many other ways of conceptualizing ideas – for example, in terms of *buildings, plants, commodities, geometry*, and *seeing*. The constant juxtaposition of such conceptual formulas in common discourse produces, cumulatively, a *cultural model* of ideas (see Figure 1).

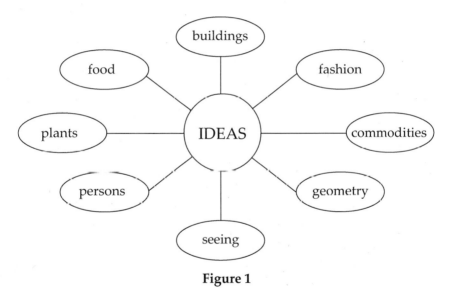

Figure 1

The gist of Lakoff and Johnson's 1980 work is that metaphor is at the basis of abstract thought and common discourse, although we are largely unaware of its presence. Everything written in this essay, too, has been structured by metaphorical cultural models. These have served us well in exposing the subject matter of semiotics. So, too, with every verbal text.

There are, of course, other figures of speech that occur in everyday discourse. But following Lakoff and Johnson's discovery of conceptual metaphors, these are now considered subcategories of the general process of metaphorization. Nevertheless, there are two that are regularly studied separately – *metonymy* and *irony* – because of their particular semantic characteristics.

Metonymy is the use of an entity to refer to another that is related to it:

1. She likes to read *Emily Dickinson*. (= *the writings of Emily Dickinson*).
2. He's in *dance*. (= *the dancing profession*).
3. My mom frowns on *blue jeans*. (= *the wearing of blue jeans*).
4. New *windshield wipers* will satisfy him. (= *the state of having new wipers*).

Synecdoche is a particular type of metonymy; it is the use of the part to represent the whole:

1. The *automobile* is destroying our health. (= *the collection of automobiles*).
2. We need a couple of *strong bodies* for our teams. (= *strong people*).
3. I've got a new *set of wheels*. (= *car*).
4. We need *new blood* in this organization. (= *new people*).

A conceptual formula of this type that requires special mention is: *the face is the person*:

1. He's just another *pretty face*.
2. There are an awful lot of *faces* in the audience.
3. We need some new *faces* around here.

It is interesting to note that metaphorical and metonymic cultural models permeate other facets of cultural expression and behaviour. The *face is the person* concept, for instance, also crystallizes in the nonverbal domain, especially in the art of portraiture. In other words, conceptual metaphors surface not only in common discourse, but also in nonverbal codes, rituals, and behaviours as well. The metaphorical formula *justice is blind*, for example, crops up not only in conversations, but also in pictorial representations. This is why there are statues of blindfolded women inside courtrooms to symbolize *justice*. The metaphorical expression *the scales of justice*, too, is evident in the sculptures of scales near or inside justice buildings. Similarly, the *love is a sweet taste* concept finds expression not only in discourse

1. She's my *sweetheart*.
2. I love my *honey*. etc.

but in rituals of love-making in Western culture. This is why sweets are given to a loved one on St. Valentine's day, why matrimonial love is symbolized at a wedding ceremony by the eating of a cake, why lovers sweeten their breaths with candy before kissing, and so on. Any ritualistic display of love will depend on what concept people infer to be more representative of a specific situation; for example, at weddings the *sweetness* concept would probably be seen to fit the situation; whereas the *physical attraction* concept would most likely be considered pertinent during other kinds of courtship performances.

Concepts and Grammar

The above discussion lays the basis for an outline of conceptual fluency theory in second-language teaching. But the question that now arises is whether or not conceptual fluency teaching is really no more than a fancy term for the study of idiomatic expressions. First, as the above examples show, the use of metaphor in discourse is not an idiomatic option. It is the basis of abstract conceptualization, forming a system of thought that permeates all of discourse. Second, conceptual fluency teaching has been extended to provide a framework for relating grammatical categories to metaphorical concepts (Langacker 1990, Taylor 1995, Danesi 1998).

As a concrete example of how the two areas are interrelated, consider the use of the prepositions *since* and *for* in sentences such as the following in English:

1. I have been living here *since* 1980.
2. I have known Lucy *since* November.
3. I have not been able to sleep *since* Monday.

1. I have been living here *for* fifteen years.
2. I have known Lucy *for* nine months.
3. I have not been able to sleep *for* five days.

An analysis of the complements that follow since or *for* reveals that those that follow since are "points in time," i.e. they are complements that reflect a conception of time as a "point" on a "timeline" which shows specific years, months, etc.: "1980," "November," "Monday," etc. Complements that follow *for*, on the other hand, reflect a conception of time as a "quantity": "fifteen years," "nine months," "five days," etc. These two conceptual domains – *time is a point and time is a quantity* – have an underlying metaphorical form, reflecting a propensity to imagine an abstract notion like "time" in terms of something concrete. These can now be seen to have a specific effect at the level of syntax by motivating a grammatical dichotomy – complements introduced by *since* are reflexes of the conceptual domain *time is a point*; those introduced by *for* are reflexes of the conceptual domain *time is a (measurable) quantity*. This is, in fact, the kind of *rule of grammar* that conceptual fluency teaching makes possible – it now relates how two specific domains of conceptualization have worked their way into the grammar. In a word, this rule stipulates how a grammatical dichotomy *reflects* a conceptual dichotomy. In French, Italian, and Spanish, on the other hand, this rule does not exist; *depuis, da* and *desde*, respectively, is used in both instances:

French

> *J'habite ici* depuis *1980.*
> *J'habite ici* depuis *quinze ans.*

Italian

> *Vivo qui* dal *1980.*
> *Vivo qui* da *quindici anni.*

Spanish

> *Vivo aquí* desde *1980.*
> *Vivo aquí* desde hace *quince años.*

and so on. Our claim is that students will be in a better position to avoid making typical "errors" such as

French

> *J'habite ici pour quinze ans.

Italian

> *Vivo qui per quindici anni.

Spanish

> *Vivo aquí por quince años.

only when they learn to conceptualize "time" in French,Italian, or Spanish, appropriately, grasping the conceptual differences between "time in English" and "time in French, Italian, or Spanish". Explaining the phenomenon of depuis, da and desde in such cases in any other way (e.g. in grammatical or lexical terms) will continue, in our view, to prove ineffectual.

Take, as one other example, the selection of certain verbs in particular types of sentences in French, Italian and Spanish. The verb *faire, fare* and *hacer* "to make" is used to convey a weather situation

> Il fait chaud. Il fait froid.
> Fa caldo. Fa freddo.
> Hace calor. Hace frío.

(literally) "it makes hot", "it makes cold." The physical state of "hotness" and "coldness" is conveyed instead by the verb *être, essere* and *estar* "to be" when referring to objects:

French

> L'eau est chaude.   L'eau est froide.

Italian

    L'acqua *è* calda.   L'acqua *è* fredda.

Spanish

    El agua *está* caliente.   El agua *está* fría.

by avoir, avere and tener *"to have" when referring to people.*

French

    Il a chaud.   Il a froid.

Italian

    Ha caldo.   Ha freddo.

Spanish

    Tiene calor.   Tiene frío.

The use of one verb or the other

    faire, être, avoir
    fare, essere, avere
    hacer, estar, tener

is motivated by an underlying metaphorical conceptualization of bodies and the environment as containers. So, the "containment context" in which the quality of "coldness" or "hotness" is located determines the verbal category to be employed. If it is in the environment, it is "made" by Nature (*Il fait chaud. Fa freddo. Hace frío*); if it is in a human being, then the body "has" it (*Il a froid. Ha freddo. Tiene frío.*); and if it is in an object, then the object "is" its container (*L'eau est froide. L'acqua è fredda. El agua está fría.*).

The point to be made here is that our unconsciously-embedded concept of "time" as a "point on a line" and as a "quantity," or of "hotness" and "coldness" as being contained in Nature, people, or things, constitute conceptual domains that have reflexes or leave reflexes in the grammars of specific languages. Knowledge of such differentiated reflexive properties is what guides competent translators implicitly when they convert one language text into another successfully. *Grammar* in conceptual fluency teaching is definable, therefore, as a system that reflects the underlying *conceptual* system guiding thought and language.

As a final consideration, any refinement or elaboration of the notion of "reflexive grammatical rule" will have to take into account the presence of different "orders" of metaphor. Take, for instance, the following conceptual models of "ideas." These models are represented by an instance frequently in common discourse by utterances such as the following:

Model 1: ideas/thoughts are food

1. What he said left a *bitter taste* in my mouth.
2. I cannot *digest* all that information.
3. He is a *voracious* reader.
4. We do not need to *spoon feed* our students.
5. That idea has been *fermenting* in me for years.

Model 2: ideas/thoughts are people

1. Darwin is the *father* of modern biology.
2. Medieval ideas are *alive* and *well*.
3. Artificial Intelligence is still in its *infancy*.
4. That idea should be *resurrected*.
5. She *breathe*d new life into that idea.

Model 3: ideas/thoughts are clothing/fashion

1. That idea is not *in vogue* any longer.
2. New York has become a center for *avant garde* thinking.
3. Revolution is out of style these days.
4. Studying semiotics has become quite *chic*.
5. That idea is old *hat*.

These sentences suggest that we conceptualize thought processes as extensions or analogues of physical objects and people. Thoughts, like food, can be taken into the mind, like clothing can be in style or not, and so on. Often, however, the conceptual process involves reference to other pre-established conceptual domains, such as, for instance, those based on Euclidean geometry:

Model 4: thoughts are geometrical figures

1. I don't see the *point* of your idea.
2. Your ideas are *tangential* to what I'm thinking.
3. Those ideas are logically *circular*.

These examples show that there are different degrees or "orders" of concepts. The *ideas are food* model, for example, is a lower-order concept because it connects a universal physical process – *eating* – to an abstraction – *thinking* – directly. But, the *thoughts are geometrical figures* model reveals a higher-order conceptualization, since geometrical figures and notions are themselves concepts.

In terms of second-language teaching, the idea would be at first to identify and catalogue the vehicles that underlie specific topics, and then match them to the grammatical categories that reflect them. So, for instance, when analyzing sentences that allude to the "hotness" or "coldness" in French, Italian or Spanish (the topic), it will be necessary to keep in mind how the conceptualization of hotness/coldness as substances that are contained in specific contexts (the vehicles) is codified into a selection rule involving the verbs *faire, avoir,* and *être* – *fare, avere, essere* – *hacer, tener. estar* – (including relevant morphological information). It is interesting to note that in French, Italian, and Spanish "being right", "being sleepy", etc. are also conceptualized as "contained" substances. This is why to say "I am right," "I am sleepy," etc. in French, Italian and Spanish one must say

French:

    J'ai raison.   J'ai sommeil.

Italian:

    Ho ragione.   Ho sonno.

Spanish:

    Tengo razón.   Tengo sueño.

Pedagogical Implications

Research conducted previously on university students of Italian (Danesi 1992, 1993a) suggests that typical classroom learners show virtually no traces of metaphorical competence, even after several years of study. The reason for this is not that they are incapable of learning metaphor, but more likely that they have never been exposed in formal ways to the conceptual system of the target language and culture. To be "conceptually fluent" in the second language the student must be able to convert common experiences into conceptually and linguistically appropriate models. At the present time there seems to be very little in second-language methodology that takes this into account.

Metaphorical competence is as teachable as linguistic or communicative competence. It can be claimed, in fact, that this can be done by simply structuring designated units of study around conceptual domains (time, weather, love, etc.), and then by teaching the appropriate grammar and communication patterns of the language as "reflexes" of these domains. If the grammatical system is viewed as a reflexive code of an underlying conceptual system, then a radical rethinking of the second-language classroom will have to be envisaged.

Actually, suggestions exist in the relevant pedagogical literature which we think fit in nicely with the idea of conceptual fluency. Masella and Portner (1981), for instance, show how the term capo for "head" can be taught as the onceptual source for *capostazione, capoluogo* and *capo d'anno; naso* ("nose") as the source for *ficcanaso, annusare,* etc. Nuessel and Cicogna (1993) suggest simply presenting students with metaphorical statements – e.g.

Lui è una volpe ("He's a fox") – and then following this up with questions designed to unravel the conceptual structure of the statements:

- What activities are common to both elements in the metaphor? (verbs)
- How are these activities carried out? (adverbs)
- What characteristics do both elements possess? (adjectives)? (Nuessel and Cicogna 1993: 324).

And Maiguashca (1988) shows how contrasting native-language metaphorical vehicles with the target language will prove to be effective in imparting conceptual fluency.

A Practical Example

In preparing instructional methodology or materials focusing on conceptual fluency, teachers should first examine the concepts to be taught. Let us take, as a case in point, the theme of "sports" in Italian. The first step is to identify the main conceptual domains that allow native speakers to deliver this concept in discourse. The following seven examples coincide with English conceptual domains (see Figure 2).

CONCEPTUAL DOMAIN	EXAMPLES IN ACTUAL DISCOURSE
fortuna (*luck*)	Quella squadra è *fortunata*. La loro vincita è *imprevedibile*.
guerra (*war*)	Quella squadra è stata *sconfitta*. Quella squadra ha un buon attacco e una buona *tattica*. Quella partita è stata una *battaglia*.
gioco (*game*)	Che bella *mossa*! Quella squadra ha *centrato*.
economia (*economy*)	Quella squadra ha *incassato* dei gol. Quella squadra ha *pagato* il gol.
alimentazione (*food*)	Quella squadra ha una *fame* di vincere. Loro sono *digiuni* di vittorie.
scienza (*science*)	Sono giocatori *sperimentati*.

Figure 2

This informs the teacher that in order for students to talk or write in a conceptually-natural way about sport in Italian, they will have to be exposed to these domains, which cohere into the following cultural model that the student must acquire (see Figure 3).

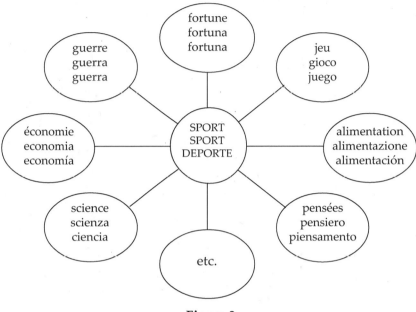

Figure 3

After this initial analysis, the rest consists in straightforward traditional pedagogy: i.e. the teacher would want to do such things as:

- prepare dialogues that exemplify this model;
- expose the students to actual sports broadcasts; highlighting how this model is employed;
- prepare exercise and activity material, whereby the students must identify the domains and explain them;
- require the students to write their own sportscast using the above as a framework;
- etc.

So, for instance, when teaching English-speaking students about the weather in Italian (the topic), it will be necessary:

1. to inform them about the conceptualization of hotness/coldness as substances that are contained in specific contexts (the vehicles);
2. to teach them how to use the verbs fare, avere, and essere as

reflexes of the vehicles (including relevant morphosyntactic information);
3.   to develop appropriate textual and practice materials based on this explanatory framework.

Considerations

There are many similar ways in which conceptual-fluency teaching can be incorporated into classroom practice. Shibles (1989), too, has shown how easily metaphorical vehicles for emotion in German can be compared to English ones for pedagogical purposes in ways that are very similar to the ones suggested here. But in our view, the most significant implication of conceptual-fluency teaching is in the area of syllabus design. How can a conceptually-based syllabus be organized? In our view, the main idea would be to identify and catalogue the conceptual domains that deliver specific topics in discourse, together with a "reflexive" analysis of the grammatical/communicative categories that encode them. This entails the development of appropriate techniques for identifying grammatical and semantic units in terms of the conceptual domains they reflect. A "conceptual syllabus" would, then, connect the verbal categories to be learned with their related conceptual domains.

Actually, the idea of making concepts the basis for the teaching syllabus was forged by the so-called "notional-functional" theorists of the early '70s (e.g. Van Ek 1975, Wilkins 1976), who deployed speech-act and notional typologies as the organizing frameworks for developing the syllabus (and more recently for developing reading skills [see also Kaplan 1978, Piper 1985, Grabe 1991, Leki 1991 on this point]). Throughout the 1970s, and for most of the 1980s, this new functionalism in language teaching was greeted with widespread enthusiasm throughout Europe and America. Unlike the traditional grammar-based methods, it provided the teacher with greater room for imparting conceptual fluency. But now that the wave of enthusiasm has passed, it has become obvious that notional-functional teaching leaves many gaps to fill and many important questions unanswered. In our view, the main problem with the "notions" delineated by the notional-functional theorists was that they were not conceived in terms of conceptual-fluency teaching. The teacher was simply given a typology of the notions with verbal illustrations. A conceptual-fluency analysis, such as the ones illustrated in this paper, was never envisaged by the functional-notional methodologists. This is not to belittle the excellent work done by those theorists. The research on metaphor that has now become so widely known was really not available to them at the time.

Conceptual-fluency teaching also entails a re-deployment of contrastive analysis as a heuristic pedagogical technique. In its original form, contrastive analysis came to be accepted both as a theory of second-language acquisition and as an organizing principle around which to plan for language teaching. The view was that the native language was a template used by the learner for deciphering and organizing the linguistic and communicative categories of the target language. Perhaps the greatest problem with contrastive analysis is that it portrays the process of second-language acquisition solely in terms of a flow from the native to the target language, assigning no active role to the role of conceptualization in this process.

With or without contrastive analysis, modern instructional techniques have been rather successful in training language learners to gain a firm control over grammar and communication. So, the issue of whether grammatical syllabi and formalistic instructional styles are more or less productive than communicative or functional ones is, in our view, a moot one.

As Savignon (1992) has suggested, it is perhaps more appropriate, and certainly more useful, to think of the two kinds of syllabi as cooperative and complementary contributors to second-language acquisition in the classroom, not as antagonistic or mutually exclusive competitors. Both these kinds of knowledge, as mentioned, are part of verbal fluency. We believe that contrastive analysis will come to have an increasingly larger role to play in the future for studying conceptual systems, not verbal ones. By documenting and analyzing many student discourse errors on the basis of their conceptual appropriateness, we envision the contrastive technique to be used as rather straightforward. Rather than contrasting verbal structures on their own, it will be necessary to contrast them in terms of the conceptual domains they reflect. The errors that result from the unconscious transfer of conceptual formulas can be labeled "conceptual transfers" (Danesi and Di Pietro 1991: 55).

An important question for future research would thus seem to be: To what extent do the conceptual domains of the native and target cultures overlap and contrast? The notion of conceptual fluency, therefore, provides second-language acquisition researchers with a convenient category for viewing certain aspects of interlanguage behaviour that cannot be explained in other ways, such as, for example, the common observation that student-produced discourse texts seem to follow a native-language conceptual flow that is "clothed", so to speak, in target-language grammar and vocabulary. The questions that a conceptually-focused conceptual analysis would ask are therefore:

- What kinds of conceptual interferences come from the student's native conceptual system? (interconceptual interference).
- How much conceptual interference is generated by the target language itself? (intraconceptual interference)?

Concluding Remarks

The second-language teacher wishing to make conceptual fluency the primary focus of teaching should take a number of things into consideration.

1. The materials chosen for a course should reflect a learning flow that starts with experiential learning techniques and ends with more analytical tasks. This sets up a learning flow from conceptualization to verbalization.

2. The teacher will always have to consider which grammatical and semantic categories reflect conceptual structures or domains. The guiding question becomes: What are the verbal clues that reveal conceptual domains? In this paper, the prepositions *since* and *for* were related to the conceptual system as reflexes of differentiated conceptual metaphors: time is a point and *time is a quantity*. The work on cognitive grammar by Langacker (e.g. 1987, 1990) and others is leading the way in showing us how to conduct extensive analyses of this type.

3. To what extent and in what ways, if any, conceptual fluency relates to, or is embedded in, the native speaker's world knowledge? It must always be kept in mind that metaphorically-shaped knowledge is probably just one possible form in which knowledge of the world is encoded and decoded by humans. As Levin (1988: 10) has aptly remarked, there appear to be many modes of knowledge:

innate knowledge, personal knowledge, tacit knowledge, spiritual knowledge, declarative and procedural knowledge, knowing that and knowing how, certitude (as well as certainty), and many other varieties.

The more appropriate goal for the teacher should be, therefore, to determine to what extent language is based on conceptual knowledge and to what extent it is based on other forms of knowledge.

4. If concepts are to be placed at the core of language courses and curricula, on what basis should they be selected and sequenced? In our view, the conceptual syllabus should be integrated with grammatical and communicative syllabi, since these latter two can be seen to reflect it. As mentioned, units in a textbook, for instance, could be planned around topics

such as "time," "love," "health," and then drafted with the "reflexive principle" in mind: i.e. with the idea that language structures (verbal tenses, prepositions, etc.) "reflect" conceptual ones.

The idea of incorporating conceptual-fluency teaching into second-language teaching is meant to be a target for further consideration and research. Not all domains of language and language learning are tied to the conceptual system, as it has been defined here. The interlanguage studies have amply documented error phenomena that are purely grammatical, communicative, etc. We should, of course, continue to assess the role played by such mechanisms in the overall process of classroom language teaching. However, in our view the notion of conceptual fluency can no longer be ignored. The work of Lakoff and Johnson and others has shown that there is a systematicity to metaphorical concepts. The process of learning the conceptual system is, arguably, identical to the one enlisted for learning grammar and communication. To ignore metaphor is to ignore a large segment of the native-speaker's competence.

References

Beck, B. 1982. "Root Metaphor Patterns." *Semiotic Inquiry*, 2: 86- 97.

Danesi, M. 1986. "The Role of Metaphor in Second Language Pedagogy." *Rassegna Italiana di Linguistica Applicata*, 18: 1-10.

Danesi, M. 1988. "The Development of Metaphorical Competence: A Neglected Dimension in Second Language Pedagogy." *Italiana*, 1: 1-10.

Danesi, M. 1992. "Metaphor and Classroom Second Language Learning." *Romance Languages Annual*, 3: 189-193.

Danesi, M. 1993a. "Metaphorical Competence in Second Language Acquisition and Second Language Teaching: The Neglected Dimension."In J. E. Alatis, ed., *Language, Communication and Social Meaning*. Washington, D. C.: Georgetown University Press, pp. 489-500.

Danesi, M. 1993b. "Whither Contrastive Analysis." *The Canadian Modern Language Review/La Revue canadienne des langues vivantes*, 50: 47-46.

Danesi, M. 1994. "Recent Research on Metaphor and the Teaching of Italian." *Italica*, 71: 453-464.

Danesi, M. 1995. "Learning and Teaching Languages: The Role of Conceptual Fluency." *International Journal of Applied Linguistics*, 5 (1995), 3-20.

Danesi, M. 1998. *Adesso: A Functional Introduction to Italian*. Boston: Heinle and Heinle.

Danesi, M. 1998. "Conceptual Iconicity and Grammatical Rules: Towards a Reflexive Grammar." In W. Pencak and J. R. Lindgren, eds., *New Approaches to Semiotics and the Human Sciences: Essays in Honor of Roberta Kevelson*. New York: Peter Lang, pp. 241-264.

Danesi, M. and R. J. Di Pietro. 1991. *Contrastive Analysis for the Contempo-*

rary Second Language Classroom. Toronto: Ontario Institute for Studies in Education Press.

Danesi, M., M. Lettieri, and S. Bancheri, S. 1996. *Con fantasia: Reviewing and Expanding Italian Language Skills*. Boston: Heinle and Heinle.

Dundes, A. 1972. "Seeing is Believing." *Natural History*, 81: 9-12.

Grabe, W. 1991. "Current Developments in Second Language Reading Research." *TESOL Quarterly*, 25: 375-406.

Johnson, M.1987. *The Body in the Mind: The Bodily Basis of Meaning, Imagination and Reason*. Chicago: University of Chicago Press.

Kaplan, R. D. 1978. "Contrastive Rhetoric: Some Hypotheses." *International Review of Applied Linguistics*, 39-40: 61-72.

Kšvecses, Z. 1986. *Metaphors of Anger, Pride, and Love: A Lexical Approach to the Structure of Concepts*. Amsterdam: John Benjamins.

Kšvecses, Z. 1988. *The Language of Love: The Semantics of Passion in Conversational English*. London: Associated University Presses.

Kšvecses, Z. 1990. *Emotion Concepts*. New York: Springer.

Lakoff, G. 1987. *Women, Fire, and Dangerous Things: What Categories Reveal about the Mind*. Chicago: University of Chicago Press.

Lakoff, G. and L. Johnson. 1980. *Metaphors We Live By*. Chicago: Chicago University Press.

Langacker, R. W. 1987. *Foundations of Cognitive Grammar*. Stanford: Stanford University Press.

Langacker, R. W. 1990. *Concept, Image, and Symbol: The Cognitive Basis of Grammar*. Berlin: Mouton de Gruyter.

Leki, I. 1991. "Twenty-Five Years of Contrastive Rhetoric: Text Analysis and Writing Pedagogies." *TESOL Quarterly*, 25: 123-143.

Levin, S. R. 1988. *Metaphoric Worlds*. New Haven: Yale University Press.

Maiguashca, R. 1988. "Quanto 'valgono' le parole straniere?" *Italiano e oltre*, 3: 136-139.

Masella, A. B. and I.A. Portner. 1981. "'Body Language' in Italian." *Italica*, 58: 205-213.

Nuessel, F. and C. Cicogna. 1993. "Narrative Texts and Images in the Teaching of the Italian language and Italian Culture." *Romance Languages Annual*, 4: 319-324.

Piper, D. 1985. "Contrastive Rhetoric and Reading in Second Language: Theoretical Perspectives on Classroom Practice." *The Canadian Modern Language Review/La revue canadienne des langues vivantes*, 42: 34-43.

Pollio, H. and B. Burns, B. 1977. "The Anomaly of Anomaly." *Journal of Psycholinguistic Research*, 6: 247-260.

Pollio, H. and M. Smith. 1979. "Sense and Nonsense in Thinking about Anomaly and Metaphor." *Bulletin of the Psychonomic Society*, 13: 323-326.

Pollio, H., J. Barlow, H. Fine, and M. Pollio, M. 1977. The Poetics of Growth: Figurative Language in Psychology, *Psychotherapy, and Education*. Hillsdale, N. J.: Lawrence Erlbaum Associates.

Russo, G. A. 1997. *A Conceptual Fluency Framework for the Teaching of Italian as a Second Language*. Toronto: University of Toronto Dissertation.

Savignon, S. J. 1992. "Problem Solving and the Negotiation of Meaning." In C. Cicogna, M. Danesi, and A. Mollica, eds., *Problem Solving in Second Language Teaching*. Welland: éditions Soleil publishing inc., pp. 11-25.

Shibles, W. 1989. "How German Vocabulary Pictures Emotion." *British Journal of Language Teaching*, 27: 141.

Taylor, J. R. 1995. *Linguistic Categorization: Prototypes in Linguistic Theory*. Oxford: Clarendon.

Van Ek, J. A. 1975. *The Threshold Level in a European Unit/Credit System for Modern Language Teaching by Adults*. Strasbourg: Council of Europe.

Wilkins, D. A. 1976. *Notional Syllabuses*. Oxford: Oxford University Press.

Winner, E. 1982. *Invented Worlds: The Psychology of the Arts*. Cambridge: Harvard University Press.

Reprinted from: Marcel Danesi and Anthony Mollica, "Conceptual Fluency and Second-Language Teaching." *Mosaic*, 5, 2 (Winter 1998): 1, 3-12.

24 What Visual Aids Can and Cannot Do in Second-Language Teaching

Hector Hammerly

Visual aids are powerfully appealing to both language teachers and students. Such aids have many advantages but also certain limitations. We should be especially leery of attempts to replace competent teachers' presentations with technological visual presentations, no matter how sophisticated the latter may be.

Language teachers have used visual aids of some kind or another since ancient times. Since the publication of the first visually oriented second-language textbook, Comenius's *Orbis sensualium pictus* in 1648, visual aids have found a relatively large number of users. Indeed, by the late 1980's it would have been difficult to come across a language teacher who did not use at least one type of visual aid in his courses.

As Brown and Mollica (1988-1989:1) correctly pointed out,

> Visuals have been used as an aid to language and the transmission of information since pre-historic times. From the paintings and drawings found on the walls of cave-dwellers, through Egyptian hieroglyphs and Chinese ideograms to modern visual extravaganzas, man has consistently made visual representations of reality. Throughout history, the world has transformed into an icon, a visual figurativization of internal and external reality. This is not surprising given the fact that sight is the strongest of the five senses.

Curiously, a rigorous definition of visual aids has never been agreed upon. Still, many in our profession consider them simply wonderful, more or less like motherhood, and neither see nor acknowledge their limitations and the practical consequences thereof.

This study attempts to deal with visual aids in language teaching with greater precision and to discuss both their advantages (which are many and have often been described) and limitations (perhaps not so numerous, but very important even though general silence surrounds them).

What Visual Aids Are (and What They Are Not)
What Visual Aids Are Not

Despite various claims and assumptions, visual aids are *not* the following:

1. *Written Language*

Whatever is a sample of written language, from one grapheme to the complete holdings of our National Library, is not a visual aid but language in its written form. We must be careful, therefore, not to succumb to the temptation certain French audiovisualist scholars have fallen into, of using the same terms *lire, lisibilité*, etc.) for reading a text and viewing images, and thus blurring the distinctions between them.

For the same reason – the need to keep two very different activities carefully apart in our minds – it would be preferable to restrict the word "literacy" to the ability to decode written language (that is, "read" in the established meaning of the term) and to use instead a new term (perhaps "visual competence") for the visual aspects that the linguistic, iconographic and cultural codes have in common.[1]

2. *Objects and Animals*

Objects, likewise, are not visual aids, although *pictures* or models of objects may be visual aids. Thus, a pencil is not a visual aid. It is an object, specifically a tool used to write with. That it can be used to demonstrate the meaning of the French word *crayon*, for example, doesn't make it any less of an object. Only a picture of a pencil would be a visual aid in this case. The same thing can be said of other objects that are often brought into the classroom, such as realia – whether menus, mantillas or money.

This argument becomes clearer when we consider *animals*. It isn't the fact that an elephant is too large to bring into the classroom that exempts it from the designation "visual aid." However small and portable, an animal is not a visual aid but an animal; only a picture or model of an animal can be considered a visual aid.

3. *People*

Carried to its illogical extreme, the view that anything visible is a visual aid led certain audiovisualists to consider people "visual aids" and the *teacher* "the most important audio-visual aid" in the classroom (Corder 1966: 33), although with appropriate materials his role was supposed to be "secondary" (*ibid.*, p. 79).

This attitude is similar to views of the teacher as a human tape recorder, a mere coordinator of the learning process, just a conversation stimulator, or a dispensable adjunct ("optional live software"?) to a computer, all teacher-demeaning views held over the years by some of the leaders of, respectively, the audiolingual, individualization, communication, and computerization movements.

Competent language teachers should reject any attempt to reduce their crucial role in the classroom, whatever movement or fad may be the source of such misguided attempts.

4. *Activities*

Things people do, from presiding over a session of Parliament to acting out a classroom skit, may have visual *impact* but are not visual aids.

5. *Media*

A consequence of limiting visual aids to nonverbal images and models is that the *means* for presenting them are not themselves visual aids. A projector is a tool that enables us to *show* visual aids. Slides, films, blackboards, flannelgraphs and computer screens are media used to display visual aids; but it is the pictures the students see – whether projected, drawn with chalk, attached, or generated electronically – that may be visual aids.

6. *Entertainment*

Pictures presented, with or without sound, only or even primarily to entertain, are not visual aids. While audiovisual entertainment may result in incidental learning, its objective is not instructional and thus it often is unsuitable for the classroom.

An *aid* is something used purposefully to facilitate the doing of something, in our case, SL learning. While our visual aids should be interesting and, if possible, entertaining, their entertainment value is clearly a matter of secondary concern.

A Definition of "Visual Aids"

Having freed the overloaded boat from much unnecessary cargo, we can now define "visual aids" more rigorously as "drawings, photos, graphics or models of a nonverbal nature used to facilitate (second language) teaching/learning."

Of course, verbal material often accompanies visual aids, whether in written (cartoons, comic strips, etc.) or spoken (film, television, video, etc.) form. The reverse is also true: visual aids often play a supporting role to verbal material. In audiovisual presentations the primary communicative function almost constantly switches back and forth between the verbal and the visual.

"Authentic" vs. "Contrived" Audiovisuals

The current push to use "authentic" audiovisuals and to minimize the use of "contrived" ones is semantically misleading and misses the point of SL teaching/learning.

It is misleading in its choice of labels: Note how loaded with positive connotations is the word "authentic" and how negative are the connotations of "contrived."

Furthermore, this trend ignores the fact that we can use audiovisuals aimed at two different audiences, native speakers and SL learners. Just labelling them accordingly as "Audiovisuals-for-natives" and "Audiovisuals-for-SL-learners" would clarify matters; of course, only the latter are visual *aid*s in our field.

Audiovisuals-for-natives are designed for viewers who are very fluent in the language and command a very large vocabulary. The viewers of audiovisuals-for-SL-learners, on the other hand, are not fluent and have precarious control of a limited vocabulary.

Thus it is hard to see how either type of audiovisual could be used effectively with the other type's audience. Natives would be extremely bored with audiovisuals-for-SL-learners, while SL learners find themselves lost and frustrated with nearly all audiovisuals-for-natives. In terms of the SL classroom, therefore, audiovisuals-for-natives should be called "Unadapted Audiovisuals" (the main connotation being "unsuitable," but there are several others) and audiovisuals-for-SL-learners should be called "Graded Audiovisuals," which could be "Learner-Designed" or "Adapted" (in either case the main connotation being "suitable").

The push for so-called "authentic" (audio) visuals, like the push for "real" communication from Day One of the SL program, is very much part of the current communication movement. Since communicationists believe that all we need to do to ensure good results is to reproduce natural language acquisition conditions in the classroom, it follows that in their view everything, from visuals to classroom activities to the noncorrection of errors, must be "real" and "authentic."[2]

Visual and Verbal Input:
Different, Noncontiguous Stimuli

It is by now well known that verbal and visual data are stored in different brain hemispheres (for about 95 per cent of the human race, verbal data storage and processing occur in the left hemisphere). Evidence of this is the finding that aphasiacs have greater difficulty in distinguishing between word meanings than between their referents (Stachowiak 1982).

Thus, neurally the pathways should be shorter -presumably being close to each other, in the same hemisphere – between a SL word and its closest native language (NL) equivalent than between either of them and their referent.

What this would do to the psychological claims underpinning the Direct Method (Franke 1884, Passy 1899, and many others), on which at least one use of visual aids is based, is not hard to imagine: the claim that the picture-SL word connection is shorter and more "direct" than the SL word-NL word connection is negated.

Their Relative Importance to Communication

It is often said that only a small percentage (between five and 15 per cent) of the meaning of communication acts is verbal and all the rest is nonverbal. While no doubt in some cases the nonverbal element is crucial, the claim seems a gross exaggeration to me.

An empirical game one can play to test the validity of the above assertion is to attend to audiovisual programs with, alternately, the audio and the video off. This "experiment" can easily be completed in one or two evenings of TV watching. See/listen for yourself. What you will notice is that the audio alone generally allows you to understand quite well what is going on, while with only the video on you are very often lost – this in a medium whose visual element is emphasized. The obvious conclusion: Words convey far more information than visuals.

Nearly three decades ago several studies have shown the greater importance of verbal input relative to visual input. While pictures may be more easily remembered than words, by secondary school verbal material is learned faster when presented verbally than pictorially. Two decades ago, Jenkins *et al.* (1967) found that college sophomores tended to encode pictures *verbally*.

Their Effect on the Imagination

Apparently verbal stimuli evoke more "sense-impression" (sensory) associations than pictorial stimuli (Otto and Britton 1965), which perhaps is just another way of saying that sound alone can result in richer mental images (does anyone still remember *The Shadow*?) than sound plus video, or that with adequate verbal stimulation the students' imagination can produce more vivid images and maybe more memorable associations than with the latest, state-of-the-art video display.

To put it another way: Do we, through the too frequent use of visuals, limit the use of our students' imagination and discourage them from the effort of having to elaborate their own mental images? Given that self-generated images and associations may be remembered better than those provided, ready-made, like baby food, we may wonder whether our teaching suffers from an over-reliance on visuals.

Their Effect on Comprehension

Pictures assist in the global comprehension of verbal material (Mueller 1980), especially if they are thematic and precede a text (Omaggio 1979). Naturally, the best global comprehension is attained when text *and* pictures are used (Kraif *et al*. 1980), as shown by our little TV "experiment."

That visual support of comprehension is mostly thematic is seen in the fact that illustrations have been found to significantly enhance 11 year-old native English speakers' comprehension of abstract passages but not of concrete ones (Moore and Skinner 1985). This too has important implications for our use of visual aids in SL teaching.

Visual Aids: General Considerations
Types of Visual Aids

As defined above, visual aids include:

1. *Drawings*

These have the advantage over photographs that one can decide precisely how much detail to show and what to highlight. Drawings include, among other things, cartoons (and comics) and maps.

- *Cartoons and comics* have been thoroughly discussed in terms of SL teaching by Mollica (1976), Brown (1977), and Marsh (1978). "Captionable" cartoons can be varied in successive interpretations. I have found wordless cartoons particularly effective as speech generators. Comics with simple verbal material, such as Snoopy and his friends (available in many languages), and later more challenging ones like Tintin and Astéryx (to mention two in French), stimulate SL practice. Of course, cartoons and comics are subject to misunderstandings arising from cultural differences, so they should be handled judiciously.
- *Maps*, preferably with other aids, can be used effectively to "take a trip" through another region or country, to locate historical or current events, and so forth.

2. *Photographs*

Scanlan (1976) has shown how to use photographs in SL teaching and how to analyze them in order to, among other things, manipulate linguistic structures and improve language skills (1980). He is aware of the "likelihood" that the students mental verbalizations will be in the NL (1976: 416). One visual medium that combines photographs or drawings with verbal material is the advertisement. Scanlan (1978), Mollica (1979), and Simon (1980) have dealt in detail with the linguistic, communicative and cultural aspects of this.

Carefully chosen photographs, especially those that are a little ambiguous or have emotional appeal, can be excellent conversation stimuli. Mollica (1992a and 1992b) has led the way in the development of this type of SL materials.

3. Graphics

There are at least seven types of graphic visuals aids, as follows:

Text modifiers such as diacritics or the use of one or a few letters with underlining, in a different size, style (bold, italic, etc.) or font have long been used as specific graphic signals.

- *General graphic devices* include lines, colours (a general visual signal used in particular by Gattegno in his *Silent Way* (1972)), and such other devices as circles, boxes (or, for that matter, any shape) and arrows, most of them, again, long part of our arsenal. The best discussion so far of "pedagogical graphics" may be Danesi's (1983).
- *Charts* also have a long history in SL teaching. Recently, the flowcharts used by computer programmers have been adapted for the teaching of SL syntax (Bryant 1983), though one wonders how readable they are for the average SL student.
- *Plans* of cities, streets, stores, houses, and rooms are useful, especially as points of reference to aid comprehension or as conversation stimuli.
- *Articulatory graphics* include face diagrams as well as special symbols that serve as articulatory pointers or reminders (Hammerly 1974-a).
- *Electronically generated non-computer graphics,* using such devices as the oscilloscope, can aid intonation, stress, and rhythm.
- *Computer-generated graphics,* which for some years have shown fine detail, can also help with stress, intonation, and rhythm – and with sound articulation.

4. Models

Two types of three-dimensional representations that are particularly useful in language teaching are models of the speech apparatus and models of places. Tree-dimensional models of the speech apparatus seem to help students visualize more realistically what is involved in the articulation of NL and SL sounds

- *Models of places* like Berlin, the Champs Elysées, a supermarket, or a typical Mexican casa can facilitate vocabulary
  practice and conversation.
  (Although models are normally included loosely under the
  term "realia," it should be remembered that this Latin word
  means "real things," which of course models are not. Models
  are visual aids, real things are not.)

A Few Problems and Possible Solutions
1. Ambiguity
The nature of perceptual ambiguity has been discussed by many,
an example being the article by Arndt and Pesch (1984). How to
reduce pictorial ambiguity has been dealt with at some length by
Corder (1966) and Wright (1976). But most verbal material cannot be represented pictorially, so visual aids are and will remain
largely ambiguous and unreliable as conveyors of the meaning of
specific words or sentences (see below). The hope that visuals
capable of conveying all meanings unambiguously would someday be developed must be considered a "pipe dream." The scientifically based "revolutionary visual pedagogies" we were supposed to look forward to in the eighties (Brown 1983:870) did not
materialize – except in the sense that the use of video and multimedia has increased. Truly revolutionary successful pedagogies
would be primarily a matter of teachers and students interacting
in more effective ways, and only secondarily a matter of applications of more sophisticated technology, for we must accept that
visuals suffer from inherent limitations.

2. Cultural bias
It has been shown repeatedly and convincingly that people from
different cultures interpret visuals differently. Pointing out the
culturally relevant features of a visual – relevant from the point
of view of both cultures, which calls for contrastive cultural analysis – is clearly the only solution to this problem.

3. Combination of separate visual and verbal material
This is done in various audiovisual media; dubbing is perhaps
the best example. In the SL classroom, captions alone, captions
plus visuals, or visuals alone can be shown as desired by using
two visual sources. As a sort of reading activity, students can
match pictures and captions, which could be on cards or, among
other possibilities, on dentists' tongue depressors (Flynn and Trott
1972).

4. Adaptation
The general unsuitability of audiovisuals-for-native-speakers for

the SL classroom has already been briefly discussed. If used, they should first be adapted to the characteristics of the SL learners involved (age in particular) and naturally to their degree of linguistic (grammatical and lexical) and communicative competence, and cultural awareness. For some such visuals systematic advance preparation of the students can compensate for lack of adaptation, but for most "authentic" visuals the amount of advance preparation needed is so great that they become useful only at a higher level of instruction.

5. *Control*

The idea of the student being increasingly self-reliant and primarily responsible for his own learning did not die in the late 70s. In fact, new technologies like the microcomputer, the VCR, and the videodisc player are making it easier, at least in theory, to place control of visuals in the hands of the learner.

However, other student-controlled technologies that have been around for many years, such as the individual 8mm film cartridge viewer, have hardly been exploited in SL teaching. Even student control of non-technological devices other than textbooks has been the exception rather than the rule in our profession, so it is difficult to tell, when, if ever, technologically advanced learner control of visuals will become a reality.

Visual Aids: Advantages and Limitations
General Advantages

1. *Atmosphere*

Visuals allow us to bring the SL world into the classroom. Every place frequented by our students should be rich in SL visuals, realia and music so as to create the atmosphere of a "cultural island."

2. *Motivation*

Visuals are an important one among the many factors that contribute to student motivation. Others include

(a) interesting and
(b) relevant content; and
(c) respect for SL learners' rights (Hammerly 1985: 211-20), such as the rights to be taught systematically, step by step; to understand what is going on in class; to be reinforced as needed; to be corrected promptly and appropriately; to have one's individual characteristics and needs taken into account; and to have input into the decision-making process.

Motivation, in short, results primarily from the evident opportunity to succeed in an interesting process of learning in which the learner has considerable input. Visuals can enhance motivation but I doubt very much that they can, by themselves, create it.

3. *Focus of attention*
A visual can draw the students' attention to most things we may want to emphasize. If visuals are simple, rather than cluttered with detail, attention can be focused on what is relevant (Corder 1966: 53). (But see General Limitation 2 below).

4. *Context*
Visuals can provide virtually all situations with their most significant non-linguistic contexts.

5. *Explanatory support*
Visual aids can help explain features of SL structure.

6. *General comprehension*
Pictures have been shown to aid general comprehension by directing attention towards a theme (Omaggio 1979) or "probable semantic area" (Dethloff 1980).

7. *Mnemonic support*
Visuals help learners retain and recall
(a) the meaning of words, etc. (Winn 1982) and
(b) the sequences in which they have occurred.

8. *Cultural insights*
Picturable cultural features are grasped better when seen than when described; for best results, however, they should be pointed out.

9. *Conversation stimuli*
This is one of the most useful functions of visual aids.

General Limitations
1. The *"Audiovisual Communication Dilemma"*
Although greater redundancy in the text and greater correlation between text and pictures result in greater clarity, less error and less ambiguity, the amount of information transmitted is reduced accordingly (Deichsel 1980). Thus in SL teaching by increasing the amount of information conveyed pictorially we reduce the amount of information conveyed linguistically, and vice versa.

2. *Focusing Attention away from Language*
This applies to both language forms and comprehension, especially listening comprehension.

- *Forms* or patterns in any component of the language must be attended to first, particulary at the moment of their initial introduction. For example, to the extent that the attention of beginners is on visual aids and their meaning, it won't be on the teacher's articulation of sounds, and as a result the imitation of sounds is bound to suffer.
- *Comprehension of the verbal message* will likewise suffer from the excessive use of visuals and from the use of many specific visuals rather than a few general ones. Specific visuals may make it unnecessary for the students to put in a real effort to understand the *language*, since apparently "to the extent that comprehension of a passage is based on visual aids it is not based on the linguistic message." (Hammerly 1985: 127).

Perhaps we should not be surprised if, at the end of a program in which visual aids are used extensively, graduates cannot follow conversations by natives. What our students need most is training in listening comprehension based on hearing only, not on hearing largely aided by seeing.

3. Unreliability in Conveying Specific Meaning

Research supports the view, that visual aids are at their weakest and, in effect, unreliable as conveyors and elicitors of the specific meanings of particular words or sentences.

- *Words*, even concrete ones, cannot be conveyed pictorially without ambiguity. An experiment (Hammerly 1974-b) revealed that even when the picture/word pairs were as concrete as *airplane, bird, deer, train,* and *tree,* university students with no knowledge of the words guessed their correct meaning only from 40 to 70 per cent of the time, while they were not sure ten to 40 per cent of the time, and they were wrong 25 to 50 per cent of the time (percentages don't add up to 100 because they varied with each of the five words).
- *Sentences in dialogues* do not fare much better. Dodson (1967: 8-9) found 30 university lecturers unable to guess the meaning of more than ten to 40 per cent of the sentences depicted in audiovisual lessons popular at the time. In research conducted from the mid-70s to the early 80s (Hammerly 1984) it was determined that experienced teachers of French could guess only an average of 54 per cent of the meaning/language conveyed by the ten frames in each of two filmstrips used in a fairly sophisticated French audiovisual textbook (Capelle and Capelle 1970).

    The fact that visuals cannot be relied upon to convey the meaning of SL words or of SL sentences in context has also been noted by several other researchers (e.g., Cole 1967, 1976). Unfortunately, it seems that many SL teachers, who of course know the SL, are so dazzled by ingenious visuals that they fail to realize that the meaning is not clear to their students, who don't know the SL.

Corder, a strong audiovisualist, saw this problem. As he put it (1966: 50): "...we can never take it for granted that what we present is immediately recognized." A few pages later (58) he added: "...our pupils must never be put in the position of needing to ask: 'What is going on here?'" Yet this is precisely what happens, much of the time, when meaning is "conveyed" monolingually, with or without visual aids, at the beginning level: learning under such conditions becomes an ongoing, frustrating guessing game.

- *Problems with the monolingual approach* to conveying meaning have already been discussed in detail elsewhere (Hammerly 1982). Suffice it to say here that monolingual methods are inefficient ("very slow") (Corder 1966: 27)); often result in vague semantization; and do not prevent the formation of SL/NL associations anyway, even when not a single word in the NL is heard in class (Sweet 1899) already observed this, and Dodson (1967: 51) called it "the eureka experience"). Too, monolingual methods are less direct than bilingual ones.

While it is understandable that the lack of multilingual materials makes a monolingual approach (usually with heavy use of visuals) necessary with linguistically heterogeneous classes such as those in ESL, even there such an approach is neither desirable nor unavoidable. When all the students in a SL class speak the same NL, a monolingual approach is no longer justifiable, either on theoretical or practical grounds; even when the teacher cannot speak the NL of the students, it is possible to arrange to convey meaning in it initially.

It is not the initial monolingual SL presentation of meaning with the aid of visuals that prevents the establishment of incorrect SL/NL associations; this can be accomplished best, instead, by actively and overtly discouraging one-to-one word "translation" (which is often mistranslation) and by relying instead on contextual equivalents, with pointers as needed. Only this – not pictures – will ensure the prompt and precise conveyance of SL meaning.

How meaning is initially introduced seems to have little to do with its subsequent internalization (Preibusch and Zander 1971). Internalization, consolidation, and expansion of meaning are a function of meaningful practice in the second language. A monolingual guessing game aided by visuals is still a guessing game, not, as some assert, communication.

The weight of available empirical evidence and of reason support the hypothesis that meaning is best conveyed by means of triads composed of

(a) contextualized SL words and sentences plus
(b) visual aids plus
(c) contextualized NL equivalents.

Using visuals enhances retention and recall, and using the NL ensures comprehension.

- *Principled bilingual teaching* in the SL classroom, which is another way of putting it, should yield the best results. This means using the NL as little as possible (certainly not to generate SL sentences) and as much as necessary (e.g., for the initial conveyance of meaning). I realize that this recommendation, which contradicts what many SL teachers believe, runs against the long-standing Direct Method tradition of Europe, and especially of France.

But principled bilingual SL teaching also has long roots, going at least as far back as the late nineteenth century. Few today seem aware that the precursor of the much-distorted and now largely rejected Audiolingual Method was bilingual, not monolingual. It followed the Sweet (1899)-Palmer (1917, 1922) – structural linguists' (1940s) route, and by the late 50s its results (which I was able to observe) were very good indeed. Even in Europe, bilingual SL teaching has made some headway, especially in Great Britain, with the work of Dodson (1967), and in Germany, taking the lead form Butzkamm (1973).

Principled bilingual SL teaching may use visual aids in many ways but it is not a reincarnation of the Grammar-Translation Method: it is also the very opposite of the "trial and error" approach to SL learning.

4. Unreliability in eliciting specific meaning

The predictability of language, even given a list of specific situations (which in itself is very arbitrary) and specific pictures, is low. The expectation of certain members of our profession, such as Corder and Wright, that someday the language which goes with specific visuals could be predicted "with a high degree of certainty" (Corder 1966: 46) will not be realized.

The best proof of this comes from SL testing. After much research, Pimsleur concluded that "even the clearest pictures tend

to elicit a variety of utterances, rather than only the one we want."
(1966: 198).

5. *Cost*

Although there has been a substantial reduction in cost over the
years, most visuals and audiovisuals are still fairly expensive,
some extremely so. The cost-effectiveness factor cannot be ignored.

Visual or Teacher Presentations

In recent years, video presentations are being promoted as being
more effective than teacher presentations (e.g. Hanley *et al.*, 1995;
Herron *et al.*, 1995). This reminds me of the audiovisual practice,
many years ago, of having the teacher present a filmstrip accompanied by an audiocassette rather than say anything herself. Furthermore, because these audiovisual presentations – whether via
video or filmstrip/audiocassette – are Direct Method monolingual presentations done strictly in the SL, they become a very
difficult and, for many students, a frustrating guessing game.

This promotion of presentations via video seems to be another attempt – there have been several – to replace the teacher,
or at least some of her important functions, with technology.
However, there will always be many things a competent teacher
can do that technology, visual or otherwise, cannot.

Although this article is not meant to discuss in detail how to
use visual aids, the strong trend to use videos for presentations
calls for the following practical suggestions:

•   While the best initial step in presenting new material might
    well be the viewing of a very short video, this should be im-
    mediately followed by a much slower review of the video,
    with the teacher observing, the class carefully and stopping
    the tape after every sentence or two for random individual
    repetition and occasional choral echoing, accompanied as
    needed by deep correction, by any bilingual clarification of
    sounds, structures or meaning the students may request or
    require , and by interaction through questions and answers,
    role playing, retelling, and so forth.
•   Visual or multimedia technology will never be able to do well
    any of the things just listed, for they all require the use of an
    intelligent, competent and *adaptable* mind – which machines
    do not and *cannot* have. While technologically aided self-
    instruction supplemented with graded conversation with a
    native speaker may be the best way to proceed when a com-
    petent teacher is not available, best results in the SL class-
    room will always be obtained by a competent, caring teacher
    aided – and at no time replaced – by visual technologies.

Conclusion

More could be written about, among other things, specific appli-cations of visual aids to the teaching of SL components, skills, cultural awareness, and literary appreciation, what the various (audio) visual media are, their relative advantages and disadvan-tages and how to use them in the SL program. But time and space are always in short supply. My hope is that through these pages the reader has become more aware of what, precisely, "visual aids" are and what they can and cannot do, and that he or she will have the opportunity (or the courage, if need be) to put this extended awareness into practice.

Notes

1.   Brown [1983: 873-7] has proposed a semiotically structured model of "visual lit-eracy" in terms of these three codes; my point is that the term "literacy" should be reserved for the written linguistic code. (An ever stronger argument can be made against the use of terms such as "computer literacy.")

2.   Natural language acquisition conditions cannot be reproduced in the classroom, as both the learners and the environment differ in major unavoidable ways. The linguis-tic results of communicative/acquisitionist/ naturalistic language "teaching" are poor. After 13 years (about 7000 hours) of French "immersion" (it isn't) graduates make very frequent errors of the most basic nature [Pellerin and Hammerly, 1986; Hammerly et al., 1994; Hammerly 1995a and 1995b]. Will communicative language "teaching" ever get a better chance to show what it can do? Does it deserve it?

References

Arndt, Horst and Helmut W. Pesch. 1984. "Non-verbal Communication and Visual Teaching Aids: A Perceptual Approach." *The Modern Language Jour-nal*, 68: 28-36.

Brown, James W. 1977. "Comics in the Foreign Language Classroom: Peda-gogical Perspectives." *Foreign Language Annals*, 10: 18-25.

Brown, James W. and Anthony Mollica, eds. 1980-1981. *Essays in Visual Semi-otics*. Toronto: Toronto Semiotic Circle.

Brown, James W. 1983. "Trends in Pictorial Pedagogics: Adding to the Ads." *The Canadian Modern Language Review/La Revue canadienne des langues vivantes*, 39: 858-888.

Bryant, William H. 1983. "Syntax Flowcharts For Advanced French Courses." *Foreign Language Annals*, 6: 469-476.

Butzkamm, Wolfgang. 1973. *Aufgeklärte Einsprachigkeit: zur Entdogmatisierung der Methode im Fremdsprachenunterricht*. Heidelberg: Quelle und Meyer.

Capelle, Janine and Guy Capelle. 1970. *La France en direct*. Waltham, MA: Ginn.

Cole, Leo R. 1967. "The Visual Element and the Problem of Meaning in Lan-guage Learning," *Audio-Visual Language Journal*, 4: 84-87.

Cole, Leo R. 1976. "Relationships Between Visual Presentations and Linguistic Items in Second-Language Teaching." *International Review of Applied Lin-guistics*, 14: 339-350.

Comenius, Johann A. 1648. *Orbis sensualium pictus*. Reprinted, Sidney: Sidney University Press, 1967.

Corder, S. Pit. 1966. *The Visual Element in Language Teaching*. London: Longman.

Danesi, Marcel. 1983. "Pedagogical Graphics in Second-Language Teaching." *The Canadian Modern Language Review/La Revue canadienne des langues vivantes*, 40: 73-81.

Deichsel, Ingo. 1980. "Quelques consequences de la cognition audio-visuelle en vue d'une méthodologie des media." *Études de linguistique appliquée*, 38: 52-64.

Dethloff, Uwe. 1980. "La réception des textes télévisuels en langue étrangère." *Études de linguistique appliquée*, 38: 106-118.

Dodson, Carl J. 1967. *Language Teaching and the Bilingual Method*. London: Pitman.

Flynn, Mary and Nora Trott. 1972. "300 Tongue Depressors." *The French Review*, 45: 6 54-656.

Franke, Felix. 1884. *Die praktische Spracherlernung auf Grund der Psychologie und der Physiologie der Sprache dargestellt von Felix Franke*. Heilbronn, Germany.

Gattegno, Caleb. 1972. *Teaching Foreign Languages in Schools: The Silent Way*. Second edition. New York: Educational Solutions.

Hammerly, Hector. 1974a. *The Articulatory Pictorial Transcriptions: New Aids to Second Language Pronunciation*. N. Burnaby, B.C.: Second Language Publications.

Hammerly, Hector. 1974b. "Primary and Secondary Associations with Visual Aids as Semantic Conveyors." *International Review of Applied Linguistics*, 12: 119-125.

Hammerly, Hector. 1982. *Synthesis in Second Language Teaching. An Introduction to Linguistics*. N. Burnaby, B.C.: Second Language Publications.

Hammerly, Hector. 1984. "Contextualized Visual Aids (Filmstrips) as Conveyors of Sentence Meaning." *International Review of Applied Linguistics*, 22: 87-94.

Hammerly, Hector. 1985. *An Integrated Theory of Language Teaching and Its Practical Consequences*. N. Burnaby, B.C.: Second Language Publications.

Hammerly, Hector. 1994. "A Picture is Worth 1000 Words and a Word is Worth 1000 Pictures.," *Mosaic*, 1, 4: 13-19.

Hammerly, Hector. 1995a. "Annotated Publication Abstracts on the (French) Immersion Approach," unpublished research paper. P.O. Box 64522, Como Lake Postal Outlet, Coquitlam, BC V3J 7V7: Lexcel Enterprises Inc.

Hammerly, Hector. 1995b. "Preliminary Results of the French Immersion Test – Home Version (FIT-HV)." Unpublished research report. Coquitlam, BC: Lexcel Enterprises Inc.

Hammerly, Hector, Monique McDonald, Trude Heift and Siok Lee. 1994. "Some Observations About the Grammaticality of French Immersion and Core French Graduates," unpublished research paper. Coquitlam, BC: Lexcel Enterprises, Inc.

Hanley, Julia E.B., Carol A. Herron and Steven P. Cole. 1995. "Using Video as an Advance Organizer to a Written Passage in the FLES Classroom." *The Modern Language Journal*, 79: 57-66.

Herron, Carol, Matthew Morris, Teresa Secules and Lisa Curtis. 1995. "A Comparison Study of the Effects of Video-Based versus Text-Based Instruction in the Foreign Language Classroom." *The French Review*, 68: 775-795.

Jenkins, Joseph R., Daniel C. Neale and Stanley L. Deno. 1967. "Differential Memory for Picture and Word Stimuli." *Journal of Educational Psychology*, 58: 303-307.

Kraif, André et al. 1980. "Compréhension de documents publicitaires TV: une approche empirique." *Études de linguistique appliquée*, 38: 82-105.

Marsh, Rufus K. 1978. "Teaching French with the Comics." *The French Review*, 51: 777-785.

Mollica, Anthony. 1976. "Cartoons in the Language Classroom." *The Canadian Modern Language Review/La Revue canadienne des langues vivantes*, 32: 424-444.

Mollica, Anthony. 1978. "The Film Advertisement: A Source for Language Activities." *The Canadian Modern Language Review/La Revue canadienne des langues vivantes*, 34,2:221-243.

Mollica, Anthony. 1979. "*A Tiger in Your Tank*: Advertisements in the Language Classroom." *The Canadian Modern Language Review/La Revue canadienne des langues vivantes*, 35: 691-743.

Mollica, Anthony. 1992a. *A Picture is worth...1000 words...*Book 1. Welland, Ontario: éditions Soleil publishing inc.

Mollica, Anthony. 1992b. *A Picture is worth...1000 words...*Book 2. Welland, Ontario: éditions Soleil publishing inc.

Moore, Phillip J. and Michael J. Skinner. 1985. "The Effects of Illustrations on Children's Comprehension of Abstract and Concrete Passages," *Journal of Research in Reading*, 8: 45-56.

Mueller, Gunther A. 1980. "Visual Contextual Cues and Listening Comprehension: An Experiment." *The Modern Language Journal*, 64: 335-340.

Omaggio, Alice C. 1979. "Pictures and Second Language Comprehension: Do They Help?" *Foreign Language Annals*, 12: 107-116.

Otto, Wayne and Gwenyth Britton. 1965. "Sense-Impression Responses to Verbal and Pictorial Stimuli." *International Review of Applied Linguistics*, 3: 51-56.

Palmer, Harold E. 1917. *The Scientific Study and Teaching of Languages. London: Harrap*. Reprinted in 1968 by Oxford University Press.

Palmer, Harold E. 1922. *Principles of Language-Study*. London: Harrap. Reprinted in 1964 by Oxford University Press.

Passy, Paul. 1899. *De la méthode directe dans l'enseignement des langues vivantes*. Cambridge, England: Association Phonétique Internationale.

Pellerin, Micheline and Hector Hammerly. 1986. "L'expression orale après treize ans d'immersion francaise." *The Canadian Modern Language Review/La Revue canadienne des langues vivantes*, 42: 592606.

Pimsleur, Paul. 1966. "Testing Foreign Language Learning." In Albert Valdman, ed., *Trends in Language Teaching*. New York: McGraw-Hill, pp. 175-214.

Preibusch, Wolfgang and Heidrun Zander. 1971. "Wortschatzvermittlung: auf der Suche nach einem analytischen Modell." *International Review of Applied Linguistics*, 9: 131-145.

Scanlan, Timothy. 1976. "A Picture's Worth a Thousand Words? Then Let's Hear Them!" *The Canadian Modern Language Review/La Revue canadienne des langues vivantes*, 32: 415-21.

Scanlan, Timothy M. 1978. "French Mail-order Catalogues as Teaching Tools: Vocabulary, Culture and Conversation." *The French Review*, 52: 217-241.

Scanlan Timothy M. 1980. "Another Foreign Language Skill: Analyzing Photographs." *Foreign Language Annals*, 13: 209-13.

Simon, Ronald H. 1980. "Images publicitaires: Images culturelles." *The French Review*, 54: 1-27.

Stachowiak, Franz-Josef. 1982. "Haben Wortbedeutungen eine gesonderte mentale Repräsentation gegenüber dem Weltwissen? Neurolinguistische Überlegungen," *Linguistische Berichte*, 79: 12-29.

Sweet, Henry. 1899. *The Practical Study of Languages*. London: J.M. Dent and Sons. Reprinted in 1964 by Oxford University Press.

Winn, William. 1982. "Visualization in Learning and Instruction: A Cognitive Approach." *Educational Communication and Technology*, 30: 3-25.

Wright, Andrew. 1976. *Visual Materials for the Language Teacher*. New York: Longman.

Reprinted from: Hector Hammerly, "What Visual Aids Can and Cannot Do In Second Language Teaching." *Mosaic*, 2, 3 (Spring 1995): 11-18.

25 A Picture is Worth... 1000 Words... Creative Activities for the Language Classroom

Anthony Mollica

Language teachers have always made use of pictorial material either to associate word and image or to have the image serve as a stimulus for conversation and discussion. The article identifies several activities whose aim is to encourage the use of pictures in the classroom.

Introduction

As James W. Brown and Anthony Mollica point out in their "Introduction" to *Essays in Applied Visual Semiotics* (1988-89:1),

> Visuals have been used as an aid to language and the transmission of information since pre-historic times. From the paintings and drawings found on the walls of the cave-dwellers, through Egyptian hieroglyphs and Chinese ideograms to modern visual extravaganzas, man has consistently made visual representation of reality. This is not at all surprising, given the fact that sight is the strongest of the five senses. Most of the information we have about the world derives from the condition of seeing.

It is precisely because the sense of sight is the strongest of all senses that we have decided to capitalize on this element and to suggest the introduction of images in the language classroom. Moreover, as Clifford T. Morgan and Richard A. King (1966:197) have concisely stated,

> Most, if not all, people experience images and images often help thinking. Some individuals have such a vivid imagination that they can recall things almost perfectly; this is called eidetic imagery.

The use of visual imagery in learning, as psycholinguists often point out, is crucial to recall mechanisms and the development of eidetic memory, and this, of course, is beneficial to language learning.

Students are frequently reluctant or even unwilling to speak in the language classroom for, quite often, the stimulus is too dif-

ficult and requires considerable research and linguistic knowledge. As we have stated elsewhere (Mollica, 1985b),

> Exchanging views on such diverse topics as "abortion", "capital
> punishment", "the role of women", and the like will not produce in
> the learner the mechanical ability to apply the target language in a
> communicatively-appropriate way to the various situations which
> make up verbal interaction. Moreover, the nature of these topics is
> such that it requires a sophisticated command of the structural and
> lexical modalities of the target language. It comes as no surprise,
> therefore, to find beginning students unwilling and unable to speak
> about these topics.

Granted, our ultimate aim should be to prepare students to
speak about these and other topics of interest to them. And, in
fact, these, and other "hot" topics of current interest, should be
introduced and discussed at an advanced stage once the students
have mastered an appropriate or comfortable command of the
language, have read widely on these subjects and/or have such
an intense personal interest that they willingly share it with their
peers and perhaps even try to impose their views on them.

The increasing research over the last decade on the development of communicative competence has made it abundantly clear
that the spontaneous use of the target language will have to be
guided and will have to be taught systematically in ways that
grammatical structures are taught. To relegate the development
of audio-oral writing skills to the "Friday afternoon conversation
class" has proven continually and consistently to be a fruitless
exercise (Mollica, 1985a).

There has, however, been an ever increasing amount of literature on the development of appropriate pedagogical strategies for the teaching and encouragement of authentic and autonomous communication in a classroom setting.

Our purpose in this paper is, in fact, to describe one of several communication-focused strategies that we have been developing and experimenting with over a number of years. We will
refer to them as "visual stimuli" because their psychopedagogical
focus is the elicitation of target language words, phrases, sentences
and entire discourse units. This discussion summarizes and refines the points made in previous studies (Mollica 1985a, 1985b,
1981, 1979a, 1979b, 1978, 1976).

The Stimulus

Psycholinguistically, a stimulus can be defined to be any
physiological or sensorial phenomenon to which an organism will
respond according to some predictable pattern of behaviour. The

"visual stimulus" has been deliberately chosen to elicit either oral or written responses, depending on the language skill teachers will wish to focus on.

It is important to note that some stimuli are better suited for oral interaction, while others are better suited for written ones; there are, obviously, still many others which are equally well suited for both oral and written activities.

The visual stimulus consists of a series of photographs which may be grouped into the following categories:

- humorous
- descriptive
- dramatic
- tragic
- cultural.

Each photograph can serve as a stimulus for discussions and compositions at various linguistic levels:

- beginning
- intermediate
- advanced.

This means that if the teacher chooses judiciously a classroom assignment based on the students' linguistic background, the same photo may be used at different levels of language instruction and will be quite appropriate in multi-level classes.

The three linguistic levels suggested above coincide with the following suggested hierarchical stages of the photograph:

- Visual Comprehension
- Personal Interpretation
- Creativity.

These three stages may be illustrated using *Photo 1* as an example. At the ***visual comprehension*** stage, students may be asked questions directly related to what is seen in the photograph. The lexical items to be elicited will be simple and the structures required to "converse" will be quite basic.

1. *How many people do you see in the picture?*
2. *What are they doing?*
3. *Name some of the items which are being used to plant a tree.*
   and so on.

At the ***personal interpretation*** stage, students may be asked to express their own opinion about the actions/scenes depicted in the photograph.

Photo: Cec Mitchell

Photo 1

1. *Why, do you think, these are people planting a tree?*
2. *Who, in your opinion, should be involved in these ceremonies?*
   and so on.

At the ***creativity*** stage, students may be asked questions focusing on their imagination and inventiveness. In some cases, teachers will want to guide the creativity process by suggesting some possible topics for consideration. At this level, some visual stimuli may be well suited to lead to further research.

1. *Write a short paragraph giving necessary information relating to the photograph. Identify*
   a. the man and the young people,
   b. the occasion for planting a tree,
   c. the location where the scene is taking place, etc.
2. *Using your research skills, find as much information as possible about tree-planting ceremonies.*
3. *Imagine that you are the anchor person for a local TV station. Give an oral account of what is portrayed by the photograph as it is being flashed on the screen.*
4. *Imagine that you are the man at the left. Write a brief speech which you would give preceding or following the ceremony, etc.*

The point to be made here is that a visual stimulus can be utilized to generate spontaneous conversation in the target language without recourse to some previously-prepared dialogue on a specific theme. Since teachers are obviously aware of the linguistic background of their students, they may wish to fuse all three stages and ask questions or suggest assignments which involve visual comprehension, interpretation and creativity.

The activities we suggest below for using photographs are not meant to be exhaustive, but rather are intended to aid the teacher to provide contextualized, meaningful oral exchanges or written assignments in the language classroom. They constitute a type of triggering device which should start conversation on a specific theme in an autonomous way.

General Pedagogical Applications

The following are some general pedagogical applications which may be used by the teacher whenever s/he feels them appropriate. They are not being presented in a pre-established hierarchical structure, but we are confident that teachers will first emphasize the speaking skill and then reinforce it with writing activities. Talking about the visual stimulus before the written assignment allows students to gather the necessary vocabulary they need as well as to help organize their thoughts in a logical sequence and thus enrich the writing activity.

Vocabulary Brainstorming

Students may be asked to do some brainstorming. For this task, students maybe divided into pairs or into a small group and asked to jot down on paper as much vocabulary as possible elicited by the visual representation in the photograph. It is obvious that each student will contribute according to his/her linguistic background and the end-result will be a comprehensive, if not exhaustive, list of varied and interesting lexical items. If the exercise is being done in a language other than English, students should be encouraged to consult a dictionary, a native speaker who may be in the classroom, or even the teacher, in order to provide as many words as possible which will enrich the speaking or writing experience.

Questions/Answers

Students may be asked to speak solely about the photograph. Teachers may decide to select only those questions based on the photo, the answers to which can be given by looking at the image. Since the teacher is aware of the linguistic background the student has, s/he will be able to choose questions which will elicit the correct response and involve the student at a certain level.

Questions/Answers activities, if logically and sequentially planned, may lead to a short written paragraph.

The Five "W"s

Teachers should constantly remind their students to attempt to answer the questions:

- Who...?
- What...?
- Where...?
- When...?
- Why...?

The answers to these and other similar questions are very suitable at the "visual comprehension" stage and, if asked often, will instill a sense of inquisitiveness in the learners and sharpen their visual acuity.

Word/Line/Paragraph Captions

Students may be asked to write a caption for the photograph. Here the students will examine the photograph and come up with an appropriate caption. This will be an excellent exercise since the students will have to compress in a short phrase or in two or three words the spirit of the scene. For example, the original photograph showing a set of twins in a fountain (*Photo 2*) was labelled "Two hot", focusing on an English pun; the original caption of the three youths sitting on a bench (*Photo 3*) was identified as "A situation well in hand". Students should be encouraged to think of both serious and humorous captions. These can come from:

- everyday language or crystallized language,
- proverbs,
- maxims,
- etc.

Photo: Zoran Milic

Photo 2

Public Speaking

The visual stimulus is also suitable for "public speaking" presentations. Students are asked to speak about the photo or use the photo as a point of departure. A discussion of ethics could be done for *Photo* 3 ("A situation well in hand").

Photo 3   *Photo*: Anthony Bruculere

Cause/Effect

Some photographs will show an effect to a given cause; others may show a cause which may produce varied effects. Students may be asked to identify either one or the other or both. See *Photo 4*.

Kim's Game

This is the popular memory game in which students are shown the photograph for a pre-determined number of seconds and then asked questions on what they saw. For this activity a copy of the photograph should be given to the students who are asked to look at it for a pre-determined number of seconds. They will then be required to turn it over and then the teacher asks a series of questions. This activity works best with photographs showing people demonstrating or protesting, with photos depicting accident scenes or with photographs which are full of details. Depending on the depth and the number of questions the teacher may wish to ask, this game can be played with practically all photos. All questions will focus on visual recall. (*Photo 5*).

Photo: Carl Turton

Photo 4

Photo: John Hryniuk

Photo 5

Newspaper Articles

Teachers may ask students to write an article for a local or school newspaper (or for a year book) based on the activities seen in the photograph. To assist each other students may be grouped together and brainstorm the lexical items and ideas or descriptions they would like to see included. Teachers may help by answering vocabulary questions or the students may seek the answers in a dictionary.

Before and After Sequence

In a discussion on cartoons, Roger Tremblay (1987) pointed out that vignettes are often pictures in a "state of imbalance"; that is, there is something which has taken place before the photo was taken and something which will follow.

Since students are provided with the "middle" photo, they should be encouraged to imagine the events which happened before and after. They will, as a result of this activity, invent or create a story with a beginning, middle and an end.

Description of events **preceding** *the scene depicted in the photograph*		*Description of events* **following** *the scene depicted in the photograph*
Before	Photo in the "state of imbalance"	After

Radio/TV Announcements

Teachers may ask students to assume the role of a newscaster and to describe verbally the activities portrayed in the photograph. In this case, obviously, the emphasis will be on the speaking.

Problem-Solving

Since photographs are in a "state of imbalance", the teacher may want to elicit from students the problem since the solution has already been shown by the photograph. *Photo 6* is a good example. Here, obviously, the little girl could not reach the fountain and enlisted the help of her sister.

Photo: Staff, *The Kitchener-Waterloo Record*

Photo 6

Writing Poetry

The photograph is also an effective stimulus for poetry writing. Many colleagues are reluctant to introduce or indeed teach poetry in the classroom and yet many students are «closet poets». They tend to be so because poetry is personal and they may be unwilling to reveal their personal feelings. If the stimulus is visual, students will focus on it rather on their personal experiences which they may not want to share and will produce very good results. Why poetry? Poetic writing demands preciseness. The word precise embodies the ideas of delineation and limit. Writing poetically helps children develop this language skill. The suggestions we are putting forth for consideration are «recipes» which students can follow with little or no difficulty. To assist them at the early stages of poetry writing, we recommend that they be asked to co-author their poetry by working in pairs or in groups. The following are some suitable examples but the choices are certainly not exhaustive:

a) *The Cinquain*

After learning the present tense and the agreement of adjectives, students may be asked to become "instant" poets by following these rules:

1.   On the first line, write down a noun: a person, a place or thing.
2.   On the line below that, write two adjectives (or two present participles, or two past participles). Separate the adjectives by a comma.
3.   On the third line, write three verbs that tell what the noun on the first line does. Separate the verbs by commas.
4.   On the fourth line, write a thought about the noun. A short sentence will be quite acceptable.
5.   On the fifth line, repeat the word you wrote on the first line or write down a synonym or some other related word.

The best way of approaching this task is to do a brainstorming of vocabulary with the entire class while the teacher or a student records on the blackboard the lexical items suggested by the class. Once the topic or title has been selected, the brainstorming begins. For example, the topic may be "Love".

•   Teachers should ask students to suggest adjectives which, in their opinion, describe the title or the topic. The answers will obviously vary; the vocabulary suggested will be drawn from each student's own linguistic background which may vary. This variation of vocabulary may very well bring to light new words; hence the activity will not only be a review of vocabulary already known to most students but also an introduction to new lexical items. Suggestions received during the brainstorming session may be:
     tender, passionate, kind, faithful, painful, friendly, confusing, hot, everlasting, fickle, romantic, exciting, emotional, sensitive, erotic, platonic, comforting, physical, sensual, wild, selfish, selfless, primal, paradoxical, fragile.
•   Ask students to suggest verbs - action words – that come to

mind when they think of "Love". Lexical suggestions may be:

protects, destroys, unites, separates, exhilarates, excites, protects, grows, changes, endures, hurts, heals, gives, shares, stimulates, burgeons, blossoms.

- Ask students to provide a thought about the topic.

  Love makes the world go round.
  Love is unconditional.
  Love is everything.
  Love is companionship.

The thought may be from a proverbial or Biblical phrase:

  Love is blind.
  Love is patient, love is kind.

from a maxim or saying:

  Lucky at cards, unlucky in love.
  Love is a double-edged sword.
  It's better to have loved and lost than not to have loved at all.

from a movie title or movie dialogue:

  Love is a many splendoured thing.
  Love means never having to say "You're sorry."

from a song:

  Love me tender, love me true.
  I love the way you love me.

or from other poems:

My love is like a red red rose.

  How do I love thee? Let me count the ways.

Ask students to provide a synonym for the topic:

  passion, affection, friendship, adoration

or an antonym:

  hate.

Some students, instead of selecting a synonym or antonym for the topic, decide to insert the name of the boyfriend or girl-friend! This is bound to create some humour in the classroom and this emphasizes the "fun" element of the activity.

Once teachers feel that they have "exhausted" the various possibilities, they should then ask students to create their own poem by following the instructions suggested above. Teachers should then ask all students to jot down the title of the poem,

"Love".

Next, teachers should ask a student to read slowly from the blackboard all the adjectives which describe the topic. Students are asked to select three adjectives from the list. It is obvious that different students will select different adjectives.

The same process – namely, asking a student to read the suggested answers written on the blackboard – is followed for the verbs (third line), the thought (fourth line) and the repetition of the topic/title or antonym for the fifth line. The reading of the lexical items on the blackboard will provide repetition to the activity.

When students have completed the task, no poem contains exactly the same vocabulary because each student has selected the lexical items of his/her choice. The poem, although done with the assistance of the entire class, becomes *personal* since it is the poem of the student who has selected the words.

Students who generally would be reluctant to share their feelings will probably do so willingly for they attribute the vocabulary as not being theirs but selected from the lists given by the class.

Since the poem deals with "love", students may decide to insert their poem in a suitable illustration, such as a heart.

Love
platonic, passionate
protects, enriches, destroys
Love is blind
Friendship

Love
sensual, mysterious
excites, endures, shares
Love is companionship
Jennifer

Students may be asked to find suitable illustrations from magazines or newspapers to embellish their written task.

Once teachers have established this as a "fun" activity, they may be encouraged to work on other types of poetry such as the following:

b) The Diamante
Students should be asked to follow these suggestions:
1. On the first line, write down a noun.
2. On the second line, write down two adjectives describingthe noun. Separate the adjectives by a comma.

3. On the third line write three participles.
4. On the fourth line, write down four nouns related to the subject. (The second two nouns may have opposite meanings from the subject.)..
5. On the fifth line, write three participles indicating change or development of the subject.
6. On the sixth line, write two adjectives carrying on the idea of change or development.
7. On the seventh line, write a noun that is the opposite of the subject.

c) The Haiku

The haiku is a Japanese unrhymed poem about nature and the seasons of the year. Several questions contained in the Teacher's Guide which accompanies the book A picture is worth...1000 words...refer to seasons. It may be appropriate for students to write a haiku poem for those photographs. The haiku has three lines and totals seventeen syllables. Students do not have to follow the syllabic count exactly but they should use a word that hints of the season of the year as they write these nature poems. The simplicity of the form of this type of poetry centers in its syllable count. The Haiku has seventeen syllables divided into lines of five, seven and five syllables. Students should keep in mind that the seventeen syllable count serves as a guide for writing a haiku; it is not a stringent, inflexible rule.

Editorials

Some photographs lend themselves quite well as a stimulus for Editorials. For example, a photo showing a child drinking from a public fountain (*Photo 7*) may lead to the importance of water in various cultures. North Americans use it to cultivate their lawns, wash their cars, etc. In many parts of the world there is a shortage of water, people drink bottled water, etc.

Bulletin Board Displays

The photographs are published in such a way so that the first large photo will serve as a basis for individual or group work. The second photo, in reduced size, with a lot of space around it, has been so designed to allow students to write/type their assignment on the page. This can then be posted on the bulletin board for display. Since the photos and the assignments will vary, this activity will provide reading material for the entire class.

Sequencing

Teachers may wish to leaf through the book and find photos

which, if placed one after another, will constitute a sequence. While each photograph may be discussed on its own merit, several photos may be grouped together to form a story. For example,

Photo 8: Drugs seized…
Photo 9: Alleged drug dealers apprehended…
Photo 10: US funds seized…
Photo 11: Canadian funds seized…
Photo 12: Reporter phones in story…
Photo 13: Woman reads events in newspaper…

Conclusion

The visual element, then, is an effective stimulus to trigger conversation in the classroom. It is by no means the only solution but it will certainly contribute to meaningful verbal and written activities. If used at different levels, it will answer the learner's linguistic needs and will provide hours of enjoyment and learning.

References

Brown, James W. and Anthony Mollica. 1988-1989. *Essays on Visual Semiotics*. Toronto: University of Victoria Semiotic Circle.

Mollica, Anthony. 1988. "Verbal Duelling in the Classroom: Audio and Visual Stimuli for Creative Communicative Activities." In Valeria Sestieri Lee, ed., *Language Teaching and Learning: Canada and Italy/Insegnare ed imparare lingue: Canada e Italia.* Ottawa: Canadian Mediterranean Institute/Roma: Centro Accademico canadese in Italia, 1988. Pp. 101- 122.

Mollica, Anthony. 1985a. "Not for Friday Afternoons Only!: The Calendar of Memorable Events as a Stimulus for Communicative Activities." *The Canadian Modern Language Review/La Revue canadienne des langues vivantes*, 42, 2 (November): 487-511.

Mollica, Anthony, 1985b. "Oral Stimuli for the Language Classroom." In Pia Kieber and Marcel Danesi, eds., *Language Teaching Strategies*, Vol. 1. Toronto: The Faculty of Arts and Science, 1985. Pp. 39-53.

Mollica, Anthony. 1981. "Visual Puzzles in the Second-Language Classroom." *The Canadian Modern Language Review/La Revue canadienne des langues vivantes*, 37, 3 (March): 583-628.

Mollica, Anthony. 1979a. "*A Tiger in Your Tank*" Advertisements in the Language Classroom." *The Canadian Modern Language Review/La Revue canadienne des langues vivantes*, 35, 4(May): 697-743.

Mollica, Anthony. 1979b. "Print and Non-Print Materials: Adapting for Classroom Use." In June K. Phillips, ed., *Building on Experience Building for Success*. ACTFL Foreign Language Education Series, Volume 10.Skokie, IL: National Textbook Company, 1979. Pp.157-198.

Mollica, Anthony 1978. "The Film   Advertisement: A Source for Language Activities." *The Canadian Modern Language Review/La Revue canadienne des langues vivantes*, 34, 2 (January): 221-243.

Photo 8

Photo 9

Photo 10

Photo 11

Photo 12

Photo 13

Mollica, Anthony. 1976. "Cartoons in the Language Classroom." *The Canadian Modern Language Review/La Revue canadienne des langues vivantes*, 32, 4 (March): 424-444.

Morgan, Clifford T. and Richard A. King. 1966. *Introduction to Psychology*. 3rd edition. New York MacGraw-Hill.

Tremblay, Roger. 1980. "La bande dessinée: Une typologie." *The Canadian Modern Language Review/La Revue canadienne des langues vivantes*, 36, 3 (March): 504-513.

Acknowledgements

For their kind permission to publish the photographs which appear in this article, I should like to thank:

Photo 1: Cec Mitchell, *The Welland Evening Tribune*

Photo 2: Zoran Milic, *The Toronto Star*

Photo 3: Anthony Bruculere

Photo 4: Carl Turton, *The Guardian Expressé*

Photo 5: John Hryniuk, *The Toronto Star*

Photo 6: Staff, *The Kitchener-Waterloo Record*

Photo 7: Ken Kerr, *Canada Wide*

Photo 8: Chuck Stoody, *CanaPress*

Photo 9: Stan Behal, *Canada Wide*

Photo 10: J. Wilkes, *The Toronto Star*

Photo 11: Rick Madonik, *The Globe and Mail*

Photo 12: Staff, *The Welland Evening Tribune*. Actor-Director Blake Heathcote in the 1991 Showboat Festival Theatre's production of *Harvey*.

Photo 13: Staff, *The Welland Evening Tribune*. Actress Teresa Kolysnyk in a scene from *The Mousetrap*.

This revised, expanded, and up-dated version contains sections from: Anthony Mollica, "Creative Writing: Poetry in the Language Classroom," *Mosaic*. 3, 1, (Fall 1995): 18-20.

Reprinted from: Anthony Mollica, "A Picture is worth... 1000 words... Creative Activities for the language classroom." In *A Picture is worth...1000 words...* Books 1 and 2. Welland, Ontario: éditions Soleil publishing, 1992. Pp. vii-xii.

26 A Picture is Worth 1000 Words and A Word is Worth 1000 Pictures

Hector Hammerly

Visual aids are very helpful in performing many peda-gogical functions in the second-language classroom. There are, however, two such functions they cannot per-form well. In some contexts, their use may even be cognitively disadvantageous. Much further research is needed on visual aids and their effects.

Pictures and visuals are not synonymous. *Visuals* is the cover term that refers to anything visible – other than writing systems, which are part of *language*. Visuals include

- *pictures* (realistic representations of objects, people, etc.);
- *graphics* (charts, diagrams, and so on); and
- *symbols* (arrows, ideographs, and so forth).

Recent books about the use of visuals in second-language teaching (Wright, 1989; Hill, 1990; Wright and Haleem, 1991) seem to accept without qualification the idea that "visuals are good for you" and simply go on to explain how to develop and use visuals. These authors do not acknowledge any limitations on the use of visuals as second language instructional aids.

There can be no question that visuals, whether still, serial, or moving, can enhance several aspects of second-language teach-ing. Among their positive contributions are their ability to

- represent sounds or structures,
- portray cultural features,
- provide situational awareness, and
- elicit verbal output – both controlled and free.

Sound and Structure Representation

The pronunciation of certain second-language sounds, especially those whose articulation is not directly observable, can be made clearer through the use of sagittal sections or pictorial articula-tory symbols (Hammerly, 1974a). Of course, only a few sounds require and benefit from such a visual approach. Using it with all sounds would be inefficient and would probably confuse the students.

(The use of a complete phonetic alphabet – a linguistic rather than a visual aid – seems unnecessary in second-language teaching. Besides, the International Phonetic Alphabet [IPA], for example, has many strange-looking symbols. Most IPA symbols are not effective reminders of the articulations they represent. The IPA is not, of course, based on the particular needs of speakers of language X trying to learn language Y and it does not provide a gradual shift from pronunciation symbols to spellings. These are all features that a good pedagogical transcription should have.)

Second-language stress and intonation can be shown visually in many ways – the best one perhaps being a scale graphic resembling a musical scale. As well, the potential of video technology to help teach pronunciation and intonation has hardly begun to be exploited. Think, for example, how useful it would be to have prerecorded videos using half the frame, then have students record the audio and video for the other half and compare the two halves.

Grammatical structures can be represented with diagrams using lines, shapes and colours, with arrows, and with other graphic devices (Danesi, 1990; Brown, 1990). It seems clear that, when properly designed and used, the various visual devices that may represent second-language sounds and structures can be very helpful. What is puzzling is that, so far, there has been very little research, that I am aware of, on their relative effectiveness in the classroom.

Culture Depiction

The use of visuals is an excellent way to convey information about all four aspects of a second culture – informational (geography, demography, institutions, and so on), behavioral (customs and everyday behaviour), achievement (heroes, artists, writers, *et al.*), and attitudinal (work ethic, ethnocentrism, xenophobia, etc.). Of course, only the visible manifestations of the second-language culture can be portrayed. With some ingenuity much can be done, whether through the use of cartoons, photographs, videos or other visual media. (In many cases, colour is essential. How would one otherwise teach that to find a mailbox one has to look for something red in Canada and something blue in the U.S.? And how about taxis in different countries? Not all are yellow.) Video can enhance the presentation of cultural information to children (Herron and Hanley, 1992). But, note that students from a different cultural background may not understand visuals very well. Tuffs and Tudor (1990) found that non-native speakers of English from Asian cultural backgrounds understood an ESL video played silently significantly less than native English speakers. There is no need to compare such radically different cultures to see certain cross-cultural difficulties. As Mollica (1994) notes, a *coffeepot* looks very different in Italy and in North America, and pictures of a Canadian university campus may be difficult to understand for Europeans, for whom a university is just buildings.

Situational Awareness

Good thematic pictures can provide awareness of important elements of a situation in which language activity occurs. They can offer the nonverbal setting or context to spoken or written language. When they perform this function, pictures provide general support to listening or reading comprehension (Mueller, 1980; Snyder and Colón, 1988), in the form of global comprehension support that is especially useful if it precedes a text (Omaggio, 1979; Dethloff, 1980) or presentation. Here the picture helps play the role of "advance organizer" (Ausbel, 1960). During the presentation of a second-language story, however, video enhances comprehension in general, but does not necessarily help understand the text itself (Baltova, 1994). I emphasize that in this function pictures provide *general* comprehension support for, as we shall see, pictures are far from adequate at conveying the meanings of *specific* words or phrases in context (Cole 1967, 1976).

Verbal Output Elicitation

The ability of pictures and other visuals to elicit verbal output has long been known. In recent years, Anthony Mollica has amply demonstrated this fact with his 1992 series of books of unusual photographs, *A picture is worth...1000 words*. These photos either tell a story or entice the imagination to invent one. They have been carefully selected for their ability to elicit conversation.Guides with questions and exercises to accompany these books are available in eleven languages.

Another visual aid I have found effective in eliciting verbal output is the "wordless" – captionless – cartoon strip that tells a story. For years I collected them and used them particularly in my intermediate and advanced classes. First, I would teach any essential new vocabulary and tell the story. Then I would ask the students questions about the story. I usually followed these first two steps twice. After that, I would ask them to tell the story themselves. Finally, they would ask each other questions about it. The same "wordless strip" could be used to tell a story in the present tense first, in the past tense later in the program, in the future tense still later, and finally as contrary to fact or from a particular point of view. This activity was very effective.

Pictures for verbal output elicitation should be chosen very carefully and used at appropriate times within a definite structural/lexical program progression. Asking students to describe scenes or tell stories for which they lack the necessary language is inviting them to make numerous errors, far more than can be corrected effectively. The result of speaking in the classroom beyond one's second-language competence is the early habituation of a very faulty inter-language, as has happened in French immersion programs (Hammerly, 1989). Careful gradation in language teaching is essential – even when using pictures.

In the four aspects discussed above – sound and structure representation, cultural depiction, situational awareness, and especially verbal output elicitation – there is little doubt that a good picture (or other visual) is worth many words, perhaps even 1,000 or more. But there are two other aspects of language teaching in which the opposite happens, that is, where a word is worth 1,000 pictures. Indeed, in those two aspects of language teaching pictures are not only unnecessary but may be harmful in a variety of ways. Moreover, a third concern is that some uses of pictures may curtail cognitive activity.

I am referring to
- the conveyance of the *specific meaning(s)* of new words and phrases,
- the elicitation of *specific* words and phrases, and
- the likelihood that providing a given picture may restrict or even eliminate, in certain activities, the generation of mental imagery.

Conveyance of the Meaning(s) of New Words and Phrases

When we know the native language of the students or have appropriate materials that allow us to address each student in his or her native language (in the case of multilingual classes), then we can use the native language to convey meaning. The use of the native language instead of pictures is much more precise and much faster. Also, it saves the students from the frustration of having to play an ongoing guessing game – a game they often lose.

To clarify what I mean by a word being worth 1,000 pictures

in conveying specific word or phrase meanings, consider the following example. Suppose we want to teach the French word *voiture* ("car") to an English speaker. A picture of a car would necessarily have to show a particular kind of car, which is, of course, misleading, for *une voiture* can be any kind of car. But the *word* "car" would transmit precisely the meaning we want to convey. And it is literally worth thousands of pictures as all the stored images of cars the student has ever seen contribute to the concept of both *car* and *voiture* – a concept the student *already* carries in his or her mind. This is certainly not a new concept that needs to be experienced physically or pictorially in order to be learned.

In attempting to convey meaning through pictures, we risk several problems. The likelihood of a narrower interpretation has already been mentioned. The opposite is also possible, though probably less likely: the learner may think of a hyponym, such as the word *vehicle* instead of *car* in our example. Or the learner may think we are trying to teach him something else, such as a colour, size, or shape. In fact, we can never be sure that the learner will interpret the picture the way we hope he or she will (Hammerly, 1974b).

Incidentally, when analyzed logically, the monolingual demonstration procedure seems downright silly: here is a grown-up teacher of English showing a book or a picture of a book and saying the inanity "This is a book" to, e.g., French-speaking students *who know perfectly well what a book looks like*! You may say the students are thereby learning the English word for "livre," but clearly all they need to readily accomplish that is for the equation book = "livre" to be made in some meaningful, informative context. Constantly trying to guess what "new" words mean in inane little sentences can hardly be a defensible activity for intelligent second-language students.

In the case of phrases and sentences that form part of an audiovisually presented dialogue, the learner may fail to understand many of the sentences. This has happened in empirical studies involving the monolingual presentation of filmstrips, even when the subjects were experienced second-language teachers (Dodson, 1967; Hammerly, 1984). The same thing no doubt happens with video presentations, although they should help make action verbs a little clearer. In fact, it has been found that the most beneficial input, as far as understanding videos is concerned, is bilingual bimodal – in the two languages and both audio and written – rather than monolingual audio (Danan, 1992).

By making overt but very brief use of the students' native

language to convey specific meanings, we can ensure that the interlingual equations the students make are correct. For even if not a single word of the first language is used in class, the students *will* make mental interlingual equations: relating the unknown to the known is an inevitable psychological process. The problem with allowing these equations to be formed covertly is that they are often incorrect – and unavailable for correction. If this matter is not dealt with openly, incorrect interlingual equations may be reinforced over a long period of time and be difficult to eradicate when the teacher finally becomes aware of them. For example, Direct Method students of French who have never heard a word of English in class say things like **fenêtre de magasin for vitrine* ("store window"), which proves that in their minds they have made the imperfect equation *fenêtre* = "window." This common phenomenon was noted by Sweet nearly a century ago (1899).

When specific meanings are conveyed in the native language, the problem just alluded to can be prevented. Oral presentations can include a clarification or warning about the limitations of the equation, as follows: *fenêtre* = "window – but a regular window, *not*, for example, a store window." Another advantage of conveying specific meanings clearly and quickly in the first language is that much time is saved by not having to spend it on slow, inefficient attempts to guess the meanings of words. Even Corder, a committed audio-visualist, admitted that monolingual methods are "very slow" (Corder, 1966:27). The time saved by conveying meanings briefly in the native language can then be spent, much more effectively, on using the words or phrases meaningfully in the second language. Of course, once new words or phrases and their meanings have been learned bilingually, pictures can be used effectively, in either a general or directed way, to help practice their communicative use.

Elicitation of Specific Words and Phrases

The second difficulty with pictures in language teaching is that they are also unreliable in *eliciting* specific words and phrases. Language test developers, to their disappointment, discovered that long ago (Pimsleur, 1966). A picture of a dog could be shown, for example, to English-speaking students of Spanish in the expectation that they would say *perro* and thereby show whether or not they controlled the sound [rr], but often some examinees would say other things, such as *animal* or *mascota* ("pet"), thus frustrating the whole purpose of the test item. This unreliability of pictures in eliciting specific words and phrases often extends, of course, to conversational output activities that may be thus attempted.

Curtailed Imagery Generation?

We should research the possibility that by providing our students with a given picture or pictures we may be asking them to be cognitively passive rather than participate actively in the process of mental imagery generation. It may be, for example, that far more images are activated or generated in reading a story than in seeing it acted out. It also seems that images one generates oneself are remembered better than those one is given. Since, more generally, ability to recall depends largely on the number and the vividness of associations, this whole question deserves study.

Conclusion

Pictures and other visuals offer numerous advantages. It has been shown that videos can profitably be used in numerous ways (Cummins, 1989; Liebelt, 1989; March, 1989; Seidler, 1989; Orban and McLean, 1990). New technologies such as the VCR and interactive video (Schmidt, 1989; Forrest, 1993) and satellite television (Oxford *et al.*, 1993; Yi and Majima, 1993) allow us to bring moving pictures into our classrooms from anywhere in the world. The integration of video (Reese *et al.*, 1988; McCoy, 1989-90) with the other elements of language programs is also beginning to be considered.

But the advantages visuals offer and the fact that for certain functions a picture is worth 1,000 words should not distract us from the empirical and logical evidence that in at least two aspects of language teaching -the conveyance of specific meanings and the eliciting of specific words and phrases – pictures are imprecise, slow and unreliable. For those pedagogical functions, just one or two words in the first language are usually worth 1,000 pictures.

Far more research is needed on visual aids, their various classroom uses, and their effects on comprehension, recall and other cognitive activities. The author hopes that this article may further encourage such research.

References

Ausubel, D.P. 1960. "The use of advance organizers in the learning and retention of meaningful verbal material." *Journal of Educational Psychology*, 51: 267-72.

Baltova, I. 1994. "The impact of video on the comprehension skills of core French students." *The Canadian Modern Language Review/La Revue canadienne des langues vivantes*, 50: 507-31.

Brown, James W. 1990. "Visual materials in contemporary French textbooks: A critique." In James W. Brown and Anthony Mollica, 1990, pp. 43-56.

Brown, James W. and Anthony Mollica, eds. 1990. *Essays in applied visual semiotics*. Toronto: Monograph Series of the Toronto Semiotic Circle, No. 3, Victoria College of the University of Toronto.

Cole, L.R. 1967. "The visual element and the problem of meaning in language learning." *Audio-Visual Language Journal*, 4: 84-7.

Cole, L.R. 1976. "Relationships between visual presentations and linguistic items in second-language teaching." *International Review of Applied Linguistics*, 14: 339-50.

Corder, S.P. 1966. *The visual element in language teaching*. London: Longman.

Cummins, P.W. 1989. "Video and the French teacher." *French Review*, 62: 411-26.

Danan, M. 1992. "Reversed subtitling and dual coding theory: New directions for foreign language instruction." *Language Learning*, 42: 497-527.

Danesi, M. 1990. "The visual display of grammatical information in L2 methodology." In Brown and Mollica 1990, pp. 57-64.

Dethloff, U. 1980. "La réception des textes télévisuels en langue étrangère." *Études de linguistique appliquée*, 38: 106-18.

Dodson, C.J. 1967. *Language teaching and the bilingual method*. London: Pitman.

Forrest, T. 1993. "Technology and the language classroom: Available technology." *TESOL Quarterly*, 27: 316-8.

Hammerly, H. 1974a. *The articulatory pictorial transcriptions: New aids to second-language pronunciation*. Blaine, W.A.: Second-language Publications.

Hammerly, H. 1974b. "Primary and secondary associations with visual aids as semantic conveyors." *International Review of Applied Linguistics*, 12: 119-25.

Hammerly, H. 1984. "Contextualized visual aids (filmstrips) as conveyors of sentence meaning." *International Review of Applied Linguistics*, 22: 87-94.

Hammerly, H. 1989. *French immersion: Myths and reality -Toward a better classroom road to bilingualism*. Calgary, Alberta: Detselig Enterprises.

Hammerly, H. 1990. "Advantages and limitations of visual aids in second-language teaching." In Brown and Mollica 1990, pp. 11-26.

Herron, C.A. and J. Hanley. 1992. "Using video to introduce children to a foreign culture." *Foreign Language Annals*, 25: 419-26.

Hill, A.A. 1990. *Visual impact: Creative language learning through pictures*. Essex, England: Longman.

Liebelt, W. 1989. "Anregungen für den Umgang mit Video im Fremdsprachenunterricht." *Praxis des neusprachlichen Unterrichts*, 3: 250-61.

March, C. 1989. "Some observations on the use of video in teaching of modern languages." *British Journal of Language Teaching*, 27: 13-7.

McCoy, E.L. 1989-90. "From *French in Action* to *Travessia*: The integral video curriculum in interactive language classrooms" *Journal of Educational Techniques and Technologies*, Winter, pp. 30-4.

Mollica, Anthony. 1992. *A picture is worth... 1000 words... Creative activities for the language classroom.* Welland, Ont: éditions Soleil publishing inc.

Mollica, Anthony. 1994. Personal communication.

Mueller, G.A. 1980. "Visual contextual cues and listening comprehension: An experiment." *The Modern Language Journal*, 64: 335-40.

Omaggio, A.C. 1979. "Pictures and second-language comprehension: Do they help?" *Foreign Language Annals*, 12: 107-16.

Orban, C. and A.M. McLean. 1990. "A working model for videocamera use in the foreign language classroom." *French Review*, 63: 652-63.

Oxford, R. et al. 1993. "Learning a language by satellite television: What influences student achievement?" *System*, 21: 31-48.

Pimsleur, P. 1966. "Testing foreign language learning." In A. Valdman, ed., *Trends in language teaching.* New York: McGraw-Hill, pp. 175-214.

Reese, L.G. *et al.* 1988. "Integrated use of videodisc for intensive Spanish language learning." *CALICO Journal*, September, pp. 69-81.

Schmidt, H. 1989. "Real conversation as a motivational factor through interactive video." *The Canadian Modern Language Review/La Revue canadienne des langues vivantes*, 45: 329-38.

Seidler, K. W. 1989. "Old wine in new bottles? A video-letter exchange project as a means of organising cross-cultural learning." *British Journal of Language Teaching*, 27: 30-5.

Snyder, H.R. and I. Colón. 1988. "Foreign language acquisition and audio-visual aids." *Foreign Language Annals*, 21: 343-48.

Sweet, H. 1899. *The practical study of languages.* London: J.M. Dent and Sons. [Reprinted in 1964 by Oxford University Press.]

Tuffs, R. and I. Tudor. 1990. "What the eye doesn't see: Cross-cultural problems in the comprehension of video material." *RELC Journal*, 21, 2: 29-44.

Wright, A. 1989. *Pictures for language learning.* Cambridge, England: Cambridge University Press.

Wright, A. and S. Haleem. 1991. *Visuals for the language classroom.* Essex, England: Longman.

Yi, H. and J. Majima. 1993. "The teacher-learner relationship and classroom interaction in distance learning: A case study of the Japanese language classes at an American high school." *Foreign Language Annals*, 26: 21-30.

Reprinted from: Hector Hammerly, "A Picture is Worth 1000 Words and a Word is Worth 1000 Pictures." *Mosaic*, 1, 4 (Summer 1994): 14-17.

27 Mnemonic Acronyms: A Memory Aid for Teaching and Learning Spanish Grammar

Frank Nuessel

Mnemonic devices are very useful to summarize and simplify grammatical rules especially when applied to many verb tenses and forms.

Introduction

The *American Heritage Dictionary of the English Language* (Morris 1979: 842) defines "mnemonic" as "a device, such as a formula or rhyme, used as an aid in remembering." We advocate the use of mnemonics, where possible, as a simple way to help students to learn particular grammatical structures.

For a history of mnemonics, there are several interesting studies. Moreover, various articles exist on mnemonics for Spanish and second-language education in general. (see references)

At the elementary and intermediate level such devices can be quite useful for students who may find that certain aspects of the grammar of Spanish are overwhelming. In these instances, a mnemonic device is often a blessing for students. Tuttle (1981) is perhaps the first person to write about this notion for Spanish in his article "Mnemonics in Spanish Class." In that essay, he talks about visual mnemonic devices such as the "shoe" verb concept for illustrating where stem changes occur in the present tense verbs. These changes occur in the first, second, and third person singular and third person plural, and when a line is drawn around these forms, they form the approximate outline of a shoe. Another sort of mnemonic device is the acronym. Morris (1979: 12) defines this notion as "a word formed from the initial letters of a name, as WAC for Women's Army Corps, or by combining initial letters or parts of a series of words, as radar from radio detecting and ranging."

Danesi (1983: 73; see also Mollica 1981: 620) notes that the visual component of any second-language learning tactic is very important. In his discussion of pedagogical graphics, or device intended to assist the student to understand and retain grammatical aspects of a second-language, Danesi (1983: 73-74) states that

> [a] pedagogical graphic is any symbol, figure, schema, diagram or chart (dots, lines arrows, circles, braces, etc.) that can be used to enrich the presentation of a grammatical point; i.e., it is a visual device that can be utilized in conjunction with, or superimposed upon, target language data in order to highlight some structural feature, relationship or process.

In the case of mnemonic acronyms, it is best to arrange the key letters of the acronym vertically and place the initial letter in capital letters and in boldface type.

Mnemonic Acronyms

In this section, mnemonic acronyms for the following discrete grammar points in Spanish will be exemplified:

1. *estar*,
2. adjective position,
3. imperfect tense,
4. object pronouns,
5. *para*, and
6. the subjunctive.

Estar

Mason (1990: 506) suggests the use of the acronym PLACE as a way to remember the use of estar reproduced here :

P osition:	Expresses the physical position or posture of a person or thing: *estar sentado, levantado*, etc.
L ocation:	Expresses where places, people, or things are located (*Estoy en Nueva York; El libro está en la mesa*).
A ction:	Expresses the result of an action or progressive (*El hombre está muerto; Estoy comiendo ahora*).
C ondition:	Expresses health and other changeable states (*estar enfermo, sucio, lleno*, etc.).
E motion:	Expresses emotions such as (*estar contento, triste, deprimido*) but one must remember that *alegre, melancólico* and *feliz* are considered inherent character traits and not simply experienced emotions that may change.

Adjective Position

The entire question of adjective position in Spanish is complex because many factors enter into the relationship of meaning and placement Contreras 1976). Tuttle (1981: 582) provides a very useful mnemonic device for remembering the usual position of adjectives in Spanish. It is LND (pronounced 'land'). Its meaning follows: Limiting adjectives precede the Noun while Descriptive adjectives follow it. Stiehm's (1978) article on teaching Spanish word order for a comprehensive overview of this complex question is an excellent study on this topic.

> **L** imiting Adjective
> **N** oun
> **D** escriptive Adjective

Imperfect

Mason (1996: 16) suggests a mnemonic device for helping students to remember under what circumstances they should use the imperfect tense. The acronym is CHEATED.

> **C** ontinuous Actions
> *He was walking in the park when I saw him.*
> **H** abitual Actions
> *Every Saturday night they would go to the movies.*
> **E** motions
> *He was happy to see me.*
> **A** ge
> *She was thirty years old.*
> **T** ime
> *It was nine o'clock.*
> **E** ndless Actions
> *The dream kept occurring.*
> **D** escriptions
> *It was a beautiful sunny day.*

Object Pronouns

At least two mnemonic strategies help students to remember where to place object pronouns in Spanish. The first is IGA (= Infinitives, Gerunds, Affirmative Commands (Quirk 2002: 903).

In the case of IGA, however, the student must keep in mind that the IG part of IGA is optional while the A part is not.

> **I** nfinitive (optional before, after)
> **G** erund (optional before, after)
> **A** ffirmative Commands

The second mnemonic device is RID (=Reflexive Indirect Direct; Quirk 2002: 904) that helps the student to recall the order of object pronouns.

R eflexive
I   ndirect
D irect

Para

While we can offer no simple and foolproof strategy for differen-
tiating por and para, it may be easier to show students the uses of
para, with its fewer and less complicated uses, and then explain
that por is used elsewhere. To this end, Mason (1992) suggests a
mnemonic device to assist students in recalling when to use either
por or para. The mnemonic acronym for the use of para is
PERFECT. Mason's acronym (1992: 198).

P urpose:	Indicates the purpose of an action (*Lo hizo para ganar dinero*)
E ffect:	Indicates the effect that something or someone has on something or someone else (*Estudia para maestro*)
R ecipient:	Indicates the person or entity that receives something (*el regalo es para mamá; el dinero es para el fondo especial*)
F uture:	Projects to a future date or event (*la tarea es para el lunes*)
E mployment:	Indicates both what something is used for or job employment (*las tijeras son para cortar; Carlos trabaja para IBM*)
C omparison:	Indicates a comparison of person or thing with others in a class (*Para un gato es muy inteligente*)
T oward:	Indicates movement toward in terms of direction (*Pablo camina para el parque*)

Subjunctive

The subjunctive mood, its forms and its uses, can be difficult to
present to students conceptually. There are a few acronyms that
help students to remember certain aspects of its formation and its
uses.

Subjunctive Verb Formation

The materials in this section derive from a session at annual meeting of the American Association of Teachers of Spanish and Portuguese (www.aatsp.org) held in Chicago August 4, 2003.

Stickles and Schwartz (2003: 1) use the acronym DISHES to
summarize those verbs whose present subjunctive is not based
on the *yo* form of the present indicative.

D	ar	dé
I	r	vaya
S	er	sea
H	aber	haya
E	star	esté
S	aber	sepa

Subjunctive in Noun Clauses

Tuttle (1981: 582; see Knop 1971: 340) suggests the acronym WEDDING as a way to remember which meaning classes of verbs take the subjunctive. WEDDING stands for the following predicates.

The WEDDING acronym thus covers noun clauses introduced by verbs of volition, emotion, desire, doubt and impersonal expressions. Likewise, it covers the use of the subjunctive in relative clauses when there is a negative antecedent or an unspecified antecedent. This acronymic mnemonic does not, however, cover instances of the subjunctive in adverbial clauses (for discussion see below).

WEDDING Acronym:	
W ill (verbs of volition such as *preferir* and so forth)	
Prefiero que Jorge llegue a tiempo.	I prefer that Jorge arrive on time.
E motion (verbs and verbal expressions of emotion such as *sentir, estar alegre de)*	
Siento que María esté enferma.	I regret that María is sick.
Estoy alegre de que puedas visitarnos.	I am happy that you can visit us.
D esire (verbs such as *querer, desear* and so forth)	
Quiero que Juan escriba la carta.	I want Juan to write the letter.
D oubt (verbs such as *dudar* and so forth)	
Dudo que llueva hoy.	I doubt that it will rain today.
I mpersonal expression (verbal expressions such as *es importante, es posible* and so forth)	
Es posible qu haya mucha gente allí.	It is possible that there will be a lot of people there.
N egative (relative clauses with negative antecedents such as *nadie, nada* and so forth)	
No hay nadie que pueda trabajar el domingo.	There is no one that can work on Sunday.
G eneralized characteristics (relative clauses with unspecified antecedents)	
¿Hay alguien que tenga la tarea de hoy?	Is there someone who has today's homework?

Impersonal Expressions

Chandler (1996) uses the acronym VOCES to indicate when to use the indicative after impersonal expressions.

Es	+ VOCES	+ *que*	´ *INDICATIVO*
Es	**v** erdad	que	*Es verdad que te quiero mucho.*
			It is true that I love you a lot.
Es	**o** bvio	que	*Es obvio que me quieres también.*
			It is obvious that you love me too.
Es	**c** ierto/c laro	que	*Es cierto que te quiero más todos los días.*
			It is certain that I love you more every day.
Es	**e** vidente	que	*Es evidente que él no te quiere como yo.*
			It is evident that he does not love you like I do.
Es	**s** eguro	que	*Es seguro que nos queremos muchísimo.*

The Use of *Que*

Wakefield (1992) employs a travel analogy as a way to help students remember when to use the subjunctive in noun clauses. She (Wakefield 1992: 200) states that

"... a sentence must contain a trigger verb indicating influence, emotion, or doubt. Two other conditions must also be made clear. There must be two clauses in the sentence indicated by a QUE, as well as a change of subject."

Wakefield then proposes a visual mnemonic namely the *"pasaporte oficial"* which has the following form reproduced here:

Pasaporte Oficial
1. *Trigger*
2. *Que*
3. *Cambio de sujeto*
Sin las condiciones de arriba, no se puede pasar a la tierra del subjuntivo

Adverbial Clause

Stickels and Schwartz (2003) provide several acronyms to address the use of the subjunctive in adverbial clauses – one of the more complex aspects of Spanish grammar.

Conjunctions which always require the subjunctive.

Stickels and Schwartz (2003: 19) use the acronym ESCAPA to refer to conjunctions which always require the subjunctive. They note with these conjunctions that you cannot escape the subjunctive.

Main Clause	Conjunctions	Dependent Clause
ANY TENSE	**E** *en caso que* **S** *sin que* **C** *con tal que* **A** *antes de que* **P** *para que* **A** *a menos que*	SUBJUNCTIVE

Conjunctions for indefinite future time or uncertainty

Adverbial conjunctions that take the subjunctive when there is an unspecified or indefinite future time, or when certainty is implied constitute another category. Stickels and Schwartz (2003: 19) use the acronym LATCHED to refer to conjunctions that take the subjective when an event has not yet taken place. These forms are not used with the past subjunctive reproduced here.

Main Clause	Conjunctions	Dependent Clause
Present,	**L** *luego que*	*Indicative* – certainty
	A *así que*	*Subjunctive* – uncertainty
Future,	**T** *tan pronto que*	
Commands,	**C** *cuando*	*Subjunctive*
All other	**H** *hasta que*	*Indicative*
tenses	**E** *en cuanto*	
	D *después de que*	

Additional Conjunctions

Stickels and Schwartz (2003: 19) use the acronym MA to refer to conjunctions that take the subjunctive when an event has not yet taken place reproduced below.

Main Clause	Conjunctions	Dependent Clause
All tenses	**M** *mientras que*	*Indicative* – certainty
	A A *unque*	*Subjunctive* – uncertainty

Concluding Remarks

The above are a few very useful acronyms for teaching selected problematic grammatical points of Spanish grammar. A useful exercise involves trying to create other mnemonic acronyms for such problematic grammatical items and structures such as: por, ser, and the preterite, to name but a few. Teacher workshops provide a good opportunity to "brainstorm" other possibilities. These memory strategies really help students to recall when and how to use challenging aspects of Spanish grammar. Very often my students tell me that they still recall these memory aids years later, and they even use them to help their own children or their siblings.

References

Atkinson, Richard C. 1975. "Mnemotechnics in Second-Language Learning." *American Psychologist,* 30: 821-828.

Chandler, Paul Michael. 1996. "Idea: VOCES: A Mnemonic Device to Cue Mood Selection After Impersonal Expressions." *Hispania,* 79: 126-128.

Contreras, Heles. 1976. *A Theory of Word Order with Special Reference to Spanish.* Amerstam: North-Holland Publishing Co.

Danesi, Marcel. 1983. "Pedagogical Graphics in Second-Language Teaching." *The Canadian Modern Language Review/La revue canadienne des langues vivantes,* 40(1): 73-81.

Higbee, Kenneth. 1979. "Recent Research on Visual Mnemonics: Historical Roots and Educational Fruits." *Review of Education Research,* 49: 611-629.

Knop, C. K. 1971. "Mnemonic Devices in Teaching French." *The French Review,* 45: 337-342.

Mason, Keith. 1990. "*Ser* vs. *estar*: A Mnemonic Device Puts estar in Its P.L.A.C.E." *Hispania,* 73: 506-507.

Mason, Keith. 1992. "Successful Mnemonics for por/para and Affirmative Commands with Pronouns." *Hispania,* 75: 197-199.

Mason, Keith. 1996. "Mnemonics for Mastering the Imperfect and Irregular Future in French, Italian and Spanish." *Mosaic,* 3(4): 16-17.

Mollica, Anthony. 1964. "Review of the Subjunctive Mood in Spanish." *The Canadian Modern Language Review,* 21, 1(October): 62-65.

Mollica, Anthony. 1965. "Review of the Subjunctive Mood in Italian." *The Canadian Modern Language Review,* 21, 2(January): 48-52.

Mollica, Anthony. 1965. "Review of the Subjunctive Mood in French." *The Canadian Modern Language Review,* 21, 3(Spring): 68-72.

Mollica, Anthony. 1981. "Visual Puzzles for the Second Language Classroom." *The Canadian Modern Language Review/La revue canadienne des langues vivantes,* 37(3): 583:622.

Morris, William, ed. 1979. *The American Heritage Dictionary of the English Language.* Boston: Houghton Mifflin.

Nyikos, Martha. 1985. "Memory Hooks and Other Mnemonic Devices: A Brief Overview for Teachers." In: P. Westphal, ed., *Meeting the Call for Excellence in the Foreign Language Classroom,* pp. 50-67. Lincolnwood, IL: National Textbook Company.

Paivio, Allan and Alain Desrochers. 1981. "Mnemonic Techniques and Second-Language Learning." *Journal of Educational Psychology,* 73: 780-795.

Quilter, Dan. 1993. *Spanish: An Analysis for Advanced Students.* New York:

McGraw Hill.

Quirk, Ronald J. 2002. "A Simplified Method of Teaching the Position of Object Pronouns in Spanish." *Hispania,* 85: 902-906.

Raugh, R, and R. C. Atkinson. 1975. "A Mnemonic Method for Learning Second Language Vocabulary." *Journal of Educational Psychology,* 67(1): 1-16.

Stickles, Leslie and Marsha Schwartz. 2003. "Subjunctive Made Easier." Presentation made at AATSP. Chicago, IL. August 4. Ms.

Stiehm, Bruce. 1978. Teaching Spanish Word Order. *Hispania,* 61: 40-434.

Tuttle, Harry. 1981. "Mnemonics in Spanish Classes." *Hispania*, 64: 582-584.

Yates, Frances A. 1966. *The Art of Memory.* Chicago: University of Chicago Press.

Wakefield, Connie Michelle. 1992. "Bridging the Communication Gap: A Passport to the Subjunctive." *Hispania,* 75: 200.

Reprinted from: Frank Nuessel, `Mnemonic Acronyms: A Memory Aid for Teaching and Learning Spanish.` *Mosaic,* 8, 2 (Winter): 21-24.

28 Teaching French Using Mnemonic Devices

John J. Janc

Mnemonic devices can make learning a foreign language more enjoyable by helping students understand, master and remember many grammatical concepts.

Mnemonic devices are basically memory aides. I have always found them useful as have those who take my classes. When trying to create one, teachers should never hesitate to give free reign to their imagination. They must play with the letters and, when necessary, look for other examples that fit the rule under consideration. Sometimes one really must "cheat" a little. Words may have to be repeated or letters used that do not fit the acronym. Teachers should regularly repeat the devices in class and should require students to memorize them when feasible. Very often, after having taught one, I give extra credit on the next quiz to those who are able to reproduce the device and explain the grammatical point that it illustrates. I then require everyone to know it by heart for the following quiz or examination. Some devices may appeal to the ear, others to the eye. Some need to be used in conjunction with another one in order to make sense. The reader will find examples of these different points below.

Adjectives

This is the traditional device used to help students remember what adjectives normally precede the noun.

> **B** eauty: *beau, joli, vilain*
> **A** ge: *jeune, nouveau, vieux*
> **N** umber: *premier, dernier, deuxième*
> **G** oodness: *bon, gentil, mauvais, méchant, vilain*
> **S** ize: *court, haut, grand, gros, long, petit*

Here is a French version of the preceding one.

> **T** aille: *court, haut, grand, gros, long, petit*
> **A** utre: *autre*
> **N** ombre: *premier, dernier, deuxième*
> **C** aract re: *bon, gentil, mauvais, méchant, vilain*
> **A** utre: *autre*
> **B** eauté: *beau, joli, vilain*

I have also used "BIG MAC" to supplement the preceding two.

BIG **M** ême
A utre
C haque

Adverbs

This device is visual in nature and is designed to help students remember that "mieux," not "meilleur," is the irregular comparative form of "bien."

bI**E**n
mI**E**ux

Adverbes of Quantity

These adverbs of quantity are followed only by "de." (PUT MAT in a CAB).

P lus	**M** oins	in a	**C** ombien
U n peu	**A** utant		**A** ssez
T ant	**T** rop		**B** eaucoup

Definite Articles

These verbs are never followed by the partitive. (PA HAD)

P référer	**H** aïr
A dorer	**A** imer
	D étester

Indefinite Articles

Two versions for this device exist because one of them may offend some people. If the predicate nominative is not modified, one uses the appropriate subject pronoun: "il(s), elle(s)." If it is modified, one uses "ce (c')."

Il est Français.   C'est un Français.

Elles sont ingénieurs. Ce sont de bonnes ingénieurs.

P arti politique	**C** itoyen(neté)
O ccupation	**R** eligion
R eligion	**O** ccupation
N ationalité	**P** arti politique

Indirect and Direct Object Promouns
The Three "As"

The three "As" are used when teaching direct objects ("compléments d'objet direct" or COD in French) because they help students recognize them. If an object is preceded by one of these words and nothing else, it is direct. If one of these words is preceded by a preposition or if there is a number, a partitive, an expression of quantity, etc. before the noun, a COD cannot be used.

A COD: Nous chantons l'/cet/ton air.

Not a COD: Nous jouons avec tes amis.

             Nous lisons trois poèmes/des poèmes/beaucoup de ces poèmes.

A rticle défini

A djectif possessif

A djectif démonstratif

This device is meant to help students learn the pattern in question. Because of its length, they are not asked to memorize it. It can be used several times: to introduce the direct-object indirect-object pattern, to teach direct object replacement, to teach indirect object placement, to teach double pronoun replacement and to teach past participle agreement.

D evoir quelque chose à quelqu'un

A ttribuer quelque chose à quelqu'un

D emander quelque chose à quelqu'un

R aconter

E xpliquer

A cheter

D ire

S ervir

P rêter

É crire

E nvoyer

D onner

M ontrer

A pporter

I ndiquer

L ire

Prepositions

The following verbs require these prepositions in French.

S ortir de   **M** onter dans
P artir de   **D** escendre de
E ntrer dans
E ntrer dans
D iriger (se) vers

These verbs are not followed by a preposition in French.

R egarder
É couter
D évisager

C hercher
A ttendre
P ayer

"RED CAP" is another version of this acronym. Some teachers replace "dévisager" by "demander." My students generally prefer the first one because of the way it sounds (it is *meant* to rime with the English pronunciation of "crêpe.")

In the passive, when describing a state of being, these past participles are followed by "de."

La route est bordée d'arbres.

La piscine est remplie d'eau.

B ordé de
R empli de
U
C ouvert de
E ntouré de

These verbs are followed by the preposition "à".

A ssister

T éléphoner
R épondre
O béir
O béir
P oser une question
É chouer
R éussir

When these verbs are followed by an infinitive, no preposition is used.

A ller	**A** imer
	P référer
D étester	**E** ntendre
E spérer	
A dorer	
D ésirer	

When these verbs are followed by an infinitive, the preposition "de" is used.

P arler	**C** hoisir
E ssayer	**O** ublier
A ccepter	**R** efuser
C esser	**P** romettre
É viter	**S** 'arrêter

When these verbs are followed by an infinitive, the preposition "à " is used (CHIRAC).

C ommencer **H** ésiter **I** nviter **R** enoncer **A** rriver **C** ontinuer

Nouns

The following nouns are masculine in the singular, feminine in the plural. "ADO" is short for "adolescent" in French.

A mour   **D** élice   **O** rgue

Pronouns

Disjunctive Pronouns

After one of these verbs, a disjunctive pronoun is used to replace a proper name or a noun designating a person.

Je pense à Paul.
Je pense à lui.
Je tiens à ma mère.
Je tiens à elle.

P enser
Ê tre
T enir

After one of these verbs, a disjunctive pronoun is used to replace a proper name or a noun designating a person. Students should be told who Édith Piaf was and that the word also means "sparrow."

P résenter (se)
I ntéresser (s')
A dresser (s')
F ier (se)

Averbial Pronouns

This device and the one that follows are based largely on sound association. Both are to be pronounced like the Japanese currency.

When "en" and all other prepositions other than "de" are followed by a noun designating a place, they are replaced by the pronoun "y."

Elles vont en France/ Paris/au concert.   Elles y vont.

Y en

When "de" is followed by a noun designating a place, it is replaced by the pronoun "en."

Ils arrivent   du Portugal.

de Rome.

du match.

Ils en arrivent.

D en

The pronoun "en" is used to replace a word following one of these words or expressions.

Adverbe de quantité

N uméro
E xpression de quantité
E xpression indéterminée
D e

When teaching the order of pronouns, students rarely forget that "y" always precedes "en" when they are told to think about the Japanese currency "yen."

Verbs: Auxiliary Verbs

When one of these verbs is followed by an object, "avoir" is used.

J'ai passé un examen.

Nous avons monté les marches.

P asser   **M** onter
U   **D** escendre
R entrer
R etourner
S ortir

This is a common device used to designate verbs conjugated

with "être." Many textbooks also use the "house of 'être'" to teach this grammatical point. They present a picture of a house with individuals illustrating many of the verbs: arriving, entering, going upstairs, coming downstairs, leaving. Another device is DR & MRS VAN DER TRAMPP.

D escendre	**D** evenir
R etourner	**E** ntrer
	R evenir
&	
	T omber
M ourir	**R** entrer
R ester	**A** rriver
S ortir	**M** onter
	P artir
V enir	**P** asser
A ller	
N aître	

Spelling and Accent Changes
Shoe/Boot/L-Shaped Verbes

This device is visual in nature. Students must imagine what a boot, a high top shoe or an "L" looks like. Teachers can draw one of each on the board. The first, second and third person singular and the third person plural forms require the same change in the present tense (both indicative and subjunctive).

comme *espérer* : célébrer, posséder, préférer, protéger, répéter, révéler, suggérer, etc.

comme *essayer* : employer, ennuyer, essuyer, nettoyer, payer, etc.

comme *acheter* : achever, élever, geler, lever, mener, peser, promener, etc.

comme *jeter* et *appeler* : chanceler, épeler, projeter, etc.

This device is oral in nature and is taught in conjunction with the next one. When the letter "g" is followed by an "a" or an "o," one adds an "e" after the "g." It is generally used when teaching verbs.

AGO

When the letter "c" is followed by an "a" or an "o," one adds a cedilla to the "c." It, too, is generally used when teaching verbs.

ACO

Irregular Conjugations

In the present tense, these verbs are conjugated as a verb from the first group is. (A COORS).

A ccueillir **C** ouvrir **O** ffrir **O** uvrir **R** edécouvrir **S** ouffrir

One uses the first three letters of the infinitive to form the present singular, the first four letters to form the plural.

M entir
I
S ortir
S entir

D ormir
I
P artir
S ervir

In order to form the singular, one eliminates the last three letters and adds the endings "s," "s", "t." In order to form the plural, one eliminates the last four letters and adds "gn" plus the endings "ons," "ez," "ent." In order to form the past participle, one eliminates the last three letters and adds a « t.»

P laindre (se) de	**C** raindre
A tteindre	**R** ejoindre
T eindre (se)	**É** teindre
	E nfreindre
A streindre qn à faire qch	**P** eindre

Negation

The second part of the negation ("pas") can be dropped with these verbs in certain situations. This device is meant to help students recognize a full negation when reading literary texts.

C esser
O ser
P ouvoir
S avoir

Conjunctions

The conjunction "à ce que" is used after these verbs.

Je tiens à ce que tu fasses la vaisselle.

  C onsentir
s'**O** pposer
s'**A** ttendre
  T enir

Tenses

Event though there is no conjunction that begins with "g," this device is most helpful when teaching students that when one verb is in the present, the other is in the present and that when one is in the future, the other is in the future. At this point, they have not learned the future perfect.

G Quand
L orsque
A ussitôt que
D ès que

P endant que
A ussitôt que
T ant que

The association of these two words occasionally helps students to know when to use the imperfect tense.

[Imparfait = Description] I.D.

If "was," "were" or "would" can be used in English to translate the French verb, the imperfect is required.

W as/Were/Would
I
M
P

This device is used in conjunction with the preceding one. The verb that directly follows the conjunction "pendant que" must be in the imperfect. The verb in the independent clause can be in either the imperfect or the preterit, depending upon the meaning of the sentence.

    Pendant que tu dormais, je dormais aussi.

    Pendant que tu dormais, j'ai regardé la télé et j'ai fait la vaisselle.

P endant que
I
M
P

The imperfect is used with the following verbs or in the following situations.

H eure	**P** endant que
U sed to	**É** motion
	A ction habituelle
W as	**V** enir de
	É motion
	D escription

Keith Mason suggests this device for helping students know when to use the imperfect while narrating in the past.

C ontinuous actions
H abitual Actions
E motions
A ge
T ime
E ndless Actions
D escriptions

Constance Knop offers this acronym for the use of the imperfect (341).

R epeated
I nterrupted
C ontinual or **C**ontinuing
H abitual

If the verb that follows "si" is in the present, the verb in the main clause can be in the present, imperative or future. When teaching body parts, I teach my students the word "pif" and the expression "faire quelque chose au pif."

P résent   **I** mpératif   **F** utur

After my students understand that a "si" clause in the present can be followed by the present, an imperative or the future, I repeat the following statements in order to help them remember the other sequences of tenses.

1. Temps simple d'un côté, temps simple de l'autre. Terminaisons de l'imparfait d'un côté, terminaisons de l'imparfait de l'autre. Si j'avais faim, je mangerais quelque chose.

2. Temps composé d'un côté, temps composé de l'autre. Terminaisons de l'imparfait d'un côté, terminaisons de l'imparfait de l'autre. Si j'avais eu soif, j'aurais bu quelque chose.

The present is used after «depuis quand.» The students have not as yet learned the imperfect.

PDQ (the chain of stores called PDQ or «Dairy Queen» or «Pretty Darn Quick»)

le **P** résent + **D** epuis **Q** uand

Moods

The pleonastic or expletive "ne" is used after these conjunctions. (CAMP)

de **C** rainte que **A** vant que **M** oins que de **P** eur que

The pleonastic or expletive "ne" is used after these verbs. (CRAP)

C raindre **R** edouter **A** voir **P** eur

Knop suggests WEDDINGS as an cronym when teaching the subjunctive.

W ill: souhaiter, vouloir; il est souhaitable, il faut
E motion: être content, heureux, ravi; il est dommage, triste
D esire: aimer, désirer, souhaiter
D oubt: douter, il est douteux, ne pas être sûr, certain, clair
I nterrogative: Croyez-vous, Pensez-vous, Trouvez-vous, Est-il sûr, certain, clair
Impersonal expressions: il est bon, essentiel, naturel, utile
N egation: ne pas croire, penser, trouver, ne pas être sûr, certain, clair
G eneral characteristics for things or people that one is not sure exists: avoir besoin, chercher, existe-t-il, y a-t-il
S uperlative

According to Knop, "The teacher may add that in a wedding two *different* persons are involved (reinforcing the idea of the subjunctive being used only with two different subjects) and that in French the 'ring' that joins these two separate people in the wedding is que" (340).

Conclusion

Mnemonic devices are very useful when teaching a new concept. Since they are primarily descriptive in nature, students must be given ample opportunity to internalize them. After they have had sufficient work with the principle involved, they will first develop monitors that lead to automatic self-correction and finally to errorless use of it. This is, after all, the ultimate goal of language instruction.

References

Knop, C. K. 1971. "Mnemonic Devices in Teaching French," *The French Review*. 45: 337-342.

Knop, C. K. 1971. "Mnemonic Devices in Teaching French," *The French Review.* 45: 337-342.

Mason, Keith. 1990. "Ser vs. estar: A Mnemonic Device Puts estar in Its P.L.A.C.E." *Hispania,* 73: 506-507.

Mason, Keith. 1992. "Successful Mnemonics for por/para and Affirmative Commands with Pronouns." *Hispania,* 75: 197-199.

Mason, Keith. 1996. "Mnemonics for Mastering the Imperfect and Irregular Future in French, Italian and Spanish." *Mosaic. The Journal for Language Teacher,* 3, 4: 16-17.

Nuessel, Frank. 2004. "Mnemonic Acronyms: A Memory Aid for Teaching and Learning Spanish Grammar." *Mosaic. A Journal for Language Teachers,* 8, 2:21-24.

Reprinted from: John J. Janc, "Teaching French Using Mnemonic Devices." *Mosaic,* 8, 3 (Spring 2004): 17-20.

29 Focus on Descriptive Adjectives: Creative Activities for the Language Classroom

Anthony Mollica, Herbert Schutz and Karen Tessar

Using examples in English, French, German, Italian and Spanish, the authors suggest a variety of activities to teach/learn/review descriptive adjectives and expand the student's active vocabulary.

Teachers are constantly searching for ways of changing formal exercises (i.e., exercises focusing on *form* into activities which focus on *communication*. One such activity which may be used to teach/drill/review descriptive adjectives is the association of an adjective with the student's name. At the same time, this is a good source for conversational exchanges. This activity has often been used as an "ice-breaker" in many initial classes at the intermediate level and has proven to be both interesting and humorous.

The activity involves the teacher's providing students with a list of adjectives listed alphabetically in the target language. The activity has worked well in both English-as-a-second-language classes and other second-language classes.

Describing Self

In this first activity, students are asked to describe themselves by associating the first letter of their name with the first letter of an adjective suggested on the list. The Teacher/Student exchange, in the target language, may resemble the following:

Teacher: What is your name?
Anthony: My name is Anthony and I am attentive.
Teacher: How do you show your *attention*?
Anthony: I always pay attention to what the teacher says…

The teacher, in asking how the student displays a particular characteristic, will change the *adjective* into a *noun*, thus expanding the vocabulary. It may be that students in providing an explanation about the characteristic with which they identify themselves may make a statement which causes laughter in the classroom. Humour should not be discounted from this activity; quite often, in fact, it is the vocabulary found in the humorous explanations which will be remembered...

Describing a Friend

A variation of the above activity may focus on a description of a student's friend.

Student: My friend's name is Ann and she is *affluent*.
Teacher: How does Ann show her *affluence?*
Student: My friend's name is Tom and he is *talkative.*
Teacher: How does Tom show his *talkativeness?*
Student: [Replies...]

Both the above and the previous activity may focus on the negative:

Student: My friend's name is *Ann* but she is not *affluent.*
Student: My friend's name is *Tom* but he is not *talkative.*

Describing Classmates

In this activity, students may be asked to name their classmates. This is particularly appropriate during the first class when students try to learn each other's names. A suitable activity is a variation of the classic *I pack my suitcase...* game. In this game, the player must identify the student's name and the adjective associated with his/her name. Each subsequent player must repeat the names previously identified and add one more to the list.

For example:

Joe: My name is Joe and I am *jovial.*
Mary: His name is Joe and he is *jovial*. My name is Mary and
    I am *morose.*
Irene: His name is Joe and he is *jovial.* Her name is Mary and
    she is *morose.* My name is Irene and I am *intuitive.*
Paul: His name is Joe and he is *jovial.* Her name is Mary and
    she is *morose.* Her name is Irene and she is *intuitive.* My
    name is Paul and I am *popular.* etc.

The activity may move faster by having the player simply repeat the name of the student and the descriptive adjective. For example,

Joe is *jovial*; Mary is *morose*; Irene is *intuitive*; Paul is *popular*; etc.

Finding a Person Who Is...

In this activity, students are given a list of characteristics for which they must find suitable students. If the teacher wishes to introduce the competitive element, the player who completes the list first is declared the winner. This activity is suitable for practising questions/answer.

The student's activity sheet may look something like this:

Find a student who is...
1.... *intelligent.*   Pamela
2.... *outspoken.*   Hans
3.... *apprehensive.*   Fidel
4.... *creative.*   Helen
5.... *helpful.*   Sophia
6.... *brilliant.*   Jennifer
7.... *optimistic.*   Karen
8.... *courageous.*   Mohamed
9.... *famous.*   Paul
10...*talented.*   David

Once a name has been associated with the characteristic and the game is over, the teacher may ask the student how he or she displays that characteristic. Suppose, for example, that the answer for the first adjective is:

Mario is intelligent.

The teacher or a student may question Mario's quality by asking:

Teacher: How do you show your intelligence, Mario?

The Ideal Companion...

In this activity, the teacher may wish to divide the blackboard or blank overhead transparency into two sections and write "The Ideal Boy" on one section and "The Ideal Girl" on the other section. Students are then urged to identify the characteristics for each. This activity is useful for a review of the formation of masculine and feminine adjectives in languages with differing adjectival forms since some qualities attributed to boys may be suitable for girls.

The activity summarizes the formation of French adjectives in the feminine form:

• To form the feminine of an adjective, add e to the masculine form (*petit, petite*).

• An adjective ending in *e* remain the same in the feminine form (*riche, jeune*).

- Some masculine adjectives ending in a consonant, double the final consonant and add *e* (*gentil Õ gentille*).
- Masculine adjectives ending in *er* change *er* to *ère* (*cher Õ chère*).
- Masculine adjectives ending in *if* change *if* to *ive* (*actif Õ active*).
- Masculine adjectives ending in *eux* change *eux* to *euse* (*curieux Õ curieuse*).
- Some masculine adjectives do not follow the above rules when forming the feminine: (*sec Õ sèche, public Õ publique, grec Õ grecque, long Õ longue*, etc.)
- Some masculine adjective have a double form in the singular. Note should be made of the feminine form (*beau, bel Õ belle*).

La garçon "idéal"	*La fille "idéale"*
riche	riche
jeune	jeune
intelligent	intelligente
gentil	gentille
curieux	curieuse
actif	active
fier	fière
doux	douce
beau	belle

My Attributes

The student may be given a list of the adjectives and be asked to check his or her attributes, positive or negative:

It is obvious that some lists are not long or varied enough to be suitable for this activity. In this case, the student may choose from the entire list (i.e. all letters of the alphabet).

Qualities I Would Like to See in...

In this activity, students identify the positive characteristics that a person of their choice should have. To provide a model, the teacher may begin the activity with any one of the following examples:

> *Teacher*: What characteristics should the Prime Minister of Canada (the President of the United States) have?
> *Student*: He or She should be decisive, incorruptible, eloquent, etc.
> *Teacher*: What qualities should your teacher have?

Student: _____

Teacher: What qualities do you look for in a political candidate? (This question may stress the positive.)

Student: _____

Teacher: What qualities do you think political candidates *actually* have? (The answers may stress the negative!)

Student: _____

Teacher: What qualities would you like to see in your future husband/wife?

(A "personalized" answer, similar to the "Ideal Boy/Girl" activity.)

Written or Oral Compositions

Of course many, if not all, of these activities can be turned into oral and/or written composition depending on the particular linguistic skill(s) the teacher wishes to emphasize.

Suggested Vocabulary

The following lists in English, French, German, Italian and Spanish are by no means exhaustive. They are presented here to save teachers hours of research time. Teachers may decide to select only items from these lists or edit these lists according to their needs.

English

A

- ☐ active / activity
- ☐ affectionate / affection
- ☐ affluent / affluence
- ☐ aggressive / aggression
- ☐ agile / agility
- ☐ agitated / agitation
- ☐ allergic / allergy
- ☐ altruistic / altruism
- ☐ ambitious / ambition
- ☐ anxious / anxiety
- ☐ apprehensive / apprehension
- ☐ arrogant / arrogance
- ☐ astute / astuteness
- ☐ attentive / attention
- ☐ autocratic / autocracy
- ☐ avaricious / avarice

B

- ☐ bashful / bashfulness
- ☐ beautiful / beauty
- ☐ bilingual / bilingualism
- ☐ bold / boldness
- ☐ boring / boredom
- ☐ brilliant / brilliance

C

- ☐ calm / calmness
- ☐ cold / coldness
- ☐ composed / composure
- ☐ co-operative / co-operation
- ☐ corrupt / corruption
- ☐ crazy / craziness
- ☐ creative / creativity
- ☐ credible / credibility
- ☐ cruel / cruelty
- ☐ curious / curiosity

D

- ☐ dainty / daintiness
- ☐ dangerous / danger
- ☐ daring / daring
- ☐ decisive / decisiveness
- ☐ delinquent / delinquency
- ☐ desperate / desperation
- ☐ destructive / destructiveness

☐ disgusted / disgust
☐ distant / distance
☐ dynamic / dynamism

E

☐ eager / eagerness
☐ efficient / efficiency
☐ egoist / egoism
☐ elegant / elegance
☐ eloquent / eloquence
☐ energetic / energy
☐ enthusiastic / enthusiasm
☐ envious / envy
☐ exasperated / exasperation

F

☐ fair / fairness
☐ famous / fame
☐ free / freedom
☐ friendly / friendliness
☐ frivolous / frivolity
☐ frustrated / frustration
☐ furious / fury

G

☐ gaudy / gaudiness
☐ good / goodness
☐ graceful / gracefulness
☐ grateful / gratitude
☐ gregarious / gregariousness

H

☐ handsome / handsomeness
☐ happy / happiness
☐ healthy / healthiness
☐ helpful / helpfulness
☐ hot-headed / hot-headedness
☐ humanitarian/ humanitarian
   ism
☐ hypocrite / hypocrisy

I

☐ idealist / idealism
☐ idle / idleness
☐ imaginative / imagination
☐ immoral / immorality
☐ impetuous / impetuosity
☐ implacable / implacability
☐ inattentive / inattention
☐ incorrigible / incorrigibility
☐ incorruptible / incorruptibility
☐ independent / independence

☐ indifferent / indifference
☐ infallible / infallibility
☐ insensitive / insensitivity
☐ insolent / insolence
☐ intuitive / intuition
☐ ironic / irony
☐ irrational / irrationality

J

☐ jealous / jealousy
☐ jocular / jocularity
☐ jovial / joviality
☐ joyful / joyfulness
☐ judicious / judiciousness

K

☐ kind / kindness
☐ kleptomaniac / kleptomania

L

☐ lavish / lavishness
☐ lively / liveliness
☐ loquacious / loquacity

M

☐ macho / machismo
☐ magnetic / magnetism
☐ maniac / mania
☐ mean / meanness
☐ misanthropist / misanthropy
☐ mischievous / mischievous
   ness
☐ morose /moroseness
☐ mysterious / mystery

N

☐ naïve / naïveté
☐ neat / neatness
☐ negative / negativitism
☐ negligent / negligence
☐ noble / nobility
☐ nonchalant / nonchalance

O

☐ obese / obesity
☐ obnoxious / obnoxiousness
☐ odd / oddness, oddity
☐ optimistic / optimism
☐ outspoken / outspokenness

P

☐ passive / passivity
☐ patient / patience

☐ pensive / pensiveness
☐ perfectionist / perfection
☐ perspicacious / perspicacity
☐ pessimistic / pessimism
☐ philanthropic / philanthropy
☐ pompous / pomposity
☐ popular / popularity
☐ proud / pride

R

☐ rational / rationality
☐ reasonable / reasonableness
☐ rebellious / rebellion
☐ reflective / reflection
☐ relieved / relievement
☐ reserved / reservation
☐ rich / wealth, richness

S

☐ sarcastic / sarcasm
☐ sceptical / scepticism
☐ scrupulous / scrupulousness
☐ sentimental / sentimentality
☐ sincere / sincerity
☐ sober / sobriety
☐ sociable / sociableness
☐ stubborn / stubbornness

T

☐ tactful / tact
☐ talented / talent
☐ talkative / talkativeness
☐ tall / height
☐ thorough / thoroughness
☐ tired / tiredness
☐ tolerant / tolerance

U

☐ underestimated/underestimation
☐ understanding/understanding
☐ up-to-date / up-to-dateness

V

☐ vain / vanity
☐ valuable / value
☐ vengeful / vengefulness
☐ vibrant / vibrancy
☐ vulnerable / vulnerability

W

☐ warm / warmth
☐ wary / wariness

☐ weird / weirdness
☐ wicked / wickedness
☐ wild / wildness
G witty / witticism, wit

Y

☐ young / youth
☐ youthful / youthfulness

Z

☐ zealous / zeal
☐ zestful / zest

French

Nouns in the following list are feminine, except where otherwise noted.

A

☐ actif, -ive / activité
☐ adorable / adoration
☐ affable / affabilité
☐ affectueux, -euse / affectuosité
☐ agile / agilité
☐ agité, -e / agitation
☐ agressif, -ive / agression
☐ aimable / amabilité
☐ ambitieux, -euse / ambition
☐ amnésique / amnésie
☐ amoureux, -euse / amour *nm*
☐ animateur, -trice / animation
G anxieux, -euse / anxiété
G apathique / apathie
☐ appliqué, -e / application
☐ appréhensif, -ive / appréhension
☐ arrogant, -e / arrogance
☐ attentif, -ive / attention
☐ audacieux, -euse / audace
☐ autocratique / autocratic
☐ avare / avarice

B

☐ bagarreur, -euse / bagarre
☐ barbare / barbarisme *nm*
☐ batailleur, -euse / bataille
☐ beau, bel, belle / beauté
☐ belliqueux, -euse / belligérance
☐ besogneux, -euse / besogne
☐ bienfaisant, -e / bienfaisance

☐ bienveillant, -e / bienveillance
☐ bilingue / bilinguisme *nm*
☐ bizarre / bizarrerie
☐ blagueur, -euse / blague
☐ brillant, -e / brillance
☐ bruyant, -e / bruit *nm*
☐ buveur, -euse / boire *nm*

C

☐ calme / calme *nm*
☐ chaleureux, -euse / chaleur
☐ champion, -onne / championnat *nm*
☐ charmant, -e / charme *nm*
☐ charmeur, -euse / charme *nm*
☐ constant, -e / constance
☐ craintif, -ive / crainte
☐ cruel, -elle / cruauté
☐ curieux, -euse / curiosité

D

☐ délicat, -e / délicatesse
☐ délicieux, -euse / délice
☐ despotique / despotisme *nm*
☐ destructeur, -trice / destruction
☐ diligent, -e / diligence
☐ diplomate / diplomatie
☐ doux, douce / douceur

E

☐ effervescent, -e / effervescence
☐ effronté, -e / effronterie
☐ énergique / énergie
☐ ensorceleur, -euse / ensorcellement *nm*
☐ enthousiaste / enthousiasme *nm*
☐ envieux, -euse / envie
☐ exceptionnel, -lle / exception
☐ extravagant, -e / extravagance

F

☐ fameux, -euse / renommée
☐ fervent, -e / ferveur
☐ fidèle / fidélité
☐ fier, -ère / fierté
☐ fou, fol, folle / folie
☐ frivole / frivolité
☐ frugal, -e / frugalité
☐ furieux, -euse / fureur

G

G généreux, -euse / générosité
G gentil, -le / gentillesse
G gourmand, -e / gourmandise
G gracieux, -euse / gracieuseté
G grossier, -ière / grossièreté

H

G habile / habilité
G hardi, -e / hardiesse
G hésitant, -e / hésitation
G honnête / honnêteté
☐ hostile / hostilité
☐ hypocrite / hypocrisie

I

☐ idéalisateur, -trice / idéalisation
☐ imaginatif, -ive / imagination
☐ immoral, -e / immoralité
☐ impartial, -e / impartialité
☐ impassible / impassibilité
☐ impertinent, -e / impertinence
☐ imperturbable / imperturbabilité
☐ impétueux, -euse / impétuosité
☐ impressionnable / impressionnabilité
☐ impudent, -e / impudence
☐ impulsif, -ive / impulsivité *n*
☐ incompatible / incompatibilité
☐ inconscient, -e / inconscience
☐ inconsistant, -e / inconsistance
☐ incorrigible / incorrigibilité
☐ indépendant, -e / indépendance
☐ indolent, -e / indolence
☐ indulgent, -e / indulgence
☐ infaillible / infaillibilité
☐ infatigable / infatigabilité
☐ ingénieux, -euse / ingéniosité
☐ inquiet, -ète / inquiétude
☐ insensible / insensibilité
☐ insolent, -e / insolence
☐ insomniaque / insomnie
☐ insoucieux, -euse / insouciance
☐ instable / instabilité
☐ instruit, -e / instruction
☐ intelligent, -e / intelligence

□ intolérable / intolérance
□ irresponsable / irresponsabilité
□ irritant, -e / irritation

J

□ jaloux, -ouse / jalousie
□ jaseur, -euse / jasement *nm*
□ jeune / jeunesse
□ jobard, -e / jobarderie, jobardise
□ jovial, -e / jovialité
□ juste / justesse

K

□ kleptomane / kleptomanie

L

□ lent, -e / lenteur
□ libertin, -e / libertinage *nm*
□ libre / liberté
□ logique / logique
□ loyal, -e / loyauté

M

□ maigre / maigreur
□ malade / maladie
□ malheureux, -euse / malheur
□ manipulateur,-trice/ manipulation
□ mélancolique / mélancolie
□ méticuleux, -euse / méticulosité
□ militant, -e / militantisme *nm*
□ misanthrope / misanthropie
□ misérable / misère

N

□ naïf, -ïve / naïveté
□ négligent, -e / négligence
□ nerveux, -euse / nervosité *n*
□ nonchalant, -e / nonchalance

O

□ opiniâtre / opinion
□ oppressif, -ive / oppression
□ opulent, -e / opulence
□ original, -e / originalité

P

□ paresseux, -euse / paresse
□ passionné, -e / passion
□ patient, -e / patience

□ perspicace / perspicacité
□ prévenant, -e / prévenance
□ prudent, -e / prudence
□ pudique / pudeur

Q

□ querelleur, -euse / querelle

R

□ radical, -e / radicalisme *nm*
□ raffiné, -e / raffinement *nm*
□ railleur, -euse / railleusement *nm*
□ raisonnable / raisonnement *nm*
□ rancunier, -ière / rancoeur
□ réactionnaire / réaction
□ renommé, -e / renommée
□ réticent, -e / réticence
□ riche / richesse
□ rude / rudesse

S

□ sage / sagesse
□ sarcastique / sarcasme *nm*
□ sauvage / sauvagerie
□ sensible / sensibilité
□ serein, -e / sérénité
□ sérieux, -euse / sérieux *nm*
□ sociable / socialité
□ somnolent, -e / somnolence
□ sophistiqué, -e / sophistication
□ soupçonneux, -euse / soupçon
□ sournois, -e / sournoiserie
□ sportif, -ive / sportivité
□ subtil, -e / subtilité
□ surexcitable / surexcitation
□ susceptible / susceptibilité
□ sympathique / sympathie

T

□ taciturne / taciturnité
□ télépathe / télépathie
□ tendre / tendresse
□ théoricien, -enne / théorie
□ timide / timidité
□ tolérant, -e / tolérance
□ tranquille / tranquillité
□ travailleur, -euse / travail *nm*
□ triste / tristesse
□ tyrannique / tyrannie

U

- [ ] ulcéré, -e / ulcération
- [ ] urbain, -e / urbanité
- [ ] usurier, -ière / usure
- [ ] usurpatoire, -trice / usurpation

V

- [ ] vacillant, -e / vacillation
- [ ] vaniteux, -euse / vanité
- [ ] vengeur, vengeresse / vengeance
- [ ] vertueux, -euse / vertu
- [ ] vexé, -e / vexation
- [ ] vieux, vieille / vieillesse
- [ ] violent, -e / violence
- [ ] voluptueux, -euse / voluptuosité
- [ ] vorace / voracité
- [ ] vulnérable / vulnérabilité

Z

- [ ] zélé, -e / zèle *nm*

German

Since only adjective forms are provided here, for space reasons, they are simply grouped alphabetically under each letter heading.

To use the German list for the activities described above, students may have first to consult a dictionary to obtain the correct form of a suitable noun.

A

abgehetzt, abwesend, aktiv, allein, alleinstehend, allergisch, allsehend, allwissend, alt, altmodisch, amüsant, angenehm, angeschnallt, anonym, anständig, anwesend, ärgerlich, arm, arrogant, artig, atemlos, aufgeklärt, aufgeknöpft, aufgeregt, aufmerksam, ausgebildet, ausgelassen, ausgeruht, ausgeschlafen

B

bankerott, bärtig, bedächtig, bedrohlich, bedroht, bedrückt, beeindruckt, beeinflußt, befangen, befriedigt, begabt, begeistert, behilflich, behindert, bekannt, beleidigt, belesen, berechnet, bereit, berühmt, beschäftigt, besonnen, beständig, blank, blau, bleich, blind, blond, borniert, bösartig, boshaft

D

dankbar, dekadent, diabolisch, dick, dickköpfig, diskret, dramatisch, draufgängerisch, dreist, dunkel, dunkelblond, dünn, durstig

E

eifrig, eigen, eingebildet, einfach, einsam, einseitig, eisern, eitel, elegant, empfindsam, energisch, enttäuscht, erwachsen, exotisch, exzentrisch

F

fähig, falsch, faszinierend, faul, feig(e), fein, feindlich, feindselig, fertig, fest, feurig, fieberfrei, fieberkrank, finster, fleißig, flink, flott, frech, frei, friedfertig, froh, fröhlich, fromm, frostig, furchtbar, furchtlos, furchtsam,

G

ganz, garstig, gehorsam, geistesabwesend, gelehrig, genial, gerecht, gesellschaftlich, gesichert, gespannt, gesund, gewiß, gewitzt, giftig, glaubhalft, gläubig, glücklich, golden, gräßlich, grau, grell, grob, groß, grotesk, gründlich, gut

H

hager, hart, häßlich, häuslich, heiser, heiß, heiter, hellblond, herrisch, herrlich, herzlich, hilflos, hilfreich, himmlisch, hinderlich, hoch, hübsch, humorlos, humorvoll, hungrig

I

impertinent, imponierend, imposant, impulsiv, indifferent, interessant, intolerant, intrigant, irrational, irr(e), irritiert, isoliert

J

jämmerlich, jovial, jubelnd, jung

K

kahl, kahlgeschoren, kahlköpfig, kalt, kapriziös, kaputt, kariert, keck, kennbar, kess, klar, klebrig, klein, kleptoman, klug, kokett, komisch, kompetent, konservativ, konventionell, kräftig, krank, kränklich, kriminell, kritisch, krumm, künstlerisch, künstlich, kurios, kurz

L

labil, lahm, lang, langsam, lästig, laut, ledig, leer, leicht, leichtfertig, leichtgläubig, leichtherzig, leichtsinnig, liberal, lieb, liebenswert, liebenswürdig, liederlich, locker, logisch, loyal, luftig, lumpig, lustig, luxuriös

M

mächtig, magnetisch, männlich, mäßig, matt, meschugge, mobil, modern, müde, mündig, munter, musikalisch, müßig, mutig, mystisch

N

nachdenklich, nachgiebig, nachhaltig, nachlässig, nachsichtig, nackt, nah, naiv, namhaft, naß, natürlich, nett, neugierig, neutral, niedergeschlagen, niederträchtig, niedlich, niedrig, nobel, notorisch, nutzlos, nützlich

O

offen, ordentlich, ordinär, originell

P

passiv, pathetisch, patzig,

pausbackig, persönlich, pfiffig, platt, plattfüßig, plump, populär, prächtig, prähistorisch, präzis, primitiv, privat, privilegiert, profan, prominent, prompt, prüde, pünktlich

Q

qualifiziert

R

rabiat, radikal, raffiniert, rar, rasch, rasiert, rational, ratlos, ratsam, rätselhaft, rauh, redlich, redselig, reel, rege, reich, reichhaltig, reif, rein, reizbar, reizend, reizlos, religiös, renommiert, reserviert, richtig, rigoros, rosig, ruhig, ruhelos, rund, ruppig

S

salopp, sanft, satt, sauber, säuberlich, sauer, säuerlich, saumselig, schal, schamlos, schauderhaft, schaurig, scherzhaft, scheu, scheußlich, schief, schläfrig, schlaff, schlank, schlapp, schlau, schlecht, schleunig, schlicht, schlimm, schmächtig, schmackhaft, schmal, schnell, schrecklich, schrill, schroff, schrullig, schwach, schwanger, schwierig, selbständig, selig, sensibel, sentimental, seriös, sicher, sichtbar, solidarisch, sorgfältig, sorglos, sorgsam, sozial, spaßhaft, spaßig, spät, spießig, sportlich, sprachgewandt, stabil, städtisch, stark, starr, steif, still, strittig, stumm, subtil, süchtig, süß

T

tapfer, taub, teuer, tief, tiefsinnig, tödlich, tolerant, toll, träge, traurig, treu, trocken, trostlos, trübe, tüchtig

U

übergeschnappt, überstürzt,

umständlich, unabhängig,
unachtsam, unauffällig,
unbegabt, unbeholfen,
unbekannt, unbelehrbar,
unbeliebt, unbescheiden,
unbesorgt, undiszipliniert,
unehrlich, unempfindlich,
unentschieden, unentschlossen,
unerkannt, unermüdlich,
unerschschrocken, unfähig,
unfreundlich, unfrisiert,
ungebildet, ungeduldig,
ungefährlich, ungefällig,
ungehorsam, ungeniert,
ungeschickt, ungeschminkt,
ungläubig, unglaubwürdig,
unglücklich, unheilbar,
unheimlich, unhöflich,
uninteressant, unklar, unklug,
unleserlich, unmodern,
unmöglich, unmoralisch,
unmündig, unmusikalisch,
unnatürlich, unordentlich,
unpersönlich, unpolitisch,
unpraktisch, unpünktlich,
unqualifiziert, unrasiert,
unregelmäßig, unsauber,
unscheinbar, unschuldig,
unselbständig, unsicher,
unterentwickelt, unterernährt,
untreu, untröstlich, unüberlegt,
unveränderlich,
unverantwortlich,
unverbesserlich, unverh eiratet,
unverständig, unvollendet,
unvollständig, unwissend,
unwürdig, unzivilisiert,
unzufrieden, unzuverlässig

V

väterlich, veraltet, verängstigt,
verantwortlich, verbissen,
verbittert, verdächtig, verehrt,
verfolgt, verführt, vergeßlich,
vergnügt, verhaßt, verheiratet,
verlobt, vernünftig,
verständig, verträglich, verwaist,
verwundbar, volljährig, vorlaut,
vornehm, vorsichtig, vulgär

W

wacker, wählerisch, wahnsinnig,

weich, weltlich, widerlich,
willenlos, willig, willkommen,
winzig, wirr, witzig, wund,
würdig, wütend

Z

zackig, zaghaft, zanksüchtig,
zappelig, zart, zartfühlend,
zärtlich, zauberhaft, zerstreut,
zimlich

Italian

All nouns listed are feminine,
except where otherwise noted

A

- [ ] affabile / affabilità
- [ ] affettuoso, -a / affettuosità
- [ ] affluente / affluenza
- [ ] aggiornato, -a /
  aggiornamento
nm
- [ ] agitato, -a / agitazione
- [ ] allegro, -a / allegria
- [ ] allergico, -a / allergia
- [ ] altruista / altruismo *nm*
- [ ] ambizioso, -a / ambizione
- [ ] amnesico, -a / amnesia
- [ ] amoroso, -a / amore *nm*
- [ ] analfabeta / analfabetismo *nm*
- [ ] ansioso, -a / ansia
- [ ] antipatico, -a / antipatia
- [ ] apatico, -a / apatia
- [ ] applicato, -a / applicazione
- [ ] apprensivo, -a / apprensione
- [ ] ardito, -a / arditezza
- [ ] arrogante / arroganza
- [ ] astuto, -a / astuzia
- [ ] attento, -a / attenzione
- [ ] attivo, -a / attività
- [ ] audace / audacia
- [ ] autocratico, -a / autocrazia
- [ ] avaro, -a / avarizia
- [ ] avvilito, -a / avvilimento *nm*

B

- [ ] balbuziente / balbuzie
- [ ] bello, -a / bellezza
- [ ] bigotto, -a / bigottismo *nm*
- [ ] bilingue / bilinguismo *nm*

- bisognoso, -a / bisogno *nm*
- briccone / bricconeria
- bugiardo, -a / bugia

C

- calmo, -a / calma
- cattivo, -a / cattiveria
- celebre / celebrità
- cleptomane / cleptomania
- cocciuto, -a / cocciutaggine
- crudele / crudeltà
- curioso, -a / curiosità

D

- degenerato, -a / degenerazione
- delicato, -a / delicatezza
- diplomatico, -a / diplomazia
- disamorato, -a / disamore *nm*
- disgustato, -a / disgusto *nm*
- disinteressato, -a / disinteresse *nm*
- disperato / disperazione

E

- efficiente / efficienza
- elegante / eleganza
- energico, -a / energia
- entusiastico, -a / entusiasmo *nm*
- esagerato, -a / esagerazione
- esasperante / esasperazione

F

- facilone / faciloneria
- famoso, -a / fama
- fastidioso, -a / fastidio nm
- fedele / fedeltà
- felice / felicità
- fiero, -a / fierezza
- frivolo, -a / frivolezza
- furioso, -a / furia

G

- geloso, -a / gelosia
- generoso, -a / generosità
- gentile / gentilezza
- giovane / gioventù
- gioviale / giovialità
- grasso, -a / grassezza

I

- immorale / immoralità

- imparziale / imparzialità
- impassibile / impassibilità
- impressionabile / impressionabilità
- imprudente / imprudenza
- indifferente / indifferenza
- indipendente / indipendenza
- infallibile / infallibilità
- innamorato, -a / innamoramento *nm*
- inquieto, -a / inquietudine
- insensibile / insensibilità
- insincero, -a / insincerità
- insistente / insistenza
- insolente / insolenza
- insopportabile / insopportabilità
- intelligente / intelligenza
- intollerabile / intolleranza
- intrepido, -a / intrepidezza
- invidioso, -a / invia
- ipocrita / ipocrisia
- irrazionale / irrazionalità
- irresponsabile / irresponsabilità
- irritante / irritazione
- irriverente / irriverenza

L

- laborioso, -a / laboriosità
- leggiadro, -a / leggiadria
- libero, -a / libertà
- logico, -a / logicità

M

- magro, -a / magrezza
- malinconico, -a / malinconia
- malizioso, -a / malizia
- maniaco, -a / mania

N

- nervoso, -a / nervosismo *nm*
- noioso, -a / noia

O

- obeso, -a / obesità
- onesto, -a / onestà
- orgoglioso, -a / orgoglio *nm*

P

- paziente / pazienza
- perspicace / perspicacia

☐ pettegolo, -a / pettegolio, pettegolezzo
☐ pomposo, -a / pomposità
☐ povero, -a / povertà
☐ pudico, -a / pudore *nm*

Q

☐ quieto, -a / quietismo *nm*

R

☐ ragionevole / ragionevolezza
☐ ribelle / ribellione
☐ ricco, -a / ricchezza
☐ risentito, -a / risentimento *nm*

S

☐ sarcastico, -a / sarcasmo *nm*
☐ sazio, -a / sazietà
☐ sciocco, -a / sciocchezza
☐ sensibile / sensibilità
☐ sentimentale / sentimentalità
☐ sereno, -a / serenità
☐ sfrenato, -a / sfrenatezza
☐ sfrontato, -a / sfrontatezza
☐ simpatico, -a / simpatia
☐ spietato, -a / spietatezza
☐ stanco, -a / stanchezza
☐ superbo, -a / superbia

T

☐ taciturno, -a / taciturnità
☐ telepatico, -a / telepatia
☐ tenero, -a / tenerezza
☐ timoroso, -a / timore *nm*
☐ tiranno, -a / tirannia
☐ triste / tristezza

U

☐ ubbidiente / ubbidienza
☐ ubriaco, -a / ubriachezza
☐ umano, -a / umanità
☐ usurpatore / usurpazione

V

☐ vanitoso, -a / vanità
☐ vendicativo, -a / vendetta
☐ veridico, -a / veridicità
☐ vittorioso, -a / vittoria
☐ volubile / volubilità
☐ vulnerabile / vulnerabilità

Z

☐ zelante / zelo *nm*

Spanish

A

☐ afable / la afabilidad
☐ afectuoso, -a / la afectuosidad
☐ alegre / la alegría
☐ alérgico, -a / la alergia
☐ altruista / el altruismo
☐ ambicioso, -a / la ambición
☐ amoroso, -a / el amor
☐ analfabeto, -a / el analfabetismo
☐ ansioso, -a / el ansia
☐ antipático, -a / la antipatía
☐ aprensivo, -a / la aprensión
☐ ardido, -a / el ardimiento
☐ arrogante / la arrogancia
☐ audaz / la audacia
☐ autocrático, -a / la autocracia
☐ avaro, -a / la avaricia

B

☐ balbuciente / la balbucencia
☐ belicoso, -a / la belicosidad
☐ bello, -a / la belleza
☐ bilingüe / el bilingüismo
☐ brillante / la brillantez
☐ bueno, -a / la bondad

C

☐ calmo, -a / la calma
☐ cariñoso, -a / cariño
☐ célebre / la celebridad
☐ cleptomaníaco, -a / la cleptomanía
☐ conmovido, -a / la conmoción
☐ cruel / la crueldad
☐ curioso, -a / la curiosidad

D

☐ delicado, -a / la delicadeza
☐ desesperado, -a / la desesperación
☐ despótico, -a / el despotismo
☐ diplomático, -a / la diplomacia

E

☐ económico, -a / la economía
☐ eficiente / la eficiencia
☐ elegante / la elegancia
☐ emocionado, -a / la emoción

- encantador, -a / el encanto
- enérgico, -a / la energía
- enfadado, -a / el enfado
- entusiástico, -a / el entusiasmo
- espontáneo, -a / la espontaneidad
- exagerado, -a / la exageración

F

- falso, -a / la falsedad
- famoso, -a / la fama
- fanático,-a / el fanatismo
- feliz / la felicidad
- feminista / el feminismo
- fiel / la fidelidad
- fuerte / la fuerza
- furioso, -a /la furia, el furor

G

- gallardo, -a / la gallardía
- garboso, -a / el garbo
- generoso, -a / la generosidad
- genial / la genialidad
- gentil / la gentileza
- goloso, -a /a la golosina
- gordo, -a / las gordura
- grosero, -a / la grosería
- guapo, -a / la guapura

H

- herido, -a / la herida
- hermoso, -a / la hermosura
- hipócrita / la hipocresía

I

- ignorante / la ignorancia
- imaginativo, -a / la imaginación
- imbécil / la imbecilidad
- impulsivo, -a / la impulsividad
- incompetente / la incompetencia
- incorruptible / la incorruptibilidad
- incrédulo, -a / la incredulidad
- indignado, -a / la indignación
- individualista / el individualismo
- inepto, -a /la ineptitud
- infeliz / la infelicidad

- inquieto, -a / la inquietud
- insolente / la insolencia
- inteligente / la inteligencia
- intrépido, -a / la intrepidez

J

- joven / la juventud
- juicioso, -a / el juicio

L

- laborioso, -a /la laboriosidad
- lascivo, -a / la lascivia
- libre / la libertad
- lindo, -a / la lindeza
- loco, -a / la locura

M

- magnánimo, -a / la magnanimidad
- majestuoso, -a / la majestuosidad
- malicioso, -a / la malicia
- misantrópico, -a / la misantropía
- monógamo, -a / la monogamia
- mundano, -a / la mundanería

N

- negligente / la negligencia
- nervioso, -a / la nerviosidad
- noble / la nobleza
- nostálgico, -a / la nostalgia

O

- odioso, -a / la odiosidad
- opulento, -a / la opulencia
- orgulloso, -a / el orgullo
- osado, -a / la osadía

P

- paciente / la paciencia
- parsimonioso, -a / la parsimonia
- pasivo, -a / la pasividad
- pedante / la pedantería
- pérfido, -a / la perfidia
- perspicaz / la perspicacia
- persuasivo, -a / la persuasiva
- pesimista / el pesimismo
- polémico, -a / la polémica

Q

☐ quejoso, -a / la queja
☐ quieto, -a / la quietud
☐ quijotesco, -a / el quijotismo

R

☐ razonable / el razonamiento
☐ radical / el radicalismo
☐ recto, -a / la rectitud
☐ rencoroso, -a / el rencor
☐ rico, -a / la riqueza
☐ rústico, -a / la rusticidad

S

☐ sarcástico, -a / el sarcasmo
☐ seductor, -ora / la seducción
☐ seguro, -a / la seguridad
☐ sensual / la sensualidad

☐ simpático, -a / la simpatía
☐ soberbio, -a / la soberbia
☐ soñador, -a / el sueño

T

☐ tacaño, -a / la tacañería
☐ taciturno, -a / la taciturnidad
☐ temeroso, -a / el temor
☐ tímido, -a / la timidez
☐ tiránico, -a / la tiranía
☐ tolerante / la tolerancia
☐ triste / la tristeza

V

☐ valiente / el valor
☐ vanidoso, -a / la vanidad
☐ vicioso, -a / la viciosidad
☐ visionario, -a / la visión

Rerpinted from: Anthony Mollica, Herbert Schutz, and Karen Tessar, "Focus on Descriptive Adjectives: Creative Activities for the Language Classroom." *Mosaic*, 3, 2 (Winter 1996): 18-23.

30 Increasing the Students' Basic Vocabulary in French, Italian, Portuguese and Spanish through English Cognates

Anthony Mollica

How can we, as teachers, facilitate the acquisition of new lexical items? How do learners acquire a wider knowledge of vocabulary? The author suggests the use of cognates as one of several strategies in teaching/learning vocabulary.

Introduction

As Robert Galisson aptly said, "Jusqu'à preuve du contraire, les mots restent bien utiles pour communiquer."And as Jana Vizmuller Zocco (1985:13) correctly points out,

> It has been tacitly assumed by many instructors that reading literary works is one of the best methods for students in advanced courses to learn new vocabulary.

and observes that

> Given the fact that students in advanced language courses possess a certain grammatical competence, one of the most pressing objectives of such a course is to help them increase their lexical competence.

Stephen Krashen (1989:440), too, concurs that

> [...] the best hypothesis is that competence in spelling and vocabulary is most efficiently attained by comprehensible input in the form of reading, a position argued by several others.

Mollica has long held the view – and reflected that view in publications (Mollica 1973, 1976; Mollica and Convertini, 1979,) – that

> The aim of the reading program [...] should be the further develop-

ment of oral and reading skills in the study of good literature. Although it is essential to read for accurate comprehension, teachers should avoid excessive grammatical analysis, word study or translation. [...] Synonyms, antonyms, definitions, diagrams, and gestures can prepare the student for a more profitable and pleasurable reading assignment. Word study should be done only to help the student understand, not as goal in itself. (Mollica, 1971:522).

Even from a quick glance at the literature available, then, we could reasonably conclude that the more one reads, the more vocabulary one acquires.

There exists, however, one unexplored goldmine: the introduction of cognates which could be presented even in the first language class

- to teach pronunciation,
- to show the affinity between English and the language being learned,
- to expand the student's vocabulary.

English-speaking students can acquire a great deal of vocabulary if they are made aware from the very first language class of the close relationship which exists between English and certain French, Italian, Portuguese and Spanish words.The endings of some English words may be changed into the other languages' endings and, as a result, a word can easily be formed in French, Italian, Portuguese and Spanish. It is interesting to note that even when a student creates an incorrect word from the English into the target language, the listener – in spite of the error – will still be able to understand its semantic meaning and hence communication will still occur.

In spite of this great source for learning and expanding the students' basic vocabulary, only a handful of authors have written on the subject:

- for French: Péchon and Howlett (1977: 33,5);
- for German: Banta (1981);
- for Italian: Mollica (1971, 2001) and Russo (2003);
- for Spanish: Madrigal (1951), Garrison (1990, Richmond (1992);
- More recently, Means has compiled three books on cognates for French (2003a), Italian (2003b,) and Spanish (2003c).

While a great emphasis has been put on cognates, deceptive cognates (faux amis, falsi amici, falsos cognatos, falsos amigos) have not been neglected. The lengthy compilation for Spanish by Diego Marín (1980) and the books for Italian by Marina Frescura

(1984) and, a decade later, by Ronnie Ferguson (1994), immediately come to mind.

In teaching German vocabulary, Banta (1981: 129) regrets the lack of emphasis which teachers place on cognates and asks,

> Do we make it sufficiently clear to our students that German and English are close relatives? Do we make them usefully aware of the linguistic community that is Western Europe and all its wide-spread former colonies? Do we really train them for intelligent guessing when they meet new words? Not really enough.

The questions that Banta raises for German are equally applicable to Romance Languages.

Garrison (1990: 509-510) believes that a list of cognates can be very productive on the very first day of an introductory class and that

> It encourages timid students by showing them that they already know many words in Spanish and that they can easily learn many more. It provides a good first lesson in pronunciation, because differences between the sound system of the two languages become dramatically apparent when cognates are compared.

And Roseanne Runte (1995: 9) stresses,

> Language is more than grammar. It is more than a way of structuring thought. It is a way of signifying our deepest feelings, our most sincere beliefs. Each time I learn a word which has no translation into another language, I feel that I have discovered a rare gift, a new idea, a fresh insight.

The following lists show several English endings which, if replaced by French, Italian, Portuguese or Spanish endings, can form a word in those languages. It is obvious that these words derive from Latin or Greek and are easily found in Romance Languages but many are also found in non-Romance Languages as well. Because these words derive from Latin or Greek, they are often referred as "Europeisms".

Space restriction sallow us to give only a handful of examples for each language and for each ending. Nevertheless, a deliberate attempt has also been made to provide different cognates for the same endings in the various languages in order to avoid repetition and to lenghten the list of examples.

We limited the selection of the suffixes to the most common.

The endings are listed in alphabetical order for easy reference. An asterisk [*] at the beginning of a word indicates a (slight) change in spelling in the target language.

From English to French

*English   French
Endings   Endings*

-able   =   -able

acceptable, curable, formidable, impeccable, improbable, indispensable, inimitable, invariable, probable, responsable, vénérable

-acy   =   -atie

aristocratie, autocratie, bureaucratie, démocratie, diplomatie, ploutocratie, suprématie, technocratie, théocratie

-al   =   -al

animal, commercial, digital, fatal, immoral, initial, local, mental, musical, national, oral, original

This list can be broken down into one in which the French words have an accent:

décimal, électoral, fédéral, général, *hôpital, idéal, légal, libéral, pénal, spécial

It should be noted that some English words which end in -al may end in -el in French

-al   =   -el

accidententel, annuel, artificiel, essentiel, exceptionnel, formel, naturel, officiel, professionnel, ponctuel, sensationnel, traditionnel, universel

Again, teachers may wish to separate those words which have an accent in French, but these are very few:

éventuel, matériel, véniel

-ant   =   -ant

abondant, assistant, constant, distant, participant, protestant, restaurant, ruminant, vacant

Note: reluctant = réticent

-ary   =   -aire

auxiliaire, bréviaire, calvaire, contraire, émissaire, honoraire, interdisciplinaire, itinéraire, militaire, *missionnaire, nécessaire, primaire, salaire, secondaire, secrétaire

-ate   =   -er

activer, agiter, animer, associer, compliquer, consolider, coordonner, dicter, formuler, illuminer, imiter, inaugurer, narrer, insinuer, terminer

Once again, teachers may wish to separate these cognates from those with an accent by creating a separate list:

aliéner, atténuer, célébrer, coopérer, déléguer, délibérer, élaborer, énumérer, exagérer, hésiter, méditer

-cal   =   -que

analytique, astronomique, classique, clinique, critique, diabolique, économique, elliptical, fanatique, logique, magique, numérique, politique, rhétorique, typique

See also **-ic = -ique**

Note: musical remains the same, musical

-ct   =   -(c)t

contrat, distinct, effet, exact, impact, indirect, instinct, objet, projet, respect, succinct

Note: dialect = dialecte, extinct = éteint, imperfect = imparfait

-ent   =   -ent

absent, agent, apparent, continent, diligent, dissident, imminent, impatient, impudent, innocent, insolent, patient, talent

Some words which end in -ent in English end in -ant in French:

-ent   =   -ant

délinquant, inconsistant, indépendant, *insuffisant

Note: efficient = efficace, obedient = obéissant, disobedient = désobéissant, student = étudiant, exponent = exposant, sufficient = suffisant

-ible   =   -ible

accessible, compatible, horrible, impossible, incompréhensible, incorrigible, irascible, possible, terrible

Note: credible = croyable

-ic   =   -ique

académique, allergique, aristocratique, catholique, capitalistique, civique, didactique, égocentrique, énergique, excentrique, laconique, pacifique panique, romantique, sceptique

-ify   =   -ifier

amplifier, clarifier, classifier, codifier, crucifier, exemplifier, fortifier, identifier, intensifier, justifier, modifier, purifier, rectifier, solidifier, vérifier

-ine   =   -ine

adrénaline, discipline, héroïne, insuline, marine, médicine, migraine, mine, sardine, vaccine, vaseline

-ist   =   -iste

antagoniste, dentiste, féministe, finaliste, journaliste, opportuniste, pianiste, radiologiste, socialiste, spécialiste

-ity   =   -ité

activité, adversité, antiquité, célébrité, communauté, diversité, facilité, formalité, localité, obscurité, priorité

-ive   =   -if

ablatif, actif, adjectif, adoptif, agressif, attractif, communicatif, contemplatif, créatif, explosif, fugitif, lucratif, négatif, offensif, positif, prohibitif, sédatif

-ize   =   -iser

agoniser, angliciser, capitaliser, centraliser, civiliser, coloniser, commercialiser, criminaliser, finaliser, formaliser, généraliser, humaniser, maximiser, organiser, pénaliser, synchroniser, terroriser, visualiser

-ly   =   -lement

*accidentellement, admirablement, *annuellement, *cordialement, cruellement, *exceptionnellement, *fondamentalement, généralement, honorablement, horriblement, *mentalement, *mortellement, *naturellement, probablement

Note: amicably = amicalement, absoleutely = absolument, completely = complètement

-nce   =   -nce

absence, alliance, assistance, confidence, différence, éloquence, existence, patience, présence, résidence, violence

See also **-ncy = nce**

-ncy   =   -nce

clémence, déficiance, émergence, fréquence, indécence, présidence, régence, urgence

-o(u)r   =   -eur

acteur, couleur, dictateur, faveur,

horreur, liqueur, mineur, moteur, odeur, orateur, professeur, projecteur, recteur, sénateur, tracteur, visiteur

Note: ténor remains the same since its origin is Italian.

-ory   =   -oire

accessoire, accusatoire, auditoire, circulatoire, conciliatoire, conservatoire, contradictoire, déclamatoire, dégoratoire, diffamatoire, exploratoire, oratoire, territoire, victoire

Note: dormitory = *dortoir

-ous   =   -eux

anxieux, curieux, délicieux, fameux, généreux, méticuleux, nerveux, odieux, précieux, religieux, *vertueux

Note: atrocious = atroce, continuous = continu, ferocious = féroce, instanteneous = instantané, posthumous = posthume, simultaneous = simultané

-sion   =   -sion

*agression compassion concession confession confusion décision division, expulsion, illusion, occasion, permission, persuasion, précision, profession, télévision, tension, transgression, version

-tion   =   -tion

action, admiration, attention, aviation, circulation, conclusion, citation, condition, connotation, conversataion, convention, correction, création, éducation, motivation, observation, ovation

-ure   =   -ure

capture, culture, cure, figure, fracture, investiture, législature, littérature, miniature, nature, température

-y*   =   -ie
*preceded by any consonant except "t"

académie, *amnistie, allergie, analogie, anarchie, autopsie, catégorie, économie, parodie, polygamie, théorie

Note: controversy = controverse, urgency = urgence, orthography orthographe

From English to Italian

English   *Italian*
Endings   *Endings*

-able   =   -abile

accettabile, impeccabile, improbabile, incalcolabile, incomparabile, inestimabile, *insaziabile, variabile

But the English ending -able can also be -evole in Italian.

-able   =   -evole

amichevole,*ammirevole, *caritatevole, *colpevole, confortevole, considerevole, convenevole, deplorevole, durevole, favorevole, notevole, onorevole, ragionevole, socievole

-acy   =   -zia

aristocrazia, autocrazia, burocrazia, democrazia, plutocrazia, teocrazia

-al   =   -ale

animale, capitale, commerciale, digitale, fatale, fondamentale, generale, *ospedale, *nazionale, orale

-ant   =   -ante

*abbondante, *costante, distante, incessante, partecipante, protestante, *riluttante, ristorante, vacante

Note: assistant = assistente

-ary   =   -ario

contrario, diario, itinerario, necessario, ordinario, *rivoluzionario, salario, sanitario, secondario, *segretario, *volontario

-ate   =   -are

attivare, agitare, alienare, alternare, animare, arbitrare, assassinare, associare, celebrare, *dettare, esitare, generare, imitare, inaugurare, narrare

-cal   =   -co

alfabetico, comico, tipico, analitico, biblico, botanico, classico, critico, cinico, economico, identico, ironico, magico, politico, retorico

-ct   =   -to, -tto

contratto, dialetto, distinto, effetto, *esatto, estinto, indiretto, *istinto, *oggetto, *progetto, *rispetto, succinto

-ent   =   -ente

delinquente, inconsistente, indipendente, insufficiente, intelligente, obbediente, resistente, studente, sufficiente

-ible   =   -ibile

accessibile, compatibile, *orrible, impossibile, inaccessibile, incorrigibile, inimitabile, irascibile, possibile, terribile

Note: sensible = ragionevole, saggio, assennato; sensitive = sensibile

-ic   =   -ico

allergico, arsenico, automatico, *cattolico, *didattico, domestico, *eccentrico, fantastico, erotico, lunatico, magico, panico, romantico

-ify   =   -ificare

amplificare, codificare, deificare, dolcificare, *esemplificare, identificare, intensificare, modificare, *semplificare, solidificare

Note: magnify = ingrandire, stupify = istupidire

-ine   =   -ina

aspirina, caffeina, cocaina, concubina, disciplina, dottrina, eroina, ghigliottina, insulina, medicina, mina, nicotina, penicillina, saccarina

Note: airline = aerolinea, chlorine = cloro, feminine = femminile, iodine = iodo, masculine = maschile, mine = miniera, sanguine = sanguigno

Some words ending in -ine in English end in -ino in Italian.

-ine   =   -ino

alpino, aquilino, bovino, canino, declino, divino, equino, felino, *fiorentino, genuino, libertino, marino, *porcospino, supino, trampolino, vaccino

-ist   =   -ista

antagonista, conformista, dentista, femminista, finalista, giornalista, musicista, opportunista, socialista

-ity   =   -ità

attività, *antichità, *ansietà, *crudeltà, difficoltà, dignità, facilità, estremità, eternità, inferiorità, moralità, *onestà, *oscenità, *ostilità, *realtà, vanità, varietà

-ive   =   -ivo

*affermativo, *aggressivo, *aggettivo, *attivo, *collettivo, comparativo, compulsivo, decisivo, definitivo, eccessivo, evasivo, negativo, offensivo, *obbiettivo, passivo, primitivo, relativo

-ize   =   -izzare

alfabetizzare, analizzare, brutalizzare, civilizzare, economizzare, familiarizzare, generalizzare, idealizzare, legalizzare, sterilizzare, terrorizzare, visualizzare

Note: acclimatize = acclimare, apostrophize = apostrofare, baptize = battezzare, criticize = criticare, eulogize = elogiare, immortalize = immortalare, recognize = riconoscere, satirize = satireggiare

-ly   =   -mente

generalmente, *intelligentemente, mentalmente, naturalmente, *probabilmente, *ufficialmente

-nce   =   -nza

assenza, alleanza, *conseguenza, *esistenza, *esperienza, influenza, innocenza, *pazienza, presenza, prudenza, residenza

-ncy   =   -nza

clemenza, demenza, deficienza, efficienza, emergenza, frequenza, indecenza, presidenza, sufficienza, urgenza

Note: agency = agenzia, fluency = fluidità, solvency = solvibilità

-o(u)r   =   -ore

*attore, collaboratore, colore, *dittatore, *direttore, favore, inferiore, *ispettore, liquore, minore, motore, odore, oratore,

posteriore

-ory   =   -orio

accessorio, conservatorio, declamaorio, derogatorio, dormitorio, illusorio, lab-ratorio, predatorio, territorio

Note: introductory = introduttivo, investigatory = investigativo

-ous   =   -oso

*ansioso, curioso, *delizioso, *favoloso, generoso, armonioso, industrioso, *geloso, luminoso, *misterioso, nervoso, numeroso, odioso, *prezioso, prestigioso, religioso

-sion   =   -sione

*adesione, *ammissione, confessione, decisione, dimensione, discussione, elisione, *esclusione, *esplosione, *espulsione, *estensione, illusione, pensione, tensione, versione

-tion   =   -zione

*azione, *amministrazione, *attenzione, benedizione, celebrazione, circolazione, conclusione, correzione, definizione, discrezione, eccezione

-ure   =   -ura

*cattura, cultura, cura, figura, *frattura,* investitura, legislatura, *letteratura, miniatura, natura, temperatura

-y   =   -ia
*preceded by a consonant other than 't'.
Note: the -i of the -ia is stressed

agenzia, allergia, amnistia, *apatia, astrologia, autopsia, autonomia, categoria, *gelosia, melodia, poligamia, simpatia, terminologia, *teologia, *teoria

Note: The *-i* in the following *-ia* endings in not stressed in nouns such as:

accademia, cerimonia, efficacia, memoria, modestia, perspicacia

From English to Portuguese

Since there is a slight change in spelling in some words between Portuguese and Brazilian [Portuguese], when two examples are given, they are separated by a [/]. The first word is Portuguese, the second is Brazilian.

English Endings		Portuguese Endings

-able = **-ável**

*aceitável, favorável, incalculável, incomparável, inevitável, inseparável, invariável, provável, memorável, *respeitável, respon- sável, sociável, variável

-acy = **-acia**

aristocracia, autocracia, burocracia, democracia, teocracia

-al = **-al**

animal, capital, comercial, digital, editorial, federal, fundamental, *geral, hospital, *nacional, oficial, oral, original, provincial, sensual, sentimental

-ant = **-ante**

abundante, constante, distante, elefante, elegante, incessante, participante, protestante, *relutante

-ary = **-ário**

contrário, diário, dromedário, itinerário, necessário, ordiná-

rio,revolucionário, secretário, voluntário

-ate = **-ar**

agitar, activar/*ativar, alienar, alternar, animar, arbitrar, assassinar, associar, celebrar, *ditar, *gerar, iluminar, imitar, inaugurar, narrar

-cal = **-co**

acústico, analítico, bíblico, biográfico, idêntico, clássico, místico, numérico, político, *prático, satírico, *teórico, típico, econômico

-ct = **-to**

contrato, dialecto/dialeto, *efeito, exacto/exato, *imperfeito, indi- recto/indireto, instinto, objecto/objeto, *respeito

-ent = **-ente**

agente, ausente, competente, continente, convalescente, delinquente/delinqüente, diferente, diligente, dissidente, eloquente/eloqüente, excelente, *iminente, *paciente, presente

Note: sediment = sedimento, sentiment = sentimento, talent = talento

-ible = **-ível**

admissível, compatível, horrível, inacessível, infalível, irascível, legível, *possível, tangível

Note: incredible = *incrível

-ic = **-ico**

acadêmico, alérgico, arsénico/arsênico, católico, doméstico, elástico, excêntrico, fantástico, erótico, mágico, pânico/pánico, romântico

-ify = **-ificar**

codificar, exemplificar, identificar, intensificar, modificar, simplificar, solidificar

-ine   =   -ina

concubina, *doutrina, guilhotina, medicina, mina

-ine   =   -ína

cafeína, cocaína, heroína

-ist   =   -ista

antagonista, conformista, dentista, feminista, oportunista, jornalista radiologista

-ity   =   -idade

actividade/*atividade, adversidade, agilidade, *ansiedade, atrocidade, brevidade, cidade, *criatividade, facilidade, identidade, infinidade, peculiaridade, possibilidade

Note: clarity = clareza, difficulty = dificuldade, nobility = nobreza, locality = lugar, penalty = pena

-ive   =   -ivo

activo/*ativo,   adjectivo/ *adjetivo, adoptivo/*adotivo, *afirmativo,   *coletivo, *comunicativo, *descri-tivo, *destrutivo, emotivo, evasivo, passivo, sedativo

-ize   =   -izar

agonizar, baptizar, capitalizar, civilizar, cononizar, *comercializar, economizar, finalizar, formalizar, generalizar, humanizar, legalizar, visualizar

Note: analize = analisar

-ly   =   -mente

*calmamente, culturalmente, *fisicamente, *logicamente, normalmente, *obviamente, oficialmente, *ralmente, *rapidamente,

*raramente,   regularmente, *relativamente, *simplesmente, *tecnicamente, *tipicamente, *tradicionalmente

-nce   =   -ncia

assistência, ausência, ciência, circunstância, correspondência, distância, desobediência, eloquência/eloqüência, existência, experiência, residência, tolerância, violência

Note: difference = diferença

-ncy   =   -ncia

clemência, continência, decência, deficiência, eficiência, emergência, exigência, freqüência, inconsitência,   indecência, infância, presidência

-or   =   -or

actor/*ator, colaborador, director/*diretor, *doutor, favor, horror, humor, inspector/*inspetor, investigador, *licor, menor, motor, *orador, posterior

-ory   =   -ório

acessório, conservatório, declamatório,   *derrogatório, dormitório, ilusório, laboratório, predatório, purgatório, território

-ous   =   -oso

*ansioso, curioso, delicioso, generoso, harmonioso, luminoso, meticuloso, misterioso, nervoso, precioso, religioso, virtuoso

Note: analagous = análogo, atrocious = atroz, continuos = contínuo, ferocious = feroz, jealous = ciumento

-sion   =   -são

adesão, admissão, confissão, conversão, decisão, dimensão,

elisão, exclusão, explosão, expulsão, extensão, ilusão

-tion = -ção

acção/ação, admiração, atenção, atracção/atração, *comunicação, destinação, edição, fracção/fração, inflação, injecção/injeção, objecção/objeção, promoção, secção/seção, tradição, tradução

ure = ura

captura, cultura, cura, figura, fractura/*fratura, *investidura, legislatura, literatura, miniatura

Note: nature = natureza

y* = ia
*preceded by a consonant other than 't'

academia, alergia, *amnistia, autobiografia, caterogia, ceremônia, diplomacia, eficácia, memória, paródia, poligamia, simpatia, *teoria

From English to Spanish

English Endings   *Spanish Endings*

-able = -able

aceptable, favorable improbable, incalculable, incomparable, inevitable, inseparable, invariable, memorable, respectable, responsable, sociable, variable

-acy = -acia

aristocracia, autocracia, burocracia, democracia, plutocracia, teocracia

-al = -al

animal, capital, comercial, editorial, digital, *excepcional, fatal, federal, fundamental, general,

hospital, *nacional, oral, original, provincial, sentimental, total

-ant = -ante

abundante, constante, distante, elegante, incesante, participante, protestante, reluctante, restaurante, vacante

Note: assistant = asistente

-ary = -ario

contrario, diario, dromedario, itinenario, necesario, ordinario, *rivolucionario, salario, *secundario, secretario, voluntario

-ate = -ar

activar, agitar, alienar, alternar, animar, arbitrar, *asesinar, asociar, celebrar, dictar, hesitar, generar, imitar, iluminar, inaugurar, narrar

-cal = -co

acústico, analítico, bíblico, biográfico, clásico, idéntico, místico, numérico, práctico, satírico, *teórico, típico

-ct = -(c)to

contrato, dialecto, efecto, exacto, imperfecto, indirecto, instinto, objeto, proyecto, respeto

-ent = -ente

agente, ausente, competente, continente, *convaleciente, diferente, diligente, disidente, elocuente, excelente, inminente, *paciente, presente

Note: sediment = sedimento, sentiment = sentimiento, talent = talento, turbulent = turbolento

-ible = -ible

admisible, compatible, horrible, imposible, inaccesible, *increíble, infalible, irascible, legible, posible, tangible , terrible

-ic   =   -ico

académico, alérgico, arsénico, católico, doméstico, económico, elástico, erótico, excéntrico, fantástico, mágico, pánico,

-ify   =   -ificar

codificar, ejemplificar, identificar, intensificar, modificar, simplificar, solidificar

-ine   =   -ina

cafeina, cocaina, concubina, disciplina, doctrina, eroina, guillotina, medicina, mina, nicotina

-ist   =   -ista

antagonista, conformista, dentista, feminista, finalista, oportunista, socialista

Note: journalist = periodista, musicist = músico, radiologist = radiólogo

-ive   =   -ivo

activo, adjectivo, adoptivo, afirmativo, colectivo, comunicativo, conclusivo, descriptivo, destructivo, emotivo, esplosivo, evasivo, pasivo, sedativo

-ize   =   -izar

agonizar, analizar, bautizar, capitalizar, civilizar, conolizar, *comercializar, economizar, finalizar, fomalizar, generalizar, humanizar, legalizar, visualizar

-ly   =   -mente

*afirmativamente,anualmente, artificialmente, automaticámente, ávidamente, *claramente, eficientemente, enteramente, especialmente, *eternamente,

finalmente, *fisicamente, probablemente, regularmente

-nce   =   -ncia

abstinencia,ambulancia, arrogancia, *ausencia, *ciencia, coincidencia, elocuencia, existencia, Francia, importancia, independencia, indiferencia, obediencia, observancia, presidencia, provincia, prudencia, tolerancia

-ncy   =   -ncia

clemencia, contingencia, decencia, deficiencia, eficiencia, emergencia, exigencia, frecuencia, inconsistencia, infancia

See also **-nce = -ncia**

-o(u)r   =   -or

actor, colaborador, director, favor, horror, humor, impostor, interior, inspector, interlocutor, investigador, licor, menor, motor, odor, orador, posterior

-ory   =   -orio

accessorio, acusatorio, conservatorio, declamatorio, definitorio, derogatorio, dormitorio, exploratorio, ofertorio, oratorio, purgatorio, territorio

-ous   =   -oso

*ansioso, armonioso, *celoso, curioso, delicioso, generoso, luminoso, meticuloso, misterioso, nervioso, odioso, precioso, prodigioso, religioso, virtuoso

Note: analagous = análogo, atrocious = atroz, continuous = continuo, ferocious = feroz, posthumous = póstumo, simultaneous = simultáneo

-sion   =   -sión

adesión, admisión,* confesión,

decisión, dimensión, elisión, exclusión,* explosión, expulsión, extensión, ilusión

-tion　　　=　　　-ción

*acción, admiración, atención, atracción, comunicación, conversación, destinación, edición, excepción, fracción, inflación, *inyección, objeción, pensión, promotción, sección, tradición

-ty　　　=　　　-dad

actividad, adversidad, agilidad, *ansiedad, atrocidad, *brevedad, *ciudad, claridad, creatividad, curiosidad, dificultad, facilidad, identidad, infinidad, peculiaridad, posibilidad

Note: nobility = nobleza, locality = lugar, penalty = pena

-ure　　　=　　　-ura

captura, cultura, cura, figura, fractura, investitura, legislatura, literatura, miniatura, natura, temperatura

-y*　　　=　　　-ia

*preceded by a consonant other than 't'.

academia, alergia, aristocracia, ceremonia, diplomacia, eficacia, memoria, modestia, parodia, poligamia

-y　　　=　　　-ía

Note: the -i of the -ia is stressed

amnistía, analogía, *anarquía, *apatía, artillería, astrología, autobiografía, autonomía, categoría, ecología, armonía, ironía, fotografía, simpatía, teoría

Pedagogical Applications

1. Teachers may decide to place these endings on bulletin boards and students add new words on a daily basis. One week could be words with the English *"ble"* ending, the next week, with the *"al"* endings, and so forth.

2. Teachers may wish to mark with an asterisk those words which in the new language have a slightly different spelling from the original English words and hence draw attention to them. Attention may also be drawn to those word by writing it in a different colour or by highlighting them.

3. Teachers should indicate to the student that nouns can be turned into adjectives, into verbs and even adverbs by changing some of the endings of the word of the target language. This activity will increase the students' vocabulary fourfold. For example,

FRENCH
noun: décision
adjective: décidé, décisif
verb: décider
adverb: décidément

ITALIAN
noun: facilità
adjective: facile
verb: facilitare
adverb: facilmente

PORTUGUESE   SPANISH
   noun: criação   *noun:* confusión
   adjective: criador, criativo   *adjective:* confuso
   verb: criar   *verb:* confundir
   adverb: criativamente   *adverb:* confusamente

4. To increase the students' vocabulary, and involve them in the use of the dictionary in the creation of new words, teachers may wish to give them a chart and ask them to complete it.

Substantivo	Adjectivo	Verbo	Adverbio
_____	_____	crear	_____
decisión	_____	_____	_____
_____	fácil	_____	_____
confusión	_____	_____	_____
_____	descriptivo	_____	_____
información	_____	_____	_____

5. Teachers may decide to ask students to make up short phrases in the very first class, thus giving the student a sense of power (in the knowledge of the new language) and a sense of satisfaction:

    Fr.   un animal intelligent
    It.   un professore competente
    Pg.   um animal inteligente
    Sp.   un restaurante famoso

6. Teachers will discover that students may not be familiar with the meaning of many of the "new" words in their own language: "ruminant, "indelible", "mendicant", etc. This activity will also increase the students' own language vocabulary.

7. Teachers may want to identify the "learned words" with the ones more commonly in use. "Mendicant" for "beggar", "velocity" for "speed", etc.

8. If the endings are presented in chart format (See Figure 1), the chart may be used for native students of French, Italian, Portuguese or Spanish to expand their English lexical knowledge. For example, native students of Portuguese can make up words from Portuguese into English. Similarly, native Spanish students may use the chart to expand their French vocabulary; native Italian students their Portuguese, etc. The students' task is reduced to identifying the word in their na-

ENGLISH	FRENCH	ITALIAN	PORTUGUESE	SPANISH
-able	-able	-abile -evole	-ável	-able
-acy	-atie	-zia	-acia	acia
-al	-al -el	-ale	-al	-al
-ant	-ant	-ante	-ante	-ante
-ary	-aire	-ario	-ário	-ario
-ate	-er	-are	-ar	-ar
-cal	-que	-co	-co	-co
-ct	-(c)t	-to, -tto	-to	-(c)to
-ent -ent	-ent -ant	-ente	-ente	-ente
-ible	-ible	-ibile	-ível	-ible
-ic	-ique	-ico	-ico	-ico
-ify	-ifier	-ificare	-ificar	-ificar
-ine	-ine -ino	-ina -ína	-ina	-ina
-ist	-iste	-ista	-ista	-ista
-ity	-ité	-it	-idade	-idad
-ive	-if	-ivo	-ivo	-ivo
-ize	-iser	-izzare	-izar	-izar
-ly	-lement	-mente	-mente	-mente
-nce	-nce	-nza	-ncia	-ncia
-ncy	-nce	-nza	-ncia	-ncia
-o(u)r	-eur	-ore	-or	-or
-ory	-oire	-orio	-ório	-orio
-ous	-eux	-oso	-oso	-oso
-sion	-sion	-sione	-são	-sión
-tion	-tion	-zione	-ção	-ción
-ure	-ure	-ura	-ura	-ura
-y	-ie	-ia	-ia -ía	-ia

Figure 1

tive language. They can then easily produce it in another or
other languages.

Conclusion

The introduction of cognates during the first few lessons of the
target language – or even at an intermediate or advanced stage of
language learning – will give students a sense of "word power"
and will make vocabulary learning/expansion from English to
French, Italian, Portuguese or Spanish much more enjoyable and
pleasurable learning experience.

References

Banta, Frank G. 1981. "Teaching German Vocabulary: The Use of English Cognates and Common Loan Words." *The Modern Language Journal,* 65 (Summer 1981): 129-136.

Ferguson, Ronnie. 1994. *Italian False Friends.* Toronto: University of Toronto Press.

Frescura, Marina. 1984. *Interferenze lessicali italiano/inglese.* Toronto: University of Toronto Press.

Garrison, David.1990. "Inductive Strategies for Teaching Spanish-English Cognates." *Hispania,* 73: 508-512.

Howlett, Fred. 1977. "Words, Words, Mere Words." *The Canadian Modern
Language Review/La Revue canadienne des langues vivantes.* Vol. 35, 4:
636-653.

Howlett, Fred and Alain Péchon. 1997. "French in Disguise." *Mosaic. The Journal for Language Teachers.* vol. 3, 3:20-23. Reprinted in Anthony Mollica,
ed., *Teaching and Learni ng Languages.* Welland, ON: éditions Soleil publishing inc., 1998. pp. 295-302.

Krashen, Stephen. 1989. "We Acquire Vocabulary and Spelling by Reading:
Additional Evidence for the Input Hypothesis." *The Modern Language Journal,*73. iv (1989): 440-464.

Marín, Diego. 1980. "Los 'falsos amigos' en español/inglés." *The Canadian
Modern Language Review/La Revue canadienne des langues vivantes,* 37,
1: 65-98.

Means, Tom. 2003a. *Instant French Vocabulary Builder.* New York: Hippocrene
Books, Inc.

Means, Tom. 2003b. *Instant Italian Vocabulary Builder.* New York: Hippocrene
Books, Inc.

Means, Tom. 2003c. *Instant Spanish Vocabulary Builder.* New York: Hippocrene
Books, Inc.

Mollica, Anthony. 2001. *"Parole per parlare:* Teaching/Expanding the Student's
Basic Vocabulary." *Italica,* vol. 78, no. 4: 464-485.

Mollica, Anthony. 1971. "The Reading Program and Oral Practice." *Italica,* 48,
4 (1971): 522-5411. The article was reprinted in *The Canadian Modern
Language Review,* 29. 1(1972): 14-21 and 29. 2 (1973): 14-21. An expanded

version appeared in Anthony Mollica, ed., *A Handbook for Teachers of Italian*. Don Mills: Livingstone Printing, 1976. Pp. 75-96.

Richmond, Dorothy. 1992. *Guide to Spanish Suffixes. How to Substantially Increase Your Vocabulary with Common Spanish Endings*. Lincolnwood, IL: Passport Books.

Runte, Roseann. 2005. "Learning Languages in the Context of Canada's Many Cultures." *Mosaic. The Journal for Language Teachers*. 2: 4: 8-11.

Russo, Antonio. 2003. *The English-Italian Lexical Converter. An Easy way to Learn Italian Vocabulary*. Ottawa: Legas.

Vizmuller Zocco, Jana. 1985. "Derivation in the Advance Course of Italian." *Inter-national Review of Applied Linguistics in Language Teaching*, 23, 1 (1985): 13-31.

Acknowledgements: I am indebted to Fernanda Adams, St. John the Baptist School, Hamilton, and Irene Blayer, Brock University, for proof-reading the Portuguese and Brazilian examples.

I would also like to express my appreciation to Frank Nuessel, Louisville University, and to Jana Vizmuller Zocco, York University, for their critical reading of the manuscript.

Reprinted from Anthony Mollica, "Increasing the Students' Basic Vocabulary in French, Italian, Protuguese and Spanish through English Cognates." *Mosaic*, 9, 2 (Summer): 21-29.

31 Games and Puzzles in the Second-Language Classroom: A Second Look

Marcel Danesi and Anthony Mollica

The use us of puzzles and games in the second-language classroom have now become intrinsic components of many approaches, and the choice of many teachers, as formats for students to review and reinforce grammar, vocabulary, and communication skills that it is difficult to imagine a workshop or a seminar without them in a teacher-education program .

Introduction

The posing and solving of puzzles, conundrums, rebuses, riddles, and the like is as old as history itself. The first surviving "think-of-a-number" puzzle dates back to an Egyptian papyrus written around 1650 BC (Wells 1992: 1). The oldest book of games in existence, known as the *Libro de juegos*, was commissioned more than 700 years ago by King Alfonso X of Castile and Leon (Mohr 1993: 11). It contains clear descriptions of how to play chess, checkers, and various card and board games. The antiquity of the puzzling instinct in human beings shows that it is a fundamental feature of the human mind. And the widespread popularity of puzzle magazines, puzzle sections in newspapers, puzzle books, TV quiz shows, game tournaments in chess, checkers, cards, etc., reveals that puzzles and games are alive and well in the contemporary human mind.

Puzzleology, to coin a term for the field that deals with the study of puzzles and games in human cultures, has enjoyed a long-standing role in the educational domain, where games, problem-solving tasks, and puzzle techniques have been the standard fare in the curricula of many school subjects for a long time. As puzzleologist James Fixx (1978: 18) once wrote, the reason for this is, no doubt, because "puzzles not only bring us pleasure but also help us to work and learn more effectively." In the area of second-language teaching, puzzleological techniques such as crosswords, word searches, scrambled words, simulations, interactive games, board games, etc. have now become intrinsic components of many approaches, and the choice of many teachers, as formats for students to review and reinforce grammar, vocabulary, and communication skills. Puzzleological activities have become such common features of commercially-available textual materials, and the topic of discussion of virtually every teacher-training seminar, that it would be impossible today to think of second-language teaching without them. They are now seen to be highly versatile techniques that serve both specific discrete-point learning tasks (*reinforcing structural and lexical knowledge*) and more interactive ones (*communication and functionality*). But it was not that long ago that the injection of this fun element in second-language teaching would have been considered a frivolous waste of time by the teaching profession. And even in today's more accepting climate, puzzleological techniques are viewed as tangential, or at best supplementary, to more mainstream techniques.

The most memory-enhancing way in which humans develop concepts, from infancy to adolescence, is through some form of recreational mental play. While the specific characteristics of such mental gymnastics might vary somewhat from culture to culture, the need to solve problems   constitutes a cognitive, cross-cultural universal.

Our purpose in this essay is to revisit puzzleology in second-language teaching, in order to give the teacher an overview of what the most relevant facts on file are *vis-à-vis* their incorporation into classroom instruction and to provide an elementary typology of puzzleological techniques for the teacher interested in incorporating them in his/her language classes.

Puzzleological Techniques and Second-Language Learning

The experimental literature dealing with the learning-efficacy of puzzleological techniques is not extensive. Outside of a few scattered attempts to assess their validity and to develop a psychologically-appropriate typology for their instructional utilization, very little has been done in the way of giving this topic a thorough empirical treatment (e.g., Omaggio 1978, 1982, Mollica 1979, 1981, Wright, Betteridge and Buckby 1979, Danesi 1979, Webster and Castonon 1980, 1985a, 1987, 1981, Rixon 1981, Rodgers 1981, Jones 1982, 1986, Palmer and Rodgers 1983, Crookall 1985, Crookall, Greenblat, Cooke, Klabbers, and Watsin 1987, Crookall and Oxford 1988, Crookall and Saunders 1989, Cicogna, Danesi, and Mollica 1992). Two clear facts have emerged from the literature.

The sketchy experimental evidence that does exist has generally shown such techniques to be supportive of language learning processes.

For such techniques to be effective, they must be designed with specific instructional/learning objectives in mind.

The empirical work of Rodgers (1981), Palmer and Rodgers (1983), and a few others (see the studies in Crookall 1985, Crookall, Greenblat, Coote, Klabbers, and Watson 1987, Crookall and Oxford 1988, and Crookall and Saunders 1989) has shown, by and large, that games are effective learning-enhancers, but that they raise several critical questions which, to the best of our knowledge, have not as yet been addressed. So, from a purely research and learning theory perspective, the general indication would seem to be that the basis for using puzzleological techniques to complement, supplement, or even completely shape the second-language teaching process is psychologically sound. Recently, Sandra Savignon (1992) has observed that such techniques have become favourites of communicative methodologists precisely because they serve the elusive goal of meaning negotiation.

But perhaps the greatest support for puzzleological techniques in second-language teaching is anecdotal evidence and common sense. The general research in educational psychology, the corpus of case studies of learners, the everyday observations of school teachers, and the common perceptions of anyone in daily contact with children and adolescents point collectively to what appears to be a fundamental requirement of learning: namely that the most memory-enhancing way in which humans develop concepts, from infancy to adolescence, is through some form of recreational mental play. While the specific characteristics of such mental gymnastics might vary somewhat from culture to culture, the need to solve problems constitutes a cognitive, cross-cultural universal. It would seem, therefore, that the logical question for second-language teaching is not whether or not to include puzzleological techniques into its repertory of instructional options, but rather how best to tap the natural tendency to solve problems in an instructionally-meaningful way. Rodgers (1981) has shown how this can be done by highlighting five properties of puzzleological techniques that are reflective of current-day practices in second-language teaching. In our view, these properties explain why they are easily insertable into the frameworks of most contemporary proficiency-oriented approaches to second-language teaching:

1. *They are competitive.*
2. *They are rule-governed* (i.e. they have a limited numbers of specific and clearly-defined rules).

3. *They are goal-defined.*
4. *They have closure* (i.e. there is a specific point at which a puzzle is solved or a game is finished).
5. *They are engaging,* in that they constantly seem to challenge the participants.

So, it would seem that puzzleological techniques are ancillary activities that can be easily used in combination with other kinds of instructional activities in. the framework of some broader methodological blueprint for second-language teaching. Rarely has anyone ventured to design a syllabus, or teaching system, aimed at making the whole second-language teaching process puzzleological in orientation. One of the few to have done so, as reported in his Ph.D. dissertation of 1992, is Mark Miller of the University of Delaware. Miller designed an entire syllabus and instructional system based on interactive game-playing. Adopting the usual experimental-statistical approach of a controlled study, he found his game-playing design to be an effective means of imparting both linguistic and communicative competence to university language students, while at the same time allowing for the maintenance of a high level of interest and motivation in the course. While this was designed only as a pilot study, it nonetheless endorses what the previous literature has been documenting in bits and pieces.

From a purely research and learning theory perspective, the general indication would seem to be that the basis for using puzzleological techniques to complement, supplement, or even completely shape the second-language teaching process is psychologically sound.

Play vs. Game

Given the paucity of so-called hard evidence in favour of the learning-efficacy of puzzleological techniques in second-language teaching, it is perhaps useful to cast a quick glance at what psychologists have to say about the use of play, problem-solving, and games in education generally. While the meaning of the word play is certainly intuitively obvious, it turns out to be a rather difficult one to define formally. It is perhaps most useful to think of play as a kind of innate and unreflective form of psycho-motor behaviour that allows children to interact in a meaningful way both with their environment and with others. It manifests itself across cultures primarily as a form of physical involvement with people and things, invariably stimulating affective and experiential responses that lead progressively to the build-up and coding of knowledge. As Munzert (1991: 37) point out:

Infants learn through exploration of the physical world by random movement, crawling, touching, and coming into direct contact with people and objects in the environment.

Culturally-structured or routinized forms of play are the games that children learn from their peers, older children, or adults in a participatory way. Spontaneous playing behaviours can occur within or outside of games. But a game always enlists some form of the play instinct. The essential requirement of a game is that it have a structure or a clearly-predictable format within which the play instinct can operate. For educational purposes one can refer to game-playing in classroom settings as a pedagogically-designed system for imparting knowledge or skill based on playing. (For a comprehensive treatment of the positive effect of games on cognitive development see, for example, Loftus and Loftus 1983).

Cognitively, game-playing invariably involves the deployment of problem-solving strategies. The goal, or end-state, of any game constitutes a problem that the child/adolescent must attempt to solve within the format of the game. This forces the learner to go from a random, experiential form of thinking to a more organized and representational one shaped by the structural elements of the game format. As Lesgold (1988: 190) observes, in order to solve a problem, the person must know what steps are possible and "how to represent the problem."

The solution path that the student discovers can be said to result from a creative strategy because the learner must use the given elements of the game to locate the path. Creativity can thus be constrained for the present purposes to mean the ability to arrange the given elements of a game or a puzzle in ways that bring about a solution to the problem posed by a game or puzzle. The arrangements will vary from individual to individual; but they will do so within the limits defined by the structural elements of the game or puzzle. Thus, unlike most popular notions of the term, creativity in game-playing or puzzle-solving involves the utilization of structures within a pre-established format. It is in coming up with the solution path that the learner is forced to explore alternative and innovative ways to use the structures to access the end-state. In this sense, therefore, it can be argued that puzzle-solving and game-playing are effective means for channelling the student's innate tendency to be creative towards some specific learning goal. As Munzert (1991: 63) has aptly remarked, creativity is an educationally-meaningful notion only if it "involves a sense of purpose coupled with action." This means that the creative act "requires that emerging ideas and thoughts be organized into new or different patterns from their previous organization" (see also Perkins 1988 for empirical studies on problem-solving creativity as purposeful behaviour; and Gowan, Khatena and Torrance 1981 for a comprehensive treatment of the associated educational implications).

Puzzle-solving and game-playing are effective means for channelling the student's innate tendency to be creative towards some specific learning goal.

Arguing from this general research base, it can be hypothesized that puzzleological techniques are effective insofar as they allow the students to come up creatively with solutions to a specific problem posed. It is in formalizing each solution through the medium of language that the students come to acquire the conceptual domains underlying the puzzle or game in terms of the language structures that express them.

It is clearly beyond the scope of the present review essay to go any further into the details of the psychology of problem-solving and game-playing and of its supporting empirical base. Suffice it to say here that it can be used to understand why puzzleological techniques constantly manifest themselves as learning-enhancing activities in second-language teaching. Extrapolating from all the discussions, anecdotal experiences, and the studies that do exist on puzzleological and game-playing techniques, the following general findings, terminological clarifications, and caveats can now be brought to the reader's attention:

It has been found necessary to distinguish between language teaching puzzles and language teaching games, since the former are problem-solving texts that require the individual learner to come up with a solution within the framework of the text, while the latter involve problem-solving activities involving group interaction, and therefore are more focused on contextual parameters.

The effectiveness of language-teaching puzzles has, to the best of our knowledge, rarely, if ever, been studied experimentally. The anecdotal evidence, however, portrays them as useful primarily as control, reinforcement, and review techniques (e.g. Mollica 1981, 1992b, Danesi 1985a, Nuessel 1994).

The research on language-teaching games (e.g. Palmer and Rodgers 1983, Crookall 1985, Crookall, Greenblat, Coote, Klabbers, and Watson 1987, Crookall and Oxford 1988, and Crookall and Saunders 1989, Miller 1992, Musumeci 1992) raises several questions that still require an answer.

1. Are they usable with all groups of students, especially since different groups and individuals respond differently to kinds and degrees of competition?

2.   Do the same kinds of benefits that have been documented in other areas of education and development over the last two decades with the use of problem-solving and game-playing techniques (e.g. Edwards, Devries, and Snyder 1972, Livingston and Kidder 1973, Devries and Slavin 1978, Loftus and Loftus 1983, Sawyers and Rogers 1994, Berk 1994) accrue in similar ways with the use of language-teaching games in second-language teaching?

3.   Do language-teaching games encourage interaction or can they inhibit classroom participatory behaviours?

Despite such *caveats* and questions, there seems to be a general feeling among users of language-teaching puzzles and language-teaching games that they foster learning, if in no other way than through the inducement of recreational states of mind.

Language-teaching puzzles and language-teaching games should be used judiciously. They should be used to motivate students and to challenge them. They should never be used as time-fillers.

A Typology of Puzzleological Techniques

Before selecting or preparing the specific language-teaching puzzles or language-teaching games for his/her course, the teacher should always keep in mind that the age, learning styles, and previous training of the students must be taken into consideration. Children can handle language-teaching puzzles that are cast in reduced and simplified form (e.g. elementary crosswords, word searches, etc.). But very young children have great difficulty in handling such language-teaching puzzles as logic puzzles, rebuses, etc. Therefore, bearing in mind that language-teaching puzzles and language-teaching games must be synchronized to the learner's age and level of competence, teachers can generally rest assured that the use of these techniques will produce favourable results:

Language-teaching puzzles are usable primarily for form-based and meaning-based language tasks, and language-teaching games for more communication-based and group interaction tasks.

Both language-teaching puzzles and language-teaching games can be easily constructed and keyed to specific and general instructional objectives. Once the learning task has been determined, the teacher can select or construct the appropriate language-teaching puzzle or language-teaching game to accomplish it.

Language-teaching puzzles and language-teaching games are

useful primarily as review, recall, reinforcement, control, and occasionally as expansion techniques.

Language-teaching puzzles and language-teaching games should be used judiciously. They should be used to motivate students and to challenge them. They should never be used as time-fillers. So, the learners should be made to understand that they are just as much a part of the course as are other kinds of exercises, drills, activities, etc. The teacher should also keep in mind that the over-use of language-teaching puzzles and language-teaching games is not desirable. To maintain interest, the teacher should always diversify the types of language-teaching puzzles and language-teaching games used together with other kinds of techniques.

Pedagogical writing in the area of language-teaching puzzles and language-teaching games within the last three decades has been rather extensive (e.g. Lee 1965, Bressan 1970, Crawshaw 1972, Wolfe 1972, Hupb 1974, Latorre and Baeza 1975, Schmidt 1977, Schloss 1977, Caré and Debyser 1978, Omaggio 1978, 1982, Wright, Betteridge and Buckby 1979, Mollica 1979, 1981, 1992, Danesi 1979, 1985a, 1985b, 1987, Hendrickson 1980, 1983, Maley and Grellet 1981, Ervin 1982, Irwing 1982, McKay 1985, Schultz and Fisher 1988, Steinberg 1991, Cicogna, Danesi, and Mollica 1992, Dickson 1992, Nuessel 1994). In general, methodologists suggest that at least three categories of these techniques can be employed in second-language teaching. These can be called as follows:

1. *form-based* language-teaching puzzles,
2. *meaning-based* language-teaching puzzles, and
3. *communication-based* language-teaching games.

This terminology attempts to synthesize into a few manageable categories the many and diverse kinds of instructional objectives suggested in the literature vis-a-vis the utilization of language-teaching puzzles and language-teaching games.

Form-Based Language-Teaching Puzzles

A form-based language-teaching puzzle focuses the individual learner's attention on language form. It is one of the most popular types of puzzeological techniques that has been in use as a regular feature in most textbooks and ancillary materials for at least three decades. Scrambled letters, crosswords, word searches, tic-tac-toe, word mazes, cryptograms, and the like make up a truly rich and broad repertory of language-teaching puzzles that can be tailored to fit specific form-based learning tasks. They are popular with both teachers and learners because they cast the reinforcement and control of spelling, grammar, and vocabulary into a challenging and recreational problem-solving format.

The following examples are suggestions that we have extracted from the literature, which we reproduce here simply to demonstrate how versatile form-based language-teaching puzzles can be. Some recent collections and discussions of such language-teaching puzzles can be found in Steinberg 1991, Mollica 1992b, and Nuessel 1994.

Word search

Danesi (1985a) created a word-search language-teaching puzzle in which he hid the French colour adjectives *rouge, noir, blanc, vert*, and *jaune*. The words can be read from left-to-right, right-to-left, up-down, and down-up. He suggests that this puzzle can be used for different objectives by simply changing the instructions for solving it. It is up to the teacher to decide which level of reading difficulty to employ. The teacher can use this puzzle for a variety of review, control and reinforcement tasks. The following are some suggested activities:

- The students can be asked simply to locate the colour adjectives in the puzzle, after having given them the words (= *simple recognition task/orthographic task*).
- The students can be asked to locate five colour adjectives in the puzzle, without telling them which ones (= *vocabulary task*).
- The students can be given definitions or incomplete sentences for each word and then asked to find the words in the puzzle (= *vocabulary review/cloze task*).
- The students can be given the feminine forms of the adjectives and then asked to locate their corresponding masculine forms in the puzzle (= *morphological task*).

The number and diversity of the instructions is limited only by the imagination and specific requirements of the teacher. All form-based language-teaching puzzles have this feature.

Mollica (in preparation) is in the process of developing for various languages a series of word-searches in which the stimulus for the hidden word is either *print* (i.e., a word), or *non-print* (i.e., an illustration) or both *print* and *non-print* (i.e., word associated with the illustration.) He arbitrarily chooses 20 words on a given topic or theme and creates the first three puzzles using both print and non-print as stimuli, followed by two puzzles in which only the visual stimulus is given (Figure 1). In this way, he is encouraging the student to learn new vocabulary or review it by going from print (word), to non-print (*illustration associated with word*) to print (*word to be found in the puzzle.*) This repetition is

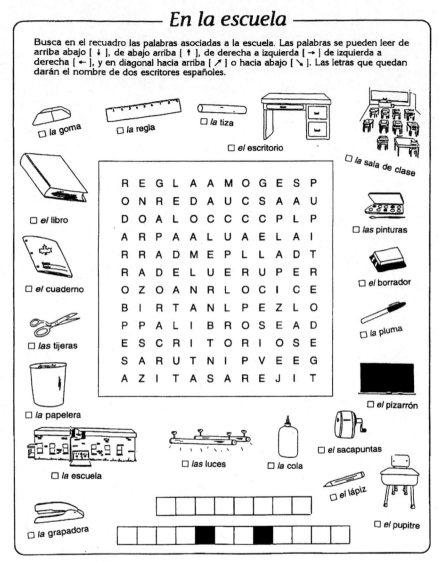

Figure 1

designed to help the student to learn or recall vocabulary. (Figure 2).

Mollica (1981b, 1982) has also created word-search puzzles in which the form reflects the theme or topic. Moreover, he suggests on "hiding" a message closely related to the theme or topic. The student solving the puzzle, therefore, cannot help but feel a sense of accomplishment in solving the puzzle but also in feeling satisfied in "finding" the related hidden message. Once all the words (*ange, berger, boules, cadeaux, cheminée, crèche, décorations,*

En route!

Trouve dans la grille les mots associés à l'auto. Les mots peuvent se lire horizontalement, verticalment, en diagonale, de droite à gauche, de gauche à droite, de haut en bas, ou de bas en haut. Transpose ensuite les lettres qui te restent pour finir la phrase ci-dessous.

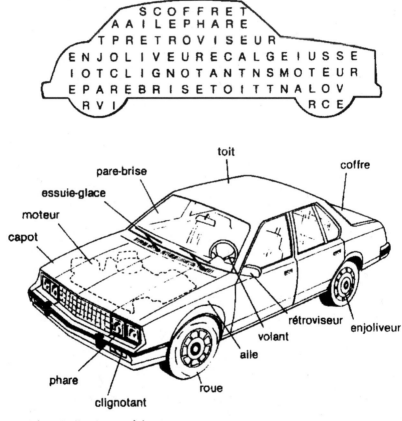

On achète de l'essence à la _____

Figure 2

étable, étoile, gui, nuit, Père Noël, renne, sapin, vœux) have been circled on the "Christmas tree", the hidden message revealed will spell out "Bonne et heureuse année." (Figure 3).

A similar word-search puzzle can be created in the shape of a heart for St. Valentine's Day (Figure 4). Again, once all the words directly related with the theme are found (*aimer, amis, amitié, amour, baisers, cadeau, cartes, chocolats, coeur, embrasser, fête, fêter, filles, fleurs, garçons, gentil, joli, lettre, rose, sourire, Valentin*), a hidden proverb

- [ ] ange
- [ ] berger
- [ ] boules
- [ ] cadeaux
- [ ] cheminée
- [ ] crèche
- [ ] décorations
- [ ] étable
- [ ] étoile
- [ ] gui
- [ ] nuit
- [ ] Père Noël
- [ ] rennes
- [ ] sapin
- [ ] vœux

```
                        B
                        O
                    B U P
                    O L È
                  N N E R S
                  E C S E A
                E I H N N P T
                U V E O O I H
              G Œ L M I Ë N R E
              U I U I T L E R E
            X O E G N A G U S E A
            T N N É É R E N N E S
          É T A B L E O C R È C H E
          T I U N B E C A D E A U X
                        É
                        D
```

Figure 3

- [ ] aimer
- [ ] amis
- [ ] amitié
- [ ] amour
- [ ] baisers
- [ ] cadeau
- [ ] cartes
- [ ] chocolats
- [ ] cœurs
- [ ] embrasser
- [ ] fête
- [ ] fêter
- [ ] filles
- [ ] garçons
- [ ] gentil
- [ ] joli
- [ ] lettre
- [ ] rose
- [ ] sourire
- [ ] Valentin

```
        D C E                 U R X
      N C A O H             O C E O S
    E S I R N E E       I S H R E S S
    B P E T S R U E L F O T U V E
    E A E E N N T R O P C T R A L
    A M I S S E C A J C O E E H L
    E M B S O R L L I V L L M R I
    G L I R E U C A D E A U I E F
      A I T A R R S V S T E A E
      R T I S S I T L S A A
      Ç N É S R R M O M
      O E U E R E O
      N G T R U
      S Ê R
      F
```

Figure 4

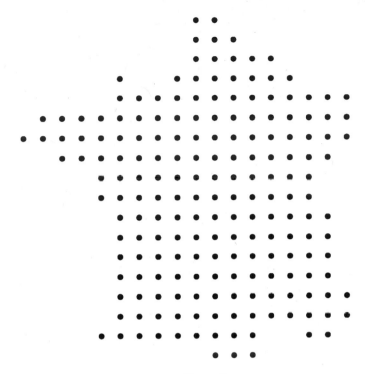

Figure 5

related to "love" will appear: "Deux choses ne peuvent pas se cacher : l'ivresse et l'amour." ("There are two things that cannot be hidden: drunkenness and love.") Mollica 1981-1982).

Hidden messages may also be used to provide cultural, linguistic, historical or geographical information (Mollica 1992c). Teachers may decide to "hide" some of the *chefs-lieux* of France (*Ajaccio, Amie, Châolon-sur-Marne, Clermont-Ferrand, Dijon, Lille, Limoges, Lyon, Marseilles, Metz, Montpellier, Nantes, Orléans, Paris, Poitiers, Rennes, Rouen, Strasbourg, Toulouse*) in the shape of the country itself (Figure 5).

But the hidden words may not necessarily always be thematic in nature. Teachers might wish to select words which are merely associated with the topic or theme. In the following word-search puzzle, (Figure 6), Mollica (1992c) includes names of rivers, mountains, cities, composers, writers, wines, as well as lexical items relating to capital "C" culture and lower case "c" culture. (*Adige, Alitalia, Alpi, Arno, arte, Bari, Barolo, Capri, Dante, Elba, esploratori, espresso, Etna, Fiat, Ionio, musicista, Papa, pecorino, Pisa, Po, poeta, repubblica, Roma, scrittori, stivale, tenori, Tevere, Torino, Verdi*). Once all the words have been found, students will realize that the hid-

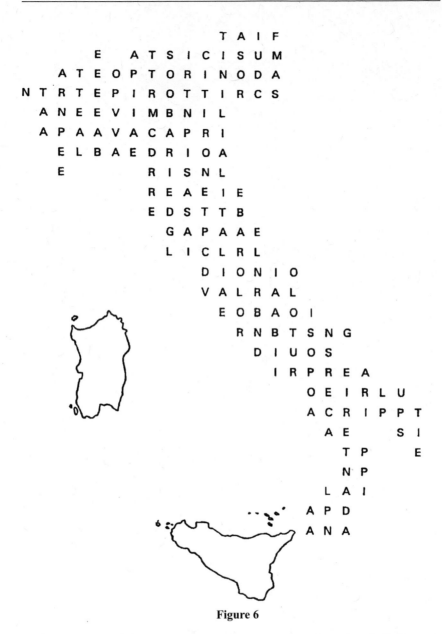

Figure 6

den message will inform them that "Dante è il padre della lingua italiana."

Crossword Puzzles

When Arthur Wynne published the first crossword puzzle in the puzzle pages of Sunday's New York *World* on December 21, 1913, he probably did not realize the instant success the puzzle was to enjoy. The biggest puzzle craze that America had ever set in motion. Roger Millington 1977: 24,25) describes the situation anecdotally. The following are some examples:

> Engaged couples announced their good news by composing appropriate crosswords and sticking them in the local paper. The Rev. George McElveen, a Baptist pastor of Pittsburgh, was the first of many preachers to use the crossword puzzle to attract bigger congregations. He announced that a large blackboard would be placed in front of his pulpit. On it was an original puzzle and the audience was required to solve it before he would begin his sermon. The solved puzzle, needless to say, proved to be the text for his sermon. In Atlantic City, crosswords were distributed in church to stir interest in a current missionary campaign in China and Persia. Churchgoers were requested, however, not to solve the puzzles during the service [...]

In December 1924, unaware the craze was shortly to achieve similar magnitudes in Britain, *The Times* took pity on America. In an articles headed AN ENSLAVED AMERICA, it noted that "All America has succumbed to the crossword puzzle." Guessing inaccurately, it continued: "The cross-word puzzle is by no means a new thing; in all likelihood it was known as long as the Civil War." *The Times* felt that the crossword was "a menace because it is making devastating inroads on working hours of every rank of society." How devastating? Well, according to their New York correspondent, five million hours daily of American people's time – most of them nominally working hours – were used in unprofitable trifling.

A great deal has been written on the crossword puzzle in the language class using the printed word as a stimulus (Mollica, 2007). In his classic study of this puzzeological technique, Dino Bressan (1970), for example, likes the crossword puzzle for the obvious contribution it can make from a linguistic point of view. "A carefully graded selection of crosswords in order of complexity," maintains Bressan, "will contribute to the acquisition of new words and phrases as well as the consolidation of previous knowledge through repetition." Bressan classifies direct-definition clues into nine different headings:

1. *Generic.* Clue: Prénom. Answer: Ils
2. *Synonymic.* Clue: Tout naturel. Answer: Inné
3. *Antonymic.* Clue: Pas fictif. Answer: Réel
4. *Allusive.* Clue: Échappe au rêveur. Answer: Réalité.
5. *Allusive-negatory.* Clue: Bien de gens ne connaissent que sa marge. Answer: Loi.
6. *Definitory.* Clue: Dont rien ne vient troubler la quiétude. Answer: Sereine.

7. *Descriptive.* Clue: Recueillent des malheureux. Answer: Asiles.
8. *Punny.* Clue: Il avait vraiment la bosse du théâtre! Answer: Polichinelle.
9. *"In" clue.* Clue: Lettres d'amour. Answer: Am.

David E. Wolfe (1972) acknowledges Bressan's worthwhile contribution and offers a number of examples "as perhaps more realizable in the language class, assuming that the crossword puzzle is teacher-prepared and is based on material previously studied by the student." One of the examples Wolfe suggests is the picture clue. "Any concrete noun which the teacher can draw, "declares Wolfe, "is appropriate as a clue, assuming the noun has been taught."

Mollica (1987, 1988a,1988b, 1991a, 1991b, 1992a), for example, has published in various languages a series of line master puzzles based on everyday vocabulary themes. These puzzles are designed to test students have mastered the vocabulary and, at the same time, provide hours of fun in or outside the classroom scene. He presents four sets of puzzles, A,B,C,D, for each theme and arbitrarily chooses twenty words for each one. Each set builds upon the previous one, reviewing the words studied and then by adding new related vocabulary words to each puzzle. The final set, D, contains all 20 illustrated words without the printed words. The following is an example for the reinforcement and control of clothing vocabulary in English (Figure 7).

As it stands this language-teaching puzzle constitutes an elementary type of exercise, whereby the beginning student will simply associate each word with its visualizable referent and then write it into the crossword arrangement. More difficult uses of this puzzle can be envisioned as follows:

1. the words can be removed from the puzzle;
2. the visual referents can be replaced by definitions, synonyms, antonyms, etc.;
3. a story containing the vocabulary can be written and the student asked to select the items that fit into the crossword arrangement; and so on.

Anagrams

The followings anagram that can be used for word recognition and spelling in Italian (Danesi 1988: 152). In this case the words to be unscrambled give common first-conjugation verbs in Italian

Anagrammando le lettere seguenti, trovare dieci verbi.

1. *g e r l e g e* (*leggere*)

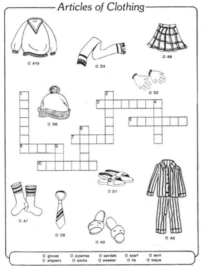

Crossword Puzzle A   Crossword Puzzle B

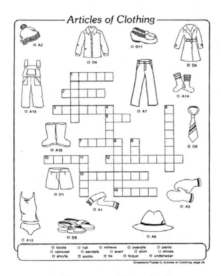 

Crossword Puzzle C   Crossword Puzzle D

Figure 7

From: Anthony Mollica, *Crossword Puzzles for Beginners*. Welland, Ontario: éditions Soleil publishing inc., 1991. Reprinted with permission of the Publisher.

2. *a l p r a r e (parlare)*

3. *a r m i p r a r (imparare)*

4. *g a r a n i m e (mangiare)*

etc.

Cryptograms

A cryptogram, such as the following, can be used for obvious word-recognition, syntactic, morphological, and discourse expectancy reinforcement and control in French (Danesi 1985a: 27). The hidden message, "L'amour est une grande illusion" translates, *Love is a great illusion.*

```
 _ '  M     U __     ___     ___     _____     _____
 1   2 3  4 5 6    7 8 9    5 10 7    11 6  2 10 12 7    13 1  1  5  8 13 4 10
```

Tic-tac-toe

A tic-tac-toe puzzle in German that has an obvious lexico-semantic focus, by which the student is expected to find three words in a line that have something in common, is the following one (Danesi 1985a: 23). The answer is three types of fruits: *Apfel, Brine* and *Pfirsich*.

Apfel	Brine	Pfirsich
Blume	Land	Baum
Hand	Kopf	Buch

Word Circle

A word-circle puzzle in Spanish, can be used to test the plural formation of nouns (Danesi 1985a: 25).

Mazes

Mazes are also useful for both oral or writing (i.e., copying) activities. The task is to visit all the French relatives only once, using the arrows as point of departure and point of return. As the student "visits" the relatives, each name can be either spoken or written out depending on the skill the teacher wishes to emphasize. Several answers are possible, thus providing variety to the activity.

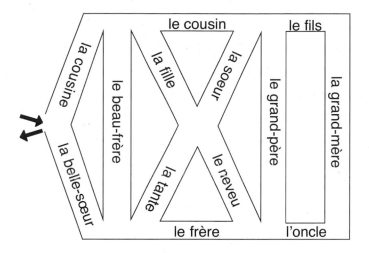

Meaning-Based Language-Teaching Puzzles

Language-teaching puzzles which focus the learner's attention on meaning are especially useful at intermediate and advanced levels. Riddles, sequences, logical deductions, and the like all allow the learner to employ the abstract language schemas of the target language fruitfully within the specific meaning domains outlined by the solution path of the puzzle.

Logical Puzzles

This type of puzzle provides factual infromation from which students draw a solution by logical thinking. These puzzles demand no technical mathematical knowledge, but "call for clear thinking and an ability to establish the logical relationships which the data presented imply." (Phillips, 1961: 2). Wylie best describes the method of obtaining a solution for such puzzles:

> By drawing clonclusions from it, and examining their consistency within the total framework of the problem, the answer is ultimately wrested from the seemingly incoherent information initially provided.

Consider as one example the following puzzle. Teachers may want to adapt this according to their teaching topics. The "professions" may be changed into "nationalities", into "food preferences," and so on.

> *MM. Martin, Blanchet et LeBlanc travaillent dans le même édifice. Ils sont banquier, avocat et bijoutier mais pas nécessairement dans cet ordre. Le bijoutier qui est l'ami de M. Blanchet est le plus jeune des trois. M. LeBlanc est plus âgé que l'avocat. Essayez ed deviner leur métier ou profession.* (Mollica, 1976: 26).

In solving this problem, Danesi (1985) suggests a table in order to keep track of the possibilities. He suggests that an X be placed in the box of the item to be eliminated; if we conclude the opposite, he suggests an O. The table for the above puzzle will be as follows:

	banquier	avocat	bijoutier
M. Martin			
M. Blanchet			
M. LeBlanc			

The third sentence leads us to conclude that M. Blanchet is not the jeweller. We can, therefore, put an X in the appropriate cell in the array to eliminate M. Blanchet:

	banquier	avocat	bijoutier
M. Martin			
M. Blanchet			
M. LeBlanc			X

The fourth sentence allows us to conclude that M. LeBlanc is not the lawyer:

	banquier	avocat	bijoutier
M. Martin			
M. Blanchet			X
M. LeBlanc		X	

Sentences three and four also allow us to deduce that M. LeBlanc is not the ajeweller. This is because the jeweller is the youngest of the three, while M. LeBlanc is at least older than the lawyer:

	banquier	avocat	bijoutier
M. Martin			
M. Blanchet			X
M. LeBlanc		X	X

A look at the table makes it clear that M. LeBlanc is the banker. We note this by putting an O in the appropriate cell and eliminating the banker possibility for the other two:

	banquier	avocat	bijoutier
M. Martin	X		
M. Blanchet	X		X
M. LeBlanc	O	X	X

We now see that M. Blanchet is the lawyer and M. Martin is the jeweller. As a result of our careful reading the final table will look like this:

	banquier	avocat	bijoutier
M. Martin	X	X	O
M. Blanchet	X	O	X
M. LeBlanc	O	X	O

Tables may become more complex with some more difficult problems involving more than three items or people.

Consider, as an example, the following logical deduction puzzle in Italian (Mollica 1992: 110).

> *Il giovane Marco Ferrara ha invitato a cena Carlo Rossi, Mario Bruni, Paolo Moretti e Gianni Martino. Purtroppo non ricorda quale professione esercitano (avvocato, architetto, chirurgo, ingegnere). Sa che...*
> 1. *Mario Bruni è più anziano dell'avvocato e dell'ingegnere.*
> 2. *Il chirurgo cena sempre da solo.*
> 3. *Mario Moretti cena spesso con Gianni Martino.*
> 4. *Il più anziano è anche il più ricco.*
> 5. *Carlo Rossi cena spesso in compagnia dell'avvocato e dell'ingegnere.*
> 6. *Gianni Martino è più anziano dell'avvocato e dell'ingegnere.*
> 7. *A Mario Bruni non piacciono le attività sportive.*
> *Sapresti dirgli quale professione esercitano questi quattro signori?*

The following table will be very useful in solving the problem.

	avvocato	ingegnere	chirurgo	architetto
Mario				
Paolo				
Gianni				
Carlo				

A table (similar to the one for the previous puzzle) can be set up to help the student keep track of the possibilities, alternatives, etc. An X in a cell indicates an elimination, and an O a finding.

It is not necessary to go into the details of the simple solution to this puzzle here. The reader will be able to figure out the answer with little difficulty. The important features to note here about the solution can be summarized in point form as follows:

These language-teaching puzzles allow the learner to become cognitively involved in the problem space created by the puzzle.

The learner must decipher the meaning of the language-teaching puzzle, making limited changes but creative ones to the components of its problem space.

By reflecting on the whole problem-solving event in conceptual and verbal ways, the learner assimilates the meaning-to-form relations that are inherent in the puzzle.

A few more examples will suffice to show the features that such puzzles embody.

Legal Cases

In a legal case such as the following French one (Mollica 1992b: 124-125), the student has to verbalize a plausible solution:

Si vous étiez le juge…

En écoutant le testament de feu M. Henri Marchand, Georges est très content d'apprendre qu'il va hériter du portefueill de son oncle. En recevant et en examinant le porte-feuille, il y trouve dix billets de cent dollars. Son cousin, jaloux, exige qu'il partage la somme avec lui. Georges soutient que son oncle lui a laissé à lui le portefeuille et, par conséquent, tout ce qu'il contient. Ce cas finit au tribunal. Si vous étiez le juge, diviseriez-vous l'argent parmi le deux cousins ou donneriez-vous la somme entière à Georges?
(Choisissez parmi vous deux avocats: un qui plaidera la cause de Georges, l'autre qui représentera son cousin).

Sequencing

In the following sequencing problem in French (Mollica 1992b: 126), students are told that two anecdotes are out of sequence:

Un mauvais écrivain et un agent de police.
1. *Arrivé à "Conclusion du test d'haleine", il inscrit consciencieusement:*
2. *Un mauvais écrivain confie à un ami:*
3. *Puis l'agent rédige son rapport.*
4. *– Tiens! Il sait déjà lire!*
5. *Un agent de police arrête un automobiliste en état d'ébriété et le conduit au poste de police.*

6. – *Quelle catastrophe! Mon fils de quatre ans a jeté au feu mon manuscrit.*
7. *"Saint Émilion 1953."*
8. *On lui fait passer tous les tests, y inclus un examen à l'alcotest.*
(Answers: *Anecdote* 1: 5,8,3,1,7; *Anecdote* 2: 2,6,4.)

More examples and discussions of meaning-based language-teaching puzzles can be found in Wright, Betteridge, and Buckby 1979, Maley and Grellet 1981, McKay 1985, Danesi 1985a and Mollica 1992b.

Communication-Based Language-Teaching Games

The literature on this type of language-teaching game is quite extensive, but the reader can consult Schultz and Fisher (1988) for a good comprehensive typology. The general definition of a language-teaching game is a problem-solving game that involves more than one learner. So, it unfolds in terms of a group-based, interactive format that focuses on language use and meaning negotiation. Games like *Charades, What's My Line?* and others (including board and card games), that create contexts in which the language is used in discourse-appropriate ways, constitute communication-based language-teaching games. Here are some examples that are self-explanatory.

Charades

Danesi (1985a: 45) proposes the following activity for charades:

Rules/Procedures:

The class can be divided into two teams once again, and the object is to guess a word or expression that a member of each team must act out in pantomime. Team members are allowed to ask questions and make statements in the target language. The words or expressions are prepared in advance by the teacher and put into a box from which each team draws. The team taking the least time overall to guess the answer wins.

Instructional Objectives/Types of Communication Skills:

By tying the words and expressions to some theme or unit, the primary objective of this game is to review vocabulary. However, since it requires the students to participate verbally in finding a solution, it also encourages the use of the language in an autonomous and meaningful way.

Family Feud

Danesi (1985a: 48) suggests that even the ever popular TV show "Family Feud" can be a source for communication-based language-teaching games.

Rules/Procedures:

> The teacher should survey a group of students on a series of general questions (your favourite colour, make of car, type of food, and so on). The frequency of each response is then tabulated. The class is divided into two teams. Ten questions are asked by the teacher in the target language and a student delegated by each team must attempt to respond to all questions within a specified time frame (for example, one minute). The answers of the two students must be different. The more popular the answer according to the survey, the higher the score. Each team then chooses a different player for the next ten questions, and the game continues as before. At the end, the scores are added up, and the team with the highest score is declared the winner.

Instructional Objectives/Types of Communicative Skills:

> This game is clearly useful in building up the ability to understand and respond to target language messages. This type of activity consequently develops fluency. Vocabulary is also practised.

Biographical Bingo

Dickson 1992: 231-232) suggests Biographical Bingo for the achievement of similar objectives.

> Played in the same way as "Find Someone who…," but uses a Bingo grid for the actions. As in Bingo, the winner is the student who finds people for 5 spaces in a row.

Questions and Answers

For a questions-and-answer activity, designed to stimulate oral participation in the classroom, Dickson (1992: 237) proposes the following:

> Form two teams. Using a large picture or map on the wall, the teacher calls out a word indicating an object or a place. One team must form a question about that object or place and the other team must answer the question. Each team wins points for correct questions or answers.
>
> *Purpose*: Students get practice in both asking and answering questions. If a picture is used, the game can review certain vocabulary. If a map is used, it could review geography.

Predicaments

For this interactive activity, Dickson (1992: 236) suggest that:

> One student leaves the room while the other students think of a

predicament such as running out of gas, the school burning down, losing their money, getting home long after their curfew, etc. The student who went out returns and asks the others in turn: "Qu'est-ce tu ferais si ceci t'arivais?" Each person must give a reasonable answer based on the predicament agreed on. The student whose answer finally reveals the predicament is "It" next.

Concluding Remarks

It is perhaps useful to conclude this essays by reviewing some of the main aspects of puzzleological techniques in second-language teaching in point form:

- These techniques have an important role to play in second-language teaching as versatile exercises, drills, etc. alongside other kinds of practice and reinforcement techniques.
- Although there is no experimental literature on the learning-efficacy of language-teaching puzzles, and only a handful of studies on the psychological effectiveness of language-teaching games, there are no indications or evidence to the contrary, namely data showing that puzzleological techniques are ineffectual or detrimental. More research is obviously required in this domain.
- Language-teaching puzzles are useful as form-based and meaning-based reinforcement and control activities.
- Language-teaching games are useful as communication-based activities.
- Although there exists some evidence that entire courses or curricula can be based on a language-teaching game approach (e.g. Palmer and Rodgers 1983, Miller 1991), by and large puzzleological techniques are useful primarily as supplementary or complementary activities that can be used in tandem with other techniques within broader methodological and curricular frameworks.
- These techniques should be given the same treatment and weight as other exercises, drills, and activities; otherwise the student will tend not to take them seriously.
- Both teacher and students must find puzzleological technique enjoyable; otherwise they will become counterproductive.
- Given all these provisions, we are convinced, as have been many teachers over the last three decades, that puzzleological techniques have as much a role to play in second-language teaching as they have been shown to have in many other areas of education.

Our purpose in this revisitation was not to be exhaustive, nor to be innovative in showing how language-teaching puzzles and language-teaching games can be incorporated into second-language teaching. Our goal was simply to highlight the diversity and versatility of these recreational forms of language and communication exercise and practice. We conclude by emphasizing one more time to the reader that puzzleological techniques do not constitute a method or an educational paradigm. They are enjoyable activities that can be used together with other kinds of practice devices for reinforcement, review, thinking, control, and communication in the classroom. All these techniques really aim to do is to achieve the same kinds of exercise and practice goals that more traditional drills and activities do. But, they inject so much fun into the process that they end up invariably fostering a positive attitude in teacher and students alike to the learning tasks at hand. And this is the primary condition for learning to occur.

References

Berk, L.E. 1994. "Vygotsky's Theory: The Importance of Make-Believe Play." *Young Children*, 50, 1: 30-39.

Bressan, D. 1970. "Crossword Puzzles in Modern Language Teaching." *Audio-Visual Language Journal*, 8: 93-95.

Caré, J.M. and F. Debyser. 1978. *Jeu, langage et créativité*. Paris: Hachette.

Cicogna, Caterina, Marcel Danesi, and Anthony Mollica, eds. 1992. *Problem-Solving in Second-Language Teaching*. Welland, Ontario: éditions Soleil publishing inc.

Crawshaw, B.E. 1972. *Let's Play Games in French*. Skokie: National Textbook Co.

Crookall, D., ed. 1985. *Simulation Applications in L2 Education and Research*. Special Issue. *System*, 13, 3.

Crookall, D. and R. Oxford, eds. 1988. *Language Learning Through Simulation/Gaming*. New York: New-bury House-Harper and Row.

Crookall, D. and D. Saunders, eds. 1989. *Communication and Simulation: From Two Fields to One Theme*. Clevedon: Multilingual Matters.

Crookall, D., C. Greenblat, A. Coote, J. Klabbers, and D.R. Watson, eds. 1987. *Simulation-Gaming in the Late 1980's*. New York: Pergamon.

Danesi, Marcel. 1979. "Puzzles in Language Teaching." *The Canadian Modern Language Review/La Revue canadienne des langues vivantes*, 35: 269-277.

Danesi, Marcel. 1985a. *A Guide to Puzzles and Games in Second Language Pedagogy*. Toronto: Ontario Institute for Studies in Education Press.

Danesi, Marcel. 1985b. *Language Games in Italian*. Toronto: University of Toronto Press.

Danesi, Marcel. 1987. "The Psychology and Methodology of Puzzles and Games in L2 Teaching." In: J. Lantolf and A. Labarca, eds., *Research in Second Language Learning: Focus on the Classroom*, pp. 107-116. Norwood, N.J.: Ablex.

Danesi, Marcel. 1988. *Manuale di tecniche per la didattica delle lingue moderne*. Roma: Armando.

De Vries, D.L. and R.E. Slavin. 1978. "Teams Games Tournaments: Review of Ten Classroom Experiments." *Journal of Research and Development in Education*. 12: 23-38.

Dickson, P. S. 1992. "Quick and Easy Games for Language Learning." In Caterina Cicogna, Marcel Danesi, and Anthony Mollica, eds. *Problem-Solving in Second-Language Teaching*, pp. 223-241. Welland, Ont.: éditions Soleil publishing inc.

Edwards, K., D.L. De Vries, and J.P. Snyder. 1972. "Games and Teams: A Winning Combination." *Simulation and Games*. 3: 247-269.

Ervin, G. L. 1982. "Using Warm-Ups, Wind-Ups, and Fillers: All of Your Class Time is Valuable." *Foreign Language Annals*, 15: 95-99.

Fixx, J. F. 1983. *Solve It*! London: Muller.

Gowan, J.C., J. Khatena, and E.P. Torrance, eds. 1981. *Creativity: Its Educational Implications*. Dubuque: Kendall-Hunt.

Hendrickson, J. M. 1980. "Listening and Speaking Activities for Foreign Language Learners." *The Canadian Modern Language Review/La Revue canadienne des langues vivantes*, 36: 735-748.

Hendrickson, J.M. 1983. "Listening and Speaking Activities for Foreign Language Learners: Second Collection." *The Canadian Modern Language Review/La Revue canadienne des langues vivantes*, 39: 267-284.

Hupb, L.B. 1974. *Let's Play Games in Spanish*. Skokie, Illinois: National Textbook Co.

Irwing, P. 1982. "Games for Use at the Intermediate Level." *The Canadian Modern Language Review/La Revue canadienne des langues vivantes*, 38: 726-727.

Jones, K. 1982. *Simulations in Language Teaching*. Cambridge: Cambridge University Press.

Jones, K. 1986. *Designing Your Own Simulations*. New York: Methuen.

Latorre, G. and G. Baeza. 1975. "The Construction and Use of EFL Crossword Puzzles." *English Language Teaching Journal*, 30: 45-55.

Lee, W.R. 1965. *Language Teaching Games and Contests*. Oxford: Oxford University Press.

Lesgold, A. 1988. "Problem Solving." In R. J. Sternberg and E.E. Smith, eds., *The Psychology of Human Thought*, pp. 188-213. Cambridge: Cambridge University Press.

Livingston, S.A. and S.J. Kidder. 1973. "Role Identification and Game Structure: Effects on Political Attitudes." *Simulation and Games*, 4: 131-144.

Loftus, G.R. and E.F. Loftus. 1983. *Mind at Play*. New York: Basic Books.

Maley, A. and F. Grellet. 1981. *Mind Matters*. Cambridge: Cambridge University Press.

McKay, S. L. 1985. *Teaching Grammar*. Oxford: Pergamon Press.

Millington, Roger. 1977. *Crossword Puzzles. Their History and Their Cult*. New York: Pocket Books.

Miller, M.C. 1992. *Two Experimental Studies of the Effectiveness of Interactive Game-Playing in the Acquisition of Japanese by American Students*. Ph.D.

Dissertation, University of Delaware.

Mohr, M.S. 1993. *The Games Treasury*. Shelburne: Chapters.

Mollica, Anthony. 1979. "Games and Activities in the Italian High School Classroom." *Foreign Language Annals*, 12: 347-354.

Mollica, Anthony, ed. 1980-1981. *Les Gamins*. Toronto: Grolier.

Mollica, Anthony. 1981. "Visual Puzzles in the Second Language Classroom." *The Canadian Modern Language Review/La Revue canadienne des langues vivantes*, 37: 583-622.

Mollica, Anthony. 1987 *Mots croisés pour les débutants*. Welland, Ontario: éditions Soleil publishing inc.

Mollica, Anthony. 1988a. *Crossword Puzzles for Beginners*. Welland, Ontario: éditions Soleil publishing inc.

Mollica, Anthony. 1988b. *Crucigramas para principiantes*. Welland, Ontario: éditions Soleil publishing inc.

Mollica, Anthony. 1991a. *Parole crociate per principianti*. Welland, Ontario: éditions Soleil publishing inc.

Mollica, Anthony. 1991b *Latin Crossword Puzzles for Beginners*. Welland, Ontario: éditions Soleil publishing inc.

Mollica, Anthony. 1992a *Palabras cruzadas para principiantes*. Welland, Ontario: éditions Soleil publishing inc.

Mollica, Anthony. 1992b. "Reinforcing Language Skills through Problem-Solving and Pencil and Paper Activities." In Caterina Cicogna, Marcel Danesi, and Anthony Mollica, eds. *Problem-Solving in Second-Language Teaching*, pp. 102-129. Welland, Ontario: éditions Soleil publishing inc.

Mollica, Anthony. 1992c. *A te la scelta! Libro primo*. Welland, Ontario: éditions Soleil publishing inc.

Mollica, Anthony. 2007. "Crossword Puzzles and Second-Language Teaching." *Italica,* 84, 1 (Spring): 59-78.

Mollica, Anthony. (in preparation). *Buscapalabras*. Welland, Ontario: éditions Soleil publishing inc.

Munzert, A.W. 1991. *Test Your I.Q.* New York: Prentice-Hall.

Musumeci, D. 1992. "Selecting Games for the Second-Language Classroom: Criteria for Multiple Functions." In Caterina Cicogna, Marcel Danesi, and Anthony Mollica, eds., *Problem-Solving in Second-Language Teaching*, pp. 242-253. Welland, Ontario: éditions Soleil publishing inc.

Nuessel, F. 1994. "Recreational Problem-Solving Activities for Teaching Vocabulary and Intermediate Spanish." *Hispania*, 77: 118-124.

Omaggio, A. 1978. *Games and Simulations in the Foreign Language Classroom*. Washington, D. C.: Center for Applied Linguistics.

Omaggio, A. 1982. "Using Games and Interactional Activities for the Development of Functional Proficiency in a Second Language." *The Canadian Modern Language Review/La Revue canadienne des langues vivantes*, 38: 515-546.

Palmer, A. and T.S. Rodgers. 1983. "Games in Language Teaching." *Language Teaching*, 16:2-21.

Perkins, D.N. 1988. "Creativity and the Quest for Mechanism." In R.J. Sternberg and E.E. Smith, eds., *The Psychology of Human Thought*, pp. 309-336.
Cambridge: Cambridge University Press.

Phillips, Hubert. 1961. *My Best Puzzles in Logic and Reasoning*. New York:
Dover.

Rixon, S. 1981. *How to Use Games in Language Teaching*. London: Macmillan.

Rodgers, T.S. 1981. "A Framework for Making and Using Language Teaching
Games." In *Guidelines for Language Games*, pp. 1-7. Singapore: RELC.

Savignon, S. 1992. "Problem-Solving and the Negotiation of Meaning in Second-Language Theory and Practice." In Caterina Cicogna, Marcel Danesi,
and Anthony Mollica, eds., *Problem-Solving in Second-Language Teaching*, pp. 11-25. Welland, Ontario: éditions Soleil publishing inc.

Sawyers, J.K. and C.S. Rogers. 1994. *Helping Children Develop through Play*.
Washington: National Association for the Education of Young Children.

Schloss, B. 1977. *Jeux linguistiques*. Toronto: OISE Press.

Schmidt, E. 1977. *Let's Play Games in German*. Skokie: National Textbook Co.

Schultz, M. and A. Fisher. 1988. *Games for All Reasons: Interacting in the
Language Classroom*. Reading: Addison-Wesley.

Steinberg, J. 1991. *Games Language People Play*. Markham, Ontario: Dominie
Press.

Webster, M. and E. Castonon. 1980. *Crosstalk: Communication Tasks and Games
at the Elementary, Preintermediate and Intermediate Levels*. Oxford: Oxford University Press.

Wells, D. 1992. *The Penguin Book of Curious and Interesting Puzzles*.
Harmondsworth: Penguin.

Wolfe, D. E. 1972. "Teacher-Made Crossword Puzzles." *Audio-Visual Language
Journal*. 10: 177-181.

Wylie, C.R. 1957. *101 Puzzles in Logic and Reasoning*. New Tork Dover.

Wright, A., D. Betteridge, and M. Buckby. 1979. *Games for Language Learning*. Cambridge: Cambridge University Press.

Reprinted from: Marcel Danesi and Anthony Mollica "Games and Puzzles
in the Second-Language Classroom: A Second Look," *Mosaic*, 2, 2 (Winter
1994): 14-22.

32 French, German, Italian and Spanish Tongue Twisters in the Classroom

Anthony Mollica

Tongue twisters are a useful source to teach pronunciation in the language classroom as well as a tool which provides moments of humour and relaxation.

Tongue twisters consist of a sequence of words whose sounds – often repeated – when spoken quickly are difficult to pronounce correctly. They probably arose from the human tendency to alliterate – putting together words with sounds – usually at the beginning of each word. Alliteration is a natural habit and the alliterative art, which predates rhyme, can be seen in such familiar phrases "When there's a will, there's a way", etc. Tongue twisters, then, are alliterative sentences in statements, in the form of a question, or in verse which, when spoken, result in a considerable oral challenge.

Nowadays, tongue twisters are regarded as a form of amusement suitable for children. In spite of this perception, they have been used for serious purposes. Speech therapists and elocutionists have often employed them to teach and/or improve a patient's or client's pronunciation. Who can forget the classic line in My Fair Lady, the musical version of George Bernard Shaw's Pygmalion, where the demanding Professor Higgins finally succeeds in getting Eliza Doolitle to pronounce impeccably, "The rain in Spain falls mainly on the plain!"

Tongue twisters are constructed in such a way that the sequence of letters, syllables or words will render quite difficult their correct pronunciation. Tongue twisters, in fact, are designed so that anyone reciting them will inevitably make errors in pronunciation.

The word "tongue twister" has an equivalent in Italian ("scioglilingua"), in Spanish ("trabalenguas"), and in German ("Zungenbrecher"), but, for some unknown reasons, it does not have an equivalent in French, a language which paraphrases it as, "mots ou phrases difficiles à prononcer". In Québec, one of Canada's provinces, it is common to use virelangue.

Tongue twisters vary in length and in format. There are some consisting of very few simple words; others are long and complex. The longest, and perhaps the most challenging tongue twister in Italian, is probably the following which appeared in the late 18th century.

Se l'arcivescovo di Costantinopoli
si disarcivesconstantinopolizzasse,
voi, vi disarcivescostantinopolizzereste
come si è disarcivescostantino-polizzato lui?

There exist variations of the above which are equally difficult to pronounce:

Se l'arcivescovo di Costantinopoli
si volesse arcivescovocostantinopolizzare,
vi arcivescovocostantinopolizzereste voi
per arcivescovoscostantinopoliz-zare lui?
(http://digilander.libero.it/tatone2001/bambini/sciglilingua.html?)

This particular tongue twister even found its way into Spain but, in that country, it has a royal twist as well as a variation:

El arzobispo de Constantinopla
se quiere desarzobispoconstantino-polizar.
El desarzobispoconstantinopoliza-dor
que lo desarzobispoconstantino-police
buen desarzobispoconstantinopo-lizador será.
(www.filastrocche.it)

El rey de Constantinopla quiere desconstantinopolizarse.
El desconstantinopolizador que lo
desconstantinopolize buen
desconstantinopolizador será.
(www.uebersetzung.at/twister/es.htm)

There are several tongue twisters which imitate this structure in both

FRENCH

Dis-moi grosgrasgrandgraind'orge, quand te dégrosgrasgrandgraind'orgeras-tu ?
– Je me dégrosgrasgrand-graind'orgerai quand tous les grosgrasgrandgraind'orge se dégrosgrasgrandgraind'orgeront.
(fr.wikipedia.org/wiki/Virelangue# Exemples _ de_virelangues)
and

SPANISH

El cielo está enladrillado.
¿quién lo desenladrillará?
el buen desenladrillador
que lo desenladrille
buen desenladrillador será.
(club2.telepolis.com/pitufasaltarina/trabalenguas/trabalenguas.htm)

Tongue twisters take a variety of forms.

1. They may appear in verse:

FRENCH

> Si ton bec aime mon bec
> comme mon bec aime ton bec,
> donne-moi le plus gros bec
> de la Province de Québec!
> (http://www.uebersetzung.at/twister/fr.htm)

> Quand un cordier cordant doit accorder sa corde,
> Pour sa corde accorder six cordons
> il accorde,
> Mais si l'un des cordons de la corde décorde,
> Le cordon décordé fait décorder la corde,
> Que le cordier cordant avait mal accordée.
> (http://www.uebersetzung.at/twister/fr.htm)

GERMAN

> Sie brauchten gar nicht umzusteigen,
> drum gab sie sich ihm stumm zu eigen.
> Doch weil verkehrt die Weichen lagen,
> fuhr man zurück im Leichen-wagen.
> (http://www.uebersetzung.at/twister/de.htm)

> Nicht alle Leute können es ertragen
> wenn Lautenspieler laut die Lauten schlagen,
> drum spielen heute laute Lauten-spieler leise Laute,
> weil manchen Leuten vor den lauten Lautenlauten graute.
> (http://www.uebersetzung.at/twister/de.htm)

ITALIAN

> Pel ritratto del trattore
> tratteggiando in trattoria
> non ho chiesto, in fede mia,
> per compenso soldi assai.
> Chè dal conto gli ho detratto
> (ciò parendomi corretto)
> i tortelli, trote e torte
> che goloso mi sbafai.
> (www.filastrocche.it)

SPANISH

> No me mires,
> que miran
> que nos miramos,
> y verán en tus ojos
> que nos amamos.
> No nos miremos,
> que cuando no nos miren
> nos miraremos.
> (http://www.uebersetzung.at/twister/es.htm)

2. They may be in dialogue form:

FRENCH

> Ta tante t'attend.
> – J'ai tant de tantes. Quelle tante m'attend ?
> – Ta tante Antoinette t'attend.
> (http://www.uebersetzung.at/twister/fr.htm)

> – Combien sont ces six saucissons-ci ?
> – Ces six saucissons-ci sont six sous.
> – Si ces six saucissons-ci sont six sous, ces six saucissons-ci sont trop chers.
> (http://french.about.com/cs/francophonie/a/tonguetwisters.htm)

GERMAN

> Beim Friseur:
> – Tag, Karl.
> – Wie geht's, Karl?
> – Gut, Karl.
> – Kahl, Karl?
> – Ja, Karl, ganz kahl.
> (http://www.uebersetzung.at/twister/de.htm)

ITALIAN

> – C'è il questore in questura a quest'ora?
> – Il questore in questura a quest'ora non c'è.
> (I librotti, *Scioglilingua*. Disegni di Walter Casiraghi. Milano: Vita e Pensiero, 1989. p. 87)

> – Buona sera. Buona sera.
> – Ha il Corriere della sera di ieri sera?
> – No. Il Corriere della sera di ieri sera non ce l'ho. Ho il Corriere della sera di stasera.
> – Buona sera. Buona sera.
> (http://digilander.libero.it/tatone2001/bambini/sciglilingua.html?)

SPANISH

> Un podador podaba la parra y otro podador que por allí pasaba le preguntó:
> – Podador que podas la parra. ¿Qué parra podas?¿Podas mi parra o tu parra podas?
> – Ni podo tu parra, ni mi parra podo, que podo la parra de mi tío Bartolo.
> (http://www.uebersetzung.at/twister/es.htm)

> – ¿Usted no nada nada?
> – No, no traje traje.
> (http://www.uebersetzung.at/twister/es.htm)

3. They may express or describe the obvious:

FRENCH

> Dans la gendarmerie, quand un gendarme rit, tous les gendarmes rient dans la gendarmerie.
> (http://www.uebersetzung.at/twister/fr.htm)

> La jolie rose jaune de Josette jaunit dans le jardin.
> (http://fr.wikipedia.org/wiki/Virelangue# Exemples _de_virelangues)

GERMAN

> Eine Diplombibliothekarin ist Bibliothekarin mit Diplom,
> eine Bibliothekarin mit Diplom ist eine Diplombibliothekarin.
> (http://www.uebersetzung.at/twister/de.htm)

> Der Zweck hat den Zweck den Zweck zu bezwecken; wenn der Zweck seinen Zweck nicht bezweckt, hat der Zweck keinen Zweck!
> (http://www.kidsaction.de/zunge.htm)

ITALIAN

> La capra che crepa a Capri
> non è più una capra di Capri.
> (www.filastrocche.it)

> Ciò che è, è;
> ciò che non è, non è;
> ciò che è, non è ciò che non è;
> ciò che non è, non è ciò che è.
> (http://uebersetzung.at/twister/es.htm)

SPANISH

> Otorrinolaringólogo trabaja en la otorrinolaringología.
> (http://www.uebersetzung.at/twister/es.htm)

> Historia es la narración sucesiva de los sucesos que se sucedieron sucesivamente en la sucesión sucesiva de los tiempos.
> (http://es.wikipedia.org/wiki/Trabalenguas)

4. They may narrate an imaginary or fictional "historical" event:

FRENCH

> Le général Joffrin nous dit :
> À Toul, ai perdu mon dentier.
> (http://www.uebersetzung.at/twister/fr.htm)

> Gal, amant de la reine, alla, tour magnanime,
> galamment de l'arène à la tour Magne à Nîmes.
> (http://www.uebersetzung.at/twister/fr.htm)

GERMAN

> Der Leutnant von Leuten befahl seinen Leuten, nicht eher zu läuten, bis der Leutnant von Leuten seinen Leuten das läuten befahl!
> (http://www.serve.com/shea/twister.htm)

Kaiser Karl konnte keine Kümmelkerne kauen, warum konnte Kaiser Karl keine Kümmelkerne kauen? Weil Kaiser Karl keine Kümmelkerne kauen konnte.
(http://www.kidsaction.de/zunge.htm)

ITALIAN

Povero pittore padovano
pitturava
per papa Pio primo
per pentitosi
per poca paga
partì
per Porta Pia.
(I librotti, 1989, p. 82)

SPANISH

El perro de San Roque no tiene rabo porque el carretero Ramón Ramiro Ramirez con la rara rueda de su carro se lo ha arrancado.
(es.wikipedia.org/wiki/Trabalenguas)

5. They may appear in the form of a question:

FRENCH

As tu été à Tahiti ?
(http://french.about.com/cs/francophonie/a/tonguetwisters.htm)

Tonton, ton thé t'a-t-il ôté ta toux ?
(http://www.uebersetzung.at/twister/fr.htm)

Je suis ce que je suis et si je suis ce que je suis, qu'est-ce que je suis ?
(http://www.uebersetzung.at/twister/fr.htm)

GERMAN

Weisst du das, dass das "das" das meistgebrauchte Wort im Satz ist?
(http://www.uebersetzung.at/twister/es.htm)

ITALIAN

Sei tu quel barbaro barbiere
che barbaramente barbasti
la barba a quel povero
barbaro barbone?
(http://junior.virgilio.it/passatempi/scioglilingua/s5.htm)

È la mamma che ti sveglia
o la sveglia che ti sveglia?
E chi è che sveglia
la mamma che ti sveglia?
(www.filastrocche.it)

SPANISH

¿Cuánta madera roería un roedor

si los roedores royeran madera?
(http://www.uebersetzung.at/twister/es.htm)
Si tu eres tu,
y yo soy yo,
¿quién es el mas tonto de los dos?
(http://www.uebersetzung.at/twister/es.htm)

6. They may be "philosophical" or "proverbial" in nature:

FRENCH

Si ça se passe ainsi, c'est sans souci.
(http://www.uebersetzung.at/twister/fr.htm)

Je veux et j'exige; j'exige et je veux.
(http://www.uebersetzung.at/twister/fr.htm)

GERMAN

Denke nie gedacht zu haben, denn das denken der Gedanken ist gedankenloses Denken. Wenn du denkst, du denkst, dann denkst du nur du denkst, aber denken tust du nie.
(http://www.uebersetzung.at/twister/de.htm)

ITALIAN

Pensa prima
parla poi
Perché parole
poco pensate
portano pena.
(I librotti,1989, p. 69)

SPANISH

De generación en generación las generaciones se degeneran con mayor degeneración.
(http://www.uebersetzung.at/twister/es.htm)

El amor es una locura
que solo el cura lo cura,
pero el cura que lo cura
comete una gran locura.
(http://www.uebersetzung.at/twister/es.htm)

7. The may describe an event:

FRENCH

Cinq chiens chassent six chats.
(www.uebersetzung.at/twister/fr.htm)

Trois tortues trottaient sur un trottoir très étroit.
(www.uebersetzung.at/twister/fr.htm)

GERMAN

Am Zehnten Zehnten um zehn Uhr zehn zogen zehn zahme Ziegen zehn Zentner Zucker zum Zoo.
(http://www.uebersetzung.at/twister/de.htm)

Im Potsdammer Boxclub boxt der Potsdammer Postbusboss.
(http://www.uebersetzung.at/twister/de.htm)

Fischers Fritz fischt frische Fische, frische Fische fischt Fischers Fritz.
(http://www.mckinnonsc.vic.edu.au/la/lote/german/materials/zbrecher.htm)

ITALIAN

Apelle, figlio di Apollo
fece una palla di pelle di pollo.
Tutti i pesci vennero a galla
per vedere la palla
di pelle di pollo,
fatta da Apelle,
figlio di Apollo.
(Martino Lironi. p. 137)

SPANISH

Tres tristes tigres tragaban trigo en un trigal.
(http://www.uebersetzung.at/twister/es.htm)

El vino vino, pero el vino no vino vino. El vino vino vinagre.
(http://www.uebersetzung.at/twister/es.htm)

8. They may state a fact:

FRENCH

Il y a deux espèces de fous :
il y a les fous ronds, et les fous carrés.
les Fourons sont carrément fous,
et les fous carrés, ca c'est un cas Happart !
(www.uebersetzung.at/twister/fr.htm)

– L'oie niche bas, la pie niche haut: où niche l'hibou ?
– L'hibou niche ni haut ni bas.
(http://www.uebersetzung.at/twister/fr.htm# O147)

GERMAN

Eine gute gebratene Gans mit einer goldenen Gabel gegessen ist
eine gute Gabe Gottes.
(http://www.uebersetzung.at/twister/de.htm)

Schnellsprechsprüche spreche ich schwer schnell.
(http://www.uebersetzung.at/twister/de.htm)

ITALIAN

Pasquale pescatore
è uno sprecone
che pesca bene
e poi la pesca spreca.
(I librotti. *Scioglilingua*, p. 74)

Sono solo

e so solo
di non essere solo
ad essere solo.
(www.viandante.com)

SPANISH

Debajo de el puente de Guadalajara había un conejo debajo de la agua.
(http://www.uebersetzung.at/twister/es.htm)

En la plaza de Constantinopla había una esquina, en la esquina una casa, en la casa un balcón, en el balcón una estaca, en la estaca una lora. La lora está en la estaca en el balcón de la casa en la esquina de la plaza de Constantinopla.
(http://www.uebersetzung.at/twister/es.htm)

9. They may appear in a story-telling format:

FRENCH

Il était une fois, un homme de foi qui vendait du foie dans la ville de Foix. Il dit :
– Ma foi, c'est la dernière fois que je vends du foie dans la ville de Foix.
(http://www.uebersetzung.at/twister/fr.htm# O19)

GERMAN

Es war einmal ein Mann, der hatte drei Söhne.
Der eine hieß Schack,
der andre hieß Schackschaw-werack,
der dritte hieß Schackschaw-werackschackommini.
Nun war da auch eine Frau, die hatte drei Töchter.
Die eine hieß Sipp,
die andre hieß Sippsiwwelipp,
die dritte hieß Sippsiwwelip-psippelimmini.
Und Schack nahm sie Sipp,
und Schackschawwerack nahm Sippsiwwelipp,
und Schackschawwerack-schackommini nahm Sippsiwwelippsippelimmini zur Frau.
(http://www.labbe.de/zzzebra/index.asp?the maid=341&titelid)

ITALIAN

C'era una volta una cincibiriciaccola, che aveva centocinquanta cincibiriciaccolini.
Un giorno la cincibiriciaccola disse
ai suoi centocinquanta cincibiri-ciaccolini:
"Smettetela di cincibiriciaccolare sempre, altrimenti un giorno non cincibiriciaccolerete più."
(http:/junior.virgilio.it/passatempi/scioglilingua/s5.htm)

SPANISH

Había una madre godable, pericotable que tenía un hijo godijo, pericotijo y tantarantijo. Un día la madre godable, pericotable y

tantarantable le dijo a su hijo godijo, pericotijo y tantarantijo:
– Hijo godijo, pericotijo y tantarantijo traédme la liebre godiebre, pericotiebre y tantarantiebre del monte godonte, pericotonte, pericotijo y tantarantijo y tantarantonte. Así el hijo, godijo, pericotijo y tantarantijo fue al monte godonte, pericotonte y tantarantonte a traer la liebre godiebre, pericotiebre y tantarantiebre.
(Enviado por Maria Fernanda Ruiz de México D.F.)
(http://www.elhuevodechocolate.com/trabale/trabale2.htm)

10. Some involve famous people:

FRENCH

Le général Joffrin nous dit :
À Toul, ai perdu mon dentier.
(http://www.uebersetzung.at/twister/fr.htm# O20)

Napoléon, cédant Sedan, céda ses dents.
(http://en.wikiquote.org/wiki/French_tongue _twisters)

GERMAN

Bismarck biss Marc, bis Marc Bismarck biss!
(http://www.mckinnonsc.vic.edu.au/la/lote/german/materials/zbrecher.htm)

ITALIAN

Torquato Tasso,
andando a spasso,
cadde in un fosso
e si fece male all'osso
del dito grosso!
(www.filastrocche.it)

SPANISH

El obispo vasco de Vizcaya busca el obispo vasco de Guipúzcoa.
(http://www.uebersetzung.at/twister/es.htm)

11. Some tongue twisters are designed so that, when pronounced very quickly, the outcome will be an obscenity.

FRENCH

C'est pas beau mais tentant de tenter de tâter, de téter les tétons de tata quand tonton n'est pas là.
(http://www.uebersetzung.at/twister/fr.htm# O36)

GERMAN

Hinter dichtem Fichtendickicht picken dicke Finken tüchtig.
(http://www.uebersetzung.at/twister/de.htm)

ITALIAN

Stiamo bocconi
cogliendo cotoni,
stiamo sedendo

cotoni cogliendo.
(www.locuta.com/gli_scioglilingua.htm; www.ac-poitiers.fr/italien/peda/sciogli.htm)

SPANISH

Tengo un tío cajonero
que hace cajas y calajas
y cajitas y cajones.
Y al tirar de los cordones
salen cajas y calajas
y cajitas y cajones.
(http://www.uebersetzung.at/twister/es.htm)

12. They may recall a grammatical structure.

FRENCH

(the present tense and past participle of *dire*):
Je dis que tu l'as dit à Didi ce que j'ai dit jeudi.
(www.uebersetzung.at/twister/fr.htm)

SPANISH

(the past participle of *"decir"*):
Me han dicho que has dicho un dicho, que han dicho que he
dicho yo. El que lo ha dicho mintió, y en caso que hubiese
dicho ese dicho que han dicho que he dicho yo, dicho y redicho
quedó, y estará bien dicho ese dicho que han dicho que he
dicho yo.
(http://www.uebersetzung.at/twister/es.htm)

(the present tense of querer):
¿Cómo quieres que te quiera si el que quiero que me quiera
no me quiere como quiero que me quiera?
(http://www.uebersetzung.at/twister/es.htm #92)

(the verb *contar*):
Cuando cuentes cuentos, cuenta cuantos cuentos cuentas,
cuando cuentes cuentos.
(www.uebersetzung.at/twister/es.htm)

13. They may be in the form of a palindrome:

SPANISH

Dábale arroz a la zorra el abad.
(http://www.uebersetzung.at/twister/es.htm)

14. Some tongue twisters, when pronounced, may indicate an
    "absurdity".

FRENCH

Mon père est maire, mon frère est masseur.
(www.uebersetzung.at/twister/fr.htm)

15. But, above all, tongue twisters are very often "nonsensical":

FRENCH

Des blancs pains, des bancs peints, des bains pleins.
(http://www.uebersetzung.at/twister/fr.htm#O74)

Seize c haises sèchent.
(http://www.uebersetzung.at/twister/fr.htm#O95)

GERMAN

Schnecken erschrecken, wenn Schnecken an Schnecken schlecken,
weil zum Schrecken vieler Schnecken, Schnecken nicht schmecken.
(http://www.uebersetzung.at/twister/de.htm)

ITALIAN

Fra le fresche frasche al fresco
fra freschi frati francescani.

SPANISH

Tras tus tres tristes tigres que triste estás Trinidad.
(www.uebersetzung.at/twister/es.htm)

As nonsensical statements, the tongue twister's main purpose in the language classroom is to stress pronunciation. There are sounds in French, German and Spanish which are difficult for Allophone s to repeat. Tongue twisters provide a humorous and less threatening way of practising such sounds. See the 3rd suggestion in Pedagogical Applications, below.

Pedagogical Applications

The following are some suggested activities focussing on tongue twisters:

1. Teachers may wish to post some tongue twisters on the bulletin board and ask students to read them from time to time.
2. Competitions can be held between two students or two groups (once the class has been divided in to half). This could be an activity used during the "warm-up"period, at the beginning of the of the lesson. It may be done a daily or intermittent basis. In either case, the activity would provide some "relaxation" at the beginning of each class.
3. Students may be asked to illustrate some of the tongue twisters and place their illustrations on the bulletin board. Other students may be asked to identify the tongue twister by looking at the illustration. The following two illustrations may be used for this activity in the French classroom for the tongue twisters "Cinq chiens chassent six chats" (Figure 1) and "Un chasseur sachant chasser sait chasser sans son chien." (Figure 2).

Figure 1   Figure 2

4. Teachers may wish to select tongue twisters to highlight different sounds as in the pronunciation of:

FRENCH

[ch] sound
Un chasseur sachant chasser sait chasser sans son chien de chasse.
(www.uebersetzung.at/twister/fr.htm)

GERMAN

[pf] sound
Pferde mampfen dampfende Äpfel. Dampfende Pferdeäpfel mampft niemand.
(http://www.schulzens.de/Grundschule/Deutsch/Zungenbrecher/zungenbrecher.html)

ITALIAN

[gli] sound
Si sbaglia il coniglio
se sceglie un giaciglio
di foglie di tiglio.
Va meglio la paglia.
(I librotti, 1989, p. 35)

the z: [dz] vs. [tz]
Una zolletta di zucchero nella tazza di zia Zita.
(www.filastrocche.it)

SPANISH

the trilled "r":
Erre con "erre" cigarro,
"erre" con "erre" barril.
Rápido corren los carros,
Cargados de azúcar al ferrocarril.
(http://www.uebersetzung.at/twister/es.htm)

5. In order to involve students even more in this language activity, teachers may wish to give them a series of words containing a similar sound from which they will create a tongue twister. For example, In Italian the words:

    sciatore, sciacquare, sciagura, scialle, sciame, scienza, scienziato, scilinguare, scimnmia, scintilla, sciocco, scioglilingua, scioperare, scivolare.

    may yield the following tongue twister:

    Lo sciocco sciatore sciava scilinguando scioglilingua.

6. An alternate or additional activity if for the students themselves to suggest both words and tongue twister.

Conclusion

Whatever the activity, tongue twisters are bound to provide moments of humour, relaxation and learning in the classroom.

Bibliography

Gianduzzo, Silvano.1991. *Lieti passatempi.* Leumann (TO): Editrice Elle Ci Di.

I librotti. *Scioglilingua.* Disegni di Walter Casiraghi. Milano: Vita e Pensiero, 1989.

Lironi, Martino. *Filastrocche, scioglilingua, canzoncine da leggere, recitare, imparare, cantare e ballare.* Milano: De Vecchi editore, 1994.

Websites

French: Search "virelangues" in www.google.fr
German: Search "zungebrecker" in www.google.de
Italian: Search "scioglilingua" in www.google.it
Spanish: Search "trabalenguas" in www.google.es

Editor's Note: A version of this article with examples only in Italian appeared in *Italiano per Stranieri* (Athens, Greece: Edizioni Edilingua) No. 3 (July 2006), pp. 4-10, with the title, "Gli scioglilingua nella glottodidattica: cenni di analisi e proposte di di attività."

Acknowledgements: I am indebted to Miriam Heusser, a student at Brock University and to Sabina Belcastro, a student at the Università della Calabria, Italy, for assisting me with the selection of the tongue twisters for German.

This is a shorter version of "French, German, Italian and Spanish Tongue Twisters in the Classroom" which appeared in *Mosaic*, 9, 3 (Fall 2007): 15-20.

Reprinted from Anthony Mollica, "French, German, Italian and Spanish Tongue Twisters in the Classroom." *Mosaic*, 9, 3 (Fall 2007): 15-20.

33 Talking off the Tops of Their Heads

Wilga Rivers

How do we develop communicative ability in a second language? We may intensify practice in the classroom (practice of patterns, practice of variations of patterns, practice in selection of patterns), but how do we engineer the great leap?

In a description of the Defense Language Institute program (1971) I read:

> After basic patterns and structures are mastered, the student can proceed to more and more controlled substitution and eventually to free conversation.

How delightfully simple it sounds! We breathe the fresh air of the uncomplicated. Our students master the basic patterns and structures; we provide them with carefully controlled practice; and hey presto! – they speaks freely in unstructured situations.

There were times, in days that seem now to belong to another age, when faith in the efficacy of structured courses and controlled drills to produce fluent speakers of another language went unchallenged. We knew where we wanted to go; we knew how to get there; we were happy with our products – or were we? And were they? Are such cries of frustration as "I can't say anything off the top of my head, it all comes out as phrases from the book" new to our ears?[1] This student complaint of the seventies sounds almost like a paraphrase of the more academic remark of 1948 that,

> while many students could participate in memorized conversations speedily and effortlessly, hardly any could produce at length fluent variations from the basic material, and none could talk on unrehearsed topics without constant and painful hesitation.[2]

Autonomy in language use

In almost a quarter of a century we have still not come to grips with our basic problem: How do we develop communicative ability in a second language?" We may intensify practice in the classroom (practice of patterns, practice of variations of patterns, practice in selection of patterns), but how do we engineer the great leap? Children learn all kinds of swimming movements while loving parents hold them, let them go a little, but are there to support them as they lose confidence; then at some moment they swim.

One moment they are nonswimmers, then they are swimmers, if only for a very short distance. The movements are the same, the activity is of a new kind – the difference is psychological. How do nonswimmers become a swimmers? They draw on their own resources; they cease to rely on somebody else's support; they become autonomous in their movements; they take off and they are swimming. How do we get our students to this autonomous stage in language use? This is the crucial point of our teaching. Until we have solved this problem we will continue to mark time, developing more and more efficient techniques for producing second-language cripples, with all the necessary muscles and sinews but unable to operate on their own. "Spontaneous expression," "liberated expression," "creative language use," "authentic communication" – the terms may vary with changing emphases in our profession: The goal seems still to elude us.

We must examine the problem at the point at which we are stalled. How can we help the student pass from the storing of linguistic knowledge and information about how this knowledge operates in communication to actual use of this knowledge for the multitudinous, unpredictable purposes of an individual in contact with other individuals? We do not need new ways to help the student acquire linguistic knowledge – we know of many from our "twenty-five centuries of language teaching"[3] and each in its heyday has seemed to be effective for this purpose. Here we can pick and choose according to our theoretical persuasion, our temperamental preferences, and our assessment of the learning styles of the particular groups of students with whom we are dealing. In any case, these students will learn according to their personal strategies in the ultimate secret of their individual personalities, even when they appear to be doing as we direct.

Essential processes in learning to communicate

We need a model of language teaching activity that allocates a full role to the student's individual learning in communication. I propose the following division of essential processes (see schema).

Ability to communicate, to interact verbally, presumes someknowledge (cognition) both in the perception of units, categories, and functions, and in the internalizing of the rules relat-

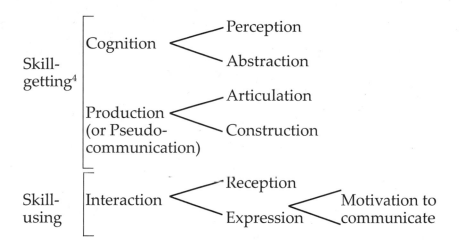

ing these categories and functions (which is a process of abstraction). I am not concerned here with how this knowledge is acquired, and I am willing to concede the validity (and probably the necessity) of a variety of approaches to this acquisition. Linguistic knowledge must, however, be acquired. In the process of acquisition students learn the production of language sequences: They learn through doing. Whether we use the terms "exercises," "drills," "intensive practice," or "activities" is immaterial; some kind of practice in putting together smoothly and confidently what they are learning is also essential. Each student must learn to articulate the sounds of the language acceptably and construct comprehensible second-language sequences by rapid associations of learned elements. No matter how much we relate these skill-getting activities to real-life situations this practice rarely passes beyond pseudo-communication. It is externally directed, not self-originating; it is a dependent, not an independent, activity. The utterances may even be original in their combinations of segments, but the students are not communicating anything that is of real import to them nor are they receiving any genuine messages from others.

This is practice in formulating messages, and as such it is valuable practice. It is near-communication with all the outward appearances of communication, but in these activities the student does not have to demonstrate that great leap into autonomy – the leap that is crucial. Our failure in the past has been in our satisfaction with students who performed well in pseudo-communication. We have tended to assume that there would then be automatic transfer to performance in interaction (both in the reception and expression of messages). We may have encouraged some sketchy attempts at autonomous interaction, but always with the supporting hand: the instructor or the native speaker leading the group, drawing the student out, directing the interchange.

Problems with drills

Wolfe suggests that progress toward autonomy is hindered by the artificiality of language learning through drills and exercises that force the student to lie. "From the point of view of true linguistic communication," he says, such "seemingly harmless sentences" as Yesterday I went to the movies, Last night I went to the game, or Last week I went to the game "border on the nonsensical."[5] I do not think this is the problem. We may even maintain that lying is a common form of real communication, but, this aspect aside, sentences in drills of this type are merely pseudo-communication, and it may be clearer to students that this is the case if they are sometimes also incredible or absurd. In a foreign-language text coauthored by the playwright Ionesco, the nonsensical, shall we say whimsical, approach to adult learning is purposefully exploited with students playing manipulatively with such sentences as

"The teacher is in the pocket of the vest of the watch";
"The crocodile is more beautiful than Mary-Jane"; and
"He says his parents are as big as the Eiffel Tower."[6]

Such manipulations are intended to force students to think of the meaning of what they are saying, which is one step toward autonomy, and pure nonsense may on occasion be more effective in this regard than the colorless, socially correct actions of Dick and Jane, or Maria and Pedro.

Communication drills

In recent writings on second-language teaching there has been increasing emphasis on communication and on what have been called communication drills. I myself have spoken elsewhere of the necessity for relating the content of drills to the student's own interests:

> Participation in the drill can be innovative: providing for practice in the repetition and variation of language segments, but with simultaneous practice in selection, as students express their own meanings and not those of a textbook writer... Practice in selection should not be considered a separate activity for advanced classes: it can and should be included in class work from the very first lessons.[7]

Moreover

many drills may be given the appearance of a game, or of elementary communication, by provoking the students into asking the teacher a series of questions in response to cues; or the items of a drill may develop a series of comments about the activities and interests of teacher and students... The more students are interested in an activity in the target language, the more they feel the desire to communicate in the language, and this is the first and most vital step in learning to use language forms spontaneously.[8]

Paulston has developed the communication drill concept in more detail.[9] She groups drills into mechanical drills, meaningful drills, and communicative drills.

In mechanical drills, there is complete control of the response so that the student does not even need to understand the drill to produce the correct response (as in simple substitution drills). Paulston suggests that if a nonsense word can be inserted as effectively by the student as a meaningful word, then the drill is of the mechanical type (for example:

"This is a box";
"Wug";
"This is a wug").

Drilling of this type is pure production: sometimes merely practice in articulation, at others in constructing an orderly sequence. As such it has its place in the initial phase of introducing a new structure or for practicing some problem of pronunciation or intonation. An example of a mechanical drill would be:

Pattern:	I'm holding a book.
Cue:	Magazine.
Response:	I'm holding magazine.
Cue:	Banana.
Response:	I'm holding a banana.
Cue:	Wug.
Response:	I'm holding a wug.

In meaningful drills, "there is still control of the response (although it may be correctly expressed in more than one way...) but the student cannot complete the drill without fully understanding structurally and semantically what he is saying." The following is an example of a meaningful drill:

Question:	When did you arrive this morning?
Answer:	I arrived at nine o'clock.
Question:	When will you leave this evening?
Answer:	I'll leave at six o'clock.

In a communicative drill, however,

there is no control of the response. The student has free choice of answer, and the criterion of selection here is his own opinion of the real world – whatever he wants to say.

This sounds like autonomous interaction, but Paulston continues:

> Whatever control there is lies in the stimulus... It still remains a drill rather than free communication because we are still within the realm of the cue-response pattern.

She gives the example: "What did you have for breakfast?" with its possibility of an orthodox response such as "I had toast and coffee for breakfast," or the unorthodox "I overslept and skipped breakfast so I wouldn't miss the bus." It is clear that the unconventional student may well turn this into real interaction, but my guess is that the majority of students, feeling insecure in their knowledge of the language and fairly certain of what the teacher expects, would remain in the area of pseudo-communication.

Palmer suggests what he calls communication practice drills.

> In communication practice (CP) drills, the student finds pleasure in a response that is not only linguistically acceptable, but also conveys information personally relevant to himself and other people.

As outlined, this is an interesting technique. Palmer maintains that "the most powerful technique at the teacher's disposal is his ability to verbally create situations which could be relevant to the student's own life and then to force the student to think about the meaning and consequences of what he would say in such situations."10 Palmer's CP drills are drills in that they center on practice of particular structures such as:

I would tell him	to	shut the door.
her		turn on the light.
them		bring some food.

He develops these, however, by a somewhat Socratic method:

Teacher: Karen, if you and Susan came to class at 8 a.m. and it was winter and the room was dark at 8 a.m., what would you tell Susan?

Karen: (with any luck at all) I would tell her to turn on the light.

Teacher: And how about you, Paul, if you were with Mary and you wanted to read, what would you do?

Paul: I would tell her to turn on the light.

Teacher: (in student's native language) You as a boy would tell a girl to do that for you?

Teacher: (continuing in the target language) Paul, if you came alone, and if I was in the room, what would you do?

Paul: I would tell you to turn on the light.

Teacher: Then I would throw you out of class.

In this type of drill Palmer is moving toward interaction in that students who give mechanically what appear to be a correct responses may well be pulled up short because they have not thought about the implications of their responses in the imposed setting. With training in such drills average students would possibly produce more original responses than in Paulston's communicative drills, because of the goad of the teacher's teasing and their natural desire to show that they had recognized the pedagogical stratagem. This type of drill teeters on the brink of interaction, but it is still in the area of pseudo-communication and production practice because the whole interchange is teacher-directed, with the specific intention of eliciting certain structures.

Using language freely for normal purposes

Where do we go from here? We must work out situations, from an early stage, where our students are on their own, trying to use the language for the normal purposes of language: establishing social relations; seeking and giving information; expressing reactions; learning or teaching others to do something; hiding intentions; talking their way out of trouble; persuading; discouraging, and entertaining others; sharing leisure activities; displaying their achievements; acting out social roles; discussing ideas; and playing with language for the fun of it.

When I say students are "on their own," I mean they are not supported or directed by the teacher: They may well be working with other students. In this type of practice students should be allowed to use anything they know of the language and any aids (gestures, drawings, pantomime) to fill out their meaning, when they are "at a loss for words."11 In this way he will learn to draw on everything he knows at a particular moment in their acquisition of the language, and to fight to put their meaning over, as they would if he suddenly found themselves surrounded by monolingual speakers of the language. This experience is not intended to replace the careful teaching of the language we already supply (the skill-getting activities we organize) but to expand it with regular and frequent opportunities for autonomous interaction (skill-using), thus making full provision for a dimension of language learning, which at present is, if not completely neglected, at least given insufficient place in our programs. As I have said elsewhere:

> Perfection at the pattern-drill level, no matter how impressive to the observer, cannot be an end in itself. It is a fruitless activity un-

less care is taken to see that the result of all this effort is the ability to use the language to express some message of one's own.[12]

In 1964, I spoke of the need for developing

that adventurous spirit which will enable the student to try to meet any situation by putting what he knows to maximum use.[13]

In 1968, I wrote

students should be encouraged, at the advanced level, to try out new combinations of elements to create novel utterances. This is what the advanced student would do were he to find himself in a foreign country. He would make every effort to express his meaning by all kinds of recombinations of the language elements at his disposal. The more daring he is in such linguistic innovation, the more rapidly he progresses.[14]

On looking back I feel it was a mistake to tag this recommendation specifically to "the advanced student" (a vague entity at best). Where we have been failing may well be in not encouraging this adventurous spirit from an early stage, with the result that the students find it difficult to move from structured security to the insecurity of reliance on their own resources, just as the young would-be swimmers cling to their mother's hand or insist on having one foot on the bottom of the pool.

In Savignon's interesting study, students in the communicative skills program (which consisted of one hour per week supplementing the regular audiolingual type of course)

were given the opportunity to speak French in a variety of communicative settings. These ranged from short (1-2 minute) exchanges between a student and a fluent speaker of French in a simulated situation to whole group discussions on topics of current interest. Emphasis was put on getting meaning across; students were urged to use every means at their disposal to understand and in turn to make themselves understood. Grammar and pronunciation errors were expected and were always ignored when they did not interfere with meaning. In other words, the experimenter and the other fluent speaker who participated in these sessions reacted to what was said, not to how it was said.[15]

One student commented:

These sessions taught me to say what I wanted to say instead of book conversations.[16]

If we compare this comment with the student's remark quoted at the beginning of this chapter it seems that these students did begin to "talk off the tops of their heads."

Autonomous interaction in the language program

Just how practice in autonomous interaction can be incorporated into the program will depend on the type of program, but incorporate it we must, giving it a substantial role in the students' learning. We must not feel that interaction practice is somehow "wasting time" when there is "so much to learn." Unless this adventurous spirit is given time to establish itself as a constant attitude, most of what is learned will be stored unused, and we will produce learned individuals who are inhibited and fearful in situations requiring language use. As Carroll has said,

> When utterances are not generated to attain communicative goals, they can hardly be rewarded by the attainment of such goals, and language learning is deprived of its true meaning.[17]

With careful selection of the activity, some genuine interaction can be a part of every lesson, even early in the learning process, with expansion of the complexity of the demands as the student advances.

Practice in autonomous interaction should be individualized in the sense that it should allow for the different ways students learn, the different paces at which they learn, the different things that interest them, and the different situations in which they prefer to learn. Students should be offered a choice of tasks (things to do, things to find out, problems to solve, situations to which to react) and then be allowed to choose their own way, their own place, time, and company, for handling them. Some may prefer to work regularly with one other person; some will prefer to work consistently with a small group; some will choose to work with the teacher. Some who are loners will prefer to work through certain situations by themselves, demonstrating their capacity as individuals (and many of these in a quiet way may outpace their fellows through sheer single-mindedness of purpose).

Students cannot be set down in groups, or sent off in pairs, and told to interact in the foreign language. Motivation to communicate must be aroused. Occasionally some fortuitous incident or combination of personalities will cause a desire to communicate something in the second language to emerge spontaneously, but in most instructional situations it will need to be fostered by the intrinsic interest of the task proposed and the students' interest in developing it. Such interest will make the interaction that follows autonomous: a genuine communication from one person to another, not just another imposed act of pseudo-communication. Because of the personal nature of the activity we are promoting, the type of reaction to be displayed will always remain consistent with the personality of the particular student. Some people are temperamentally incapable of interacting with a babble of words; to force them to do so is to force them back into pseudo-communication and into mouthing learned phrases. The quality of the interaction will be judged by other criteria: ability to receive and express meaning, to understand and convey intentions, to perform acceptably in situations and in relations with others.

Earlier I suggested various natural uses of language in interaction that can be incorporated in this type of activity. Here I will expand on these and set down a few elaborations of each.[18] A imaginative teacher will think of many others.

1. *Establishing and maintaining social relations:* greetings between persons of the same and different age and status; introductions; wishes for special occasions; polite enquiries (with attention to the permissible and the expected questions in the culture); making arrangements; giving directions to strangers; apologies, excuses, refusals, mild rebukes, hedging (the gentle art of noncommunication); encouraging, discouraging, and persuading others. Students may be sent to find out from a monolingual native speaker (or one who pretends to be monolingual) how these are enacted in the cultural context of the language being learned.

2. *Seeking information* on subjects for which students have some basic vocabulary. (At some point finding out specific technical vocabulary can be part of this type of interaction). Once again the native speakers or informants involved act as though they were monolingual. The information may be useful for (1), for (3), for (4), for (8) or even for (11).

3. *Giving information* about oneself, one's background, one's country, or about some subject in which one is proficient. The student may be giving information to other students learning to do or make something (4), or passing on information gained in (2). Simulated settings like bank or airline counters, customs desks, workshops, or restaurants may be used where the students are confined to the school setting.

4. *Learning to do or make something.* The possibilities here are limitless. The pressure of intensive courses can be relieved by organizing actual sessions in the second language where students work with real-life materials and activities (sports, physical exercise, hobbies, crafts, music, dance, cooking, making clothes).

5. *Expressing one's reactions.* Students can be put in real situations or simulated situations where they have to react verbally throughout a television show, at an exhibition of pictures or photographs, or during a friendly sharing of slides.

6. *Hiding one's intentions.* Each student may be given a mis-

sion that must not be revealed under any provocation but must be carried out within a given period of time. This type of activity carries purposeful use of the language beyond course hours as students try to discover each other's missions.

7. *Talking one's way out of trouble.* Simulated or real situations of increasing verbal difficulty should be set up where students must use their wits to extract themselves from some dilemma.

8. *Problem solving.* A problem may involve (2) or (4), or even (6) and (7). The problem presented should be an active one whose solution requires verbal activity or enquiry. As early as 1953, Carroll posed the question whether aural-oral methods might not be more successful if, instead of presenting the student with a fixed, predetermined lesson to be learned, the teacher created a 'problem-solving' situation in which the student must find... appropriate verbal responses for solving the problem," thus being early forced "to learn, by a kind of trial-and-error process, to communicate rather than merely to utter the speech patterns in the lesson plans.[19]

9. *Sharing leisure activities.* Students should have the opportunity to learn and become proficient in the games and diversions of the target culture. They should be able to participate in verbal competitions. Where there are special activities associated with festivals or national holidays these should be engaged in.

10. *Conversing over the telephone.* This is always difficult in a second language and should be practiced early. The student should use a phone book in the second language and, where possible, make actual calls enquiring about goods, services, or timetables for transport. The help of monolingual contacts outside the course should be enlisted. (Some incapacitated persons and older people living alone would enjoy participating in this type of communication.) This activity can be linked with (2) or (8) and will often involve (3).

11. *Entertaining others.* The student should be given the opportunity to use their natural talents or encouraged through role-playing sessions and skits to act out in front of a group. They may conduct a radio call-in programs or a TV talk or game show. Groups of students may prepare and present radio or TV commercials (these may involve more or less talking interspersed with mime and are therefore very suitable for the early stages of a course). A continuing serial story, with episodes developed successively by different groups, keeps interest alive.

12. *Displaying one's achievements.* Students may tell the group about what they did in (4), (5), (6), (7), or (8), or they may present and explain special projects. This can be a regular culminating activity to draw together more individualized efforts at interaction.

13. *Acting out social roles.* In our social life, we are continually acting out roles: the hostess, the guest, the employee, the leader, the impressive achiever, the long-suffering noncomplainer. Improvisations, where students act out various roles in relation to each other, are not only useful and interesting but also provide a cover for those more inhibited students who do not mind expressing feelings and viewpoints when they are presumed to be those of others. These activities also bring in aspects of (1), (3), (5), (7), and (11).

14. *Discussing ideas and optinions.* This is one of the most frequent verbal activities in any language. It can be linked with understanding the target culture and similarities and differences in ways of acting and reacting between speakers of the first and second languages. Discussion groups, debates, panel discussions, lecturettes or oral reports with questions and comments from the listerners, and frequent classroom discussion of second-language material read or seen are obvious ways to develop this ability, which also involves (2), (3), (5), and (8).

15. *Playing with language.* This is another frequent activity of all language users. We love jokes, puns, word games, crossword puzzles, and so on. Students can make up poems and learn nonsense and counting rhymes. Charades, in which students act out the various syllables of a word and then the complete word, are useful. As students go further, they become interested in word histories and word formation and learn to create their own words in acceptable ways. They also learn to distinguish levels of language (formal from familiar, standard usage from slang and jargon) and become familiar with regional and subgroup variants.

All of these activities will obviously not be possible for all students from the earliest stage of learning. The teacher will select and graduate activities from these categories so that the attitude of seeking to communicate is developed early in an activity which is within the student's growing capacity. An impossible task that bewilders and discourages students too early in their language learning is just as inhibiting of ultimate fluency as lack of opportunity to try what they can do with what they know.

Noncorrective approach to interaction

Some people will have deep-seated doubts about accepting such an approach, because they foresee that the student will make many errors that may become ingrained and ineradicable. It was because of such problems that many turned away from the direct method, seeking something more systematic that would seem to ensure more accurate production. Unfortunately, the emphasis on correct production at all times and the firm determination to create a learning situation where students would not make mistakes seems to have led to an impasse for many students. If we wish to facilitate the "great leap" into autonomous communication that I have described, then a change of attitude toward mistakes during interaction practice is imperative. It is during production (or pseudo-communication) practice that immediate corrections should be made. It is then that we should make the students conscious of possible errors and so familiarize them with acceptable sequences that they are able to monitor their own production and work toward its improvement in spontaneous interaction. In interaction practice we are trying to develop an attitude of innovation and experimentation with the new language. Nothing is more dampening of enthusiasm and effort than constant correction when students are trying to express their own ideas within the limitations of their newly-acquired knowledge of the language. What is required is that the instructor note silently the consistent and systematic errors made by each student (not slips of the tongue and occasional lapses). These errors will then be discussed with students individually at a time when the instructor is helping them evaluate their success in interaction, with particular attention being paid to those types of errors that hinder communication. Such an analytic session may be conducted from time to time with a tape of an actual communication sequence, the student or group of students being asked to detect errors in their own spontaneous production and suggest corrections and improvements.20 This technique makes the students more alert to their own mistakes and to other possibilities for expressing their meaning that they have not been exploiting.

Many of the types of activities listed may have already found their place in our courses. The originality of the approach lies not so much in the novelty of the activities as in the way in which they are approached. To develop autonomous control of language for communication we must at some time allow the student autonomy, and, conversely, we must discourage dependence. We must give students practice in relying on their own resources and using their ingenuity, so that very early in their language learning they realize that only by interacting freely and independently with others can they learn the control and ready retrieval essential for fluent language use. As Jespersen once said,

> The first condition for good instruction in... languages would seem to be to give the pupil as much as possible to do with and in the ... language; he must be steeped in it, not only get a sprinkling of it now and then; he must be ducked down in it and get to feel as if he were in his own element, so that he may at last disport himself in it as an able swimmer.[21]

Let's work it out

1. Take some structural pattern drills from the textbook you have been using and try to turn them into meaningful drills. Now try to rewrite them as communicative drills. Try these out on others in your group. What did you learn from this exercise?

2. Design some classroom conversational practice as pseudo-communication (that is, "near communication with all the outward appearances of communication"). What would you have to do to convert these activities into genuine communicative interaction?

3. Design some role-playing activities for practice in establishing and maintaining social relations, talking one's way out of trouble, and acting out social roles.

4. Draw up some lists of words and expressions in the second language that students would need to know to express various kinds of reactions (appreciation, frustration, hesitancy, suspicion, enthusiasm, etc.). Begin to use these with the class you are teaching.

5. Plan in detail some leisure activities in which students can use the language with each other in a purposeful way. (These may be for a club, festivity, national celebration, dinner, or international day, among others.)

Notes

1. *The Advisor* (Teacher-Course Evaluation, University of Illinois, 1970-71), p. 122.

2. F. Agard and H. Dunkel, *An Investigation of Second-Language Teaching.* Lexington, Mass.: Ginn, 1948, p. 288.

3. L. Kelly, 25 *Centuries of Language Teaching.* Rowley, Mass.: Newbury House, 1969.

4. I have borrowed the division into skill-getting and skill-using from Don H. Parker, "When Should I Individualize Instruction?" in *Individualization of Instruction: A Teaching Strategy,* ed. Virgil M. Howes. New York: Macmillan, 1970, p. 176.

5. D. L. Wolfe, "Some Theoretical Aspects of Language Learning and Language Teaching," *Language Learning.* 17 (1967): 175.

6. M. Benamou and E. Ionesco, *Mise en Train.* New York: Macmillan, 1969: "Le professeur est dans la poche du gilet de la montre," p. 44; "Le crocodile est plus

beau que Marie-Jeanne," p. 114; "Il dit que ses parents sont aussi grands que la Tour Eiffel," p. 141.

7. "From Skill Acquisition to Language Contro," chap. 3 of Rivers, *Speaking in Many Tongues: Essays in Foreign-Language Teaching,* 3rd ed. Cambridge: Cambridge University Press, 1983; or *TQ* 3 (1969): 12.

8. *Teaching Foreign-Language Skills,* 2nd ed. Chicago: University of Chicago Press, 1981, p. 110. See also 1st ed., p. 109. Italics not in the orignial.

9. C. B. Paulston, "Structural Pattern Drills: A Classification," *Foreign Language Annals.* 4 (1970): 187-93.

10. Adrian Palmer, "Teaching Communication," *Language Learning.* 20 (1970): 55-68.

11. S. Savignon used this technique in her "Study of the Effect of Training in Communicative Skills as Part of a Beginning College French Course on Student Attitude and Achievement in Linguistic and Communicative Competence," unpublished Ph.D. dissertation, University of Illinois at Champaign-Urbana, 1971, since published as Communicative Competence: An Experiment in Foreign-Language Teaching. Philadelphia: Center for Curriculum Development, 1972.

12. Rivers, *Teaching Foregin-Language Skills,* 2nd ed., pp. 110-11. See also 1st ed., p. 109.

13. *The Psychologist and the Foreign-Language Teacher.* Chicago: University of Chicago Press, 1964, p. 78. Italics not in the original.

14. *Teaching Foreign-Language Skills,* 1st ed., p. 201. Italics not in the original.

15. Savignon, *Communicative Competence,* p. 25. On pp. 28 and 29 are listed a variety of communicative tasks used during the practice sessions. Savignon acknowledges her indebtedness to L. A. Jakobovits, *Foreign Language Learning: A Linguistic Analysis of the Issues.* Rowley, Mass.: Newbury House, 1970, chap. 3, for guidelines in defining these tasks. Jakobovits was the director of Savignon's study.

16. Savignon, *Communicative Competence,* p. 30.

17. J. B. Carroll, "Conscious and Automatic Processes in Language Learning," *The Canadian Modern Language Review/La Revue canadienne des langues vivantes.* 37 (1981): 471.

18. These activities are described in greater detail in Rivers et al., the *Practical Guides,* chap. 2, with many suggestions for their implementation. Many of the activities listed in the Index of these books under Games are also appropriate.

19. J. B. Carroll, *The Study of Language.* Cambridge, Mass.: Harvard University Press, 1953, p. 188. Italics in the original.

20. This is one of the techniques employed in Curran's Counseling-Learning/Community Language Learning approach.

21. Otto Jespersen, *How to Teach a Foreign Language.* London: Allen and Unwin, 1961, p. 48. Originally published in English translation in 1904.

This is a revised version of a paper delivered at the Defense Language Institute English Language Branch, lackland Air Force Base, Texas, on June 30, 1971, (TESOL Project). Originally published in *TESOL Quarterly*, 6 (1972):71.81.

Reprinted from "Talking off the Tops of their Heads." *Mosaic,* 7, 1 (Fall 1999): 3-10. By permission of Prof. Wilga Rivers.

34 The Five-Step Performance-Based Model of Oral Proficiency

Rebecca M. Valette

What can language teachers learn from the football coach? The author presents a five-step model which can be used to organize instruction so that the focus is on performance, that is, on using the second language for real-life communication.

Although we second language teachers have been unanimous in proclaiming "oral proficiency" as one of our major goals of instruction, there has been much debate as to how this goal is best achieved. For instance, how important is it to provide "comprehensible input" in the classroom? What is the role of grammar and/or linguistic analysis? Are drill and practice activities useful? How much time should be spent on simulated oral communication activities: role play, information gap activities, conversational exchanges? How and when should teachers engage in error correction? The current interest in "authentic assessment" is forcing all of us to focus on evaluating the outcomes of our second language courses. In doing so, we will need to adopt a "performance-based curriculum" in which our success and that of our students will be measured in terms of how well they can use the second language for communication in real-life situations.

The term "performance-based instruction" evokes, and perhaps appropriately so, the image of a sporting event, such as a football game. Indeed, at the secondary school level, the one faculty member who is the most rigorously evaluated in terms of student performance or student outcomes is usually the football coach. Almost every weekend during the fall season, coach and players focus their attention on outcomes, or performance, namely on how well they will play in the "real" game against another school in their league. During the week, however, there is training and practice of various sorts.

In order to elaborate a second-language model for performance-based instruction based on the football analogy, we must

closely observe how young people learn to play football. At first,
a child is happy to zigzag down the lawn carrying the ball. But
soon the young player needs to learn what real football is by:

- watching actual football games,
- learning the rules of the game, and
- drilling the skills, such as throwing, receiving, blocking and
  running.

  Furthermore, the young player needs to gain experience in:

- scrimmage practice, and
- participating in actual games.

Clearly a young player who cannot understand the game on
television, who cannot catch a pass, and who does not know what
is meant by "offside", may have fun "playing football" with
friends, but certainly is not "proficient" at the game.

Of course, there are levels of performance in football, each
with its corresponding levels of proficiency. In the United States,
young players participate in the Pop Warner League. Then they
may play junior high varsity and senior high varsity, before moving to university varsity, and perhaps even professional football.
Each level becomes more complex and more challenging.

Common to all levels of football, however, is the emphasis
on performance. The focus is on playing the game well, that is,
responding creatively and effectively to situations as they develop
on the field and initiating new moves and strategies as needed.
Then, during the following week, the performance in the previous game is closely studied and criticized. There is training and
practice, with much of the practice time spent on drills, building
strength, and developing accuracy of execution of plays and routines. Daily workouts are not simply scrimmages followed by
congratulations. Even the scrimmage sessions are followed by
close critiques, in an effort to improve performance the next time.

Building oral proficiency in a foreign language is very similar to building proficiency in football. In the Five-Step Performance-Based Model outlined on the next page, the first four steps
each contribute to preparing students for the last step which is
using the language for actual communication with native speakers.

Step 1. Guided Observation:

Listening to the Spoken Language

In Step 1, the students come into contact with the second language
as it is spoken in authentic situations. At its most difficult, this

Steps	Oral proficiency	Football
1. Guided Observation	Listening to the spoken language	Watching actual football games
2. Guided Analysis	Learning how the language works	Learning the rules of the game
3. Guided Practice	Building the skills	Training: drill and practice
4. Simulated Performance	Participating in guided conversations and role play	Scrimmage practice
5. Performance	Speaking in real-life situations	Participating in actual games

means listening to conversations between native speakers, watching television, listening to the radio, etc. Listening to thesecond language in its most authentic manifestation is like going to a professional football game: people unfamiliar with the game have no idea what is going on, people with some notions of football follow the main movements of the game, avid fans know the players, the plays, the signals, and can analyze not only what did happen but what might have happened. At the highest level of comprehension, listening to authentic speech, like attending professional football games, requires an awareness and a sensitivity to cultural connotations and allusions.

The learner needs guidance in developing this initial skill of comprehension.

- At a beginning level, Step 1 consists of listening to the ssecond second language in its most authentic manifestation is like going to a professional football game: people unfamiliar with the game have no idea what is going on, people with some notions of football follow the main movements of the game, avid fans know the players, the plays, the signals, and can analyze not only what did happen but what might have happened. At the highest level of comprehension, listening to authentic speech, like attending professional football games, requires an awareness and a sensitivity to cultural connotations and allusions.

- At a beginning level, Step 1 consists of listening to the simplified but none the less real language of contrived and/or scripted spoken materials. This type of activity might include TPR (Total Physical Response) activities, listening to simplified narrations, watching videos scripted for language learners but filmed on location by native speakers. This activity is like attending a Pop Warner league game, where one can observe the main features of football in a less complex environment.

- At a more advanced level, this step will include listening to authentic material that has been specifically selected or edited so as to be more comprehensible. Usually this means listening to authentic material with the opportunity of stopping and replaying parts of a recording, perhaps even using captioned versions of a video to enhance comprehension. This is like watching a football game on television where instant replays and charts help clarify the action.

What the students understand from the material they are watching and/or listening to is often termed *comprehensible input*. With language learning as with football, the focus must be on moving from a general notion of what is going on to increasingly more accurate levels of comprehension and more precise appreciation of the complexities of the language.

The better a student understands a second language, the more effectively that student will eventually be able to participate in a conversation, just as the more a young player understands the game of football, the better that player will eventually be able to perform on the field.

Step 2. Guided Analysis:

Learning How the Language Works

In Step 2, students learn how the second language is put together, how it works.

- At first, attention is focused on isolated, individual elements, such as the sound system, syntax patterns, grammatical structures, and vocabulary. This is like learning the rules of football, such as what type of movements are considered "clipping" or "holding" and what penalty such calls carry.
- Then students are expected to recognize and understand the elements in the context of a spoken message: can they make phonemic distinctions, can they hear a gender marker and tell whether a noun is feminine or masculine, can they notice whether a verb is in the preterite or the imperfect, are they aware of the use of a subjunctive or the choice of a particular

adjective and do they know how this affects the meaning of what is said. This linguistic analysis is similar to the football player or spectator recognizing an offside movement when it occurs during a game without waiting for the referee to make the call.

Study of the language itself has traditionally been the focal point for second language instruction. Many types of techniques have been developed: inductive and deductive presentations, charts and paradigms, grammars of various sorts (e.g., classical, structural, transformational), mnemonic devices, illustrated vocabularies, flash cards, etc. In the context of the Five-Step Performance-Based Model, these activities constitute one of the five essential steps, but they must be viewed in the context reaching Step 5, which is the ability to use the second language in authentic oral communication situations.

Step 3. Guided Practice:

Building the Skills

In Step 3, the students move from understanding and learning to actually manipulating elements of the spoken language.

*   At first, students learn to handle short meaningful phrases, for example, giving their names, exchanging greetings, describing the time and weather. Practising these brief contextualized and meaningful phrases is like tossing the football and encouraging a young player to catch it and run.

*   Then, students begin to drill and practice the second language more intensively, often by concentrating on specific elements in isolation. They may repeat verb forms, or practice difficult sounds like the French /y/, or mimic sentence intonations. They may identify colours, recite numbers, name objects on a transparency. These non-contextualized, word-level activities may be compared to the football team's push-ups, blocking practice, and running drills.

*   Finally there are the meaningful, contextualized activities where students respond to guided questions and various oral and printed cues to produce correct sentences. This is similar to drills where the football team runs through plays, with a focus on careful, accurate performance.

The above types of guided language-learning activities are not goals in themselves, but enabling outcomes. Their mastery enables learners to speak the language more effectively, just as precise drill and practice helps football players to perform more effectively during the game.

Step 4. Simulated Performance:

Participating in Guided Conversations and Role Play

In Step 4, students have the opportunity to use, in simulated conversational exchanges and role play situations, the new words, phrases and patterns they have learned. The emphasis is on self-expression and conveying information fluently in a meaningful context. Much as one might try to have these exchanges resemble real-life conversations, for example by using props to establish a café scene or a TV game show, teachers and students both recognize that the context is artificial. This type of language practice is similar to football scrimmage practice. In scrimmage, the players divide into two teams and play against one another: it may look like a real game from a distance, but everyone knows that it is not. Scrimmage gives the players the opportunity of running their plays in a game-like context where the focus is on performing effectively.

An important aspect of scrimmage practice is that although the coach allows the game to go on uninterrupted, he/she afterwards brings the team together to analyze weaknesses, criticize poor moves, and outline further drill and practice activities. The scrimmage practices may even be videotaped to allow the players themselves the opportunity of seeing how they performed and where they need to improve. Similarly, Step 4 activities in language classes can be rendered much more effective if they are followed up by analysis and individualized suggestions for additional practice.

Step 5. Performance:

Speaking in Real-Life Situations

Step 5, represents the ultimate desired outcome of the Performance-Based Model of Oral Proficiency. This is the point where students have the opportunity to use the second language for real communication in an authentic situation. The type of situation may vary: e.g., the student is abroad or in an area where the language is spoken and uses the language to order food or ask for a service; the student has a casual conversation with an exchange student or with members of a host family abroad; the student makes a telephone call to request information. At this step, as one becomes increasingly proficient, one needs to be aware of the more complex aspects of communication, including cultural values and expectations, linguistic registers, and conversational characteristics such as turn-taking.

In real communication, as in the real football game, the "clock is running." One cannot start over, one must continue playing. The aim is to communicate as effectively as possible within existing constraints.

After the communication event, like after the game, the student can try to recall what went well and what caused comprehension to break down. Often the teacher is not available, and the "performance" was not recorded, unless the communication event was videotaped or recorded. In the latter case, there may be the opportunity for teacher and student to review the performance and use this diagnostic information to plan for other learning activities.

Conclusion

The five steps described above are not simply moved through once in sequential order. In second-language acquisition as in learning to play football, there is a continuous upward spiralling as students improve their skills. As students move from elementary to more advanced levels, they grow to understand more complex speech, to learn about more difficult structures, to acquire a more extensive vocabulary, to practice these new linguistic aspects in more challenging activities and more complex simulated conversational exchanges. Each of the steps, however, continues to play an important role and none should be omitted.

It is particularly important to recognize that scrimmage practice is meaningless unless the players demonstrate during practice that the running backs know how to hold the ball, that the quarterback can pass the ball with some degree of accuracy, and that the pass receivers know how to catch it. Similarly, it is the role of the language teacher not to engage students in Step 4 (Simulated Performance) activities until they demonstrate at Step 3 (Guided Practice) that they can pronounce the language so as to be understood by native speakers, and that they have a reasonable control of the vocabulary and structures with the role-play activity will require.

In conclusion, one might reflect on the respective roles of the teacher and the coach. The good coach is constantly asking for more demanding and more precise effort from the players, but both coach and players know that they are working together to perform well in the next game. The coach is task-master, judge and trainer, as well as facilitator and provider of encouragement and praise. The coach knows that player self-esteem is linked to a job well done, a game well played. Similarly, the effective teacher in a performance-based language program must maintain high expectations, provide appropriate practice activities, and also motivate students to want to express themselves well so that they, too, begin to view themselves as effective second-language speakers.

Editor's Note: This text has been abridged and adapted from the opening chapter of the 1994 Northeast Conference Reports. Cf. Rebecca M. Valette, "Teaching, Testing, and Assessment: Conceptualizing the Relationship," in Charles Hancock, ed., *Teaching, Testing, and Assessment: Making the Connection* (Lincolnwood Illinois: National Textbook Co., 1994), pp. 1-42.

Reprinted from: Rebecca M. Valette, "The Five-Step Performance-Based Model of Oral Proficiency." *Mosaic*, 2, 2 (Winter 1995): 1-5.

35 Immersion: Why Not Try Free Voluntary Reading?

Stephen Krashen

Immersion programs have not given comprehensible input a real chance. The author suggests reading as one of the solutions.

In recent years, observers of immersion programs have been very concerned about the finding that immersion students do not speak the second language perfectly, even after years of participation.[1] There is the widespread conviction that the solution lies in focusing more on form and using more direct teaching of grammar. I maintain that this conclusion is premature and that immersion programs have not yet given comprehensible input a real chance.

We can explain the "imperfection" of immersion easily without abandoning the Input Hypothesis. As others have pointed out, immersion students are exposed to a limited range of input and have no peer interaction. In addition, immersion has never attempted to exploit one of the best sources of comprehensible input: free voluntary reading. There is an enormous amount of research that confirms that free voluntary reading is the source of a great deal of our reading ability, our writing style, our ability to use complex grammatical constructions, our vocabulary, and much of our spelling ability (Krashen, 1993). Students who participate in free voluntary reading programs in school, such as sustained silent reading, typically outperform traditionally taught comparison students on a variety of measures of literacy competence (second language studies of in-school free reading include Elley and Mangubhai, 1983; Elley, 1991; Pilgreen and Krashen, 1993), and that more reading outside of school is associated with more literacy development (second language studies include Tudor and Hafiz, 1989; Cho and Krashen, 1994; Constantino, 1994).

Immersion children do not read for pleasure in their second language. Romney, Romney and Menzies (1995) reported no relationship between the amount grade 6 immersion students said they spent reading in French, and their scores on a test of reading comprehension. The reason for this result is that the children hardly read at all in French: "They spent an average of 3 1/2 minutes a day reading French books and one minute reading French comics, magazines, and newspapers..." (p. 485). In comparison, they averaged 26 minutes per day reading English books and seven minutes reading English language comics, magazines and newspapers. When asked to name their favourite French authors, only 3% of the students could name an author; in contrast, 81% were able to name their favourite English author.

There is, in addition, no clear evidence that focusing on form is effective. I have argued that focusing on form leads typically to short-term gains for limited aspects of language, and these gains are apparent only on   form-based measures; the knowledge gained in this way does not become part of true linguistic competence (Krashen, 1992, 1994a, 1994b).[2]

In light of the overwhelming evidence that free reading is a powerful source of language competence, the finding that immersion children do not do free reading, and the lack of clear evidence for focusing on form, one is led to the conclusion that free reading should at least be considered as an option. Students interviewed by Romney et al. explained why they didn't do much reading in French: there was little for them to read in French that was both interesting and comprehensible. The solution to this problem means assembling collections of interesting (and comprehensible) books in the second language, providing some sustained silent reading time, reading good stories to students in class, and discussing good books in class. This is certainly an easier, more pleasant, and more promising route than doing more activities that focus on the conditional and Imperfect.[3]

Notes

I should like to thank Jeff McQuillan for helpful comments on an earlier draft of this paper.

1. One often reads that immersion students have "fossilized." Harley and Swain (1984), however, conclude that for the early French total immersion students they studied, "there is currently no evidence that immersion students' interlanguage stops developing... while growth towards target language norms in productive language may seem remarkably gradual, we find at any grade level...that there is new development relative to earlier grades" (p. 300). Duchesne (1995) arrives at a similar conclusion. In a study of errors of French immersion students from grades 1 to 6, he found that while some errors did remain, "les erreurs, en général, diminuent en fréquence d'année en année... on obtient une image beaucoup plus dynamique et optimiste de la situation que celle que dessine la fossilisation." (p. 527). Improvement slows down after grade three, but continues to take place.

2. Studies specifically done with immersion students have not made the case for focusing on form: Harley (1989) provided grade six French immersion students with

eight weeks of special instruction on the *imparfait/passé composé* distinction. Her experimental groups averaged 11.9 hours of work on this comparison, while control groups did less than half that amount. Experimental students scored significantly better on two out of three (form-based) measures, but differences on one measure (the cloze test), while significant, were small (less than 3%), and delayed post-testing done three months later revealed no significant differences among the groups.

In Day and Shapson (1991), seventh graders focused on the conditional for six weeks and showed better gains than a comparison group on two out of three measures, but tests were form-based, and delayed post-testing was done 11 weeks after the treatment ended. This interval may have been too short: As noted above, Harley's subjects' gains disappeared after three months. Using adult subjects, White (1991) reported that gains from conscious learning were lost when subjects were tested one year later. Scott and Randell (1992)'s adult subjects showed clear declines in performance on consciously learned aspects of French grammar four weeks after post-testing. Their subjects studied each grammar rule for only four minutes while Day and Shapson's subjects had three periods per week of instruction for six weeks. Working much harder, however, may only delay the inevitable).

In Lyster (1994), grade 8 French immersion students showed some gains in the use of *tu/vous* after 12 hours of instruction over five weeks, and held these gains at delayed post-testing one month later; as in Day and Shapson, this interval may have been too short. Improvement in another feature of politeness and polite closings in letters did not endure to the post-testing. One post-test, a multiple-choice test, clearly focused students on form, and the others, involving written and oral production, had elements of form-focus as well, as students taking these tests had just experienced a great deal of instruction on just those forms required on the tests (e.g. the written task required students to write an informal letter and a formal letter).

Salomone and Palma (1995), in a study of French immersion in the United States, assert that "increased attention to students' grammatical competence...has made this particular immersion school even more successful" (p. 232), but provide no data. In their thorough analysis of six teachers' implicit theories and classroom behaviour, there is no mention of free voluntary reading in French. Duchesne (1995) suggests that immersion students' improvement in certain structures (e.g. agreement of possessive adjectives) was due to an increased emphasis by teachers on these structures, but without a comparison group that did not receive instruction, there is no evidence this is so.

In at least one instance in Salomone and Palma's report, "grammar instruction" was really "language appreciation." Mr. Loffland, the principal, explained: "We're teaching a lot more grammar now. I was observing in an upper-grade classroom, and the children were conjugating 12 verbs. They loved it. One boy couldn't do the *passé composé* of *lire* so I said: 'Jason, j'ai...' and he said, 'lu.' They know it intuitively." (Salomone and Palma, p. 230). What Mr. Loffland observed was language performance, not language acquisition or language learning: Jason had already acquired the correct form, and Mr. Loffland elicited it.

I find it very hard to believe that the children love grammar instruction. McQuillan (1994) asked 49 adult second language students who had participated in extensive reading about their preferences: 84% said that reading was more pleasurable than grammar, and 78% felt reading was more beneficial than grammar, suggesting that once students do it, they like it and understand its benefits. In addition, there is a great deal of evidence that children enjoy hearing stories and reading books that they select on their own (Krashen, 1994b).

3.   It has been pointed out, most recently by Tarone and Swain (1995), that immersion children lack competence in the nonacademic, conversational style of the second language. Light reading might be of help, because it contains a great deal of everyday language. For some evidence, see Cho and Krashen (1994).

References

Cho, K.S. and Krashen, S. 1994. "Acquisition of vocabulary from the Sweet Valley Kids series: Adult ESL acquisition." *The Journal of Reading*, 37: 662-7.

Constantino, R. 1994. "Pleasure reading helps, even if students don't believe it." *The Journal of Reading*, 37: 504-5.

Day, E. and Shapson, S. 1991. "Integrating formal and functional approaches to language teaching in French immersion: An experimental study." *Language Learning* , 41: 25-58.

Duchesne, H. 1995. "Évolution de d'interlangage chez les élèves de la 1re à la 6e année en immersion française." *The Canadian Modern Language Review/ La Revue canadienne des langues vivantes*, 51: 512-536.

Elley, W. and Mangubhal, F. 1983. "The impact of reading on second language learning." *Reading Research Quarterly*, 19: 53-67.

Elley, W. 1991. "Acquiring literacy in a second language: The effect of book-based programs." *Language Learning*, 41: 375-411.

Harley, B. 1989. "Functional grammar in French immersion: A classroom experiment." *Applied linguistics* 10: 331-359.

Harley B. and M. Swain. 1984. "The interlanguage of immersion students and its implications for second language teaching." In A. Davies, ed., *Interlanguage. Edinburgh*: Edinburgh University Press. pp. 291-311.

Krashen, S. 1992. "Under what circumstances, if any, should formal grammar instruction take place?" *TESOL Quarterly*, 26: 409-411.

Krashen, S. 1993. *The Power of Reading*. Englewood, Colorado: Libraries Unlimited.

Krashen, S. 1994a. "The input hypothesis and its rivals." In N. Ellis, ed., *Implicit and Explicit Learning of Languages*. London: Academic Press. pp. 45-77.

Krashen, S. 1994b. "The pleasure hypothesis." In J. Alatis, ed., *Georgetown Round Table on Languages and Linguistics*. Washington, DC: Georgetown University Press. pp. 299-322.

Lyster, R. 1994. "The effect of functional-analytic teaching on aspects of French immersion students' sociolinguistic competence." *Applied Linguistics*, 15: 263-287.

McQuillan, J. 1994. "Reading versus grammar: What students think is pleasurable and beneficial for language acquisition." *Applied Language Learning*, 5: 95-100.

Pilgreen, J. and Krashen, S. 1993. "Sustained silent reading with English as a second language high school students: Impact on reading comprehension, reading frequency, and reading enjoyment." *School Library Media Quarterly*, 22: 21-23.

Romney, J.C., D. Romney, and H. Menzies. 1995. "Reading for pleasure in French: A study of the reading habits and interests of French immersion children." *The Canadian Modern Language Review/La Revue canadienne des langues vivantes*, 51: 474-511.

Salomone, A. and E. Palma 1995. "Immersion grammar: A changing portrait of Glenwood School." *Foreign Language Annals*, 28: 223-234.

Scott V. and S. Randell. 1992. "Can students apply grammar rules for reading textbook explanations?" *Foreign Language Annals*, 25: 357-367.

Tarone, E. and M. Swain. 1995. "A sociolinguistic perspective on second language use in immersion classrooms." *The Modern Language Journal*, 79: 166-178.

Tudor, I. and Hafiz, F. 1989. "Extensive reading as a means of input to L2 learning." *Journal of Research in Reading*, 12: 164-178.

White, L. 1991. "Adverb placement in second language acquisition: Some effects of positive and negative evidence in the classroom." *Second Language Research*, 7: 133-161.

Reprinted from: Stephen Krashen, "Immersion: Why Not Try Free Voluntary Reading?" *Mosaic*, 3, 1 (Fall 1995): 1, 3-4.

36 Four Approaches to "Authentic" Reading

Rebecca M. Valette

Currently, schools and colleges are witnessing a renewed interest in the teaching of reading within the foreign language curriculum. However, there is a lack of consensus as to what reading is and how reading comprehension skills are best taught (by the teacher) and acquired (by the student). Given the present increasing concern for "authentic assessment", it is incumbent upon us to look at the types of readings our students are likely to encounter in the "real" world and how they will interact with them.

In their daily life, people encounter wide varieties of reading texts which vary from one-word signs and short ads to lengthy informational articles, from the entertaining features found in illustrated magazines to several hundred pages of straight text in a novel or biography. Not only do these texts look different from each other, but, as people read them, they do so for different purposes and use different reading strategies.

In order to prepare students for reading second language materials once they leave our classrooms, we not only need to select "authentic materials", we need also to try to replicate "authentic conditions". We should ask ourselves:

- When would people normally read this type of text?
- Why would they normally read it?
- What reading techniques would they probably use as they read it?
- What would they do after they have read it?

An analysis of common reading texts in the light of the above considerations would indicate that there are four main approaches to real-life reading comprehension, each of which activates different pre-reading, while-reading and post-reading activities:

Four Approaches to "Authentic" Reading
Approach 1: Reading in a Daily-Life Context

- realia

- advertisements
- instructions
- notes
- forms
- e-mail, etc.

Approach 2: Reading for Information
- newspaper articles
- reference works
- internet, etc.

Approach 3: Reading for Pleasure
- "light" reading:
- magazine features and articles.

Approach 4: Participatory Reading
- "serious" reading:
- short stories
- novels
- plays
- poetry.

Note that not all four approaches must be taught in a given course, nor are all students interested in all approaches. (For example, a person who is not planning to go abroad may be less interested in Approach 1. A student of international law would be more interested in Approach 2).

Approach 1: Reading in a Daily-Life Context

In our modern world, people use their reading skills constantly as they go about their daily activities. Our contemporary civilization requires that people be "functionally literate", that is, that they be able to read and interpret a wide variety of printed messages, ranging from signs and product names to menus, from bus schedules to movie announcements, from help-wanted ads to headlines, from printed instructions to notes or e-mail from colleagues or friends.

Foreign language learners who intend to visit or reside in a community where that second language is spoken need to acquire similar functional reading skills. In addition to being able to read the texts aloud (a necessary factor, for example, in ordering food from a printed menu), and to understand the relevant vocabulary, students need to know how the culture works so that they interpret the texts correctly. For example, in consulting a railroad schedule, readers must understand how times are expressed, what different types of trains appear on the listing, which days each train runs, which services are offered, etc. In addition, many types of print materials, such as classified ads and movie schedules, also require that the reader be familiar with frequently used abbreviations.

In a daily-life context, reading is done for a purpose: one is making one's way around a city, one is looking for a specific type of restaurant, one is trying to decide which movie to see. The aim is to find and focus on the relevant information, and to interpret it accurately. (It is not common practice to waste one's time reading the irrelevant sections).

Pre-Reading Activities

Within the classroom, activities based on realia and similar documents should duplicate authentic reading tasks. Functional reading is almost always purposeful, rather than random. This focus should be reflected in the pre-reading activities. (Teachers will want to avoid artificial questions, such as "What information do these realia contain?")

Prompt students by setting the scene. For example: "Here is a movie listing from a French newspaper. You and your friends want to see *Cyrano255* tonight. Find out where the movie is playing and when the last show starts."

Encourage students to create their own scenarios. For instance, have pairs of students decide what type of food they would like to eat for supper, and then distribute a listing of restaurants so that they can decide where to go.

While-Reading Activities

In functional daily-life reading, students need to skim and scan in order to find the information they need. It is just as important that they know which things to skip, so that they economize their efforts.

- As students read a listing with several options, have them check off those which they want to consider and cross out those which are inappropriate. For example, have them look for vegetarian dishes on a menu, trains that run on Sundays, hotels that accept pets.
- Have students write down the information they are looking for. For instance, if they are planning to see *Jean de Florette*, they can list the movie theatres where the film is playing and note the times of the showings.
- Prepare and distribute a chart or grid on which students will note specific information. For example, they could take a page

of rental ads from a newspaper and classify each of the listings by number of rooms, size, availability of an elevator, etc.

Post-Reading Activities

In a daily-life context, reading activities are typically followed by
some sort of action: one reserves a hotel room, one buys a train
ticket, one decides which movie to see or which apartment to visit.
In the classroom, post-reading activities most frequently take the
form of a conversation or a rôle-play, although in some situations
written responses are also appropriate.

- Have students discuss with one another which apartment they
  would like to rent and why, basing their conversation on the
  real estate listings they have been consulting.
- Have students prepare an appropriate rôle-play, based on the
  documents they have read. For instance, after reading a newspaper schedule of concerts, students can phone the hall to
  reserve seats for the performance they have selected.
- Have students fill in a visa form or a job application form
  that they have been studying.

Approach 2: Reading for Information

The purpose of this type of reading is to expand one's knowledge. The reader is motivated to get more information on a certain topic and thus searches out appropriate sources. In the area
of current events, people reading for information usually turn to
newspapers. For example, they may have heard about a robbery
and want more details, or they would like to get the full report on
a sports event or an international confrontation. For less current
topics, people in need of information turn to reference works
(almanacs, encyclopedias, now often via internet), professional
journals, and non-fiction books of all sorts.

Whereas functional literacy is activated only within the setting of the culture of the second language, the students' ability to
read for information can also be put into practice in an Anglo
context. Students in immersion courses and in programs fostering "languages across the curriculum" are often asked to refer to
second-language materials. At the university level, students may
consult texts in a second language as part of their coursework in a
variety of fields such as business, international law, history or
journalism (cf. Lange 1994).

In reading for information, the readers select what they are
going to read on the basis of the specific questions they would
like to have answered. Their purpose is to expand their knowledge. If one text does not contain all the information they are look-

ing for, they search out and read additional sources. Sometimes their reading opens up new areas of exploration or new fields of investigation.

Pre-Reading Activities

Clearly the preparatory step in reading for information is to formulate the appropriate questions. What information do the students expect to find in the text?

- Show the reading to the class (for example, a newspaper article about a plane accident), and have the students work together in small groups to draw up a list of related questions, such as: When did the accident occur? How many casualties? How many people were saved? Why did the accident happen?
- Present the class with the topic of the reading (for example, bull-fighting), and have the students first generate a list of related questions, and then rank these questions in order of importance.
- Prepare a list of statements, some accurate and some not, concerning the topic of the reading (for example, French Impressionism, or the voyages of Jacques Cartier). As a pre-reading activity, have students indicate which of the statements they think are true and which are false.

While-Reading Activities

As the students read for information, they are actively looking for answers to previously established questions. Because the focus is on content, and not skill-building, it is important that the reading material be accessible to the students. Depending on the level of the class and the difficulty of the text, it may be necessary to provide reading helps: glosses, a bilingual dictionary, etc. If reading is done in class, the teacher can move around the room acting as a resource person, explaining what certain words and phrases mean.

- If students have prepared a list of questions, have them fill in the answers that they find while reading the text. Then have them place a large question mark next to those questions which the text did not address.
- Have the students refer to a list of true/false statements as they read the text. For each true statement, they are instructed to underline the corroborating sentences in the selection. For each false statement, they are to underline the contradictory information.
- Have students surf the internet to find answers to a series of

questions. For each site where they find an appropriate answer, they write down the internet address and (if possible) print out the information they have found.

Post-Reading Activities

Since the goal of reading for information is to expand one's knowledge, one generally learns new things. In addition, it is not unusual to find that the reading has inspired some additional questions.

- Have students each list the most interesting fact that they learned from the reading, together with one follow-up question they would like to explore.
- If the text did not answer all the pre-reading questions the students had prepared, encourage them (if appropriate) to do further research on the topic.
- Have students list other things they would like to find out about as a result of having read the text. These may turn out to be somewhat tangential topics. (For example, an article on Lafayette's rôle in the American Revolution might spark an interest in locating on a map all the cities in the United States named in Lafayette's honour).

Approach 3: Reading for Pleasure

Reading for pleasure, or "light" reading, is what people do while waiting at the doctor's office or before falling asleep at night or at other leisure moments. They flip through a magazine, and look at the various articles and features: some are informative, some give advice, some take the form of self-tests or letters to a confidential advisor who offers professional help, some treat more serious topics such as environmental concerns or archaeological findings, others reveal incidents in the lives of celebrities or offer uplifting tales of heroism. An average reader often has many magazines to choose from: news magazines, detective magazines, sports magazines, fashion magazines, science magazines, etc.

The style in these articles and features is typically straightforward and does not require reader interpretation. Any background information the reader might need is made explicit within the article itself.

When flipping through a magazine, second-language readers, like first-language readers, read those articles and features that have attracted their attention. If a person is struck by some interesting points, he or she might decide to discuss these with a friend, either by describing the content of the article or by reading salient passages aloud.

Pre-Reading Activities

In the "real" world, it is the reader who decides what magazine to look at and which articles to choose. Illustrations and typography play an important role in the selection process. In order to make pre-reading activities as "authentic" as possible, it is important that readings be presented with their original art and layout.

- Typically readers select an article because they have some notion as to its content. Similarly, students who are "reading for pleasure" should be encouraged to try to discover the content of an article before they read it.
- Have students look at title and illustrations and try to guess or brainstorm what the article is about.
- Have students look at the format of a magazine selection and try to guess what type of article or feature it most likely is (story? biography? self-test? advice column?).

While-Reading Activities

Very quickly students will discover whether their guesses about the theme and the format of the article are correct. Magazine pieces are meant to be transparent. More importantly, the actual reading of the article is meant to be relaxing, and so it is essential that students understand what the text is saying. (Students do not need to understand every word, but they should have a fairly accurate notion of the basic content.) In the "real" world, people do not usually have a dictionary available while reading a magazine: if a text is too hard, they simply stop reading it. In "light" readings prepared for classroom use, unfamiliar terms and expressions should be glossed or footnoted so that students find the reading experience to be a pleasurable one.

- As students read, encourage them to find and note down one or two interesting things they would like to discuss or share with others.
- If the reading is a self-test, have students actually take the test and then analyze their scores.
- Since articles are often written in a casual or colloquial style, encourage students to note down new words or expressions that they would like to incorporate into their active vocabulary.

Post-Reading Activities

Reading for pleasure is largely a private experience. Sometimes, however, one is eager to share with others the main points of what one has read, or some interesting trivia one has picked up. In this sense, magazine articles often act as a catalyst for conversation.

- Have students in pairs or small groups engage in conversation about an article they have just read.
  ("Did you see that article on...?
  It says that...
  What do you think?")
- Have students select a sentence or short passage they find interesting and read it aloud to their partner.
- If the magazine article consists of a set of interviews, the students can compare the various views presented and indicate which of the interviewees they tend to agree with, or which of the people they would like to spend an evening with, etc.

Approach 4. Participatory Reading

Participatory reading, or "serious" reading, goes beyond the acquisition of information or new knowledge. The texts, whether fiction (such as short stories, plays, novels, poetry), or non-fiction (such as essays and critical pieces), have been written so as to require the reader's personal involvement. Frequently these readings assume a certain background knowledge on the part of the readers, and then provide a new interpretation or an original view. More often than not, they function as a springboard for deeper reflection about some aspect of the human condition.

Literary texts are meant not only to be read, but also to be re-read. Of course, on the first reading, the readers need to discover WHAT is being narrated or expressed. Then, on a second reading, they may wish to explore HOW the author creates an effect or portrays a character or develops a theme.

Frequently literary readings elicit a personal response on the part of the reader. Some students may even be inspired to create related texts of their own.

Pre-Reading Activities

In the "real" world, one rarely reads a book or a story without some sort of background knowledge about the work; either one has seen the corresponding movie, or one has read a review, or a friend has recommended a book because of its humour or its surprise ending. In addition, when American readers read works by contemporary American writers (especially writers of the same socio-economic milieu), they have a common bond: they share a similar cultural background and are sensitive to the same cultural referents. In order to appreciate a work written at a different historical period or for a different ethnic group, and especially a work written in a second and as yet somewhat unfamiliar language, most readers require additional background information in order to approach the reading task in a natural way.

- Have students look at the illustrations and read a blurb on the author (and the work) to get a general idea of the theme, the locale and the time period. Book jackets are excellent for this activity.
- Use posters, maps, pictures, documentary films, etc., to familiarize the students with the background information that the author expects them to possess. (For example, students would more readily relate to Camara Laye's *L'enfant noir* if they could see pictures of village life in West Africa in the 1930s. Similarly, before presenting Ronsard's *Ode à Cassandre*, the teacher could show a poster of a Renaissance castle like Chenonceau, and have students see how the flower gardens are at a certain distance from the castle itself; this allows them to realize that the poet, by inviting Cassandre to come admire a rosebush, is in reality enticing the young woman to go with him to a fairly secluded area where the two can be together without being disturbed).

If appropriate, help students anticipate what the crux of the reading will be so as to involve them from the outset with the development of the plot. (For example, in introducing Diop's *L'Os*, you could have students imagine a more contemporary scene. "You are living in a remote country and your family in the States has just sent you a package of brownies. You are about to enjoy this unexpected treat when a friend arrives. Since you do not want to share the brownies – after all, they were sent to you!, – you try to get your friend to leave. What approach would you take?")

Together with the students, read the opening paragraphs (or scenes or lines) and help them determine the general tone or mood of the work. If the opening is particularly descriptive (as in Mérimée's *Mateo Falcone*), focus briefly on the essential elements (e.g., the fact that the Corsican *maquis* offers an excellent hiding place for outlaws). Then encourage the students to move on to the actual story.

While-Reading Activities

The most important consideration as students are reading a work of fiction is that they all understand what is happening. Vaguely getting the "gist" is not enough. Nor is it helpful for students to approach such a reading in a dogged linear fashion word by word, for the author's meaning almost always goes far beyond the actual sentences. At the most basic level, students need to know who is where and how the plot is developing. (In the real world of "authentic reading", if one does not understand what is going on in a novel or a play or a story or a poem, one simply puts the book down).

Since the goal of participatory reading activities is to simulate a positive reading experience, we might do well to let students determine what formats make the story the most accessible
for them. A few might be challenged by guessing meanings and
reading an unglossed text. Some might prefer glosses in the second language, while others might opt for glosses in English. Some
might like to have an end vocabulary for quick reference, while
others would be happier consulting their own dictionary. Still
others would be most comfortable reading with a bilingual text.
When using a bilingual text in class, students should be encouraged to discuss the reading in the second language. The presence
of a facing-page English equivalent means that the teacher no
longer needs to check whether certain words and phrases have
been understood, and is free to focus on the story itself, the themes,
the plot development, the author's style. (In the "real world" there
is no such thing as "cheating" while reading – either one is reading or one is not. For many second-language learners, a bilingual
text is an excellent way of approaching a text that would otherwise be above their heads).

- Divide a longer text into scenes or meaningful segments. In
  some anthologies, the editors introduce each scene of a story
  with a brief title which functions as an advance organizer,
  cuing a key element or theme. (Cf. Valette and Renjilian-
  Burgy, 1993.) If you wish, you might give a short title to each
  scene. At the end of each segment, ask a few questions to
  check general comprehension, and then have students in small
  groups try to anticipate what will happen next. This can be
  done as a game, with groups writing out their guesses and
  placing them in an envelope. After the class has read the next
  segment, the guesses are taken from the envelope and read
  aloud. How many groups guessed correctly what would happen?

- For each segment of the reading, prepare a résumé of the action in which you insert four or five errors. As students in
  pairs read the summary, they are instructed to underline and
  correct the errors. (This error-correction technique can also
  be used as an oral activity. One student begins to summarize
  what happened, but inserts an error. The classmate who first
  hears the error interrupts to correct the inaccurate sentence,
  and then continues the summary, eventually inserting a new
  error, which in turn is corrected by another alert classmate,
  and so forth).

- To check whether students understand descriptive passages,
  have them work in small groups to sketch out the scene as if
  they were going to film it. This type of activity leads to lively

discussion and a close reading of the text. When all the groups are finished, have them compare their sketches. (For example, in reading Camus' *L'Hôte*, you might have students draw the floor plan of the school teacher's living quarters).

- For certain types of readings, it is valuable for students to hear the text as they are reading it. By giving a dramatic reading of the selection the teacher can significantly enhance the students' comprehension. Poetry, especially, comes to life when read aloud, as do prose texts written in dialect or with idiosyncratic phonetic spelling (for example, Queneau's *Zazie dans le métro*).

Post-Reading Activities

- Since participatory reading by its very nature requires student involvement, literary texts are an excellent springboard for the development of writing activities. In addition, with certain genres such as plays and song lyrics, it is not only appropriate but almost essential that students hear the texts performed.
- Have students present the story they have read from a different angle. (For example, after reading Maupassant's *En voyage*, students could imagine they were the Countess and write diary entries describing her trip from Russia to Menton, or they could imagine themselves as her admirer and narrate the story of her death from his point of view).
- Have students extend the story, imagining a follow-up scene which they act out as a dialogue. (For example, after reading Michelle Maurois' *Le Bracelet*, students can invent a conversation between the young girl and the shopkeeper's mysterious fiancé).
- If your language laboratory has a collection of literary recordings, make a tape of two or three different actors interpreting the same text (for example, a poem of Prévert). Have students determine which interpretation they prefer and why.
- If a poem that the students have read in class has been put to music, or if the poem consists of the lyrics of a song, play the corresponding piece in class. Ask students how the music influences or changes their interpretation of the text. (For example, after listening to Zachary Richard's stirring rendition of *Réveille*, students become emotionally drawn to the tragic history of the Acadians).
- As a class project, take students to see the actual performance of a play or the movie version of a novel they have read.
- Give students the opportunity to develop their own artistic interpretation of a work they have particularly enjoyed. These

projects may take many forms: for instance, a poster depicting the mood of a play, a series of photos to accompany a poem, an original poem inspired by one read in class, a montage of musical selections to accompany a scene from a play, a video version of a dramatic episode, a dancer's interpretation of the protagonist's emotions, etc.

Readings of the types described in these four approaches have been used by teachers for decades, as have many of the suggested techniques. What characterizes these four approaches, however, is that the emphasis throughout the corresponding activities is not on what Rivers (1975, p.4) calls "skill-getting" (that is, the "learning-to-read" component of the second-language class), but rather on the "skill-using" (the often neglected "real reading" component). Their aim is to simulate the "authentic" reading experiences that second-language learners will engage in when one day they have the opportunity to interact with real texts in the real world. Some of these reading approaches and their corresponding techniques are being tried in current textbooks. See for example Freed and Knutson (1989) for Approach 1; Davies et al. (1990) for Approaches 1 and 3; Valette and Valette (1995a, 1995b) for Approaches 2, 3 and 4.

References

Barnett, Marva A. 1988. *Lire avec plaisir: Stratégies de lecture.* New York, NY: Harper and Row.

Been, Sheila. 1975. *"Reading in a Foreign Language Teaching Program."* TESOL Quarterly 9,3: 233-242.

Bernhardt, Elizabeth B. 1986. *"Reading in the Foreign Language,"* pp. 93-115, in Barbara H. Wing, ed. *Listening, Reading, and Writing: Analysis and Application* [1986 Northeast Conference Reports]. Middlebury, VT: Northeast Conference.

Davies, Evelyn, Norman Whitney, Meredith Pike-Baky, and Laurie Blass. 1990. *Task Reading.* Cambridge, Eng.: Cambridge Univ. Press.

Freed, Barbara and Elizabeth Knutson. 1989. *Contextes: French for Communication.* Cambridge, MA: Newbury House.

Grellet, Françoise. 1981. *Developing Reading Skills: A Practical Guide to Reading Comprehension Exercises.* Cambridge, Eng.: Cambridge Univ. Press.

Lange, Dale L. 1994. *"The Curricular Crisis in Foreign Language Learning."* ADFL Bulletin, 25, 2: 12-16.

Mackay, Ronald, Bruce Barkman and R.R. Jordan, eds. 1979. *Reading in a Second Language: Hypotheses, Organization and Practice.* Rowley, MA: Newbury House.

Nance, Kimberly A. 1994. *"Developing Students' Sense of Literature in the Introductory Foreign Language Literature Course."* ADFL Bulletin, 25, 2: 23-29.

Omaggio Hadley, Alice. 1993. *Teaching Language in Context*. 2nd edition. Boston, MA: Heinle and Heinle.

Papalia, Anthony. 1987. *"Interaction of reader and text"*, pp. 70-82, in Wilga M. Rivers, ed., *Interactive Language Teaching*. Cambridge, Eng.: Cambridge Univ. Press.

Rivers, Wilga M. 1975. *A Practical Guide to the Teaching of French*. New York: Oxford Univ. Press.

Rivers, Wilga M. 1981. *Teaching Foreign-Language Skills*, 2nd ed. Chicago: Univ. of Chicago Press.

Rivers, Wilga M. 1987. *"Interaction as the Key to Teaching for Communication*, pp. 1-16, in Wilga M. Rivers, ed., *Interactive Language Teaching*. Cambridge, Eng.: Cambridge Univ. Press.

Shrum, Judith L. and Eileen W. Glisan. 1994. *Teacher's Handbook: Contextualized Language Instruction*. Boston, MA: Heinle and Heinle.

Swaffar, Janet K., Katherine M. Arens and Heidi Byrnes. 1991. *Reading for Meaning: An Integrated Approach to Language Learning*. Englewood Cliffs, NJ: Prentice Hall.

Valette, Jean-Paul and Rebecca M. Valette. 1995a. *À Votre Tour: Intermediate French*. Lexington, MA: D.C. Heath.

Valette, Jean-Paul and Rebecca M. Valette. 1995b. *Discovering French -Rouge*. Lexington, MA: D.C. Heath.

Valette, Rebecca M. 1994. *"Teaching, Testing, and Assessment: Conceptualizing the Relationship"*, pp. 1-42, in Charles R. Hancock, ed. *Teaching, Testing, and Assessment: Making the Connection* [1994 Northeast Conference Reports]. Lincolnwood, IL: National Textbook.

Valette, Rebecca M. and Joy Renjilian-Burgy. 1993. *Album: Cuentos del mundo hispánico*, 2nd. ed. Lexington, MA: D.C. Heath.

Wiggins, Grant. 1994. *"Toward More Authentic Assessment of Language Performances"*, pp. 69-86, in Charles R. Hancock, ed. *Teaching, Testing, and Assessment: Making the Connection* [1994 Northeast Conference Reports]. Lincolnwood, IL: National Textbook.

Reprinted from: Rebecca M. Valette, "Four Approaches to "Authentic" Reading." *Mosaic*, 4, 2 (Winter 1997): 1, 3-7.

37 Teaching Writing in Elementary and Intermediate Language Classes: Suggestions and Activities

Frank Nuessel and Caterina Cicogna

General recommendations to incorporate writing into the curriculum with four specific examples of particular writing tasks.

Introduction

The traditional concept of the four skills (listening/ understanding, speaking, reading, and writing) and their conventional classification into the receptive (listening/ understanding, reading) and the productive skills (speaking, writing) persists in language teaching today. The prevailing methodological philosophy in vogue has often determined the curricular attention accorded to one or all of these linguistic abilities.

Of the four skills, writing is perhaps the one aptitude that receives the least attention in the elementary and intermediate language class. Magnan (1985:109), for example, observes that "writing has become a neglected skill in language courses." Explanations for the "second-class status" of this skill are varied (see also Dvorak , 1986; Omaggio, 1986; Magnan, 1985, for discussion):

1. a shift in emphasis caused by the advent of audio-lingualism with its stress on oral production;
2. a frequent, albeit erroneous, assumption that this skill will be developed in some other course;
3. the notion that students have already learned how to write in an English composition course, and that they can transfer this knowledge automatically to a language situation (see Dvorak 1986:151-153; Krashen 1984:38 for a discussion that such similarities, in fact, exist);

4. the belief, expressed by some instructors, that they do not know how to develop and enhance their students' writing abilities; and
5. the notion that writing proficiency is not necessary in a language class in the first few years.

Despite a tendency to neglect the skill of writing, this linguistic ability is perhaps more rigorously evaluated than the other three skills because its relative permanency permits the reader to scrutinize every aspect of this form of communication. In this regard, Allen and Valette (1976:285) have observed that:

> Writing may well be considered the most difficult of the language skills. People are flattered when a foreigner tries to speak their language, and they tend to tolerate a light accent and occasional awkward expression with good grace. The speaker's personality makes a greater impression than the accuracy of his or her spoken language. But a letter is judged more severely on its purely linguistic merits. Even errors in spelling and grammar are not easily excused, even if the meaning is clear and the handwriting attractive and legible.

Furthermore, Chastain (1976) captures the fact that writing enhances and reinforces the other linguistic skills when he observed that

> writing […] helps to solidify the student's grasp of vocabulary and structure and complements the other language skills.

In a curriculum guideline, the Ontario Ministry of Education (1980) echoes Chastain's remark and comments further

> Students should write to practice and consolidate their grasp of structures and vocabulary; they should also write to express their own ideas as early as possible.

The Purposes and Process of Writing

Robert M. Terry (1989:43) cites Magnan (1985) who states that writing has two basic purposes, namely,

*   "as a *support skill* (class and homework exercises to practice grammatical forms and structures, vocabulary and spelling) and
*   as a *communicative skill* (to inform, relate, question, persuade, etc.)."

Many language instructors continue to focus on the end product of writing, despite the fact that most experts in rhetoric and composition now advocate writing as a process. Process-orientation in composition places emphasis on this skill as a developmental ability which consists of a progressive series of editorial stages of revision, improvement, and, ultimately, a concluding product.

Tricia Hedge (1988:21) views the act of writing as a series of steps in a chain which can be summarized in the following seven stages:

1. Initial motivation
2. Assembly of ideas
3. Planning and outlining
4. Note-taking
5. Preparation of a first draft
6. Revision and replanning of the initial draft
7. Formal presentation of the final product.

According to Hedge (1988:21), the above linear representation of the act of writing amounts to an oversimplification of the writing process. For this reason, Hedge (1988:21) defers to Smith (1982) who describes this task as an unordered set of deletion, substitution, and movement operations that ultimately lead to a finalized version. Hedge (1988:21-23) further notes that many rhetoricians categorize the writing process into to three separate modules:

1. Pre-writing activities.
   A. Determination of the purpose.
   B. Determination of the audience.
2. Writing and rewriting.
3. Editing.

These general facets of writing need to be kept in mind when dealing with specific writing assignments in the language class room situation. In fact, time dedicated to an "introduction to writing as process" will ultimately be well-spent since such an orientation will familiarize students with writing and help attenuate fears about this type of assignment.

Types of Writing Tasks

Writing, of course, has many different purposes and functions:

- to persuade
- to inform
- to motivate
- to analyze
- to criticize
- to warn
- and so forth.

In addition, written discourse is varied in its manifestations and may include a wide spectrum of formats, styles, and registers (see Grellet 1981:3-4, cited in Omaggio 1986:125 for a comprehensive listing of written communication formats) exemplified in the following partial enumeration:

Literary pieces

(poems, essays, short stories, drama, and so forth).

Personal communication

- letters
- post cards
- telegrams
- notes

Newspaper and magazine formats

- advertisements
- classified section
- weather forecasts
- and so forth.

Instructions

- recipes
- directions
- and the like.

General Recommendations for the Incorporation of Writing into the Language Curriculum

The following is a series of general suggestions to the instructor to facilitate the development of writing skills in the language classroom. These recommendations will surely contribute to making the subsequent writing task more interesting and more rewarding for all concerned.

1. Make available examples of "authentic" writing samples so that students will become familiar with an appropriate format for the specific assignment given by the instructor.
2. Control the length of the assignment. Short, manageable writing assignments provide students with a sense of accomplishment, especially in the initial writing exercises. Moreover, brief writing tasks make students realize that they can be successful in carrying out writing assignments.
3. Provide students with guided composition tasks. Specify a logically ordered set of individual questions to be answered. This building-block approach to writing may seem simplistic. In the initial stages of writing, however, students will be able to produce short, cohesive writing samples. At a later stage, exercises in sentence-combining activities may be imple-

mented (Cooper, Morain, and Kalivoda 1980) to develop more sophisticated writing techniques.

4. Specify the audience for the particular writing task. The intended audience may be known (communication with a friend, assignment for a course), or unknown (an essay for a publication to be read by a large and unknown readership).
5. Include selected vocabulary related to the writing assignment on a separate sheet of paper.
6. Vary the writing formats. Grellet (1981:3-4, cited in Omaggio 1986:125) has noted the wide variety of writing purposes and functions. Such diversification also helps students to be able to read diverse written communication formats.
7. Synchronize the writing assignment with the appropriate lesson in the textbook with respect to vocabulary and grammar.
8. Avoid the use of a red marking instrument. For revision purposes, use any contrasting colour except red in order to avoid its negative connotations (Semke 1984).
9. Include positive commentary about the well written parts of the writing assignment.

Specific Examples of Writing Tasks

The following four suggestions for types of writing activities contain explicit recommendations designed to facilitate the writing objective with a minimum of difficulty. Each item contains a general account of the specific task together with an ordered list of operations necessary to complete the assignment.

Telegrams

The preparation of a telegram requires students to make very succinct statements about important matters. This type of writing assignment means students must communicate a message quite tersely.

1. Provide students with the following situations or scenarios (Di Pietro 1987):
   a. You are in Rome. You have lost your wallet and you need to have money wired to you immediately.
   b. You send a congratulations notice to your parents for their twenty-fifth wedding anniversary.
   c. You congratulate your sister on the birth of a child.
2. Provide students with a "telegram form" for writing the appropriate message.
3. Provide spaces (underlines) for a message of ten, fifteen, twenty, or thirty words to ensure that students comply with the requirement for conciseness.

Recipes

Food preferences and preparation are important elements of any culture. This assignment is best synchronized with grammar on commands, and food vocabulary, and the basic format is applicable to any culture. This type of assignment also provides students with an opportunity to learn about the culinary habits and preferences of another culture (time of meal, place of meal, types of food, and so forth).

1. Ask students to write a recipe for a specific dish.
2. Review commands.
3. Include a selected sheet of vocabulary for food and the specific verbal activities related to recipes (stir, beat, cut, and so forth)
4. Use the names of specific recipes to provide a sense of the types of dishes possible with attention to the order of presentation in a multi-course meal.

Post Cards

The task of writing a post card to friends or family members can be an interesting activity for students because it involves imagination, fantasy, as well as some research to gather factual information about a particular locale. Moreover, this form of directed writing activity is relatively short, hence students do not perceive it to be an impossible writing exercise.

We advocate the introduction of post cards from various locales to add a realistic dimension to this task. The post cards may be reused by making a photocopy. Assign students as many different post cards as is feasible. The format of this written exercise follows:

Directions to students:

1. Provide exemplary post cards (originals or photocopies).
2. Address the card.
3. Write the date.
4. Write a post card to a friend, family member, parents, boyfriend, girlfriend. Include the appropriate salutation.
5. Indicate where you are.
6. Note the significance of the photograph or other graphic element on the reverse of the card (panorama of city, place of local, national, or international, historical interest).
7. Tell what you are doing (visiting relatives, sightseeing, studying, conducting business, and so forth).
8. State your overall reaction to the trip (exciting trip, fast-paced, fun, demanding, and so forth).

9. Mention how the weather is (rain, snow, cold, hot, mild).
10. Indicate when you are returning home (month, date, time).
11. Provide an appropriate closing.
12. Select from items 3-8 above. Be brief since the amount of writing space on a post card is limited.

Directions and map-making

The preparation of a map is a task that everyone does on occasion. One map-making activity that is quite common is the preparation of a map for someone who does not know how to go to your home.

1. Advise students to tell a classmate how to get to their home from the school/university.
2. Prepare an explicit map.
3. Write out clear and comprehensive instructions on how to drive from the school/university to the house/apartment in question.
4. Provide an appropriate vocabulary sheet (cardinal directions, words for street, highway, and so forth.)
5. Advise students to use personal commands, or the second person singular verbal forms.

Conclusion

The suggestions provided in this short article are by no means exhaustive. They do provide, however, a good start for a language skill which is often neglected.

References

Allen, Edward David and Rebecca M. Valette. 1976. *Classroom Techniques: Foreign Language and English as a Second Language.* New York: Harcourt Brace Jovanovich.

Chastain, Kenneth. 1976. *Developing Second-Language Skills: Theory to Practice.* Chicago: Rand McNally.

Cooper, Thomas, G. Morain, and T. Kalivoda. 1980. *Sentence combining in second language instruction.* Language in Education: Theory and Practice Series, Volume 31. Washington, DC: Center for Applied Linguistics.

Di Pietro, Robert J. 1987. *Strategic interaction: learning language through scenarios.* Cambridge: Cambridge University Press.

Dvorak, Trisha. 1986. "Writing in the foreign language." In *Listening. reading and writing analysis and application*, ed. by Barbara Wing, 145-167. Middlebury, VT: Northeast Conference.

Grellet, Françoise. 1981. *Developing reading skills.* Cambridge: Cambridge University Press.

Hedge, Tricia. 1988. *Writing.* Oxford: Oxford University Press.

Krashen, Stephen D. 1984. *Writing research. theory. and applications*. Oxford: Oxford University Press.

Magnan, Sally Sieloff. 1985. "Teaching and testing proficiency in writing: skills to transcend the second-language classroom." In *Proficiency, curriculum, articulation: the ties that bind*, ed. by Alice C. Omaggio, 109-136. Middlebury, VT: Northeast Conference.

Ministry of Education, Ontario. 1980. *French Core Programs 1980*. Toronto: Ministry of Education, Ontario.

Omaggio, Alice C. 1986. *Teaching language in context: proficiency-oriented instruction*. Boston: Heinle and Heinle.

Semke, Harriet D. 1984. "Effects of the red pen." *Foreign Language Annals*, 17:195-202.

Smith, Frank. 1982. *Writing and the writer*. London: Heinemann.

Terry, Robert M. 1989. "Teaching and evaluating writing as a communicative skill." *Foreign Language Annals*, 22:43-54.

Reprinted from: Frank Nuessel and Caterina Cicogna, "Teaching Writing in Elementary and Intermediate Language Classes: Suggestions and Activities." *Mosaic,* 1, 2 (Winter 1993): 9-11.

38 Students' Empowerment: E-mail Exchange and the Development of Writing Skills

Christine Besnard, Charles Elkabas and Sylvie Rosienski-Pellerin

The teaching approach described in this paper tries to make second-language learning more attractive to students by placing them at the centre of their own learning experience.

"I was given the possibility of expressing myself in French without being told exactly what to write. Indirectly, I learned a great deal of vocabulary and expressions."

"I had the chance to practise my skills on an informal yet academic basis."

"I wanted to do my best because somebody else rather than my prof would be reading my work."

(Students' comments)

Can we make second-language (henceforth L2) learning more authentically communicative, more interactive and more socially based? As experienced educators, we know for a fact that in spite of the communicative "revolution", the development of writing skills in the foreign language classroom remains artificial, hence the lack of motivation of many students. While teaching a second-year French writing course at the university, we looked into new technologies in order to make language learning socially grounded, experiential, and therefore more meaningful to the students. In 1992-93, we decided to develop a computer-assisted language learning (CALL) writing course in which corresponding via e-mail (i.e., electronic mail) with peers from another institution could turn writing practice and the study of grammar, vocabulary and style into an enriching experience.

Theoretical Background

Research in cognitive psychology, pedagogy and language teach-

ing and learning has placed considerable emphasis on real communication (written and oral) in second language learning. Canale
and Swain (1980), Ellis (1990), Guntermann and Phillips (1981),
Rivers (1972), Savignon (1983) and Terrell (1984), among others,
have all stressed the importance of engaging students in true and
meaningful interactions. Indeed, for communication to be authentic, the student needs to communicate with a "real" person (a peer,
a friend, the registrar, a journal editor…) and not with the teacher,
as it is usually done in language courses. As stressed by Meirieu
(1987:57), written practice should not be studied as such, but be a
means to an end, and should not have as its sole purpose
evaluation and grading by the professor. Littlewood (1984:97)
insists that as language teachers,

> we should try to insure that learners are always aware of the com-
> municative value of what they are learning. For example […] we
> should create communicative contexts in the classroom; learners
> should be helped to use the language   for expressing their own
> personal needs and their own personality…

It has also been reported that most language students at the
university level wish to be engaged in a more "experiential approach" to the language that allows them to share their personal
experiences and discuss their projects, likes and dislikes (Corbeil,
1992:497). Indeed, the importance of the social aspect of language
learning has never been as highly stressed as it has been over the
last two decades: researchers agree that social interaction is a key
component to language acquisition.

Though computers can jeopardize the establishment of interaction in the classroom (students are hypnotized by the screen,
and the computer becomes a physical barrier between students),
we believe that computers can still be used as powerful social
tools. Even if word-processing and most language softwares do
not, as such, lead to interaction in the classroom, when they are
integrated in activities that promote interaction, they become most
socially effective. As Johnson (1991:62) argues: "it is not computer
use that creates social effects, but the way teachers structure classroom interaction involving computer use."

Project Description
When it started in 1992-93, our experimental project involved 8
participants on a voluntary basis. These students (four from the
University of Toronto matched with four from York University)
had chosen to complement their regular second-year course load
by maintaining a bi-weekly e-mail correspondence in French.

Since 1993, this e-mail exchange, along with the use of word-processor and electronic writing tools *(Hugo Plus, Le Correcteur 101, La Disquette linguistique, Collins On-line French-English Dictionary*, etc.), have been fully integrated into the program of our second-year writing courses in both institutions. It involved a total of 20 participants in 1993-94 and now counts more than 30 students. Although the use of e-mail in second language learning and teaching is not new, building a whole course around the interactive use of computers and e-mail is rather original; in our project, e-mail is not a complement to the course (such as bulletin-boards, group discussions around the course content, etc.) but the main component of written language practice. The professors responsible for this exchange do not correspond with the students but are the facilitators for their correspondence. As for the textbooks assigned (composition guides, grammar manuals, etc.), they are mainly used as reference.

Exchange Procedure and Course Content

At the beginning of the academic year, each student is provided not only with the course material but also with a kit which includes:

- the project outline and the protocol to be followed in every exchange
- the technical steps to access university network   and to use e-mail
- a summary of basic word-processing features.

As stated in the exchange protocol, in their bi-weekly correspondence, students have to follow these five steps:

1. acknowledge receipt of letter
2. answer partner's questions on various matters
3. react to previous mail and/or ask for clarifications
4. write a content-based composition corresponding to the type of writing studied in class (self-portrait and autobiography, description of urban and natural surroundings, film and book reviews or play critiques, analysis of national and international news, etc).
5. add a personal note.

To prepare students for each exchange, the professor introduces the linguistic tools (vocabulary, grammar, tips on writing techniques, etc.) needed for specific topics as indicated in step (4) of the protocol. Students are then asked to write a letter to their correspondent focusing on that particular topic. They will type the first draft of their letter at home or in the computer laboratory in order to bring it to the next class where, with the help of the instructor, they will edit it and improve it, using the in-class computers. This second stage is most important since it allows for interaction and cooperation between peers, and between students and teacher; students constantly ask peers for help regarding word-processing as well as grammar, vocabulary and style. It should also be pointed out that in addition to work done during this time slot, some students find it necessary to consult with the professor before or after class. Once the letter is completed and corrected, it is the responsibility of the student to send it by e-mail before the deadline agreed on in the protocol.

As to the receipt of the partner's letter, it is once again the student's responsibility to check his/her mail, retrieve it and print it. Occasionally, students bring their letters to class and willingly share some of the content with peers (photographs, anecdotes, funny stories, "emoticons", etc.).

Research has shown that language learning is facilitated when topics dealt with in the classroom take into consideration students' experience, interests, needs and emotions which, in fact, are part of their daily life. Therefore, exchanges between our students focus on the following subjects or themes in this specific order:

- (auto)biographical information
- family life
- studies and career
- leisure, hobbies and interests
- current affairs (national and international)
- controversial topics.

As for grammar, it is not taught for grammar's sake but as a means to achieve better understanding and communication. Thus, we choose topics which we know will generate the need for the study of particular grammatical aspects of the language.

Students' Evaluation of the Exchange Project

During the second year of the project, instructors from both institutions handed out questionnaires to the students who participated in the exchange for its evaluation. Their feedback proved to be most useful. Not only were we encouraged to find out that the project was highly rated, but students' comments also provided us with a better understanding of their learning experience.

To students, the main benefit of this experience was a dramatic improvement of their writing skills which they attributed to the fact that they were writing to fellow students and not for the instructor. Indeed, several of them felt that their work would be scrutinized by their partners and wanted to measure up to their level. They also considered this experience to be a refreshing one since it gave them the opportunity to practise their written French in a more authentic and creative way, thus making learning more challenging than usual. They felt that the project expanded beyond the limits of the classroom and allowed them to exchange personal ideas in an authentic way and to establish new friendships. Students said they also developed more confidence in their computer skills.

Students were stimulated by the fact that their correspondent would enjoy receiving an interesting and well written letter through e-mail. They felt free to express themselves without "being told exactly what to write". They also liked the fact that their textbooks were peripheral rather than central to their learning experience and that the process of letter writing provided them with the opportunity to focus not only on the grammatically correct but also on the importance of expressing themselves clearly.

Though answers were in large part very positive, students pointed out some weaknesses in the project. Technical problems which delayed the processing and the transmission of letters at the beginning of the year received most of the criticism. Another area of disappointment was that they felt left out or ignored when not receiving a letter from their partner. Some students were also frustrated by the lack of time allotted to reply to their correspondent.

When asked whether the work on computer should be done before, during or after class, most students said they favoured working on the computer during classtime because instructors and peers could help; some even suggested that an optional additional hour be offered to compensate for the lack of time. However, others pointed out that doing most of the work outside of the classroom would provide them with more time to consult all sorts of resources (i.e. dictionaries, spell checks, language manuals, etc.) and would thus leave classtime for the correction of errors. This last remark is understandable, considering the fact that the majority of students chose to write first a draft on a piece of paper before typing it and improving it on the computer. Students who elected to type their letters directly on the computer found editing easier; it saved them time and enabled them to do quick spell checks and synonym searches. Most importantly, when asked how this exchange program made them work on their written French differently from the previous years, students mentioned that:

a) editing was not left to the last minute but became a regular practice, thanks to easy access to learning aids;

b) they spent more time correcting their mistakes and organizing their ideas to ensure that their message was properly understood;

c)   having a partner to correspond with enabled them to produce very personalized work since they shared their experiences, compared viewpoints, explored different subjects, and related their ideas in a more authentic and direct style;

d)   by receiving their partner's letters, they became aware of the latter's writing style which, in turn, influenced their own.

Reflections on Teaching and Learning via E-mail

Three years of observation of students at work with the computers, combined with our analysis of the project, led us to the following conclusions which, we hope, will guide other instructors who wish to embark on a similar venture.

a. Advantages of E-mail

Some advantages of L2 teaching and learning via e-mail are:

* the use of second language is more authentic – learners become aware of its communicative values since they write to a real audience;
* the content of letters is more interesting, dynamic and spontaneous than essays to the professor; students want to write more and do not hesitate to put in extra time;
* L2 learning is done in context;
* students compare their partner's writing skills with their own and try to do better;
* students benefit from facilitated and quicker use of learning aids (electronic dictionary, grammar and spell checks, thesaurus…);
* students familiarize themselves with new   technologies;
* the social setting is more congenial and leads to better social interaction between peers;
* motivation is enhanced;
* learning is more autonomous – students take added responsibilities and work on their own in the computer laboratory.

b. Challenges of E-mail

The following are some of the challenges of L2 teaching via e-mail:

* technical problems;
* limitations of software (not enough interaction);
* difficulty in adapting this kind of experience to a traditional curriculum;
* difficulty in scheduling exchanges between two institutions with different calendars;

- difficulty in meeting the needs and objectives of two different institutions, two curricula and two groups of learners;
- students not respecting the exchange protocol (not replying to the previous letter);
- students not respecting the time schedule;
- partners feeling left out when not receiving answers;
- possible lack of commitment from students;
- students dropping the course (and leaving their partner);
- danger of unfortunate mismatching of partners.

c. Role of Student

Some new responsibilities of the student will be:

- student becomes more self-disciplined;
- student is more autonomous;
- student must be willing to take more responsibilities (educational commitment);
- student takes more initiatives;
- student has more control over the content of the exchange;
- student is often placed in situations where cooperation with peers is needed (will ask for or provide help);
- student is committed to his/her own learning as well as to his/her partner's learning.

d. Role of Teachers

Teachers will face new responsibilities:

- teachers become facilitators and mediators (learning process is no longer teacher-centred but learner-centred);
- teachers should model the use of learning tools such as grammar books, dictionary, computer-assisted learning material, etc.;
- they should ensure, on a regular basis, that students respect the schedule and protocol;
- they should outline at the beginning of the year the working habits and strategies students are expected to develop in order to maximize this unusual learning experience;
- they should ensure that technical support is provided;
- teachers become consultants both in and out of the classroom;
- they should view themselves as less of an authority figure.

e. Advantages

The main advantages to this new approach to L2 teaching are:

- it generates 3 simultaneous types of interaction;
- among students (exchange of information, ideas, comments, laughter, etc.);

- between students and professor (students can instantly and more easily make changes to the text after the professor's critical reading);
- between students and computer (thanks to computer learning aids such as spell check, thesaurus);
- it is more efficient;
- instant printing;
- technical speed;
- easy deleting, cutting and/or pasting;
- students work at their own speed;
- it brings novelty into the classroom and stimulates learners.

f. Disadvantages

Some disadvantages are:

- technical problems can take too much time away from classroom work;
- exchanging personal letters may make group work impractical;
- corrections by the professor tend to become editorial (pinpointing of details) since the size of the screen prevents the reader from getting an overall picture of the text;
- computers tend to become a physical barrier between the professor and students as well as between students themselves;
- some students and professors may suffer from technophobia;
- the use of technology cannot be imposed on every instructor.

Pre-Test and Post-Test Results

In 1993-1994, students participating in this exchange were given a set of tests at the beginning and at the end of the year. The same tests were also administered to control groups in both institutions. These tests had two components: grammar (fill-in the blanks questions) and style (lexical and syntactical improvement).

Before proceeding with the results, we would like to point out that in our two institutions the second-year writing course focuses on the improvement of style and syntax through intensive writing. We would like to add that we were also fortunate to have two small participating groups in the exchange (12 and 8 students) and that on one campus the course amounted to a total of 33 hours whereas on the other campus it amounted to a total of 60 hours.

The following results represent the average marks received by students who wrote both tests: 24 students in the control group and 17 in the exchange group.

Although the format of the test did not reflect the type of

writing the exchange groups practised throughout the year, it was administered with the intention of checking whether the exchange groups acquired the same grammatical, lexical and syntactical skills as the control group. In this respect the project was successful since the exchange group performed better than the control group. (They obtained an average of 63.52% for grammar and 67.35% for style against 61.74% and 60.28%, respectively.) It is worth pointing out that, even though the emphasis was placed on written practice rather than on grammar, test results show that grammar skills improved even more than writing skills. (An increase of 12.40% against an increase of 9.90% for style.)

These good results encouraged us to maintain this second-year writing course centred around an e-mail exchange. We are now in our fourth year, and it is our intention to pursue our testing in order to develop new strategies which could further enrich our experience.

Conclusion

While communicative teaching is difficult to achieve within the limits of the traditional classroom setting, this experience has gone beyond our expectations: students discovered common past experiences, exchanged ideas and advice on various matters, expressed their feelings and moods, and some even sent pictures via e-mail. From a pedagogical point of view, this learner-centred approach highly motivates students from beginning to end and seems to be particularly beneficial to their acquisition of the French language.

As educators conducting this project, we were particularly interested in finding out what led to its success. We believe that the main factors behind the students' renewed interest in the study of a second language are: real communication, social context, integration of technology in the classroom, and interaction between students and between students and the professor.

Our computer-assisted exchange is structured in such a way that all students are involved in a common project which they feel proud of. We also insure that the course is socially based by structuring it around written correspondence dealing with issues which motivate students because they are truly communicative. This project has proven to be particularly enriching from a pedagogical and human point of view.

As confirmed by Nathan (1985), Neu and Scarcella (1991) and Phinney (1989), students using word-processing in writing classes develop positive attitudes and more confidence toward their own writing. Indeed, it is worth noting that in two different surveys

(Neu and Scarcella [1991] and the authors of this article), students have indicated that since they can easily access learning tools such as spell checks, thesaurus, etc. they do not hesitate to take risks in writing and editing and therefore become more comfortable with their use of the language. Their motivation leads them to spend considerably more time improving their texts from a linguistic and organizational perspective. As pointed out by Neu and Scarcella (1991:171),

> being able to make changes, to examine the altered work, and quickly to change it back to the original form, if desired, provides a psychological freedom that stimulates students' creativity, their exploration of ideas, and their evaluation and revision of those ideas.

Another source of motivation is the new relationship which is established between students and professor. Indeed, the use of computers is bound to affect the role of the teacher:

> In the computer-based writing class, students come to view the teacher as the consultant, technician, or resource person who can be called upon not only to help them solve writing problems but also to help fix technical problems, such as the failure of the printer. (Neu and Scarcella, 1991:173).

As we have observed in this exchange, this relationship is all the more different in that both students and professor have a common enemy/friend: the computer.

References

Canale, M. and Swain, M. 1980. "Theoretical Bases of Communicative Approaches to Second-Language Teaching and Testing." *Applied Linguistics*, 1 (1):1-47.

Corbeil, G. 1992. "Complémentarité des cours de langue à l'école secondaire et à l'université: existante ou inexistante?" *The Canadian Modern Language Review/La Revue canadienne des langues vivantes*, 48 (3): 497-511.

Ellis, R. 1990. *Instructed Second Language Acquisition – Learning in the Classroom*. Oxford: Basic Blackwell.

Guntermann, G. and J. K. Phillips. 1981. "Communicative Course Design: Developing Functional Ability in All Four Skills." *The Canadian Modern Language Review/La Revue canadienne des langues vivantes*, 37 (2):328-343.

Johnson, D. M. 1991. "Second Language and Content Learning with Computers." In *Computer-Assisted Learning and Testing. Research Issues and Practice*, ed. P. Dunkel, pp. 61-83. New York: Newbury House.

Krashen, S. D. and T. D. Terrell. 1983. *The Natural Approach: Language Acquisition in the Classroom*. New York: Pergamon Press.

Littlewood, W. T. 1984. *Foreign and Second Language Learning – Language Acquisition Research and its Implications for the Classroom*. Cambridge: Cambridge University Press.

Meirieu, P. 1987. *Apprendre... oui mais comment*. Paris: ESF éditeur.

Nathan, J. 1985. *Micro-Myths: Exploring the Limits of Learning with Computers*. Minneapolis: Winston Press.

Neu, J. and R. Scarcella. 1991. "Word Processing in the ESL Writing Classroom – A Survey of Student Attitudes." In *Computer-Assisted Language Learning and Testing. Research Issues and Practice*, ed. P. Dunkel, pp. 169-187. New York: Newbury House Publishers.

Phinney, M. 1989. "Computers, Composition and Second Language Teaching." In *Teaching Languages with Computers: The State of the Art*, ed. M. Pennington, pp. 81-96. La Jolla, Ca: Athelstan.

Rivers, W. 1972. "Talking off the Tops of their Heads." *TESOL Quarterly* 6: 77-81.

Savignon, S. 1983. Communicative Competence: Theory and Classroom Practice. Reading, Mass.: Addison Wesley.

Terrell, T. D. 1984. "The Natural Approach to Language Teaching: An Update." *The Modern Language Journal*, 41 (3): 460-479.

Reprinted from: Christine Besnard, Charles Elkabas and Sylvie Rosienski-Pellerin "Students' Empowerment: E-mail Exchange and the Development of Writing Skills." *Mosaic,* 3, 2 (Winter 1996): 8-12.

39 "Dear Santa ..." Santa Claus Helps with Communicative Competence

Carmela Colella and Anne Urbancic

How do we stimulate and encourage students to write compositions in the target language? The authors suggest a successful activity which includes students at both the elementary and university level.

Have teachers ever considered why so much sarcastic humour has been directed towards the stereotypical first composition of the school year? Inevitably, "What I did on my summer vacation" becomes the students' initiation for the writing exercises in the academic year to follow. We do interesting things on our summer vacation, but we loathe writing about them, just as we loathed writing about them when we were students. It is only now as we prepare and lead workshops for teachers of international languages [Italian] that we have begun to question why this, and other similar titles, are so unappealing to the learners, and do not inspire, do not motivate them at all.

We are clearly not the only ones who wonder, and who would like some guidance in teaching composition in our classes. In a recent series of workshops for teachers of elementary level Italian, the participating teachers were offered workshops on various topics, including the development of writing competence. These activities are equally applicable to other languages.

As Second Language Acquisition (SLA) Instructors, we know that we must ensure the development of all aspects of communicative competence. In some cases this is easier said than done. For example, the integration of conversation is readily achieved in the language class. But what of the development of communicative competence through composition? As Alice Omaggio Hadley (2001: 337-38) observes:

> It is important to consider ways to integrate writing with practice in listening, speaking, and reading so that language skills are not artificially separated. An integrative approach provides students with opportunities to use the language they are learning in authen-

tic communication while solidifying control of various aspects of the new language through writing as a support skill. Even when writing activities are used simply as a pedagogical aid, they can be structured in ways that help students to produce cohesive and coherent discourse.

We asked ourselves, therefore, "How can we teach or include composition in an interesting way, integrating it into the other tasks that we require of students? How can we make the writing exercise relevant for the students? Can we provide a real reader, besides ourselves, for our students' work?"

The answers to such questions are also at the basis of the ACTFL promotion of the Five C's, that is, the five standards for foreign language learning. In other words, how can our composition exercises involve Communication, Cultures, Connections, Comparisons and Communities?

We considered which one of the five C's the students would find most appealing. From a previous writing exercise undertaken in conjunction with learners at Università degli Studi di Roma – Tor Vergata[1] we knew that the immediate interest for students was to make a connection with a real reader. Students told us they needed to know that what they wrote created an uncontrived link between them and another person. Every teenager with a computer and MSN knows this; they are able to multi-link, thereby creating several levels of connections simultaneously. Websites such as "Friendster" or "Facebook" and others, so familiar to our students, have a similar intent. But how can we translate such an activity into the classroom? And even more difficult, how do we take this into the SLA classroom where connections must be made in another language?

We suspected that connecting with a real reader in another language would have other repercussions. The most exciting aspect of the Rome-Toronto exchange was not only the sharing of two cultures but the fact that there was also a visible growth, a maturing of the students' world view together with an awareness of the effect their modes of expression had on others. In discussing the importance of making connections through writing, Guy Allen (2002: 281) concurs:

> The act of filling the page with the meaning the writer chooses to put into the world alters the writer's relationship to self and world. The writer becomes conscious of consciousness and at once defines and transcends a situation. The writer acts upon the world, and in so doing produces a changed world and a changed self in the world, a self that takes responsibility for deciding what meaning is.

It was our hope to arrive at a writing exercise which would

enable our SLA students to reflect on language and on their role in the learning process through the exercise.

Given that their knowledge of Italian is at the low to mid novice level, what simple but relevant writing exercise could our students be assigned? And subsequently, how could we model the same exercise for teachers of Italian at the elementary level?

Letter writing can be presented in various ways just as letters can be formal, friendly, business, long short, fun, serious. What all letters have in common is the intention for a reader, someone who is not the writer or the student's language teacher. In other words, letters make a real connection with someone else. We have extensive experience with epistolary archives and we knew letter writers from the past not only made a connection with a long ago addressee but also with us today. Letters from the past made us part of another community, allowing us to compare a community of decades ago with our community today. We hoped that the teachers in the workshop would also see the benefits of creating a community of students. Thus we decided that the 5 C's (communication, cultures, connections, compari-sons, and communities) would be the focus of our letter writing workshop.

We began by presenting a theoretical overview of letter writing, including conventional protocols in Italian formal and informal correspondence. We decided not to focus on business correspondence. We also looked at theoretical considerations of letter writing, including works by Patrizia Frescaroli, Maria Cristina Giongo, Stefano Godani and R. M. Mata; these and others can be found on the website created previously in collaboration with Nicla Gargano (http://www. chass.utoronto.ca/~ngargano/corsi/corrisp/corrispondenza. html). Our workshop participants, in groups of 4-5, produced templates for letters for specific grade levels from JK to grade 8, including templates for birthday greetings, thank you notes and special occasion correspondence. The groups then shared their work with the other participants. In the discussion following, we also considered ethical issues such as how much and what kind of information about the child ought to be included. The participation of elementary or high school students in activities such as these must be closely monitored by the teacher; for safety and liability reasons teachers must ensure that letters do not contain personal information which may specifically identify the child other than by name.

Taking advantage of the early November workshop date, we then proposed a further assignment. We suggested that the teachers have their students write letters to Santa Claus, *Babbo Natale*. Not surprisingly, many of the teachers had already planned for this task. Most were aware that their pupils would be writing to Santa Claus at North Pole, HO HO HO. They knew that the English-speaking Santa Claus would actually answer the letters, thanks to the volunteers of Canada Post. Their concern was that no one would answer the Italian *Babbo Natale* letters. How delighted they were then to hear the second part of the assignment which involved not them, but the first year beginner and intermediate level students of Italian attending Brock University. What we proposed was that the letters from the elementary school children would be received and answered by students at the university. For the latter group, this assignment would constitute one of the four compositions required by the course.

In our first attempt there were several stumbling blocks. Fortunately the attitude of the students, both elementary and university level, was not one of them; both groups eagerly, animatedly, and willingly took up the task. Their teachers demonstrated a similar excitement towards the project.

Since we wanted to share the results of this task with other educators, we first consulted with the Chair of the University Ethics Research Committee and discovered that a written release from both the university students and also the parents of the participating elementary school children was required.

When we announced to the university students that their next composition assignment would involve replying to letters written by children learning Italian at the elementary school level, great murmurs of interest and excitement followed. We had given them a task which they not only found challenging but also engaging. Furthermore, they found it personally meaningful and relevant. Once the students had received and read their letters from the children, they expressed much concern about ensuring that they properly understood the contents of the letter. But in fact, deciphering the hand writing of the young learners proved more challenging than the Italian text. As a result we took time to review target specific vocabulary (especially toys and video games), we brainstormed ideas, possible replies and helpful Christmas expressions. We decided as a group that all the letters were to have a similar appearance so that the children would understand that they all of them came from the same *Babbo Natale* and that no one's *Babbo Natale* was better than any one else's. This naturally led to a brief lesson on the conventions of letter-writing in Italian. Alice Omaggio Hadley (2001: 282) confirms that:

> [v]arious conventions of written language that distinguishes it in style and tone from spoken discourse can be learned and practiced. Second language writing instruction that is carefully planned can

help students learn more about the composing process itself, a recursive, problem-solving activity that has the potential to affect students' writing and thinking skills in their native language, thus extending the benefits of language study well beyond the limits of the second-language classroom.

The exercise of answering the *Babbo Natale* letters also lent itself to a welcome discussion of the cultural differences in celebrating Anglo-Canadian Christmas, Italian Christmas and Italo-Canadian Christmas. The mythical figure of the *Befana* charmed our university students and many included a reference to her in their replies. The most original was from a student who wrote:

> Grazie per la tua lettera di natale [sic]. Ho notato chi [sic] il tuo italiano è molto buono. È migliore del mio. La Befana mi ha insegnato l'italiano così posso rispondere alle lettere che ricevo in italiano.

> *[Thank you for your letter. I noticed that your Italian is very good. It is better than mine. The Befana has been teaching me Italian in order that I may reply to those letters I receive in Italian in the same language.]*

A letter with another very interesting integration of the mythical old witch stated,

> Ho parlato con la Befana e lei mi ha detto che vuole aiutarmi a trasportare i tuoi regali – va bene? Spero che sí perche [sic] lei conosce il percorso più veloce per arrivare alla tua casa!

> *[I have spoken to the Befana who has informed me that she would like to help me with your gifts – is this O.K. with you? I hope it is, because she knows a short-cut to your house!]*

After reading these letters we were confident that a cultural connection had been made and hoped that the cultural reference was meaningful to the elementary level pupils as well as to the university students.

Further ethical issues arose when we discussed the content of the letters: should the answer from *Babbo Natale* promise the children their desired gifts? Our students decided that they ought not to agree to provide the gifts requested by the child. Imagine the conundrum of our student who received a request for either a puppy or a little baby brother for Christmas. Here was a letter requiring a rather creative response. The child had written:

> Caro Babbo Natale,
> [...]Sono un bambino bravo e studio l'italiano. Sotto l'ablero [sic] di Natale vorrei travare [sic]: un fratellino o un cagnolino. Spero che mi porterai i regali che ti ho chiesto. Tanti baci e tanti auguri.
> *[Dear Santa Claus,*
> *... I am a good boy and study Italian. Under my Christmas*

tree I would like to find a little brother or a puppy. I hope you will be able to bring me the gifts I have requested.
Many kisses and best wishes.]

The reply from the university student brilliantly dealt with the request for a puppy but obviously the issue of the little brother proved to be much more complicated to contend with and was tactfully ignored:

> [...] Quest'anno non sono sicuro se posso portarti quello che mi hai chiesto perché tutti i cagnolini non vogliono lasciare i loro fratelli e sorelle per Natale. Però prometto che tutto ciò che troverai sotto l'albero quest'anno sarà divertente e ti piacerà molto. [...]

> *[I am not certain that I can bring you what you have requested because the puppies do not want to leave their brothers and sisters at Christmas. I promise that everything you will find under the tree this year will be fun and you will enjoy it all very much...]*

The students also decided that in their replies no reference to parents or family be made. They agreed not refer to past Christmases or make any statement the child might know to be untrue.

Aware that the children would read their letters during class time, and driven by a sense of duty and responsibility towards these young learners of Italian, 80 university students left their classes that week motivated to do their best. The grade assigned for the composition became of secondary importance, surpassed by the greater concern to please and surprise the young children. To our great satisfaction in grading the replies, we discovered that the university students had made extensive use of the dictionary and had also included (accurately we might add) grammatical structures not yet discussed in class.

Richard J. Light (2001: 65) tried a similar experiment in his English essay writing class and we were pleased to discover that we more or less had arrived at the same conclusions:

> the student writers learn a great deal from writing for an audience of their peers. Traditionally, when students write papers for a professor, they assume they are writing for an expert on the topic. Therefore they may not bother to explain assumptions or to spell out every argument in detail. Writing for fellow students [or for younger students] requires a different approach and a different authorial voice. Several students report that the first time they were asked to do this they struggled for days thinking about how to change their presentation. Writing for a real audience [...] is very different from writing only for a professor to get a grade.

Omaggio Hadley (2001: 317-18) also has advice about the evaluation process for written assignments. She notes:

[o]pinions about how and when to evaluate student written work vary widely. For example, some researchers, scholars, and practitioners recommend that we respond primarily to content and not to form. Others suggest that we respond to both form and content, with some scholars recommending that response to form be reserved to the final draft and others preferring to respond to formal features throughout the process. There seems to be consensus that involving students in their own correction is helpful [...] and that a combination of teacher-, peer- and self-evaluation might yield the most successful results.

Taking our cue from Omaggio Hadley, we included peer editing. Prior to submitting the composition, the university students spent 20 minutes of class time proof reading each other's work, commenting on the content and making necessary revisions. Only then did the students submit their reply from *Babbo Natale* for grading. Since students wrote their names on the replies they had proofread, we happily noticed the contribution and suggestions of their peers as we read their work. We corrected the grammatical errors and ensured that the content was culturally and age appropriate and then assigned a grade. We returned the assignment to the university students along with instructions for making the necessary changes. We also provided special Christmas stationery.

As we approached the end of a long fall term, the excitement in the university class was palpable. Of the eighty letters assigned, seventy five were returned as requested. Several students volunteered to write extra letters for those children who did not have a reply.

Perhaps our description of this project thus far seems overly optimistic. There were indeed problems, not the least of which the five students who forfeited their grade. In addition, imagine our consternation when in a last minute review before sending the letters on, we discovered that not all the required corrections had been made appropriately. Too late to have students rewrite their letter, and unable to make the corrections by hand, we were compelled to devise a creative solution quickly. What to do? The answer came as we reviewed one of the letters which mentioned a visit by the *Befana* to the North Pole. As a result, we asked the elementary teachers read to their class a letter from the *Befana* informing the children that they should overlook any mistakes of Italian grammar and spelling present in the letters because Santa Claus was just starting to learn Italian. From a logistical perspective, we also regretted not having required a complete class list from the elementary school teachers to facilitate the distribution of the responses and to better organize the task.

Would we do this exercise again? Definitely! Not only would we repeat the *Babbo Natale* task but we would consider other letter exchanges on different themes. We discovered that we had included in one exercise the 5 essential standards of foreign language learning promulgated by ACTFL and that we had done this at two levels. The students communicated their knowledge of Italian without being aware of having done so; they created two communities which shared this knowledge, one at the elementary school level and one at the university level. Aware that there were real readers to the letters, students on both sides made an extra effort to connect in a meaningful way with their reader. We must confess, that we chuckled when we read the replies by the university students, the same students who grumbled about memorizing verbs or doing other such tasks, but who encouraged the young language learners to continue with their study of Italian and spoke to them of the importance of knowing a foreign language. Wise comments similar to the following could be found in many of the letters:

Sono allegro tu è [sic] impari un'altra lingua perché ti aiuta a fare amici in tutto il mondo.

[I am pleased that you are learning another language because it will help you make friends around the world]

or

[...] sono molto contento di sentire che studi l'italiano.

Spero che ti piace imparare l'italiano perché è una bella lingua, ed è molto importante continuare a studiare l'italiano perché troverai nel futuro che viene molto conveniente sopra tutto con la tua famiglia e anche con me.

[I hope you enjoy learning Italian because it is a beautiful language, and it is very important to study Italian because you will discover that in the future it will be very useful especially with your family and also with me.]

One student felt compelled to remind a child that Christmas was not about being greedy and receiving a lot of things but that the festivity was an opportunity to celebrate with family and friends.

In addition, for the elementary school children the connection extended to their parents who, in a post-task survey about the exercise, undertaken by one of the teachers, commented that they were "happy", "surprised" "impressed", "excited" and our favorite, thought it was a "cool idea". This exercise presented three cultures in contact with each other: Anglo-Canadian, Italian and Italo-Canadian. This task allowed appropriate proficiency level comparisons in syntax, morphology and lexis. It offered development in interpersonal, interpretive, and presentational (i.e. letter writing format) communication. Most of all it was fun!

At the end of the task, we basked in a wonderful sense of accomplishment; all the children had received their replies and almost all the letters were submitted on time. The crisis of the uncorrected errors had been averted and all had finished well. Determined to verify that this sense of accomplishment was justified we anonymously solicited comments on the task from the university students who participated. We hoped that Light's (2001: 64) impression that students identify the courses that had the most profound impact on them as courses in which they were required to write papers, not just for the professor, as usual, but for their fellow students as well, would hold true for this task. We were not disappointed. The overwhelmingly positive feedback encouraged us to continue to make connections and to share our experience. We read comments similar to the following over and over again:

> I thought this exercise (writing as Santa) was imaginative and fun. I enjoyed the practical application of Italian to this activity!;

> This writing assignment was fun. It was a different activity, and I found it to be a change of pace. It was fun to know that a child who is also learning Italian will be reading my work.;

> This was a good activity. By doing it, it was not only a good opportunity to learn, but it was also fun, and purposeful. It was a nice change for a composition. I enjoyed it!;

> This writing assignment was very fun. It allowed me to really connect with the Italian language. Writing about something I could relate to helped me to actually enjoy doing an assignment for this class. It made me realize everything I've learned.;

> I found this assignment to be a challenging one. It helped me to use vocabulary I was not familiar with, therefore I had to put time and effort into it. With the knowledge I had from the course, plus other vocabulary I was able to practice verbs and sentence structures. I think it was a good idea to put our knowledge into a real situation like this.

The task had truly been successful and we had managed to motivate, and involve the students in a manner that had never before taken place in our language classes.

In the years since this experiment first took place we have have repeated it annually always with the same level of personal and academic satisfaction for all groups involved.

Bibliography

Allen, Guy. 2000. "Language, Power and Consciousness" in *Writing and Healing. Toward an Informed Practice*, edited by Charles M. Anderson and Marian M. MacCurdy. Urbana, Ill: National Council of Teachers of English.

Frescaroli, Patrizia. 1994. *Cosa dire o scrivere in ogni occasione*. Milano: De Vecchi.

Giongo, Maria Cristina. 1987. *La frase giusta per ogni circostanza*. Milano: De Vecchi.

Godani, Stefano. 1998. *Cosa dire e scrivere in ogni occasione*. Genova: Gulliver Libri.

Light, Richard J. 2001. *Making the Most of College: Students Speak Their Minds*. Cambridge, MA.: Harvard UP.

Mata, R. M. 1977. *La moderna corrispondenza privata e commerciale: la lettera che "sfonda"*. Milano: De Vecchi.

Omaggio Hadley, Alice. 2001. *Teaching Language in Context*. 3rd ed. Boston: Heinle and Heinele. Thomson Learning.

Note

1. During the academic year 2004-05, students in an intermediate Italian class at Brock University exchanged e-mails with students studying English for Special Purposes at the Università degli Studi di Roma – Tor Vergata. The Canadian students wrote e-mails in Italian to the Tor Vergata students, who in turn replied in English and corrected the Italian grammar. The Brock students reciprocated by correcting the English grammar in the e-mails sent by the students from Rome.

Reprinted from: Carmela Colella and Anne Urbancic, "Dear Santa... Santa Claus Helps with Communicative Competence." *Mosaic,* 9, 1 (Spring 2007): 21-25.

40 Gestures and Language: Fair and Foul in Other Cultures

Joanne Wilcox

Using the correct body language abroad can lessen the risk of failure in personal and business relationships. It's worth careful examination before you pack your bag.

Gestures often communicate faster and better than oral language in getting a point across. The deaf recognize this and transfer ideas and images with grace and beauty, using arms and hands and fingers and here and there a bit of body language thrown in.

A story about the deaf will help make the point. I grew up in the shadow of a tree-laden granite slope called Island View south of Halifax. Island View overlooks St. Margaret's Bay and one of the islands viewed on a clear day is Shut-in Island, along with the nearby community of Peggy's Cove and the most-photographed lighthouse in the world.

Because my uncle suffered total deafness since birth, around our house during his visits, sometimes with friends, lip-reading was our method of conversation. I recall his caution at one point not to "mouth" Island View to a newly-met deaf person at any time, since it might lead to delight or surprise or outright shock. Try it! If you form your lips and say "Island View," your mouth will confuse the lip-reader with three words of considerably greater impact: "I love you."

It's a great lesson why we should not tread on unfamiliar turf without knowing the pitfalls in both oral language and body language. It's important that we pick up the general rules of the new territory. Equally important, it should tell us that any attempt by North American business to establish liaison with peoples in other cultures must be examined with care. Items to be checked would include dress codes, gift-giving and receiving, where to sit at dinner – and at the conference table – where and when your spouse fits in, what days or seasons the government offices are closed and/or the local banks. And much, much more.

And, of course, translation. Faultless translation is essential to a business relationship in most cultures. Even where it is apparently not essential, the passing of a fully translated front-and-back business card is a pleasant and courteous thing to do.

Knowledgeable officials in the export business know this. The President of the Business Council on National Issues, Thomas d'Aquino, summed it up nicely:

> Good products and services and vigourous salesmanship are cornerstones of successful exporting. Combine these with knowledge of foreign cultures, languages and business practices, and then you will have the winning edge.

It's sound advice. Yet the truth is North Americans are slow learners when it comes to executive manners and business etiquette abroad. As mentioned, the minimum courtesy when visiting another country on business would seem to be a business card in that country's language, and knowing how to use the body to deliver it. Yet, except for visits to Japan, where in Tokyo some 12 million business cards are exchanged daily, such a courtesy is uncommon with Canadians.

It needs preparation. When you plan your trip, envision your first meeting with your own countrymen at the embassy, and your meeting with your new strategic partner, the bank manager, and the customs people you'll be dealing with. In Tokyo, for example, cards are exchanged in a greeting ceremony of respect and welcome called *aisatsu*. It is important that the card-offering be accompanied by gestures. Here's how it's done:

- Your business card is called *meishi*.
- The seller presents first to the buyer.
- Hold your card Japanese-side up.
- Put the card forward with both hands with your thumbs on the upper side, present it while bowing moderately. Sometimes, the Japanese will receive your card with both hands.
- Cards are presented preferably while standing.
- Receive your contact's card in the same manner.
- When received, read and examine the card carefully. This is an important mark of courtesy; to simply take it and shove it into a pocket or wallet without examining it is offensive to the giver, as would be the case in any culture.

Business cards are winners. Consider this example.

I gave a client some treasured information on Japanese culture a few years ago. He had an international moving company, and was vying with a few large competitors on a job to move a Japanese family from Canada back to Japan. When he arrived at the address, he greeted the lady of the house with a dignified bow from the waist, offering his business card with both hands. As soon as he stepped foot in the home he immediately took off his shoes and put them in order by the door. The woman was so delighted by his efforts to make her comfortable by using her traditions, he got the job.

The point is that being culturally sensitive to body movement as well to language is a pleasant and very civilized way to get the edge on the competition.

When approaching your target market, it is quite natural that the first item to examine is your use of the language. This does not mean that you have to be fluently bilingual; just get to know a few key words like "Hello", "Please", "Thank you" – that kind of thing. You should also have your correspondence translated into the native tongue for ease of understanding. Accentuate the positive.

In making language arrangements, it's always wise to have a reliable source do the work. But to look on the negative side by way of example, executives very often fall into a trap, such as word that the secretary's second cousin took a course in the language seven years ago and that "she'll be able to do it for us." To make this point stick, here are some words that were quite likely put into English by someone like the secretary's second cousin living in another country:

- In a Bangkok cleaning shop is the sign: "Drop your trousers here for best results."
- In an Acapulco hotel: "The Manager has personally passed all the water served here."
- A slogan in China for "Pepsi comes alive" became: "Pepsi brings your dead ancestors back from the grave."
- ... and then there's the folded card that looks like a sandwich board, commonly called a "table-tent", found on the bedroom

Fred Chardtrand, *Canadian Press*
President George Bush's "Thumbs"

dresser at a hotel in the Orient. On one side it noted the following: "Our proud bell-captain will be pleased to take your luggage and send it off in all directions" while on the other side the hotel pointed out: "Guests are welcome to take advantage of our chambermaids."

The point is made. It's risky business to arrange your translation "in-house". To have the prospective buyer or strategic partner in the target market pass it around the office for a good laugh at your expense is surely risk enough.

Most travellers have some notion of the pre-travel checklist. You'll want to think about clothing, gift-giving, where to sit at the conference table, dinner etiquette, and a lengthy list of such matters. But we find that in most cases even those who have thought out some of these needs beforehand have given little thought to a vitally important item: even the world's top politicians have passed by consideration of when and when not to use common North American gestures and body language. Be aware that gestures as well as language goofs can cause a giggle.

A few years back, George Bush's presidential visit to Australia was coming to a successful conclusion as he walked up the stairs to his aircraft for the trip home. Then he paused, turned to the crowd and, with a sweeping gesture, gave Aussies something to think about for years: the thumbs-up sign.

Greg Gibson, *Associated Press*
President Bill Clinton's "OK sign"

North Americans consider this a nice thing to do. In some regions Down Under, however, it's an obscenity worse than giving the finger.

Advice on such body language has been put together in a scholarly work at Oxford University in *Gestures: their origins and meanings* by Desmond Morris, Peter Collett, Peter March and Marie O'Shaughnessy (published by Jonathan Cape). They note that the thumbs-up sign can have this offensive application in certain countries in Europe, while in both Europe and North America it can mean victory or approval.

- All countries have sensitive spots. In Indonesian and in some other cultures in southeast Asia, you have a problem if you're left-handed; one never uses the left hand to give or receive anything. The left hand is always kept aside to be brought out for cleaning purposes in the washroom.
- In Saudi Arabia, a million dollar deal can be lost if you cross your legs. In the Saudi culture, if the sole of your foot shows, you are telling your host he is beneath a dog. In some parts, the people believe that the dangling foot is the devil pointing at them.
- The Japanese would much rather you didn't blow your nose anywhere in a public place. To do so in a dining room can put an end to negotiations right away.
- Better not scratch your cheek with your forefinger. It may

resemble the "cheek screw". When the hand is rotated in this way it means crazy in Germany, and effeminate in Spain. However, in Italy it means good.

- In European countries particularly, the forearm jerk can be an aggressive sexual insult or sexual comment. In this display, the clenched fist is jerked forcibly upwards; the jerked arm is bent at the elbow and, as the jerk is performed, the other hand is slapped down on the upper arm, as if something is checking the upward movement.

- In a rap session following a seminar on gestures, a Greek person in the audience pointed out that the way we use the head to make a "yes" or "no" is precisely the oppositive in Greece. Over there, the up-and-down nod of the head means "no", while the side-to-side shake means "yes".

Not all gestures are foul. Tap your fingers gently on the table in Taiwan following a meal, and it signals your appreciation of the event.

And some have mixed meanings. The gesture of "pursing the hand" is common in the Mediterranean countries, particularly in Italy. The fingers are straightened and brought together in a point facing upwards. This can be a what-are-you-talking-about query, or praise or approval, or sarcastic criticism.

What is called "The Ring" in some countries is our OK sign, thumb and forefinger forming a circle, with the remaining three fingers aloft. During President Bill Clinton's trip to Russia earlier in 1994, citizens attended a Town Hall meeting in Moscow and got a first hand look at the President's "ring" during an animated oration he was giving at the time. Clinton may have thought it was OK, but to Russians it was a shocker. The OK sign over there, and in a number of other countries, is an "orifice symbol". If the president had been a run-of-the-mill tourist in a Moscow pub, he could have had his nose flattened and ended his evening in a Moscow slammer.

Social gaffes like these can be embarrassing, and a politician or business executive has little room to claim: "Nobody told me." It just won't wash. The President got off lightly. Even a minor miscue can kill a meeting or ruin a deal.

Think you know your international etiquette? If you're planning a trip, try the following quiz. If you do all right, *bon voyage*. If you goof, it's time to bone up.

1. When in Taiwan, you offer thanks for a good meal by:
    (a) Inviting the chef into the dining area with the suggestion that all present raise their glasses to that person's success in marriage.

(b) Tapping your fingers lightly on the table.

(c) Lighting a peach-coloured candle that you ask the head waiter to deliver to the table at the conclusion of the meal.

2. A gift of flowers is appropriate in Mexico. The flowers should be in the favourite floral colour of the people, that is:

(a) Red, symbolizing the great tomato crop.

(b) White, the international symbol of purity.

(c) Yellow, for the sun god that has been so kind to Mexico's tourist industry.

3. If offered a drink in the Netherlands prior to a business discussion, you should:

(a) If you're a woman executive, place it between your knees and hold it there for 30 seconds. If a man, flatten your hand and hold the drink on your upright palm for 30 seconds.

(b) Accept it without ritual of any kind.

(c) Decline, stating that you want to carry on with business, and when you've made the sale you'll pick up the tab all around.

4. In the Peoples' Republic of China, a superb gift to offer your host is:

(a) A T-shirt with the image of your country's leader stamped on it.

(b) A small clock with white-gloved Mickey Mouse hands pointing the time.

(c) A vase or basket arrangement from a local florist.

5. When paying a restaurant tab in Japan, be sure to include a tip in this manner:

(a) Kiss the signed credit card receipt with the tip shown clearly on it and present it to the head waiter.

(b) Put the tip in cash in a decorative envelope and give it to the head waiter, who will then distribute the cash to the appropriate staff.

(c) Ask to see the chef and go to the kitchen to present that person with the tip money in a manila envelope in coins only.

6. When greeting your host/hostess in India, you will:

(a) Firmly grab his/her right hand in greeting as you would in Canada, and shake it vigorously.

(b) Click your heels once, then point the toes of your shoes together and bow.

    (c) Press your own two palms together in greeting.

7. When meat or a vegetable on your plate looks somewhat different from what the dining room back home would serve, you would:

    (a) As a conversation opener, show interest by asking wether the dish features an endangered plant or animal species.

    (b) Suggest that you'd like to repay your host's kindness if you could just find a Pizza Delight or a Harvey's in town.

    (c) Cut it into bite-sized pieces and eat the meal placed before you.

8. In Sweden, when asked for your title and the full name of your company:

    (a) Say you'll write the information in English on the placemat to give it a personal touch.

    (b) Offer to send a fax when you get home.

    (c) Have a business card with you that bears a translation for all pertinent information, including telephone and fax numbers.

9. You've just completed a presentation and the sale looks like a sure thing. You then put your material back in your briefcase and:

    (a) Extend an offer to meet everyone at the bar downstairs and exercise your elbow and wrist to make a drinking gesture.

    (b) Put thumb and forefinger together to form the "okay" circle, and leave the room.

    (c) Say thank you in both your language and theirs, and leave.

10. In Kuwait, when coffee is offered:

    (a) Drink two cups with your right hand, then decline a third by shaking your cup slightly before returning it to the server.

    (b) After each cup, tug at your earlobes in a brief gesture of thanks.

    (c) Take off your right shoe at the start of the coffee service, place it upside down on the floor directly in front of your host until you have finished coffee, and then return it to your foot.

The Answers

1. Avoid A and C. They're apt to start people talking. It's correct to tap your fingers on the table. Choose B.

2. Forget the sun god and the tomato nonsense. To Mexicans, yellow flowers connote death, and red flowers cast spells. On the other hand, white flowers remove spells, so B wins the day.

3. Accept the drink without fuss. B is the choice you'd make, an essential part of business culture in the Netherlands.

4. Try C, the floral arrangement. The gift of a clock is a symbol of bad luck in China, and the T-shirt is, well_a bit Mickey Mouse in its own right.

5. B. The tip in the decorative envelope reflects knowledgeable behaviour and is much appreciated. A and C are out of the question.

6. It's proper to press your own palms together. A and B are in bad taste. Choose C.

7. C might seem like a tough one to handle, but it has to be done. When abroad, eat what's placed in front of you.

8. A and B might lose you some goodwill marks. Go with C, in any country visited, and make sure you have the translation service prepare your cards before you jet away.

9. C wins again. Better stay away from using the "okay" sign in any country; it can be the equivalent of the obscene finger gesture, or just not understood.

10. A is the correct coffee ritual. B is useless, and C is a real loser, since to show the bottom of one's shoe or foot is very rude indeed; this kind of behaviour could result in your early departure from Kuwait.

Next time you plan a trip, somewhere on your checklist between "garments" and "gift-giving", place the reminder: "gestures."

Editor's Note: For additional incorrect translations, read Richard Lederer'anecdotes in Anthony Mollica, "*Traduttore, traditore!*: Beware of Communicative Incompetence!," *Mosaic*, Vol. 3, 4: 19-20. The list is reproduced in the revised and up-dated article, "Language Learning: The Key to Understanding and Harmony", Chapter 1 in this volume.

Photos: Courtesy Canadian Press
Illustrations: George Shane
Reprinted from: Joanne Wilcox, "Gestures and Language:Fair and Foul in Other Cultures." *Mosaic*, 2, 1 (Fall 1994): 10-13.

41 Teaching to the Test: Principles of Authentic Assessment for Second-Language Education

Edwin G. Ralph

Educators typically recoil at the phrase, "teach to the test." Yet, this article supports that injunction as being valid for second language teachers – provided that certain conditions are met.

A recent trend that has appeared on the agenda of school re form in several countries is centered on the raising of national educational standards and on the implementation of comprehensive evaluation of students' learning performance. A divisive issue emerging from this movement deals less with whether these assessments will influence classroom teaching and learning – because they will (Marzano, Pickering, and McTighe, 1993; Zessoules and Gardner, 1991) – but more with what types of assessments should be used (Worthen, 1993). A fear is that if these "new" assessments are merely a rehash of the traditional standardized, multiple-choice, norm-referenced type, then teachers will tend to mirror a similar type of instruction in their classroom practice. As a consequence, it is believed that their students' learning will tend to reflect corresponding characteristics, such as low-order thinking, memorization of discrete items, and inability to apply this knowledge in real-world situations (O'Neil, 1993).

The purpose of this article is to demonstrate, however, that the practice of "teaching to the test" is not inappropriate – provided that "the test" is one that meets the criteria of "authentic assessment" as described in the current literature of education reform (Wiggins, 1993). The term "authentic assessment" like many reform notions in education is a new label for an old practice that has been used by good teachers throughout history (Cronin, 1993; Perrone, 1991).

Authentic Assessment: What is it?

Authentic Assessment, "direct assessment", "process testing", or "performance assessment" (Herman, Aschbachers and Winters 1992, Worthen 1993) refers to the otherwise known as "alternative assessment" application of generic formulae, is not considered as revolutionary by current second language educators, as it may be perceived by some other members of the educational establishment. In fact, evidence for the pursuit of such goals as learners' communication competence, language proficiency, and practice in real life situations has been observable in second language education for several years. This evidence has been manifested on several fronts:

- internationally (Girard, Huot, and Lussier-Chasles, 1987);
- nationally, through the establishment of the National Core French Study (Tremblay, 1992);
- provincially, through the formation of several governments' recent second language curriculum policies and guidelines (Diffey, 1991); and
- commercially, through several publishers' dissemination of applicable educational materials (e.g., Jean, 1991).

A further line of support bolstering the fact that the field of second language education has embraced the concept of authentic learning/assessment is the acknowledgment of this phenomenon by recognized experts in the area of authentic learning. Wiggins (1992, 1993), for instance, has complimented second language educators for designing tasks and tests to assist beginning second language students to move progressively from a crude grasp of the complex whole of a communication act to a more sophisticated grasp of the experience. He advocates:

> We need to generalize from [second language] courses, which get the learner speaking and listening in context immediately and working toward the ultimate criterion of fluent contextual performance (Wiggins, 1993, p. 203).

Thus, this emphasis in current second language education–whether in core or immersion programs of ESL, FSL, Heritage languages, or First Nations' languages – on engaging students in experiential/global learning and assessment activities is a major goal worth pursuing and perfecting. However, for the benefit of second language teachers, who may be entering the profession, or who may be at various stages in their teaching careers, this present paper seeks to identify some of the key principles and practices of authentic assessment as it is applied in the daily practice of second language instruction.

Key Principles of Authentic Assessment

A synthesis of the current research literature related to authentic assessment reveals four key principles characterizing this process (Herman, 1992; Marzano, Pickering, and McTighe, 1993).

Constructivist Learning

Authentic assessment is built on current learning theories espousing cognitivist developmentalist assumptions, whereby learners participate individually and with others in various learning and assessment activities that require personal meaning-making, and reflective and self-regulated interpretation. Students demonstrate their performance by engaging in realistic, motivating communicative tasks.

Although authentic assessment stresses students' production of holistic, unique, and complex linguistic tasks involving a synthesis of higher-order thinking, it does not ignore the performance of lower level skills or discrete linguistic elements. However, the traditional drill skill, mechanical/ algorithmic language activities are used sparingly, and essentially play a supporting role en route to helping learners to progress developmentally toward becoming both accurate (i.e., mechanically correct) and proficient (i.e., communicatively comprehensible) second language users (Valette, 1993). Skilled second language teachers reflectively and effectively supplement students' holistic language experiences (e.g., communicative functions and notions) with occasional language study exercises (e.g., grammatical structure/pronunciation). Moreover, the latter is subordinated to the former, in that the language study component tends to be used to advise learners how to improve the accuracy of their particular second language productive (speaking/writing) skills (Tremblay, 1992).

Communicative Tasks

A learning/assessment task illustrating this cognitive/constructivist principle is one that will engage students in specific functional/notional scenarios appropriate for their age, their interest(s), and their level of linguistic competence. For example, a possible activity for 9 and 10 year old second language students, with 3 to 4 years prior experience in a core second language program, is one that the present author found to be effective in his own teaching practice. Students are requested to prepare and present a role-play, in pairs, of a typical after-school telephone conversation. They would be given clear directions about using recent material presented in class, and everyone would be clear that students would be evaluated on their use of second language, their acting ability, and their creativity "…to make up statements that reflect the intended meaning of the text" (Nemni and Lecerf, 1990, p. 14).

Integration of Teaching/ Learning/Assessment

A second principle of authentic assessment is that the components of teaching, learning, and assessment are considered as an integrated whole. Because the cognitivist-constructivist approach emphasizes learners' performance of tasks that demonstrate what they know and are able to do in real-life situations (or meaningful simulations of the same), then it follows that any of these tasks – whether they take the form of informal practice-sessions, or of more formal performances, projects, portfolios, or tests – are eligible to be evaluated in any second language class period. However, students must be informed of this procedure at the beginning of the course, and periodically throughout the school term (Nemni and Lecerf, 1990). Thus, the traditional distinction between "the test" and "a learning task" is purposefully blurred, so that all classroom activities including individual assignments and group tasks are evaluated and make up part of student grades for reporting purposes.

Regardless whether each second language learning experience is, by nature, formative (ongoing) or summative (terminal), or discrete or integrative, or norm or criterion referenced, or formal or informal, it is crucial that both students and teachers should know clearly what the particular content and performance standards are for each of these tasks (Jean, 1991; Palmer Wolf, LeMahieu, and Eresh, 1992). Moreover, Wiggins (1993) asserts that all authentic assessment whether "task" or "test" should provide enticing, stimulating challenges for learners in which they are   engaged in meaningful communicative situations. An example of such a specific second language situation could involve having students conduct and analyze a survey of their peers' typical daily dietary intake, or of their physical activity patterns, and then to present the findings formally to the class via oral and/or project formats in the second language. Again, these tasks would be evaluated according to specific predetermined and clearly stated criteria.

Productions of Unique Simulations

Because of normal logistical constraints that exist in schools, second language teachers may be forced to contrive authentic simulations that are somewhat artificial, but that "feel real" to students (Wiggins, 1992, p. 27). For instance, the present author has had several groups of his former middle-years second language students successfully plan, prepare, and perform the following dramatic skits complete with second language dialogue, taped sound effects and background music, appropriate costumes, and stage props and lighting: "A Missed Aircraft Hijacking," "Fractured Fairy-tales," "Former TV Heros," "Cinderfella and His Godfather," and "At the Movies."

In keeping with authentic performance principles, these students were assessed on both their individual and group use of the second language, their dramatic participation, and their involvement (including their fulfillment of their responsibility to prepare their own costumes and props). Inevitably, this author also found that learner motivation increased toward second language course specifically, and toward the second language generally, as a result of having students to participate in these meaningful but simulated learning tasks (Ralph, 1987, 1989).

Quality and Coverage of Content

A third standard characterizing authentic assessment is that the performance tasks must not only be consistent with the current trends advocated in the curricular field, but that they also must be representative of the key elements of the discipline (Herman, 1992). With respect to second language education in Canada in recent years, the National Core French Study (Lapkin, Harley, and Taylor, 1993) has provided a major impetus both for provincial governments (Lazaruk, 1993), and for publishers (Nemni and Lecerf, 1990) to help revise policies and create materials based on the concept of having students to use language meaningfully in true communicative contexts. Thus, provincial second language guidelines (Diffey, 1991; Saskatchewan, 1988) as well as contemporary published programs (e.g., Jean, 1991; McConnell and Collins, 1989), promote learners' integration of the analytical/technical with the communicative/function aspects of second language acquisition. The goal is that these "communicative situations are made as real as possible in the classroom" (Saskatchewan, 1988, p. 218).

In pursuing the ultimate content objective of helping students to function both fluently *and* accurately in the four second language skills (Valette, 1993), teachers are faced with the perpetual challenge of creating learning and assessment activities that have an appropriate blend of language experience and language study. Current experts in the field are agreed that this optimum mix is best reached when second language educators embed learning and assessment activities in units or themes appropriate for specific age groups. Students take part in natural and authentic language experiences as they encounter a variety of interesting tasks related to these broad themes. Thus, learners are actually put into real-life communication situations where they have to use the second language in a personal, direct way – rather than first having to learn several discrete language skills, and then trying to apply them in a new setting (Duplantie, Hullen, and Tremblay, 1992).

Activities Related to Students' Lives

These second language learning and/or testing activities are designed to tap into learners' own life experience and interests. A further example used with middle years students might be to develop (and later to assess) their listening comprehension of actual TV or radio news/ sports/weather reports (or simulations thereof) delivered by a native second language speaker. By answering a set of oral and/or written questions about the report, students would demonstrate several skills: their global understanding of the content, their knowledge of specific facts presented in the broadcast, and their ability to deduce/analyze/interpret these facts. Further, to demonstrate their second language oral production skills they could be assigned to create, prepare, and present a simulated TV or radio report of their own. These resulting role-plays could also be audio or videotaped in the classroom setting and would be assessed not only for the technical aspects of second language grammar and usage, but also for student participation/initiative/creativity.

The present author has found through his 30 years' experience in education from the elementary to adult levels as second language teacher, school principal, school district second language coordinator, university professor, and supervisor of teacher interns – that such stimulating activities meet two key goals. They not only help motivate students and reenergize teachers toward the second language program, but these tasks seem to have an effect on reducing negative attitudes among certain students who may have been formerly categorized either as "reserved, retiring, or recalcitrant," or as "rambunctious, rude, or rebellious" (Ralph, 1982, 1987, 1989, 1993, in press). The positive reinforcement received by students as a result of their participating in a successful authentic performance contributed to an increase in their more favourable acceptance of the second language course.

Quality and Fairness of Standards

A fourth principle of authentic assessments that the assessment process always seeks to produce accurate results upon which to permit fair and sound decisions and conclusions about student performance, teacher effectiveness, and program quality.

However, a persistent dilemma for all educators, including those in second language teaching, is to design learning and assessment activities that optimize both the validity (i.e., fidelity to the criterion situations that maximize learners' freedom to respond appropriately in real communicative contexts) and the reliability (i.e., consistency, precision, and standardization of results). Because many traditional assessment formats tend to decontextualize and decompose knowledge into isolated, generic, or simplistic responses, educators advocating the authentic approach seek to reduce these deficiencies by devising alternative standards and tasks that allow for more pluralistic, diverse, and idiosyncratic performance by students (Wiggins, 1993). The latter reflect the complexities involved in confronting ambiguous communication scenarios in the real world of students' lives.

The principle undergirding our best current understanding of second language acquisition and assessment emphasizes the integration of both the analytical *and* the global dimensions of second language learning. Research by Stern (1982), by the National Core French Study (Tremblay, 1992), by provincial ministries of education in Canada (Diffey, 1991), and by the American Council on the Teaching of Foreign Languages (Wiggins, 1993) has resulted in the publication and dissemination of accepted second language proficiency guidelines – empirically grounded in clearly described traits characterizing the performance of learners at various stages of second language abilities.

Moreover, there exists a variety of scoring descriptors, evaluation formats, and assessment frameworks, as well as several actual second language tests that have been piloted and normed on target groups similar to the individuals being tested (Lapkin, Argue, and Foley, 1992). Thus, second language educators currently have a choice among several trustworthy assessment sources, some of which are: the above instruments; materials provided by provincial ministries and/or local school divisions; tests included in the second language programs from commercial publishers; teachers' personally created materials and activities; and combinations of the above.

Quality Assessments

An example of an authentic learning or testing task that seeks to gauge students' second language receptive and productive skills would be for the teacher to arrange time to conduct an oral second language interview with each of the students in a class. Learners would be forewarned, for instance, to be prepared to respond to oral questions from a "TV talk-show host" from another country. The purpose would be for "the interviewer" to record the interview and to take it back for later telecasting in the interviewer's nation, in order to generate interest among similarly aged students to come to visit the interviewee's school in Canada. The interviewee would have been told previously thus to expect to use persuasive and enthusiastic responses in order to motivate these potential viewers to come to Canada.

The interviewer's questions would reflect what Howard (1980) calls a "semi free" format, in that specific topics and/or questions would not be pre-specified for the respondent; and that the interviewee would be expected to make use of previously learned second language material presented and practised in class, such as Canadian geography, descriptions of weather, buildings, families, and school- and home-life. During the activity, respondents would be assessed globally for their integration of the communicative, grammatical, and sociolinguistic dimensions of second language, as well as for their overall knowledge of the topic and their linguistic versatility.

Fairness in the assessment of each of the above learning/testing tasks would be secured if the evaluators ensured that they would incorporate the following criteria:

- to develop and use scoring rubrics based on accepted second language models or templates that would indicate both exemplary and nonexemplary performances (the latter illustrating typical errors for each age/stage of second language development);
- to assess students' grammatical/technical second language skills, such that these mechanical aspects would be regarded as important – but not as sufficient aspects – in learners' demonstrations of their proficiency in realistic and relevant second language communication;
- to delay key decisions regarding learner, teacher, program, and context matters, until a variety of learning/assessment tasks would be collected in order to provide a composite profile of results; and
- to align all such learning/assessment activities with the second language program's objectives, as well as to apply the authentic assessment philosophy, principles, and practices in their daily instructional routines.

Second-Language Education on Track for Authentic Assessment

This article has indicated that our contemporary knowledge of effective second language education is based on the cognitive view of learning, in which learners actively construct personal understanding in a holistic manner as they engage in actual communicative activities. Because the processes of teaching, learning, and assessment of learning are so closely and intimately tied, and because the latter directly affects both of the former processes, then it is essential that second language educators ensure that all of their assessment practices both guide, and are guided by, the specified student-learning tasks for each level, and the accompanying performance standards for these tasks. In the light of this key assumption, Marzano, Pickering, and McTighe (1993) aptly conclude that it is essential that the authentic assessment task "...reflects good instructional practice, so that teaching to the test is desirable" (p. 13).

Thus, "the test" virtually represents any second language activity derived from the experientially-oriented thematic approach that prepares students "for real world language use" (Lapkin, Harley, and Taylor, 1993, p. 486). At this point in time, second language education has already embraced this concept, and may second language educators continue to implement and to improve these authentic learning tasks in the daily routines of their classrooms!

References

Cronin, J. 1993. Four misconceptions about authentic learning. *Educational Leadership*, 50, 7: 78-80.

Diffey, N. 1991. Provincial curriculum guidelines in core French. *Canadian Modern Language Review/La Revue canadienne des langues vivantes*, 47: 307-326.

Duplantie, M., J. Hullen, and R. Tremblay. 1992. *Guide pédagogique: Élans 2e. première partie*. Anjou, Québec: Centre Éducatif et Culturel, Inc.

Girard, C., D. Huot, and D. Lussier-Chasles, D. 1987. "L'évaluation de la compétence de communication en classe de langue seconde." In Pierre Calvé and Anthony Mollica, eds., *Le français langue seconde: Des principes à la pratique*. Welland, Ontario: Canadian Modern Language Review.

Herman, J. 1992. "What research tells us about good assessment." *Educational Leadership*. 49, 8: 74-78.

Herman, J., P. Aschbacher, and L. Winters. 1992. *A practical guide to alternative assessment*. Alexandria, VA: Association for Supervision and Curriculum Development.

Howard, F. 1980. "Testing communicative proficiency in French as a second language: A search for procedures." *The Canadian Modern Language Review/La Revue canadienne des langues vivantes*, 36:272-289.

Jean, G. 1991. *Entre amis 1: Teacher's Guide*. Scarborough, Ontario: Prentice-Hall.

Lapkin, S., V. Argue, and D. Foley. 1992. "Annotated lists of French tests: 1991 update." *Canadian Modern Language Review/La Revue canadienne des langues vivantes*, 48:780-807.

Lapkin, S., B. Harley, and S. Taylor. 1993. "Research directions for core French in Canada." *The Canadian Modern Language Review/La Revue canadienne des langues vivantes*, 49:476-513.

Lazaruk, W. 1993. "A multidimensional curriculum model for heritage or international language instruction." *Mosaic*. 1, 1 :13-15.

Marzano, R., D. Pickering, and J. McTighe. 1993. *Assessing student outcomes*. Alexandria, VA: Association for Supervision and Curriculum Development.

McConnell, G., and R. Collins. 1989. *D'accord 2: Teacher's Guide*. Don Mills, Ontario: Addison-Wesley.

Nemni, M., and B. Lecerf. 1990. *Bienvenue 3: C'est parti! Teacher's Guide*. Scarborough, Ontario: Prentice-Hall.

O'Neil, J. 1993. "The promise of portfolios." *ASCD Update*. 35, 7: 1, 5.

Palmer Wolf, D., P. LeMahieu, and J. Eresh. 1992. "Good measure: Assessment as a tool for educational reform." *Educational Leadership*. 49, 8: 8-13.

Perrone, V. 1991. "Introduction." In V. Perrone, ed., *Expanding student assessment*, pp. vii-xi. Alexandria, VA: Association for Supervision and Curriculum Development.

Ralph, E. 1982. "The unmotivated second-language learner: Can students' negative attitudes be changed?" *The Canadian Modern Language Review/La Revue canadienne des langues vivantes*, 38:393-502.

Ralph, E. 1987. "Motivation et étude d'une langue seconde: Peut-on modifier une attitude négative chez les élèves?" In Pierre Calvé and Anthony Mollica, eds., *Le français langue seconde: Des principes à la pratique*. Welland, Ontario: Canadian Modern Language Review.

Ralph, E. 1989. "Research on effective teaching: How can it help second language teachers motivate the unmotivated learner?" *Canadian Modern Language Review/La Revue canadienne des langues vivantes*, 46:135-146.

Ralph, E. 1993. "Beginning teachers and classroom management: Questions from practice, answers from research." *Middle School Journal*. 25, 1: 60-64.

Ralph, E. (in press). "Middle and secondary second language teachers: Meeting classroom management challenges via effective teaching research." *Foreign Language Annals*.

Saskatchewan Education. 1988. *Core French: A curriculum Guide for Grades 7-12*. Regina: Saskatchewan Education.

Tremblay, R. 1992. "Second languages in Canadian education: Curriculum concerns." *The Canadian Modern Language Review/La Revue canadienne des langues vivantes*, 48:811-823.

Valette, R. 1993. "The challenge of the future: Teaching students to speak fluently and accurately." *The Canadian Modern Language Review/La Revue canadienne des langues vivantes*, 50:173-178.

Wiggins, G. 1992. "Creating tests worth taking." *Educational Leadership*. 49, 8: 26-33.

Wiggins, G. 1993. "Assessment: Authenticity, context, and validity." *Phi Delta Kappan*. 75:200-214.

Worthen, B. 1993. "Critical issues that will determine the future of alternative assessment." *Phi Delta Kappan*, 74:444-454.

Zessoules, R., H. Gardner, H. 1991. "Authentic assessment: Beyond the buzzword." In V. Perrone, ed., *Expanding student assessment*, pp. 47-71. Alexandria, VA: Association for Supervision and Curriculum Development.

Reprinted from: Edwin G. Ralph, "Teaching to the Test: Principles of Authentic Assessment for Second-Language Education." *Mosaic,* 1, 4 (Summer 1994): 9-13.

42 The Problem of Passion and Culture

Roseann Runte

Culture defines us as humans and offers us the possibility to identify ourselves, pursue greatness and espouse universal values. Language is, with other forms of communication, both the expression of culture and the tool which changes culture. Education is essential to preserve and affirm our culture and the continuation of civilization. The most important investment we can make is in education, research, creativity, the arts and sciences, for they represent power and offer our lives meaning.

Myths of an Arcadian land of milk and honey, of Paradise lost in a distant past, are common in many cultures. The moment of perfect innocence does not exist in human memory, yet we imagine a time of peace and harmony when there was no need for clothing. The strategically placed fig leaf was, it is generally agreed, necessitated by the loss of innocence and the birth of self-consciousness and shame.

Culture is thus born of shame, of fear, of possessiveness as much as of love of others. To mediate fear and self-consciousness, society requires a kind of social contract and group culture defining what is permitted and what is preferred. This partially unwritten contract assures us of the freedom to create while it also poses limits to our creativity. The contract is continually improved by and enforced by education. Those without access to education, such as women in the eighteenth century, complained that they were taught only how to wear fig leaves when they wanted to learn science, politics, and art.

Culture is the vehicle that allows expression of our lives, ideas, and ideals. It is also the boundary which limits the direction, speed, and distance the vehicle will travel. Culture is like a pen that allows us to write and, like paper, which limits our writing to the page. If we are born in a culture which reads from right to left, we will orient our thoughts accordingly. If we are born in a culture which respects all forms of life, we will take care not to step on the spider that another might not even perceive. Culture is thus, in Lockean terms, learned: but the existence of overriding concepts of Beauty and Truth, of Perfection and of Innocence, indicate that there are universal ideals which underlie all cultures and unite all peoples.

Culture is also geographically determined. Peoples who live in the desert will have different vocabularies, different ideas from those who know only the tropical rainforest or the Arctic Circle. In one culture, water will have a greater value than in another. In one culture, colour will be prized, while in another music will be highly developed. Culture is economically, scientifically, and technologically driven while at the same time the economy, science, and technology are driven by culture. The capability of producing leisure time and musical instruments will determine the musical culture of a people. A people with a culture which prizes work may have a greater economic success. Economic development which runs counter to a regional culture is rarely successful. Culture can represent an escape from technology. However, technology can also offer the means of escape or provide the subject for artistic expression.

The French poet, Jean de La Fontaine, wrote a biography of Aesop who was both a fable writer and a slave. In this narrative, Xantus, Aesop's master, orders Aesop to buy the very best for a dinner party. Aesop chooses nothing but tongue, which he serves in a variety of sauces, saying that "tongue is the link for civil life, the key to the sciences, the organ of truth and reason." Some time later, Xantus is expecting some disagreeable guests and asks Aesop to get the worst food possible for dinner. Once again Aesop serves only tongue, indicating that tongue or language is "the mother of all debates, the nurse of all trials and the source of all divisions and wars." The two menus substantiate the abstract concept of language and offer a delicious metaphor for the possibilities and limits of language.

Language is par excellence, the expression of culture and a cultural vehicle which forms people. In Canada, we need only think of the passion which the subject of language rouses to understand the negative aspect, and we need only read one of the great works of Canadian literature to conceive of the grandeur possible. Language and culture offer us structures by which to iterate a logical argument and to order our ideas. Ironically, these very structures arouse such emotion that we lose our ability to reason when it comes to discussing them. In grammar, the most common expressions are those which have changed and are changing the most dramatically, becoming both simplified and subject to regional variations. The less frequently employed forms of language do not change and become archaic and are eventually no longer understood and fall into oblivion. Yet, people will insist that their language is impervious to change, that they do not have an accent (everyone else does), that if others want to communicate with them, they can just learn their idiom.

There are moments of transcendent passion which are offered through artistic expression. The great poem, painting, dance, musical piece, or idea can transform our lives. The Abby of Melch is a damp, dark medieval structure on a hillside in a pastoral setting outside Vienna. In February it was both damp and miserably cold. As they doubtless did centuries ago, monks stood at tables in the library transcribing by hand the contents of leather-bound volumes. In a windowless chapel, a solitary monk played Bach by heart on the organ. Suddenly the music ceased to wash over the listener. It entered every fibre of his being, vibrating the very strings of his heart. It was no longer cold and damp. The medieval stones are timeless confederates in sharing the secret of the monk's joy, of the listener's enlightenment. Such moments of transcendent beauty and passion doubtless recompensed the monks' lives of deprivation. Such moments have the power to change lives. They are moments that educators share with students. This is why educators are fortunate and why they are more than mere dispensers of knowledge and methods. This is also why teaching is such a great challenge.

Passion is not simply the moment of discovery: the "eureka moment." It is the search for knowledge which, as Emerson said, brings great pleasure and which provides a universal motive for human existence. All human beings are conscious of their mortality and of the limits of their knowledge. All human beings have innate concepts which are larger than their experience. These factors provide the universal motivation to seek truths, the elusive truth, longevity, the fountain of youth, perfection.

All culture is not peaceful and all passion is not transcendent. There is a culture of violence and horror. Just as it may be human to seek the eternal and universal, it is also human - if we believe philosophers such as Bergson and the evidence offered daily by the newspapers - to seek the thrill of horror. Culture as a medium for expression may lend its tools to this end. Just as the modern symphony can express the jarring, clanking, and unpleasant (to some) noise of construction, science can apply its discoveries to the extinction of life. Passion may just as well be for evil ends as for good. War is caused by poor reason and is fought by passion. The passions for power or lucre are just as strong as the passion for peace. The difference lies in the application of logic. The attempt to increase power or wealth through violence is a displacement of values. Human life must logically be more important than wealth.

The problem humanity faces is that we need passion to drive us on, to spur us to new discoveries which will enable an increasing world population to survive on earth. We also need culture as a vehicle of expression and as a means to temper, to regulate our passions and to refine their expression. In the most elemental of examples, Thomas Wolfe posited that it is far better to have demolition derbies or boxing matches than massive annihilation and war: Yet, how can we encourage culture without limiting the possibilities of science and art, without creating prejudice? How can we encourage creative passion, providing freedom, while limiting the expressions of violence and horror which appear inevitably to accompany human endeavour, punctuating our history with unfortunate wars and conflicts along with the moments of great achievement and inspiration? The problem and the solution both lie in the fact that culture is born simultaneously from the concepts of beauty and fear. People need one another to produce an economy of leisure that permits the flowering of art and science which is a basic human need, as much as food and shelter. It is the need for beauty which makes people save for the future, which makes them invest in science. This means that the pursuit of knowledge is not only necessary for human happiness but for human existence.

People also need one another for protection, and they need an organization which limits freedoms to protect individuals and the group. This means that to meet our fears, we need laws, and we accept their enforcement. Every society has written and unwritten laws which are enforced by custom and by legislation.

It is frequently said that education is the key to changing the world, to creating a culture of peace. Education can simply reinforce the values of a single group, or it can contribute to changing those values. Education could focus on the common experiences, values, pains, pleasures, and words of all cultures. It should be the task of intellectuals in this world of increasing internationalization to discover these links. Since understanding and knowledge eliminate fear, translations of writings from one language to another should be fostered. Technology should be employed to unite people in a conversation which will overcome the problems of distance and geography. We need to teach the next generation that the joy of understanding and discovery is the true measure of wealth. The eighteenth-century French philosopher

Denis Diderot hoped that all philosophers would be kings and that all kings would be philosophers. Today our goal might be that all citizens would aspire to be poets. Then language would not be fossilized poetry, as Emerson said, but language would simply be poetry and thus transcendent.

The word "culture" comes from the Latin *cultura*, meaning tending, cultivating. Culture is thus not static. It is a process, and it involves education and care. The future of humankind requires the cultivation of our mental and moral gardens as well as the world's resources, which will provide the support necessary for life and living. André Malraux wrote that culture is not inherited, it is conquered. This is truly and happily an idea of the past, of an age when imperialistic nations could collect artefacts and peoples, absorbing and classifying them in museums and laboratories. It once was possible for some to declare themselves the arbiters of taste and cultural values for others. Today, we have learned that culture is not automatically inherited. It is not conquered - neither is it for sale or capable of being purchased. Culture must be pursued with passion, individually and in groups, and the joy of the pursuit can change the world.

Power is not wealth but art, literature, music, poetry, science. The closest human beings come to eternity and to universality is in the pursuit of knowledge, in the creative expressions of our deepest thoughts. Voltaire wrote that future generations would remember civilizations only for their scientific and artistic creations. Artistic and scientific creations have fostered human life and made life possible. Wei Jungshen, a Chinese electrician who spent years in jail for having composed essays arguing for democracy, declared "Writing kept me alive" (*The Courage to Stand Alone*, 1997). Similarly, a professor at Glendon College recounted that she survived the Nazi prisoner-of-war camp because of books. They provided her another world into which she could escape and live. When she died years later, she left her library to the university, so others could share the same hope, pleasure, and inspiration.

The greatest positive changes in the world have occurred as expressions of human will, not by the force of arms but by the force of words. The Berlin Wall was broken down and Apartheid was voted down by people inspired by the words of poets, prophets, politicians, friends, and neighbours. The world will never forget Martin Luther King's dream, so powerful that it transcended his death and changed a nation. Language can be passionate and can inspire passion. It is the instrument of culture. It can also transform culture. The pen is indeed mightier than the sword, having the power to transform positively while the sword can only elimi-nate, annihilate, augmenting fear which in turn will result in the reduction of liberty that is necessary for the pursuit of knowl-edge.

Perfection, truth and beauty, eternity and universality, are elusive goals. Utopia is, by its very definition, impossible. How-ever, it is this very impossibility which intrigues and inspires and makes our lives interesting and possible. The resolution of the problem of passion and culture lies in humankind's natural pro-pensity to seek the eternal qualities we can probably never pos-sess. The key to world peace and understanding, to the continua-tion of human existence on this globe, lies in accepting and sup-porting this pursuit as the central goal of society. The support of education, research, creativity, the arts and sciences must be con-sidered the most important investment humanity can make in the future.*

*Reprinted from: "The Problem of Passion and Culture," *Queen's Quar-terly,* Vol. 107, No. 1, Spring 2000. By permission of Prof. Roseanne Runte.

Reprinted from: Roseann Runte, "The Problem of Passion and Culture." *Mosaic,* 9, 3 (Fall 2007): 12-14.

43 Teaching Culture in the Foreign Language Classroom

Nelson Brooks

There is general agreement that culture should be taught in a language course, but just what this means is unclear. To rough out a definition of culture that will be immediately useful to language teachers, statements are made as to what culture is not, viz.: geography, history, folklore, sociology, literature, civilization. A list of proposals invites discussion and development of the meanings of culture leading to wide professional acceptance.

Foreword

The purpose of this paper is to define and describe culture in terms that will be meaningful to classroom teachers of foreign languages, especially in the earlier phases of instruction. No attempt is made to portray culture for the literary scholar nor for the scientist in psychology or linguistics or anthropology. In each of these disciplines the concept must be developed according to the needs and insights of those immediately concerned. Whether or not the concept presented here is fully satisfactory to those who practice these disciplines is irrelevant. We have reached a point at which foreign language teachers must themselves decide what is to be understood by and done about culture as it relates to their professional responsibilities.

There is, at the same time, no intention of showing for these adjacent fields any less respect than in the past, or anything other than appreciation and approval of their aims and accomplishments. This is especially true of literature. The ideas and proposals set forth here are offered in full confidence that the goals now being pursued in language classes will continue to result in the presence of more and better prepared students in literature courses.

In learning a foreign language the words themselves count less than what they mean. The meaning of a word is, at bottom, the segment of personal or societal life to which it refers. The in-

tent of this paper is to find ways of studying how language is
linked to the way of life of which it is so significant a part, as well
as ways of appreciating the attitudes and values of users of language that bind them so firmly to the culture in which they were
nurtured.

The Problem

Our greatest immediate problem is that we are uncertain about
what we mean by the word culture. For decades our profession
has announced its intention of teaching culture. Teachers want to
teach culture. Many have done so and continue to do so, with
results that are more or less satisfactory. There has been a cultural dimension discernible in textbook materials for a long time.
Its form has varied from the inclusion of a few footnotes to the
preparation of an entire approach entitled "cultural" and incorporating culture as a principal factor.

Yet the need remains for a definition of culture that is widely
agreed upon and is meaningful in terms of events in a language
classroom. Well-intended phrases that relate cultural studies to
the desire for peace and friendship among nations need to be
amplified with specific detail. The classroom teacher is entitled
to say: "Better international understanding is a noble aim and I
am for it. But what should I be doing at nine-fifteen on a Tuesday
morning in my language class that will help bring it about?"

It appears that a suitable concept of culture needs first of all
to be made explicit. It should then be communicated to those who
prepare materials for classroom teaching and be reflected in plans,
selections, exercises, and recommendations. It should also be
communicated to those who teach and those who are preparing
to teach so that they may know what is meant by the term culture
as they deal with language learning and with examples of literature. The concept should be set forth in such a way that it may be
grasped by students as well as teachers, first of all to understand
what it is, then to see how the insight applies to those whose language is being learned.

The needed concept of culture should be expressed in terms
that will be usable by those who teach and learn in schools as
well as in colleges. It is during the early phases of language instruction that the inclusion of culture is at once the most significant and the most baffling. As every year passes an increasing
number of students have their first encounter with another language in the schools, while colleges deal less with monolinguals
and more with the advanced phases of language study and with
literature. We are approaching a time when the teaching of the
beginning phases will, in college, be principally for those who

are already competent in a language other than their mother tongue.

Cultural anthropologists are by now reasonably clear as to what they mean by the word culture, at least in their discipline. What the word means to the humanistic scholar, however, still remains diffuse and ill-defined. While anthropologists have a deep respect for language competence and recognize in language a most important component of culture as they conceive of it, they are motivated by no strong desire to influence the teaching of foreign languages one way or another. In this their outlook differs notably from that of humanistic scholars, many of whom feel that in the academic world language studies should be illuminated by and oriented toward one field only: literature. At the same time the linguistic scientist often takes the position that whatever is said or done about language, even language learning, should bear his stamp of approval. These varying winds of doctrine and cross currents of opinion and research make heavy going for classroom teachers. They are entitled to feel that their understanding of the problem should be clearly expressed.

Need for Solution

The desire for a cultural accompaniment to language acquisition has long been felt though only vaguely understood by the great majority of language teachers. There is little need to exhort them to teach culture; their willingness is already manifest. But there is a need to help them understand what meaning they should assign to the word culture and how it can become significant and fruitful in a sequence of years of language study. There is a need for materials especially prepared for the teaching of culture and for tests that will measure the learner's progress in acquiring information and sensitivity in this area.

But it may well be asked whether the need for a more precise definition of culture is so widely justified after all. Is this really a central issue in providing students with control of a foreign language, which is, at bottom, the teacher's essential task? Is anything more than incidental encounter with and random reference to cultural matters required in establishing the language skills? Will special emphasis upon culture not be wasteful of precious class time and end by giving the student less rather than more of what he is entitled to expect from his language course? Should not the language class concern itself with language proper and postpone cultural matters until the student has greater maturity and greater language competence? There are already available many texts with a cultural ingredient in their total content: is it really necessary to do more than is already being done?

An immediate answer is that the proper time for the beginning of cultural understanding is important. Because of the large decrease in population in language classes with each succeeding year of advancement, the concept of culture can be communicated to only a relatively small number of students unless this is done in the earliest phases of their instruction. As the analysis of language in both its externalized and internalized forms is carried forward, it becomes increasingly clear that we have not taught even the beginnings of a foreign language unless we have taught what it means to those whose native language it is. The mere recording in new linguistic forms of one's native culture hardly justifies the effort involved in becoming adept at all the rules and practices of another language. But we cannot know what the new language means to the native speaker until we know in some systematic and fairly extensive way the meaning he attaches to the words and phrases he uses.

When the learner puts his newly acquired language to use he soon finds that there are overtones of meaning that are not captured by skills, grammar, or lexicon. If a student speaks to a teacher and uses forms of pronoun, verb, and possessive adjective that are in the second person singular, he will have committed a serious error that is either laughable or impertinent. But it is an error that nothing in pronunciation, grammar, or vocabulary can help him correct or avoid. Such a mistake is related not to any theory of language but to a theory of language users. This, of course, moves the problem out of linguistics as such and into culture. This amounts to saying that instruction in a foreign language, even at the start, remains inaccurate and incomplete unless it is complemented by appropriate studies in culture.

The study of culture in the foreign language classroom appears to be a matter of greater importance than we have hitherto supposed, due to the nature of language and to the circumstances encountered in learning a second language in formal education. This importance is intensified if we look closely at the full range of language as a means of communication.

In theoretical terms, we may analyze language in action into three distinct bands: syntactic, semantic, and pragmatic. By syntactic we refer to the grammar of sounds, marks, forms, and orders of words, and their relationshop to each other. It has been succinctly defined by Charles Morris as the relationship of signs to signs. The semantic area is immediately adjacent to the syntactic. Here we study how signs mean what they mean and how the modifications in the syntactic area bring about parallel modifications in meaning. This has been defined by Morris as the relation of signs to things signified. In the third area, the pragmatic, we may study the manipulation of syntax and semantics by an actual user of language. A new element is now introduced, for language at this point acquires a unique coloring and bias depending upon what the individual brings to the language act in terms of his age, status, attitude, intent, and similar factors. A spoken interview or a personal letter will tell us something about both the writer and his language that is not to be discovered by searching out in the dictionary the words he has employed or in a grammar the constructions he has used.

There are two principal ingredients in the individual's contribution to language in action. One is biological, having its origin in the genetic heritage of the speaker; the other is social, having its origin in the beliefs, habits, and practices of those with whom the individual comes in contact. These result in the cultural dimension of language, without which it remains, in an important way, wanting.

There are other less radical yet equally valid reasons for the systematic pursuit of cultural studies throughout the language course. An incessant problem in all classroom work is the involvement of the student's interest, attention, and active participation. A prime source of these motivating factors is the student's awareness of his own growth in mastering a new mode of symbolic expression. This source of motivation is especially powerful at the start of the language course, and often provides, in itself, sufficient forward thrust to keep the learner working at a productive rate for a long time. Another source of motivation, different in nature, but equally forceful, is the satisfying of an eager curiosity about what life is like in other places, in other climates, in other times. Information as to what it is like to be a member of another societal group is again precisely what is meant by systematic study of culture. A third source of motivation is the pleasure to be derived from the writings of talented authors whose works, either literary or expository, have an esthetic attractiveness and a humanistic appeal to which the young are sensitive, often to a remarkable degree, provided the manner of presentation is of the appropriate sort.

Up to Now

References that can be termed cultural are of course to be discovered in almost any activities of language teachers and in any materials printed for student use. But up to now there have not been very many serious attempts to deal with the subject of culture in language instruction at a professional level and in a systematic way.

It may be useful to classify what has been done in the follow-ing manner:

a)   Individual authorship
b)   Research projects
c)   Teacher training and retraining programs
d)   College courses
e)   Standard tests
f)   Conferences and seminars supported by professional groups and followed by the distribution of printed reports.

At the level of individual authorship we find culture included, sometimes incidentally, sometimes in a purposeful and sustained way in many language texts and reading texts. In addition, not a few books have been published with the unique intent of por-traying the culture of a given foreign country. A number of col-leges and universities have offered courses for students who are already quite competent in language and who wish to pursue stud-ies that are not exclusively literary in nature but in which litera-ture is one of many facets of the target culture that are the subject matter of the course.

A landmark in professional attention to the role of culture in language instruction was the seminar held in the summer of 1953 at the University of Michigan. This seminar was supported by the Modern Language Association and resulted from a proposal presented to the Association by Albert Marckwardt in December 1952. The subject of the seminar was: "Developing Cultural Un-derstanding through Foreign Language Study." The participants were: R.W. Brown, J.E. Englekirk, D.H. French, M.C. Johnston, V.H.W. Lange, A.H. Marckwardt, R.L. Politzer, A. Sommerfelt, and B.W. Wheeler. Present also as junior assistants were L.R. Criminale and J.A. Davies. There were daily sessions during the four weeks from 29 June to 24 July. French, German, and Spanish, in addition to English, were selected as the languages to be repre-sented. A twenty-three page summary report of discussions, find-ings and recommendations appeared in PMLA in December 1953.

The seminar was interdisciplinary, based upon the realiza-tion that only thus could the subject be properly dealt with. Most of the problems we now face were foreseen at that time and many excellent recommendations were offered. There was, however, little immediate effect of the publication of this report. For lack of funds, for lack of organizational facilities and personnel, perhaps most of all for lack of professional readiness for the problem in the terms in which it was presented, no widely based changes of significance came about as a result of this seminar.

A few years later, in the spring of 1960, the Northeast Conference on the Teaching of Foreign Languages selected as the topic for its yearly discussions and reports: "Culture in Language Learning." Several committees considered and wrote about aspects of this matter and, as is customary, their formal reports were printed and distributed widely in the area served by this conference. The views of both scientists and humanists are expressed in these reports, which are characterized by rather unsuccessful efforts to synthesize in a way useful to classroom teachers a number of points of view that differed widely in content, perspective, and basic analysis.

Under the auspices of the NDEA, a research project for the examination of cross-cultural contrasts comparing the United States with a number of European countries was launched in 1959. Though classroom pedagogy was not the immediate concern of this research, the ultimate use of its findings in the preparation of teaching materials and in the training of teachers as well as upon classroom programs was envisaged from the start.

Other research projects linking cultural studies to language instruction have also been supported by NDEA funds, notably the project under the direction of Howard Nostrand at the University of Washington.

Culture has played an important role in two other types of activity. One is the inclusion of a section on Culture and Civilization in the battery of seven tests that comprise the MLA Proficiency Tests for Teachers and Advanced Students. The other is the inclusion of culture as a major topic in the programs of the NDEA Institutes, both summer and academic year, presented on a long list of college and university campuses in each successive year beginning in 1959.

From a review of these projects, activities, and reports, two conclusions stand out in sharp clarity: there is an imperative need for a definition of culture in all its meanings. Even greater is the need for a synthesis of culture as viewed by the scientist on the one hand and by the humanist on the other into an orderly and coherent program that can be meaningful in terms of the daily happenings in language classes at the earlier stages of instruction.

Clarification of Concepts

Since a precise statement of what culture is in terms of classroom instruction will obviously be difficult, a degree of clarification may result from making some remarks about what culture is not. If they seem exaggerated, the overstatement is a consequence of the fog of confusion that now surrounds us. We shall make rough approximations knowing that they will inevitably need modification and refinement.

Culture is not the same as geography. The latter is a study of the surface of the earth, of its land and water areas, its temperature and climate, its mineral deposits and sources of power and fuel, its plant and animal life, and its characteristics that are favorable or unfavorable to human life. Though the study of geography began with the Greeks, geography itself is as old as the earth, and thus far older than the human culture which is our present concern. Geography is the stage upon which the drama of human culture is played. But the play's the thing, not the scenery. Geography can at best be no more than the material surroundings in which culture takes root, flourishes, and comes to fruition.

Culture is not the same as history. Of course everything has a history – even history – and human culture is no exception. But our reference is to the discipline of history, whose purpose is to tell the story of the past. It does this with the most careful reference to existing documents, these being almost exclusively in the form of written records. There is some recognition of monuments, building, and artifacts, but in the main history is a matter of printed and written documents. The historian establishes with the greatest care the authenticity of prime sources, then collates, sifts, selects, interprets, and evalutates in terms of a coherent and meaningful pattern. Events that occurred before there were written records are called pre-history, which incorporates, to no little extent, conjecture and deduction. In general, it is fair to say that history goes back no further than the invention of writing, an event of the fifth century B.C. Though much younger than geography, human culture is vastly older than history, for culture appears at present to go back in time the greater part of two million years.

Culture is not the same as folklore, the systematically studied customs, legends, and superstitions that are transmitted in an informal way from one generation to another by means of oral communication. Tales of heroes, songs, dances, home remedies, childhood games and pastimes all loom large in folklore. These matters are important in that they are a part of the common experience of the young and serve to establish a sentimental bond among the members of a cultural group who have shared them in early life. At times they may serve to reflect national aspirations, attitudes, and values. There is no doubt of the worth of folkways as colorful and characteristic expressions of a societal group, and they can be very useful in the understanding of primitive societies. But folklore can provide only a limited and partial view of what we mean by culture.

Culture is not the same as sociology, a discipline that dates from the early nineteenth century. Sociology is the science of human groups, viewed essentially in their collective aspects. Usually noted are the family, the patterns of social classes or strata, the economic system, the legal system, the political system, and the organization and function of religious communities. Sociology seeks to formulate the laws governing the behavior of large numbers of people, and since its inception it has been interested in the general rather than in the specific. Broad generalizations, statistical analyses, and studies of the characteristic similarities and differences in the groups that make up a composite social order are its principal concerns. Sociology is, of all the social sciences, the most closely related to cultural anthropology. Yet the distinction between the two fields continues to be more sharply noted, a fact reflected in the growing number of separations in the academic world of Sociology and Cultural Anthropology into individual departments of study.

Culture is not the same as literature. Both the creation and appreciation of literature rest upon esthetic values which have at their very core patterns of preferment and rejection that are at marked variance with the totality of experience in which culture has its roots. A literary work presents a personal perspective on the predicaments of human life, upon which is superimposed – if it really is literature – a floodlight of intent, effect, and affect that is the very essence of fine art. Some of our most incisive penetrations into the ethos of a given culture come to us through the efforts of the literary artist. Yet in the nature of things, literature can supply us with but a part – though clearly a most valuable part – of what needs to be taught under the heading of culture.

Above all, culture is not the same as civilization. The distinction between these two presents a major problem for teachers and students alike. The word civilization itself, constructed upon the Latin word for the inhabitant of a town or city, is perhaps the best starting point in establishing essential differences. Civilization deals with an advanced state of human society, in which a high level of culture, science, industry, and government has been attained. It deals mainly with cultural refinements and technological inventions that have come about as the result of living in cities and thickly populated areas. Though the effects of civilization may have spread far and wide throughout an entire society, it is fair to say that civilization develops in and emanates from those areas in which persons of diverse classes live together in large numbers, permitting advancements and improvements in all walks of life that are not possible when family groups live in relative isolation. Consider the not unusual circumstance in which two young lovers express their affection for each other over the telephone. The instrument they are using is clearly a device that could have come into being only through the development of civilization. But the attitudes and sentiments the young people express, and the language they use to express them, belong not only to civilization but to culture, for they are events and systems of another order with a very different and far longer history.

Having said with this much emphasis and detail what culture is not, it is now time to attempt to say what it is. In doing this we do not deny the proximity of all the foregoing areas to the one we shall identify as culture. Nor do we deny the important interrelation of each of them to culture as well as to each other. Indeed, our intention is not to cut off culture from these other matters but rather to focus our perspective in such a way that a foreground is clearly outlined and is sharply contrasted with the background to which it refers and relates.

The most important single criterion in distinguishing culture from geography, history, folklore, sociology, literature, and civilization is the fact that in culture we never lose sight of the individual. The geography, for example, of mountains, rivers, lakes, natural resources, rainfall, and temperature is quite impersonal and would be what it is whether people were present or not. It is only when we see human beings in this geographical picture and observe the relationship between their individual lives and these facts and circumstances of the earth's surface that our perspective becomes what we may call cultural. The census, so important in sociology, serves to count people, identify age groups, occupations, and salaries, to quantify types of dwellings and plumbing. But such information does not really become cultural until we see related to it a dark-haired sixteen-year old boy named Henry, tall for his age, who lives in one of these houses, goes to high school, and works part-time at a lunch counter, looks forward to college and a career in electronics, and who writes lyrics for the school paper.

With this criterion in mind, we come to grips with the dilemma of definition. The Humpty Dumpty approach ("When I use a word, it means just what I choose it to mean – neither more nor less") must give way to a more normal use of the verbal symbol. It is the fate of some words to have a number of meanings that are not only sharply different but at times contradictory. Such a word is culture. We find it used in reference to raising blueberries, improving one's speech, listening to string quartets, and training children in infancy. We find it used to refer to a nation's total character, thought, and action. We call cultural that which stands out as the best that people do; we also call cultural everything they do, and everything they think and believe as well. Clearly, no single word can mean all these things at once.

When dictionaries list an assortment of meanings for a given word, they assign a number to each one, then define it. We adopt this prodecure for the word culture in order to separate its various meanings and relate them to each other.

Culture – biological growth
Culture – personal refinement
Culture – literature and the fine arts
Culture – patterns for living
Culture – the sum total of a way of life

It is not necessary to say very much about the first three meanings, nor about the last one, for they are all in general use and familiar enough. It is culture, that is the least well understood, yet the most important in the early phases of language instruction. We define it as follows:

Culture refers to the individual's role in the unending kaleidoscope of life situations of every kind and the rules and models for attitude and conduct in them. By reference to these models, every human being, from infancy onward, justifies the world to himself as best he can, associates with those around him, and relates to the social order to which he is attached.

There are certain basic dimensions in the pattern of human existence that are the same everywhere for everyone and always have been ever since man became man. Culture deals with man as a human animal as well as with man as man. It must talk about cleanliness and sanitation and the personal needs of food, sleep, and shelter. It must not only answer the question: Where is the bookstore? It must also answer the question: Where is the bathroom? Obtaining food and drink, finding protection against the weather and a place to sleep, communicating with those near us, taking care of the young and the sick or injured, continuing the race, being a child to parents and a parent to children, seeking an outlet for emotional urges and expression of intellectual activities, from idle curiosity to mechanical and artistic invention – all these are the terms according to which human life is lived. They are the constants of the human predicament. Of course they relate to the variable factors of geography, history, economics, civilization, and the others we have named, but these constants are always present for every living human being to deal with no matter how the variables may change, grow stronger or weaker, disappear entirely or dominate completely.

In culture, interest is centered upon the area where social pattern and individual cónform meet and interrelate. (The proposed noun cónform comes from the verb confórm, on analogy with cónduct from condúct, cóntrast from contrást, a procedure common in English.) Many factors contribute to shaping the social pattern into what it is, and quite as many contribute to making the individual what he is. What is central in culture, is the interchange and the reciprocal effect of each upon the other. It is in these terms that we look to history, geography, sociology, linguistics, and psychology for background information that is indispensable. Yet we remember that they are but the casting and the stage setting for the drama of interaction that we call culture.

We reiterate that culture focuses upon the individual and the many social circumstances into which he must fit, upon the pattern of accommodation and the personal conform. What is important in culture is what one is "expected" to think, believe, say, do, eat, wear, pay, endure, resent, honor, laugh at, fight for, and worship, in typical life situations, some as dramatic as a wedding or a court trial or a battlefield, others as mundane as the breakfast table or the playground or the assembly line. And just as important is the extent to which that expectation is met. There can be no doubt that throughout life the force and prestige of the cultural model exert a powerful influence upon what the individual thinks and does. But important also, though in inverse ratio is the effect the individual has upon the model with which he is expected to comply. Small though this influence is, it is the principal origin of social change.

The proper adjustment of individual impulse and action to socially approved behavior is learned in great detail quite early in life, though with little awareness of recommendations to be followed, just as language, with all its complexities, is learned early in life without awareness of rules or formal instruction. Though individual human needs are constant the world over, because men everywhere are physiologically and psychologically the same, there are a thousand reasons why the patterns emerging from the interaction of personal need to group-approved behavior will differ, often very widely, from one locality to another. This is precisely what gives the study of culture its special quality and interest. It is also what makes it indispensable in the learning of another language, for a complete understanding of the new language is possible only in terms of the uniqueness of the patterns for living of those whose language it is.

While man as an animal has certain physiological needs that must be satisfied daily, man as man has certain emotional and spiritual needs that also require daily satisfaction. At all ages, man craves companionship and affection. He needs to satisfy his innate curiosity and to symbolize in various ways. He needs to give expression to the exploratory and creative urges within him. He is never wholly sufficient unto himself, but needs to share his life with others. Culture is the area of this sharing process. No individual could create culture by himself; no individual escapes having the imprint of his culture deeply pressed upon him. One of the purest examples of the results of man's association with man is language. Not to recognize language, the simple ability to communicate in words, for the amazing creative process that is is, and to denigrate it instead, is to fail to recognize the very fulcrum upon which all humanism rests.

From the point of view of language instruction, culture may upon closer inspection be resolved into two distinct and complementary areas: formal culture and deep culture. Formal culture defines the individual's relationship to the refinement in thought, action, and surroundings of culture. It defines his relationship to the wide range of esthetic expressions of culture, poetry and prose, the theatre, painting, the dance, architecture, and artistry in whatever form. It relates him to the displays of heroism and leadership in word and deed that are known to all. It relates him also to the multiple and interrelated structures of social organization, economic effort, and professional discipline, and to the outward manifestations of politics and religion of culture. The features of formal culture are easily discernible in the total pattern of the social group and are actively present in or are accessible to the awareness of the individuals who are in it.

In formal culture, the social order turns to the individual, singles him out, and focuses upon him the attention of a small group or large. He is named, orally or in print or both, and comment is made upon his new status, his personal accomplishments. Note is taken of his achievements in the past or his prospects for the future. Such events are infant baptism, birthday celebrations, confirmation ceremonies, the awarding of diplomas and degrees in school and college, the winning of prizes of many sorts, engagement and marriage, appointment and election to rank or office in professional, social, and political organizations, citations for bravery in military life, for accomplishments in civil life and the academic world, and for artistic creations – and finally funerals.

We cannot overlook the negative counterpart of the foregoing, in which the individual is singled out for censure and punishment because of flagrant disregard of what the community expects. A child is punished by being banished from the family table or by being given a place of humiliation and shame in school; an adult, by being expelled from the organization of which he is a member, by fine or imprisonment or even death if his acts are legally reprehensible. In all these instances too, the individual is pointed out, named, and brought to the attention of all concerned.

Deep culture functions in a different way. It is a slow, persistent, lifelong process that begins in infancy, and although its effectiveness is most notable in childhood it never really ceases. There is no naming of the individual, no focusing of public attention upon private behavior. Indeed, there is almost no awareness that the process is taking place. But through continued association with others the individual gradually accommodates his way of observing, speaking, eating, dressing, gesturing, thinking, believing, living, and valuing to that of those around him.

There is no reason why the facts of history and geography, the data of economics and sociology, information about and examples drawn from literature and the fine arts should not find their way into the content of language courses to the extent that they do not detract from the principal business at hand: language learning. But until such information has been related to a boy or a girl, a man or a woman with a name, a position in life described, and with a personal interest in and relation to the facts presented, we are not yet within the territory identified as culture. Whether this person is someone in real life or a character in fiction is not important. What is important is to see an individual relating to the people and the life around him. As long as we provide our students only with the facts of history or geography, economics or sociology, as long as we provide them only with a knowledge of the sophisticated structures of society such as law and medicine, or examples and appreciative comments on artistic creations such as poems, castles, or oil paintings, we have not yet provided them with an intimate view of where life's action is, where the individual and the social order come together, where self meets life.

In retrospect it may seem that our analysis is perhaps too detailed and serves only to complicate an already complex situation even further. But realism suggests that if culture is taken to mean all that is subsumed under the five different definitions, then our task is impossible and we would do better to admit it and abandon the pretense. If, however, culture is taken to mean first of all and principally definition four, with as much of definitions three and five as can reasonably be added as the learner's competence increases, then the task, though still prodigious, at least becomes manageable.

The Profile of a Culture

In 1953 two anthropologists, Edward T. Hall, Jr., and George L. Trager, issued a pre-publication edition of a work entitled The Analysis of Culture. The authors were then at the Foreign Service Institute of the Department of State in Washington, D.C. Their purpose was, as scientists, to develop an outline or map according to which any culture could be analyzed and described.

In 1959 one of the authors, Edward T. Hall, published a book entitled The Silent Language, which is an amplification of The Analysis of Culture. In its simplest form the scheme upon which their presentation is based is a list of ten focal points of critical importance in the fabric of a culture's makeup. These ten points are plotted in two dimensions, horizontal and vertical, yielding a checkerboard or grid with 100 slots or squares, each marking a salient point in cultural analysis. This list is as follows:

1. Interaction
2. Association
3. Subsistence
4. Bi-sexuality
5. Temporality
6. Territoriality
7. Learning
8. Play
9. Defense
10. Exploitation

This is indeed a fascinating list, purporting as it does to mark the principal points in the web of human existence.

Under 1. *Interaction*, we see man interacting with all that he finds in the environment that surrounds him.

Under 2. *Association*, we see him associating with his fellows in the family, in study and sports groups, in clubs and guilds, and in many other ways.

In 3. *Subsistence*, we see him gaining the requirements of living: food, dwellings, clothing.

Under 4. *Bi-sexuality*, we see the two sexes characterized according to the different things they learn, the occupations they engage in, the lives they lead as men or women, and the ways in which they relate to each other as individuals and as groups.

In 5. *Temporality*, we consider the time concept and all that this means in the passing of the hours, the cycle of days and nights, of months and seasons, and their effect upon human living.

Point 6. *Territoriality*, treats of space in terms of a room of one's own, nearness to one's neighbors, the street on which one lives, property of one's own, boundaries, frontiers, and other matters that have to do with space and our relation to it.

7. *Learning,* includes what we learn informally and unconsciously (this comprises a large part of our behavior and our thought) as well as what is learned in formal education in childhood and in later life.

8. *Play,* is concerned with games, sports, amusements, recreations, and pastimes for all ages.

9. *Defense,* deals with our means for defending that which we value and our innate responses that lead us to protect what we consider ours or that which we feel merits our action to defeat aggression.

Finally, 10. *Exploitation,* studies our control over things, our handling of tools and resources, our development in technology and engineering.

This is a stimulating analysis, and The Silent Language can be warmly recommended as useful reading for any language teacher. At the same time, we are likely to feel that this analysis has many of the limitations that characterize a great part of scientific thought in America today. There are many matters that are not brought up for consideration which may appear to those who teach the young equally important in mapping or charting the way of life of a people or a nation. Without denying the value of the ten points listed above, we may propose another list of matters that appear central and critical in the analysis of a culture. Our list is as follows:

 1. Symbolism
 2. Value
 3. Authority
 4. Order
 5. Ceremony
 6. Love
 7. Honor
 8. Humor
 9. Beauty
10. Spirit

An analysis of *Symbolism* would tell us not only about a nation's language but also about its literature and art, its myths, its politics, and its religion.

Under *Value* we would consider personal preference and rejection, conscience, morality, and philosophy.

Under *Authority* we would note whose word is accepted and

acted upon at various ages in one's life and in various situations and circumstances.

Under *Order* we would study what dispositions there are toward a clear, methodical, and harmonious arrangement of thoughts and things in the life of both individual and community.

Ceremony would focus our attention upon the almost excessive human fondness for elaborate dress and complicated ritual, for congregations great and small on occasions gay and solemn.

And what analysis of culture would be complete without discussing *Love*, whether it be the attachment of parent and child, of husband and wife, the devotion of one friend to another, or the attitude of an individual toward a supreme being? Even if we see in love no more than the reciprocal of aggression, it would appear to merit a place in our list.

Under *Honor* we would consider the high standards of personal conduct that give evidence of our attitude toward ourselves, our families, our friends, our country.

Under *Humor* we would note not only how important and popular is the sense of what is witty, comic, and laughable but also what is found to be humorous and how this varies from one age group to another and from one culture to another.

Under *Beauty* we would seek for and describe in the products of man's brain and hand that which is over and above the practical and the utilitarian, and marks a striving toward innovation and perfection, and is an indication of the esthetic sense which man is motivated to express.

Finally, under *Spirit* our attention would be turned upon the evidence of man's awareness of himself as man, the special human capacity whereby his thoughts may range in time and space far from the situation in which he finds himself, contemplating both reality and non-reality, and permitting him to pursue the eternal quest of what it is that he is.

Culture in the Classroom

How can the transition be made from these theoretical matters to the active, crowded, noisy, vital, potentially chaotic, and potentially eager reality that is the classroom?

A class session is a notable example of culture. Here the forces of formal as well as deep culture are exerted strongly upon the individual. Here he learns for the first time about many of the social models he will eventually face and what his attitude and behavior regarding them is expected to be. There is a prescribed location and décor, a typical atmosphere, a complicated pattern of rapport between peers and persons of unequal station. There is a task at hand to be accomplished together with stated and valued rewards when the pattern and the expected cónform mesh and fit.

It is a special characteristic of the foreign language classroom (when its purpose is to teach communication) that one language is superimposed upon another, producing a result not unlike a double exposure in photography. Ideally the original picture quickly fades as the second picture slowly establishes itself in clarity and detail. Of all the elements of the target culture, the most typical, unique, and challenging, yet the most easily available, is the target language. Its authentic use from the beginning is therefore a most valid cultural objective.

This recommended use of language brings us to an analysis of the classroom as a situation. We ask the usual questions: Where are we? Who is present? What is the interrelationship between one person and another? What are the special features and circumstances of the location? Upon what is attention focused? How is language used and how does it reflect the various factors in the environment? When those present address each other, are the forms used intimate or polite? If proper names are spoken (everyone has at least a half-dozen), which ones are used and by whom? If a name is preceded by a title, what title and which part of the name? What formulas of politeness appear, what requests, what directives? To all these questions neither grammar nor semantics has an answer. They are not matters of language but of language users. As such they are cultural, and rightly observed they can give a cultural dimension to every language class beginning with the first day.

In comparing and contrasting the mother culture with the target culture we may expect to find similarity in the types and range of social models that are to be adjusted to. Differences are less likely to appear in the hierarchy of models than in the details of expectation and the manner of cónform. In this we may see a deeper significance in the establishing of a cultural island in the classroom. Posters, pictures, maps, signs, and realia of many kinds are all helpful. But they remain peripheral to the main features of the situation we are concerned with. What is central is the use of language, the role being played by each of those present, where people stand or sit or how they move about, their attitudes, their gestures, whether the students speak singly or in unison, how permission to speak is asked for and granted, whether replies are memorized or created, how answers are approved of or disapproved of and corrected, what ensues when expected patterns of deportment are not conformed to. The fact that many of these details are different in the target culture gives them an interest and an appeal that easily invites attention and participation on the part of those whose mother tongue is English.

The next important concern is to see how language itself is studied and learned in the target culture, and to imitate or make appropriate adaptations of such procedures in our American classrooms. This concern has to do with the correctness of pronunciation, the rightness of grammatical forms, orthography, and semantic selections. It has to do with all the various skills, particularly of writing, with the role of literary texts in language learning, and with the analysis of language structure. It has to do with the dyadic of language, a behavior pattern which involves far more than question and answer and takes us into the mutual exchange of utterance and rejoinder, which is the commonest form of overt language behavior the world over.

The element of culture that is closest to language, though at bottom non-linguistic, is music. Alike in so many ways, there are basic differences between language and music that result in the listener's always knowing whether the person to whom he is listening is speaking or singing. The reason for this is that vocal music is based upon rigorously enforced patterns of tempo, rhythm, and pitch, all so different that if the message conforms to one it cannot conform to the other. Singing inevitably does violence to the norms of speech in length of sounds, in dynamic stress, and in pitch phonemes. Although music can be of little aid in phonology and syntax, this does not mean that it cannot be moderately helpful in semantics. But the chief value of music lies elsewhere. The non-linguistic characteristics of music are culturally valuable essentially for their originality and their uniqueness, when they are authentic to the culture in which they developed. Music is welcomed in the language class not because it teaches language but because it represents other elements of culture in a most appealing form.

The human voice and the printed line are not the only vehicles of culture available in the language classroom. The physical menace of a towering mountain, the sound of a waterfall, the three-dimensional facade of a cathedral or a castle, the interior of a powerplant or a capitol building, the taste of a sparkling wine or the odor of a perfume shop cannot be made an immediate experience of the classroom. But pictures can go a long way toward suggesting and acting as surrogate for such detalis of the target culture. Again, care must be exercised. What is selected for presentation must be authentic, typical, and important; otherwise false impressions may be created. Pictures have been widely used, and rightly so, in presenting culture. But if pictures are to be effective in culture, they must in every case relate the cultural configuration to individual participation. It is not enough to see a market display of fruits and fish and vegetables; we need to see the vendor and a client engaged in a transaction. It is not enough to see the facade of a school and some empty classrooms; we need to see a class in session and observe the posture and attitude of teacher and students. It is not enough to see a picture of a busy street scene in a large city; we need to see a closeup of a pedestrian waiting, more or less patiently, for the signal to cross. It is not enough to see a painting displayed in a museum; we would also like to see the artist in his studio working at an unfinished canvas.

Culture, especially as it is reflected in the use of language, is the dominant feature in the basic course. But as the student advances from one level of language learning to another the nature of instruction in culture changes and develops. In the second phase, culture continues to be a principal concern, but the learner now has enough language competence to appreciate comments about and discover and preceive for himself significant matters in culture. As the learner progresses in his reading, he will, if the right things have been done in the basic course, find an added dimension of cultural significance in the stories he reads, in the characters that are depicted, and in the situations that are developed. He will find cultural values reflected in what the author chooses to talk about, to have his characters say and do, to have the reader understand, infer, and react to in his presentation. In this second phase, the learner should begin to understand what is being aimed at in the cultural objective and to see how there can be both a scientific interpretation and a humanistic interpretation of cultural matters. He should begin to be made aware that he too lives in a culture and that these analyses can appropriately be made of his own way of life as well as of that of a foreign country.

In phase three there can be a systematic study of the target culture along the lines suggested in the section of this paper entitled "The profile of a culture." Literary and non-literary works can be read with both analysis and synthesis in mind, enabling the learner to interweave and interrelate the triple objectives of this phase: the perfecting of the control of language skills, an acquaintance in depth with a significant number of literary works of the highest order, and a sophistication in cultural awareness, insight, and sympathy with regard to the way of life of those whose language he is studying.

Proposals

Proposal I

That the concept of culture as herein defined be reviewed, perfected, and confirmed professionally in a representative and supportive way. That the statement of this concept then be given wide circulation so that it may be made available to teachers in service, teachers in training, authors of materials for classroom instruction, and authors of tests of progress and achievement in language courses.

Proposal II

That materials be prepared to teach students the various meanings of the word culture and how they may expect to identify it in the language they learn and the books they read – and how a better understanding of their own culture may result from this study.

Proposal III

That materials be prepared to help teachers know about, analyze, and teach culture in the foreign language in which they are giving instruction.

Proposal IV

That materials be prepared to help teachers give instruction concerning the target culture in English.

Proposal V

That materials be prepared to show how elements of the target culture are embedded in the target language itself.

Proposal VI

That teaching dialogues be prepared that are based not only upon basic matters of linguistic structure and semantics but equally upon situations that are authentic and important in the target culture.

Proposal VII

That the distinction between culture and the other meanings of culture be sharpened, and that all areas receive appropriate attention at the proper time and in a suitable way according to the gradually increasing competence of the language learner.

Proposal VIII

That culture be generally recognized as a specific goal from the early phases of language instruction onward, with all that this implies in terms of the preparation of materials, the training and retraining of teachers, classroom procedures, and measurement.

Proposal IX

That increased attention be given to the role of pictures in language instruction, recognizing that while pictures cannot teach the sounds or the structure of a language, they can often show with remarkable success what language stands for. Sharper distinctions are necessary than have been made in the past concerning the power of words to generalize and the power of pictures to particularize.*

Bibliography

[A partial listing of books and articles that deal with the problem of teaching culture or are representative of sources from which basic concepts may be derived.]

Barzini, Luigi. 1964. *The Italians*. New York: Atheneum.

Beaujour, Michel, and Jacques Ehrmann. 1967. "A Semiotic Approach to Culture." *Foreign Language Annals*, 2:152-163.

Benedick, Ruth. 1934. *Patterns of Culture*. Boston: Houghton Mifflin.

Boas, Franz. 1963. *The Mind of Primitive Man*. New York: Crowell-Collier.

Brooks, Nelson. 1966. *Culture and Language Instruction*. New York: Harcourt, Brace and World.

Brooks, Nelson. 1964. "Language and Culture." *Language and Language Learning*, pp. 82-96. New York: Harcourt, Brace and World.

Brown, R.W., et al. 1953. "Developing Cultural Understanding Through Foreign Language Study: A Report of the MLA Interdisciplinary Seminar in Language and Culture." *PMLA*, 68:1196-1218.

De Madariaga, Salvador. 1928. *Englishmen, Frenchmen, Spaniards*. London: Oxford University Press.

De Tocqueville, Alexis. 1946. *Democracy in America*. New York: Knopf; Vintage Books, 1954. (First published in 1835.)

Edgerton, M., Jr. 1965. "The Study of Languages: A Point of View." *Liberal Education*, 51,iv:1-9.

Fisher, Glen. 1956. *Philosophy and Science in Foreign Affairs: The Behavioral Science Component. A Foreign Service Institute Training Document*. Washington, D.C.: Department of State.

Fleissner, Else M., *et al.* 1964. "Four Cultures." *Selective and annotated bibliographies. PMLA*, 79,iv,part 2: 18-49.

Hall, E.T., Jr., and George L. Trager. 1953. *The Analysis of Culture*. Washington, D.C.: Pre-publication edition.

Hall, Edward T. 1959. *The Silent Language*. New York: Doubleday.

Henle, Paul, ed.1958. *Language, Thought, and Culture*. Ann Arbor: University of Michigan Press.

Hsu, Francis L.K. 1953. *Americans and Chinese: Two Ways of Life.* New York: Schuman.

Kluckhohn, Clyde. 1949. *Mirror for Man.* New York: McGraw-Hill.

Kroeber, A.L. 1953. *Anthropology Today.* Chicago: University of Chicago Press.

Kroeber, A.L. and Clyde Kluckhohn. 1952. *Culture, a Critical Review of Concepts and Definitions.* New York: Random House, Vintage V-226. (First published by Harvard University, 1952.)

Lado, Robert.1957. *Linguistics Across Cultures.* Ann Arbor: U. of Michigan Press.

Lenneberg, Eric H., ed. 1964. *New Directions in the Study of Language.* Cambridge, Mass.: M.I.T. Press.

Lévi-Strauss, Claude. 1966. *The Savage Mind.* London: Weidenfeld and Nicolson.

Linton, Ralph. 1936. *The Study of Man: An Introduction.* New York: Appleton.

Mead, Margaret. 1942. *And Keep Your Powder Dry.* New York: Morrow.

Mead, Margaret and Rhoda Métraux. 1953. *The Study of Culture at a Distance.* Chicago: University of Chicago Press.

Morris, C. 1956. *Varieties of Human Value.* Chicago. University of Chicago Press.

Murdock, George P., *et al.* 1950. *Outline of Cultural Materials.* New Haven, Conn.: Human Relations Area Files.

Northeast Conference on the Teaching of Foreign Languages. 1960. *Culture in Language Learning.* Reports of the Working Committees, 1960. G. Reginald Bishop, Jr., ed. Princeton, NJ: Princeton University Press.

Nostrand, H. L. 1967. *Background Data for the Teaching of French.* Seattle, WA: University of Washington.

Opler, M.E. 1945. "Themes as Dynamic Forces in Culture." *American Journal of Sociology,* 51:198-206.

Parsons, Talcott. 1954. *Essays in Sociological Theory: Pure and Applied.* New York: The Free Press.

Sapir, Edward. 1956. *Culture, Language and Personality.* Berkeley: University of California Press.

UNESCO. 1953. *Interrelations of Cultures: Their Contributions to International Understanding.* Paris.

Vygotsky, L. S. 1962. *Thought and Language.* Cambridge, Mass.: Michigan Institute of Technology Press.

Whorf, B.L. 1956. *Language, Thought, and Reality.* Cambridge, Mass.: Michigan Institute of Technology Press.

Wylie, Laurence. 1966. *Deux Villages.* Boston: Houghton Mifflin.

Wylie, Laurence. 1964. *Village in the Vaucluse.* New York: Harper.

Wylie, Laurence *et al.* 1961. *Six Cultures. Selective and annotated bibliographies.* New York: Modern Language Association.

Yale French Studies. 1966. *Structuralism.* Nos. Thirty-six and Thirty-seven. New Haven, CT: Yale French Studies.

*This study was supported in its preparation with MLA/ERIC funds provided by the U.S. Office of Education (NDEA, Title VI).

The article appeared in *Foreign Language Annals,* vol. 1, 3(March 1968): 204-217. It is reprinted with permission of C. Edward Scebold, Executive Director of ACTFL.

Appendix

The following is taken from:
Nelson Brooks, *Language and Language Learning: Theory and Practice.* New York: Harcourt Brace World, 1964, pp. 90-95.

Greetings, Friendly Exchange, Farewells
- How do friends meet, converse briefly, take their leave?
- What are the perennial topics of small talk?
- How are strangers introduced?

The Morphology of Personal Exchange
- How are interpersonal relationships such as differences in age, degree of intimacy, social position, and emotional tension reflected in the choice of appropriate forms of pronouns and verbs?

Levels of Speech
- In what ways are age, provenance, social status, academic achievement, degree of formality, interpersonal relations, aesthetic concern, and personality reflected in the standard or traditional speech?
- Patterns of Politeness.
- What are the commonest formulas of politeness and when should they be used?

Respect
- Apart from overt expressions of deference and discipline, what personages and what cultural themes, both past and contemporary, are characteristically held in sincere respect?

Intonation Patterns
- Apart from the selection, order, and form of words themselves, what overtones of cadence, interrogation, command, surprise, deference, and the like are born exclusively by the dynamics of pronunciation? (For example, the French *Vous vous en allez ce soir* may be pronounced in such a way that it is clearly ei-

ther a statement, a rejoinder, a question, an order, or a sentence read by a child from a book.)

Contractions and Omissions

* What words or sound are normally telescoped into contractions (for example, can't) or frequently dropped altogether (for example, the French ne) in spoken speech?

Expletives

* What words and intonation patterns are commonly used to enliven one's speech by way of commentary upon one's own feelings or actions, those of the person addressed, or the nature or behavior of other elements in the immediate situation?

Types of Error in Speech and their Importance

* What errors is the speaker of English likely to make in the new language?
* What is the relative seriousness of these errors in the new culture? (For example, in French, a mistake in the gender of a noun is deeply disturbing, but the failure to make a past participle agree, if noticed at all, is readily condoned.)

Verbal Taboos

* What common words or expressions in English have direct equivalents that are not tolerated in the new culture, and vice versa?

Written and Spoken Language

* Aside from richness of vocabulary and complexity of structure, what are the commonest areas of difference between spoken language and writing?

Numbers

* How are numbers pronounced, spelled, represented in arithmetical notation, written by hand, and formally printed in ways that are peculiar to the new culture?

Folklore

* What myths, stories, traditions, legends, customs, and beliefs are universally found among the common people?

Childhood Literature

* What lyrics, rhymes, songs, and jingles of distinct aesthetic merit are learned by all young children?

Discipline
- What are the norms of discipline in the home, in school, in public places, in the military, in pastimes, and in ceremonies?

Festivals
- What days of the calendar year are officially designated as national festivals?
- What are the central themes of these occasions and what is the manner of their celebration?

Holidays
- What is the usual thythm of work days and days off?
- What do young people do with their days off?
- Observance of Sunday.
- How does Sunday differ from weekdays with regard to what an individual does or does not do, may or may not do?

Games
- What are the most popular games that are played outdoors, indoors, by the young, by adults?

Music
- What opportunities are offered the individual for training and practice in vocal and instrumental music?

Errands
- What are typical errands that a young person is likely to be asked to do, either at home or in school?

Pets
- What animals are habitually received into the home as pets?
- What is their role in the household?

Telephone
- What phrases and procedures are conventional in the use of the telephone?
- What is the role of the private telephone in the home?
- Where are public telephones to be found and how is the service paid for?

Comradeship
- How are friendships and personal attachments likely to be formed and what provisions are made for fostering comradeship through clubs, societies, and other group organizations?

Personal Possessions
- What objects are often found decorating the bureau and walls of a young person's bedroom?
- What articles are likely to be discovered in a boy's pocket or a girl's handbag?

Keeping Warm and Cool
- What changes in clothing, heating, ventilation, food, and drink are made because of variations in temperature?

Cleanliness
- What is the relation between plumbing and personal cleanliness?
- What standards of public hygiene and sanitation are generally observed?

Cosmetics
- What are the special conditions of age, sex, activity, and situation under which make-up is permitted, encouraged, or required?

Tobacco and Smoking
- Who smokes, what, and under what circumstances? What are the prevailing attitudes toward smoking? Where are tobacco products obtained?

Medicine and Doctors
- What are the common home remedies for minor ailments?
- What is the equivalent of the American drugstore?
- How does one obtain the services of a physician?

Competitions
- In what fields of activity are prizes awarded for success in open competition?
- How important is competition in schools, in the business world, in the professions?

Appointments
- How are appointments for business and pleasure made?
- What are the usual meeting places?
- How important is punctuality?

Invitations and Dates
- What invitations are young people likely to extend and receive?

- What formalities are involved?
- What is the counterpart of "dating" in the United States?

Traffic

- How does vehicular traffic affect the pedestrian?
- What are the equivalents of traffic lights, road signs, cross-walks, safety islands, parking meters, hitchhiking?

Owning, Repairing, and Driving Cars

- Are young people interested in gasoline motors?
- Are they knowledgable about them?
- What is the role of the car in family life?
- What are the requirements for obtaining a license to drive?

Science

- How has modern science affected daily living, inner thought, conversation, reading matter?

Gadgets

- What mechanical devices are commonly found in personal use, in the home, in stores, and in travel?

Sports

- What organized and professional sports are the most popular and the most generally presented for the public?

Radio and Television Programs

- How general is the use of radio and television and what types of programs are offered, especially for young people?

Books

- What are the facts of special interest concerning the printing, punctuation, binding, selling, and popularity of books?

Other Reading Matter

- In addition to books, what types of reading matter, such as newspapers, weeklies, magazines, and reviews, are generally available and where can they be bought or consulted?

Hobbies

- In what individaul hobbies are young people likely to engage?

Learning in School

- What course of study is usual for an individual of a given age and academic orientation when compared with that of a student in similar circumstances in the United States?

Homework and Learning in the Home
- What is the importance of homework in formal education?
- What is taught at home by older members of the family?

Penmanship
- What styles of handwriting are generally taught and used?
- What kinds of writing tools are available at home, in school, in public places?
- What are the conventions concerning the writing of dates, the use of margins, the signing of names?

Letter Writing and Mailing
- How do letters customarily begin and end?
- How are envelopes addressed?
- Are there typical kinds of personal stationery?
- Where are stamps bought?
- Where are mailboxes found?

Family Meals
- What meals are usually served en famille?
- What is the special character of each meal, the food eaten, the seating arrangement, the method of serving dishes, the general conversation?

Meals away from Home
- Where does one eat when not at home?
- What are the equivalents of our lunchrooms, cafeterias, dining halls, lunch counters, wayside inns, restaurants?

Soft Drinks and Alcohol
- What types of nonalcoholic beverages are usually consumed by young people and adults?
- What is the attitude toward the use of beer, wine, and spirits?
- What alcoholic drinks are in frequent use at home and in public?

Snacks and Between-meal Eating
- Apart from the normal trio of daily meals, what pauses for eating or drinking are generally observed?
- What is the customary hour and the usual fare?

Cafés, Bars, and Restaurants

- What types of cafés, bars, and restaurants are found and how do they vary in respectability?
- Yards, Lawns, and Sidewalks.
- What are the equivalents of American back yards, front lawns, and sidewalks in residential and business areas?
- What is their importance in the activities of young people?

Parks and Playgrounds

- Where are parks and playgrounds located and with what special features or equipment are they likely to be provided?

Flowers and Gardens

- Of what interest and importance are flower shops, house plants, gardens for flowers and vegetables in town and in the country?

Movies and Theaters

- Where are moving picture houses and theaters to be found?
- What procedures are involved in securing tickets and being seated?
- What can be said of the quality and popular appeal of the entertainment?

Races, Circus, Rodeo

- What outdoor events are in vogue that correspond to our auto or horse races, circuses, and similar spectacles?

Museums, Exhibitions, and Zoos

- What types of museums, exhibitions, and animal displays are generally provided and what is their role in the education of the young and the recreation and enjoyment of adults?

Getting from Place to Place

- What facilities for travel are provided for short distances about town or from one city or part of the country to another, by bus, rail, or airplane?

Contrasts in Town and Country Life

- What are some of the notable differences in dwellings, clothing, manners, shopping facilities, public utilities, when life in town is compared with life in the country?

Vacation and Resort Areas

- What areas have special climate, scenery, or other natural features that make them attractive for vacation?

Camping and Hiking
- How popular are summer camps, camping, hiking, and cycling trips, and what organizations are especially interested in their promotion?

Savings Accounts and Thrift
- In what ways do banks or other organizations provide for the deposit of small amounts of money by individuals?
- To what extent and in what ways are young people encouraged to practice thrift?

Odd Jobs and Earning Power
- What kinds of chores and odd jobs are young people expected or permitted to do?
- If these are paid for, how is the individual reimbursed?
- To what extent are regular paying jobs made available to younger persons?

Careers
- What careers have strong appeal for the young?
- How important is parental example and advice in the choice of a career?
- What financial help is likely to be forthcoming for those who choose a career demanding long preparation?

Reprinted from: Nelson Brooks, "Teaching Culture in the Foreign Language Classroom," *Mosaic*, 7, 2 (Winter 2000): 3-17.

44 Teaching Culture in a North American Context: An Introductory Note

Anthony Mollica

In his widely-read, often-quoted article on "Teaching Culture in the Foreign Language Classroom," Nelson Brooks (1968:204) proposes a list of matters that appear central and critical in the analysis of culture. His list is as follows:

1. Symbolism
2. Value
3. Authority
4. Order
5. Ceremony
6. Love
7. Honour
8. Humour
9. Beauty
10. Spirit

> An analysis of *Symbolism*, [suggests Brooks] would tell us not only about a nation's language but also about its literature and art, its politics, and its religion. Under *Value* we would consider personal preferences and rejection, conscience, morality and philosophy. Under *Authority* we would note whose word is accepted and acted upon at various ages in one's life and in various situations and circumstances. Under *Order* we would study what dispositions there are toward a clear, methodical, and harmonious arrangement of thoughts and things in life of both individual and community. *Ceremony* would focus our attention upon the almost excessive human fondness for elaborate dress and complicated ritual, for congregations great and small on occasions gay and solemn. And what analysis of culture could be complete without *Love*, whether it be the attachment of parent and child, of husband and wife, the devotion of one friend toward another, or the attitude of an individual toward a supreme being? Even if we see in love no more than the reciprocal of aggression, it would appear to merit a place in our list. Under *Honour* we would consider the high standards of personal conduct that give evidence of our attitude toward ourselves, our families,

our friends, our country. Under *Humour* we would note not only
how important and popular is the sense of what is witty, comic and
laughable but also what is found to be humorous and how this varies from one age group to another and from one culture to another.
Under *Beauty* we would seek for and describe in the products of
man's brain and hand that which is over and above the practical
and the utilitarian, and marks a striving toward innovation and
perfection, and is an indication of the aesthetic sense which man is
motivated to express. Finally, under *Spirit* our attention would be
turned upon the evidence of man's awareness of himself as man,
the special human capacity whereby his thoughts may range in time
and space far from the situation in which he finds himself, contemplating both reality and non-reality, and permitting him to pursue
the eternal quest of what it is that he is.

For Brooks, then, *ceremony* occupies an important place in the
teaching of culture.

"Halloween," "Thanksgiving," "Valentine's Day,"
"Mother's/Father's Day" are essentially North American celebrations. So why are we trying to impose a North American cultural
tradition on a target language other than English? The reason is
quite simple. North American students attending English-speaking classes celebrate these festivities by being involved in a number of practical hands-on activities. It seems, therefore, pedagogically sound to draw from this highly motivational source with
which the English-speaking students are familiar.

To assist teachers and instructors of various languages who
may not be very familiar with these topics, a rubric in *Mosaic*,
"Teaching Culture in a North American Context", has been providing background information on a number of these "ceremo-
nial" cultural topics.

The information has been presented in both prose and dialogue format. It is obvious that information presented in dialogue
form obviously lends itself much more easily to conversation and
discussion than the more intricate narrative or descriptive prose.

The information – whether in prose or in dialogue – is meant
to be used as a springboard for further research and activities.
The section on "Halloween", for example, provides the background in prose. That same information has been used to recall –
in a humorous way – the origins and the reasons for the celebration of "Halloween." Teachers may want to involve their students
by having them act out the "interview" or even ask a group of
students to videotape it. The latter activity would enlist the participation of a larger group since it would involve "actors," "di-
rectors," "stage-hands," "producers" in the video production.
Students should be encouraged to use the target language during
the staging or production of the "interview."

This type of activity will involve not only students who are good language students but also students who – although they may not excel in the target language – feel their participation as being important in the success of the production.

As the late H. H. Stern (1983: 4) pointed out,

> In the last few years a new view of language acquisition has re-sulted partly from research on second-language learning and partly from the immersion experience. It underlines the fact that a lan-guage cannot be learned by formal practice alone. Much of it is learnt in the process of doing something else while using the language.

In essence, Stern is paraphrasing the old adage:

"Tell me and I forget.
Show me and I know.
Involve me and I learn."

Calvé (1985: 278) echoes similar sentiments when he states that

> ce n'est qu'en communiquant qu'on peut apprendre à communi-quer.

Involvement is the key idea in Stern's quotation, in the adage, and in Calvé's remark. And, if we accept the twin principle that we learn best by doing and that we speak when we want to say something or when we want to obtain information which is of interest to us, then the stimulus proposed above will fulfill these two functions.

References

Brooks, Nelson. 1968. "Teaching Culture in the Foreign Language Classroom." Foreign Language Annals, 1, 3 (March): 204-217.

Calvé, Pierre. 1985. " Les programmes de base: des principes à la réalité." *The Canadain Modern Language Review/La Revue canadienne des langues vivantes*, 42, 2 (November): 271-287.

Stern, H. H. 1983. "And Cinderella may yet go to the Ball: A personal view of the past, present and future of Core French." *Dialogue. A newsletter on the Teaching of English and French as Second Languages*. Toronto: Council of Ministers of Education, Canada. 2, 1 (November): 1-4.

45 Teaching Culture in a North American Context: Halloween Revisited

Anthony Mollica, Marjolaine Séguin, Raffaella Maiguashca and Natalia Valenzuela

Editor's Note: In Volume 1, No. 1 of *Mosaic*, we published some historical background to *Halloween*. That information is now followed by interviews with a "Witch". The three dialogues which follow, however, contain some interesting "twists":

- the French Witch threatens to turn our intrepid journalist into a rabbit!...
- the Italian witch is in North America as part of an ANSI delegation (the National Association of Italian Witches!)... and complains about the working conditions...
- the Spanish interviewer is ill-at-ease for interviewing a Witch for the first time...

Halloween

Halloween, celebrated every year on the 31st of October, is a custom which dates back more than 2000 years. The current name, which originates from the English expression *All Hallows' eve*, was not coined until much later on. In North America, Irish immigrants introduced several rituals characteristic of this holiday.

Originally, Halloween was celebrated by the Celts who were then living in Great Britain and in northern France. Traditionally, on October 31st which marked the eve of the Celtic new year, the Celts remembered Samhain, the master of Death. They believed that Samhain allowed the dead to return to earth during the ceremony; hence, the notion of ghosts on Halloween.

Marked by superstitions, Halloween has been associated with numerous mysterious rituals. In an attempt to see into the future, the evening was spent practising witchcraft around fires which were destined to scare away evil spirits. In modern times, traces of these beliefs are still noted by the presence of witches.

Pumpkins which are hollowed out, carved and lit are another reminder of this distant era. In fact, an Irish legend relates how Jack, a miser, could not go to Heaven and was even refused entry to Hell because he played tricks on the devil. As a result, Jack was condemned to roam the earth day and night with his lantern. Thus originated the expression *Jack-o'-lantern*.

The custom of going from house to house in search of candy dates back to the beginning of the Christian era. Originally, Irish peasants, in the name of Saint Columba, would call on the neighbouring houses, reminding others to bring pork and lamb meat to the evening's celebrations. Later, the poor began to beg from house to house. Nowadays, children enjoy "trick or treating" their neighbours, asking for candies.

More recently, following UNICEF's initiative, a new custom has been adopted whereby Canadian children collect money for children of under-developed countries. This has proven to be a wonderful way to help those who are less privileged than ourselves.

Over the years, accidents have unfortunately become a part of Halloween. Security projects have been launched so that certain dangers would be eliminated in the large cities. For example, children are advised to wear white or light-coloured costumes so that drivers are better able to see them at night. In addition, children are urged to wear make-up on their faces instead of wearing masks which would hinder their vision. Younger children should be accompanied by an adult and should eat only candy which is wrapped in sealed paper.

Entrevue avec une sorcière

Sorcière: C'est bien vous qui m'avez fait voyager sur mon balai magique pour que je vienne vous parler des origines de l'Halloween?

Mosaic: C'est exact, très chère sorcière Barbara Cadabra. Merci infiniment d'avoir accepté mon invitation. (Il faut être poli avec les vieilles sorcières pour qu'elles ne nous jettent pas de mauvais sort!)

Sorcière: Chut! Si vous parlez dans mon dos, je vais vous transformer en lapin.

Mosaic: Bon, revenons à nos moutons.

Sorcière: Quoi? Vous préférez devenir un mouton?

Mosaic: Pas du tout! Je disais simplement, revenons au sujet de l'Halloween. Vous en êtes bien la spécialiste, non?

Sorcière: Bien sûr! Commençons par le commencement. Le mot *Halloween* nous vient de l'expression anglaise *All Hallows Eve* qui veut dire Veille de la Toussaint.

Mosaic: Hum… Toussaint… Toussaint… Il y a le mot *saint* là-dedans, n'est-ce pas?

Sorcière: Mais oui! La Toussaint est une fête catholique en l'honneur de tous les saints.

Mosaic: Alors, si on fête l'Halloween le 31 octobre, cela veut dire qu'on fête la Toussaint le 1er novembre.

Sorcière: C'est bien ça et on fête l'Halloween depuis près de 2000 ans.

Mosaic: Oh! C'est donc bien vieux l'Halloween!

Sorcière: Attention! Du respect pour la vieillesse.

Mosaic: Pardon!

Sorcière: Comme vous disiez tout à l'heure, revenons à nos moutons! Il y a très longtemps, les Celtes qui vivaient en Grande Bretagne et dans le nord de la France célébraient la fin de leur année le 31 octobre.

Mosaic: Le jour de l'Halloween?

Sorcière: Pas tout à fait. À cette époque-là, ils célébraient Samhain, le maître de la mort. Ils croyaient que Samhain avait le pouvoir de faire revenir les morts sur   la terre cette nuit-là.

Mosaic: Vous me faites peur avec ces histoires de fantômes!

Sorcière: Hi, hi, hi! Vous comprenez maintenant pourquoi on parle encore de fantômes le soir de l'Halloween.

Mosaic: Et pourquoi alors parle-t-on aussi de sorcières à l'Halloween?

Sorcière: Voyez-vous, mes ancêtres les sorcières ont toujours essayé de prédire l'avenir et plus particulièrement le soir du 31 octobre.

Mosaic: Vous cherchez à me faire peur avec vos histoires de sorcellerie.

Sorcière: Mais non! Je veux juste vous expliquer que mes ancêtres les sorcières effrayaient les mauvais esprits en pratiquant leur magie secrète autour du feu.

Mosaic: Si vous continuez, je ne vais pas sortir de chez moi le soir du 31 octobre.

Sorcière: Tant pis! Vous ne pourrez pas admirer toutes les citrouilles illuminées de votre quartier.

Mosaic: Mais j'aime les citrouilles! Est-ce qu'elles ont une vieille histoire elles aussi?

Sorcière: Avez-vous déjà entendu parler de la légende irlandaise de Jack et sa lanterne?

Mosaic: Jack et sa lanterne... Cela me dit quelque chose.

Sorcière: Et bien voici! Ce Jack était un misérable avare qui avait joué beaucoup de mauvais tours au diable. À sa mort, il n'a pas pu aller ni au Paradis ni en Enfer.

Mosaic: Ne me dites pas qu'on l'a renvoyé sur la terre?

Sorcière: Précisément! Là, il a été obligé d'errer jour et nuit avec sa lanterne à la main.

Mosaic: Si je comprends bien, la lanterne de Jack est l'ancêtre des citrouilles illuminées qui invitent les enfants à aller sonner aux portes des maisons.

Sorcière: C'est ça! Vous savez, il y a très longtemps, les paysans irlandais allaient aussi de maison en maison.

Mosaic: Pour demander des bonbons?

Sorcière: Non, non. Ils allaient chez leurs voisins pour leur rappeler d'apporter du porc et de l'agneau à la fête d'un de leurs saints préférés appelé Saint-Columba. Par la suite, ce sont les pauvres qui se sont mis à mendier de porte en porte.

Mosaic: Alors, c'est sûrement pour cela que les enfants qui sonnent à nos portes aujourd'hui nous disent "La charité s'il vous plaît!"

Sorcière: Et oui, cette courte phrase nous rappelle les mendiants irlandais.

Mosaic: Cela explique donc aussi les petites banques que l'UNICEF distribue dans les écoles pour que les élèves d'ici ramassent de l'argent pour les enfants des pays plus pauvres.

Sorcière: Vous commencez à comprendre bien des choses.

Mosaic: Le soir de l'Halloween, je crois que j'irai faire une promenade en voiture dans les rues pour voir tous les beaux costumes. Peut-être que quelques enfants me donneront des bonbons.

Sorcière: Attention, mangez seulement ceux qui sont enveloppés!

Mosaic: N'ayez crainte, je connais les règles de sécurité pour les bonbons et pour les costumes aussi. Par exemple, il paraît qu'il est préférable de porter un costume de couleur claire et de se maquiller au lieu de porter un masque.

Sorcière: C'est la simple logique, non? De cette façon les automobilistes peuvent mieux voir les enfants dans la rue et les enfants peuvent mieux voir autour d'eux.

Mosaic: Mais vous, sorcière Barbara Cadabra, vous portez une robe, une cape et un chapeau tout noirs. Si je me promène en voiture, je ne pourrai pas bien vous voir.

Sorcière: Cela ne fait rien. Hi, hi, hi. Moi, je suis une vraie sorcière et vous, *abracadabra*, si vous ne me respectez pas, je vais vous changer en lapin.

Mosaic: Non!

Intervista con una Strega

Mosaic: Buonasera, Signora Strega!

Strega: Buonasera!

Mosaic: Innanzi tutto vorrei ringraziarla per averci concesso questa intervista. Per noi lettori di *Mosaic*, questa è un'occasione molto speciale. Non capita tutti i giorni di poter parlare a una Strega...

Strega: Anche a me non capita spesso di parlare con studenti e docenti di lingua italiana. Il piacere è tutto mio!

Mosaic: Beh, noi vorremmo farle alcune domande sulla festa di Halloween... Ormai la festa si avvicina. È alla fine di ottobre, no?

Strega: Sì, certo. Il 31 ottobre per essere esatti. Io sono arrivata qui dall'Italia con qualche giorno di anticipo... e mi sto appunto preparando per la grande serata.

Mosaic: Dall'Italia? Ma è venuta da sola?

Strega: No, faccio parte di una delegazione inviata dall'ANSI (Associazione Nazionale Streghe Italiane) per partecipare a questo Halloween 1996. Siamo in tredici a rappresentare l'Italia.

Mosaic: Ma, scusi, in Italia non si festeggia Halloween?

Strega: No, da noi non esiste questa festa! C'è una ricorrenza simile in questo periodo, il giorno dei morti, il 2 novembre... Però è molto diverso: la gente va al cimitero a visitare i morti, poi la sera c'è la tradizione di mangiare le castagne arrosto, di pregare insieme per i morti, di ricordarli... Ma noi streghe non interveniamo in queste attività.

Mosaic: Ma allora, scusi, signora Strega, Lei non conosce bene la tradizione di Halloween...

Strega: Come no, la conosco benissimo! Prima di venire qui ci hanno fatto seguire un corso intensivo di lingua e cultura inglese. E poi ci hanno fatto anche un "training" speciale per poter partecipare alle attività che si svolgeranno qui, in Nord America.

Mosaic: Ah, ho capito. Bene, allora, per cominciare vorremmo farle una domanda di tipo linguistico. Da dove viene la parola *Halloween*?

Strega: Viene dall'espressione inglese *All Hallows' Eve*. Questa tradizione è stata introdotta in Nord America dagli immigranti irlandesi ma risale a un periodo molto più antico. Infatti originariamente Halloween era un rituale celebrato dai celti, un popolo antico che viveva in Gran Bretagna e nella Francia del nord. Durante la notte del 31 ottobre, che per loro segnava la vigilia di capodanno, si credeva che le anime dei morti tornassero sulla terra. Ecco perché ci sono i fantasmi, le streghe... Capisce?

Mosaic: Sì, capisco. Però mi deve spiegare una cosa: le streghe esistevano anche in passato?

Strega: Ma certo che esistevano! Anzi, Le dirò, in passato noi streghe avevamo un ruolo molto più importante di adesso. La notte di Halloween ci riunivamo intorno al fuoco, passavamo tutta la notte a ballare, a fare incantesimi e magie... Eravamo molto potenti allora: gli spiriti maligni avevano paura di noi... (*sospiro*) Quelli sì che erano bei tempi!

Mosaic: Beh, anche oggi ci sono rimaste tracce di questi riti antichi...

Strega: Sì, è vero... Per esempio, l'abitudine di svuotare le zucche e ritagliare una faccia che assomiglia a una strega, e poi illuminarle dal di dentro con una candela o con una lampadina. Questo ricorda la leggenda inglese di *Jack-o'-lantern*, il fantasma di un uomo avaro che, dopo la morte, è stato condannato per sempre a vagare sulla terra con la sua lanterna.

Mosaic: Ah sì, questa storia me la ricordo...

Strega: Jack era un tipo molto avaro e per questo non era stato ammesso in Paradiso. Però anche all'Inferno non l'avevano accettato perché aveva fatto dei brutti scherzi al diavolo...

Mosaic: Sì, proprio così...

Strega: E poi c'è anche "Trick or treat"... I bambini mascherati vanno di casa in casa chiedendo dolci e caramelle... o minacciando di fare brutti scherzi se rimangono a mani vuote. Sono sicura che questa è la parte più divertente per loro...

Credo che piacerebbe molto ai bambini italiani!

Mosaic: Ma qual è l'origine di questa usanza?

Strega: Anche questa deriva da un antico costume irlandese. I contadini la sera andavano dai loro vicini a chiedere cibo e bevande per la festa della notte.

Mosaic: L'unica parte nuova, allora, è la raccolta dei soldi per l'UNICEF, non è vero?

Strega: Sì, questa è un'iniziativa moderna. Mi sembra molto bella perché i bambini, mentre si divertono, sanno di aiutare altri bambini meno fortunati di loro.

Mosaic: E mi dica, Signora, cosa ne pensa, Lei, dei brutti episodi che si sono verificati negli ultimi anni durante la notte di Halloween?

Strega: Penso che sia un vero peccato. Comunque, sono state proposte delle regole di sicurezza che dovrebbero diminuire il pericolo. Per esempio, i bambini più piccoli devono essere accompagnati da un adulto, i dolci devono essere controllati accuratamente, e così via. Io suggerirei anche ai bambini di truccarsi invece di mettersi una maschera.. Le maschere possono impedire di vedere chiaramente, specialmente di notte.

Mosaic: Certamente! Dunque, Signora Strega, Lei rimarrà qui in Nord America con le sue colleghe fino alla notte di Halloween. E dopo, mi dica, ha intenzione di trattenersi ancora qualche giorno?

Strega: Eh, purtroppo non possiamo assolutamente permettercelo. Per ragioni professionali dobbiamo rientrare in Italia al più presto. Abbiamo molto da fare nei prossimi due mesi...

Mosaic: Come mai?

Strega: Beh, ci sono soltanto due mesi prima di Natale, e poi arriva subito il 6 gennaio, il giorno della *Befana*... Noi streghe italiane siamo molto occupate in quel periodo.

Mosaic: Perché? Cosa succede il 6 gennaio? Chi è la Befana?

Strega: Il 6 gennaio è appunto la festa della Befana, cioè dell'Epifania. È una festa molto importante per noi streghe, e per i bambini naturalmente. Vede, la Befana è una donna vecchia e brutta, una strega insomma, che va in giro per le case, scendendo per il camino, a cavallo di una scopa, e porta i regali ai bambini...

Mosaic: Ma i regali, scusi, non li porta Babbo Natale?

Strega: Sì, certo. Però in certe parti d'Italia, a Roma per esempio, la tradizione della Befana è ancora molto sentita. La sera precedente la gente sta alzata fino a tardi, la città è tutta illuminata, c'è chiasso per le strade... E poi il 6 gennaio è un giorno festivo in Italia. Non c'è scuola. Non si lavora...

Mosaic: Ah! Beati voi! Da noi invece il 6 gennaio non è festa. Dunque, Signora Strega, vedo che Lei e le Sue colleghe siete molto occupate...

Strega: Altro che occupate! E per stipendi bassissimi, mi creda. Infatti è molto probabile che facciamo sciopero...

Mosaic: (*incredulo*) Sciopero? Ma avete un sindacato?

Strega: Eccome! Il SINSI (Sindacato Nazionale Streghe Italiane) al momento è in trattative per gli aumenti salariali...

Mosaic: Veramente?!

Strega: Eh, sì. Anche le condizioni di lavoro sono inaccettabili: orari quasi sempre notturni, il fumo e l'aria sporca dei camini, e poi queste scope così scomode... Non le dico il mal di schiena durante il volo Roma-Toronto!

Mosaic: Eh, capisco...

Strega: Alle soglie del 2000, nel boom della tecnologia, giriamo ancora con queste scope antiquate: senza cellulari... senza stereo... Insomma è una vita da cani!

Mosaic: Beh, noi le auguriamo tutto il successo professionale possibile, Signora Strega. E poi le facciamo doppi auguri: *Buon Halloween e Buona Befana!*

Strega: Grazie!

Mosaic: Grazie a Lei, Signora, per essere venuta e per averci detto tante cose interessanti. Speriamo di rivederci...

Strega: Sì, arrivederci!

Entrevista con una Bruja

Mosaic: Muchas gracias, estimada señora Bruja, por consentir en darnos esta entrevista con *Mosaic:*. Sé que está haciendo frío y entiendo que ha venido en su escoba. ¿Está tiritando? (*Preguntado con cara de preocupación.*)

Bruja: No, no, no... No tienen que preocuparse. El placer es mío. Tengo la costumbre de viajar en escoba hasta cuando nieva, no me molesta. Así me da la oportunidad de presentarles informaciones sobre la historia y las tradiciones de la fiesta de Halloween.

Mosaic: De acuerdo. Ahora quiero preguntarle... Perdóneme, señora Bruja, por mirarle así con tanta curiosidad; es que nunca he visto una verdadera bruja de tan cerca.

Bruja: (*sonrisa tímida*) Sí, entiendo... todos los mortales suelen mirarme así.

Mosaic: Me imagino que estará muy ocupada preparándose para esta gran fiesta. ¿Podría decirme por qué sólo le vemos una vez al año?

Bruja: Pues la verdad es que las brujas siempre estamos merodeando allí, lo que pasa es que recibimos una mayor publicidad en fines de octubre, hasta en día de Halloween que es el día 31.

Mosaic: Se estarán preparando las brujas por todo el mundo, ¿verdad?

Bruja: No. la fiesta de Halloween es esencialmente una tradición norteamericana, aunque nació en Europa hace más de 2000 años. Lo que se celebra todavía en España, en Italia y en Francia es el día de los muertos, el día 2 de noviembre. Pero es algo distinto. La gente suele ir a visitar a sus muertos en cementerios para recordarlos. Pero las brujas no entramos en esta costumbre.

Mosaic: Bueno, interesante saberlo. ¿Qué significa la palabra *Halloween*?

Bruja: Se originó de la expresión inglesa *All Hallows' Eve.*

Mosaic: Y ¿quiénes fueron los que iniciaron esta costumbre en Norte América?

Bruja: Fueron los inmigrantes irlandeses que introdujeron en Norte América varios rituales característicos de la fiesta. Pero al principio el día de Halloween fue celebrado por los Célticos que vivían en Gran Bretaña y en el norte de Francia.

Mosaic: ¿Qué celebraban los Célticos?

Bruja: El día 31 de octubre era el día de la noche vieja para los Célticos. Veneraban a Samhain, el patrón de la muerte. Creían que gracias a Samhain, durante la ceremonia de la noche vieja, reaparecían los muertos. De allí vino la noción de fantasmas el día de Halloween.

Mosaic: ¿Entonces nos dice que existían brujas en aquella época?

Bruja: Si, como no. El día 31 de octubre, las brujas – mis abuelas y mis bisabuelas – se reunían al rededor del fuego para tratar de ver el futuro, utilizando brujería. Se creía que el fuego asustaba a los espíritus del mal. Hoy los rastros de esta creencia se manifiestan en el surgimiento de la popularidad de brujas la noche de Halloween.

Mosaic: Pero si las brujas no hacían más que ver el futuro, ¿por qué en Norte América le tenemos tanto susto?

Bruja: Me alegra de que usted me haya hecho esta pregunta. Las brujas tenemos una mala reputación, gracias a las películas de Hollywood. Claro que existen algunas que tienen mal carácter pero no todas somos tan irritables.

Mosaic: ¿Me dices que Usted nunca ha transformado algún desgraciado en sapo por haberla molestado?

Bruja: Lo mejor hubo unas ocasiones en las cuales he tenido que enseñarles una lección a algunos granujas que me molestaban. Pero a mí no me gustan los sapos. Cuando tengo que cambiarles en algo, les cambio en murciélagos. Pero no tengo malas intenciones. Mis encantos no duran más de diez minutos. Pero dejemos de hablar de estas tonterías. No quiero asustarla.

Mosaic: Ha, ha, ha... yo no me asusto *(cara blanca de miedo)*. Bien pues entonces *(aclarandóse la garganta)* ¿Cómo se daría cuenta un turista de que el día de Halloween es una gran fiesta en Norteamérica?

Bruja: Existen decoraciones características de la fiesta. La más popular es el jack-o'-lantern que la gente exhibe en sus casas. Son calabazas vaciadas, limpiadas, talladas e iluminadas de dentro con bombillas o candelas.

Mosaic: ¿Qué tiene que ver esta costumbre con fantasmas?

Bruja: Según una leyenda irlandesa, había una vez un avaro llamado Jack. Al morir, le negaron la entrada al cielo por su avaricia; y tampoco le admitieron en el infierno por haberse burlado del diablo. Resultó que el espíritu del difunto Jack fue condenado a rodear el mundo eternamente con su linterna, sin poder jamás descansar. De allí nació la expresión *Jack-o'-lantern*.

Mosaic: ¿Qué nos puede decir acerca de la costumbre de *"Trick or treat"*?

Bruja: Esta es una costumbre para los niños. Van de casa en casa, disfrazados y pidiendo dulces. A principios de la época cristiana, los campesinos irlandeses visitaban a sus vecinos para recordarles traer carne de puerco y de cordero a las celebraciones de la noche. Después, los pobres empezaron a mendigar de casa en casa pidiendo limosna. Hoy, en Norte América, niños van vestidos de brujas, fantasmas y personajes populares, de casa en casa pidiendo caramelos.

Mosaic: ¿Ha cambiado esta tradición desde que empezó en Norte América?

Bruja: Sí. Recientemente, gracias a una iniciativa de UNICEF, la tradición adoptó una nueva costumbre. Además de caramelos, los niños piden dinero para países menos afortunados. Así los niños se divierten mientras ayudan a los que más lo necesitan.

Mosaic: ¿Nos puede ofrecer más informaciones acerca de la fiesta de Halloween que no le he preguntado?

Bruja: Sí. Háy algo muy importante que le quiero decir. Desafortunadamente, resulta que varios accidentes también forman parte de la fiesta e iniciativas de seguridad han sido presentadas para eliminar ciertos peligros. Aquí tiene unos consejos que les ayudarán a los niños a divertirse y a evitar accidentes: Niños que van disfrazados deben llevar ropa de color blanco o claro para que los motoristas les puedan ver fácilmente... En vez de llevar máscaras, es mejor que los niños se disfrazen pintándose la cara. Así, no se impide su vista, y pueden evitar situaciones peligrosas... Niños pequeños deben ser acompañados por un adulto en caso de emergencia imprevisto... Se debe comer sólo caramelos que son bien envueltos y sellados, y se debe examinar minuciosamente toda la fruta que reciben.

Mosaic: Muchísimas gracias, Señora Bruja. Le agradecemos su tiempo y sus informaciones.

Bruja: No hay de que. Espero que todos los niños pasen un día de fiesta divertidos.

Pedagogical Suggestions

The following are some suggested activities for Halloween. They are not presented in any order or difficulty. Teachers will know the linguistic background of the students and will select only those activities appropriate to the age and linguistic level of the class. The suggestions are by no means exhaustive; the teacher will undoubtedly think of others!

Follow-up Activities
Teacher-initiated Activities:

1. Identify and explain any difficult vocabulary found in the text. Use synonyms, antonyms, cognates, definitions and illustrations to do so.

2. Ask comprehension questions based on the text. Use the following key words (known in English as the five "W"s):

- *Who...?*
- *What...?*
- *Where...?*
- *When...?*
- *Why...?*

Student-initiated Activities:

1. You have been asked to prepare a poster on "Safety on Haloween." Prepare a list of suggestions you will give to children going out "trick-or-treating" on Halloween. (This will be a good review of the imperative.) For example:

   - Wear light-coloured clothing.
   - Paint your face instead of wearing a mask. (Masks often block your vision.)
   - Have an adult accompany you when "trick-or-treating."
   - Examine apples, pears and other fruit very carefully be fore eating it.
   - Eat only wrapped candies.
   - etc.
   - Illustrate the poster.

2. Ask one of your classmates to play the role of the witch. Imagine you are a reporter. Interview the "witch" and obtain from her as much information as possible on the origin of Halloween. (For an effective interview, the "witch" will have to be familiar with the historical information about Halloween provided in the above paragraphs.)

3. Interview Jack-o'-lantern. Try to find out what trick he played on the devil. Make the interview as humourous as possible.

4. You have been given a pumpkin. Draw the pumpkin on a sheet of paper. Then draw on the pumpkin a face which is happy, sad, angry or scary. Colour it accordingly.

5. Tell your classmates or write about the first time you went out "trick-or-treating" in your neighbourhood.

6. Write an imaginary story entitled, "The Haunted House." Tape the story and use spooky sounds to obtain the desired effect.

7. Some people are superstitious. What superstitions exist in your target culture? List them. What superstitions exist here in Canada? The following are some examples:

   - Walking under a ladder.
   - Black cat crossing your path.

- Breaking a mirror.
- Spilling salt.
- Friday, the 13th.
- Giving knives as gifts (if you do, you generally give a penny for good luck with the gift).

Some superstitions, symbols of good luck:

- Breaking china.
- Rabbit's foot.
- Horseshoe.
- Four-leaf clover.

8. Imagine someone has sent you one of the photographs which appears below. Describe it to your classmates.

Photo: Wanda Goodwin, *Canada Wide*   Photo: Wanda Goodwin, *Canada Wide*

9. Draw a mask you would like to wear at a Halloween party.
10. Prepare a bulletin board on "Halloween."
11. Prepare a pumpkin pie from a recipe you find in a book.
12. Have you ever read a ghost story? Have you ever heard one? Tell your classmates about it.
13. The suffix *phobia* comes from the Greek word phobos meaning fear. Find the equivalent suffix in your language and explain the fear. Here are some irrational fears some people have:

- *agoraphobia* = fear of public or open spaces.
- *claustrophobia* = a morbid fear of being in confined spaces.
- *arachnaphobia* = fear of spiders.
- *xenophobia* = fear or dislike of strangers or foreigners.

What other fears do you know? List them.

14. Do a research project and find out more about the Celts.

15. Have you ever played a trick on someone? Tell your class-mates about it. If you have never played a trick on anyone, tell about a trick someone played on the TV program, *TV Bloopers and Practical Jokes*.

Editor's Note: The Pedagogical Suggestions included in this article have been drawn from Anthony Mollica, "Teaching Culture in a North American Context: Halloween." *Mosaic*, 1, 1 (Fall 1993): 20-21.

Reprinted from: Anthony Mollica, Marjolaine Séguin, Raffaella Maiguashca and Natalia Valenzuela, "Teaching Language in a North American Context: Halloween Revisited." *Mosaic*, 4, 1 (Fall 1996): 18-22.

46 Teaching Culture in a North American Context: Thanksgiving

Anthony Mollica

Through a "time-machine" interview, we were able to reach a Pilgrim and ask him a few questions about Thanksgiving Day.

Mosaic: The tradition of a Thanksgiving festival at harvest time is an ancient custom. We know that the oldest harvest festival is that of the Succoth, the Jewish Feast of the Tabernacles. The Romans held a nine-day feast dedicated to Demeter, the goddess of agriculture. The pre-Christian Druid priests of Britain held a "harvest home" celebration, a feast after the last crops were reaped and stored for the long winter months ahead.

Pilgrim: Yes, that's true. And so did the people in Egypt, China, Japan, India and Africa. They even gave some of their best foods to their gods as part of their celebration.

Mosaic: Our modern-day Thanksgiving, however, originated with you, the Pilgrims.

Pilgrim: Yes, the first American Thanksgiving was celebrated in 1621 at the Plymouth Colony in Massachusetts.

Mosaic: Who initiated the custom of this celebration?

Pilgrim: It was William Bradford's idea. Mr. Bradford was the Governor of our colony at that time.

Mosaic: What was the reason for this celebration?

Pilgrim: Governor Bradford ordered a day of Thanksgiving for surviving the very hard times the new settlers had gone through.

Mosaic: To what hard times are you referring?

Pilgrim: Less than a year before, we had landed on the shores far from our native England. During the first winter, half of the group died. For a time it looked as if no one would survive.

Mosaic: You led a somewhat comfortable life in England. What reasons led you to leave that country?

Pilgrim: It was mostly for religious reasons.

Mosaic: Kindly explain.

Pilgrim: As you know, at that time, the Church of England stood between Catholic and Protestant religions. The Anglican services were filled with ritual. We were told what to believe.

Mosaic: And you opposed the Church's views?

Pilgrim: We wanted to study the Bible and decide for ourselves what to believe. Some people made fun of us for wanting to "purify the church" and they nicknamed us "Puritans." Many of us still went to the Church of England, but also met se-. cretly in homes to study the Bible and listen to sermons. Some of us were prepared to leave the Church right away.

Mosaic: What did you do?

Pilgrim: Some with enough courage did break away. One such group had been meeting in William Brewster's home in the village of Scrooby. When eventually we did separate from the Church, life became harder and harder for us.

Mosaic: What steps did you take to alleviate your hardships?

Pilgrim: In 1607 we decided to move to Holland, where we could worship as we pleased. But leaving England was a real problem.

Mosaic: Why a problem?

Pilgrim: England would not issue passports to "traitors", and the voyage would be expensive. No one, except William Brewster, had much money. In spite of such obstacles, by 1608 about 125 of us had reached Holland.

Mosaic: Why Holland?

Pilgrim: The Dutch were tolerant, peace-loving and kind. In Holland we could worship as we pleased.

Mosaic: Where did you first settle?

Pilgrim: We first settled in Amsterdam, but then moved to Leyden, a centre for the spinning and weaving of woollen cloth. We managed to make a living and support our new church. But after more than ten years of this life, we became restless.

Mosaic: Why the restlessness?

Pilgrim: In England most of us had been farmers. In Holland, farmland was scarce and expensive. What's more, our children were forgetting the English language and the English ways. Some of our children were even losing respect for the Sabbath. And at this time, a war was also brewing between the Dutch and the Spanish.

Mosaic: And so you decided to leave Holland for the New World?

Pilgrim: Precisely. In September 1620, we set sail on the *Mayflower*, and after almost three months at sea we spotted land. We landed at last on the rock-bound shores of a strange and lonely coast and named the land New England. I still recall that cold December day very vividly.

Mosaic: Life must have been very difficult in the New World.

Pilgrim: Yes. During the first winter, many of my friends died. But in spite of the hardships, we survived as a colony and our gratitude led us to hold a time of Thanksgiving.

Mosaic: Who was invited to this first celebration?

Pilgrim: All the colonists and the native Americans who lived nearby shared this great feast.

Mosaic: What had the native Americans done for you?

Pilgrim: They had helped us to survive, showing us new and wonderful foods so we wouldn't starve. They even taught us to gather cranberries, to plant corn, to hunt wild turkeys, and to dig for clams. Of particular help was Chief Massassoit and his tribe.

Mosaic: Was he invited to the celebration?

Pilgrim: Of course! He came with ninety of his fellow tribesmen. It was a larger crowd than we had expected but we welcomed them. Four of our marksmen had been sent out to hunt game for the occasion and they had returned laden with wild turkeys, quail and other game. Chief Massasoit had sent his best hunters into the forest and they had shot five deer. We had plenty of food for everyone.

Mosaic: Did this Thanksgiving immediately become a yearly celebration as we know of it today?

Pilgrim: No, it took many years for Thanksgiving Day in America to become the permanent and regularly observed holiday we know today. In 1789, President George Washington issued a proclamation urging Americans to celebrate Thanksgiving. But, it was Sara Josepha Hale who is credited with the establishment of this national holiday.

Mosaic: What did Mrs. Hale do?

Pilgrim: She wrote thousands of letters to those who, she felt, would be of help to her cause. She wrote to governors of states urging them to make Thanksgiving an annual holiday in their states. She even wrote to President Abraham Lincoln, sending him a copy of President Washington's original declaration. As a result of this campaign, Mrs. Hale was granted an interview with President Lincoln in 1863. The President subsequently declared the last Thursday in November an annual, Thanksgiving Day.

Mosaic: Was this date widely accepted?

Pilgrim: The custom since 1863 has been for the President to issue a proclamation setting the day of Thanksgiving. The date was set for the fourth Thursday in November. Some of the New England States had opted to celebrate it the last Thursday in November (whenever November had five Thursdays). It was 1941 when a joint resolution of Congress proclaimed that after the year 1941, the last Thursday of November would be set aside to celebrate Thanksgiving.

Mosaic: The situation is different in Canada, isn't it?

Pilgrim: You're right. In Canada the first Thanksgiving was celebrated by the city of Halifax in 1763. Its citizens wanted to express their gratitude for the Treaty of Paris whereby France yielded Canada to Great Britain. On October 9, 1879, the Canadian Government proclaimed the first Thanksgiving as we know it to-day. Canadians celebrated it for the first time on November 6, 1879.

Mosaic: As you well know, our Canadian Thanksgiving falls in October. What is the explanation?

Pilgrim: Following World War I, Thanksgiving and Armistice Day were both celebrated on the same day. In 1931, "Armistice Day" was changed into "Remembrance Day" and so it was decided to celebrate Thanksgiving in October to avoid two major holidays in the same month.

Mosaic: And so Canadians celebrate Thanksgiving in October?

Pilgrim: As of 1953, Thanksgiving is celebrated the second Monday in October.

Mosaic: How do the United States and Canada celebrate Thanksgiving?

Pilgrim: Canadians celebrate it the same way as Americans. There is a dinner to which family and friends are invited. But we in the United States hold parades, and watch football games.

Mosaic: Thank you. You've been very helpful with your information on Thanksgiving.

Pedagogical Suggestions

1. Illustrate all the key words from the text either by bringing into class illustrations or by drawing them yourself.
2. Write a short paragraph about what Thanksgiving means to you.

3. Research and speak briefly on the following:

   (a) President George Washington

   (b) President Abraham Lincoln

   (c) Sara Josepha Hale.

4. **Mosaic** was able to record a soliloquy by a turkey... Create a similar monologue from the point of view of

   (a) a Pilgrim

   (b) a native American.

Le soliloque du dindon

Être ou ne pas être rôti:
voilà la question!
Depuis 1621,
mes ancêtres et toute ma famille tremblons
dès qu'approche l'automne...
glou... glou, glou... glou,
«Et pourquoi donc?»
À cause du massacre
de l'Action de grâce,
qui se célèbre
le deuxième lundi d'octobre au Canada,
et le dernier jeudi de novembre aux États-Unis.
Lors de la première célébration
de la fête de l'Action de grâce,
nos ancêtres sauvages
ont été décimés
par les Indiens;
mais depuis l'arrivée des Pèlerins,
on nous élève pour nous sacrifier
en ce jour funeste.
Dès l'heure de notre naissance,
glou... glou...
nous connaissons notre sort
tragique,
notre destin fatal
et l'heure exacte de notre
exécution...
La guillotine, malheureusement,
nous attend.
On nous coupe la tête.
On nous plume.
On nous congèle.

Quelle coutume barbare!
Avant de nous manger,
ces inexorables êtres humains
nous farcissent
et trempent notre chair
dans la sauce de canneberges.
Puis, ils se gavent
à s'en rendre malades.
Quelle honte!
Quel scandale!
Quelle horreur!
Mais pourquoi toujours nous?
Pourquoi pas les canards?
Ou même les sales vautours?
glou... glou...
Quand je pense que nous sommes
d'innocents végétariens...
Quel outrage!
je suis bien d'accord...
Il faut remercier Dieu
pour toutes les bénédictions
reçues pendant l'année
et pour la bonne récolte...
mais pourquoi ne pas fêter
cet événement
le 32 octobre?

Reprinted from: Anthony Mollica, "Teaching Culture in a North American Context: Thanksgiving." *Mosaic*, 2, 1 (Fall 1994): 21-22.

47 Teaching Culture in a North American Context: Hannukka

Louise Lewin and Perla Riesenbach

The Story of Hannukka

About 2100 years ago, the land of Israel, then called Judea, was ruled by the Greeks. Their king, Antiochus, tried to force the Jews in his kingdom to worship his people's Greek gods. It was forbidden to practise the Jewish religion. Those who were caught were killed. Antiochus had a powerful army who punished those who disobeyed his orders.

A spiritual leader named Mattatias, together with his five sons and other brave Jews, formed a small army to fight for their rights and freedom to practise the Jewish religion. The Jewish people were ready to risk their lives rather than give up the right to worship their God.

Upon Mattatias' death, his son Judah became the leader of the revolt. The Jews continued the battle against Antiochus and his army. Judah is considered the hero of Hannukka because his blows were hard and strong like those of a hammer. This is the reason he was given the name Judah Maccabbee. (Maccabbee means hammer in Hebrew.)

After many battles, the Jews were finally victorious. After their victory, Judah and his army returned to the Temple in Jerusalem. The Jews had to clean and purify the Temple. They had to remove the statues of Greek gods that Antiochus had placed there. Only then was the Temple restored to its former beauty.

It was the 25th day of the Hebrew month of Kislev when the Jews were finally able to pray in their Temple. They needed some oil to light the Menorah to start their prayers. They found a small amount of oil which appeared to be enough for only one day. To their amazement, this small amount of oil continued to burn for eight days. This is considered a miracle of Hannukka.

The Jews were grateful for several reasons. With a small army, they defeated Antiochus' powerful army. They recaptured their

Temple and they regained their freedom to worship their God. For these reasons, Hannukka is considered a celebration of liberty and heroism.

To commemorate the miracle of the oil which lasted eight days, every year the Jews light candles during the eight days of Hannukka. This is the reason Hannukka is referred to as the Festival of Lights.

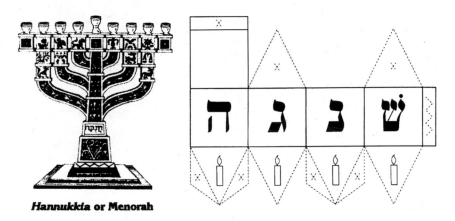

Hannukkia or Menorah

The Celebration of Hannukka

Hannukka is celebrated every year for eight days according to the date on the Jewish calendar (25 Kislev to 2 Tevet). This usually corresponds to a date in late November or December. This year, 1994, Hannukka will begin on November 28. The hannukka candles are placed in a special type of candelabra called Hannukkia in Hebrew. This Hannukkia is more commonly referred to as a Menorah. It has nine candle holders. The first candle is lit on the eve of the first day. The candle-lighting takes place every night after dark, except on Friday night. A servant-candle, (called *shamash* in Hebrew), always placed higher than the others is used to light the other candles. The first night, the *shamash* lights one candle; the second night, the *shamash* lights two candles and so on until the eighth night when the *shamash* and all the eight candles are lit. The lit Hannukka candles are meant to be placed in the window or other spots where they may be seen by others, who will be reminded of the tale they tell.

Hannukka is very much a celebration that involves the children. They play with a special spinning top called *dreidel* which has four sides. Each side has a Hebrew letter on it: Nun, Gimel, Heh, Shin. The Hebrew letters stand for the words: "A great miracle happened there". ("There" refers to Israel.). The children play with raisins, pennies, toothpicks or any other collection of small items. The children take turns spinning the Dreidel and usually play by the following rules:

- if the *dreidel* falls on Nun, the player gets nothing.
- if the *dreidel* falls on Gimmel, the player takes the whole pot.
- if the *dreidel* falls on Hay, the player takes half the pot.
- if the *dreidel* falls on Shin, the player puts in one.

Food

No celebration is complete without food, and Hannukka is no exception. As "oil" is the important symbol of Hannukka, the foods that are eaten have been fried in oil. A very popular dish is potato pancakes, *latkes*, in Yiddish. (See recipe below). The pancakes are eaten with sour cream and apple sauce. The other traditional dish is jelly doughnuts, which have also been fried in oil, thus continuing the theme of oil.

Gifts

The children traditionally receive a small sum of money at this time. The Yiddish term for this is "Hannukka gelt". Little packs of chocolate coins are also popular at this time. These days, in many families, the children receive gifts for Hannukka.

Hannukka is a time for celebration. Parties with families and friends are held throughout the holiday. Hannukka can easily be incorporated into a language class activity at this festive time.

Suggestions for Activities

1. Draw a Hannukkia.
   Place the left hand on the left side and trace along the four fingers. Repeat with the right hand. To obtain flame, the students can draw and colour each flame.
2. Make a *dreidel*.
   Cut along the dots. Fold along the lines and glue where marked X. See illustration below.
3. Draw and send a postcard to a Jewish friend. The card can have the drawing of a Hannukkia or a dreidel on the front. The message can be as simple as "Happy Hannukka".
4. Riddles
   I am small. I produce flames. I can be lit. What am I?
   I was found in the Temple. I burned for eight days. What am I?
   The children play with me during Hannukka. I can turn. What am I?
   I am delicious. I am served with apple sauce. What am I?

5. The following is a recipe for latkes that can easily be made at school. Note that since hot oil is required to make this recipe, the students should be closely supervised.

Ingredients:

2 large potatoes

half of an onion

1 (beaten) egg

1/2 teaspoon of salt

half cup of flour

oil (enough to coat the pan)

apple sauce and/or sour cream

Method:

Peel and grate the potatoes. Peel and grate the onion. Stir the beaten egg and salt. Add the flour, a bit at a time, mixing well. Coat the pan with the oil and heat it until it sizzles. Pour the mixture into the pan. Brown one side, then the other. Serve with apple sauce and/or sour cream and enjoy!

6. For intermediate and senior levels.

Hannukka falls at a time of year when values and feelings such as hope, charity and friendship surround our everyday life. It is a good opportunity to share during Hannukka the values that are attached to this Jewish holiday, but more importantly to relate these values to other religions, faiths, and cultures. The following suggestions for group activities attempt to do so.

Hope:

Terry Fox and Rick Hansen are Canadian heroes today because they did not lose hope. In small groups, students can talk about these heroes and can think of other people that they consider as heroes. They can tell each other the stories of these people who did not lose hope.

Charity:

It is important to give. One can give many things such as clothing, money, food, and time. In small groups, students can list what can be given, what organizations, organized charities (UNICEF, etc.) are available. Given the time allotted for such activities, in a secondary school class small groups can organize, with the help of their teacher, a charity project in their class and/or in their school.

Friendship:

Many questions need to be answered when it comes to friendship. How can one make friends? What are the characteristics of a good friend? Of a best friend? How does it feel when one is rejected by a group? Students can share their experiences with this complex relationship.

Peace:

After discussing the meaning of the concept of peace, students can find the word peace in as many languages as possible.

Tradition:

There are many traditions associated with Hannukka. Every person has traditions, whether it be a family, religious, or food tradition. The students can share:

a. One of their traditions.
b. A recipe that represents their own culture. (*Latkes* is the one which is related to Hannukka).
c. The class can compile the recipes brought by each student and publish a multicultural recipe book.

Reprinted from: Louise Lewin and Perla Riesenbach, "Teaching Culture in a North American Context: Hannukka." *Mosaic,* 1, 2 (Winter 1993): 20-21.

48 Teaching Culture in a North American Context: The Chinese New Year

Cheng Luo

Introduction

One of the most significant developments in second language (SL) learning in recent years has been the recognition of the close relationship between language and culture. Among the questions that are often asked by teachers regarding the teaching of culture are: *what* to teach and *how* to teach it. The answer, especially to the first question, depends, among other things, upon how we define *culture*. According to Brooks (1982: 20-21), culture may be defined as the *best* of everything in human life, e.g. the observable Culture MLA (music, letters, and arts); or as *everything* in human life, that is, the nonobservable Culture BBV (belief, behaviour and values). While neither perspective is sufficient for giving a full definition of culture, many SL teachers seem to emphasize MLA more than BBV. If this is indeed the case, then it appears that a more balanced approach is needed in teaching culture, such that both MLA and BBV receive due attention in the SL teaching/learning process.

This article addresses the above issue by looking at a particular cultural event: the Chinese New Year. The reason for selecting this event is twofold:

* major cultural festivals like the Chinese New Year encompass both MLA and BBV;
* some festivals manifest the close relationship between language and culture.

In addition, ethnographic description on the Chinese New Year and how people celebrate it will be provided, both for information purposes and as the basis of suggested language and cultural activities for the Chinese as a second language class.

The Chinese New Year

Of all the Chinese festivals, the Chinese New Year, also known as the Spring Festival, is the most important and most celebrated. It is the first day of the year according to the Chinese lunar calendar, which works somewhat differently from the Christian Gregorian (solar) calendar. Because of this, the exact date of the Chinese New Year varies from year to year: somewhere between January 15 and February 20 on the solar calendar. For 1995, it falls on January 31.

Origin

The Chinese have celebrated their New Year for about 5,000 years. The traditional term for the event is 過年 *Guo Nian*, literally "to get over Nian". According to an ancient Chinese legend, *Nian* was a fierce animal that came out to devour people on the last night of the year. Once *Nian* went to a village where someone was cracking a whip. At the sound, *Nian* ran away. When it got to the next village, *Nian* saw some red clothes that had been hung out to dry. Again, it was scared away. At the third village, the sight of a fire once again kept *Nian* from the villagers. Now that people knew what *Nian* was afraid of, they set off firecrackers, put up red spring couplets on doors (see Suggested Activities, section 4), and hung out lanterns on the same night every year, in order to "get over Nian". This practice, together with the people's ever-renewing wish for a better life in the new year, formed the tradition of Chinese New Year celebrations.

The Chinese Zodiac

Celebration of a particular New Year is based on a 12-year cycle on the Chinese zodiac, with each year named after an animal that represents an Earthly Branch. 1995 marks the year of the Pig. The animal ruling the year of one's birth becomes that person's animal sign and is believed to influence his or her character and destiny. For example, those born in the year of the Pig (1947, 1959, 1971, 1983, 1995) are said to be honest and brave. Traditionally, decisions about marriage, friendship, business, etc. are made according to the guidelines of one's animal sign. The Appendix shows a horoscope of the Chinese Zodiac. Beginning with the Mouse, the cycle reads counter-clockwise.

Stories about the zodiac animals abound. According to one, the Heavenly Jade Emperor once invited twelve earthly animals to his palace the next day to become zodiac animals. Among the invited was the Cat, who at the time was a good friend of the Mouse. Early the next morning, the Mouse, who had not been invited, went with the other animals without waking up the Cat. Just before they entered the Heavenly Gate, the Mouse jumped onto the horn of the Ox, who happened to lead the team, and was the first to be seen and appointed by the Jade Emperor. By the time the Cat woke up and hurried to the Heavenly Palace, all the zodiac animals had already been named. Furious, the Cat vowed to revenge itself on the Mouse who has since been its arch enemy.

Preparations

Household preparations for the New Year start about one week before the New Year. These include house cleaning, festival shopping, making new clothes, window decoration (with paper cuttings), hanging New Year pictures, writing spring scrolls, and preparing festival food, including *jiaozi* and New Year cakes. It is a common practice to put on the door an upside down character (*fu* "福 happiness"), because "upside down" (倒 *dao*) in Chinese sounds the same as the word for "arrive" (到 *dao*). The intention is to elicit 福倒了 *Fu dao le* "The *happiness* is upside down", which is interpreted as "Happiness has arrived."

New Year's Eve

The New Year's Eve is the time for all the family members, including those away from home, to come together to share a sumptuous feast, to drink a toast to each other's happiness, to give out "lucky money" in red envelopes to children and to stay up throughout the night chatting, playing games or watching special TV programs. When the clock strikes midnight, a new round of firecrackers is set off, people bid farewell to the old year, cheer the coming of the new, and eat 餃子 *jiaozi*, a kind of stuffed dumplings whose pronunciation comes from the phrase 交子 *jiao zi* "reach midnight", and which symbolizes smooth transition into the new year.

New Year's Day

On New Year's Day, people put on new clothes, offer ritual homage and thanksgiving to their ancestors and gods, pay respects to senior members of the family, wish each other good luck, and exchange gifts. Then they go out to bring New Year greetings to their friends and relatives. Favoured greetings include 恭喜發財 *Gongxi facai* "Wish you great fortune" and 新年好 *Xin nian hao* "Happy New Year". The New Year feast, which is shared with visiting relatives and friends, is as sumptuous as the New Year's Eve feast, and must include a course of whole fish to symbolize a surplus year to come, because, again, "fish" (魚 *yu*) sounds like "surplus" (餘 *yu*).

Throughout the festival, the crackling of firecrackers continues, and dragon and lion dances are performed on the streets. In some areas, the festivities last about two weeks till the Lantern Festival.

Suggested Activities

1. Stories

Stories about the Chinese New Year, such as "Guo Nian" and "How the Mouse became a zodiac animal", may be told to the students, who may then roleplay the story. Advanced students may, under the teacher's guidance, write down their own version of the story in the form of a short play and then act it out.

2. The Lunar Calendar

A Chinese lunar year consists of 12 months, five of which have 29 days and seven have 30 days. There is a leap year about every three years which contains an extra month. 1995 happens to be a leap year with an extra August. Students may compare the different ways the Chinese lunar calendar and the western solar calendar work and, in small groups, work out the corresponding dates of the Chinese New Year on the solar calendar for the next two or three years.

3. The Chinese Zodiac

Using the horoscope (see Appendix), students may work in groups to find out each other's animal sign, alleged character and destiny, as well as the do's and don'ts for individual students according to the Chinese zodiac. It should be pointed out to the students, however, that the alleged do's and don'ts, as well as the characterization, are merely cultural beliefs and do not have to be taken literally. In addition, students may also discuss and compare animal images in Chinese and other cultures.

4. Spring Couplets

These are the poetic couplets written vertically on red scrolls in strictly symmetrical forms,   with a short phrase written horizontally as a conclusion. The content expresses such themes as thanksgiving, prosperity, newness, goodwill and social or natural harmony. These couplets are a good source of folk literature that may be appreciated by advanced students through guided analysis of sample couplets such as:

The right scroll:

五	谷	豐登 辭	舊	歲
wu	gu	feng-deng ci	jiu	sui
five	crop	abound	farewell-to	old	year

"Farewell to the old year in bumper harvest of the five crops."
The left scroll:

六畜　　興 旺 迎　　新　春
liu xu　　xing-wang ying　　xin　chun
six animal　　thrive　　welcome new spring

"Welcome in the new spring with thriving prospect of the six animals."
The horizontal scroll:

年　　年　　有　　餘
nian　nian　you　yu
year　year　have　surplus

"(There's) surplus year after year."

5. Colours

Colours have culture-specific symbolic meanings. For example, *red* in Chinese symbolizes happiness, luck or success, and is the favoured colour for festivals, weddings, opening ceremonies, etc. Students may discuss the symbolic meanings of different colours in Chinese and compare them to those of other cultures they are familiar with. The following is a short list of common colour terms and their symbolic meaning in Chinese (Luo 1992). Other colour-meaning correspondences can be elicited from the students.

Colour	*Meaning*	*Example*	
red	happiness	wedding dress	紅運
	luck	*"red luck"*	
yellow	noble	royal colour	
white	purity	"innocent"	清白
	sadness	funeral dress	
green	life		
black	wickedness	"black gang"	黑幫

6. Linguistic Preferisms

These are socio-psychologically favoured expressions, especially at festival times, for example:

- 恭喜發財　Gongxi fa cai "Wish you great fortune"
- 萬事如意　Wan shi ruyi "Everything as you wish", 福到了 *Fu dao le* "Happiness has arrived", and
- 年年有餘　*Nian nian you yu* "Surplus year after year."

Also to be noted is the number "eight" (八, *ba*), which rhymes with the word for "(fortune) expansion" (發 *fa*) and therefore gains popularity among Chinese. These and other similar expressions tell about cultural beliefs and values of the Chinese, and should be made known to the students, who can then use them, first in simulated, and then in real, communicative situations.

7. Window Decoration

The traditional art of paper cutting is most popularly used in New Year window decoration. Students may learn to paper cut simple patterns from demonstrations by invited folk artists or by following instructions in relevant books.

8. Making *jiaozi*

There is no festival without food. A popular food for the New Year is *jiaozi*, whose symbolic meaning is explained under New Year's Eve, above. The teacher may give a demo on how to make *jiaozi* and ask the students to make some on their own. Where feasible, tasting of other New Year food such as the New Year cake and spring rolls will also enrich students' cultural experience.

Conclusion

The major themes of the Chinese New Year include thanksgiving, wish for prosperity, newness, and social cohesiveness (kinship, friendship, etc.), which reflect the cultural belief, behaviour, and values (BBV) of the Chinese. On the other hand, music, letters and arts (MLA) are reflected in such festival elements as dragon or lion dances, spring couplets, and paper cut window decoration. Such a balance provides not only rich input of cultural content (i.e. what to teach) for the language classroom, but also an appropriate source for enriched language learning activities (i.e. how to teach).

Appendix
Horoscope of the Chinese Zodiac

The Chinese Zodiac consists of a 12-year cycle, with each year named after a different animal that distinctly characterizes its year. Many Chinese believe that the year of a person's birth is the primary factor determining that person's personality throughout his lifetime. To learn about your Animal Sign, find the year of your birth in the sequence below.

Mouse/Rat

1936, 1948, 1960, 1972, 1984, 1996.

You are ambitious yet honest. You like to invent things and are a good artist. Prone to spend freely. Most compatible with Dragons and Monkeys; least compatible with Horses.

Ox

1937, 1949, 1961, 1973, 1985, 1997.

You are dependable, patient, and bright, with strong ideas to inspire others. You can be happy by yourself, yet make an outstanding parent. Marry a Snake or a Rooster. The Sheep will bring trouble.

Tiger

1938, 1950, 1962, 1974, 1986, 1998.

You are aggressive, courageous, candid, and sensitive. People respect you for your deep thoughts and courageous actions. Look to the Horse and Dog for happiness. Beware of the Monkey.

Rabbit

1939, 1951, 1963, 1975, 1987, 1999.

Luckiest of all signs, you are talented, good-natured and articulate. Affectionate yet shy, you seek peace throughout your life. Marry a Sheep or Pig. Your opponent is the Rooster.

Dragon

1940, 1952, 1964, 1976, 1988, 2000.

Healthy, energetic, and passionate, you make a good friend because you listen to others carefully. Your life is complex. Marry a Monkey or Rabbit late in life. Avoid the Dog.

Snake

1941, 1953, 1965, 1977, 1989, 2001.

You are wise and a passionate lover of good books, food, music and plays. Though lucky with money, you are vain and high tempered. The Rooster or the Ox is your best sign.

Horse

1942, 1954, 1966, 1978, 1990, 2002.

You are hard-working, cheerful, popular and attractive to the opposite sex. Yet you are often ostentatious and impatient. You need people. Marry a Tiger or a Dog early, but never a Mouse.

Sheep

1943, 1955,1967, 1979, 1991, 2003.

Elegant, inquisitive, and creative, you have good taste and make a good artist. Yet you are timid and prefer anonymity. You are most compatible with the Pig and the Rabbit, but never the Ox.

Monkey

1944, 1956, 1968, 1980, 1992, 2004.

An enthusiastic achiever, you are intelligent, funny and good at solving problems. But you are easily discouraged and confused. Avoid Tigers. Seek a Dragon or a Mouse.

Rooster

1945, 1957, 1969, 1981, 1993, 2005.

A pioneer in spirit, you are talented, hard-working, and a deep thinker in questing after knowledge. You are selfish and eccentric. Rabbits are trouble.

Dog

1946, 1958, 1970, 1982, 1994, 2006.

Loyal, honest and a good secret-keeper, you work well with others. You are generous yet stubborn, and sometimes selfish. Look to the

Horse or Tiger. Watch out for Dragons.

Pig

1947, 1959, 1971, 1983, 1995, 2007.

Noble, chivalrous and honest, you make a good student for always finishing projects or assignments. Your friends will be lifelong, yet you are prone to marital strife. Avoid other Pigs. Marry a Rabbit or a Sheep.

References

Brooks, N. 1982. "The analysis of foreign and familiar cultures," in R.C. Lafayette, H.B. Altman and R. Schulz, eds., *The Culture Revolution in Foreign Language Teaching*, 19-31. Skokie, Ill.: National Textbook Co.

Cheng, H-T. 1976. *The Chinese New Year*. New York: Holt, Rinehart and Winston.

Luo, C. 1992. "Culture in vocabulary," in G. Irons and T.S. Paribakht, eds., *Make Changes, Make a Difference*, 171-186. Welland, Ontario: éditions Soleil publishing inc.

Robinson, G.N. 1985. *Crosscultural Understanding*. New York: Pergamon.

Modern Chinese: Beginner's Course, Vol. 3. Beijing: Beijing Language Institute Press.

Traditional Chinese Culture in Taiwan (2nd ed.), 1991. Taipei: Kwang Hwa Publishing Co.

Reprinted from: Cheng Luo, "Teaching Culture in a North American Context: The Chinese New Year." *Mosaic*, 2, 2 (Winter 1994): 23-26.

49 Teaching Culture in a North American Context: Ukrainian Easter

Tania Onyschuk

Background

*K**hrystos Voskres!* (Christ is risen!) then *"Voistynu Voskres!"* (Indeed He is risen!) are the joyous greetings heard on Ukrainian Easter morning and throughout the Easter season. It is a happy time when families and the community join together to celebrate Christ's Resurrection.

This year Ukrainian Easter will fall on May 1. Most other Christian churches will already have celebrated Easter a month earlier. The difference occurs because Ukrainian religious holidays follow the Julian calendar and not our present-day Gregorian one. Thus, Ukrainian Easter can be on the same day or up to five weeks later than Easter of other churches.

Ukrainian Easter has many rich traditions that have developed over a long period of history. Some of these date back to pre-Christian rites greeting spring. In springtime people saw regrowth and re-birth everywhere. The earliest signs of spring were the returning birds, which built nests and laid eggs that hatched into new birds. People believed birds brought spring on their wings. This is why the egg became an important part of spring festivities.

With the coming of Christianity in the tenth century, the spring rituals were transformed into Easter traditions and given Christian meaning. Today's Ukrainian Easter traditions, while deeply religious, contain many elements that can be traced back to the joyous greeting of spring.

The Sunday before Easter (Palm Sunday) is known as Willow Sunday. There are no palm trees in Ukraine, so the willow was chosen because it was thought to have healing powers. After the pussy willows are blessed in church, people, and children in particular, tap each other with the willows saying, "Be as tall as the willow, as healthy as water, and as rich as the earth". The blessed willows are then placed behind religious pictures in the home or planted. They are never thrown away.

The week before Easter is spent in preparation. On the evening of "Pure" Thursday, Ukrainians attend a special Passion service and return home with lighted candles, which are used in the Easter celebrations. On "Passion" (Good) Friday a special shroud is laid out in church. Everyone fasts during Friday and Saturday in remembrance of Christ's fast.

Paska

During these days special Easter breads are baked, *krashanky* (one-coloured eggs) and Easter baskets are prepared. "*Babka*" is a tall, round bread that is light, sweet and rich. "*Paska*" is a round bread topped with symbolic decorations in the form of a cross or a circle symbolizing eternal life.

Pysanka Symbols

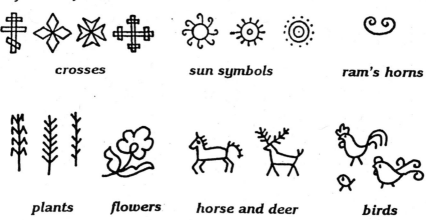

crosses   **sun symbols**   **ram's horns**

plants   **flowers**   **horse and deer**   **birds**

On Easter morning, there is a sunrise service, after which all the Easter baskets containing the special breads, butter, cheese, ham, sausage, horseradish, salt, *krashanky* and Easter eggs are blessed. The rows of baskets containing embroidered cloths, artistically arranged food, colourful Easter eggs and candles are a lovely sight. Each family then hurries home to break the fast. The meal starts with the family sharing one blessed egg, as a symbol of family strength and unity. The food in the Easter basket is only part of the meal that includes cheesecakes and many baked sweets.

In the afternoon, families gather in the church yard or parish hall for Easter games and *hahilky*. *Hahilky* are choral dances performed by girls and young children. The children then play games using *krashanky* in egg rolling contests or tests of the eggs' strength. The winners get to keep the coloured eggs. On Easter Sunday everyone tries to give and receive a beautifully decorated Easter egg.

Easter Monday is called "Wet" Monday. After the church service, young people squirt or drench each other with water. This commemorates the persecution suffered by early Christians. Traditionally, girls presented each boy that doused them with water with an Easter egg.

Ukrainian Easter Eggs – Pysanky

The most famous of Ukrainian Easter traditions are the lovely and intricate *pysanky*. What may seem like decorations on the eggs, are actually symbols with special meanings. If you know the meaning of these symbols, you can read the respective meaning of each egg. That is why in Ukrainian you don't make *pysanky*, you "write" them.

The oldest symbols are circles that represent the sun and symbolize eternal life. Crosses represent the four corners of the world and Christ's Resurrection. Horses and deer symbolize wealth, birds, a fulfilment of wishes. Flowers and plants symbolize growth. Ram's horns represent strength.

Colours also have symbolic meanings. Red symbolizes love, green – health, youth and spring. Yellow brings with it the warmth of the sun and represents happiness. Orange is symbolic of strength. Brown depicts the wealth of the earth. Black is a sad colour, but when combined with white, symbolizes safety. Purple suggests patience and trust.

Pysanky are "written" using hot bees' wax, dyes, and a special writing tool, which is a small metal cone attached to a stick. The melted wax flows through the tip of the cone onto the egg. The parts of the egg that are covered in wax will remain white. The egg is next dipped into the lightest dye, usually yellow. Then parts of the yellow egg are drawn upon with wax. These parts will stay yellow. Afterwards, the egg is dipped in orange dye and the process is repeated to the final colour. The egg is placed in a heated oven to melt the wax. The result is a multicoloured *pysanka*.

Suggestions for Activities
a. General Activities

Since Ukrainian Easter is a time of joy and renewal, the suggested activities can be incorporated into language classes as part of an "Easter-around-the-world-theme" or as part of a unit on spring.

1. Make a *krashanka*.

    Use hard-boiled white eggs. Prepare food colouring or special dyes in glass jars. Add a tablespoon of vinegar to each jar of dye. Dye each egg a different colour. Use the *krashanky* in games or as decorations.

2. Make a natural green dye.

    Use a young branch from an apple tree (don't destroy more branches than necessary).

    Shave the bark from the branches to make about 2 cups of bark shavings.

    Cover with water, add 1 tsp. of alum and simmer gently for 1 hour.

    Cool and add 2 tbsps. of vinegar. Place an egg for about 2 hours in the dye. The egg will be light purple. After the egg is removed from the dye, it will start turning light green.

3. Make an Easter card.

    Use Ukrainian *pysanka* symbols to make a card with special wishes for a friend. Remember that the symbols and colours have certain meanings. Explain the meaning of your wishes inside the card.

4. Play Ukrainian Easter games.

    Each child will need a *krashanka*. Set up races in groups of four to see whose egg rolls the farthest. Have the finalists race each other. The child whose egg rolls the farthest is the winner.

5. Write a story.

    Long ago, people did not know the scientific reason for changes from season to season. Imagine you are a person living long ago. Write a story about how and why spring comes.

b. Activities for Higher Levels

6. Write a *pysanka*.

    Invite to class someone who is experienced in writing Easter eggs to instruct and help the students. This person should be able to obtain all the necessary materials. Set aside at least 2 hours for this class.

7. Traditions and beliefs associated with Ukrainian Easter can be used as the starting point for group activities and discussions that share and compare traditions and beliefs of other cultures, faiths and religions.

Calendar

Many cultures make use of different calendars to determine the time of religious or cultural celebrations. Ukrainians use the Julian calendar. Small groups of students can research a calendar that may be relevant in their lives. A display can be set up of the various calendars.

Symbols

Symbols appear in many aspects of our lives. They also play an important part in most celebrations, rituals, religious and cultural holidays. Each student can share a symbol from his/her experience and explain its meaning or significance. This sharing may lead to a discussion of humanity's need for symbols and how their use affects our lives.

The egg is an important symbol of Ukrainian Easter. Is the egg also a symbol in other cultures? Students can list cultures, celebrations or festivals where the egg is used as a symbol. If there is interest, they can make charts comparing and contrasting the various symbolic meanings of eggs.

Spring

The coming of spring and the rebirth and regeneration of nature is an important part of the celebration of Ukrainian Easter. Today our planet has difficulty in regenerating itself. The class can list various reasons why our planet may be in danger. The students may also wish to organize a spring project that will help nature regenerate itself, for example, tree planting, recycling or clean-up projects.

Reprinted from: Tania Onyschuk, "Teaching Culture in a North American Context: Ukrainian Easter." *Mosaic,* 1, 3 (Spring 1994): 21-22.

50 Teaching Culture in a North American Context: Valentine's Day

Anthony Mollica, Marjolaine Séguin and Natalia Valenzuela

Through a "time machine" interview, we were able to reach Cupid, the Roman God of Love, and ask him a few questions about St. Valentine's Day.

Mosaic: I am delighted that you've accepted to be interviewed…As the mythological Roman God of Love, you should be able to provide our readers with a wealth of background information about St. Valentine's day.

Cupid: Yes, of course. This is a celebration which began in Rome more than 2000 years ago with the feast of Lupercalia, celebrated every February 15 to ensure protection from wolves.

Mosaic: Why was this feast so important to the Romans?

Cupid: The celebration was in honour of the God Lupercus, the Roman shepherd's protector against ravaging wolves. These fierce, hungry animals lived in the woods that covered most of the land. They killed sheep and goats. The wolves were so bold that even the farmers and their families were not always safe.

Mosaic: And so each year the Romans had feasts to honour Lupercus and thank him for his protection. But what has this to do with Valentine's Day?

Cupid: At the time of the *Lupercalia* – as the feast to honour Lupercus was called – the people feasted and danced and played games. When the young men wanted partners for the dances and games, they drew the names of the girls out of a bowl. These girls would be their partners. Often these girls became the young men's sweethearts.

Mosaic: I understand that these festivities changed with the advent of Christianity.

Cupid: Correct! With the advent of Christianity, the Romans no longer believed in Gods such as Lupercus, and priests tried to do away with this pagan ritual. The people did not want to give up this celebration, however, and so the church fathers decided to keep this holiday in the middle of February...with some changes.

Mosaic: To what changes are you referring?

Cupid: At these feasts, the people were asked to honour a man of the church, St. Valentine, who was beheaded on February 14.

Mosaic: Who was this Valentine?

Cupid: Valentine – or rather *Valentinus* – was a priest who lived in pagan Rome around the year 270 A.D. He was imprisoned for defying the laws of Emperor Claudius.

Mosaic: What laws did he defy?

Cupid: Claudius had considerable difficulty in recruiting men to serve as soldiers in his wars. The men preferred not to leave their wives, families and sweethearts to fight in foreign lands. And so Claudius declared that no more marriages could be performed and that all engagements were to be cancelled. Valentine believed that this edict was against the laws of God and nature, so he performed Christian marriage ceremonies secretly. When Emperor Claudius discovered what Valentine was doing, he had the priest arrested and sentenced to death.

Mosaic: There is another legend surrounding this incident...

Cupid: Ah, yes! One legend tells that while Valentine was in prison, he restored the sight of the jailer's blind daughter, who brought him food and tried to cheer him up. Legend has it that before dawn on the morning of his execution, he wrote her a farewell note in which he spoke of the bond of affection between people, and he signed the message, "From your Valentine."

Mosaic: I understand that there is a possible third source for the origin of the feast.

Cupid: Yes... Another possibility for the naming of February 14 as a courtship day may have come from an old belief that birds choose their mates on that day, and that man, whose thoughts generally turn to love about the same time of the year, would do well to imitate the birds. Doves and pigeons mate for life and therefore were used as a symbol of "fidelity".

Mosaic: And so, through the centuries, these rituals all merged together?

Cupid: Yes. The modern St. Valentine's Day is a day dedicated to lovers, a time to exchange sentimental greeting cards and love words of never-ending adoration.

Mosaic: February 14 was designated as a feast day by the Catholic Church, was it not?

Cupid: Yes. In 496 A.D. Pope Gelanius named February 14 as St. Valentine's Day. In fact, St. Valentine became the patron saint of lovers; but in 1969 this celebration was dropped from the Roman Catholic calendar.

Mosaic: True. But, nevertheless, the exchange of cards and some traditions continued throughout the years...

Cupid: Some historians trace the custom of sending verses on Valentine's Day to a Frenchman named Charles, Duke of Orléans. Charles was captured by the English during the Battle of Agincourt in 1415. He was taken to England and thrown in prison. It is believed that on Valentine's Day he sent his wife a rhymed love letter from his cell in the Tower of London.

Mosaic: Sending Valentine cards to-day is a common occurrence...

Cupid: Quite right... The custom of sending Valentine cards began in the early 1800s. In fact, it was Esther A. Howland, a Mount Holyoke College student in Worcester, Massachussetts, to craft the first cards in the United States. Her idea was an immediate success; so much so, that she hired a staff of young women and set up an assembly line to produce the cards. Miss Howland's business was so successful that she is reported to have built it into a $100,000 a year business! Some cards were hand painted...others were decorated with dried flowers, lace, feathers, imitation jewels. Some even featured a fat Cupid or showed arrows piercing a heart. Needless to say, I was not pleased with the way I was portrayed... (*smiling*) being fat, I mean...

Mosaic: I've seen several illustrations of you represented as a chubby, naked, winged boy with a mischievous smile. You appear with a bow and a quiver of arrows by which you transfix the hearts of youths and maidens. I am sure you are probably responsible for the union of many famous couples.

Cupid: I should like to take credit for their union and not for their separation! I certainly do not want to be held responsible for the separation of royal couples... or for the many divorces taking place in the entertainment world...

Mosaic: I can appreciate your point of view. We all want to appear successful in our line of work. And, certainly, your line of work has created many jobs... particularly in the production of Valentine cards which are manufactured on an enormous scale today...

Cupid: Yes... There is a Valentine for everyone – sweetheart, spouse, children, parents, teachers. In terms of the number of greeting cards sent, Valentine's Day ranks second only to Christmas!

Mosaic: That reminds me... I have a lot of cards to send I appreciate your taking the time out during your busy schedule to talk to us about the background for this important celebration. (*seeing Cupid getting ready to place an arrow in his bow*) Please don't... hope that on this occasion I can remain unscathed from your arrow...

Cupid: All right. On this occasion, I'll let you get along with your work and not have your thoughts turn to love. But next year!...

Entrevue avec Cupidon

Cher Jean,

le directeur de la revue Mosaic me demande de vous informer que nous allons travailler ensemble pour interviewer Cupidon au sujet de la Saint-Valentin. Je vous donne donc rendez-vous à 16 heures demain après-midi à l'entrée du Pavillon des crocus du Jardin Botanique. Vous pourrez facilement me reconnaître. Je porterai une rose à la boutonnière. Au plaisir de faire votre connaissance.

Marie.

Numéro de télécopieur [222] 222-2222

Le lendemain à 16 heures.

Jean arrive au Pavillon des crocus et voit une femme qui porte une rose à la boutonnière. C'est sûrement elle! Elle est assise sur un banc, élégamment vêtue. Il s'approche d'elle et, tout à coup, il sent comme une piqûre dans sa poitrine.

Jean: (*timidement*) Pardon, Mademoiselle,... vous êtes bien...

Marie: (*toute souriante*) Marie. Oui, c'est moi. Merci d'être à l'heure. Je suis un peu pressée cet après-midi et je n'ai pas encore repéré notre ami Cupidon mais il ne devrait pas tarder.

Cupidon: (*caché derrière les crocus, rit tout bas*) Les gens croient toujours que je suis en retard mais, en réalité, j'arrive toujours avant eux. Il le faut bien si je veux utiliser mes flèches discrètement. J'attendrai encore un peu pour voir l'effet de celle que je viens juste de lancer dans le coeur de ce jeune homme.

Jean: Hum!... C'est un beau Pavillon... (*à part*: et Marie est une belle fille)

Marie: Oui, notre ami Cupidon l'a choisi car les crocus sont les fleurs officielles de la Saint-Valentin.

Jean: Je croyais que les roses étaient les fleurs de prédilection de la Saint-Valentin.

Marie: Les roses ont toujours été le choix par excellence de plusieurs amoureux dans le monde entier, mais les crocus sont les fleurs officielles de la Saint-Valentin car elles annoncent l'arrivée du printemps.

Cupidon: (*sortant de sa cachette*) Les crocus sont aussi un rappel de l'histoire de Valentin lui-même!

Marie: Cupidon, te voilà enfin! Mais d'où viens-tu? Je ne t'ai pas vu arriver.

Cupidon: (*taquin*) Ah, je ne révèle pas tous mes secrets! Je m'excuse d'être en retard. J'avais un autre rendez-vous avec Radio-Canada. Que veux-tu, en février, je suis très occupé. Tu n'es pas seule aujourd'hui, Marie?

Marie: Tu as un bon sens de l'observation, Cupidon! Je te présente Jean, un nouveau rédacteur de la revue *Mosaic*. Le directeur nous envoie faire une recherche sur la Saint-Valentin et j'ai pensé que tu serais la meilleure personne pour nous aider.

Cupidon: Très bon choix en effet! Écoute, il faut d'abord que je finisse ce que j'ai commencé à te dire au sujet de Valentin. C'était un très bon médecin de la Rome Antique et il paraît qu'il a guéri miraculeusement une jeune fille aveugle un jour avant son exécution.

Jean: L'exécution de la jeune fille aveugle?

Cupidon: Vous êtes bien impatient, jeune homme! Non, l'exécution de Valentin lui-même. L'Empereur Claudius lui a fait couper la tête car il mariait des jeunes gens en cachette.

Marie: Les médecins mariaient les gens dans la Rome Antique?

Cupidon: Tu es impatiente, toi aussi, Marie. (*à part:* L'impatience est un ingrédient qui se marie très bien avec mes flèches!) J'ai oublié de te dire que Valentin était prêtre en plus d'être médecin.

Marie: Mais je ne pouvais pas deviner cela, moi.

Cupidon: Bien sûr que non, Marie. Excuse-moi.

Jean: Très bien, mais pourquoi alors mariait-il les gens en cachette?

Cupidon: Il faut savoir qu'à cette époque, l'Empereur de Rome avait besoin de beaucoup de soldats et il avait remarqué que ceux qui étaient mariés préféraient rester à la maison avec leur épouse et leur famille. Il avait donc interdit les fiançailles et les mariages.

Jean: (*offusqué*) Mais cela n'a pas de sens d'empêcher les coeurs de s'aimer!

Cupidon: Je suis bien d'accord avec vous!

Marie: Alors l'empereur s'est fâché et a fait tuer Valentin pour cette raison-là?

Cupidon: C'est une des versions que nous a laissées l'histoire mais il paraît qu'il y aurait eu sept personnes nommées Valentin.

Marie: Six autres Valentins?

Cupidon: Et oui, mais je suis pressé aujourd'hui. Je ne crois pas que j'aurai le temps de tout vous raconter. (*Il regarde la porte d'entrée.*) D'ailleurs je dois m'absenter pendant deux secondes. À tout de suite! Ne bougez pas d'ici!

Jean reste interloqué. Marie sourit.

Jean: Mais où est-ce qu'il va comme ça?

Marie: Tu ne connais pas encore notre cher Cupidon. Tu vois le couple qui vient de rentrer?

Jean: Les jeunes habillés en jeans?

Marie: Oui.

Jean: Mais je ne vois pas Cupidon.

Marie: C'est çá son astuce! Il se cache toujours pour lancer ses flèches d'amour.

Cupidon: (*de retour*) Bon, excusez-moi, mais les affaires urgentes ne peuvent jamais attendre. Ce charmant petit couple avait besoin d'un philtre d'amour. Grâce à moi, ils seront irrésistiblement attirés l'un vers l'autre.

Marie: Dis donc, Cupidon, toi aussi tu travailles en cachette, comme notre ami Valentin?

Cupidon: Tu sais, tout ce que je fais c'est de lancer la première flèche. Le reste, je n'en suis pas responsable. (*à part*: heureusement!...)

Jean: Bon, écoutez, tous les deux. Nous sommes venus ici pour faire une entrevue et il nous reste très peu de temps. Cupidon, laissons faire les six autres Valentin mais dis-moi une chose. Je croyais que la Fête de la Saint-Valentin venait de traditions païennes, bien avant Jésus Christ.

Cupidon: Dis-donc Marie, ton copain est bien informé! En effet, dans la Rome antique, on célébrait à la mi-février une fête païenne appelée Lupercales.

Marie: Et quelle est la relation avec la fête des amoureux?

Cupidon: Bonne question! Ce jour-là, on mettait le nom de jeunes filles dans une boîte et celui de jeunes hommes dans une autre boîte et on tirait au sort deux noms.

Jean: Qu'est-ce qui arrivait aux deux personnes?

Cupidon: Ils sortaient souvent ensemble pendant le reste de l'année.

Marie: Cupidon, est-ce qu'il y a aussi une histoire à propos des oiseaux?

Cupidon: Bien sûr, Marie! Au Moyen-Âge, on pensait que c'était le 14 février que les oiseaux s'accouplaient et construisaient leur nid.

Marie: Il me semble qu'il fait encore bien froid en février pour s'accoupler. Enfin...

Jean: Cupidon, tous ces faits historiques sont bien intéressants mais que peux-tu nous dire ton rôle à toi dans cette Fête de la Saint-Valentin?

Cupidon: Je ne peux pas vous révéler tous mes secrets, mais si je vous dis que mon nom vient d'un mot latin qui veut dire "désir", vous pourrez tirer vos propres conclusions.

Marie: Cupidon, la Saint-Valentin, ce n'est pas seulement pour les amoureux. Si j'ai envie d'exprimer mon amitié ou mon appréciation pour des personnes que j'aime bien, comme ma soeur, ma mère ou mon professeur, ça me semble l'occasion appropriée.

Cupidon: *Et oui, de nos jours, on envoie des cartes aux personnes qu'on aime et ce ne sont pas nécessairement des demandes en mariage comme c'était le cas dans le passé. Oh, Oh! Je vois des jeunes coeurs tout prêts à être transpercés. Vous m'excuserez, mais je dois voler au devant de ces jeunes gens. Merci pour l'invitation. À bientôt!*

Jean: *Il ne va pas revenir?*

Marie: *Cette fois-ci, je ne pense pas. Il faudra attendre à l'année prochaine pour lui parler à nouveau.*

Jean: (un peu nerveux) *En attendant, on pourrait peut-être aller quelque part pour rédiger notre article sur la Saint-Valentin. Au restaurant du Jardin Botanique peut-être.*

Marie: *C'est que…je n'ai pas beaucoup de temps…*

Cupidon, caché derrière elle, lui lance une flèche invisible.

Marie: *Ahï!*

Jean: *Qu'est-ce qu'il y a?*

Marie: *Rien. Une piqûre de moustique probablement.*

Jean: *Alors, le restaurant?*

Una entrevista con Cupido

Mosaic: Buenos días y bienvenido, Señor Cupido. Me alegro mucho de tenerle aquí para hablarnos de la fiesta de San Valentín.

Cupido: El gusto es mío, señora. Si me hubieran dicho que estaría hablando con una mujer tan guapa (*dándole una mirada de arriba a abajo*) habría traído mis flechas amorosas…

Mosaic: Gracias, pues a mí, sí, me advirtieron que Ud. es muy encantador y que le gusta coquetear con las mujeres.

Cupido: Así es. Me gusta todo lo romántico (*acercándose a la mujer*).

Mosaic: Dígame Sr. Cupido lo que lo que significa su nombre.

Cupido: Soy uno de los dioses mitológicos y la palabra "cupido" significa "deseo" (*tomando la mano de la mujer*).

Mosaic: (*extricando calmamente la mano y aclarándose la garganta*) Hablamos de otra cosa. ¿Cuál es el origen del día de San Valentín?

Cupido: Pues la verdad es que hay varias interpretaciones acerca del origen de esta fiesta. Su espíritu romántico decidirá la que más le guste.

Mosaic: Sí, de acuerdo. Me parece que es una fiesta antigua, ¿no?

Cupido: Sí, el día de San Valentín que celebramos hoy nació de una tradición pagana de la Roma antigua. Se celebraba entonces la fiesta de *Lupercalia*. La gente honraba al dios Lupercus, el cual era responsable de proteger a los pastores y a su rebaño de lobos afamados que rodeaban por las afueras de Roma.

Mosaic: Entonces... ¿era más bien una fiesta pastoral?

Cupido: De una parte, sí, pero también se celebraba la fertilidad y veneraban a los dioses romanos *Juno y Pan*.

Mosaic: ¿Cuáles eran las costumbres asociadas a la fiesta de Lupercalia?

Cupido: Había una tradición muy simpática. Cada doncella escribía su nombre y un mensaje romántico en una carta. Luego, ponían todas las cartas en un gran cacharro. Después los mancebos del pueblo, uno a uno, escojían una carta. Así, los jóvenes se juntaban. Claro que yo tuve que ayudarles a enamorarse.

Mosaic: Es una tradición lindísima, hasta sería divertido hacerlo hoy día; pero ¿quién fue San Valentín?

Cupido: En tiempos romanos, durante el reino del Emperador Claudius II Gothicus, había un curandero cristiano muy conocido llamado San Valentín, que también era uno de los primeros sacerdotes cristianos. El ser cristiano era algo de valientes puesto que en esa época perseguían a los cristianos por sus creencias.

Mosaic: ¿Y nada más que por ser cristiano le encarcelaron?

Cupido: No era tan sencillo. El Emperador Claudius buscaba desesperadamente a soldados para luchas en sus guerras, pero los hombres no cumplían porque no querían dejar a sus mujeres o a sus novias. Claudius se enojó y declaró que no habría más bodas. Era ilegal casarse. Todos los noviazgos fueron cancelados.

Mosaic: ¡Que triste! Me imagino que los enamorados se desesperaron...

Cupido: (*Diciendo "no" con la cabeza*) No necesariamente. El padre Valentín creía que la nueva ley era injusta y por lo tanto, en secreto, él casó a varias parejas.

Mosaic: Eso sí que es romántico. Y por eso le encarcelaron a San Valentín ¿verdad?

Cupido: Según una versión de la historia, sí, cuando Claudius se enteró que le esteban engañando, le encarceló y le condenaron a muerte; pero también hay otra leyenda... la de la hija del carcelero.

Mosaic: Sí, conozco esta leyenda. La niña estaba ciega, ¿verdad?

Cupido: Así era. Un día vino un carcelero a visitar a Valentín, para ver si él pudía ayudar a su hija y devolverle la vista. Valentín trató de sanar a la niña y, mientras tanto el rumor de su cristiandad, su reputación de curandero, y el hecho de que seguía casando a la gente, llegó a oídos de Claudius. Valentín fue condenado a muerte.

Mosaic: ¿Y por eso santificaron a Valentín?

Cupido: Paciencia… hay más. Unas horas antes de morir, Valentín le mandó una carta a la niña ciega. Al abrir la carta hubo un milagro. ¡Ella la leyó! Le había vuelto la vista. Pronto todos se enteraron y Valentín fue considerado un santo. El mismo día le asesinaron. Era el día 14 de febrero.

Mosaic: Increíble. ¡Qué emocionante! Hasta me trae lágrimas a los ojos. (*sacando de su bolsa un pañuelo*).

Cupido: Sí. Santificaron a San Valentín y en 496 D.C el Papa Gelasius declaró el día 14 de febrero día de San Valentín. El cristianismo ya era aceptado, y querían depaganizar la fiesta de Lupercalia.

Mosaic: He oído que en 1969 el día 14 de febrero fue dejado del calendario litúrgico. ¿Es cierto?

Cupido: Sí es cierto. Pero aunque no es una fecha religiosa sigue siendo una fiesta popular.

Mosaic: ¿Cuáles son las costumbres del día de San Valentín hoy día?

Cupido: Es el día de los amantes y de los enamorados. Se suele enviar cartas románticas, flores, mensajes de amor y chocolate a la persona da la que estamos enamorados.

Mosaic: Ud debe de estar muy ocupado puesto que se acerca el día 14 de febrero.

Cupido: Estoy siempre ocupado. No olvide que la gente no se enamora del un día al otro. Hasta me parece que hoy la gente tarde aun más en enamorarse.

Mosaic: ¿Porque dice eso?

Cupido: Tuve recientemente a un hombre que cuando le percé el corazón de una de mis flechas amorosas, en vez de alegrarse ¡se fue al médico quejándose de indigestación! ¡Y fíjese que mis flechas son de mayor calidad!

Mosaic: No sabía que había diferentes grados de flechas.

Cupido: Sí, hay que tener mucho cuidado. Sino la gente se enamora pero de pronto dejan de amarse. Con las flechas de mayor calidad, la gente sigue amándose por toda la vida.

Mosaic: Veo la importancia de la calidad de las flechas. Y aunque podré hablar con Ud. todo el día, no tenemos más tiempo. Muchísimas gracias por la visita y le deseo un día de San Valentín estupendo.

Cupido: (*besándole la mano*) Señora, ha sido un encanto conocerla y compartir estas informaciones con Ud. Espero que la próxima vez que nos encontremos, yo tenga mis flechas... (*tirándole un besito*).*

*The Authors wish to express their appreciation to Daphne Tunks for researching some of the background information contained in this "interview".

Reprinted from: Anthony Mollica, Marjolaine Séguin and Natalia Valenzuela "Teaching Culture in a North American Context: Valentine's Day." *Mosaic*, 4, 2 (Winter 1997): 23-26.

51 Teaching Culture in a North American Context: Mother's Day/Father's Day

Anthony Mollica and Tania Sterling

Through a "time-machine" interview, we were able to reach Anna Jarvis and ask her a few questions about Mother's Day.

Mosaic: Miss Jarvis, you are credited as being the driving force behind Mother's Day which is celebrated in the United States, in Canada and in many other parts of the world. How did this idea originate?

Anna Jarvis: As you probably know, the custom of holding a festival in honour of motherhood is very old. The ancient Greeks worshipped the goddess Cybele, the mother of the gods. The custom was later introduced into Rome about 250 B.C., and on the Ides of March the festival continued for three days. But these festivals were entirely different from the one I proposed in honour of mothers.

Mosaic: How was your suggestion different?

Anna Jarvis: I felt that at least one day a year should be identified when sons and daughters should pay a tribute to their mothers.

Mosaic: What steps did you take to achieve this?

Anna Jarvis: As you know, my mother died on May 9, 1905. In succeeding years, I held memorial services and encouraged other sons and daughters to remember their mothers in a similar way. I arranged for a special mother's day service in one of the churches and everyone was asked to wear a white carnation.

Mosaic: I understand that the custom of wearing a white carnation was later modified...

Anna Jarvis: Yes, that's true. There were so many requests for white carnations that florists could not meet the demand... Florists soon discovered that people wanted something more colourful...

Mosaic: What was the solution?

Anna Jarvis: Eventually a distinction was made between those whose mothers were still alive and those whose mothers were dead. The red carnation was worn by sons and daughters whose mothers were still alive, while the white carnation was worn by sons and daughters whose mothers had passed away.

Mosaic: Was the idea of celebrating Mother's Day readily acceptable?

Anna Jarvis: It appears so. The suggestion of honouring one's mother appealed to the imagination of others, and services were held in more churches the next year. As you know, the city of Philadelphia where I was born, was the first city to observe formally the celebration on May 10, 1908. But I wanted to make this day a national holiday and lobbied with our politicians...

Mosaic: How did you go about it?

Anna Jarvis: I wrote thousands of letters to influential persons suggesting that a day be chosen to honour and remember our mothers.

Mosaic: How did the various politicians respond to your request?

Anna Jarvis: They were quite positive and encouraging. President Woodrow Wilson was so enthusiastic about it that on May 9, 1914, following the adoption of a resolution by Congress, he issued a proclamation declaring that the second Sunday in May be observed as Mother's Day.

Mosaic: Yes. I recall President Wilson stating that this day was to be regarded "as a public expression of our love and reverence for the mothers of our country."

Anna Jarvis: The idea spread like wild fire to countries such as Afghanistan, Costa Rica, Spain, Italy, England, Sweden, Denmark, China, Mexico to mention only a few. In India, for example, Mother's Day was established as a memorial to the wife of the political and spiritual leader Mohandas K. Gandhi.

Mosaic: You must be very pleased with the dissemination of this celebration which had humble origins.

Anna Jarvis: I was particularly pleased that sons and daughters soon got into the habit of making little gifts on this day to their mothers. I do emphatically deplore, however, the commercialism which eventually infested this day of tribute.

Mosaic: I would like to move on to another tribute: the one established to honour fathers. Could you provide us with some background information?

Anna Jarvis: I'd be very pleased to. You know, however, that I had nothing to do with this. The idea was originated by Mrs. John Bruce Dodd from Spokane, Washington, in 1909.

Mosaic: Were Mrs. Dodd's reasons in wanting to establish a day to honour her parent similar to yours?

Anna Jarvis: There are some minor differences. Mrs. Dodd wanted to honour her father who had successfully reared a family of children after the death of their mother.

Mosaic: How did she go about it?

Anna Jarvis: I am told that she wrote to the Rev. Conrad Bluhm, president of the Spokane Ministerial Association and proposed that the third Sunday in June be set apart for honouring fathers.

Mosaic: What was the reaction?

Anna Jarvis: The congregation immediately approved the proposal, and the first celebration was held in Spokane in June 1910.

Mosaic: Was there any difference between the celebration of Father's Day and Mother's Day?

Anna Jarvis: The only major difference that immediately comes to mind is the flower used. Sons and daughters were asked to wear a red rose if their father was alive and a white one if he was deceased. You will recall that the carnation is the symbol for Mother's Day.

Mosaic: Was the rose the first choice as the symbol?

Anna Jarvis: Actually, members of the Martin W. Callener Bible class of Wilkinsburg, PA, had suggested the dandelion in 1924, as "the more it is trampled on, the more it grows," but its use did not become general.

Mosaic: Did the Father's Day celebration spread as quickly as Mother's Day?

Anna Jarvis: Not quite. In 1911, the celebration was discussed in Chicago as if the idea was new. A dispatch from Vancouver, Washington appearing in the Portland *Oregonian* in 1913 believed that the celebration for Father's Day had originated there.

Mosaic: When did the celebration officially come into general use?

Anna Jarvis: If I am not mistaken, it was in 1934.

Mosaic: Thank you, Miss Jarvis, for all this useful information.

Pedagogical Suggestions

Following are some suggested activities for Mother's Day/Father's Day. They are not presented in any specific order of difficulty. Teachers will know the linguistic background of their students and will select only those activities appropriate to the age and linguistic level of the class. These suggestions are by no means exhaustive; teachers will undoubtedly think of others.

1. Send a singing telegram to your Mother/Father expressing your best wishes for the Day. (The telegram may be live or pre-recorded on audiotape.)

2. Send a balloon-o-gram (with a secret message inside the balloon).

3. Create a menu and take your parent breakfast in bed.

4. Design a ticket and mail it to your parent inviting him/her to attend a scene (or scenes) you will perform at your house depicting why your parent is so special to you.

5. Imagine that the idea of Mother's/Father's Day originated with you. Write a letter to a politician urging him/her to lobby to have it declared a national holiday.

6. Your local newspaper is having a contest for the Best Mom/ Best Dad. Write a short paragraph about the qualities of your parent and submit it to the contest.

7. Write a poem for your parent expressing your love and your gratitude for what he/she has done for you.

8. Make a placemat and get it laminated for the kitchen table.

9. Design a Best Mother/Best Father Certificate. List at least three reasons for this "award".

10. Using the information from the Jarvis "interview" printed above, write in your own words a short paragraph about the origins of Mother's Day/Father's Day.

11. Write an Editorial indicating reasons why sons and daughters should celebrate Mother's Day/Father's Day.

12. Interview several people (on audiotape, if possible) and ask them what they think of Mother's Day/Father's Day celebrations.

13. Design a Happy Mother's/Father's Day card and write a message in one of the languages you are currently studying.

14. List a dozen adjectives which best describe your parent.

15. Make a series of drawings illustrating the activities in which your parent is frequently involved.

16. Imagine that you are Anna Jarvis and have the opportunity to meet President Wilson. Select a partner to play the role of the President and try to persuade him to establish a day to celebrate Mother's/Father's Day.

[Text by Anthony Mollica; Pedagogical Suggestions by Tania Sterling.]

Reprinted from: Anthony Mollica and Tania Sterling, "Teaching Culture in a North American Context: Mother's Day/Father's Day." *Mosaic*, 1, 4 (Summer 1994): 22-23.

Contributors

Janis L. Antonek is Assistant Professor, Department of Curriculum and Instruction, University of North Carolina at Greensboro, where she teaches and oversees the FL and ESL methodology programs.

Jill Bell is Assistant Professor in the Faculty of Education, York University, where she teaches courses on language and literacy.

Christine Besnard is Associate Professor of French. She teaches at Glendon College, York University, North York, Ontario.

Nelson Brooks was Associate Professor of French, Yale University, Director of Summer programs, and Director of the Summer Language Institute, at the time this article was published.

Paul Cankar, MA, is instructor of Spanish at St. Michael's High School in Austin, Texas. His interests include learner strategies and the development of proficiency-based materials.

Nicholas J. Cepeda is currently an assistant professor in psychology at York University in Toronto and an assistant project scientist at the University of California, San Diego. He teaches educational psychology and investigates practical, theoretically-based methods for improving learning and long-term retention in the classroom.

Kenneth Chastain is Professor of Spanish, Department of Spanish, Italian and Portuguese, University of Virginia, Charlottesville, Virginia.

Caterina Cicogna is Education Officer, Office of the Consulate General of Italy, Toronto, Ontario.

Carmela Colella is Assistant Professor of Italian at Brock University. Her research interests include second-language methodology, teacher ducation, and digital humanities. She is currently creating humanities research tools and a multimedia language learning object for Italian.

Marcel Danesi is Professor of Semiotics and Applied Linguistics ,Victoria College, University of Toronto and Adjunct Professor at the Università della Svizzera Italiana of Lugano, Switzerland.

Richard Donato is Associate Professor of Foreign Languages in the School of Education at the University of Pittsburgh, Pennsylvania.

Philip Donley has taught Spanish at the University of Texas at Austin, Southwestern University, and Austin Community College. His interests include language anxiety and teaching critical thinking skills. He often conducts seminars in anxiety-reduction and critical thinking.

Charles Elkabas is Professor of French at Erindale College, University of Toronto. He has published several articles on the new technology in language teaching.

Hector Hammerly is Professor of Applied Linguistics and teaches in the Linguistic Department, Simon Fraser University, Burnaby, British Columbia.

Cher Evans-Harvey is Assistant Professor, Faculty of Education, Nipissing University, where she teaches courses in methodology for French as a second language.

Peter J. Heffernan is Professor of Education at the Faculty of Education, University of Lethbridge, Alberta, with primary responsibility for second-language teacher preparation.

John J. Janc received a Doctorat de troisième cycle from La Sorbonne Nouvelle and a PhD from the University of Wisconsin, Madison. He has been teaching French at Minnesota State University, Mankato, for twenty-eight years. He has been actively involved in teacher preparation and TA supervision. He has published numerous article dealing with the French Language and teaching it.

Stephen D. Krashen is Professor of Education at the University of Southern California. It has always been his desire to write a paper in which both the footnotes and the references were longer than the actual article.

J. Clarence LeBlanc is a retired high school and university second-language teacher who maintains his passion for teaching, and its administrative and political dimensions. He was a member of the National Core

French Study and chaired the Culture Syllabus Task Group.

Louise Lewin teaches methodology courses in French as a second language at the Faculty of Education, Glendon College, York University.

Cheng Luo holds a Ph.D. in Linguistca and TESL from the University of Manitoba. He is currently teaching at Brock University.

Raffaella Maiguashca is Associate Lecturer at York University where she teaches Italian language and methodology courses.

Anthony Mollica is Professor emeritus of Education, Faculty of Education, Brock University, St. Catharines, Ontario and Professor (status only), University of Toronto at Mississauga.

Frank Nuessel is Professor of Linguistics at the University of Louisville, Louisville, Kentucky.

Tania Onyschuk is an instructor in charge and coordinator of Ukrainian classes at Our Lady of Sorrows, Metropolitan Separate School Board, Toronto.

Anthony Papalia was a former Chair, Faculty of Educational Studies, SUNY, Buffalo. At the time of his death in 1988, he was Professor in the Faculty of Educational Studies, SUNY, Buffalo.

Sylvie Rosienski-Pellerin is Associate Professor of French and teaches at Glendon College, York University, North York, Ontario.

Edwin G. Ralph is Associate Professor of Education, College of Education, University of Saskatchewan, Saskatoon, Saskatchewan.

Merle Richards is Associate Professor of Education, Faculty of Education, Brock University, St. Catharines, Ontario.

Perla Riesenbach teaches French as a second language at Leo Baeck Day School, Board of Jewish Education, Toronto.

Wilga Rivers is professor of Romance Languages and Literature emerita, Harvard University. As a coordinator of Romance Languages she improved the offreings in French, Italian, Portuguese, Romanian and Spanish, She is the author or coautor of some thirteen books and nearly 80 articles. She is a recognized national and international authority in the psychological and linguistic aspects of language teaching.

Roseann Runte, is President of

Carleton University. She is a former President of Old Dominion University, Norfolk, VA. Professor, author, and poet, she is a former principal of Glendon College, York University and a former President of Victoria College, University of Toronto. Dr. Runte is the only woman in Canada ever to be President of an English and French University. She has published four volumes of creative writing, edited ten books and has written over one hundred articles on subjects ranging from the environment to regional economic development, education to literature, second- language acquisition to women's issues. She is a member of the World Parliament of Cultures.

Sandra J. Savignon is Professor of Applied Linguistics at Penn State University where teaches courses in second-language acquisition, language and gender and World Englishes. Prior to going to Penn State in 1997, she was professor of French and of English as an International Language at the University of Illinois where she founded and directed a multidisciplinary doctoral program in Second Language Acquisition and Teacher Education (SLATE). She is the author

of *Communicative Competence: Theory and Practice* (Mc Graw-Hill, 1997), *Interpreting Communicative Language Teaching: Contexts and Conerns in Teacher Education* (Yale University Press, 2002) and numerous articles.

Herbert Schutz is Professor of German and Chair, Department of Slavic Studies, Brock University, St. Catharines, Ontario.

Marjolaine Séguin is a teacher currently enrolled in the French as a second-language program, Brock University.

Tania Sterling teaches French as a second language at Canadian Martyrs, Burlington, Ontario.

H. H. Stern is professor emeritus in the Department of Curriculum of the Ontario Institute for Studies in Education (OISE), University of Toronto. He was the founding director of the Modern Language Centre of OISE, a position he held from 1968-1981. He is the author of several books and research reports on language teaching.

Karen Tessar is a student completing her B.Ed. at the Faculty of Education, Brock University, St. Catharines, Ontario.

G. Richard Tucker is professor of Applied Linguistics at Carnegie Mellon University, Pittsburgh, Pennsylvania.

Anne Urbancic teaches language, culture and literature in the Department of Italian Studies and is also the co-ordinator for VIC ONE Frye and Pearson Streams. Her teaching and research interests have an interdisciplinary focus and include second-language pedagogy, late 19th/early 20th century Italian literature and semiotics.

Natalia Valenzuela is completing her B.Ed at the Faculty of Education, Brock University.

Rebecca M. Valette is Professor of Romance Languages at Boston College. She is past President of the American Association of Teachers of French.

Joanne Wilcox is President of Multilingual Communications for Management (MCM), Manotick, Ontario. MCM specializes in translation and cross-culture business etiquette.

Zofia Wodniecka is currently a postdoctoral fellow in Ellen Bialystok's laboratory, at York University and Rotman Research Institute in Toronto. She teaches cognition and psycholingui-stics and investigates bilingualism from these perspectives. She examines cognitive processes underlying second-language use and enhancement of executive function in bilingual populations.

Also available from
éditions Soleil publishing inc.

FRENCH

BK-133 Le présent

BK-138 Le futur

BK-136 Le calendrier

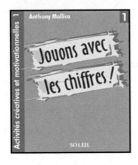

BK-131 Jouons avec
les chiffres

BK-135
À l'école

BK-097 La presse à
l'école

BK-201 Mots croisés
pour les débutants

BK-067 Une image
vaut...1000 mots... 1

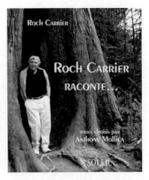

BK-229 Roch Carrier
raconte...text+2 Cds

BK-003 Parole
crociate per
principianti

BK-114 Opera Italian!

BK-233 Parliamo con
la pubblicità
(includes DVD)

BK-069 Una immagine
vale... 1000 parole... 1

BK-144 Attività
lessicali 1

BK-145 Attività
lessicali 2

SPANISH

BK-036 ¡Escoge tú!

BK-070 Una imagen
vale... 1000 palabras... 1

BK-075 Una imagen
vale... 1000 palabras... 2

For more publications in French, Italian, Spanish, English,
German, Latin, Portuguese, etc...
visit us at: www.soleilpublishing.com